Handbook

Since the *Handbook of Counselling* was first published, counselling has undergone a period of rapid growth and change. This, the second edition, has been revised and thoroughly updated with the addition of six new chapters, making it a comprehensive and up-to-the-minute guide to counselling theory and practice. The contributors, all experienced practitioners, reflect the diversity and also the coherence of counselling today. They examine the principles of counselling, the issues affecting practice, and consider how the profession is likely to develop in the future.

The handbook is divided into five parts: Introduction, Arenas, Settings, Themes, and Issues. Part 1 focuses on the current and future development of counselling and examines counselling in the context of the lifecycle. Part 2 describes the main arenas in which counselling occurs: individual couples, family and group counselling. Part 3 focuses on counselling in different settings including private practice, voluntary settings, education, medical contexts, and organizations. Part 4 covers specific topics ranging from gender, race, and sexual orientation to career counselling and counselling for trauma and post-traumatic stress disorder. The final part focuses on research and evaluation, counsellor–client exploitation, and other professional issues affecting counselling.

Published in association with the British Association for Counselling, the *Handbook of Counselling* provides a definitive source of information and guidance for counsellors both in training and practice.

Stephen Palmer is Founder Director of the Centre for Stress Management, London. He is former Managing Editor of *Counselling*, the journal of the BAC and has written widely on the subject of counselling and stress management. He is a Fellow of the British Association for Counselling. **Gladeana McMahon** is a counsellor, trainer, and supervisor in private practice, London. She is the author of *Starting your own Private Practice*.

Handbook of counselling
Second edition

Edited by Stephen Palmer
Associate editor Gladeana McMahon

Published in association with the British
Association for Counselling

London and New York

First published 1989 by Tavistock/Routledge

Second edition published 1997
by Routledge
11 New Fetter Lane, London EC4P 4EE

Simultaneously published in the USA and Canada
by Routledge
29 West 35th Street, New York, NY 10001

Routledge is an imprint of the Taylor & Francis Group

Reprinted 1998, 1999 and 2000

© 1997 British Association for Counselling

Typeset in Times by J&L Composition Ltd, Filey, North Yorkshire
Printed and bound in Great Britain by T. J. International Ltd, Padstow, Cornwall

British Library Cataloguing in Publication Data
A catalogue record for this book is available from the British Library

Library of Congress Cataloguing in Publication Data
Handbook of counselling / edited by Stephen Palmer and Gladeana McMahon. –
2nd ed.
p. cm/
    Includes bibliographical references and indexes.
    1. Counselling–Great Britain. I. Palmer, Stephen, 1955–.
II. McMahon, Gladeana, 1954–.
BF637.C6H312 1997
158´.3–dc20   96–44637

ISBN 0–415–13951–1
ISBN 0–415–13952–X (pbk)

For Maggie, Kate, Tom and Mike for their patience. To our colleagues, supervisors, students and clients from whom we have learnt so much about counselling. And to Michael Megranahan who died soon after completing his chapter for this book.

Contents

Figures, tables and boxes

Figures

Tables

Boxes

Contributors

Diane Bailey is currently Director, Equal Opportunities, at the Open University, seconded from her substantive post of Senior Counsellor in which she develops and manages student support services. She has taught and researched extensively in Higher Education and at the National Institute for Careers Education and Counselling, and has written widely on educational guidance and open learning. Currently she is co-opted on to the Lead Body for Advice, Guidance, Counselling and Psychotherapy.

Elsa Bell has been working formally as a counsellor with young people since 1975 and in student counselling since 1979. She has been Head of Counselling at Oxford University since 1990. She is the former Chair of the Association for Student Counselling and the British Association for Counselling and is currently Chair of the UK Register Executive Committee and the Counselling and Psychotherapy Development Group of the Lead Body for Advice, Guidance, Counselling and Psychotherapy. She is a Fellow of Kellogg College, Oxford; the British Association for Counselling, and the Royal Society of Arts.

Tim Bond is a Staff Tutor in Counselling, University of Durham and is a former chairperson of the British Assocation for Counselling (1994–96). His publications include *Standards and Ethics for Counselling in Action* (1993) and other books and articles on professional issues associated with counselling and multidisciplinary work.

Jocelyn Chaplin is a feminist psychotherapist, artist, writer, trainer and mother. Jocelyn has been in private practice for twelve years. She has taught and led workshops in many places including The Woman's Therapy Centre and the City University, co-founding the Serpent Institute to train counsellors in both humanistic and psychodynamic traditions within a framework of goddess spirituality. Jocelyn has published widely including *Feminist Counselling in Action* (1988).

Grahame F. Cooper, Ph.D., is UKCP registered as a sexual and marital psychotherapist and as a psychoanalytic psychotherapist. He is in private practice in Birmingham as a psychotherapist and as a supervisor. He holds the Westminster Pastoral Foundation Certificate in Psychodynamic Supervision. He has served as Chair of the British Association for Sexual and Marital Therapy and of the West Midlands Institute of Psychotherapy. He has written papers on aspects of counselling and on ethics and has also contributed chapters to *Sex Therapy in Britain* (1988) and the first editon of *The Handbook of Counselling* (Routledge, 1989).

Roslyn Corney is Professor of Psychology at the University of Greenwich. Previously she was a senior lecturer at the Institute of Psychiatry and the Department of Psychological Medicine, St Bartholomew's Hospital. Her research has mainly focused around mental health issues in general practice, in particular the evaluation of psychological treatments. She has recently edited *Communication and Counselling Skills in Medicine* (1991) and co-edited *Counselling in General Practice* (1995), both published by Routledge.

Sue Culley, MA, is an independent consultant, with a particular interest in the application of counselling skills and theory to workplace issues. Currently working in change-management programmes, equal opportunity and harassment awareness, she also contributes to Employee Assistance Programmes as Clinical Director with Focus Ltd.

Peter Dale, Ph.D., is a BAC accredited counsellor and counselling supervisor in Hastings, East Sussex. His doctoral research explored clients' and therapists' perceptions of the therapeutic process with adults who were abused as children. He has also worked for the NSPCC for many years and since 1986 has been manager of NSPCC East Sussex.

Windy Dryden is Professor of Counselling at Goldsmiths College, University of London. He has authored or edited over 100 books including *Facilitating Client Change in Rational Emotive Behaviour Therapy* (1995) and *Daring to be Myself: A Case of Rational-Emotive Therapy*, written with Joseph Yankura (1992). In addition, he edits twelve book series in the area of counselling and psychotherapy including the *Brief Therapy and Counselling* series and *Developing Counselling*. His major interests are in rational emotive behaviour therapy, eclecticism and integration in psychotherapy and, increasingly, writing short, accessible self-help books for the general public.

John Foskett is an Anglican priest and pastoral counsellor who has been a member of APCC and BAC since their inceptions in the 1970s. He was chaplain to the Bethlem Royal and Maudsley NHS Trust, where he was the organizer of the first supervision and consultation course for pastors and therapists. He is actively involved in the European and International Pastoral Care and Counselling movements and has a special interest in mental health practice and theory. He is author of *Meaning in Madness* (1984) and co-author of *Helping the Helpers* (1988).

Paul Hitchings, M.Sc., is a chartered counselling psychologist and a UKCP integrative psychotherapist. He works in private practice as a counsellor, supervisor consultant and trainer. He is also a staff member at Metanoia Institute where he teaches on the Person-Centred Counselling and the Integrative Psychotherapy programmes.

Patrick Hughes, Ph.D., C.Psychol., M.Inst. Group Analysis, UKCP, conducted and developed Diploma and Masters courses in the psychology and practice of counselling over a period of twenty years at the University of Reading. Since his retirement, he has continued to practise as a group analyst and counselling psychologist, and has also acted as examiner and consultant to a large number of counsellor training courses.

Michael Jacobs, MA, is Director of the Counselling and Psychotherapy Programme in the University of Leicester, Fellow of the British Association for Counselling, a registered psychotherapist, and a trainer and supervisor. His books include *The Presenting Past* (1985), *Psychodynamic Counselling in Action* (1988), *D. W. Winnicott* (1995), and *The Care Guide* (1995).

Jennifer M. Kidd, Ph.D., C.Psychol., AFBPsS, is a senior lecturer in the Department of Organizational Psychology, Birkbeck College, University of London. Prior to this she worked as a career counsellor in further education and as a research fellow at the National Institute for Careers Education and Counselling. She is a chartered occupational psychologist and her main areas of research and publication are career guidance and career development.

Colin Lago, (DASE, Keele), M.Ed. is Director of the Counselling Service at the University of Sheffield. He originally trained as an engineer before becoming a youth worker in London and a teacher in Jamaica. He has published training videos, papers and books, some of these with Joyce Thompson (see below). He is a former chairperson of both the Association for Student Counselling and RACE, and has recently been awarded a fellowship of the British Association for Counselling. Colin and Joyce are co-authors of *Race, Culture and Counselling* (1996).

Pittu Laungani is a Reader in Psychology at South Bank University, London. His major research interests are in the field of cross-cultural psychology of health, illness, death and bereavement. He has written and edited five books, the most recent being *Death and Bereavement Across Cultures* (Routledge, 1996).

John McLeod is Professor of Counselling Studies at Keele University. His interests encompass narrative approaches to counselling and psychotherapy, the evaluation of counselling outcomes, and the relevance of research for practice. Recent publications include *An Introduction to Counselling* (1992) and *Doing Counselling Research* (1994).

Gladeana McMahon is a BAC accredited counsellor and recognized counselling supervisor, a BABCP accredited cognitive-behavioural psychotherapist and is UKCP registered. She has run a private practice since 1988 providing counselling, training, and counselling supervision and has worked in a variety of voluntary, medical, statutory and private-sector settings. She is author of *Starting Your Own Private Practice* (1994).

Mike Megranahan was a psychologist and European Operations Director for EHR. He was Chair of the Association for Counselling at Work and of the Employee Assistance Professionals Association. He was presented with an award for his contribution to employee assistance programmes development in Britain. Widely published, he was also Editor of *Employee Counselling Today* and *Employee Assistance Programme International*.

Stephen Palmer is a chartered counselling psychologist, a UKCP registered psychotherapist and a certified supervisor of rational emotive behaviour therapy. He is Founder Director of the Centre for Stress Management, London. He was formerly Managing Editor of *Counselling*, published by the British Association for Counselling (BAC) and vice-chair of the BAC publications sub-committee. He is a BAC Fellow and is widely published on counselling and stress management. His recent books include *Counselling: The BAC Counselling Reader* co-edited with Sheila Dainow and Pat Milner (1996), and *Dealing With People Problems at Work* with Tim Burton (1996).

Barbara Pearce, B.Sc. (Maths), is Director of CCDU Training and Consultancy (formerly the Counselling and Career Development Unit) at the University of Leeds. Although fully supportive of individual work within counselling she is particularly interested in applying counselling skills within an organizational framework, a focus for the work of CCDU over the last twenty years. In this context counselling is an important management tool and the basis of many generic organizational skills.

Bernard Ratigan, Ph.D., is Consultant Adult Psychotherapist and Director of Training in Nottingham Psychotherapy Unit and also co-ordinates the HIV Psychotherapy Service in the Department of Genito-Urinary Medicine, City Hospital, Nottingham. He is a member of the Training Committee of the South Trent Training in Dynamic Psychotherapy, a UKCP registered psychoanalytic psychotherapist, a BAC accredited counsellor and a member of the Association for Lesbian, Gay and Bisexual Psychologies. His major clinical interests are in working with gay men, forensic psychotherapy and group therapy. He has written a number of papers on group therapy, HIV and homosexuality.

Jane Read is an accredited member of the British Association of Sexual and Marital Therapy, and a psychotherapist registered with the United Kingdom Council for Psychotherapy. She is Associate Director of the M.Sc. and Diploma training programmes in Human Sexuality at St George's Hospital, London. Jane Read has a special interest in people with fertility problems, and is the author of several articles on fertility and sexuality issues, as well as *Counselling for Fertility Problems* (1995). Jane has over twenty years experience of working with sexual, relationship, and fertility issues.

Fred Roach, Ph.D., AFBPsS, C.Psychol., is a consultant clinical psychologist and Listed Law Society Directory of Expert Witness. One of his main therapeutic interests is cognitive behavioural therapy, including hypnosis and brief psychotherapy. He is currently Head of Psychology Specialty for Alcohol and Substance Misuse, and Forensic Psychology Services within Surrey Heartlands NHS Trust. Dr Roach also runs a private counselling, assessment and psychological treatment service through his forensic and clinical psychology consultancy.

Thomas A. Schroder, M.Sc, C.Psychol., is a clinical psychologist/psychotherapist. He is currently working for Southern Derbyshire Mental Health (NHS) Trust, heading the Psychology Specialty of a multidisciplinary Psychotherapy Service. His previous appointments include a spell as Regional Tutor consultant with the National Marriage Guidance Council (now Relate). He teaches psychotherapy at Derby University and on the South Trent Training in Dynamic Psychotherapy.

Michael Scott, Ph.D., C.Psychol., AFBPsS, is a chartered counselling psychologist and recent author of *Developing Cognitive-Behavioural Counselling* (1995) and *Counselling for Post-Traumatic Stress Disorder* (1992) as well as numerous papers. He is a consultant psychologist to, amongst others, ICI and Merseyside Police and also works in the NHS in primary care. In addition he is Honorary Research Fellow in the Department of Psychology at the University of Manchester.

Julia Segal, MA, is Senior Counsellor at the Central Middlesex Hospital Multiple Sclerosis Unit, Central Middlesex Hospital, London and is active within BAC. Since 1979 in her counselling, teaching, and writing she has sought to find ways in which the ideas of the psychoanalyst Melanie Klein can be used to make sense of thoughts, emotions, and behaviour in every-day situations.

Catherine Shea, Lecturer in counselling at the University of Durham, started her professional life in social work, going on to train and work as a counsellor in a variety of contexts – marriage, student and drug/alcohol counselling in particular. She has also at various levels pursued further academic study in the areas of literature and theology. Her current research interests draw on both these elements of her experience. She is currently writing on the use of 'self' in qualitative research and on the interface between theatre and therapy.

Eddy Street, Ph.D., is a chartered clinical and counselling psychologist. He is currently Consultant Clinical Psychologist at the Children's Centre, Llandough Hospital Penarth, Vale of Glamorgan, where he works thera-peutically with children and families. His private practice is focused on marital and individual counselling and supervision. He has taught exten-sively on themes-related skills development and the 'self' of the counsel-lor. His published work include *Counselling for Family Problems* (1994) and *Brief Therapeutic Consultations* (1996) written with Jim Downey.

Léonie Sugarman is a chartered occupational psychologist with a parti-cular interest in issues of life-span development. She is Senior Lecturer in Psychology at University College of St Martin, Lancaster. She has been on the editorial board of the *British Journal of Guidance and Counselling* for many years, and Associate Editor since 1986.

Carole Sutton is a chartered counselling psychologist and Principal Lec-turer in Psychology at De Montfort University, Leicester, where she teaches psychology and counselling skills. She is particularly interested in the evaluation of practice and is a former Chair of the Research Panel of the British Association for Counselling. Her publications include *A Hand-book of Research for the Helping Professions* (1987) and *Social Work, Community work and Psychology* (1995).

Kasia Szymanska is a chartered counselling psychologist and a UKCP registered psychotherapist. She is an Associate Editor of *Counselling Psychology Review* and works as a psychologist, trainer, and supervisor. Her particular areas of interest include therapist and client sexual contact, anxiety and stress management.

Joyce Thompson was born and spent her childhood years in Jamaica. She spent all her working life in the UK and has recently retired to Jamaica from a post as Senior Education Manager with the West Lambeth Health Authority. She is a former chairperson of RACE (Race and Culture Education and Counselling), a sub-committee of the British Association for Counselling. Upon retirement she received lifelong membership of BAC in recognition of her outstanding services over the years.

Richard Velleman is Director of Research and Development and Head of the Addictions Service with the Bath Mental Health Care Trust. He is also Senior Lecturer in Psychology at the University of Bath. His research and practice interests centre on the families of problem drinkers and drug users, the use of volunteer counsellors in the substance abuse fields, the development of counselling practice, and the evaluation of services for people with alcohol and drug problems. He was a member of th Alcohol Concern Executive from its formation in 1983 until 1991, and spearheaded the creation of the current Volunteer Alcohol Counsellors Training Scheme. He has written on *Counselling for Alcohol Problems* (1992) and is currently writing a book on the children of problem drinkers.

Susan Wallbank, NDD, Dip.Soc., is Counselling Coordinator for Cruse Bereavement Care with special responsibility for the management of the Cruse Bereavement Line. She has written extensively on various aspects of bereavement. Her work includes *The Empty Bed - Bereavement and the Loss of Love* (1992), *Facing Grief - Bereavement and the Young Adult* (1991) and *Counselling by Letter* (1994). She represents 'nearly there' voluntary organizations on the United Kingdom Register of Counsellors Executive Committee.

Ray Woolfe is course director for the Diploma/MA in Counselling at Keele University and is the author of many articles and a number of books on counselling and counselling psychology. He has recently published a *Handbook of Counselling Psychology* (with Windy Dryden).

James Wright is a senior consultant with human resources consultants Focus Ltd., whom he joined from the commericial sector with experience of personnel management and development. His current responsibilities include management of Employee Assistance Programmes. James' counselling training began with the psychodynamic approaches, developing further into the cognitive-behavioural, particularly rational emotive behaviour counselling.

Foreword

In counselling, the personal issues of one party, the client or clients, are held in mind by another, the counsellor, and worked on together. The same process happens in psychotherapy. In a rapidly changing world where old social certainties no longer hold sway, where difference easily stimulates fear and suspicion, and where the gulf between the 'haves' and the 'have nots', the technologically skilled and the unskilled, the socially supported and the isolated, the genetically favoured and the disadvantaged, widens, these alterations to the fabric of our society undermine the readiness of one person to aid another and erode the institutions that used to provide such action. While in nature collaboration and symbiosis are as successful evolutionary strategies as competition, the latter is being elevated into *the* political metaphor for our time.

Despite these changes, the capacity for social concern is not extinct. New institutions have evolved to express social interest. One of these is the British Association for Counselling. Over the twenty years of its life, the Assocation has been concerned with the well-being of the activity which we call counselling, evolving standards for practice and training, pressing forward the elaboration of theory, and latterly becoming more active in testing the validity of practice through research. The intention is to develop the field of counselling so that clients can receive ethical, appropriate and effective counselling. This handbook reflects the breadth of the field and provides a systematic guide to mode or arena of practice, the special requirements of particular settings, and themes to be considered in work where race, gender and disability, to mention but three, are crucial dimensions.

Counselling is a human activity which attests to the willingness of one person to help another in their psychological journey through life. The work is not easy. In entering into a counselling relationship, the counsellor opens him or herself to an empathic experience of the hopes, fears and doubts of the client, the set-backs and the strivings, the joys and the sadnesses. The counsellor puts at the service of the client this empathic understanding, a professional attitude, varying degrees of training and practical experience, and the insights of their own experience of living.

There is much to learn. Either in the role of volunteer or paid counsellor, theory, practice, ethics and research have to be studied. The *Handbook* provides a detailed, overview of the field. I commend it to trainees who are beginning a demanding professional journey and the trained who want to maintain their skills.

Mark Aveline
President,
British Association for Counselling

Preface

Why a handbook of counselling? In the past three decades counselling has become a profession. Many thousands of individuals are either working as counsellors or using counselling skills in a variety of settings. Both the beginner and the experienced counsellor need a reliable handbook to turn to for background information or guidance at some time in their career. This book provides a 'state-of-the-art' overview of the theory and practice underlying the mainstream world of counselling. It will interest trainers and supervisors working in the field of counselling as well as the layperson wishing to learn about different aspects of counselling.

The first edition, the *Handbook of Counselling in Britain*, was published in 1989 and edited by Windy Dryden, David Charles-Edwards and Ray Woolfe. This second edition, with the shorter title *Handbook of Counselling*, has been fully up-dated and revised. Six additional chapters have been included covering topical subjects such as brief counselling and trauma counselling. The *Handbook* seeks to offer a comprehensive review of the main fields of counselling activity in Britain today, and is published in association with the British Association for Counselling (BAC). The book has almost forty contributors and each chapter reflects their individual opinions. Understandably their views may not necessarily represent the views of BAC.

The handbook is divided into five parts: Introduction, Arenas, Settings, Themes, and Issues. To give a degree of coherence, each chapter in Parts Two to Five (with the exception of Chapter 31) has an organizing framework consisting of Principles, Issues, and Future Developments.

In the Introduction Ray Woolfe focuses on the present and future of counselling in Britain. In Chapter 2 Léonie Sugarman and Ray Woolfe discuss counselling in the context of the lifecycle. In Part Two the practice of counselling is described as it occurs in the major arenas, i.e. individual, couples, family, and group counselling. In Part Three there are nine chapters focusing on counselling in different settings, including private practice, the voluntary sector, education, medical settings, and organizations.

The last chapter in this part concentrates on brief counselling and includes counselling in time-limited settings. In Part Four, thirteen thematic topics are covered ranging from gender, race, and sexual orientation to careers counselling and counselling for trauma and post-traumatic stress disorder. Finally, Part Five focuses on three issues: research and evaluation in counselling, counsellor–client exploitation, and an overall picture of the professional issues in counselling.

I have included in the appendices the current (1997) BAC codes of ethics for counsellors, the use of counselling skills, for supervisors of counsellors, and for trainers in counselling and counselling skills. Appendix 5 covers the ethical guidelines for monitoring, evaluation, and research in counselling. Even if the reader is not a member of BAC these codes of ethics may provide useful guidelines into what is now considered a minimum standard of practice for individuals involved in the field of counselling.

As stated previously, this book has been published in association with BAC. One of the original aims of BAC, laid down in 1976 and later incorporated into the organization's Memorandum in 1987 when it became a company limited by guarantee with charitable status is:

> to promote and provide education and training for counsellors working in either professonal or voluntary settings, whether full or part time, with a view to raising the standards of counselling for the benefit of the community and in particular for those who are the recipients of counselling.

The *Handbook of Counselling* helps to maintain BAC's commitment to this original aim. It provides useful information for BAC's 15,250 individual and 908 organizational members.

Details about individuals or agencies offering counselling services or about training courses in counselling or counselling skills have not been included as such information frequently changes. However, if you seek current details you should contact the British Association for Counselling at 1 Regent Place, Rugby, Warwickshire, CV21 2PJ.

Stephen Palmer

Abbreviations

ABC	Association of Black Counsellors
ACW	Association for Counselling at Work (BAC)
APCC	Association for Pastoral Care and Counselling (BAC)
ASC	Association for Student Counselling (BAC)
ASMT	Association of Sexual and Marital Therapists
BAC	British Association for Counselling
BACUP	British Association for Cancer United Patients
BPS	British Psychological Society
CCDU	Counselling and Career Development Unit (Leeds University)
CEPEC	Centre for Professional Employment Counselling
CIE	Counselling in Education (BAC)
CMS	Counselling in Medical Settings (BAC)
COSCA	Confederation of Scottish Counselling Agencies
CRUSE	National Organization for the Widowed and their Children
CVPE	Certificate of Pre-vocational Education
DFEE	Department for Education and Employment
DHA	District Health Authority
EAP	Employee Assistance Programme
EAPA	Employee Assistance Professionals Association
FPC	Family Practitioner Committee
IPD	Institute of Personnel Development
ISDD	Institute for the Study of Drug Dependence
MS	Multiple sclerosis
MSC	Manpower Services Commission
NHS	National Health Service
NLP	Neuro-linguistic programming
NMGC	National Marriage Guidance Council (now known as Relate: National Marriage Guidance)
PAPI	Perception and Preference Inventory
PSRFC	Personal/Sexual/Relationship/Family Counselling (BAC)
RACE	Race and Cultural Education in Counselling (BAC)

SEPI	Society for the Exploration of Psychotherapy Integration
TA	Transactional Analysis
TC	Training Commission
TVEI	Technical and Vocational Education Initiative
UKCP	United Kingdom Council for Psychotherapy
WPF	Westminster Pastoral Foundation
YTS	Youth Training Scheme

Part one

Introduction

Chapter one

Counselling in Britain: present position and future prospects

Ray Woolfe

Introduction

The aim of this chapter is to provide an account of the nature and range of counselling as it is practised in Britain in the mid 1990s. This process will encompass discussion of the major issues facing counselling at the present time. In particular, the chapter aims to:

(1) offer a definition of counselling and discuss its universality;
(2) examine the extent to which it is legitimate to regard counselling as a homogeneous, unitary activity;
(3) comment upon the major counselling paradigms;
(4) explore the boundary between counselling and related disciplines;
(5) identify the settings in which counselling is practised, the counsellors and their clients;
(6) outline and discuss key issues within counselling at the present time;
(7) articulate the role played by the British Association for Counselling.

Defining counselling

Counselling is still a relatively new activity. The British Association for Counselling, now widely recognized as the voice of counselling in Britain, came into being as recently as 1977 having metamorphosized out of a Standing Conference for the Advancement of Counselling. This in its turn had been created in 1970 through the auspices of the National Council for Voluntary Organisations.

In the intervening years, counselling has come a long way, yet there is still no copyright or patent on the use of the term. In common parlance, it is frequently understood as a form of advice giving and this is legitimized by the continuing practice of dictionaries, one of which defines counselling as 'specifically a therapeutic procedure in which a usually trained person adopts a supportive non-judgemental role . . . or gives advice on practical problems' (Brown 1993). The term is now widely employed in this manner.

For example, in the area of business and finance, one comes across references to such activities as debt counselling and double-glazing counselling.

Perhaps this is not surprising and, in a slightly odd way, a compliment to the influence of counselling. At root, counselling is based upon communication, listening and interpersonal skills. These are essential in a wide range of interpersonal situations, not least in helping activities. Many helping activities arise spontaneously as when a friend, relative or colleague suddenly confronts us with a personal problem or stressful issue. These skills then come into play. However, the key difference between events such as these or the approach of the company representative lies in intentionality. Counselling differs from friendship in that its focus is not on the provision of tea and sympathy or on advice giving and it differs from selling in that its aim is not to manipulate another person into making a purchase.

In contrast, counselling is an activity engaged in deliberately, with a clear intention and operating according to a clearly defined set of rules.

> People become engaged in counselling when a person, occupying regularly or temporarily the role of counsellor, offers or agrees explicitly to offer time, attention and respect to another person or persons temporarily in the role of client.
>
> (BAC 1985: 1).

The use of the term 'explicitly' is, according to the same document, 'the dividing line between the counselling task and *ad hoc* counselling and is the major safeguard of the rights of the consumer' (BAC 1985: 2).

This definition of counselling provides a framework or reference point around which further discussion about the state of counselling in Britain can take place. Counselling requires rigorous definitions if it is to avoid the danger of becoming vague and diffuse. It is particularly necessary given the existence of an accreditation scheme for counsellors within BAC and even more importantly in light of the existence of the United Kingdom Register for Counsellors.

Having made this point, it is also neccessary to indicate that the use of precise definitions and the development of professional boundaries raises a number of important issues with which counselling generally and BAC in particular will continue to wrestle. These derive primarily from the fact that the activity of counselling is not confined to the work carried out by those people formally designated as counsellors. This is reflected in the title of BAC: an organization for *counselling* and not just for *counsellors*. Many people, paid and voluntary, with a vast variety of titles and forms of professional identification would claim to be practising counselling in the course of their work, though their primary identification might well not be 'counsellor'. Some of them have had considerable counselling training.

Without their contribution, counselling would be a very restricted and exclusive activity.

In practice, the distinction between the activity known as counselling and the practice of counselling skills within another form of contract may not always be easy to draw. This may particularly be the case in situations where counsellor and client hold other roles in relation to each other. For example, a manager may have the task of acting as counsellor to a worker for whom s/he has line management responsibility; or a tutor may counsel a student with whom s/he has a teaching role. The BAC definition attempts to resolve such conflict by emphasising that 'clarification of the opportunity offered, in a way that the client can understand, differentiates the counselling task from other mutual responsibilities in the perception of both client and counsellor' (BAC 1985: 2). However, the tidiness of such theoretical definitions may not always be easy to replicate in the complex and often confusing empirical world in which we live.

Professional boundaries

The previous discussion addresses the need to distinguish between situations in which there is a clear counselling contract as opposed to those in which counselling skills are practised without such a contract. In short, this represents a boundary issue concerning what is and what is not counselling. However, there is another key boundary issue for counselling concerning its relationship to cognate professional disciplines, particularly psychotherapy and counselling psychology. In considering this topic, it is appropriate to remember that while historically there are clear differences, operationally the differences have become muddled (Carroll 1991).

Counselling and psychotherapy

There is long running debate about the difference between counselling and psychotherapy. There are those such as Patterson (1974) who conclude that there are no essential differences and Truax and Carkhuff (1967) use the terms interchangeably. However, the following points are often made in attempts to differentiate between the two processes. They do not necessarily represent the views of the author of this chapter. Inevitably, there is some overlap between the individual views.

(a) Psychotherapy is concerned with personality change whereas counselling is concerned with helping an individual to utilize his or her own coping resources (Tyler 1967). Clarkson (1994) suggests that psychotherapy can be seen to emphasize intervention, treatment and reconstruction whereas counselling has an enabling and facilitating focus. However, Nelson-Jones (1982) argues that mobilizing coping resources might well be considered as personality change.

(b) Psychotherapists work with people who have histories of pathology and psychological disturbance. In contrast counselling involves a process of problem solving with people who are basically emotionally healthy but who are being confronted by a temporary life problem or issue, related to a crisis or developmental stage.

(c) The focus of work for many psychotherapists is the transference between the two parties and the unconscious world of the client; the past life of the client re-experienced in the present. In contrast, counsellors work in a person-centred manner with the here and now relationship between therapist and client as the lynchpin.

(d) Psychotherapy is a long-term process, whereas counselling essentially has a short-term focus.

(e) Psychotherapy training is based upon personal analysis combined with the development of diagnostic and analytical skills. In comparison, counselling training is concerned less centrally with personal analysis and more with the process of goal setting and the tasks involved in achieving these. This view of counselling would be supported by the emphasis placed in counselling training over the past fifteen years on the work of Gerard Egan.

(f) Psychotherapy practice is rooted in psychodynamic theory, whereas the theory underpinning counselling is largely derived from and inspired by humanistic writers such as Carl Rogers.

(g) Psychotherapists work largely in clinical and medical settings, while counsellors work across a wider range of arenas, including educational institutions and the workplace. It follows that psychotherapists tend to refer to patients, while counsellors talk about their clients. On the other hand, an increasing number of counsellors have found employment within the primary health care setting.

There can be no final answer to the question of whether counselling and psychotherapy are one and the same thing. In examining the difference, Clarkson (1994) lays emphasis upon the focus of psychotherapy being what she describes as 'revolutionary change' as opposed to the 'evolutionary change' which is the concern of counselling. She sees each as emphasizing different skills, goals and methodologies. However, rather than debating the validity or otherwise of this point of view, it seems more constructive to emphasize personal identity and to reflect that in the world in which we live, some people identify themselves as counsellors, others as psychotherapists and some as both. For example the United Kingdom Council for Psychotherapy, which was founded in 1993 contains eight sections:

• Psychoanalytic and Psychodynamic Psychotherapy
• Behavioural Psychotherapy

- Family, Marital, and Sexual Therapy
- Humanistic and Integrative Psychotherapy
- Hypnotherapy
- Analytical Psychology
- Psychoanalytically Based Therapy with children
- Experiential Constructivist Therapies

It does not seem fanciful to suggest that members of the behavioural section for example might have more in common with cognitive-behavioural counsellors than they do with members of many of the other sections. The same could be said about almost every section. Personal identity is arguably more important than a theoretical debate over whether we are referring to the same or different activities. In the final resort, attempts to resolve the issue in terms of some overarching theoretical plan are probably futile. There are some differences, as Clarkson indicates, but both enterprises lay stress upon valuing the client as an individual, listening in an accepting and non-judgemental fashion and fostering the capacity for self-help. In practice as opposed to theory, such differences as do exist often lie in relatively mundane concerns with the nature and length of training, the settings in which people work and the problems and issues with which they are typically confronted.

Counselling and counselling psychology

Counselling psychology is a relative newcomer to the therapeutic scene, but one whose relationship with counselling is interesting to explore, particularly as it throws light upon some of the strengths and weaknesses of counselling in Britain at the present time. The historical development of counselling psychology in Britain since its first appearance in 1982 as a section within the British Psychological Society has been charted by Woolfe (1990 and 1996). He has identified a number of key factors underlying this development and its rapidity. These include:

- an increasing awareness among psychologists of the importance of the helping relationship as a significant variable in working with people;
- a growing questioning of the medical model of working with people across a wide range of helping professionals and corresponding acceptance of a more humanistic value system;
- an increasing emphasis in the work of helpers on promoting well-being rather than responding to sickness and pathology;
- a developing awareness of the need for a more articulated scientific basis for counselling.

Consideration of these factors illustrates both the strengths and the weaknesses of counselling in Britain (as well as the underlying strengths and weaknesses of psychology). On the one hand we can observe the strong roots of counselling in a humanistic value system and the increasing acceptance of this value system. On the other hand we can note its traditional lack of rigour in its approach to evaluating its own practices. (Barkham and Barker 1996, McLeod 1995, Elton Wilson and Barkham 1994). Evaluation is all too often still of the intuitive, hunch variety.

The underlying dynamic behind the growth of counselling psychology lies in a perceived need to bridge this gap, to understand counselling as both a science and an art. This has involved the development of a more interactive, process based, qualitative research methodology; see for example Toukmanian and Rennie (1992), McLeod (1994) and Barker *et al.* (1994). The development of research methods courses within Masters programmes in counselling is a reflection of this dynamic.

Counselling psychologists are first and foremost psychology graduates and underlying their practice is an emphasis upon the systematic application of psychological knowledge founded in a base of empirical research. It is argued, with some justification, that this knowledge base and understanding of research methodology is not accessible without a psychology degree.

It is appropriate to point out at this point that counselling psychology has its own boundary issues particularly concerning clinical psychology. Indeed, as some clinical psychology services now offer counselling to purchasers such as primary health care practices, there would appear to be points at which counselling and clinical psychology overlap. The overlapping of professional boundaries certainly does not end here. Many community psychiatric nurses provide counselling services and the list could be extended to include social workers, probation officers, occupational therapists, speech therapists and psychiatrists. This list is not exhaustive.

As with psychotherapy, the boundaries between counselling and counselling psychology are blurred and inexact. However, there seems no purpose in arguing whether these boundaries should or should not exist. The fact is that they are there and their existence is due to historical circumstances which cannot be changed. There are now over 250 chartered counselling psychologists listed in the Register of Chartered Psychologists held by the BPS. Therefore this group would appear to be a significant force in counselling practice in Britain at the present time.

Different traditions within counselling

What emerges from the previous discussion is that in examining the relationship between counselling and cognate disciplines, it is important to acknowledge their origins in different cultures, traditions and bodies of knowledge. However, even if we leave aside psychotherapy and counselling psychology, contemporary practice within counselling itself is anything but homogeneous and, on the contrary, manifests enormous diversity.

Dryden's handbook of individual therapies in Britain (1990) contains accounts of twelve major theoretical approaches:

- Psychodynamic (Freudian)
- Psychodynamic (Kleinian)
- Psychodynamic (Jungian)
- Adlerian
- Person-Centred
- Personal-Construct
- Existential
- Gestalt
- Transactional Analysis
- Cognitive
- Behaviour

Within this list, at least three major traditions are represented and each has influenced contemporary counselling practice in its own way. The following accounts are deliberately brief and concentrate on offering a flavour of the critique levelled at each paradigm plus a comment or two about its strengths.

The analytical/psychodynamic tradition

The analytical/psychodynamic tradition is frequently parodied as being a relic of nineteenth-century thought characterized by biological determinism, a pessimistic view of human nature, male-centredness, and a paternalistic and cold relationship between therapist and client. However, much of this criticism treats knowledge as something that is fixed and unchanging and fails to take account of the vast changes which have taken place in analytical and psychodynamic theory and practice.

Object relations and attachment theory have had an enormous influence on contemporary attitudes and understanding within this tradition, influenced by workers such as Bowlby (1969, 1973), Winnicott (1965) and Kohut (1971). The approaches associated with their theories of self- and ego-development form part of the basic training of most counsellors. The idea that the past influences the present and that crises in the present derive from unresolved developmental conflicts is heavily influential in much counselling practice even amongst those who would not define themselves primarily as psychodynamic counsellors. The notions of transference and counter-transference and of working with the transference also inform the work of many counsellors.

In addition, the paradigm is based upon a well-developed theory of child development. While there may be dispute about aspects of this theory, about the existence of stages of psycho-sexual development for example and about the importance of sexuality in the growing child, the fact that there is a detailed theory of personality development distinguishes it in particular from humanistic approaches.

The cognitive-behavioural tradition

The cognitive-behavioural tradition reflects the influence of mainstream psychology. The basic idea is very simple. Behaviour is seen as the product of learning; therefore that which is learned can be unlearned. People respond to stimuli, often quite unconsciously, and the response will, if reinforced, be likely to persist. This applies to all areas of life. For example people can learn to be helpless if their helpfulness is reinforced by significant others expressing sympathy and paying them lots of attention (Seligman 1975). Eysenck (1976) suggests that we should look at the symptoms of those in need as the product of learned behaviour.

Over the past ten years, the work of behavioural counsellors has widened to incorporate the role of cognition. This involves examining the relationship between the way in which a person labels his or her situation and his or her subsequent emotional and behavioural reaction to that situation. Thus, for example, a person who appraises a forthcoming examination as a potentially catastrophic event is more likely to experience anxiety problems when it takes place than the person who perceives the event as a challenge. In this formulation, the concept of 'appraisal' is critical (Lazarus 1978). A variant of cognitive-behavioural therapy that has received much attention, inspired by the work of Albert Ellis (1962), argues that behaviour can be changed by encouraging the client to dispute irrational beliefs, thus enabling him to think more logically and rationally.

The behavioural paradigm has been heavily criticized as de-humanizing individuals by ignoring internal processes such as feeling and thinking. While the addition of cognitive factors dilutes this criticism, it is still argued that the approach focuses on alleviating symptoms rather than causes and ignores deeper, underlying issues. It is also argued that the rather directive, teaching style of the therapist is contrary to the non-directive philosophy which is widely held to be central to the value system which underlies counselling.

On the other side of the coin, the approach has the great merit of not blaming the client if the work is not making progress. It is common practice among counsellors to argue that if a particular therapy does not work, then the client is unsuited to that therapy. In contrast, the cognitive-behavioural position is that if the therapy does not work, it is because there is something wrong with the method used and that this needs to be adapted. Such research as there is on counselling outcomes indicates that, at least in the short term, cognitive-behavioural therapies appear to be more effective than other therapies across a wide range of conditions including anxiety states, phobias, and depression.

The humanistic tradition

The person-centred approach is inspired by the work of Carl Rogers (1951) and in particular the importance placed upon the so-called core conditions of empathy, unconditional positive regard (warmth) and authenticity/congruence/genuineness. Person-centred practice derives from the philosophy of humanistic psychology, which has been described as a 'third-force' in psychology (Maslow 1968; Rowan 1976). Its primary characteristic is its optimistic view of human nature. Thus the object of the person-centred approach is to help the person to become what s/he is capable of becoming or, as Maslow put it, to achieve 'self-actualization'.

A strength of the humanistic approach lies in the respect it affords the individual. It takes the view that each person knows what is best for them. This value base leads to the development of the notion of the therapist as a facilitator and of counselling as a process of authentically being with the client in the here and now rather than something one does to or for the client. The humanistic value system has been enormously valuable in offering a corrective to the medical model of helping based upon notions such as illness, symptoms, labelling and emotional neutrality. In addition, while it was Rogers himself who coined the term 'core conditions', these are now widely accepted across the counselling world and elsewhere as the basis of an effective working alliance between counsellor and client.

On the negative side, concepts such as 'fully functioning person' and 'self-actualisation' emerged out of the leisured, affluent, optimistic world of Californian America in the 1950s and '60s. However they have a somewhat hollow ring to them in the world of the late twentieth century, in which issues such as homelessness, physical and sexual abuse of women and children, unemployment, and racial prejudice feature strongly. Maslow's well-known pyramid of need (Maslow 1968) would suggest that without a base of physical and emotional security, emotional development is difficult if not impossible. Moreover, there is little empirical evidence to support the notion that people are somehow intrinsically good. Finally, there is an increasing emphasis in counselling on models of time-limited therapy for which more directive, focused procedures are usually advocated (Murgatroyd and Woolfe 1982).

Egan and the spirit of the age

Arguably the most influential figure in the field of counselling training over the past fifteen years has been Gerard Egan. Egan has built upon the work of Rogers by embedding his ideas in a hierarchical, stage model which lays great emphasis upon action to achieve goals. In doing this he also takes on board behavioural concepts such as rewards and reinforcements. Egan's book on the skilled helper first appeared in 1975 and has run to five editions (Egan 1994).

The success of his work lies in its congruence with the spirit of the age, particularly its emphasis upon the acquisition of skills and upon acting and doing rather than just developing self-awareness. The development of a National Vocational Qualification in counselling represents a logical result of an emphasis upon counselling as a series of skills in action rather than as a way of being with a client. More generally, this discussion illustrates the desirability of locating all counselling theory and practice in its social, economic and political context (Woolfe 1982). Without in any way diminishing the value of time-limited therapy, it is logical to argue that the contemporary interest in brief therapy reflects a society in which through-put and value for money are emphasized. The work of Freud and Rogers and indeed of all writers is rooted in their respective cultures and reflects the values of these cultures.

A patchwork quilt

Not all the approaches listed by Dryden (1990) fit easily into one of the three paradigms outlined above. Some writers would link the humanistic and existential traditions even though they have rather different views of human nature, others would separate them. Some would argue for a fourth paradigm based upon a transpersonal and spiritual dimension (Rowan 1990). Transactional analysis is influenced both by analytical developmental theory and by a social-psychological concern with the analysis of social as well as intra-psychic transactions. Gestalt theory is seen by Patterson (1986) as deriving from a mixture of Gestalt psychology (a concern with configuration and integration), an existential emphasis upon individual responsibility for thoughts, feelings and actions in the here and now, and from Zen Buddhist concerns with people discovering their true natures. Placing therapies into categories is not always simple.

In a contemporary world often described as post-modernist (Woolfe 1995) where grand theories are out of fashion and where the emhasis is upon flexibility, it is perhaps not surprising to find that eclecticism and integration increasingly feature strongly in discussions of methodology. Perhaps the day of the pure theory is drawing to a close.

An emerging profession

Counselling is a broad church. It includes people who work full-time as counsellors, people who work part-time and people who work voluntarily. It includes those who are in salaried employment and those who are self-employed. It includes those whose primary professional identification is as counsellors and those whose primary identification lies elsewhere but who counsel in the course of their work. It includes those who would claim to be counsellors and those who would be regarded primarily as employing counselling skills. It includes people who are accredited by the British Association for Counselling and those without this qualification. It includes people who work in statutory agencies, people who work in agencies in the private sector and people who work in voluntary agencies. It includes those who identify strongly with a particular theory or school and consider other theories inadequate, if not downright bad, and those who take a more open, eclectic stance. It includes those who have undertaken large amounts of personal development work, including experience as a client, and those who have not. It contains those who are radical and have a concern with the social implications of counselling and those with a more conservative viewpoint who argue that counselling is about personal not political change. It includes those whose focus is on counselling as a professional activity and those who perceive counselling in missionary terms as a gift to be given.

Inevitably within such heterogeneity, there are different and sometimes competing interests and priorities. A past executive officer of BAC identified a key task of the organization as reconciling a 'tension between the pulling-together spirit and divisiveness' (Charles-Edwards 1988).

Considering the organization in the round, Charles-Edwards suggests that those with most energy for BAC have tended to be employed counsellors and consequently the organization's energies have been disproportionately geared to full-time counsellors rather than those employing counselling or pastoral care skills in their work. He goes on to suggest that there is a danger within BAC of fostering the concept that counselling should become highly professionalized, which would result in those not formally trained being squeezed out. He percives this as a threat to what he describes as the 'ecumenicism' of BAC.

These words were written in 1988 and the growth in the organization in the intervening period from around 4,000 to over 12,000 individual members (BAC 1995: 4) seems to offer evidence that these dangers have been avoided. On the other hand, the emergence of a register provides a new challenge in holding counselling together.

United Kingdom Register of Counsellors

The Register represents an attempt to create a single, nationally recognized system of professional self-regulation. A significant impetus to this process came from the desire to protect counsellors in terms of future job mobility in the light of the move towards an open labour market within the European Union. However, other powerful forces were and still are at work. These include the need to protect and inform the public, provide employers and insurance companies with information about counselling standards and offer experienced counsellors recognition of their competence. Overall, the Register goes some way towards answering the criticism frequently levelled at counselling, that it is an unregulated profession.

The existence of the Register alongside others such as those of the United Kingdom Council for Psychotherapy and British Psychological Society raises the need for interdisciplinary dialogue about the comparability of training programmes and qualifications.

Accreditation

An accreditation scheme for individual counsellors is now well established within BAC. In addition accreditation schemes have also come into being for individual supervisors and trainers. On top of this, a course recognition scheme underpins the development of standards in counselling training courses. There can be no question, therefore, that accreditation of individuals and recognition of training programmes has a firm and secure base and in an emerging profession is here to stay. These schemes are buttressed by a series of codes of ethics and practice for counsellors, users of counselling skills, supervisors, and trainers.

Nevertheless, as this chapter has indicated, there is always likely to be a tension between, on the one hand, the professionalized end of counselling and, on the other hand, those who emphasize the use of counselling skills. In addition there are those who lay emphasis upon counselling as a movement espousing particular values rather than a profession. In a survey of the views and attitudes of BAC members carried out in 1993 (BAC 1993), the main dissatisfaction with the organization concerned the accreditation process which was described as slow, secretive and prone to mistakes.

The balance between the various interest groups within counselling is not static and the present situation is perhaps best summarized by Frankland (1995) speaking as Chair of the BAC Individual Accreditation Group:

Until recently accreditation has often triggered hostility and carping criticism of the motives and standards of those who created, developed and currently work within the scheme. At last I sense a more positive feeling: that we have something valuable, operated by sound people with honourable motives which will always need some adjustments but which deserves to be supported as a flexible and worthwhile system of identification of mature professional practitioners.

National Vocational Qualifications

It would not be appropriate to write a chapter on the state of counselling in Britain without some mention, albeit a brief one, of National Vocational Qualifications. This has generated an enormous amount of debate within the world of counselling. On the one hand the argument has been that to reduce the complexities of counselling to a set of skills-based competencies is dehumanizing and/or impossible. It fails to take into account the values and personal dispositions which are such a key feature of counselling. On the other hand it has been argued that explicit definition of competencies is necessary if counselling standards are to improve and counselling is to receive more central government support. The development work of the National Lead Body for Advice, Guidance, Counselling and Psychotherapy demanded an enormous amount of energy from the world of counselling and standards have been defined and will gradually become included in qualifications.

It is possible to speculate that counselling training programmes will become increasingly focused on the delivery of a National Vocational Qualification. Funding incentives are likely to facilitate this process.

It is too early as yet to talk about the success or failure of NVQs as they relate to counselling. However, it does seem appropriate to offer a personal view that the work done within the Lead Body has exceeded the expectations of many in the sophistication with which it has been able to identify elements of competence in counselling without losing sight of the importance of the counsellor's values and attitudes.

Counselling sectors

The extent to which counselling is a broad church can be seen by looking at the various divisions which exist within BAC. This provides information about the groups of people who deliver counselling and about the cohorts who receive it. The divisions are as follows:

- Association for Counselling at Work (ACW)
- Association for Pastoral Care and Counselling (APCC)
- Association for Student Counselling (ASC)
- Counselling in Education (CIE)
- Counselling in Medical Settings (CMS)
- Personal, Sexual, Relationship, Family (PSRF)
- Race and Cultural Education in Counselling (RACE)

In the accounts which follow, some information about divisional aims has been culled from unpublished and undated (c.1995) documentation sent by BAC to all individuals who apply for membership, entitled 'Invitation to Membership'.

Association for Counselling at Work

This division has over 800 members (BAC 1995: 9) and reflects the growth of interest in counselling in the workplace. Its aim is to promote the practice of counselling and the use of counselling skills in work-related settings.

This is arguably one of the fields in which there is most potential for the employment of counsellors. The development of employee assistance programmes (EAPs) has been facilitated by the realization that counselling is a relatively cheap option in facilitating the health of stressed employees. Reddy (1987) suggests that in-company counselling services pay off in commercial terms and that the number of such schemes is growing, though still small in relation to the USA where over 4,000 companies operate EAPs. However a baser motive for development arises from the growing fear companies have of being faced with litigation for damage to emotional health, and as a requirement for the provision of insurance. More positively, a number of large organizations in Britain have established in-house counselling schemes and there is evidence that these have been successful in reducing absenteeism and lowering levels of stress. Extensive research has been carried out on a scheme established by the Post Office (Cooper *et al*. 1990).

The spread of a free counselling service to shop-floor workers would appear to offer enormous potential in spreading the availability of counselling across a much wider section of the population than is able to access it at the present time.

Association for Pastoral Care and Counselling

This division, together with the Association for Student Counselling, was founded in 1970 as an informal association of people involved in training for pastoral care and counselling. Thus it existed before the establishment of BAC in 1977. It is concerned to raise standards both in the teaching and the exercise of pastoral care and counselling within the community. It aims to draw upon the insights of theology as well as the social sciences. It has a history of providing support for those practising pastoral care in Christian and Jewish contexts (BAC 1995: 9).

Association for Student Counselling

Founded in 1970, it now has over 700 members (BAC 1995: 10). Its aim is to promote student counselling as an integral aspect of the educational process within institutions of further and higher education. Over the years student counselling has probably been the most professionalized sector of counselling, providing full-time paid employment for a significant number of counsellors. This professionalism is manifested in the fact that the division, uniquely within BAC divisions, has its own accreditation scheme.

However, the financial crisis facing further and higher education in the mid-1990s has had an impact upon student counselling services and at the present time there is a growing and unfortunate tendency for educational establishments to replace their full-time counsellors with people employed on a sessional basis.

This tendency, if that is what it is, is regrettable. Counsellors working within large organizations such as universities are in a unique position to act as internal systems consultants. They are able to perform a developmental as well as a remedial role through being in a position to provide feedback to management about the impact of organizational structure and functioning upon the emotional welfare of its personnel (Ratigan 1989). The stresses experienced by students confronted with financial problems, poor housing conditions and the prospect of eventual unemployment makes any move away from full-time counsellors doubly unfortunate.

Counselling in Education

The membership of this division includes a range of people working in educational settings: teachers and lecturers, youth and community workers, advisors, administrators and inspectors, counsellors in schools and colleges, and educational support workers. The division operates a system of regional support groups to which almost a third of its membership belong (BAC 1995: 10). These are intended as a corrective to the isolation which many members feel in their places of work.

In the early days of counselling, there was frequent discussion about the developmental as opposed to the remedial function of counselling. A number of counsellors were appointed in schools and this appeared to be a promising domain for the future employment of counsellors. In the intervening years, financial pressures on schools have halted this process and the early promise has not materialized. Nevertheless, counselling has continued to maintain a firm foothold in schools and colleges.

Counselling in Medical Settings

This division has over 1300 members (BAC 1995: 11) and together with the field of workplace counselling, primary health care represents the likeliest area of expansion of opportunities for counsellor employment.

The division, however, covers the whole spectrum of medical settings including hospitals. general practice and health centres. In addition to those workers whose primary identification is as counsellor or psychotherapist it includes within its membership representatives of such groups as nurses,

health visitors, doctors, administrators, chaplains, social workers and complementary health practitioners.

As in the case of CIE, the division is addressing the sense of isolation
reported by members by setting up a regional networking scheme to
provide support and a forum for the exchange of information. This concern
with countering isolation is perhaps a reflection of the fact that many
graduates of counselling training courses are beginning to work independently on a freelance basis.

Personal, Sexual, Relationship, Family

The division has over 1000 members and with such an encompassing title
incorporates a wide range of interests and groups. Many of its members are
likely to practice professionally as counsellors and psychotherapists, while
at the other end of the spectrum it would incorporate counsellors working
on a voluntary basis in agencies such as Relate or Cruse. The division acts
as a pressure group for the promotion of professional interests.

Within counselling generally, the meaning of the terms 'professional'
and 'voluntary' is more complex than might appear at first sight. The
former is often treated as a superior state to the latter and a division is
drawn between paid and unpaid. Yet many voluntary workers are highly
trained, highly skilled and highly experienced. Counselling has a long
history of using volunteers and of voluntary agencies. For their part,
voluntary agencies may employ some paid workers either on a part-time
or full-time basis. Increasingly, with the decline in public subsidies, voluntary agencies are needing to become profit-making organizations, in order
to improve and sometimes just to maintain services to their clients. There is
also an issue of whether trainees in voluntary organizations should not be
made to contribute towards the cost of their training in that many use this
added value in order to seek paid employment elsewhere.

Race and Cultural Education in Counselling

This is the youngest of BAC's divisions and has 236 individual and 38
organizational members (BAC 1995: 12). The primary focus of the division
is on issues of race, including culture as it impinges on issues of race. Its
concerns include monitoring and confronting racism in the world of counselling and encouraging the development of race-related training methods
and materials and to facilitate cultural education in counselling.

The emergence of this division is to be greatly welcomed and it directs
us more generally towards a consideration of counselling as culturally
located in a particular time and place. Concepts such as 'fully-functioning
person' (Rogers 1951) and 'self-actualization' (Maslow 1968) have a
slightly hollow ring to them if one is the victim of racism, sexism, unem-

ployed or homeless (see Dryden *et al.* 1989). A society where the dominant ideological position of the New Right asserts that problems are rooted in individual motivation and attitudes rather than in social and economic factors poses a danger for counselling. This is that counselling becomes a substitute for social change and that counsellors may get sucked into a collusive process in which social problems come to be reframed as caused by lazy, deviant, awkward or under-socialized individuals and families. In this way, counselling runs a risk of being part of the problem as well as part of the solution.

Conclusion

In the eqiuivalent chapter of the first edition of this book (Dryden *et al.*.1989), the dilemmas involved in the move towards greater profession-alization of counselling were articulated. The move towards codification and standardization may be a crucial component of public recognition of counselling, but it poses the danger that many people will feel marginalized and left outside the 'new' boundaries. This dilemma is still there and will not go away as counselling begins to emerge as a profession with its own register of approved counsellors.

Chester (1985: 6), discussing the changes which were taking place in the then National Marriage Guidance Council, referred to the development of the organization from a 'marriage movement to service agency'. He defines the difference between the two in the following terms: 'the former has values to promote and members to affirm them, whilst the latter has objectives to achieve and personnel to implement them'. Here in a nutshell is encapsulated the steady process which counselling is experiencing. A point has now been reached where it is debatable whether it is appropriate to describe the patchwork quilt of counselling as a movement.

The world of counselling has become a complex enterprise, far broader than the work carried out by people with a formal designation as counsel-lors. However, each group has something to contribute. Without the com-mitment of professional counsellors, whose work often shades into psychotherapy, to improving standards of training, practice and supervi-sion, counselling would be a diffuse activity, lacking integration. Without the contribution of those people not designated as counsellors but who use counselling skills in their work, the benefits of counselling would be spread much more thinly throughout the population. Without the army of volun-teers working in community settings, many of whom perceive counselling skills as a vehicle for promoting self-confidence as a first step along the road to social change, counselling would become inward looking and less socially progressive.

The challenge for BAC in the years ahead will be to contain all these disparate and potentially centrifugal forces.

References

Barker, C., Pistrang, N. and Elliott, R. (1994) *Research Methods in Clinical and Counselling Psychology*, London: John Wiley.

Barkham, M. and Barker, C. (1996) 'Evaluating Counselling Psychology Practice' in R. Woolfe and W. Dryden (eds) *Handbook of Counselling Psychology*, London: Sage.

BAC (1985) *Counselling: Definition of Terms in use with Expansion and Rationale*, Rugby: BAC.

——(1993) 'Membership Survey 1993', *Counselling* 4(4): 243–4.

——(1995) 'Annual Report 1994/1995', Rugby: BAC.

Bowlby, J. (1969) *Attachment and Loss: Vol. 1 Attachment*, Harmondsworth: Penguin.

——(1973) *Attachment and Loss: Vol. 2 Separation*, Harmondsworth: Penguin.

Brown, L. (ed.) (1993) *The New Shorter Oxford English Dictionary*, Oxford: Oxford University Press.

Carkhuff, R. R. (1969) *Helping and Human Relations*, New York: Holt, Rinehart and Winston.

Carroll, M. (1991) 'Counsellor Training or Counsellor Education?: A Response', *Counselling* 2(3): 104–5.

Charles-Edwards, D. M. (1988) 'Counselling Management and BAC', *Counselling* 6(3): 3–11.

Chester, R. (1985) 'Shaping the Future: from Marriage Movement to Service Agency', *Marriage Guidance* Autumn, 5–15.

Clarkson P (1994) 'The Nature and Range of Psychotherapy' in P. Clarkson and M. Pokorny (eds) *The Handbook of Psychotherapy*, London: Routledge.

Cooper, C. L., Sadri, G., Allison, T. and Reynolds, P. (1990) *Counselling Psychology Quarterly* 3(1): 3–11.

Dryden, W. (ed.) (1990) *Individual Therapy: A Handbook*, Buckingham: Open University Press.

Dryden, W., Charles-Edwards, D. M. and Woolfe, R. (eds) (1989) *Handbook of Counselling in Britain*, London: Routledge.

Egan, G. (1994) *The Skilled Helper*, Pacific Grove, Ca.: Brooks Cole.

Ellis, A. (1962) *Reason and Emotion in Psychotherapy*, New York: Lyle.

Elton Wilson, J. and Barkham, M. (1994) 'A Practitioner-Scientist Approach to Psychotherapy' in P. Clarkson and M. Pokorny (eds) *The Handbook of Psychotherapy*, London: Routledge.

Eysenck, H. J. (1976) (ed.) *Case studies in Behaviour Therapy*, London: Routledge and Kegan Paul.

Frankland, A. (1995) 'An Invitation to Accreditation: Steps Towards an Emerging Profession', *Counselling* 6(1): 55–60.

Kohut, H. (1971) *The Analysis of the Self*, New York: International Universities Press.

Lazarus, R. (1978) 'The Stress and Coping Paradigm', University of California, Berkeley (mimeo).

McLeod, J. (1994) *Doing Counselling Research*, London: Sage.

——(1995) 'Evaluating the Effectiveness of Counselling: What we don't know', *Changes* 13(3): 192–200.

Maslow, A. H. (1968) *Towards A Psychology of Being*, Princeton NJ: Van Nostrand.

Murgatroyd, S. J. and Woolfe, R. (1982) *Coping with Crisis: Understanding and Helping People in Need*, London: Harper and Row.

Nelson-Jones, R. (1982) *The Theory and Practice of Counselling Psychology*, London: Holt, Rinehart and Winston.

Patterson, C. H. (1974) *Relationship Counselling and Psychotherapy*, New York, Harper and Row.

——(1986) *Theories of Counselling and Psychotherapy*, New York: Harper and Row.

Ratigan, B. (1989) 'Counselling in Higher Education' in W. Dryden, D. Charles-Edwards and R. Woolfe (eds) *Handbook of Counselling in Britain*, London: Routledge.

Reddy, M. (1987) *The Manager's Guide to Counselling at Work*, London: Methuen and the British Psychological Society.

Rogers, C. R. (1951) *Client-Centred Therapy*, London: Constable.

Rowan, J. (1976) *Ordinary Ecstasy: Humanistic Psychology in Action*, London: Routledge and Kegan Paul.

——(1990) *What is Humanistic Psychology?*, London: Routledge.

Seligman, M. E. P. (1975) *Helplessness: On Depression, Development and Death*, San Francisco: W. H. Freeman.

Toukmanian, S. G. and Rennie, D. L. (1992) *Psychotherapy Process Research*, Newbury Park, Ca.: Sage.

Truax, C. R. and Carkhuff, R. R. (1967) *Towards Effective Counseling and Psychotherapy*, Chicago: Aldine.

Tyler, L. (1967) *The Work of the Counselor*, New York: Appleton-Century Crofts.

Winnicott, D. W. (1965) *The Family and Individual Development*, London: Tavistock.

Woolfe, R. (1982) 'Counselling in a World of Crisis: Towards a Sociology of Counselling', *International Journal for the Advancement of Counselling* 6: 167–76.

——(1990) 'Counselling Psychology in Britain: an Idea whose Time has come', *The Psychologist: Bulletin of the British Psychological Society* 12: 531–5.

——(1995) in I. Horton, R. Bayne and J. Bimrose (eds) 'New Directions in Counselling: A Roundtable', *Counselling* 6(1): 34–5.

——(1996) 'The Nature of Counselling Psychology' in R. Woolfe and W. Dryden (eds) *Handbook of Counselling Psychology*, London: Sage.

Chapter two

Piloting the stream: the life cycle and counselling

Léonie Sugarman and Ray Woolfe

Introduction

The life course of each of us can be thought of as a river. On occasions turbulent, but at other times calm, it flows in a particular general direction whilst deviating here and there from a straight and narrow path. It meets and departs from other rivers or streams along the way, having a momentum of its own whilst both influencing and being influenced by the environment through which it flows. In the counselling encounter the lives of client and counsellor touch each other at a particular point in the life cycle of each. Each will be working, both inside and outside the counselling relationship, implicitly and explicitly, and with varying degrees of ease and success, on his or her developmental tasks – that is, those 'physiological psychological, and social demands a person must satisfy in order to be judged by others and to judge himself or herself to be a reasonably happy and successful person' (Chickering and Havighurst 1981: 25). Each phase of the life course has its own developmental tasks, the successful achievement of which contributes to personal happiness and to the successful management of later tasks. Failure contributes to unhappiness, social disapproval and/or later difficulties. This view of the life cycle is like a glue which binds together the experience of the helper and the client, and of the disparate concerns raised by clients at different life stages. The client's development tasks will often be the *raison d'être* of counselling.

Change is the basic raw material of counselling. Yet there is only one kind of change that can be said, with certainty, to be experienced by each and every human being and that is the change associated with ageing. It is an inexorable fact of human life that we are born; that the process of ageing begins at the moment of birth; and that sooner or later we die. While we die at different ages, a majority of people, at least in the developed western world, will arrive there by a process of growing through childhood into adolescence, and via early and middle adulthood into old age. Together with gender, race, and class, age is a key defining characteristic of personal and social identity. It is not for nothing that the counsellor, after eliciting the name and address of the client, will then ask the question 'what is your age?' It follows, therefore, that the process of counselling would be enhanced by the existence of a conceptual framework that offers an understanding of the changes associated with ageing. Such a framework is provided by the notion of 'life-cycle development'; a concept which attempts to articulate what happens to individuals as they grow and develop and move through the various periods of life.

Although each individual is unique, there is a developmental sequence through which individuals pass as they move through life. At each stage of development there is a need for new knowledge and skills to be acquired. Counselling may be relevant at any stage of development, but particularly at the point of transition from one stage to another, where the potential for stress but also for personal change may be greatest.

Age and change

Change is implicit when we talk about the life course. We are not just human beings, we are young, adolescent, middle-aged or elderly human beings. While our gender and our ethnic and social origins remain with us, we need constantly to engage in a subjective process of re-evaluating what the process of ageing means.

Some clients may approach a counsellor with an issue which is explicitly age-related: a person may be frightened of growing old; be left with a feeling of loss as children grow up and leave home; or simply experience a vague sense of purposelessness as life passes by. Phrases to describe such states have developed in the vernacular. Thus, we talk of the 'empty nest syndrome', the 'mid-life crisis', or the 'male menopause'; of people being 'old before their time'; or of being 'mutton dressed as lamb'. All these reflect assumptions about age-related or age-appropriate concerns and behaviours. Other issues which clients bring to counsellors may have a less explicit and more subtle association with age or life stage. Thus, a couple in their mid-forties might seek help with a marital issue concerning one spouse's infidelity. They will almost certainly raise questions about feeling bored with the same partner after sixteen years of marriage and how it feels still to be found sexually attractive.

It may be the absence of an anticipated change or development that provides the focus of a counsellor's work with a client. Thus, parents of a teenager with a severe learning difficulty may feel trapped and helpless that their child will never be able to leave home. They cannot look forward to the freedom from routine parental responsiblities that usually accompanies the later years of life. Similarly, a twenty-year-old student may feel trapped because he or she cannot afford to leave home, yet feels that by this age an individual ought to be independent. The counsellor's task once again is to explore with the client the origin of this belief system. In each case the client has implict and often explicit expectations about what life should be like at a particular point in time. These expectations are reflected in hopes, fears and fantasies. Through helping clients to explore these grey areas, the counsellor assists them to clarify the origins of their expectations and the extent to which they are realistic.

Perhaps for most of us, much of the time we realize that change is occurring slowly, gradually, and inexorably; and in an approximate kind of way we remain in tune with it. Almost without conscious awareness we adjust our dress, language, behaviour and attitudes so that what we expect of ourselves is in a rough kind of congruence and harmony with what others expect of us. Through this incremental, quantitative change we maintain a sense of continuity. It lends a sense of coherence to our overall life story, linking the more notable changes and events into a composite whole (Hermans 1992).

Life events and marker points

The process of change encompasses a large number of significant life events, some already referred to, which both demand and denote change, and which serve as marker points in an individual's life. Frequently these marker events entail a change in status or role, and may signal to the individual that he or she is either 'on time' or 'off time' with regard to society's norms and expectations (Neugarten 1977).

People may face crises in their lives if such markers or normative events do not take place, or take place at the 'wrong' time. Thus, for example, a young person may find it impossible to get a good job; a couple may find they are not able to conceive the child they want, whilst another may conceive a child at the 'wrong' time, for example in their early teens, or when the woman has just started a new job. Counsellors are not unfamiliar with such cases. They are also familiar with age-related issues such as the client's sense of despair – 'by my age I should have . . .', or personal ageism – 'I can't do that at my age.' In all those instances the counsellor may assist the client to understand the source and derivations of such age-related assumptions, and the ways in which these influence current feelings and behaviour. Are these age-related beliefs an accurate expression of reality and of the individual's personal values; or are they the injuctions of society's norms which, with the help of a counsellor, the individual might seek to challenge? More generally, the counsellor can be said to have a role in encouraging clients to examine the stereotype of adulthood and ageing which informs their thinking.

Age and personal identity

An individual's personal identity is intimately bound up with the notion of age. It provides a peg on which to hang a notion of who and what we are. Since counsellors are centrally concerned with a client's sense of identity, they are, *ipso facto*, also involved with the variable we know as age. Our sense of age gives us an indication of what is expected of us by others in terms of behaviour, dress, attitudes, relationships and so on.

While growing older affects us physically, intellectually and emotionally, we are not always aware of what is happening to us. Often it takes some kind of critical event to teach or remind us that we are living life against a moving backcloth of time and ageing. It may be a major life event such as having a heart attack or becoming a grandparent that draws our age to our attention. Alternatively, small incidents – like being called 'Sir' or 'Madam' for the first time, being turned to for advice, or being offered a seat on a bus by a younger person – can be infused with a personal meaning for our sense of identity which far outstrips their objective significance. Sometimes the realization that we have not, as it were, kept up with the passage of time can be startling, emotionally upsetting, and, perhaps, challenging. This is often associated with the dawning awareness that we are in some way 'out of step' with our peers or with what we assumed our life would be like at a particular age. We might, for example, realize that, unlike us, most of our contemporaries have moved on from their first job and are driving cars, not motor bikes. Chancing upon an old diary, letter or acquaintance may remind us that we had expected to be doing something quite different 'by now'. Our sense of age and identity is infused with this social component – how we stand in relation to others and to the social norm. We are not, however, always brought up short by these reminders of ageing and of time passing.

Stages theories of development

Most people can readily divide their own or a 'typical' life span into a number of phases or stages. These will often be linked both to age (childhood, adolescence, early adulthood etc.) and to significant life events (going to school, leaving home, becoming a parent). Theorists of human development have often followed suit, focusing in addition on a range of psychological processes that accompnay such stages – for example psychosocial crises (Erikson 1950) or cognitive structuring of the world (Piaget 1976). These theories have a number of implications for the work of the counsellor. They provide circumstantial evidence of the psychological issues being faced by clients at different life stages (Thomas 1990). They also provide a reminder about the importance of seeing an individual client's emotional needs as rooted in an affective and cognitive developmental process which began at birth.

Stage-based accounts of human development typically focus on different 'developmental tasks' (Havighurst 1972) to be addressed at different life stages. Failure to confront and manage these tasks effectively may result in difficulty in moving satisfactorily through later stages. When psychodynamic theories of counselling refer to clients having 'unresolved conflicts', they are describing the way in which just such a failure may create problems for the individual long into the future. Erik Erikson, one of the most influential theorists in this field, suggests that the growth of the ego involves the sequential and cumulative emergence of personal strengths. Although each characteristic may always exist in some form, there is a time when the development of each assumes special importance.

Erikson's work hypothesizes the existence of eight stages and thus eight possible crises. The first four are rooted in childhood and we have not the space here to do more than simply name them. They are Basic Trust versus Basic Mistrust; Autonomy versus Shame and Doubt; Initiative versus Guilt; and Industry versus Inferiority. They are related to Freud's Oral, Genital and Latency stages of development. The resolution of each crisis leads respectively to the development of hope, will, purpose and competence. The fifth stage is concerned with Identity versus Role Confusion and is typically a characteristic of adolescence. This is a phase when the work of the counsellor is concerned with client issues such as sexual identity, autonomy from parents, and developing a coherent set of values.

Erikson sees adulthood as containing three stages, each with its own crisis or turning-point: Intimacy versus Isolation; Generativity versus Stagnation; and Ego Integrity versus Despair. The first adult crisis is concerned with the need to establish intimate relationships. This involves a fusing of identity with another person, as, for example, in marriage. This stage is characteristic of the early twenties and its central feature is a mutual search for a shared identity through the development of the ego characteristic of love. Unless this takes place, it becomes difficult for the individual to move to the next stage, whose crisis involves the need to be creative and to give of oneself to other people; for example to one's children, friends, colleagues, or the community in general. The ego quality that is developed here is that of care. If this fails to occur, the result is stagnation and self-absorption which makes much harder the overcoming of the final challenge, which involves coming to terms with life as finite and one's one and only life. The successful resolution of the crisis at this stage generates Wisdom. Neugarten (1977) invites us to think about the period of middle age in terms of 'time left to live'. Emotional problems in old age arise if the individual sees life as a chapter of failures and missed opportunities.

This kind of stage theory is helpful to counsellors because it indicates how current crises faced by individuals can reveal flaws in the resolution of earlier crises. In other words, the past is often revealed in the present and the work of the counsellor is directed towards examining the link between the client's past experience and present modes of operating in the world.

It is important not to take this kind of stage theory too literally, as covering every individual and every culture. This would be too mechanical an interpretation of a model which we would describe as a useful guide to our thinking. Normative accounts of human development are written not on tablets of stone, but on the shifting sands of time; and it is somewhat ironic that as interest in such accounts has increased, so their likely accuracy for any one individual has declined. Neugarten and Neugarten (1986) point to the blurring of distinctions between life periods that has occurred in our society and resulted in 'the fluid life cycle' (Hirschhorn 1977). Thus for many people education and training is no longer confined to childhood and the early adult years, and more people undergo major career changes than ever before. An increasing number of people not only marry, but divorce, remarry, and possibly re-divorce. Women's childbearing years can extend over a quarter of a century or more, and first-time grandparents may be aged from about thirty-five to well over seventy.

Since social, cultural, technological and historical changes inevitably render obsolete detailed accounts of a typical life cycle, it may be more helpful for the counsellor to develop a broad-brush understanding of the life course. Thus Levinson (1986; Levinson *et al.* 1978) in addition to identifying the developmental tasks characterizing different life stages, also points to a more overarching pattern – the life course as an evolving life structure characterized by a series of alternating structure-building and structure-changing phases. The structure-changing phases are major transition points, during which we question earlier decisions, change direction and in one way or another sever links with at least some aspects of our past. Such disruptions to our accustomed ways of being can be disconcerting to ourselves and those with whom we live and interact. Problems in accepting and resolving such disruptions may well be what propels clients into counselling. To see such upheavals as inevitable and healthy can rid them of some of their terror. The focus on intervention can then be construed as maximizing the developmental potential of such structure-changing phases, rather than trying to minimize their impact in order to minimize the change required of the individual. This has been described as a developmental rather than a disease perspective (Danish, Smyer and Novak 1980). Such upheavals, despite, or perhaps because of their potential for growth, can be stressful and draining. Levinson offers the prospect of relief from this turmoil during the structure-building phases which, though not devoid of change, are concerned with implementation of decisions and consolidation of changes – periods of calm, as it were, between the storms.

Gould (1978), another stage theorist, also identifies a common theme running through different life stages. He depicts adult development as the sequential relinquishment of erroneous assumptions developed as guiding principles during childhood. Thinking about the life cycle in this way helps the counsellor to become clearer about the possible nature and origins of some of the problems with which he or she is characteristically presented. Thus, for example, failure to resolve the so-called 'mid-life crisis' (associated with the second of the three adult stages) may invite exploration not just of what has happened to the client in his or her thirties and forties, but also of how the individual's psyche has become rooted and formed at earlier stages. As Gould puts it, the concern of the counsellor is with the emergence, confrontation and transcendence of childhood consciousness.

The family life cycle

In thinking about the life cycle, it must be remembered that individual development takes place in a social context and in particular within the institution we know as the family. Thus, when we talk about the developmental needs of an individual, we are referring to needs which exist alongside those of other people with whom we have ongoing intimate relationships, some of whom are at different points in their life cycle.

A point made by Street in his discussion of family counselling in Chapter 5 of this volume is that the developmental needs or tasks of different family members may conflict. Thus, just as one or both parents feel ready and able to decrease career involvement in order, as resigning politicians often say, 'to spend more time with their family', it may be that the children with whom they want to spend more time are struggling to loosen their ties to the parental home. Similarly, the trend for delaying parenthood until the mid-thirties or even the forties means that middle-aged adults may be coping simultaneously with the demands of both young, dependent children and frail, dependent parents. It is not merely the practicalities of such tasks that can cause problems, but the necessary psychological and emotional adjustments. Furthermore, the young children and the elderly parents will also have their own adjustments to make. The traditional nuclear family where the father is in full-time work and the mother is at home caring for two dependent children is no longer the norm. Thus, the traditional six-stage family cycle of unattached young adult, newly married couple, family with young children, family with adolescents, launching children and moving on, and the family in later life (Carter and McGoldrick 1989) may not reflect the anticipated or actual family life cycle of many clients. Families must negotiate the impact of factors such as divorce, remarriage, step-families, single parenthood and same sex partnerships.

Haley (1973), an influential figure in the field of family counselling, has suggested that family psychopathology is the result of disruption or dislocation in the unfolding of the life cycle of the family. As in the individual model, families are seen as passing through critical stages, each one involving important developmental tasks. A problem is viewed 'as a developmental impasse which occurs when the family is struggling to negotiate developmental transition' (Bennun 1988: 15). The key point is that at every stage, each member of the family system and each subsystem (such as parents, children, father/daughter, mother/son) have needs which if not resolved will generate difficulties.

Problems are created when the family becomes locked into rigid patterns of problem-solving and the unproductive expenditure of ever-increasing amounts of energy. The family is then stuck and the unfolding of the life cycle is disrupted. Counselling involves supportively 'unbalancing' the family, so as to force its members away from the rigid patterns of communication and interaction in which it has become set (Haley 1980). Such therapeutic work in the area of family life-cycle development illustrates the value of employing a life-cycle approach in the setting of clinical practice and indicates how the former can inform the latter. In doing so, it highlights the potential of a life-cycle perspective for the counsellor working with an individual client.

Principles of intervention

Whilst recognizing that human development is grounded in a web of family and other relationships, our focus in this chapter is on the role of the counsellor in the context of the individual life cycle. So far we have indicated why the concept of the individual life cycle might be important for counsellors and suggested that without an awareness of its existence, the counsellor is limiting his or her understanding of the client's cognitive and emotional concerns. We have already explored some of the implications of such a perspective for the work of the counsellor. We now intend to look at these in a more systematic fashion, by examining four specific principles of intervention which seem to emanate from the idea of life-cycle counselling: self-empowerment as the goal; life-event or transition processes as the focus; developmental, eclectic counselling as the strategy; and the 'system' as well as the individual as the target.

Goal: self-empowerment

The assumption of developmental potential throughout life is no stranger to the practice of counselling or the value system of counsellors but, even so, it does beg the question of what we mean by development – especially in the adult years when self-evident criteria of physical, social and intellectual maturation may be less apparent. A more subtle or, indeed, a quite different concept of development is needed unless we are simply to say that any change and any life-course pattern constitutes development.

The counselling literature is replete with potential candidates for the basis of such a definition. Formulations concerning the nature of the healthy personality permeate the literature on counselling. Discussions of, for example, the 'fully functioning person' (Rogers 1961) or the 'self-actualized person' (Maslow 1962) revolve not around static end-states but rather around dynamic ways of being. Thus, it is more appropriate to talk of the developing rather than the developed person – with an emphasis on process and direction rather than merely outcome.

Hopson and Scally (1980) make a distinction between 'change' and 'development'. While change offers a potential for development, it is not in itself a sufficient condition for development to take place. It is possible, for example for a person to change in a way that inhibits or prevents development. As Hopson and Scally make clear 'for a change to be developmental there needs to be a movement towards a greater realisation of personal potential; namely, acquiring new skills, increasing self awareness and clarifying one's values' (ibid.: 183). Their operational definitition of development is based on the notion of the individual becoming more self-empowered, that is 'more proactive, less dependent upon others, valuing the integrity of others as well as themselves, more in charge of themselves and their lives' (ibid.: 183).

Hopson and Scally's concern with promoting as well as describing self-empowerment leads to a definition of the developing person which at the same time provides a set of targets for counsellors. Central to the concept of self-empowerment is the belief that in any situation there are always alternatives, even though none may be desirable; that is, we always have a choice. Self-empowered living involves the ability to identify these alternatives; to choose between them on the basis of personal values, priorities and commitments; and to act on these choices in order to implement them. A further dimension of self-empowered behaviour is the ability to facilitate the self-empowerment of others, enabling them to live more self-empowered lives.

Hopson and Scally focus on five attributes needed in order to become more self-empowered: awareness, goals, values, life skills and information. In addition to the more commonly mentioned need for awareness of self and others, there is the need for healthier systems in which to live and work. In talking of goals they do not mean vague or highly abstract aspirations such as the wish to be happy. Rather, they mean specific concrete outcomes – for example, 'I wish to expand my social life' or 'I wish to gain two promotions within the next five years' – which can form the basis of action planning. The specification of goals, whilst being necessary, is not a sufficient indicator of self-empowered behaviour. The goals must be the individual's own goals, consistent with his or her well-considered values. Hopson and Scally describe such goals as commitments. Not all goals would mark the person as more rather than less self-empowered. To be defined as such the values on which the goals are based must be consistent with many of the criteria of self-actualization or maturity. These values centre around self-respect and respect for others; responsibility for self; and the assumption that oneself, others and systems all have the potential to change.

The notion of counselling which emerges from this analysis, based upon the assumption of life-long change, places an emphasis on the development of generic skills which can be transferred from one situation to another. Thus, for example, a client who has some understanding of the coping process involved in grieving a death would be better able to cope with the loss involved in, say, unemployment or retirement or just growing older and losing one's youth than a client who does not have this understanding. Counselling from this perspective has the goals of encouraging client self-awareness and values clarification, and of teaching creative problem-solving skills. Placing it in a life-cycle framework directs attention to the blocks to client learning that may be found in both the helper's and the client's stereotypes about age, ageing, and age-appropriate behaviours.

Focus: life events

Life events are processes or transitions as well as markers. Evidence from a number of sources suggests that a fairly typical sequence of responses will tend to follow the onset of a critical life event. Perhaps the best-known example is with regard to the bereavement process (see Chapter 22). Others include the response to major surgery or to job promotion (Parker and Lewis 1981). More generally Hopson (1981; Hopson and Adams 1976) identifies a sequence or cycle of seven phases as typically accompanying a wide range of critical life events, both positive and negative. First is a period of immobilization or shock, a sense of being overwhelmed, unable to plan or think logically. This gives way to a minimization phase where the existence of the change or its impact is denied or at least minimized. Third is a period of self-doubt, frequently showing itself as depression, but possibly through other emotions such as anger or frustration. The next stage is reached as the individual begins to become able to accept the post-transition reality. This is followed by a period of testing as the individual begins to spread his or her wings in this new situation. Next comes a phase of seeking for meaning in the changed way of being and, finally, the transition can be said to be complete when the individual has internalized these new realities and meanings.

The idea of a cycle contained within the transition sequence emphasizes the inherent potential for growth and provides pointers to the counsellor, who can adapt the style and type of intervention to the client's stage in the process. Progress will not necessarily be smooth. There may be much vacillation between stages, and no definitive units of either time or degree of response can be given to any one phase. The fourth stage (accepting reality) is, however, something of a watershed in that it marks the point at which the individual begins to come to terms with and deal creatively with the change. Supporting, or perhaps sometimes pushing, the client into this confrontation can be a turning point in the counselling relationship at which the whole emphasis becomes more forward-looking. Of course, timing is of the essence; too early, and the confrontation risks plunging the client further into the depths of depression with no immediate prospect of relief.

The transition cycle, with its emphasis on coping with change and managing loss, is particularly compatible with a life-cycle perspective. Growing up and growing older involve major gains, but also major losses. We are aware of losing our childhood sense of the world as a magical place; we become aware of losing our sense of not having responsibilities for others; we lose our feeling of youthful vigour, energy and vitality; we experience the loss of children as they leave home; we lose the identity of being a worker when we retire – the list is endless. Each event involves the individual in a process of grief work which, if completed successfully, enables that individual to work through the transition in such a way as to feel emotionally fulfilled and not left with a sense of crisis. Coping with change involves working through a process of grieving for what is lost; counselling from a life-cycle perspective can be seen as a process of engaging with clients to review, reassess and, possibly, reauthor their life story (Sugarman 1996).

Strategy: developmental, eclectic counselling

A life-cycle perspective encourages a broad, encompassing mind set – the antithesis of narrowly focused specialisms. It also adopts a relativistic perspective on 'truth', accepting the potential validity of a range of conceptual approaches to the life cycle. It is a world view which encourages eclecticism – the use of approaches and methods from a range of situations and settings (Norcross and Grencavage 1989). Furthermore, the concept of the life cycle helps to provide a theoretical rationale for choice of methods, shifting the emphasis towards a more integrationist postion.

Counselling from a life-cycle and, hence, a life events perspective frequently involves helping clients manage transition. Different counselling interventions may be denoted depending on the stage the client has reached in the transition sequence outlined in the previous section. Egan, in what has been termed (Inskipp and Johns 1984) a model of developmental eclecticism, describes the helping process as a series of three hierarchical stages. This sequence of stages is compatible with the intervention needs of clients at different stages in the transition cycle. In the most recent version of his model (Egan 1994), the stages of helping are described as:

(1) establishing the present scenario;
(2) establishing the preferred scenario;
(3) getting there.

The first stage is exploratory and the first step within it involves helping clients to tell their story. During the transition phases of shock, minimization and self-doubt (depression) the client will need time to allow the fact of the transition to sink in. Self-esteem and the sense of the world as a predictable place may be rocked, particularly if the life event was unpleasant and unexpected. The non-judgemental acceptance and the focus on exploration which pervade the helper–client relationship at this point is of particular importance. It is a person-centred, non-directive step during which the client's goal is self-exploration and the helper's goals are understanding and relationship building. It can counter the range of feelings the client may experience at this stage – panic, urgency to do something, paralysis. 'Look before you leap' could be an aphorism for the work done during this phase.

It is possible for individuals to become stuck in the early phases of a transition – never, for example, coming to terms with the death of a loved one, the children's departure from home, or being dropped from the firm's football team. If the transition is to be an experience from which the client learns and grows then he or she needs, at some point, to move on from the period of taking stock. The later steps of stage 1 of the helping model are indicated here: identifying and challenging blind spots, and searching for what Egan calls 'leverage', that is, identifying and working on issues, concerns or opportunities that 'will make a difference' to clients' lives. If clients have been unable of their own volition to move on from the bottom of the self-doubt or depression phase of the transition sequence, this work on blind spots and leverage may help propel them into the 'recovery' phases.

Stage 2 of Egan's model of helping involves helping clients to examine what a better future might look like. This involves accepting the reality of the change or life event and beginning to let go of the past – the fourth phase of the transition sequence. 'Nothing ventured, nothing gained' might be the adage here. Following this, clients may require help in translating preferred scenarios into concrete agendas. In other words, objectives or goals have to be set which, when translated into action, will turn the desired futures into reality. Goal setting is, like the transition stage of letting go, a watershed. Both involve a shift in attention from the past to the future – a looking forward to what might be rather than, or at least as well as, looking backwards to what is no more. By the end of Egan's second stage, clients should know what they want to accomplish even if they do not yet know how to achieve the desired goal.

The third and final stage of Egan's model is based upon achieving the identified goals through the development and implementation of action plans. In the language of the transition sequence it can be seen as setting the scene for systematic rather than haphazard 'testing'. 'If you don't know where you're going, you'll probably end up somewhere else', the title of David Campbell's (1974) book on life-career planning, captures the tone of this stage. The final stages of the transition sequence, 'search for meaning' and 'integration', can be addressed, either directly or implicitly, through the processes of evaluation and termination of the helping relationship.

Ivey (1986) considers client development during counselling in a somewhat different way which is explicitly informed by an understanding of human cognitive developmental stages. He sees development as the aim of counselling and psychotherapy: 'Change, growth, creativity, transformation, and evolution are all about development. Staying put, refusing or being unable to change are what development is not' (ibid.: 28). Furthermore, Ivey proposes that the development which occurs in adult clients during therapy recapitulates that of children working through the Piagetian stages: sensori-motor, preoperational, concrete operational, and formal operational. Different therapeutic interventions can promote change and movement at different points through this sequence. Through all this, Ivey sees life, and therapy, as a dynamic process rather than as means to a particular end. Both are about journeys rather than destinations.

Target: systems as well as individuals

A number of writers in this book point to the responsibility of the counsellor to act as an agent not just of personal change, but also of systems change. This view is of particular relevance in a discussion of life-cycle change and counsellor response. The counsellor informed by this perspective will be concerned with prevention as well as cure; in particular with challenging social sterotypes about adulthood in order to demystify them, rather than just responding to adults who arrive with age-related issues to discuss. Institutional change is also an integral notion underlying the goal of empowering clients to take greater control over their own lives. There is a real danger that counselling can become a vehicle for helping people to adjust to social systems which are themselves pathological and may well generate problems for individuals in the first case. It is just such a perspective which has encouraged many feminist therapists to question how far the traditional family is a system in which the rights of women have been abused and whether it is appropriate to help women to adapt to such a situation (see Chapter 16 by Chaplin). Adopting such a perspective has a number of implications for the work of counsellors. At the very least it highlights the desirability of allowing clients to share experiences with each other in groups, so that a conceptual and personal understanding can be reached of how the cognitive and emotional repertoires of individuals are rooted in their social contexts.

Conclusion

We have sought in this chapter to examine the importance of age and life stage in the construction of an individual's personal identity and to illustrate ways in which this knowledge influences the practice of the counsellor. It is unlikely that there will ever be counsellors working in Britain who style themselves primarily as life-cycle counsellors. However, this in no way detracts from the importance of the subject. There can be few counsellors who are unaware of the importance of the life cycle as an issue in their work and our hope is that this discussion has elevated the topic to a more conscious position in their awareness. Our belief is that a greater focus by counsellors on developmental work will reduce the amount of remedial work in which they are currently engaged.

References

Baltes, P. B., Reese, H. W., and Lipsitt, L. P. (1980) 'Life span developmental psychology', *Annual Review of Psychology* 31: 65–110.

Bennun, I. (1988) 'Systems theory and family therapy' in E. Street and W. Dryden (eds) *Family Therapy in Britain*, Milton Keynes: Open University Press.

Campbell, D. P. (1974) *If You Don't Know where You're Going, You'll Probably End Up Somewhere Else*, Niles, Illinois: Argus Communications.

Carter, B. and McGoldrick, M. (1989) 'Overview: The changing family life cycle – a framework for family therapy' in B. Carter and M. McGoldrick (eds) *The Changing Family Life Cycle*, 2nd edn, Boston: Allyn and Bacon.

Chickering, A. W. and Havighurst, R. J. (1981) 'The life cycle' in A. W. Chickering *et al.* (eds) *The Modern American College: Responding to the New Realities of Diverse Students and a Changing Society*, San Francisco, California: Jossey-Bass.

Danish, S. J., Smyer, M. A. and Nowak, C. (1980) 'Developmental intervention: Enhancing life-events processes' in P. B. Baltes and O. G. Brim (eds) *Life-Span Development and Behavior* vol. 3, New York: Academic Press.

Egan, G. (1994) *The Skilled Helper: a Systematic Approach to Effective Helping*, 5th edn, Monterey, California: Brooks/Cole.

Erikson, E. H. (1950) *Childhood and Society*, New York: Norton.

Gould, R. L. (1978) *Transformations: Growth and Change in Adult Life*, New York: Simon & Schuster.

Haley, J. (1973) *Uncommon Therapy: The Psychiatric Techniques of Milton H. Erickson*, New York: Norton.

——(1980) *Leaving Home*, New York: McGraw Hill.

Hermans, H. J. M. (1992) 'Telling and retelling one's self-narrative: A contextual approach to life-span development', *Human Development* 35: 361–75.

Havighurst, R. J. (1972) *Developmental Tasks and Education*, 3rd edn (1st edn 1948), New York: David McKay.

Hirschhorn, L. (1977) 'Social policy and the life cycle: a developmental perspective', *Social Service Review* 51: 434–50.

Hopson, B. (1981) 'Response to the papers by Schlossberg, Brammer and Abrego', *Counselling Psychologist* 9(2): 36–9.

——and Adams, J. (1976) 'Towards an understanding of transition: defining some boundaries of transition dynamics' in J. Adams, J. Hayes, and B. Hopson (eds) *Transition: Understanding and Managing Personal Change*, London: Martin Robertson.

——and Scally, M. (1980) 'Change and development in adult life – some implications for helpers', *British Journal of Guidance and Counselling* 8(2): 175–87.

——(1981) *Lifeskills Teaching*, London: McGraw Hill.

Inskipp, F. and Johns, H. (1984) 'Developmental eclecticism: Egan's skills model of helping' in W. Dryden (ed.) *Individual Therapy in Britain*, London: Harper & Row.

Ivey, A. E. (1986) *Developmental Therapy: Theory into Practice*, San Francisco, California: Jossey-Bass.

Levinson, D. J. (1986) 'A conception of human development', *American Psychologist* 42: 3–13.

——and Darrow, D. N., Klein, E. B., Levinson, M. H. and McKee, B. (1978) *The Seasons of a Man's Life*, New York: Knopf.

Maslow, A. H. (1962) *Towards a Psychology of Being*, Princeton, New Jersey: Van Nostrand.

Murray Parkes, C. (1972) *Bereavement*, London: Tavistock.

Neugarten, B. L. (1977) 'Adult personality: towards a psychology of the life cycle' in L. R. Allman and D. T. Jaffe (eds) *Readings in Adult Psychology: Contemporary Perspectives*, New York: Harper & Row.

——and Neugarten, D. A. (1986) 'Age in the aging society', *Daedalus* 115(1): 31–49.

Norcross, J. C., and Grencavage, L. M. (1989) 'Eclecticism and integration in counselling and psychotherapy: Major themes and obstacles', *British Journal of Guidance and Counselling* 17: 227–47.

Parker, C. and Lewis, R. (1981) 'Beyond the Peter Principle: managing successful transitions', *Journal of European Industrial Training* 5(6): 17–21.

Piaget, J. (1976) 'Piaget's theory', in P. Neubauer (ed.) *The Process of Child Development*, New York: Meridian.

Rogers, C. R. (1961) *On Becoming a Person*, London: Constable.

Sugarman, L. (1996) 'Narratives of theory and practice: the psychology of life-span development', in R. Woolfe and W. Dryden (eds) *Handbook of Counselling Psychology*, London: Sage.

Thomas, R. M. (1990) *Counseling and Life-Span Development*, Newbury Park, California: Sage.

Part two

Arenas

Chapter three

Individual counselling

Windy Dryden and Stephen Palmer

Introduction

Most counselling that takes place in Britain today probably occurs within the one-to-one arena[1] of individual counselling. While it is advantageous for counsellors to follow the general principle of meeting clients' preferences for being seen within a particular counselling arena to enhance the development of a good working alliance, each arena (individual, couple, family, and group counselling) has its advantages and disadvantages. What, then, are the particular therapeutic merits of individual counselling? Dryden (1984) interviewed a number of counsellors whose views on this topic are presented below.

(1) Individual counselling, by its nature, provides clients with a situation of complete confidentiality. It is indicated therefore when it is important for clients to be able to disclose themselves in privacy without fear that others may use such information to their detriment. Some clients are particularly anxious concerning how others, for example in group counselling, would react to their disclosures, and such anxiety precludes their productive participation in that arena. Similarly, clients who otherwise would not disclose 'confidential' material are best suited to individual counselling. As in other situations, transfer to other arenas may be indicated later when such clients are more able and/or willing to disclose themselves to others.

(2) Individual counselling, by its dyadic nature, provides an opportunity for a closer relationship to develop between counsellor and client than may exist when other clients are present. This factor may be particularly important for some clients who have not developed close relationships with significant people in their lives and for whom group counselling, for example, may initially be too threatening.

(3) Individual counselling can be conducted to best match the client's pace of learning. Thus it is particularly suited for clients who, due to their present state of mind, or speed of learning, require their counsellor's

full individual attention. This is especially important for clients who are quite confused and who would only be distracted by the complexity of interactions that can take place in other therapeutic arenas.

(4) Individual counselling is particularly therapeutic when clients' major problems involve their relationship with themselves rather than their relationship with other people.

(5) Individual counselling may be particularly helpful for clients who wish to differentiate themselves from others – for example, those who have decided to leave a relationship and wish to deal with individual problems that this may involve. Here, however, some conjoint sessions with their partner may also be helpful, particularly in matters of conciliation (Gurman and Kniskern 1978).

(6) Individual counselling may also be the arena of choice for clients who want to explore whether or not they should differentiate themselves from others – for example, those who are unhappy in their marriage but are not sure whether to work to improve the relationship or to leave it. The presence of the other person may unduly inhibit such individuals from exploring the full ramifications of their choice.

(7) It can be helpful for counsellors to vary their therapeutic style with clients in order to minimize the risk of perpetuating the client's problems by providing an inappropriate interactive style. Individual counselling offers counsellors an opportunity to vary their interactive style with clients free from the concern that such variation may adversely affect other clients present.

(8) Individual counselling is particularly beneficial for clients who have profound difficulties sharing therapeutic time with other clients.

(9) Individual counselling may also have therapeutic merits but for negative reasons. Thus, clients may benefit by being seen in individual counselling who may not be helped from working in other arenas. Therefore, clients who may monopolize a counselling group, be too withdrawn within it to benefit from the experience, or who are thought too vulnerable to gain value from family counselling can often be seen in individual counselling with minimal risk.

If these are some of the therapeutic merits of individual counselling, then who is actually offering this service? Nelson-Jones (1995: 4–5) suggests that there are four main categories of individuals who might view themselves as employing counselling skills and knowledge:

(1) helping service professionals e.g. counsellors, counselling psychologists, social workers, career officers;

(2) voluntary counsellor who work in numerous voluntary settings;

(3) people using counselling skills as part of their jobs, e.g. doctors, teachers, nurses, clergy;

(4) informal counsellors in daily relationships such as work colleagues,

friends, partners or family. (Cowen (1982) has suggested that empathic networks can also include bartenders and hairdressers too.)

Principles

It should be noted that individual counsellors in Britain vary according to the theoretical orientation that they bring to the work. While research on the theroretical allegiances of individual counsellors in Britain is needed, it is likely that most work within either the psychodynamic tradition (Freudian, Kleinian, Jungian, object relations), the humanistic tradition (person-centred, Gestalt, transactional analysis) or the cognitive-behavioural tradition (behavioural, cognitive, rational emotive behavioural), or are eclectic (e.g. multimodal) and/or integrative in approach (in that they draw upon the principles and methods of some or all of the above traditions). Although members of the British Association for Counselling may not necessarily accurately reflect therapeutic loyalties in Britain, in a survey (BAC 1993) of their members the following results were found: 60 per cent practised psychodynamic counselling; 57 per cent practised person-centred counselling; 19 per cent practised cognitive/cognitive-behavioural counselling. The total percentages add up to over 100 as many of the counsellors who took part in the survey practised more than one approach to counselling.

In this section, however, a 'common factors' approach is adopted and some of the principles are highlighted with which most individual counsellors are likely to agree (Frank 1985).

The relationship in individual counselling

Most counsellors would probably agree that the relationship between client and counsellor is an important therapeutic factor in individual counselling, even though different counsellors may point to different features of this relationship as having particular therapeutic value.

Individual counsellors endeavour to form a relationship with their clients that is characterized by mutual trust and respect, and in which clients feel safe enough to disclose and explore their concerns. When counsellors are experienced by clients as being understanding, genuinely concerned with their welfare, and on their side, then there is a much greater likelihood that clients will benefit from the counselling process than when these experiences are absent (Truax and Carkhuff 1967). In addition, when counsellors are experienced by their clients as either over-involved (intrusive) or under-involved (cold, detached and withholding) in the counselling process, these factors have been shown to be associated with client harm (Grunebaum 1986). Therefore counselling can be 'for better or worse'; what has the power to be healing has also, in less skilled hands, the power to be harmful (Strupp et al. 1977).

While the quality of the relationship between counsellors and clients is likely to be a central feature of individual counselling, it may not always be sufficient for a good outcome. When it is sufficient, what is likely to occur is that clients are helped by their counsellors' empathic understanding, genuine concern and respect to engage in a fruitful period of emotional release and self-exploration, where they begin to lose their fear of looking within themselves and begin to explore different aspects of themselves and their life situation. It also happens that they begin to view themselves, other people, and the world differently, and begin to move towrds accepting themselves as fallible human beings with strengths and weaknesses. They may also begin to identify hidden resources within themselves that they may be able to use spontaneously outside the individual counselling arena to improve relationships and in the service of their personally held goals.

Other clients may require more active help from their counsellors. Some may require, for example, that their counsellor offer a different perspective within which they can begin to view themselves, others, and the world differently. Yet others may require that their counsellor help them acquire new skills with which they can experiment ouside counselling sessions (see Palmer and Dryden 1995). When these 'additive' ingredients are a feature of effective counselling, however, they are generally rooted in the facilitative qualities of the relationship discussed above.

Interestingly, researchers have recently moved away from investigating the effects of the facilitative conditions upon the counselling relationship and have concentrated instead on the therapeutic alliance. Barkham (1996: 53) states, 'While the facilitative conditions have been viewed as a possible mechanism of change, the therapeutic alliance is best viewed as a mechanism which enables the client to remain in and comply with treatment'. Horvath and Symonds (1991) undertook a meta-analytic review of twenty-four studies and concluded that the alliance was positively related to therapeutic outcome. Therefore it could be concluded that for effective counselling both the facilitative conditions and a good therapeutic alliance are beneficial.

A focus on the whole person

Even when clients bring a specific problem to counselling, their counsellors may offer them an opportunity to widen the focus of exploration to other arenas of their life (unless counselling is being offered in a time-limited setting). This is due to the shared view among counsellors that clients are complex 'whole' people. Ideally, however, counsellors do not seek to impose their 'wholistic' views on their clients, and if the latter want only to work on a delineated problem their wishes are respected.

If clients do wish to make use of such invitations to widen the focus of exploration, then the arena of individual counselling is particularly facilitative. In this arena the absence of other clients means that counsellors can offer their full time and attention to their individual clients who are encouraged to take an unhurried look at themselves in the total context of their lives.

A focus on the whole person not only means that clients can explore, should they wish to, any aspect of their lives, but also that counsellors should pay attention to different aspects of their clients' functioning. They may, however, be constrained by their theoretical perspectives (see section on Issues below). While individual counsellors are noted by the emphasis they place on clients' feelings, they may also focus on their clients' thoughts and attitudes, behaviours and skills, images, dreams and fantasies, relationships (direct exploration of the relationship with the counsellor and indirectly with other people), sensations and physiological responses (if they have the requisite skills and knowledge). Such a focus also means that counsellors should neither lose sight of the interconnections among these different aspects of client functioning nor of the fact that the person is more that the sum of her or his parts.

This focus on clients as whole people and on their different but inter-connecting modes of functioning can be more easily undertaken in individual counselling than in other arenas where (a) the presence of other clients may emphasize the relationship between the client and others, and (b) time constraints may restrict the focus of exploration to a smaller number of modes of client functioning.

Explanatory frameworks and tasks

A preoccupation of some research into counselling has been to pit one approach or method against another to determine which is more effective. However, it appears that different counselling approaches yield comparable results (Luborsky *et al.* 1975; Smith *et al.* 1980). One reason for this equivalence is that relationship variables are common across different counselling approaches, although it is also likely that clients find value in a diverse range of approaches. In addition, Smith and associates found that the average treated individual did better than 80 per cent of non-treated individuals. In other words, counselling is better than no counselling except of course when it leads to harm (see Chapter 29 for a fuller discussion of research issues). However, some leading psychologists such as Lazarus (see Dryden 1991) have suggested that the Smith *et al.* study was method-ologically flawed and should be ignored as it failed to include a large number of relevant studies. Lazarus asserts that other meta-analyses did show differences (see Wilson 1985). If we consider the more recent litera-ture, some studies have highlighted variations in the effectiveness of different approaches in the treatment of specific disorders. For example, Butler *et al.* (1991) found cognitive-behavioural therapy superior to behaviour therapy in the treatment of generalized anxiety disorder. We return to the issue of relative effectiveness under future developments (see p. 54).

Frank (1985) has noted that each approach to counselling involves an *explanatory framework* (a conceptual scheme that provides an explanation for clients' concerns and for what is considered therapeutic) and a set of *tasks* (in which both clients – inside and outside the counselling room – and counsellors – inside the counselling room – engage in the service of clients' goals). In rational emotive behavioural counselling, for example, the explanatory framework centres on the important role that irrational beliefs play in explaining clients' concerns. The tasks dictate that counsellors should help clients to identify, challenge, and change (through thought and deed) these irrational beliefs in the counselling session and that clients should practise this same sequence both within and between counselling sessions (Ellis 1994).

It is likely that in effective individual counselling, counsellors and clients agree (albeit most often at an implicit level) (a) on an understanding of the clients' problems, and (b) to undertake to carry out their respective tasks in the service of clients' goals. The degree to which each participant accommodates to the other's view of the client's concerns is unknown but it is probable that the client is more likely to adopt and work within the counsellor's explanatory framework than vice versa. It is difficult, thus, to imagine a psychodynamic counsellor, for example, agreeing with a client that the latter's relationship concerns are explained by a lack of social skills and even less likely that such a counsellor would actually teach the client these skills (although psychodynamic counsellors may well refer clients to other counsellors for social skills training: see Chapter 12).

Extending this argument, ineffective counselling may occur when counsellor and client fail to agree to use a similar explanatory framework. Thus, using the above example, if the client maintains the stance that his or her problem is due to a lack of social skills and the counsellor considers it to be explained by the client's conflict with authority figures, then unless one accommodates to the view of the other or the two arrive at an explanation that somehow encompasses both viewpoints, progress is not likely to occur. In fact, the counsellor's intransigence is likely to lead to early termination of counselling.

Similarly, progress may be hindered in the realm of tasks. Thus, for example, clients may not understand the tasks they are asked to perform and/or how these relate to their goals, or they may not be able or willing to carry them out. Counsellors, on the other hand, may not be skilful at carrying out their own tasks and/or may not succeed in helping their clients to engage productively in their tasks. Counsellors may negotiate or set tasks that overwhelm the client instead of just being sufficiently challenging. This also hinders progress.

Some counsellors deliberately set out to educate their clients in their explanatory framework and the tasks recommended by their approach to counselling, while other counsellors do not do this. In the latter case, the client is likely to learn about this implicitly. One person who went to consult a person-centred counsellor, for example, was initially puzzled regarding what she was expected to do as a client, but came to realize that her role was 'to talk about my feelings'. She soon experienced some benefit from counselling and her puzzlement ended. In the scheme employed here, at first she did not know the nature of her tasks but came to see that she was expected to engage in the task of 'talking about feelings'. The benefit she experienced led her to understand one aspect of her counselling's explanatory framework: 'talking about feelings is therapeutic'. This encouraged her to continue to engage more deeply in this helpful process. This does of course raise the ethical issue of whether she entered counselling with informed consent.

There is an important connection between 'explanatory framework', 'task', and 'relationship' variables. A good counselling relationship may help the client and counsellor to share a similar explanatory framework and an agreed set of tasks but it is not a sufficient condition for this to occur. One client remarked that he found his counsellor very understanding and concerned with his development, but claimed that he needed more active help than 'just talking'. 'I needed explicit help to change my behaviour in the real world but she didn't give me this.' On the other hand, a client may agree with the counsellor's explanatory framework and agree to perform the tasks implicit in the counselling approach but may not benefit from the process because a good working relationship has not been developed. Thus, for example, the client may not experience his or her counsellor as understanding or may feel judged negatively.

To summarize, effective individual counselling probably involves the development of a good relationship between counsellor and client, a shared agreement to employ a useful explanatory framework concerning the client's problems and what is therapeutic, and successful execution of helpful mutually agreed tasks.

The process of individual counselling

While it should be remembered that individual counsellors bring different orientations to their work, it is likely that most practitioners would concur with the view that counselling is a process and that different interventions are more salient at different points in this process. Since space does not permit a thorough examination of this viewpoint from different theoretical perspectives, we will illustrate this principle with reference to the work of Gerard Egan (1986, 1994), whose impact on the work of counsellors of individuals in Britain has been noteworthy (Inskipp and Johns 1984).

Egan's view is that counselling is a developmental process and that different counsellor skills are needed at different stages in the process. He further notes that the success of this developmental process depends on the extent to which the client experiences the counsellor as offering high levels of the core relationship conditions discussed earlier (see p. 11). Egan's developmental model, as described in Chapter 2, should be seen as a flexible guide for intervention rather than as a rigid approach that should necessarily be used with all clients.

Given the above, in the early stage of the process counsellors strive to develop a good working relationship with their clients and to help them explore their concerns in increasingly concrete and clear terms. Then clients are helped to develop new perspectives that form the basis for later constructive action. In the next stage, counsellors help their clients to set and commit themselves to goals based on the emerging new perspective of the previous stage. Finally, counsellors encourage their clients to achieve their goals by helping them to

(a) develop a range of strategies for action;
(b) evaluate and choose from among these strategies;
(c) formulate action plans;
(d) implement these new strategies in appropriate areas of their lives.

While Egan (1994) outlines specific skills that counsellors require to help them carry out the tasks of each stage, counsellors who employ such a developmental model may use a broader range of skills than those discussed by Egan in the service of each stage's tasks. Whether counsellors are competent at using different skills at each stage will depend partly on their training experiences (and partly on their personal inclinations and temperament). Indeed, it follows from this model that counsellor training programmes need to train their students in a broad range of skills if they are to help their clients across the entire developmental cycle of counselling.

Issues

The discussion in this section will centre on two issues that the authors consider to be important and worthy of public debate. First, the issue concerning the relationship between individual counselling and other counselling arenas will be discussed. While counsellors work predominantly in individual counselling, they may also work in other arenas and thus need to consider both the limitations of individual counselling and the pros and cons of clients moving among different arenas. The second issue concerns the differences among various theoretical approaches to individual counselling. This issue will be presented 'as if' a debate between counsellors from different therapeutic orientations were to occur. This debate may help counsellors to appreciate the variation in different counsellors' approaches – an appreciation which is necessary if counsellors are to explore the possiblities and limitations of eclecticism and integration (to be discussed in Future Developments, p. 51).

Relationship with other counselling arenas

As was noted in the previous section, counselling can take place in a number of arenas (individual, couple, family, and group). One question that emerges here concerns which arena is appropriate for which clients at which stage of the counselling process. In order to answer this question an appreciation of the contraindications (as well as the particular therapeutic merits) of individual counselling is necessary. The following points again emerged from Dryden's (1984) discussion with a number of counsellors.

Contraindications for individual counselling

(1) Individual counselling may be contraindicated for clients who are likely to become overly dependent on the counsellor. In these cases dependency can become so intense as to lead to client determination, in which events unfold according to previous causes and not the clients' free will. These clients may be more appropriately helped in group counselling where such intense dependency is less likely to develop due to the fact that the counsellor has to relate to several other people.

(2) Individual counselling, by its dyadic nature, can involve a close inter-personal encounter between client and counsellor and as such may be contraindicated for those clients who may find such a degree of in-timacy or the prospect of such intimacy unduly threatening and where the likelihood of overcoming this is poor.

(3) Individual counselling may be contraindicated for clients who find this arena *too* comfortable. Based on the idea that personal change is often best facilitated in situations where there is an optimal level of arousal, individual counselling may not provide enough challenge for such clients. In this context, Ravid (1969) found that it may be unproductive to offer individual counselling to clients who have had much previous individual counselling but still require therapeutic help.

(4) Individual counselling may not be appropriate for clients for whom other arenas are deemed to have greater therapeutic value. Clients who are shy, retiring and afraid to take risks, for example, are more likely to benefit from group counselling (if they can be encouraged to join such a group) than from the less risky situation of individual counselling. In addition, partners who can productively use the con-joint situation of couple counselling often benefit more from this arena than from working in individual counselling. This is particularly true when they have both committed themselves to remain in and to improve their relationship.

Having outlined some indications and contraindications for individual counselling, we should like to stress that these are guidelines only and not relevant in all cases. In addition, we have stated elsewhere (Palmer and Dryden 1995: 200) that depending upon the experience and clinical acumen of the counsellor, clients with a number of contraindications may still benefit from individual counselling. Perhaps the best way of determining whether a client will benefit or not from this arena is in fact for counsellors to work with their clients in individual counselling and to monitor their response to it, although a 'reception' or initial interview should aim to establish which of the available arenas is best for that client.

Movement between counselling arenas

Once the counsellor and client have decided to work in individual counselling, this does not mean that the client will remain within it throughout counselling. Thus, a client may be first seen in individual counselling and then join a counselling group once their intrapsychic concerns have largely been dealt with and their interpersonal concerns have come more to the fore. Indeed, some clients may be seen in individual counselling and group counselling conjointly. This can be valuable when clients need to work on a one-to-one basis and discuss at length their personal reactions to their experiences in the group. However, it should be noted that some counsellors argue that the conjoint use of individual and group counselling inhibits clients from dealing with their experiences of the group *in* the group.

Should a client's individual counsellor also be his or her counsellor in another arena? Since initially clients in group counselling are generally strangers to each other, this issue can largely be explored and decided on the basis of the client's feelings and opinions alone. However, when movement from individual counselling is being considered, it is often inadvisable for the client's individual counsellor to act as counsellor to the convened couple or family. One reason for this is due to the fact that the counsellor–client dyad has a history, the content of which is unknown to the other partner or family members. The latter may feel, as a result, that the counsellor may have a stronger alliance with the client than with them and the development of a productive counselling relationship among participants in the couple or family counselling arena may thus be inhibited. (This phenomenon can also occur in group counselling but is much less likely to be an inhibiting factor on the ensuing group process.) The longer the client has worked in individual counselling, the more likely it is that this will be an issue for the other client(s). Also, given that the client's partner or other family members are part of the client's everyday world, the client may find sharing the counsellor in the new arena much more difficult than he or she would with strangers in group counselling.

In addition, issues of confidentiality may add to this tension. For example, if a counsellor has been working with a woman in individual counsel-ling, he or she is bound to keep confidential material that has arisen in that arena. If the counsellor then were to see the woman and her husband in couple counselling, the husband would know that the counsellor could not disclose this material and may feel the three-person alliance to be unba-lanced against him. Equally the counsellor may inadvertently reveal con-fidential material in the couple counselling arena which was previously gleaned from the individual counselling. This could adversely affect the counsellor's relationship with the woman as well as raising ethical con-cerns. Such issues need to be kept firmly in mind when discussing move-ment among counselling arenas with clients (see Chapter 31 for an in-depth discussion of professional issues in counselling).

Different emphases among differing approaches to individual counselling

In the first section of this chapter, some general principles were outlined about individual counselling that arise from taking a 'common factors' approach (Frank 1985). However, it is important not to deny that there are differences among the various approaches to individual counselling that are currently practised. These differences may make it difficult for counsellors with diverse orientations to communicate effectively with one another unless these differences are understood and, if possible, accepted. Appli-cants to training courses, in particular, need to understand these differences if they are to make informed decisions concerning their choice for initial counsellor training. In addition, if the field is to move towards an integra-tive or eclectic position, an appreciation of the different emphases in the major counselling traditions will facilitate the exploration of the possibi-lities and limits of integration and eclecticism in individual counselling. This will be considered more fully in the final section of this chapter.

Modality focus

Although it was argued earlier that many counsellors adopt a whole-person focus in their work, various counselling approaches place differential emphasis on the seven modalities of human functioning (Lazarus 1989) outlined in the section on Principles (i.e. behaviour, affect, sensation, imagery, cognition, interpersonal relationships, and physiological function-ing). Thus, humanistic approaches to counselling focus particularly on affect, phenomenally based cognitions about self, and interpersonal rela-tionships; psychodynamic approaches do not place a direct focus on any of the modalities but look for the existence of unconscious conflict as it is manifested in the modalities; while cognitive-behavioural approaches tend to emphasize cognition, imagery, and behaviour while considering affect to be the product of cognitive processes.

Image of relationship

The major traditions within counselling tend to consider the relationship between counsellor and client in different ways. Psychodynamic approaches view the counsellor–client relationship as an 'as if' one where the emphasis is on perceptual, affective, and interactional distortions; where, for example, the client unconsciously views and relates to the counsellor 'as if' the latter were a significant person, usually from the client's past. The 'real' relationship between counsellor and client is considered to be important but as a backdrop enabling the counsellor and client to stand back and reflect on the meaning of the client's distortions.

In the humanistic approaches (and particularly so in person-centred counselling) the emphasis is on the real, here-and-now relationship between counsellor and client which is seen as the major vehicle for therapeutic change. The important curative factor in the person-centred approach is the client's experience of the counsellor as a person in his or her own right who is understanding and genuinely concerned for the development of the client. The focus on the 'as if' quality of the relationship is consequently played down.

In cognitive-behavioural approaches, the relationship between counsellor and client is regarded as a real present-centred relationship which serves as a facilitative backdrop to the successful execution of a set of important therapeutic tasks. Such counsellors are likely to view themselves primarily as educators whose major role is to help clients acquire cognitive and behavioural skills that they then practice between counselling sessions.

Time and space focus

Counsellors from the major traditions also differ concerning the focus they place on issues of time and space in engaging their clients in exploration in counselling. With respect to time counsellors may facilitate clients' exploration of their past, present, and/or future. With respect to space, some counsellors may place a greater emphasis on interaction within the counselling relationship, while others may focus more on clients' lives outside the counselling sessions.

Psychodynamic counsellors tend to view clients' functioning in terms of the latters' past experiences and encourage them to understand that their present and future aspirations are coloured by their past. In addition, they tend to seek clues to their clients' current relationship difficulties in terms of the clients' relationship with their counsellors (the transference relationship). When the transference relationship is manifest, this is then linked to clients' past and present relationships outside the counselling arena. This dual focus is well expressed in the title of Jacobs' (1986) book on psychodynamic counselling, *The Presenting Past*.

Person-centred counsellors (who probably represent the majority of humanistic counsellors) tend to work in the time and space frames determined by their clients. Thus, they weave between the present, past and future time frames and between the 'in here' and 'out there' space frames. Gestalt counsellors, on the other hand, tend to emphasize the 'here-and-now' space and time frames in their work and endeavour to help the focus on these frames as far as possible.

Cognitive-behavioural counsellors tend to work within the present and future time frames and focus more on their clients' outside experiences than on their experiences within the counselling room, although the latter focus is not neglected when it becomes salient. In the same way, the client's past is not neglected when he or she wishes to focus on this time frame.

At present, counsellor training programmes tend to be based on one of the major traditions as listed above. Whether this will continue in the future depends on the extent to which counsellors can explore how far eclectic and integrative counselling is possible.

Future developments

Eclecticism and integration

It is likely that in future individual counsellors will continue to become increasingly interested in exploring the prospects and possiblities of eclecticism and integration. Eclecticism defines the practice of counsellors who claim to choose what appears to be best from diverse counselling systems, sources and styles. Eclectics often state a dislike for working within a single orientation, select from two or more theories, and believe that no present theory is adequate to explain or predict all of the phenomena that counsellors observe (Norcross 1986).

Integration, on the other hand, refers to the process of incorporating parts into a whole and stresses the formulation of a perspective on counselling that emphasizes common factors within a generally accepted overarching framework. Integrationists, like eclectics, are disenchanted with a single theoretical approach to counselling but are more preoccupied than eclectics with integrating the endeavours of counsellors from disparate schools.

There are indications that the trend away from single counselling systems is beginning to get underway in Britain; for example, the number of integrative counselling courses is slowly increasing and there exists a growing network of members of the British Institute of Integrative Psychotherapists. However, a caution is in order at this point. To call oneself an eclectic or an integrationist reveals nothing about one's mode of practice. These terms may be fashionable but it is important that they do not obscure undisciplined practice. Indeed, eclectics, for example, are often perceived as muddle-headed individuals who are too sloppy or lazy to develop a sound set of theoretical principles to guide their work (for further discussion see Owen 1996). It may be that for the development of a mature eclecticism or integrationism in individual counselling to occur practitioners need to have (a) sound initial training in one theoretical approach while being exposed to the merits of other approaches, or (b) sound initial training in one theoretical approach followed by sound training in another theoretical approach, or (c) a sound training in one eclectic approach such as Lazarus' (1989) multimodal counselling or a sound training in an integrative approach of counselling, for example, that based on Egan's (1994) work. However, such developments will also be enhanced by a much-needed growth in more advanced training courses in counselling (in both the public and private educational sectors) where experienced practitioners might come together to explore the possibilities of eclecticism and integration.

The issues they might explore could include the development of

(a) a set of common principles, couched in acceptable language, that would form the basis of further exploration;
(b) a matrix of modalities of client functioning that would facilitate comprehensiveness in individual counselling. Lazarus (1989) has outlined one such matrix: behaviour, affect, sensation, imagery, cognition, interpersonal relationships, and physiological functioning;
(c) salient dimensions of client variability to enable counsellors to consider how they might vary their practice in response to such client variability. Beutler (1983), for example, has argued that symptom complexity, level of client reactance (to therapeutic influence), and style of defence constitute important dimensions along which clients vary and which merit a differential counsellor response. To this list might be added an understanding of clients' learning styles and how they may warrant modifications in counselling approach;
(d) a schema for counsellor decision-making allied to a taxonomy of salient dimensions of client variability that would help practitioners make decisions concerning, for example, variations in interactional style, modifications in the therapeutic alliance, and selection among a set of counselling methods and techniques.

Putting these points together in a consistent and productive manner constitutes an immense task, but we predict that exploration along these lines will enable counsellors to discover the advantages and disadvantages of eclectic and integrative practice.

Individual counselling is a particularly appropriate arena in which the development of these ideas can be explored. Thus, for example, if counsellors are going to consider how to vary their approach to clients across the counselling process then this is best done, at least initially, in the arena of individual counselling where practitioners do not have to consider the impact that such variation might have on other clients present.

Specialized versus generalized counselling

Most individual counsellors working in Britain today are likely to be generalists but with one or more particular specialisms. They are trained (within the constraints of particular counselling orientations) to offer general counselling to clients with a range of concerns and difficulties, but in the course of their work may come to specialize in working with a particular group of clients. As shown elsewhere in this volume, working with particular client groups involves a detailed knowledge of the specific concerns and issues that face these groups. However, to what extent does working with particular client groups involve modification of one's general counselling approach? There is a need to translate careful delineation of particular clients' problems and issues into the development of specific counselling interventions targeted for use with these clients and we predict that this is one area in which individual counselling will develop in the future. If the development can be harnessed to those in the area of eclecticism/integration, then the likelihood that a personalized counselling approach can be offered to clients who have both specialized needs (with regard to their concerns) and individual needs (with respect to their learning styles, and so on) will be increased.

Addressing the 'plastic bubble' effect

Critics of individual counselling have argued that there is a danger that a kind of 'plastic bubble' surrounds work that is done in this counselling arena, in that the work may become isolated from the realities of the client's life. While we have shown that movement between different counselling arenas can (and, some would argue, should) occur to obviate this effect, what can the counsellor do to weaken the boundary between individual counselling and the client's everyday life? We foresee that individual counsellors will increasingly grapple with this problem, especially as issues of accountability and effectiveness with respect to counselling in general and individual counselling in particular come increasingly to the fore in British society. It is likely, then, that individual counsellors will experiment with modifications in their approach, such as (a) incorporating interventions that *specifically* address the generalization issue (i.e. how clients can specifically use their counselling-inspired gains in their daily lives), and (b) utilizing interventions that treat absent significant others 'as if' they were present. Bennun's (1985) description of doing marital counselling when only one partner is present is a good example of this latter trend. In the next section we focus on a specific area to illustrate how counselling and the training of counsellors cannot stand still and how outside forces such as service purchasers are likely to demand changes.

The drive for efficiency and effectiveness

With more counsellors working in time-limited settings, we suspect that they will experience increasing pressure from service purchasers to provide an efficient and effective service. Accountants are less concerned about what methods are used as long as costs can be reduced or maintained at acceptable levels. In the future clients may only have the 'luxury' of extended counselling to explore a variety of issues in the private practice sector, whilst counselling in the National Health Service and general practice will be relegated to helping people with specific problems such as phobias and depression. Anecdotally, we have already noticed that more students are attending our courses to learn cognitive-behavioural approaches as they wish to work in time-limited or brief counselling settings (see Chapter 15).

Very few counselling training courses devote much time to either time-limited or brief counselling. We wonder how many counsellors who work in time-limited settings or offer brief counselling have actually received formal extended training in this type of work and receive supervision from supervisors who also have been formally trained in this area. This raises the ethical issue of counsellors offering a service beyond their level of competence (see Appendix 1 for the BAC Code of Ethics and Practice for Counsellors). As service purchasers start to realize this, perhaps in the future more will start demanding that their counsellors have formal training in this type of work. Accredited counsellor status alone may not be sufficient.

Interestingly, as the majority of individual counselling is usually short-term whether by choice or due to early termination, training courses may start reflecting this and give more guidance to students on the inherently brief nature of counselling. Over the next decade we may start to see different approaches to counselling adapt to the market needs of the service purchasers and, more importantly, its individual customers.

Research into the therapeutic benefits to the client of accredited counsellor status

At the moment the counselling and related therapeutic professions in Britain are holding much in store for various forms of recognized status: the BAC have accredited counsellors, the UKCP have registered psychotherapists and the BPS have chartered counselling psychologists. However, contrary to popular belief, there is no research evidence showing that accredited, registered or chartered practitioners are any more effective therapeutically than non-qualified practitioners. Also research has not confirmed that recognition or advanced qualifications lead to less counsellor abuse of clients. In fact the converse has been shown in America for similar professions (see Chapter 30). These issues may become more important if 'astute' service purchasers wish to reduce overheads by employing less qualified counsellors. If this was to become an issue then we may well see members of professional therapeutic bodies insisting that the bodies finance a research programme into the relative effectiveness of recognized and non-recognized practitioners.

Conclusion

To what extent these and other developments in individual counselling will occur depends on the willingness of counsellors to

(a) adopt an experimental attitude to their work;
(b) read widely the literature on counselling;
(c) maintain an ongoing continuing professional development programme by attendance on suitable courses;
(d) learn from each other's innovations.

Despite some of the negative and misleading media hyperbole that the field of counselling has received in recent years (see Bond 1996), with the great efforts being made by the new profession to 'clean up its act' the future prospects for individual counselling look most promising.

Note

1 In this chapter we use the word 'arena' to refer to the setting of individual, couple, family, and group counselling.

References

BAC (1993) *BAC membership survey*, Keele: Mountain & Associates.
Barkham, M. (1996) 'Quantitative research on psychotherapeutic interventions: methodological issues and substantive findings across three research generations'

in R. Woolfe and W. Dryden (eds) *Handbook of Counselling Psychology*, London: Sage.

Bennun, I. (1985) 'Unilateral marital therapy' in W. Dryden (ed.) *Marital Therapy in Britain, Volume 2: Special Areas*, London: Harper & Row.

Beutler, L. E. (1983) *Eclectic Psychotherapy: A Systematic Approach*, New York: Pergamon.

Butler, G., Fennell, M., Robson, P. and Gelder, M. (1991) 'A comparison of behavior therapy and cognitive-behaviour therapy in the treatment of Generalized Anxiety Disorder', *Journal of Consulting and Clinical Psychology* 59: 167–75.

Bond, T. (1996) Watchdog: Letter from the Chair to BAC members. *Counselling* 7(2): 97.

Cowen, E. L. (1982) 'Help is where you find it', *American Psychologist* 37: 385–95.

Dryden, W. (1984) 'Therapeutic arenas' in W. Dryden (ed.) *Individual Therapy in Britain*, London: Harper & Row.

——(1991) *A Dialogue with Arnold Lazarus: 'It Depends'*, Milton Keynes: Open University Press.

Egan, G. (1986) *The Skilled Helper: A Systematic Approach to Effective Helping*, 3rd edn, Monterey, CA: Brooks/Cole.

——(1994) *The Skilled Helper*, 5th edn, Monterey, CA: Brooks/Cole.

Ellis, A. (1994) *Reason and emotion in psychotherapy*, (revised and updated) New York: Birch Lane Press.

Frank, J. D. (1985) 'Therapeutic components shared by all psychotherapies' in M. J. Mahoney and A. Freeman (eds) *Cognition and Psychotherapy*, New York: Plenum.

Grunebaum, H. (1986) 'Harmful psychotherapy experience', *American Journal of Psychotherapy* 40(2): 165–76.

Gurman, A. S. and Kniskern, D. P. (1978) 'Research in marital and family therapy' in S. L. Garfield and A. E. Bergin (eds) *Handbook of Psychotherapy and Behavior Change*, 2nd edn, New York: Wiley.

Horvath, A. O. and Symonds, D. B. (1991) 'Relation between working alliance and outcome in psychotherapy', *Journal of Counseling Psychology* 38: 139–49.

Inskipp, F. and Johns, H. (1984) 'Developmental eclecticism: Egan's skills model of helping' in W. Dryden (ed.) *Individual Therapy in Britain*, London: Harper & Row.

Jacobs, M. (1986) *The Presenting Past*, London: Harper & Row.

Lazarus, A. A. (1989) *The Practice of Multimodal Therapy*. Baltimore: Johns Hopkins University Press.

Luborsky, L., Singer, B., and Luborsky, L. (1975) 'Comparative studies of psychotherapy: is it true that "everyone has won and all must have prizes"?', *Archives of General Psychiatry* 32: 995–1008.

Nelson-Jones, R. (1995) *The Theory and Practice of Counselling*, 2nd edn, London: Cassell.

Norcross, J. L. (1986) 'Eclectic psychotherapy: an introduction and overview' in J. C. Norcross (ed.) *Handbook of Eclectic Psychotherapy*, New York: Brunner/Mazel.

Owen, I. (1996) 'Are we before or after integration?', *Counselling Psychology Review* 11(2): 12–18.

Palmer, S. and Dryden, W. (1995) *Counselling For Stress Problems*, London: Sage.

Ravid, R. (1969) 'Effect of group therapy on long-term individual therapy', *Dissertation Abstracts International* 30: 2427B.

Smith, M. L., Glass, G. V. and Miller, T. I. (1980) *The Benefits of Psychotherapy*, Baltimore, MD: Johns Hopkins University Press.

Strupp, H. H., Hadley, S. W., and Gomes-Schwartz, B. (1977) *Psychotherapy for Better or Worse: The Problem of Negative Effects*, New York: Aronson.

Truax, C.B. and Carkhuff, R. R. (1967) *Toward Effective Counseling and Psychotherapy: Training and Practice*, Chicago: Aldine.

Wilson, G. T. (1985) 'Limitations of meta-analysis in the evaluation of the effects of psychological therapy', *Clinical Psychology Review* 5: 35–47.

Chapter four

Couples counselling

Thomas Schröder

Introduction

The first English-language account of couple therapy was published just over sixty years ago. At that time, the concerns of marital partners were generally seen as an obstacle to individual therapeutic work. Now, the predominant view has shifted towards regarding couples counselling as one important option among others. In Britain this development has been underlined by the foundation of the National Marriage Guidance Council (today Relate) in 1947 – a direct consequence of the rapid growth in the marriage counselling movement – and of the Family Discussion Bureau (today the Tavistock Institute of Marital Studies) in 1948. While there are various ways of helping couples (as will be discussed below), it is *conjoint* work, where both partners are seen together, which is most clearly distinguished from other forms of counselling. Therefore, much of the following discussion will pertain to this modality.

Although this chapter adopts an integrative point of view, there are two biases which need to be declared. First, my own clinical orientation is predominantly psychodynamic, and it would be surprising (and somewhat disconcerting) if this had not influenced my views. Second, couples counselling will be treated here as an endeavour in its own right, separate and different from family counselling. This issue has been somewhat controversial. Gurman, Kniskern, & Pinsof (1986), in an authoritative review of the field, asserted that 'marital therapy (is) now viewed by most clinicians as a subspeciality of family therapy'. However, the latest edition of the same review (Alexander, Holtzworth-Munroe and Jameson 1994) now concludes that such a postulated 'underlying coherence is elusive at best', citing research which 'emphasizes the differences, not the similarities, of marital therapy and family therapy'.

Apart from their historically separate development it is the nature of the therapeutic relationship which, in my view, distinguishes these forms of therapeutic work from each other, and, indeed, from other modes of counselling.

Unlike individual and group counselling, where the development of the important relationship(s) can be observed from their beginnings, in couples counselling the strongest initial relationship in the room is pre-established and independent of the counsellor. This affords opportunities as it allows the counsellor to disengage in order to observe the couple's patterns of interaction. It also presents obstacles as disorientating interactional pressures are exerted which derive from the couple's joint history rather than the current circumstances. This situation is also encountered in family counselling. The crucial difference lies in the fact that in marital work counsellors cannot make an alliance with one partner without necessarily excluding and isolating the other, whereas in family work they may 'join' (make an alliance with) a subsystem, leaving other family members to support each other. Working with a co-therapist mitigates but does not eliminate this special feature of counselling couples.

Much of the literature concerning helping couples with their relationship problems makes reference to 'marital therapy' or similar terms, raising the question of whether one might usefully distinguish between 'counselling' and 'therapy'. As in other therapeutic modes the answer will differ according to the context in which the work is carried out (for example, 'voluntary' vs. 'professional' or 'supportive' vs. 'curative') and to the theoretical model followed. In this chapter no distinction is drawn between couple counselling and therapy, although it should be borne in mind that working with couples, like any other therapeutic activity, can be practised at various levels of depth and sophistication.

While the vast majority of couples coming for help are heterosexual and married, the basic principles of couple counselling apply equally to unmarried and homosexual pairs, and terms like 'spouse', 'partner', 'marital counselling', or 'couple work' will be used interchangeably and taken to apply generally. This is not to deny that, for instance, gay couples face special issues arising from, among other reasons, their minority status. However, the commonalities between dyadic relationships far outweigh such special features, a fact which is acknowledged in the practice of most agencies offering help to couples.

Principles

Settings

Today, couples counselling in Britain is offered by a spectrum of agencies. This ranges from specialist services, such as the Tavistock Institute of Marital Studies or Relate, through more generalist counselling organizations which offer help to couples as one among several options, to Social Services and Health Service settings in which the primary focus may well be on individual symptoms or family problems rather than on marital issues. To which of these agencies a couple presents will largely depend of their own initiatives and views of the problem.

The decision to seek counselling help for marital problems does not come easily to most couples and typically indicates that the informal social resources – such as friends or families of origin – available to both partners have already been drawn upon without effecting the desired help. (For a discussion of the informal and formal aspects of a 'help-seeking career', see Brannen and Collard (1982)) However, if the couple are clear about the source of their troubles, they are likely to seek out or be referred to a specialist service. Otherwise, they may seek clarification and referral from their general practitioner or other persons trusted to know (such as clergy) or contact a generalist service for advice. In either case the couple counsellor can draw on an initial understanding that what is required is marital work and can act in a context sympathetic to this approach.

The situation is somewhat different in agencies which do not see marital work as their primary concern. Couples will have presented there because they did not construe problems as lying within their relationship and the marital counselling comes about either as an adjunct to other interventions (for example, dealing with a child's problems) or because the focus on one partner's psychological or somatic symptoms has not been fruitful. Some of the problems arising from this in the counselling process are discussed below, but in addition couple counsellors may be faced with the task of justifying their approach to sceptical colleagues or bewildered referrers.

Diagnostic criteria

Once the couple have made their way through the various stages of seeking help and are established as presenting with a problem between them rather than with individual difficulties, the question arises as to which form of help is most appropriate for them. There are five basic options:

(1) the couple can be engaged in individual work (where partners are seen separately by different counsellors);
(2) collaborative counselling (where partners are seen separately by different counsellors who communicate with each other about the couple);
(3) concurrent mode (i.e. the couple are seen separately by the same counsellor);
(4) conjoint work with one or two counsellors;
(5) they may be assigned together with other couples to conjoint group-work.

The choice between these options might well be based on theoretical considerations. Grunebaum, Christ and Neiberg (1969) suggest a three-stage model for diagnosis and treatment planning. First, they seek to establish whether the couple are committed to working on the marital difficulties. If not (for instance, if the partners come to the decision that they wish to end their relationship rather than seek to improve it), they recommend individual or collaborative work. For those couples who are committed to tackling their joint problems, the second diagnostic question concerns the locus of symptoms. If there are serious difficulties outside as well as inside the relationship, the authors favour concurrent counselling which affords the opportunity of working on different individual problems as well as on couple issues. If most of the difficulties arise from within the relationship, the final question concerns chronicity. For those couples whose problems are acute and relatively recent (often arising from a transition point in the life-cycle of the couple), the recommendation would be for conjoint work whereas couples with long-standing, chronic problems are considered to benefit from groupwork.

While to my knowledge there is no empirical support for this rather prescriptive model, it has some practical appeal and it meshes well with developmental concepts. From the vantage point of individual development one would ask if partners (who from a psychodynamic understanding are assumed to have chosen each other because of a shared level of immaturity) had progressed enough in their own individuation to be able to tolerate the complications of conjoint counselling, especially the triangular relationship arising in work with a single counsellor. Looking at the development of the couple, one would ask if – regardless of whether they had formally contracted a marriage or not – both partners had actually progressed beyond the 'premarital' or 'courtship' phase with its inherent denial of interdependency and were thus committed to working conjointly on shared problems; or whether – at the other end of the spectrum – their relationship had come to the end of its life and was in fact 'emotionally dead', thus precluding the option of useful conjoint work.

So far, the available evidence from empirical research is too sketchy to form a coherent basis for decisions in treatment planning. However, there are indications that individual counselling for marital problems may well be an ineffective strategy (for the empirical evidence see Gurman *et al.* (1986); for a dissenting clinical view see Bennun (1991)). The decision between the various options will in reality often be made on the basis of practical considerations such as available resources or skills and personal preferences of the counsellor. Furthermore, many practitioners will feel free to mix modes; for instance by contracting some concurrent individual sessions with a couple seen in conjoint counselling if the partners become temporarily too preoccupied with their own individual needs to focus on their relationship.

An integrative conceptual framework for conjoint counselling

Considering the variety of conceptual approaches – some of which are discussed below – currently used by marital counsellors and therapists, it may seem premature to adopt a single, integrated frame of reference. However, I do believe that there is enough common ground between the various schools of thought in their practice of working with couples to allow us to construct such a framework without losing or obscuring what is of value in their differences. The relatively short history of the field has helped to avoid the establishment of entrenched positions and one might thus broadly characterize the current situation as one of diversity of theory and convergence of practice.

In the model used here, which is described in more detail in Schröder (1991), interventions in couple counselling are seen as happening within a therapeutic frame provided by the *working alliance* (with the attendant continuous monitoring of the therapeutic relationship) and the *therapeutic contract* (with the attendant formulation and continuous reformulation of the couple's problem). The temporal sequence, as outlined by Ables and Brandsma (1977), consists of: Forming a Working Alliance → Agreeing a Therapeutic Contract → Making Therapeutic Interventions. In marital counselling, where working alliances tend to be more difficult to maintain than, for example, in individual work, this sequence may need to be worked through repeatedly by the counsellor who may have to focus on repairing the working alliance with one partner and restating the contract before being able to proceed with interventions.

Maintaining a stable frame, in the way outlined below, is not only central to conjoint counselling regardless of theoretical approach; it is in itself the main intervention of counsellors operating at a basic level of competence – invariably necessary, but often sufficient to help couples with relatively mild and recent problems. Basic interventions, of the type described below, which have face-validity and are therefore readily understood (though not always adhered to) by clients, require an intermediate level of training and are used by counsellors of different theoretical persuasions, whereas 'specialist interventions' are usually highly specific to a particular theoretical approach, often require a specialist level of expertise, and are not described in this chapter.

Alliance issues

The importance of establishing a good working alliance for the successful outcome of any therapeutic endeavour is well documented, even though definitions vary. What is discussed here rests on the following premise:

> The working alliance consists of an understanding between counsellor(s) and clients that

- there is a joint therapeutic task to be done collaboratively,
- to carry out this task requires an atmosphere of trust,
- the potential social aspects of the relationship will have to be set aside for the benefit of the task.

Other issues often connected with the alliance, such as establishing joint goals, are dealt with below in the section on contracting.

The process of establishing, maintaining, and, if necessary, repairing the working alliance is familiar from individual counselling. Indeed, some ascribe a major therapeutic influence to the gradual disillusionment and adjustment to reality brought about by repeated minor alliance breakdowns and repairs. However, the maintenance of an alliance is nowhere as central to the counselling process as in conjoint couples' work, especially if there is only one counsellor involved. From a developmental point of view one might argue that it is the difficult and often traumatic transition from two-person to three-person relationships (where the latter entail all the new potential for rivalry, jealousy, competition and exclusion which the former lack) which is reawakened in the counselling room; and, indeed, some couples experience marital problems in connection with the birth of the first child, which raises similar issues (see Clulow 1982). From the counsellors' perspective it is the sheer difficulty of trying to relate to two people at the same time – often in the face of determined efforts by one or both partners to form an exclusive relationship – which makes for the challenge and the special opportunities in triadic couple work.

While experienced counsellors will have a number of means at their disposal to mitigate the stresses of a triadic relationship (such as disengaging from the couple, addressing them jointly, balancing attention given to each partner), the fact remains that the quality of the alliance is based on subjective experience; giving equal time to both partners may be satisfactory for one, but not feel anything like enough for the other. Ultimately, what is required of both spouses is the capacity to set aside their own needs temporarily in order to have those of their partner attended to. In successful marital counselling this achievement will serve the couple well in the future. If either partner cannot tolerate the temporary deprivation entailed in triadic work, they fulfil one of the exclusion criteria for this form of counselling.

Contracting

After the establishment of a satisfactory working alliance with both partners, the agreement of a therapeutic contract becomes possible. Explicit contracts tend to promote a feeling of security but may foster dependence; agreements which are left largely implicit underline the clients' competence and autonomy but may be confusing and anxiety-provoking. Finding the right balance will depend on client needs as well as on the personal style of the counsellor; however, if the terms are not even clear in the counsellor's mind they are unlikely to have been successfully established with the couple.

It may seem trivial to restate the central premise, namely that the work in hand is couple counselling and that the focus is therefore primarily between the partners rather than with either one of them. However, it is surprising how easily this basic principle can be 'forgotten' in the heat of the session, and it may well be helpful for counsellors to be able to refer back to an explicit agreement when trying to refocus a couple on their primary task.

Some counsellors routinely state at the outset of work what they see as the responsibilities of the parties involved; others rely on the fact that their conduct within the session makes their assumptions sufficiently clear. What is important is that deviations from the counselling framework do not go unchallenged. If, for instance, the couple start acting as if it were the counsellor's role to decide who was right and who was wrong in one of their arguments, a comment or demonstration that this is not in the range of the counsellor's responsibilities, but that adopting a neutral stance is, will prevent the session from becoming a mere repetition of the partners' domestic quarrels.

Time-limited couple counselling is becoming more widely practised, especially in professional settings, and trial periods of a few weeks are popular. Practical reasons, such as the lengths of waiting lists, are probably as responsible for this trend as clinical experience or research demonstrating the efficacy of briefer contracts. While it is welcome that counselling is thus made available to a larger number of clients, it is disturbing to note that gross average treatment lengths (which tend to be between five and six sessions), drawn from a great number of disparate cases, are sometimes regarded as normative figures prescribing the 'optimal' number of sessions for every couple. As with other features covered by the contract, what matters is that decisions do not result from unreflected routine, but from a careful assessment of the needs of specific clients.

Formulation.   Naturally, couples will present their counsellor(s) with their own ideas as to what their difficulties are about. Frequently, partners' views will differ considerably as both are convinced that problems would all but disappear if only it were possible to persuade the other to be more reasonable. While the couple's formulation will inevitably be restricted (if they had a comprehensive understanding they might already have successfully dealt with their problems themselves), it is nevertheless based on their personal experience. The counsellor's task is therefore not one of discounting or replacing the views of the couple on the nature of their predicament, but rather (as in any other form of counselling) one of adding a different perspective or meaning.

Inevitably, counsellor's formulations of problems will depend upon their theoretical backgrounds, but there are some common principles. One of these concerns an understanding that the actions of the couple are inter-dependent and that their disparate views may well represent two different angles of the same cycle of events (system-orientated counsellors would say that the couple punctuate the same sequence differently). Hence, a husband (for the purpose of an example, it could equally be the wife) might claim that the trouble always starts when his wife takes to going out at night. As a result he becomes concerned, starts questioning her when she comes home, but is met with what he feels to be indifference. He therefore takes issue with her when she plans to go out next and, in the face of her reluctance to listen, is moved to make his point more forcefully. Rather than considering his wishes she absents herself even more frequently and a major row, which has been building over weeks, finally erupts. If only she would show more consideration, none of this need ever happen. His wife, for her part, might say that things go quite smoothly until her husband has one of his jealous turns. He then starts persecuting her with unreasonable questions and generally makes the atmosphere at home so miserable that she is compelled to go out to let him simmer down. However, far from becoming calmer, he seems to take positive pleasure in getting at her and, try as she might to get out of his way to avoid a row, it finally erupts. If only he could get a grip on himself, none of this need ever happen.

If the counsellor can successfully convey to the couple that their own disparate stories are representing different angles on the same interactional sequence to which both contribute and which both escalate with ever more determined efforts to pursue what they think would resolve the conflict (while probably attributing sinister motivations to their partner), a major step towards a better understanding of their problems has been achieved. It is then dependent on the counsellor's theoretical persuasion whether the formulation is left there or elaborated in terms of the links between the collusive pattern and the partner's experiences in their families of origin, or of the maladaptive beliefs the partners hold, or of the costs and benefits they see themselves as accruing in the relationship.

Another widely shared principle in formulating a couple's problems is the acknowledgement of natural stresses arising from different stages in the couple's life cycle (a concept popularized by Sheehy (1976)). It is far from obvious to many couples coming for help that quite normal and predictable events such as setting up house together, coping with the first baby, supporting ailing parents, having children at the adolescent stage, seeing the last child leave home, or dealing with the changes brought about by retirement, require adjustments from both partners which may well lead to the emergence of conflicts which could hitherto be contained. The same, of course, holds true for unexpected changes such as redundancy. If, for instance, a couple had operated a division of labour by which one partner would go out to paid work and the other concentrate on the household, the working partner's loss of job – be it through retirement or redundancy – and consequent re-entry into the domestic sphere (hanging about in the kitchen all day) will threaten both their identities and make it even harder to cope with the greatly increased hours of forced togetherness. Having their attention drawn to life-cycle issues will often come as great relief to a couple; it 'normalizes' their distress and diminishes feelings of shame and guilt.

In the literature on marital difficulties several attempts to classify couples into recurring types can be found. Some of these supposedly stable matchings, for instance the so-called 'obsessive/hysterical marriage' have at one time or other attracted closer attention. In practice, couple typologies have little to contribute to the formulation of a particular case. Their value may rather lie in allowing counsellors faced with difficult couples to recognize aspects of their own clients in these descriptions and in reassuring them that they are not alone in their struggles.

Interventions

The following paragraphs will list some of the main areas of intervention available to the couple counsellor. It would be regrettable, however, if this created the impression that couple counselling could proceed in a technological fashion, delivering packaged interventions to the clients once the ground has been cleared by alliance-building and contracting. Couple counselling, in my view, is primarily about listening to the client couple's leading concerns, and interventions are of use only if they speak to those concerns.

Interpretation. Not all counsellors would say that they are using interpretations in their work, especially if they understand the term as being restricted to statements which are intended to 'make the unconscious conscious'. However, if the word is used in a wider sense, probably most counsellors would recognize interpretations as an aspect of their own practice. One might view them as explanatory statements which are related to the process of formulation in that the counsellor's understanding of the couple's problem is conveyed in a piecemeal fashion. Which part of the formulation is thus communicated may depend on the particular aspect of their problem which the clients are demonstrating at the moment, or on their counsellor's sense as to what they are currently 'ready to hear', i.e. what they can admit to themselves or to each other.

Apart from conveying what the counsellor understands already, interpretations can serve to enhance or modify the formulation if they are used as hypotheses about the couple's difficulties which need to be explored and which can be confirmed, discarded, or reformulated. Taking this point of view one might almost say that the counselling process has come to an end when the complete formulation has been elicited and communicated by the counsellor and understood by the couple; however there is probably no end to improving formulations, so indications as to when to end counselling will have to be sought from elsewhere.

Aiding communication.   Difficulties in communication are one of the most visible signs of marital distress and many couples will describe their problems in this fashion when they first come for help. As the ways in which partners fail to talk to each other are readily observable in the counselling room, communication appears as a fruitful area in which to concentrate the therapeutic work. It should be borne in mind, however, that 'communication difficulties' is largely a descriptive rather than an explanatory concept. The question of the 'why' rather than the 'how' of miscommunication becomes relevant as soon as the counsellor's efforts to help the couple to talk more effectively fail to meet with success. At this point it often emerges that partners respond to each other not on the basis of the current interaction but according to the pre-established 'set' originating from an earlier phase in the couple's joint history or from previous relationships – especially those in their families of origin. Dicks (1967) first drew attention to the phenomenon of people being initially attracted but ultimately repelled by seeing a disavowed aspect of themselves represented in their spouses.

If such internal obstacles can be dealt with, a whole spectrum of ways of promoting effective communication is open to the counsellor, ranging from active techniques, such as inviting the partners to role play each other in an argument, to relying on the counsellor's listening stance to serve as a model for the couple. It is also worth taking note of the extent to which partners try to make use of the counsellor to channel their communications as a measure of how much the couple are used to talking to each other directly and how much they tend to involve third parties.

Aiding negotiation.   In order to make use of the opportunities which counselling affords, it is essential for the couple to give up a combative mode of being with each other and to adopt a negotiating stance instead. In the long run this stance will be important in helping them to resolve their day-to-day conflicts if they decide to stay together, or to effect a separation in which the damaging consequences are minimized. Relinquishing a combative mode does not mean that spouses are required to forget about their dissatisfactions. On the contrary, in order to be able to negotiate with others as to how and how far both their needs can be met, it is important that both partners accept their responsibilities not only for having been part of the problems but also for contributing towards their solution. This requires both to become aware of their needs and wants and to express them in specific terms which can be met by their partner. Thus, 'you never take my wishes into account and I am not going to stand for it any longer' may be useful ammunition in marital fighting; something like 'I want you to ask me before you accept an invitation for both of us, because I feel put down if you don't' is more useful in starting a joint negotiation. If the process becomes stuck at this point, counsellors may need to attend to aiding communication (see above) first.

Although the couple will bring current conflicts which may well be resolved during the course of counselling, the actual issues are mainly of value as examples demonstrating how to negotiate, since the couple cannot hope to begin to cover all possible areas of differences in the counselling work. Some couples may find it initially helpful to write down their agreements, but the practice of detailed behavioural contracting with reward or penalty points attached to a list of desired or unwanted actions is probably rare today. In any case, it seems preferable to use ways of negotiating which the clients are likely to carry on using once their counselling has finished.

If adopting a negotiating stance was easy, couples would do so without coming to counselling. Apart from a backlog of unaired grievances, partners have often come to a point where neither is prepared to make the first step. To help them shift into a more constructive mode requires tact and patience on the part of their counsellor and often takes considerable time.

Termination. Unless the ending occurs prematurely, following an irretrievable breakdown of the working alliance, termination is a distinct phase of couple counselling. It is therefore remarkable that so little is written about it, even less than in the literature on individual counselling. Separation and loss are of course universally painful areas, but perhaps it is the parallel between the breaking of the therapeutic bond and the potential breakup of the couple which make termination particularly difficult to contemplate in this context.

There is a spectrum of views on the permanence of endings. This ranges from a 'curative' stance with an expectation that ideally termination should be absolute and the couple should not be in contact with the counsellor again, to a 'health maintenance' stance with an expectation that termination is provisional and allowing for repeated but less intensive periods of counselling. The 'absolute' position has to balance the advantages of facing separation issues squarely with the drawbacks of the possible sense of failure and deprivation engendered if some issues remain unresolved. The 'provisional' position has to weigh the benefits of doing the minimum necessary against the risks of fostering dependency in a couple which is never given the message that they can now manage on their own.

As in individual work, there is a practical and an emotional task to be done around termination:

- for the counsellor to hand back and for the couple to accept the previously shared responsibilities of observing, reflecting on, and if necessary changing their interactions;
- for both parties to break the attachment by acknowledging that the
counselling relationship was important and will be lost, but has now
become unnecessary.

Complications are similar to those arising in individual work, for
instance the approaching ending may be heralded by the couple relapsing
into ways of interacting which previously had been overcome.

Specific to the termination of marital counselling is the necessary withdrawal from a three- (or four-) person relationship back into the dyad,
leaving the couple with the issue as to how much they are in future going to
make use of third parties in order to regulate the distance between them.

Issues

Areas of debate

Even though the practice of couple counselling shows evidence of many
unifying features, there are, of course, areas about which opinion is
divided. Some of the issues which give rise to current debate within the
field are discussed below.

Different theoretical approaches

Theoretical differences are important despite the tendency among many
counsellors and therapists to embrace the label 'eclectic'. For the field as a
whole, a true integration needs well elaborated theoretical positions to
draw on; for each counsellor a secure internal framework is a vital prerequisite for assimilating new and different ideas.

Theoretical views of couple counselling can be differentiated according
to the main therapeutic persuasions, which in turn draw on theories of
dyadic relationships, varying widely in their sophistication and elaboration.
In fact, as I have argued elsewhere (Schröder 1985), the relative importance conceptually afforded to the couple provides the central criterion
which distinguishes the various schools of thought. These can therefore be
located on a continuum: on one end we find cognitive approaches, such as
rational emotive behaviour therapy, focusing on the individual's maladaptive cognitions which may be changed without reference to a partner.
Further along we find the client-centred view of spouses aiming for individual congruence to provide optimum conditions for personal growth for
each other. Next on the spectrum lie behavioral approaches which concentrate on the interaction between the couple, making individual satisfaction

contingent on the partner's response. Yet further along we find the psychodynamic view of the couple as a psychic entity with shared fantasies and collusive defences derived from the 'fit' of their individual histories (for an elaboration see Willi (1982)). Systemic approaches which emphasize the couple's role as subsystem of families and wider social contexts would also be placed right at this end of the continuum.

With this model in mind, we can understand theoretical differences as deriving from different ways of looking at couples. Not surprisingly, altering the angle of vision affords a different vista; a useful fact to bear in mind when our familiar outlook does not allow us to see the problems of particular clients clearly.

Co-therapy

Whether to use one or two counsellors in the conjoint work with couples is a theoretically and practically controversial question. There seems to be little empirical evidence that foursomes in marital counselling result in greater therapeutic benefits, but most studies do not take account of differential client groups. Many counsellors like the idea of working in pairs but are restricted by the pressure of waiting lists and the shortage of available co-workers. This frequently precludes the setting up of a stable counselling partnership, which would maximize therapeutic potential, and as a result regular co-therapy in conjoint couples counselling is often confined to specialist settings.

Practical constraints apart, the question remains if co-therapy should be regarded as the modality of choice. As mentioned above, establishing a working alliance is easier in a foursome than in triadic work. Furthermore, working in a pair reduces the risk of gender-based distortions. Another factor in the decision may be found in the theoretical persuasion of the counsellor:

- From a social learning point of view the opportunity for modelling presented by counselling in pairs is as obvious as the danger of unwittingly presenting to the clients an example of a dysfunctional partnership. Sophisticated behavioural counsellors might therefore be expected to prefer co-working.
- From a systemic point of view the additional worker would probably be better employed as a live supervisor in the room or behind a one-way screen. Counsellors who are grounded in this approach might therefore see little value in working with a co-therapist.
- From a psychodynamic viewpoint, the mirroring of the client couple's conflicts by the counsellor couple is an important source of information and the containment of one pair's anxiety by the other a powerful therapeutic factor (for a striking illustration of these issues see Skynner

(1979)). The danger lies in the possibility that co-workers who are unaware of enduring conflicts among themselves may well end up working them out through their clients – to the detriment of the latter. However, if proper space for reflection can be made, the richness and flexibility of interaction which co-therapy allows makes it the preferred mode of working for psychodynamic counsellors.

It would be regrettable if scarcity of resources were to marginalize co-working in conjoint counselling completely. However, in reality it will probably be of most importance with more difficult clients and in settings which are invested in training, research, or theory development.

'Convening' a couple

This term, taken from the vocabulary of family counselling, is meant to describe a situation in which the counsellor has made a unilateral decision that conjoint work would be appropriate and proceeds to persuade the couple accordingly. If one takes a strategic perspective on the helping process (for instance Haley (1976)), and therefore sees all interventions as directive and designed to persuade, there is only the technical problem of circumventing possible reluctances. From other points of view it seems ethically questionable to impose a focus which the couple did not choose.

At the diagnostic stage a recommendation for conjoint work when only one partner has presented with problems, however well founded theoretically, may well convey the message that the counsellor places greater value on the relationship than on individual needs. Feminist writers have been particularly alert to the possibility that couple counselling may present yet another instance where women's needs of individual space and attention are discounted in favour of concentrating on marriages which generally afford greater psychological protection to men.

There is a strand of opinion recommending convening a couple when individual work has become stuck, especially if there is evidence that the partner at home in some way 'sabotages' therapeutic gains. The resulting problems for the working alliance are formidable and, practical circumstances allowing, it may well be better to bring in a co-therapist or have the couple work taken on by a different counsellor.

Wider applications

Preventive work with couples

Within the health services the current trend towards prevention and education is unmistakable if still comparatively weak. Within the counselling field, Relate (formerly National Marriage Guidance Council) has shown considerable commitment to educative work, but otherwise, prevention is still largely an untapped area in Britain.

Preventive efforts have been brought to bear at various points in the life cycle of the couple, each resulting in a clearly discernible area of work such as relationship education in schools, marriage preparation, preparation for parenthood, and marriage enrichment. However, the only consistent effort has been in the field of marriage preparation, which derived much of its impetus from the Church. Marriage enrichment, while gaining ground in North America, is still in its infancy in Britain and there may well be cultural obstacles, such as the widespread reservation to discuss intimate relationships, which will impede its development here.

Common to preventive work is its emphasis on the non-pathological ordinary aspects of couple relationships. This can present a difficulty for counsellors who are trained to direct their attention towards the dysfunctional aspects of their clients' interactions, even though they may include information-giving and education in their counselling work. It has therefore been argued that preventive work requires an educational rather than a counselling background. However, counsellors can draw on their knowledge and experience of human development and, given adequate preparation themselves, may find prevention a welcome addition to working with distressed couples.

Conciliation and divorce counselling

Conciliation, meaning the structured arbitration of a dispute between couples (usually following separation or divorce), is a fast-growing area. Once exclusively the domain of the probation service, the field has over the past fifteen years witnessed the emergence of a number of specialized agencies which since 1983 can be affiliated to an umbrella organization. The boundaries with family counselling are diffuse as children are often involved in the conciliation process.

Different models of practice have emerged, ranging from strictly task-centred mediation to counselling which includes the exploration of interpersonal conflicts and established patterns. Common to all is the emphasis on conciliation rather than reconciliation – that is to say, the acceptance of the couple's decision to break up and the attempt to deal with the consequences of this decision in a non-adversarial manner which is normally precluded by the legal system.

Divorce counselling is an altogether wider area which includes therapeutic goals such as emotionally supporting the partners through their breakup and preparing them for new relationships. While one might argue that this would be well within the brief of traditional couple counselling, it seems that clients prefer to discuss the end of their marriage in a setting different to those which are commonly held to be devoted to 'marriage mending'.

The possible savings to the Legal Aid budget effected by the avoidance of protracted legal battles have been cited as a compelling reason for increased funding of conciliation and divorce counselling services. Whether such savings are in fact achieved has recently been the subject of intense debate. It would not be surprising if in the long run such rational considerations were outweighed by the ideological stigma easily attached to services which expressly do not aim to keep couples (and families) together.

Future developments

The future of counselling couples cannot be separated from developments in the entire therapeutic field. There is, however, one feature which distinguishes marital work: the voluntary sector is strongly represented and is probably dominant in terms of number of cases seen. Arguably, this has led to the relative neglect of couple counselling in professional settings – one or two specialist establishments notwithstanding. This has been more than offset by the vigorous growth of work in the voluntary sector (which has the advantage of preventing couples from being defined as 'patients' or 'official' clients with all the potential for a pathological 'career' which such labelling entails). Such growth will inevitably lead to voluntary agencies becoming more professional, increasing their expertise, refining their quality assurance and accreditation systems, and ultimately charging market rates for their services. This trend, which has already been in evidence in Relate's transition from 'social movement' to 'service agency', is increasingly blurring the distinction between the two sectors.

Training opportunities in couple counselling are in Britain mainly provided by Relate: National Marriage Guidance. Its former link with the Institute of Marital Studies was an excellent example of a broad-based voluntary organization drawing on the expertise of a specialist professional agency and has had beneficial spinoffs for the probation service and other social work agencies. It would be desirable if other approaches could draw on similar specialized centres and if couple work took a more prominent role in the training of helping professions.

One area deserving more sustained attention is that of conjoint couples' groups. Perhaps counsellors are overawed by the logistics of setting up such ventures or by the complex interplay of dyadic and group relationships. In any case, the therapeutic opportunities afforded to couples who are able to combine individual and relationship work warrant more widespread interest in this neglected field.

Both the voluntary and the professional sector are currently under the same pressure towards steadily increased cost effectiveness. At worst, this presages a continuing trend towards high turnover/low intensity counselling carried out by inexpert workers briefly trained in 'core skills'. At best, it will engender a more widespread interest in clinically meaningful evaluation and in briefer, focused approaches to couple counselling. However, proficiency in brief work demands training and experience beyond that required in ordinary counselling and proper evaluation has costs both in time and energy. Given the prevailing climate, it will take the combined efforts of both voluntary and professional sectors to keep developments from being guided by a search for expediency rather than quality.

References

Ables, B., and Brandsma, J. M. (1977) *Therapy for couples*, San Francisco: Jossey-Bass.

Alexander, J. F., Holtzworth-Munroe, A., and Jameson, P. (1994) 'The process and outcome of marital and family therapy: Research review and evaluation' in A. E. Bergin and S. L. Garfield (eds) *Handbook of psychotherapy and behavior change*, New York: Wiley.

Bennun, I. (1991) 'Working with the individual from the couple' in D. Hooper and W. Dryden (eds) *Couple Therapy: A Handbook* Milton Keynes: Open University Press.

Brannen, J., and Collard, J. (1982) *Marriages in trouble*, London: Tavistock.

Clulow, C. (1982) *To have and to hold*, Aberdeen: Aberdeen University Press.

Dicks, H. V. (1967) *Marital tensions*, London: RKP.

Grunebaum, H., Christ, J., and Neiberg, N. (1969) Diagnosis and treatment planning for couples, *International Journal of Group Psychotherapy* 19: 185–202.

Gurman, A. S., Kniskern, D. P., and Pinsof, W. F. (1986) 'Research on the process and outcome of marital and family therapy' in S. L. Garfield and A. E. Bergin (eds) *Handbook of psychotherapy and behavior change*, New York: Wiley.

Haley, J. (1976) *Problem-solving therapy*, San Francisco: Jossey-Bass.

Schröder, T. A. (1985) 'A psychodynamic practitioner's point of view' in W. Dryden (eds) *Marital therapy in Britain*, London: Harper and Row.

——(1991) 'Approaches to couple therapy' in D. Hooper and W. Dryden (eds) *Couple Therapy. A Handbook*, Milton Keynes: Open University Press.

Sheehy, G. (1976) *Passages: Predictable crises of adult life*, New York: Dutton.

Skynner, R. (1979) 'The family therapist as family scapegoat (postscript)', *Journal of Family Therapy*, 1: 20–2.

Willi, J. (1982) *Couples in Collusion*, New York: Aronson.

Chapter five

Family counselling

Eddy Street

Introduction

Families and their functioning always seem to be at the centre of any discussion about the social ills of society and how 'care' should be administered by the community. It appears as if the family is perceived as both the cause of, and the solution to, a great many problems. Even though it has been evident for some time that the family is the main socializing agent of a community, it is only in more recent decades that the family has warranted its own 'theory', 'policy', or even a special kind of counselling. Following the Second World War a new emphasis was placed on the importance of family life for, although there is no formal 'family policy' in Britain, the majority of our legal, financial and social legislation has been based on the notion of the 'normal' nuclear family. These policies rest on the view that the family is the basic social unit in society and that, apart from educational provision, the state should work to uphold the sanctity of the family and should not in normal circumstances intervene in its functioning. Given this major emphasis on the way in which our society and its provisions have been constructed it is not surprising that many professional workers who are involved in dispensing a vast range of welfare and care services find themselves offering help and advice to families. An element of this help will make use of counselling approaches, involving as they do the ecouragement of self-evaluation, problem solving and change.

We can regard the topic of family counselling as covering such situations as a health visitor discussing with young parents how they might help their 6-month-old child to adopt a different sleep pattern; or an educational psychologist talking to a divorced mother about her 15-year-old son who persistently plays truant; or a community nurse listening to the problems of caring for a demented elderly lady looked after by her married daughter; or a psychiatric nurse suggesting to the wife of a depressive man some strategies for dealing with him and her children; or a general practitioner talking to an elderly couple who care for their 29-year-old chronically mentally ill son. In essence, all these situations involve the care of

one generation by another and sometimes that care is dispensed co-opera-
tively by two or more adults and sometimes it is dispensed by one adult
alone. Whatever the practicalities of the situation it does involve one
person at one time (but not all the time) being able to deal with his or
her own needs in such a way that the needs of another are met. Naturally,
these circumstances create reactions in the care giver, the person who is
receiving the care, and those other people who are intimately involved in
this care-giving situation. Family counselling can, therefore, occur in a
multitude of settings but it will always involve these same central elements.

Principles

Guiding theoretical principles of family counselling

Individuals and the family life cycle

Human development is interactional, i.e. it is a process in which the
behaviour of one person is meshed with the behaviour of another. It also
cannot merely be confined to that time of life known as childhood, but has
to be seen as a lifelong process. Not only do adults affect the development
of a child but, by virtue of the reciprocity of interaction, a child affects the
development of adults. From this it is a small step to note how adults,
within the context of their relationships, affect the development of each
other. Development, therefore, is a process that occurs throughout life and
is of essence relationship bound.

Central to this view of the life-embracing and interactive nature of
development is the concept of the developmental task. These are tasks
which face all individuals at stages of the life cycle. They are tasks which
have to be dealt with so that the next set of tasks on the path of development can be approached. As the 'family' is the principal primary group for
the majority of people in western culture, it represents the principal context
in which individuals face developmental tasks. Families are composed of
individuals as well as couples; they are composed of children as well as
parents. The task of family life itself is to balance the need of individuals,
of the marriage, of adults, of children, in such a way that there is a blending
together which allows the needs of all to be met more or less simultaneously. When this occurs the tasks facing the individuals and the family
present as enjoyable experiences rather than as problems, and there is the
time and emotional energy to confront and adaptively deal with any unforeseen or unfortunate event that may occur.

At a general historical and cultural level, we all face similar life tasks,
and it therefore becomes possible to map out those issues that a family may
have to face throughout the life of its individual members. Hoffman (1989)
argues that development is not a continual process but one characterized by

transformations, changes and the sudden appearance of functional patterns that simply did not exist before. The timing and nature of developmental shifts cannot be predicted, though predictions can be made about the issues and the direction of organization that will take place. What becomes an issue is how the family adapts and deals with its own changes. Street (1994a) has outlined the tasks that face the individual, the marital pair both as a couple and as parents at different stages of the life cycle. Each set of tasks is different but it is possible for each to be met in a manner which is synchronized with the other sets of tasks. Family life is therefore characterized by the balancing of differing needs. These needs, by virtue of the way in which life changes, will be altering and modifying over time.

Influences of past, present and future

In facing the tasks that arise for themselves, individuals and families use two types of information to set about problem solving. They use the historical information they have about how they, as members of a particular family, set about dealing with life's issues. They also make use of information that they acquire in the here-and-now. This will include their hopes and fears about how the future will evolve for them. Obviously these types of information are dynamically related.

Historical influences are principally concerned with the developing notion of the 'self'. As a process the self cannot be considered to be something that follows rigid patterns. The current conception based on social constructionism is that notions of the self shift and change through an individuals's life (Gergen 1991). As children we all acquire a sense of who we are through our relationship with our parents. We develop our view of ourself in terms of the relationships that are constructed for us in our families of origin. The set of relationship patterns that is established internally when we are children becomes the templates that we use when we are adults, but templates that may alter as life itself changes. Elements of these templates will refer not only to adult relationships but also to our own parenting relationship, i.e. the relationships we construct with our children.

In the ongoing hurly-burly of daily family life, family members will be attempting to do their best to maximize pleasant events in their world and to minimize unpleasant events. In this sense, much of behaviour is cognitively directed to anticipated future events. In order to decide what is pleasant or unpleasant they will be using their current awareness as well as the view of events handed down historically. Once the decision of the pleasantness or unpleasantness of events is determined, individuals then act in a way that the behaviourists have well described. A considerable amount of family behaviour can therefore be considered to be contingency based. It has to be remembered, however, that the determinants of what is considered a positive or negative contingency are determined by past experiences and future anticipations. To an outsider some interaction that occurs in families may be considerd to be definitely noxious, for example persistent outbursts of anger; but for the individuals concerned, definitions of 'love' may involve someone being frequently very angry. As our sense of worth and lovableness is determined by our past learning history, then we will seek out experiences that reinforce that sense of self even though, to someone else, they may appear negative. The way in which present behaviour is construed and then put to use is therefore an important element in the way in which families establish their particular way of interacting.

The family as an open system

As the family is a social unit there is a need to conceive of its operation in terms of activity as a social group. Workers with families have tended to base their view on General Systems Theory (Kerr 1981). This holds that the family is a functioning operational system comprising of interrelated parts, all of which combine to influence its total functioning. It naturally still considers the individual but events are studied within the context in which they occur, with attention being placed on connections and relationships rather than on individual characteristics. The family is seen as being composed of 'subsystems', such as individuals, the parental subsystem, the sibling subsystem, men and women subsytems (fathers and sons, mothers and daughters), with each subsystem contributing to the functioning of the total family system. Some subsystems are hierarchically related in that the efficient operation of one determines the operation of another; in particular, an efficient parental system determines whether the children (sibling) system functions appropriately. It has been argued that the marital subsystem is hierarchically related to the parental subsystem, for the marital pair will need to have a 'good enough' marriage in order for them to function as 'good enough' parents.
Families need a means to cope with change and they differ in the extent to which they are able to adapt and accommodate to changing circumstances. Some will remain rigid, with both their internal and external boundaries and their rules of behaviour remaining the same, even though the situation demands an alteration. Other families are so loose in their boundaries and have so few rules of relating that they deal with the world in a chaotic fashion and, consequently, there is permanent change where stability would be of assistance (Olson et al. 1989). In order for the family to begin to accommodate to life's events, there needs to be communication both between and within subsystems. Communication is the means by which family members develop a collective view of the tasks that face them. The boundaries of a family, in fact, define the flow of communication within

that system. Thus, if communication is not occurring, the boundaries are inevitably rigid and impermeable so that individuals or other subsystems are isolated. When communication is excessive but unheard, it merely becomes 'noise' in the system. In these circumstances boundaries fail to differentiate between subsystems: in this case confusion reigns for family members as they are unsure of which subsystem they belong to; and they may even be confused as to the nature of their identity as the boundary between self and others is unclear. This has been termed an 'undifferentiated ego mass' by Bowen (1979) and indicates a serious distortion of communication that may require help of a special nature so that it can be unravelled.

A feature of the functioning of systems is feedback, which is the process whereby a system takes information from itself in order to determine the next event. Feedback therefore involves a system using its own activity to determine what its next activity shoud be. This briefly outlines what is termed circular causality or circularity, which views the origin or development of family behaviour as arising from the interactions between the various subsystems of the family itself. This is particularly important when considering family problems, for the origin and particularly the maintenance of problems can be viewed in terms of circularity. The emphasis is therefore on mutual causality. Since each part of the family system continually influences all the other parts, the focus is on the overall pattern of relationships rather than just one element of those relationships; and issues of 'blame' in the family therefore change when one adopts the view of circular causality.

The counsellor as part of the system

As the family is a social group that is continually in interaction with its immediate social environment, at various points in time, different individuals and groups from the world at large will be incorporated into its system. This certainly occurs when a counsellor meets with family members to discuss difficulties they may be facing. The manner of this process takes as its context the 'definition' of the problem. The majority of counsellors will come from agencies that, in the eye of the public world, will have a clear definition of the problem. Thus, for example, a family being asked to see a psychiatrist is quite likely to assume that this is because someone is to be seen as psychiatrically ill and they, the family, may be antagonistic to this. In some contexts the family may willingly accept the agency's definition of the problem, but in other contexts, the family will attempt to have its definition of the problem accepted by the counsellor. Within the 'counselling system', interaction in the initial stages of contact occurs in the mutual search for a common definition.

As there is this mutual search for a definition of the problem that is addressed through counselling, it is possible that the activities of the counsellor may not always assist the family. The offer of counselling always implies that an input from outside the family is needed. As the counsellor is incorporated into the system then it may be that the family believes it can only deal with its difficulties if its members are involved with a counsellor. In other circumstances the family can pressurize or manipulate the counsellor to adopt its definition of the problem and this can result in the maintenance of a difficulty with nothing changing. Thus, for example, parents of an adult with severe learning difficulties can persuade a community nurse that they need constant visiting because of the nature of their child's disability, and even though the nurse has a different view of the disability, the constant visiting reinforces the parents' perception and does not effect changes through the counselling process. The counsellor in these circumstances is offering 'more of the same' (Watzlawick *et al.* 1974) in a fashion that does not assist the change process.

As counsellors can be incorporated into systems in unhelpful ways it is important that the position of counsellor is maintained such that it can be helpful to all concerned. This position of being both a member of a system and an 'objective' outsider can be easy under some circumstances, but in others, the counsellor will need to make use of colleagues and seek the advice of consultants to ensure that the appropriate stance *vis-à-vis* the family is maintained.

Practical principles of family counselling

Street (1994a) has outlined the skills necessary to maintain the principles of family counselling and grouped them to include (i) assessing the present situation, and (ii) moving towards constructive aims.

Assessing the situation

In assessing the situation prior to embarking on the direction of counselling, counsellors need to be aware of the following important facets of the family situation.

Life cycle issues. The counsellor requires an awareness of the life-cycle issues that are confronting the family. Different families have different histories and these influence the issues that the family faces through life. For example, the age of the parents when a handicapped child was born to them may be very relevant to how they face the task that lies in front of them, illustrating how the counsellor will need to be curious about how the future could unfold for a particular family. In the above example, a younger couple may, at some point in the future, consider what would happen if they had another child, whilst an older couple will have to consider a different set of future tasks. By bringing to the fore the issues as part of the life cycle, the family faces the problems they have within the context of their own situation; this allows the family to experience the counselling situation as a personal one for themselves. Workers who offer family counselling often find that many of the problems they meet involve primarily dealing with life-cycle issues and the adaptations that are necessary for a particular family's situation.

Family meaning of difficulties.   The counsellor will need to acquire an understanding of the meaning that the family holds of their difficulty. In many situations the family will have an unhelpful perception of the meaning of particular acts. They may believe, for example, that elderly people with dementia can be in more control of their behaviour than they are in fact capable of. Similarly, young parents often ascribe intentionality to an infant's spontaneous behaviour when it is not developmentally possible for the child to commit those acts in an intentional way. In another situation, there will be no 'right' or 'wrong' understanding of the behaviour and there may in fact be several explanations. Thus, for example, an 8-year-old boy's misbehaviour may be considered to be due to his poor relationship with his stepfather and to the poor discipline offered by both parents. In this case the counsellor will seek to clarify the exact meaning the family has of the behaviour and indeed whether or not there are any conflicting views held by different family members. It is important for the counsellor to establish the ideology of the family with regard to the difficulty it faces. This ideology may also include notions of who is and who is not willing to help the family (see Street and Downey 1996).

Interactive sequences.   The counsellor should establish the interactive sequence in which the problem behaviour is embedded. It needs to be remembered that what is defined as the 'problem' is in fact only one element of the family's interaction and that the events both prior to and following the 'problem' are just as much causal to the distress everyone feels as the actual difficulty itself. The counsellor therefore needs to establish how each family member thinks, feels and acts before and after the problem appears. Different types of difficulties will necessitate differing emphasis on the 'before' and 'after' in the interactive sequence. Hence, when a child misbehaves there is reason to look at the events which led up to the misbehaviour, for in this case the misbehaviour may be construed as being contingent on behavioural acts, say, between the parents. In the case of an adult with a brain injury the problem behaviour itself – for example, sudden memory lapses – may not be the consequence of any discernible event but the reactions of family members to the lapses. In the stream of interactive behaviour the counsellor has to assist the family in determining an appropriate 'punctuation' or order of its members' behaviour. This is helpful as it is an arbitrary decision as to what will be perceived as being the 'beginning' or 'end' of any series of interactive events. It is this process of mutually constructing a beneficial punctuation of interaction that, in an important way, marks out the family counselling approach from other approaches.

Moving towards constructive aims

The general aims for the family counsellor are to assist the family in forming a realistic view of the task that faces them, then assisting them in constructing a strategy to deal with the task and of then supporting them whilst it is ongoing. In order to meet this general aim the counsellor should ask four questions, the answers to which will guide the content of the counselling process.

(1) **Does the family have information on which to base an appropriate view of the task?** In many situations family members will be operating on insufficient knowledge about the difficulty that faces them. It is the counsellor's task to ensure that their knowledge is appropriate. In the case of someone suffering from schizophrenia some family members may believe that delusive thoughts can be argued away by reason, and every time a delusion is expressed, they may become angry and spend a good deal of time trying to discuss the reality of the situation. Some of the most effective programmes for helping families with a member suffering from schizophrenia involve an education phase (Birchwood and Smith 1987). Family members are sometimes given prepared leaflets and talks so that they are aware of the problem with which they are dealing. Many young families are quite ignorant about the behaviour of infants and young children and need help to become aware of this. Similarly, most families do not have appropriate notions of the likely course of chronic physical illnesses and the way in which treatment will affect them (Nichols 1987). Subsidiary questions that the counsellor will need to ask are 'Is the manner in which the information is imparted effective for a problem of this nature?' and 'Do family members have a view of the problem that is flexible enough to accept new information that could result in them changing their behaviour?'. The answers to these questions may affect the direction that counselling will take for particular families. Some families will be found to have considerable difficulty in recognizing and assimilating new information; such may be the problems of these families that the focus of the counselling approach may be on the system of communication itself.

(2) **Is the communication in the family clear and open or does it need to be clarified?** Much of the behaviour that takes place within families

is based upon how each person interprets the behaviour of the other family members. When a difficulty or a crisis emerges, a situation is created which is not typical for the family; in that sense it is 'new'. Under these circumstances, any one person's acts may convey messages which are not appropriately received or understood by others. It is important to appreciate that this type of communication may or may not be verbal. The counsellor's task is to ensure that each family member, as far as possible, is able to appreciate the nature of the communication that he or she is making so that other family members can be clear about the way in which the communication affects themselves. In doing this the counsellor will be unravelling the 'ideology' of the family that surrounds the particular problem they are facing. The meaning that each family member places on the acts of each other and of themselves needs to be discovered. Once this has been done the counsellor can set about the task of ensuring that the communication (both verbal and non-verbal) that takes place is clearly understood as it is intended.

(3) **Is it possible to specify the needs of everyone in the family?** Even though a difficulty presents itself primarily through one person, each family member is affected by it. The family task therefore is to deal with the particular difficulty whilst ensuring that the needs of all other family members are being met. The task for the individual is to ensure that his or her personal needs are met in a way appropriate to family functioning as well as him/herself. It is in this situation that the counsellor joins with the family in helping its members to balance the needs of all. When families face difficulties it is often found that some members feel they have to put their own needs too much to one side to meet the needs of another person encountering a difficulty. In these circumstances negotiations have to occur on the interactive themes of inclusion, control and intimacy (Doherty *et al.* 1991). Depending on which theme is central at that time, the counsellor's task is therefore to bring to discussion what each individual feels they need themselves in order that they can deal with the task that faces them generally. In some situations the counsellor will need to use knowledge of child development to be sure that the needs of the children are clearly understood by all.

In this part of the counselling process the family is being assisted to be aware of the way personal needs affect the solving of a problem. Thus, for example, a married daughter who is caring for her ageing parent may require her husband to deal with particular aspects of their children's care, and this couple may need the help of their brothers and sisters to offer respite care, so they may be relieved occasionally. In this case, if the daughter requires help from her brother, it naturally introduces into the counselling situation how the needs of the brother are to be seen and met. He may for example have certain perceptions and feelings about how his mother is being cared for which may affect the ease with which he can assist his sister; and these then become elements to the general family situation that need to be taken into account.

(4) **What negotiations for adaptations to change need to be made?** Once the family has acquired a clearer idea of the task that faces its members and how this task affects their particular family, it may become apparent that some changes will be required. Such changes in behaviour in any one member will obviously have implications for others. The family will need to investigate the alternative paths of change in order to become aware of the implications of each action. The process takes the form of family members saying 'If I do this then what will you do?', or 'If you do that then I would think . . .', or 'What will happen if we decide to do . . .?'. The counsellor can help the family during this process by holding on to an overall view of the task, so that the discussion that takes place does not lose its context. It may well be that the counsellor will suggest possible alternatives as the family considers the changes that could be made. It should be remembered that not all counselling situations involve a change in behaviour: many merely involve the opening of awareness, the acceptance of what is happening, and, in these situations, using the availability of the counsellor's support.

The answering of these broad questions frames the activity of the counsellor. Not only does this apply to the overall counselling process which may occur over many sessions, but it also outlines what needs to occur moment by moment. In order to assist each individual in the family the counsellor needs to hold on to a view of the family as a single entity. In order to assist the family as a whole the counsellor needs to hold on to a view of each person functioning in his or her own particular way and requiring respect for his or her own individuality. It is the balancing of these paradoxical positions that represents the personal challenge to the family counsellor.

Issues

Within any field of counselling, particular activities seem to draw attention to the ideology, ethics and practice of the counsellor. In family counselling, workers are very sensitive about questions regarding the 'identity' of the client. Can the client be regarded as the family unit alone or are separate people within that unit all individual clients? There are occasions when counsellors need to be mindful of the position and role of individuals in the family; this is especially the case with children and to some extent with women. At the core of this issue is the debate concerning the tenability of holding on to a view of the family as a unit or whether the needs of particular individuals have to take priority. In order to review the ethical, ideological and practical issues concerned with this debate three areas will be surveyed.

Divorce and conciliation

The increase in divorce in society has resulted in many children beginning life in one family and then continuing it in a family that has changed its composition by divorce and remarriage. There is evidence that children who maintain contacts with both natural parents in a non-conflictual context are well-adjusted (Robinson 1991). The Children Act 1989 emphasizes the need for both parents to continue to be involved, maintaining their responsibility to their child. A situation is therefore created of attempting co-operative parenting between adults whose marital relationship has broken down and between whom there possibly exists residual hostility and mutual distrust. It can often happen that difficulties ensue not only in the usually traumatic immediate pre- and post-divorce period but also for a considerable time following this. Parents individually will often seek someone in a counselling role in order to recruit him or her in a conflict between them and their previous partners concerning issues usually related to their children. The counsellor is therefore faced with a situation in which past family conflicts affect the present-day functioning of a system that can no longer be considered to be a family but which still requires co-operation over particular tasks. There are several dangers in undertaking this conciliation role (Kruk 1993; Robinson 1993). The first problem invariably concerns the strong pressures that exist to place the children in the 'power' positions, i.e. implying that, as children, they have a definite choice about this particular problem – for example, how often they will visit their father – and that these choices can be acted upon in a rational way. Although the amount of say children have in these issues varies with their age, the counsellor needs to operate on the premiss that the task at hand is to move towards a negotiated balance of everyone's needs and, in this respect, the views of children have to be regarded within the context of the development-enhancing maintenance of generational boundaries. A second danger is to be 'recruited' on one parent's side; and this again brings to the fore the need for the counsellor to make clear to clients the ethics on which his or her practice is based. In the case of the above example, the counsellor may need to inform the mother that the father has the right as a natural parent to see his children: not only is this an ethic that determines how the counsellor behaves, it is in fact the reality of the situation. The third danger in this type of 'family' counselling is the attempt to deal with 'old' issues through the means of the here-and-now problem. In any divorce there are naturally many unresolved issues between the partners: it has to be assumed that the couple decided on separation as a means of dealing with all those issues between them that did not seem resolvable within the marriage. In the post-divorce period elements of these issues may become 'replayed' through the negotiations that need to occur about arrangements for the children. It is important for the counsellor to convey to each parent that he or she has an appreciation of the situation that led to the person adopting the attitude being taken, but it is then important to move on to discuss the present problem purely in the context of the new 'family' situation, i.e. a family separated by divorce. If this is borne in mind it then becomes possible to deal with the here-and-now interaction in such a way that a negotiated solution is found that is acceptable to all. These later themes are particularly important when one considers the natural process by which stepfamilies operate – themes and processes with which counsellors may be invited to assist (Robinson 1991; Robinson and Smith 1993).

Meeting the needs of children: involvement with families that neglect and abuse

There is clearly a need for families who are neglectful and abusive to be offered help. Such is the complexity of the emotional and interpersonal factors of these cases that it is beyond the scope of this chapter to detail the varieties of assistance that families could require. However, at some point in their contact with a helping agency a worker may be offering help of a counselling nature to such a family. It may well be that through the counselling process a family reveals the presence of abuse, and a counsellor therefore needs to be very clear about the issues of confidentiality that these cases raise. An essential principle vigorously held within counselling is that of the confidentiality between client and counsellor. The counsellor in the first instance will have to determine who is the client – is it the child or is it the family? Clearly counsellors cannot allow themselves to be placed in positions where the dilemma of who is the client has not been satisfactorily resolved and cannot be resolved. Knowledge of abuse often involves the prospect of a child being removed from a family. To make decisions concerning whether or not a child should be taken from a family because his or her development is being seriously affected is not something that the counsellor can take into account during counselling. Sometimes also, the family may be legally obliged to be involved in particular agencies and it could be that a form of counselling is offered to them: under these circumstances the clients cannot be considered to be voluntary, and this places the counsellor in particular difficulties. These are discussed by Crowther *et al.* (1990). Often information acquired about the abuse during 'counselling' could have a bearing on the management of the case by the

agency. Clearly, when clients cannot be deemed to be presenting themselves for counselling solely as a result of their own motivation, then the
issue of control in counselling is brought to the fore (White *et al.* 1993).

To deal with some of these dilemmas there certainly needs to be an
appropriate definition of roles worked out by the agencies and the professionals concerned. This would make it clear to the workers and family alike
as to who has responsibility for what and the rules of discussion that frame
different worker/family interactions. Issues connected with the care of
children raise a variety of complex questions and they can only be adequately addressed if the worker embarking on counselling is well prepared
for any situation in which the ethics of counselling may be called into
dispute. Street (1994b), for example, has discussed the therapeutic issues in
cases of child–parent separation which has been termed 'developmental
closure', a feature of many abusive situations. Issues concerning the way
family systems view child abuse focus around the failure of many to take
into account the gender-based differences in families of physical, social
and economic power (James and Mackinnon 1990). Particular forms of
treatment have now been designed to address gender issues (see White *et
al.* 1993).

Women in families

It is now viewed that sexual inequality is a major source of conflict and
distress in families and, as seen above, this inequality can affect the way
particular phenomena are dealt with by professionals. The roles that
women are given in families are seen as systemically according them
less status and power than men and hence their lives are less satisfying.
It is typically the case that, in families where sacrifices have to be made in
order to provide an appropriate level of care for a family member, women
are those who make and are usually required to make, those sacrifices. It
can therefore be argued that family counselling on whatever issue often
merely supports the unequal role of women and does little to change the
basic inequality that exists. It has been argued (Goldner 1985) that sexual
inequality has been ignored in family work because of the dominance of
systems theory as an explanatory account of family structure and functioning. This argument views systems theory as adopting a particular historical
view of the family, namely that of the 1950s. Here the family was seen as a
haven and sexual inequality was perceived as a harmonious complementary
arrangement in which men and women presided over separate but equal
worlds. Goldner (1991) has continued her critique of this issue and
reviewed the effect of post-modernism on feminism and family therapy.
She notes that the outcome is a move away from conflict-based thinking to
co-operative ideas based on a co-evolved narrative.

Clearly, the counsellor must be aware of the political and social context in which the modern family operates. It is one in which questions of power and sexual inequality are very much to the fore (Perelberg and Miller 1990; Speed and Brew 1995). The external world will therefore have some very important influences on how family members will perceive their role and how they will attempt to negotiate the meeting of their needs. The issue is whether or not the counsellor should foster the process of thinking about sexual inequality or whether he or she should allow the family to deal with it in their own way, knowing that some may choose the usual sexual stereotypes. Families require of their counsellor genuineness concerning the principles on which practice is based and these principles should very easily be capable of being put into operation through the process of counselling. If during counselling, for example, it transpires that violence has occurred between partners the counsellor could inform them that this is unacceptable and that, if it continues, then particular types of advice would be given and action taken to prevent its recurrence. One cannot assume that any decision or issue is more the province of one person rather than another because of the power of that person in the family. The counsellor should start from the basis that equal power sharing occurs at every moment through the counselling process and that the family's reaction to this will determine whether any issues surrounding sexual inequality become a part of the context of the counselling.

Future developments

At the core of family counselling is a dilemma that faces the counsellor about the relationship between the individual and the family. On the one hand there is the view that the individual is so much a part of the family and that the individual's behaviour is so influenced by the activities of the family that, at all times, one should view the unit to be helped as the 'system' (Haley 1976). Alternatively, there are those who view the links between the individual and the family as being of varying strengths under particular conditions (Holmes 1985). These latter workers are therefore able to discuss the indications and contra-indications of family counselling, determining it as being appropriate in some circumstances but not others.

That there are basically two ways of considering family counselling has naturally led to developments in different directions though paradoxically these developments eventually pose identical problems for counsellors. For those who do not overly stress the 'systems' aspect but emphasize the family *per se*, the developments initially lie in ensuring that family issues are given due weight when an individual presents with any type of stress or difficulty (Orford 1987). Clearly, the ability to offer even a minimal amount of family counselling at a time of crisis will have considerable beneficial effects. In this area there continue to be developments in the context of providing counselling in situations where there is ill health

(Street and Soldan 1995; Black 1989) and 'family systems medicine' grows apace.

The counselling of the family, however, is not limited merely to crises as there are a growing number of other areas in which the skills and knowledge of family counselling can be applied. Thus, for example, the last decade has seen significant changes in attitude, support and responsibility towards children and teenagers with disabilities, encouraging living in ordinary family environments rather than in large institutions. This particularly affects the many foster and adoptive families who have to be recruited to help move some of these children out of inappropriate care. These families have to adjust to a new member with very particular and special needs and often they will encounter their own doubts and insecurities as well as doubts and scepticism from their wider social network. As the need for more substitute families increases, the preparation and support the new family will require will be considerable: an important family counselling input will clearly be necessary for this group.

Another direction of development springs from a growing awareness of the need for preventive-type interventions, particularly with regard to the problems that can arise from parenting young children. There has been a growth in the use of behavioural approaches to children's problems (Crane 1995). These have been heavily based on the 'triadic model', which involves the worker developing a relationship with the carer of the child rather than with the child. The development of this particular approach has necessitated the use of counselling skills in the process of assisting the parenting relationship. It has been continually argued that the health, education and social services devote little attention to equipping people with the knowledge to anticipate problems or the skills to solve or manage them. Instead, families are required to identify themselves through a problem, which casts them in an inadequate or passive role, rather than as people able to specify some of their immediate needs, and seeking ways in which to meet those needs. If such arguments are accepted, which seems to be happening slowly, then clearly this is an area in which family counsellors will have a major contribution to make. Grief (1994), for example, has outlined how family therapy ideas can be used in parenting groups in schools, providing an example of how innovative approaches challenge the notion of 'treatment' sessions as being the primary means of assisting families.

Family counsellors may therefore find that the needs of the families they see lead them into involvement with community action and wider political considerations. De'Ath (1988) has argued that those workers assisting with families cannot avoid becoming involved in issues of social policy. Naturally, counsellors always need to be mindful of their role as well as being aware of the limits of counselling *per se*, but certainly here is a 'growth' area for family counsellors in which the question of the boundaries of counselling as an activity will clearly be raised.

The other view of family counselling places stress on the system's properties of the family as a social group. This view holds that the family systems perspective is a total orientation and that it is possible and indeed desirable to hold this view and practise its skills across all situations. Taken from this perspective, the developments in family counselling are indeed wide ranging and cover numerous situations in which 'counselling' could be possible. Stated another way, the development proposed by this view is that family counselling is not the response to a particular situation (the family), but is in fact a school of counselling based on an understanding of human systems. This approach then leads on to a focus on the interface between the systems of the families and the organizations/agencies with which they have to deal. Counsellors can then become actively involved in the problems that are posed by the attentions given to a family by a particular public agency. This move in focus shifts the assumption that it is the family that is the problem. The family may have great difficulties but the greatest of them all can be the unhelpful attentions of professional helpers. Dimmock and Dungworth (1985), for example, have illustrated how it is possible to effect some change in the 'problem' by involving a number of the family's social networks (professional and non-profes- sional) in discussions about how to assist with the family. This is an attempt to apply the notion 'working with the system' in a wider sense and to use the understanding of this wider context for the benefits of particular individuals.

Following on from this approach has been the development of workers offering a variety of forms of consultation to agencies and organizations themselves. Wynne et al. (1986) and Campbell et al. (1991) outline the practical steps necessary to provide an input to organisations so that they may meet their aims more efficiently. These developments again take the counsellor out of the counselling room and one-to-one relationship and clearly place him or her in the wider social context – a context in which the influence of 'political' issues in their broadest sense are felt. Workers from the 'orientation' viewpoint are therefore willing to involve themselves in complex organizational issues as they believe that their pespective of the system can assist the individuals's performance in a wide range of activ- ities not necessarily related directly to the family. Indeed it may well be that some workers from this perspective cease to apply their skills to care- giving organizations and become active with organizations that are ulti- mately concerned with typical business and financial goals.

Both conceptions of 'family' counselling contain dilemmas and dangers in the manner in which they may develop. There can readily be a shift from counselling to advocacy and from this to other forms of social intervention. On the other hand there may be a movement towards the ethics of the market place. As always, counsellors need to keep in the forefronts of their minds the ethics and values that they hold and consider these in conjuction with the variety of roles they may be required to perform. As with all new developments, ultimately the question raised is how counselling is to be defined and practised. In terms of the theoretical development in family counselling Walsh (1993) notes 'there is a clear shift . . . from a deficit model informing counselling to one that emphasises resources, moving the counsellor from the analysis of what went wrong to being involved in a search for what can be done to enhance functioning, be it of the family or otherwise.' In this respect it is noticeable that there is a gradual coming together of counselling approaches with the person-centred (Rogerian approach) being extended by those working with families (Gaylin 1993) and adapted to a systemic framework (Street 1994). Pinsof (1994) additionally presents a means of integrating individual and interactive approaches thereby allowing the counsellor to construct a practice and personal style that involves working with individuals, couples and families.

Conclusion

It is, or course, a truism to say that we are all part of a family. Families provide the context in which we attempt to meet our needs, which are by their very nature relational. Given the extent that our families, however composed, have such an influence on our adjustment to the wider world, it is little wonder that many of the problems and worries of life are based within its confines. Yet it also offers the solution to many difficult situations. The problems that families present and the potential for care and support they offer are enormous. No worker, regardless of discipline or theoretical persuasion, can avoid the ways in which families can affect and influence particular circumstances. It would seem necessary for all workers to have some understanding of family processes and functioning. Our thinking has for too long been dominated by a view of human distress as being the product of processes internal to the individual. It is important for all workers to have an appreciation of the forces and influences of the family on the individual and, in particular, it is essential that workers come to be able to tap the potential of these forces for the well-being of all. It is, therefore, essential that counsellors who in any way deal with families have knowledge of the systems' properties of families so that they may make interventions based on an awareness of the family as a whole. There is now a considerable body of knowledge concerning family functioning and all counsellors should be able to draw upon this. If we neglect the power of families we do so at our peril; if we can tap its tremendous resources we make available to our clients a natural means of care and support of infinite possibility.

References

Black, D. (1989) 'Life threatening illness, children and family therapy', *Journal of Family Therapy*, Special issue, Spring 1989: 81–102

Birchwood, M. and Smith. J. (1987) 'Schizophrenia and the family' in J. Orford (ed.) *Coping with Disorder in the Family*, London: Croom Helm.

Bowen, M. (1979) *Family Therapy in Clinical Practice*, New York: Jason Aronson.

Campbell, D., Draper, R., and Huttington, C. (1991) *A Systemic Approach to Consultation*, London: Karnac Books.

Crane, D. R. (1995) 'Introduction to Behavioural Family Therapy for families of young children', *Journal of Family Therapy* 17: 229–42

Crowther, C., Dare, C., and Wilson, J. (1990) '''Why should we talk to you? You'll only tell the court?'' On being an informer and a family therapist', *Journal of Family Therapy* 12: 105–22

De'Ath, E. (1988) 'Families and their differing needs' in E. Street and W. Dryden (eds) *Family Therapy in Britain*, Milton Keynes: Open University Press.

Dimmock, B. and Dungworth, D. (1985) 'Beyond the family: using network meetings with statutory child care cases', *Journal of Family Therapy* 7: 45–68.

Doherty, W. J., Colangelo, N., Hovander, D. (1991) 'Priority Setting in Family Change and Clinical Practice: The FIRO Model', *Family Process* 30: 227–40.

Gaylin, N. L. (1993) 'Person-Centred Family Therapy' in D. Brazier (ed.) *Beyond Carl Rogers*, London: Constable.

Gergen, K. (1991) *The Saturated Self*, New York: Basic Books.

Goldner, V. (1985) 'Feminism and family therapy', *Family Process* 24: 31–47.

—— ——(1991) 'Feminism and Systemic Practice: Two critical traditions in transition', *Journal of Family Therapy* 13: 95–104.

Grief, G. L. (1994) 'Using Family Therapy Ideas with Parenting Groups in Schools', *Journal of Family Therapy* 16: 199–208.

Haley, J. (1976) *Problem Solving Therapy*, San Francisco: Jossey-Bass.

Hoffman, L. (1989) 'The Family Life Cycle and Discontinuous Change' in B. Carter and M. McGoldrick (eds) *The Changing Family Life Cycle: A framework for Family Therapy*, (2nd edn,) Boston: Allyn and Bacon.

Holmes, J. (1985) 'Family and individual therapy: comparisons and contrasts', *British Journal of Psychiatry*, 147: 668–76.

James, K. and Mackinnon, L. (1990) 'The ''Incestuous Family'' Revisited: A critical analysis of family therapy myths', *Journal of Marital and Family Therapy* 16: 71–88.

Kerr, M. (1981) 'Family systems theory and therapy' in A. Gurman and D. Kniskern (eds) *Handbook of Family Therapy*, New York: Brunner/Mazel.

Kruk, E. (1993) 'Promoting Co-operative Parenting After Separation: a therapeutic/intervention model of family mediation', *Journal of Family Therapy* 15: 235–62.

Nichols, K. A. (1987) 'Chronic Physical disorder in adults' in J. Orford (ed.) *Coping with Disorder in the Family*, London: Croom Helm.

Olson, D. H., Russell, C. S., Sprenkle, D. H. (1989) *Circumplex Model: Systemic Assessment and Treatment of Families*, New York: Haworth Press.

Orford, J. (1987) 'Integration: a general account of families coping with disorder' in J. Orford (ed.) *Coping with Disorder in the Family*, London: Croom Helm.

Perelberg R. and Miller, A. (1990) (eds) *Gender and Power in Families*, London: Routledge.

Pinsof, W. (1994) 'A synthesis of family and individual psychotherapies', *Journal of Family Therapy* 16: 103–20.

Robinson, M. (1991) *Family Transformation Through Divorce and Re-Marriage: A Systemic Approach*, London: Routledge.
——(1993) 'Comment on Promoting Co-operative Parenting After Separation', *Journal of Family Therapy* 15: 263–72.
Robinson, M. and Smith, D. (1993) *Step by Step: Focus on Stepfamilies*, Hemel Hempstead: Harvester Wheatsheaf.
Speed B. and Brew, C. (eds) (1995) Gender, Power and Relationships, London: Routledge.
Street, E. (1994a) *Counselling for Family Problems*, London: Sage.
——(1994b) 'A Family Systems Approach to Child–Parent Separation: "developmental closure"', *Journal of Family Therapy* 16: 347–66.
Street E. and Downey, J. (1996) *Brief Therapeutic Consultations*, London: Wiley.
Street, E. and Soldan, J. (1995) 'Chronic Illness and Disability' in J. Ketley and G. Marsh (eds) *Counselling in Primary Health Care*, Oxford: Oxford University Press.
Walsh, F. (1993) *Normal Family Processes, 2nd edn*, New York: Guilford Press.
Watzlawick, P., Weakland, J., and Fisch, R. (1974) *Change: Principles of Problem Formation and Problem Resolution*, New York: Norton.
White J., Essex, S., and O'Reilly, P. (1993) 'Family Therapy, Systemic Thinking and Child Protection' in J. Carpenter and A. Treacher (eds) *Using Family Therapy in the 90s*, Oxford: Blackwells
Wynne, L. C., McDaniel, S. H., Webber I. T. (eds) (1986) *Systems Consultation: A New Perspective for Family Therapy*, New York: Guilford Press.

Chapter six

Counselling in groups

Bernard Ratigan

Introduction

Aristotle wrote that human beings are, by nature, social animals. Yet the
lay person's view of counselling is that it is in essence an individual
activity, or more properly, dyadic: client and counsellor. Although psychotherapy and counselling emerged as individualist disciplines, in the
second half of the twentieth century there has been an enormous growth
in the use of group methodologies in a variety of settings. The range is wide
and includes:

- formal, long-term groups designed to help bring about major changes in
  members' functioning;
- brief but intensive groups;
- skill training and staff support groups;
- groups with a focus on helping members solve, resolve, or accept problems, make adjustments, or cope with trauma.

Group counselling covers a wide gamut.

This chapter surveys the major theoretical and clinical perspectives
underpinning various forms of group counselling. It includes some descriptive material to illustrate the nature of the counselling process as it can
occur in group settings. Issues in group counselling are considered, including the goals of the group, inclusion and exclusion factors, the role of the
group counsellor, the 'work' of group members, the development of different types of group over time, how change actually occurs in groups, the
limitations of the various types of groups, and effective leadership profiles.
There follows a review of the different purposes for which counselling and
counselling skills are used in groups and an attempt to identify the different
types of group setting where counselling has a part to play. The chapter
concludes with a consideration of likely future developments. These
include questions to do with training, the increasing use and appropriateness of group counselling, and the convergence of methodologies.

Principles

All the major theoretical approaches to individual counselling and psychotherapy are represented and practised in group counselling. This chapter takes as the primary differences between counselling and psychotherapy the following: length of time over which the group meets, the depth at which the members' material is treated, the use of transference, and the purposes for which the group is convened. A pragmatic distinction is preferred in which counselling emphasizes work with non-patient groups, is of shorter duration, with little explicit use of the transference and where there is a greater degree of task orientation. Throughout the chapter, though, these distinctions will be continually blurred and the literature of psychotherapy and counselling equally utilized.

The history of group counselling is not extensive and has developed rapidly in the second half of the twentieth century (Roberts 1995). During the Second World War attempts were made to develop group treatments for soldiers which led to important work at the National Training Laboratory at Bethel, Maine in the USA and the Tavistock Clinic and the Tavistock Institute in London (Trist and Murray 1990; Trist and Murray 1993; Lyth 1988 a and b). The application of psychoanalytic insights to group processes provided one of the major perspectives in group counselling (Foulkes and Anthony 1957). The work of Rogers was also of significance in the development of group counselling. From his work with individual clients important ideas evolved about the nature of human development and necessary conditions for growth and change which have profoundly affected group counselling (Thorne 1988). Humanistic psychology has a strong base in group methodologies, as for example with Gestalt and psychodrama. The development of stress counselling groups is reported in Palmer and Dryden (1995).

Group counselling offers a fundamentally different experience to the client from that of individual one-to-one counselling. In his magisterial work, Yalom (1995) identified eleven factors which distinguish the curative factors operating in group counselling and provide a background to all its forms:

(1) The instillation of hope is central to all forms of psychological therapy, and to religion and medicine.
(2) Universality: one of the most significant learnings by members of groups is that they are not alone in either their experience or concerns.
(3) Imparting of information: although in the beginning group members often expect that, as in school, they will be taught facts, they come to realize that this is of relatively small importance.
(4) Altruism: group membership often releases in participants previously hidden or forgotten capacities for helping others.
(5) The corrective recapitulation of the primary family group: groups can

help members to work through and in some ways heal hurts sustained in earlier life.

(6) Development of socializing techniques: participation in a group provides the opportunity for learning, and practising, different ways of relating to others in a live setting.

(7) Imitative behaviour: by watching others' behaviour and listening to them, group members can discover their own distinctive personal styles.

(8) Interpersonal learning: through interaction with others, members are often able to grow and change. Groups provide an opportunity for both emotional and cognitive understanding.

(9) Group cohesiveness is the result of all the forces acting on the memories to remain in a group and is not a curative factor *per se* but a necessary precondition for effective change.

(10) Catharsis and ventilation of feelings are not themselves sufficient for change, but may play a significant part in the process and can therefore also be curative factors.

(11) Existential factors such as the need to take responsibility for oneself, the fact of individual isolation, contingency, the inevitability of mortality, and the capriciousness of existence are all themes which are often more easily tackled in group settings rather than in individual therapy.

In one of the most significant pieces of large-scale research in this field Yalom established what members of groups themselves saw as the most helpful factors. In order of importance they were:

(1) discovering and accepting previously unknown or unacceptable parts of myself;

(2) being able to say what was bothering me instead of holding it all in;

(3) other members honestly telling me what they think of me;

(4) learning how to express my feelings;

(5) the group's teaching me about the type of impression I make on others;

(6) expressing negative and/or positive feelings towards another member;

(7) learning that I must take ultimate responsibility for the way I live my life no matter how much guidance and support I get from others;

(8) learning how I come across to others;

(9) seeing that others could reveal embarrassing information and take other risks and benefit from it helped me to do the same; and

(10) feeling more trustful of groups and other people.

Applications

There are a wide variety of types of groups in existence ranging from those in clinical settings offering long, slow treatment to educational and management training settings with short lives and focused agendas. Historically, the group-analytic movement established a model of groupwork in which a group of strangers would come together on a weekly or twice-weekly basis, often over a period of years, with the leader (usually called the 'conductor') acting as analyst to the group (Roberts and Pines 1991). The conductor would usually only comment on the group process in so far as it revealed the transference material emerging in the free associations of the group members (or patients) about themselves, the other members, and, especially, the leader. It will be seen that such groups are derived from the psychoanalytic ideas of Freud and the theory underpinning them owes much to the work of Bion (1961).

In contradistinction to analytic groups are those derived from the work of Rogers, who eschewed what he saw as the deterministic ideas of Freud and instead emphasized the importance of the personal encounter between client and therapist in both individual and group settings. From using these ideas in small-scale encounter groups in the 1960s, Rogers and his associates have extended the concept of group counselling through to much larger gatherings of people from widely diverse ethnic and language backgrounds. Similarly, the group-analytic perspective has developed methods for exploring the big issues that divide and exercise people. Some of the most exciting developments in groupwork ideas and practice in the 1990s have demonstrated the power of groups to facilitate communication between people otherwise separated by conventional barriers of nationality, class, ideology, sexual orientation, gender, race and language.

Psychology and education combined to produce a range of group methods which employ theories based upon cognitive-behavioural and social-learning approaches. One of the increasingly widely practised forms of groupwork is assertiveness training. Although there are a number of models in existence the unifying idea behind them is that individuals working together in a group with a leader are systematically trained to develop skills which will help them in their relationships with others. There is considerable emphasis on participants identifying situations in their own lives in which they are not assertive – that is, in which they are passive or aggressive. By enacting these scenes with tuition from the leader and the active support and encouragement of other group members standing in as significant others in the participant's life, skills are acquired (Dickson 1982).

Assertiveness training is of particular interest because it includes within it a number of other methodologies, for example instruction and psychodrama. When groupwork ideas were first being contemplated in the years before and during the Second World War, group leaders would sometimes give lectures on aspects of mental health. This practice has now dwindled with the realization that the kinds of changes being worked for in group approaches need something more powerful than information and instruction. Psychodrama has a long and distinguished history. Originating with Moreno's theatre of the mind, it owes more than a little to Freud's psychoanalytic ideas, especially with regard to the importance of dreams, but it has become widely disseminated in most forms of groupwork, training, and education through the practice of role-play. There does, of course, exist the pure form of psychodrama with its own training and applications. It is an especially potent form of group counselling because of its immediacy, the role of the director (*sic*), and its capacity for getting at traumatic material in group members' lives, current and past (Blatner 1973). It is especially applicable in forensic settings. Because it is such a powerful, and potentially explosive, medium it requires specialist training and supervision.

Among some of the most significant changes that have taken place in western society this century have been those in the relationships between men and women. The women's movement is essentially founded upon ideas that have been arrived at in groups. Single-sex groupings are not, of course, new. Indeed, through much of human history boys and girls have been educated and trained in single-sex groups and much human activity is carried out separately. What is especially interesting in terms of group counselling is that both women's and men's groups are now regularly convened to develop and raise consciousness and to give their members the context and possibility of exploring issues that are hard or impossible in mixed-gender settings. In viability, one of the perennial issues in single-sex counselling groups is the emotional and sexual emotions between members. This century has begun to see the recognition of the complexity and range of human sexuality and sexual orientation. Well-run groups provide safety for people to explore the often painful parts of themselves which may have lain unrecognized or hidden for years and sometimes decades. Such exploration can have the most profound implications not only for the group member but also for his or her partner, parents, children and friends.

As has been mentioned, group therapy really began to take shape during the Second World War as part of the treatment given to those suffering neurotic disorders. It is in other total and neo-total institutions that group counselling has grown, if not flourished. In the prison system, for example, there has been some recognition of the power of groups as a therapeutic agent of change. Two particular modalities are worthy of special note. Psychoanalytically derived groupwork methods are used to treat some of the most disturbed and disturbing prisoners (Cox 1978). Methods derived from psychodrama are also practised in work with prisoners. Again, the focus on drama seems to give such methods a special significance and power. Although there are very few psychiatric therapeutic penal facilities in Britain, there is a need to expand groupwork treatments to make them available on a much wider basis.

Groups, then, are having an increasingly important impact on the treatment of the emotionally disturbed and ill. Even in organically orientated psychiatric units there is recognition of the importance of establishing a therapeutic milieu, even if this proves difficult in practice (Whitely and Gordon 1979). Therapeutic communities all have group therapy at their centre and out-patient groups are routinely organized in NHS specialist psychotherapy departments as well as increasingly by community mental health teams (Hinshelwood 1987; Kennard 1983). Another important development is the range of self-help groups in the community. Examples abound: groups for alcohol and other substance abusers, for those with eating disorders, for the bereaved, those traumatized by violence or sexual attack or abuse, for the recovering mentally ill, for those affected by HIV, for those coming out as gay or lesbian, for those who consider themselves to be sexual compulsives, for the divorced and many others. Although some of these groups would eschew notions of leadership on ideological grounds, they are, of course, subject to many of the same dynamics and processes as more formally convened groups with trained, professional leaders. Indeed, it is clear that as in any other form of therapy the important distinction is not between the professional and the amateur but between the more effective and less effective leader.

Lastly, groups are used extensively in training for the therapeutic and other helping professionals such as social work, education, and management. It is increasingly recognized that the formation of people for such professions requires more than cognitive learning and specialist skills. The power of the group can be utilized to show beginners the need for personal knowledge which, paradoxically, is often best acquired in interaction with others. The painful process of change and the acquisition of personal insight and sensitivity is often enhanced and made more powerful by the exposure to the group experience.

Issues

Goals of the group

Counselling groups are convened for many reasons although it is important that they are convened for a purpose. What the group is for will condition how it is conducted, led or facilitated. Group counsellors have themselves to understand the group's purpose so that they can make this explicit to the participants. Of course, stated and actual goals can diverge considerably and once groups begin they develop a life, culture and personality of their own which is as likely to fluctuate as is any human being.

The role of the leaders

Group counsellors have important but often subsidiary roles when compared with their individual colleagues. The work starts with the conception of the group, when it is called into being and for what purpose the group is convened. Group counsellors have many important housekeeping and boundary-holding functions. They need in particular, to ensure that the potential client population is aware of the availability of the group. There are key questions about selection:

- is the group appropriate for all those who would wish to join?
- what are the criteria for selection?
- what is the optimum size of the group, the maximum and the minimum?
- over what period of time will the group meet and meet and how frequently?
- how long will sessions be?
- once started is it open so that new members may join as some leave, or is it closed?
- where will the group meet?
- are there rules or guidelines about the participants meeting outside sessions and what is to happen if this does happen?
- what are the rules about confidentiality?
- what are the rules about smoking, eating or drinking in sessions?
- what is the policy to be on absence and its notification?
- what supervision arrangements do group counsellors need to support their work?

This list is not exhaustive and the reader is referred to Whitaker (1985) for an extended discussion of these and related issues.

The work of the counsellor includes many external functions which, though of apparently small significance, do much to ensure an efficiently and carefully run group with a good therapeutic culture. Examples of these include getting and keeping the same room each week; ensuring that there are enough chairs and that the chairs are there for every session in the same configuration. Small matters but of great importance.

Once the group has begun, the work of the counsellor will vary depending on his or her primary theoretical orientation, the purposes for which the group is convened, and the particular point it has reached in its developmental natural history. In all groups, though, counsellors will play particular attention to both what is said and not said, to helping the group stay in the here-and-now and to boundary matters like time, breaks and endings. Two important concepts of relevance are holding and leverage. Holding refers to that special quality of relationship that a leader has with the group which parallels that of the good (enough) parent able to communicate to the infant and child that they are viewed unconditionally. Through reliability and a non-retaliatory stance the leader can help to sustain a productive therapeutic atmosphere. By applying the principles of leverage the effective leader can identify just how much force to apply where and for how long to maximize change. It is a skill acquired with experience under supervision and from making inevitable mistakes.

There are a variety of special elective techniques. One of which is the use of written reports. After each session the counsellors write an account of what they have observed. This provides an opportunity for the participants to relive the session, for insights and changes to be underscored and emphasized, for learning to be reinforced and it can help members see that the group is an orderly process with direction leading to gains (Yalom *et al.* 1975; Aveline 1986). It is usual for the report to be written by the therapist immediately after each session and posted to group members. Participants often display a range of emotions about the reports which can become an important part of the group process.

Groups are complicated and suffused with complex interactions. Two leaders are almost always better than one. They provide support for each other, they are able to adopt differing roles in the group at different times, one perhaps more active than the other, and they are able to offer to the group and each other differing perspectives on what is going on. For mixed-gender groups it is particularly helpful if the leaders are of different genders: many issues relating to male–female relationships, to parents, and sexuality can thus be given greater prominence.

The final issue facing group leaders is that of supervision. The powerful forces at work in any therapeutic relationship are multiplied many times over in a group. It goes without saying that group leaders must themselves have embraced the training tripos of theoretical instruction, a personal experience of group membership and of doing supervised work. Supervision is necessary from the moment the idea of the group is conceived and called into being. One of the advantages of having two leaders is that peer supervision is much easier to arrange. Some kind of supervision is, however, essential for the well-being of the group and the leaders.

The work of group members

The 'work' of participants in groups will vary with the purpose of the group. One of the unifying concepts throughout most group modalities is that of remaining in the here-and-now. This means trying to say what members are experiencing in the present moment. This is especially difficult for most neophyte group participants and requires considerable effort, as many human interactions avoid this. A good group culture can be invaluable in transmitting the importance of staying in the here-and-now. Members soon sense when the group is not 'working' and say so.

The basic ground rule for group members is uninhibited conversation. This is the group equivalent of free association in individual work. It is an encouragement for continued communication in the face of antagonism. Conflict, both within and between members, is one of the distinctive features of most forms of group counselling. The asymmetry of the power relationship between counsellor and client in one-to-one work is transformed in group counselling, so that in groups clients can often more quickly experience and express angry or fearful feelings towards leaders. A member who attacks a leader may be a spokesperson for others and the public character of the occasion tends to ensure that retaliation will not take place. Further, in individual work, the only source of information is the counsellor; in a group, the other members also serve as sources of feedback, as models, as guides and as encouragers.

The expression of anger can be a particularly useful medium of learning, growth and healing, especially with those people who have been traumatized, have never learned how to express their anger adequately, or have become skilled at converting it into depression or some psychosomatic condition. Members' anger with one another and with the leaders, is often an important turning point for both the individuals concerned and for the group's development as a therapeutic agent for change. Although painful, being angry with one another is often a way of saying 'I am taking you seriously', and even 'you are important to me'. For those group participants who experience themselves as more or less unimportant, to be able to get close to saying these words can be profoundly significant.

Group members tend to discover that in many ways they are more similar to each other than they expected. Behind the masks of everyday life, of surface coping, even the most seemingly well-adjusted group members will usually have undercurrents to explore. Sullivan's (1953) one-genus postulate, 'everyone is much more simply human than otherwise', although conceived in the context of individual psychotherapy, seems even more apt in the context of groups.

The distorted views that group members have of themselves, other members and leaders provide one of the richest sources of material for productive work in a group. The distortions are a result of the life experiences of the participants. Frank (1974) has identified two, mirror and transference reactions, that are especially common, important and useful. Mirror reactions are those where group members tend to detect and disapprove of traits in someone else that they deny in themselves. In the group they can be helped to see them as their own. Transference reactions occur when members inappropriately transfer on to or put into other participants or the leaders those feelings which are, or more usually were, appropriate to others in their lives. Through the process of the 'reflective loop' members can be helped to see and work through their distortions and difficulties over and over again. Members of groups come to demonstrate what Frank has called their 'assumptive world'. Instead of merely talking about their life and concerns they *become* them and so demonstrate them in the group. In the group they create the relationships and the difficulties which they experience in the outside world. The group can then become a workshop or laboratory where steps can be taken to change with the powerful support of the other group members and the leaders.

How groups develop over time

Counselling groups, like other forms of life, have a natural history: a beginning, a middle and an end. Early sessions are often characterized by hesitancy, fear, dependency, difficulties in staying in the here-and-now, and high expectations. It is a time for building group norms that emphasize the importance of openness and sharing but not too much too soon. Sometimes it is more useful if participants are able to hold back on what seems very pressing until a sufficient degree of trust has been built up. Likewise, confrontations, although important and often therapeutic in effect, are often the characteristic of the more established, safer atmosphere of the mature group. In these matters there is usually a tension between the need to disclose and the fear of disclosure: done too soon and a fragile therapeutic alliance can be destroyed; left too late, and an anti-therapeutic culture may preclude any real sharing and be very difficult to shift.

In more mature groups, participants are gradually able to free themselves of inhibitions and resistances to talking openly, more able to stay in the present and more able to give and receive feedback and to exercise autonomy both within and outside the group. There is also an increasing ability to risk doing the things, being the person they wish, and sharing the words and feelings which are hard to express but which are necessary for change and growth.

In groups derived from cognitive, behavioural, Gestalt and psychodramatic modalities, the development is much more determined by the leader. In all forms of groups, however, there comes a moment which, if seized, can result in sharp changes of attitude or behaviour. One of the Greek words for time, *kairos*, better expresses the power of the auspicious moment. It is very much a feature of counselling in groups and links this kind of work with drama and ritual.

All groups have to face issues to do with ending. Even in long, open groups in which members stay as long as they need, there are endings. Most counselling groups are of fixed length and a well-run, mature group will be helped to face the questions of ending well in advance of it actually happening. It is a time for reflection on the gains made, the insights, the sense of belonging, the good and the bad times shared. It is also a time for sadness, loss, anger and frustration. The well-run group will be helped to face these issues and to work through them. As in individual work, breaks and endings will generate many, often lost or repressed, memories of other losses experienced by group members in the past. Members will be surprised at the powerful feelings encountered and, with help from peers and therapists, be able to speak of them and work through the pain of the losses.

How change occurs

There are a variety of factors at work in groups which facilitate, and inhibit, change. Ideally, participants come to see themselves more fully and are able to try out new ways of being and relating to others and thinking about themselves and their worlds. In the safety of the group they are offered space and time which can provide the context in which these changes can occur. It is a complex (and not fully understood) nexus of factors which both allows the participants to experience the safety necessary for change to occur and for the anxiety or tension which is the spur to move towards change (Yalom *et al.* 1975; Bloch and Crouch 1985). Developments, learning, insight, and growth occur in an episodic rather than a linear manner. Merely being in the group is clearly not sufficient for change to occur; involvement in other processes, such as risking saying what one is feeling, sharing secrets, giving and receiving feedback, catharsis, confrontation, modelling, and the corrective emotional experience can all be important. An important process in group counselling is the reflective loop of doing, looking back on what was done, and then understanding. As groups mature, members often take over this function from leaders.

Limitations of counselling groups

Group counselling provides a therapeutic and learning environment in which many human problems can be worked on to good effect. People for whom a one-to-one relationship is essential will not benefit from groups. Those who will probably not do well in groups are those suffering from psychotic illness and severe depression, those who can only see their difficulties in physical terms, the paranoid who are overly suspicious, the narcissistic who need all the attention for themselves, and the schizoid who are too cut off from other people. Once people have been helped to move from these categories, group work can often provide an important and potent ingredient in their return to well-being. In essence, groups are more for interpersonal rather than intrapersonal development (Ratigan and Aveline 1988).

It is also often difficult to persuade potential participants that a group really is the treatment of choice and not a second best to individual therapy. The culture of individualism in our society is often strongly embodied in those with difficulties, especially interpersonal difficulties.

The power and flexibility of group counselling is that it can be used to help participants over a whole range of concerns. There are very few people who could not benefit from the forum for open genuine communication which group counselling can provide.

Future developments

Human beings are born into group life and need other people for physical and emotional nourishment, sustenance, and hope. Although the history of counselling has emphasized work with individuals, it is becoming clear that group work will become more significant. There are many reasons for this. It appears that not only are groups somewhat more economic, they can sometimes provide a more effective form of help than individual work. The empirical work to establish this, fraught with many methodological difficulties because of the complexities of what goes on in groups, is yet to be fully undertaken (Bednar 1970).

What is clear from observation is that in a group a person is able not only to describe difficulties but, when they are of an interpersonal nature or have an interpersonal dimension, they can also demonstrate them. Groups are good at mobilizing a range of sources of help, not least other group members. Apart from the boundary and housekeeping functions of the leaders, group members can be helped to become peer therapists to each other. The acts of sharing and being of assistance to others in the group is well documented as giving great benefit to the participants (Yalom 1995).

As our society seemingly becomes more fragmented and individuals experience the trauma of alienation, there is an increasing need for the use of psychological techniques to help construct what so-called simple or primitive societies did naturally through social structures and rituals (Roose-Evans 1994). We need to help ourselves create mechanisms which provide safe space and dedicated time to ensure our physical, emotional and spiritual well-being and growth. In a society which is rapidly changing, where individuals and families are often separated, where there are conflicting values, goals and identities on offer, counselling in groups can assist in bringing people to, and keeping them at, a psychologically healthy state. One of the most simple yet profound satisfactions reported by group members is that of 'just being together'.

It is possible to discern powerful centrifugal forces in our society which make contact between people harder to make and to sustain. Urbanization, changing patterns of domestic and family life, a widening understanding of the concept of 'family', the increasing specialization of function, and the increasing pace of life are the important factors at work. Yet there is an insatiable thirst for contact between human beings.

Although it may seem fanciful or wishful thinking, the principles embodied in group counselling can be seen as offering one, perhaps one of the few, ways in which conflict between people of different genders, nations, classes, races and so on can be helped towards resolutions without resort to violence. In the context of the group, human beings can be helped to meet each other as persons in what the Jewish writer Martin Buber called the 'I–thou' encounter. In the group setting, participants can, in principle, begin to explore what lies behind these categories, what reality is for the human beings actually present in the room, what their assumptive worlds are, and begin to challenge some of the distortions which impede free communication between people and have occasionally disastrous human consequences. Black/white, male/female, lesbian-gay/heterosexual, Catholic/Protestant/Jew/Muslim/atheist: the list of seemingly irreconcilable dichotomies seems endless. The powerful and primitive forces at work in all human interactions can, in a well-run group, be experienced, understood, contained and, perhaps, modified. Mechanisms such as scapegoating, splitting, denial, projection, and many others are all powerfully at work in the microcosm of the group and in the macrocosm of the relations between states. My hope is that exposure to group processes may help to improve our world by helping group members to see that what is happening in the group also happens in relations between peoples, states and cultural groups.

The convergence of group-counselling methodologies

Predicting the future in any field of human endeavour is foolhardy, but at the moment the dominant ideologies in group counselling are psychoanalytic (Hyde 1988), humanistic, and cognitive-behavioural (Alladin 1988). The impression is that outside of the major training institutes there is a considerable degree of pragmatic eclecticism with, perhaps, a predominance of post-Rogerian person-centred approaches. These are often stiffened with aspects of Yalom's existential and interpersonal ideas, sometimes with episodes owing something to psychodrama and Gestalt. The whole being is held together with a theory owing not a little to the seminal work of the group analysts.

Whilst the protagonists of the different modalities might well stake claims for doctrinal purity, the future could well see a merging of approaches. This might come about as a result of practitioners themselves being confronted by intractable group situations which show their existing formulations and practices to be inadequate. The process of convergence may also be accelerated by an increase in the numbers of training programmes through which novices and more experienced practitioners progress. It is not unusual for group leaders to have been exposed to many forms of group before settling to one that makes sense for them and their group members.

Although some research has been undertaken on the effectiveness of one approach as against others and the suitability of approaches for different groups and purposes, much still remains to be done and the field is still wide open.

Conclusion

This chapter has reviewed group counselling in Britain as it appears to one practitioner currently working in the NHS and who has been heavily influenced by person-centred, existential, and psychoanalytic ideas. Others with differing orientations would, doubtless, have given different accounts. What is clear is that group counselling has come a very long way in the last fifty years and that it has an exciting and productive future ahead. It is likely to become not only much more important within counselling, but also within society as a resource for personal development in, for example, education, community development, religion, and in the workplace, as well as in clinical settings. People live in groups: should they not then be treated in groups?

References

Alladin, W. (1988) 'Cognitive-behavioural group therapy' in M. Aveline and D. Dryden (eds) *Group Therapy in Britain*, London: Routledge, pp. 115–39.

Aveline, M. (1986) 'The use of written reports in a brief group psychotherapy training', *International Journal of Group Psychotherapy* 36: 477–82.

Aveline, M. and Dryden, W. (eds) (1988) *Group Therapy in Britain*, London: Routledge.

Bednar, R.L. (1970) 'Group psychotherapy research variables', *International Journal of Group Psychotherapy* 20: 146–52.

Bion, W. R. (1961) *Experiences in Groups and Other Papers*, London: Tavistock.

Blatner, H.A. (1973) *Acting-In: Practical Applications of Psychodramatic Method*, New York: Springer.

Bloch, S. and Crouch, E. (1985) *Therapeutic Factors in Group Psychotherapy*, Oxford: Oxford University Press.

Cox, M. (1978) *Structuring the Therapeutic Process*, Oxford: Pergamon Press.

Dickson, A. (1982) *A Woman in Your Own Right*, London: Quartet.

Foulkes, S.H. and Anthony, E.J. (1957) *Group Psychotherapy: The Psychoanalytical Approach*, London: Penguin Books.

——(1989) *Group Psychotherapy: The Psychoanalytical Method*, London: Penguin Books.

Frank, J. (1974) *Persuasion and Healing*, revised edn, New York: Schoken Books.

Hinshelwood, R. D. (1987) *What Happens in Groups: Psychoanalysis, The Individual and the Community*, London: Free Association Books.

Hyde, K. (1988) 'Analytic group psychotherapies' in M. Aveline and W. Dryden (eds) *Group Therapy in Britain*, London: Routledge.

Kennard, D. (1983) *An Introduction to Therapeutic Communities*, London: Routledge.

Lyth, I. M. (1988a) *Containing Anxiety in Institutions: Selected Essays*, vol. 1, London: Free Association Books.

——(1988b) *The Dynamics of the Social: Selected Essays*, vol. 2, London: Free Association Books.

Palmer, S. and Dryden, W. (1995) *Counselling for Stress Problems*, London: Sage.

Ratigan, B. and Aveline, M. (1988) 'Interpersonal group therapy' in M. Aveline and W. Dryden (eds) *Group Therapy in Britain*, London: Routledge.

Roberts, J. P. (1995) 'Reading about group psychotherapy', *British Journal of Psychiatry* 166: 124–9.

Roberts, J. P. and Pines, M. (eds) (1991) *The Practice of Group Analysis*, London: Routledge.

Roose-Evans, J. (1994) *Passages of the Soul: Ritual Today*, Shaftesbury, Dorset: Element.

Sullivan, H. S. (1953) *The Interpersonal Theory of Psychiatry*, New York: Norton.

Thorne, B. (1988) 'The person-centred approach to large groups' in M. Aveline and W. Dryden (eds) *Group Therapy in Britain*, London: Routledge.

Trist, E. and Murray, M. (eds) (1990) *The Social Engagement of Social Science, volume 1: The Socio-psychological Perspective*, London: Free Association Books.

——(1993) *The Social Engagement of Social Science: A Tavistock Anthology, volume 2: The Socio-Technical Perspective*, Philadelphia: University of Pennsylvania Press.

Whitaker, D.S. (1987) *Using Groups to Help People*, London: Routledge.

Whitely, J.S. and Gordon, J. (1979) *Group Approaches in Psychiatry*, London: Routledge.

Yalom, I.D. (1995) *The Theory and Practice of Group Psychotherapy*, 4th edn, New York: Basic Books.

Yalom, I.D., Brown, S. and Bloch, S. (1975) 'The written summary as a group psychotherapy technique', *Archives of General Psychiatry* 32: 605–13.

Part three

Settings

Chapter seven

Counselling in private practice

Gladeana McMahon

Introduction

Numbers

Nobody knows how many counsellors operate their own private or independent practice in the United Kingdom since there is no compulsion to register with any official body in order to practise. Any statistics quoted can be 'guestimates' at best and indicative only. Feltham (1995a) quotes an article in *The Sunday Times* of 26 July 1993 claiming a figure of 30,000 paid counsellors/therapists, 140,000 volunteer counsellors and 2 million people using counselling skills. However, this would include employed as well as self-employed counsellors and presumably cover a range of therapies not all of which would fall under the heading of counselling as it is generally understood. Syme (1994) concentrates her attention on the number of counsellors in the *Counselling and Psychotherapy Resources Directory* published by BAC, which lists some 2,300 entries in 1995. However, as she points out, this overlooks the very large numbers of independent practitioners who choose for one reason or another not to advertise their services through the BAC *Directory*. This may include, for example, those who appear in the *National Register of Psychotherapists* which currently lists some 3,100 practicing psychotherapists who have met the training requirements of organizations recognized by and affiliated to the United Kingdom Council for Psychotherapy. The overlap between these two lists is surprisingly low.

Geographical distribution

As Syme (1994) has observed, the distribution of independent counsellors and psychotherapists across the country is far from being in proportion to the population (the same is probably true of employed counsellors and psychotherapists). The range is enormous. In the North and North West postal districts of London there is an independent counsellor or psychotherapist to every 2,000 people. In Scotland and Northern Ireland it is one for every 60,000 people. There are five times more independent counsellors and therapists listed in the North West London postal district alone than in the whole of Scotland. Similar patterns are evident across the country with London and South East England enjoying the lion's share of private counselling and psychotherapy services and clearly able to support such numbers of fee-charging practitioners.

About 1 in 5 entries on average in the *BAC* Directory also appear in the *Register of Psychotherapists*. If this overlap is subtracted together with the number of psychotherapists listing an employer's address and those practising overseas, a total number of around 4,400 emerges. This, perhaps, represents a closer estimate of counsellors and psychotherapists who have a sufficiently serious commitment to self-employment as to obtain a listing in one or other of these directories. It is also worth noting that any overlap with the *Register of Chartered Psychologists* appears to be negligible.

There will of course be a significant number of practitioners who appear in no register or directory, the majority of whom are probably in employment but run a small, part-time practice and may have aspirations to independent practice at an appropriate time. This number could lie in the range of 5,000–10,000. In addition, there are a number of registers within the complementary medicine and hypnosis fields which contain details of hypnotherapists and counsellors who do not overlap either.

Gender

It is well known that the majority of independent counsellors and psychotherapists are women. The BAC *Directory* gives a split of 76 per cent women to 24 per cent men; the *National Register of Psychotherapists* 67 per cent women to 33 per cent men.

Theoretical orientation and approaches

Amongst entries in the BAC Directory, the main theoretical orientations or approaches listed are:

Psychoanalytic/psychodynamic   48 per cent
Cognitive-behavioural   12 per cent
Humanistic   46 per cent
Transpersonal   11 per cent
Eclectic/integrative   36 per cent

(The percentages do not sum to 100 per cent because many entries list two or more approaches.)

Here, again, there are significant regional variations, with psychoanalytic/psychodynamic orientations prevailing in London and up to the Midlands, and Humanistic orientations prevailing strongly in the far North and far West and still prevailing but less strongly in the remainder of the country. Amongst entries in the National Register of Psychotherapists the picture is different again as follows:

Psychoanalytic/psychodynamic   48 per cent
Humanistic and integrative   25 per cent
Family   13 per cent
Hypnotherapy   5 per cent
Cognitive-behavioural   9 per cent

If a comparison was to be made with BAC entries by removing hypnotherapy and family therapy the indications would be:

Psychoanalytic/psychodynamic   59 per cent
Humanistic and integrative   30 per cent
Cognitive-behavioural   11 per cent

It may be possible to draw a tentative conclusion here: that independent practitioners trained in and utilizing psychoanalytic/psychodynamic approaches are more likely to see themselves as psychotherapists. Those using humanistic or integrative approaches are more likely to see themselves as counsellors.

Principles

The foregoing section, in business terms, would be called market research, ie. finding out about likely customers and competitors, the market share of product groups and the likely demand for counselling or psychotherapy services. Sad though the conclusion might be, the reality is that any counsellor who attempts to start a private practice in a sparsely populated and/or economically poor area is not likely to do very well financially. Feltham (1995b) describes well the economic stress of running a private practice in East London.

Market research is only one of several business disciplines useful to any self-employed person, counsellor or otherwise. Business planning, accountancy, marketing and administration (or the absence of these) all play a significant part in determining the success or failure of a private practice however good the individual counsellor may be. A comprehensive guide to these matters is given by McMahon (1994).

There are relatively few publications dealing with the business side of running a private counselling practice. Some counsellors even think it is unethical to run a practice and charge people directly for what could be claimed are mental health or welfare problems more properly dealt with through the taxation system and the National Health Service (Pilgrim 1993). It could be argued, not unreasonably, that because of inadequate state recognition or support, counselling remains a service available generally only to those who can afford it and perhaps, more cynically, as a service offered solely by white middle-class practitioners to predominantly middle-class clients.

As a counter argument it could be claimed that, as a relatively new 'product' entering the welfare market, counselling has yet to establish itself as conferring sufficient benefits and value for money to claim recognition at a national level. Hence, until this happy day arrives why not let the 'product' develop and mature, sponsored by those who can afford the development costs? To turn the ethical argument around completely, it could also be claimed that private practitioners are, and always have been, from Freud onwards, risk-takers, innovators and pioneers who have helped to develop counselling into what it is today and, perhaps, that only private practice allows the counsellor the freedom to develop therapies without the bureaucratic or theoretical orientation constraints imposed by employers.

Turning again to business principles, it is often claimed that the purpose of any business is to make a profit. In the case of a counsellor in private practice this would mean sufficient income left over for the counsellor to live on after the expenses of running the business and the claims of the Inland Revenue have been met. Although accountants might disagree, this is a misguided concept. Profit is a by-product of doing the right things and is essentially only a financial monitoring measure which may impress the bank manager.

So, what are 'the right things'? First, the counsellor needs a good product to offer. This means a thoroughly competent, professional service delivered to high ethical standards. There is no room for the second rate, the exploitative and the greedy, which harm client, counsellor and the profession. A good product requires years of training and development and a high level of personal motivation on the part of the counsellor. Training, supervision and, possibly, personal therapy need to continue throughout the counsellor's working career. One can only be impressed by Francesca Inskipp (1993) embarking on a three-year diploma in psychosynthesis at the age of sixty-eight!

Second, the product needs to be properly 'packaged' and carry an 'after-sales' service. This means that the therapeutic relationship does not merely encompass the forty-five to sixty minutes of dialogue between counsellor and client. It involves all forms of communication outside the counselling session, the travel to and from the counsellor's premises, the premises itself, the counselling environment, security, confidentiality, punctuality, after-hours accessibility, the nature and form of the contract between counsellor and client, and the development of trust and care. Many of these aspects would fall under the heading of 'customer care' in a business context and emphasize the respect due to a client or customer, without whom the business would cease to exist.

Third, the product needs to be brought to the attention of those likely to benefit from it. This is what many people believe to be marketing though advertising and promotion are only two aspects. A counselling service can be advertised either directly to potential clients or indirectly through potential referral sources. Again, a comprehensive review can be found in McMahon (1994).

In the early days of setting up a private practice the counsellor may have to depend on communication channels such as *Yellow Pages*, *Thomson Directory*, circulars and local advertisements to generate demand. As the practice develops, networking, referrals from employers, GPs and other counsellors, and personal recommendation are likely to take over as the counsellor establishes a professional reputation and a higher profile in the area.

Fourth, fees need to be set at a level perceived by the client or customer as representing value for money. From a purely economic point of view an optimum level would be that which generates just sufficient demand to fill the hours the counsellor is willing or able to devote to client counselling. A counsellor has a limited productive capacity and, typically, twenty to twenty-two hours per week of actual client contact are all that can be spared or are, indeed, healthy. However, factors such as the client group serviced, whether long- or short-term counselling, type of counsellor training, experience, and stamina all affect the number of weekly client-contact hours that can be safely undertaken. The British Association for Counselling is currently considering setting upper limits of client-contact hours for their members. Additional hours are required for activities such as continued professional development, supervision, administration (e.g. casenotes, writing to GPs), marketing, and financial administration which could easily bring the total number of working hours to forty.

Fifth, the range of products on offer need to be decided on. Training and experience determine the range of clients and types of presenting problems the counsellor is competent to deal with. The counsellor has a duty of professional care to clients and the initial assessment session can be crucial in determining whether to continue with a client or make an appropriate referral elsewhere. The novice counsellor may be tempted to think that the suicidal, psychotic or severely disturbed client can be handled where, perhaps, the medical profession appears to have failed. Reality can teach some harsh and painful lessons in such cases.

In mature practices, the counsellor is likely to have diversified away from a total dependency on a client caseload and may be involved in other counselling-related activities such as supervision, training, writing or media work.

Sixth, the counsellor needs to exercise control over the financial and administrative aspects of the practice. A separate bank account and frequent banking, regular and accurate book-keeping, control of business expenditure, up-to-date filing systems and records and the prompt dealing with correspondence, etc., may not be obvious priorities for a self-employed counsellor but they cannot be ignored and time needs to be allocated each day to keeping on top of administrative tasks.

Seventh, a regular review of the practice is required and investment decisions taken, both in terms of continued training for the counsellor and in terms of equipment. Alterations to premises, repairs, refurbishing and decorating may also be required. These days, equipment may include one or two telephone lines, an answering machine, a fax and a personal computer and printer with a range of appropriate software. Counselling itself continues to develop with new therapies emerging such as the multi-modal model (Lazarus 1989, Palmer and Dryden 1995) and with developments within established therapies. Just as the medical profession needs to keep abreast of new surgical techniques and new drugs so the counsellor needs the stimulation and knowledge which come from new ideas and approaches.

Business planning

Most of the seven requirements listed above can be contained and described in a business plan, which has two components:

(1) A statement of business objectives
(2) A description of how these objectives are to be achieved

Such a plan might cover a typical period of 1–3 years and may be applied to any sort of business and is, perhaps, particularly applicable to small businesses and the self-employed who are starting a new business. The reason for this is that 80 per cent of new businesses fail within the first five years. However, if the would-be entrepreneur had been sufficiently disciplined to draw up a business plan, the typical problem of inadequate cash flow could have been spotted before the business was even started and plans made accordingly, including the possible decision not to start the business at all!

A statement of business objectives is relatively straightforward and might read something like: 'To run a successful private practice in counselling and counselling-related activities within the British Association for Counselling's Code of Ethics and Practice' (see Appendix 1). The word 'successful' can be interpreted as the individual wishes but unless the counsellor has other income or financial support it would normally include making sufficient income (after expenses and taxes) to live on. The word also suggests the achievement of a good professional reputation.

The major part of a business plan is more time-consuming and is devoted to answering four main questions:

(1) Is there likely to be sufficient potential demand for the counsellor's services?
This is answered by market research with consideration of the following:

- the catchment area
- geography (density of population, physical barriers etc.)
- socio-economic characteristics of the population
- competitors and competing services (who are they? location? types of services offered? how successful? etc.)
- typical fee rates charged for the area
- numbers of potential clients
- ease of travel to the counsellor's premises

(2) Does what the counsellor offers seem credible and acceptable to potential clients and referral sources?
Under this heading might be listed:

- personal qualifications, training, accreditation, experience, reputation, code of ethics
- type and range of services offered
- premises (location, suitability, general environment)
- business administration
- fact sheet
- terms and conditions of business (fees and how paid etc.)
- client contracts, records, confidentiality
- indemnity insurance, premises insurance
- appointments

(3) How does the counsellor intend to translate potential demand into actual demand and to what level?

- advertising (media, directories, *Yellow Pages* etc.)
- promotion (leaflets, letters, talks etc.)
- networking and personal contacts
- forecast numbers of client sessions each month

(4) What are the financial implications of setting up and running a private practice in counselling and what arrangements need to be made to ensure its viability?
This is the crucial question for most aspiring private practitioners and it is far better to carry out a serious evaluation in advance of giving up paid employment. In all probability, the private practitioner will suffer a serious drop in income in the first few years and, at the same time, incur extra expenses: premises related costs, telephone bills, postage, training, purchase of equipment etc. There are no paid holidays or sick leave, no

employer's superannuation schemes. On a personal level some sacrifice of living standards is likely and there is always the fear that business will dry up.

The exercise which will convey the most useful information answering the financial question is the cash forecast. It needs to be done on a month-by-month basis along the lines of the example below:

The example illustrates the hypothetical case of a counsellor with a modest income requirement (drawings of £750 per month to live on) and a modest business expenditure, typically £400 per month. The business builds up from a lowish base to the equivalent of about 20 clients per week paying £20 per session. In months 1 and 2 around £3,000 is spent on setting up the consulting room. In month 11 a holiday is taken which increases drawings and reduces income. In this example the counsellor would have needed at least £5,000 in savings or a loan to survive. For those with higher personal expenditure or business expenses this initial capital might need to be £10,000 or more. If a bank loan is required, the production of a well thought out business plan is likely to impress the bank manager.

Ongoing financial requirements include:

- daily entry of income and expenditure in a day or cash book
- monthly totalling and reconciliation to the bank statement
- monthly calculation of likely income tax liability and putting aside (DIY PAYE!)
- monthly analysis of expenditure under appropriate headings in an expenditure analysis book
- orderly storage of all expenditure receipts
- annual submission of books and receipts to the auditor for preparation of annual accounts

Table 7.1 Example of a cash forecast

Month	I Income	E Expenditure	D Drawings	I-E-D Cash Flow	Cumulative Cash Flow
1	500	2,300	750	− 2550	− 2550
2	700	1,200	750	− 1250	− 3800
3	800	400	750	− 350	− 4150
4	1000	400	750	− 150	− 4300
–	–	–	–	–	–
–	–	–	–	–	–
10	1600	400	750	+ 450	− 2500
11	300	200	1250	− 1150	− 3650
12	1700	400	750	+ 550	− 3100
–	–	–	–	–	–

Much of the initial risk in starting a private or independent practice can be eliminated by starting a part-time practice whilst retaining full or part-time employment. This allows a degree of 'market-testing' to be carried out from the comparative safety of a secure income and may permit savings to be built up to finance any shortfall in income in the early stages of full-time practice.

Developing the independent practice

As the chief executive of the business (as well as the production manager, marketing manager, office manager, book-keeper and probably the reception-tionist as well), the independent counsellor needs to step back from the practice at intervals and review how well (or badly) things have gone.

How has the business plan worked out in practice? Has demand been above or below expectation? What unforeseen problems have arisen which need dealing with? Has the counsellor managed to cope personally, professionally and business-wise? What opportunities have arisen which deserve closer investigation? Is the business moving in a direction in tune with the counsellor's aspirations or longer-term objectives? The answers to these questions will determine the actions which need to be taken and help to ensure the survival and development of the practice.

As the practice matures and the practitioner's competencies extend in range and depth through experience and continued training the counsellor may develop an interest in helping other less experienced counsellors, either through supervision or training, or possibly through writing books or articles for journals, or perhaps through active membership of professional groups and associations. Providing the counsellor is trained in group facilitation skills, groupwork can help the counsellor increase both profits and interest areas. For example, six people at £15 per ninety-minute session would make the counsellor's hourly rate £60 as opposed to perhaps £30 for individual counselling.

Career development in employment tends to involve the acquisition of greater managerial responsibility through internal or external promotion. In solo independent practice the counsellor has already taken this jump and has total managerial responsibility for the practice – its organization, control, finance, and the delivery of a professional service to approved standards.

Development in terms of management can involve the employment of others, particularly if the counsellor cannot alone meet the demands placed on the practice. In the first instance this may involve contracting out the non-counselling tasks such as premises cleaning, book-keeping, and typing. This is straightforward enough. However, if the practice employs a receptionist and other counsellors as employees then regard needs to be paid not only to the ability of the counsellor to motivate and supervise, in a managerial sense, but also to employment law and the employment rights of individuals, the collection and payment of tax and national insurance for employees, registration for and payment of Value Added Tax, and probably the acquisition and running of larger premises, the payment of business rates, etc.

In such cases the counsellor inevitably becomes more of a manager and less of a direct service provider. Control of the professional content of counselling and quality standards becomes more difficult; client problems are replaced by managerial problems. Group practice is possible, as in the medical, legal, and accountancy professions. This has the advantage of spreading the cost of overheads and allows a degree of daily professional and managerial support but has the disadvantage of potential conflict and the generation of 'political' problems if practitioners are not well suited to working together.

It is not possible to duplicate the individual counsellor, and the counsellor/client relationship is generally so personal and so crucial to the therapeutic process that counsellor autonomy is, understandably, jealously guarded. It may be for this and for other reasons, given above, that private practice tends to remain the province of individual independent practitioners.

Professional development, though, can and needs to continue with the aim of achieving professional excellence. Hard though this is to define, the respect of fellow practitioners and the personal gratitude and recommendation of clients remain good indicators of such achievement.

Issues

Client protection and accreditation

It would be an arrogant private practitioner who, looking back over years of professional training and experience, would claim never to have made mistakes in the assessment and treatment of clients, however good their motivation and personal integrity might have been. How many mistakes or even instances of malpractice might occur if the counsellor lacked training, experience or supervision and possibly did not even subscribe to an acceptable code of ethics and practice?

Which professions contain a higher proportion of incompetent or corrupt individuals? The highly trained and regulated, for example medical doctors, nurses, airline pilots or the less highly trained and regulated, for example politicians, estate agents, insurance sales staff (prior to their regulation)? The freedom to practise independently without bureaucratic regulation may be a wonderful thing for the would-be practitioner. It may not be so wonderful for the gullible, trusting, and vulnerable client.

Who would knowingly or willingly undergo brain surgery for a tumour from an insufficiently trained and inexperienced person? Yet the counsellor deals with the contents of the brain, opening up closed or little-used connections, developing unused portions or entering fresh data in an attempt to change attitudes, behaviour or understanding. These are serious responsibilities and should not be undertaken lightly or by those who do not know what they are doing.

It is well recognized that unregulated private practice carries the greatest potential dangers for the client (Syme 1994), as indeed it probably does in any other profession dealing with individual clients who are not in a position to judge the competence or integrity of the practitioner. Different professional bodies have differing views on what constitutes basic standards. For example, for a number of years the BPS has insisted that counselling psychologists who wish to become chartered must have 40 hours of personal therapy, whereas the BAC will only be asking for such a requirement from 1998 onwards. There are also differences in the recommended ratio of supervision hours to client-contact hours between these two organizations. Employers of counsellors would normally insist on explicit minimum standards of training, practical experience, personal therapy and ongoing supervision or possibly provide such training and supervised practical experience as well as ensuring adherence to approved codes of ethics and practice. The existence of an employer with stated standards of ethics and practice also permits complaints to be dealt with and the sanction of dismissal for unacceptable practice. With, perhaps, lesser impact, membership of one of the organizations comprising the United Kingdom Council for Psychotherapy entails the possible sanction of loss of membership for proven malpractice as does membership of the British Association for Counselling.

None of these measures, though, prevents the setting up or continuation of a private practice. The British Association for Counselling's guidelines for private practice suggest that the counsellor needs to meet at least the requirements for BAC accreditation. However, by October 1995, there were only 883 BAC accredited counsellors, probably about one in five of those practising independently. Even in these cases it is arguable as to whether the requirements are sufficient. For example, there is no requirement for the counsellor to have dealt with a wide variety of clients or the range of presenting problems which can occur typically in independent practice. It is also becoming increasingly well recognized that a total dependency on one theoretical orientation alone is not always sufficient to deal effectively and efficiently with the needs and the financial and time constraints of the client or perhaps of the client's employer. Few counsellors are trained in brief therapy yet most counselling is probably brief in nature. For example, workplace counselling and counselling carried out in GP surgeries are usually no more than six sessions in duration.

Perhaps, more crucially, the accreditation procedure does not look, in any real sense, at the actual therapeutic interactions between counsellor and client, relying for this aspect on two 1,000-word case studies as written up by the counsellor. Whilst it would not be possible for the accreditation panel of five accredited counsellors to sit in on client sessions it would be possible to tape sessions (after providing for client anonymity) and for the panel to view or listen subsequently. Alternatively, the counselling session could be simulated with one or more of the panel acting as a client with the remainder of the panel observing and taking notes. This could be supplemented by oral questions as is suggested in the recent proposals for a National Vocational Qualification in counselling. In Britain the BAC procedure for accrediting supervisors does involve direct observation of the aspiring supervisor in action and it may be for this reason that the procedure has yielded only some fifty to sixty accredited supervisors in the whole of the United Kingdom. By contrast, in the United States, the Albert Ellis Institute for Rational Emotive Behavior Therapy requires the supervisor to be observed and assessed supervising a group of supervisees over a four-day period.

It must be better to have a rigorous and thorough accreditation process producing accredited counsellors of proven and broadly based competence if the term 'accredited counsellor' is to achieve the professional status and recognition that professionals in other fields enjoy. High standards always command respect even if their adoption means that fewer counsellors achieve accredited status

Although the limited research findings available appear to show that training and personal therapy have no impact on therapeutic outcome, it would be naive to believe that all that is needed is a co-operative client and a therapist with the right personal qualities. It is my contention that the lack of evidence demonstrates the scant research in this area. Most counselling supervisors and counsellors are able to state quite clearly the ways in which training and a period of personal therapy have influenced therapeutic practice for the benefit of the client. Symanska and Palmer (see Chapter 30) suggest that the statutory registration of counsellors may not necessarily stop all professionals from abusing their clients. However, the mistake may lie in believing that if statutory registration will not totally eradicate counsellor–client exploitation then it serves no purpose at all. It is my contention that statutory registration would deter some counsellors from exploiting their clients in the same way that the risk of detection and subsequent prison sentences deter some people from committing crimes. The fear of being 'struck off' and not being able to earn a living would act as a deterrent to some. This statement cannot currently be validated, in the same way that the numbers of people kept out of criminal activity by the fear of detection cannot be evaluated. However, just because these claims cannot be substantiated does not mean they have no relevance. Rationalization of training, the creation of national standards, rigorous accreditation procedures, and statutory registration all have their part to play in protecting both clients and counsellors.

Insurance

For the protection of both the counsellor and client two forms of insurance are virtually mandatory in private practice. Indemnity insurance is required to allow compensation to be paid to a client in cases of proven malpractice or negligence without bankrupting the counsellor. Public liability insurance is also required to cover accidents to clients whilst on the counsellor's premises. These matters are covered extensively by Bond (1993).

Counsellor protection and survival of the practice

Care needs to be taken about the personal safety of the counsellor and the experienced practitioner will tend to recognize danger signals and take appropriate action. Clients of either sex with a violent history are generally to be avoided unless other adults are close at hand during counselling sessions. For this reason, referrals from reliable sources are generally safer than self-referrals where no information is available on the client and the assessment and initial sessions are generally more critical until the two-way process of trust and respect has been established. If the counsellor is regularly in a vulnerable situation the use of a small portable alarm may be advisable. Some systems can be quite deafening in a small room. In addition, counsellors may benefit from attending a self-defence training course. Such precautions, together with the use of personal alarms and/or panic buttons with alarms attached to the local police station, help to keep the counsellor physically safe. It is important to remember that there are no procedures or safeguards that provide total safety. The possibility of attack is perhaps most realistically seen as an occupational risk which at best can be limited.

More generally applicable is the matter of counsellor health and the achievement of a satisfactory balance between client counselling, other counselling-related work, training, supervision, possibly personal therapy, professional contacts, a social life and last but not least, adequate rest and relaxation. In a busy private practice the temptation always exists to try and squeeze in a few more clients, either because they are people the counsellor wishes to help and knows can be helped or possibly because the counsellor needs the income to live on.

It requires considerable personal discipline and effort to maintain such a balance and over-work is a serious problem. Not only does the counsellor suffer if ill-health results and income is lost but client therapy is interrupted which is also detrimental.

Such a situation is more likely to occur if the counsellor is undercharging clients. It would be better, from the point of view of the counsellor's health and the quality of therapy to the client, to have twenty clients each paying £25 in a week than forty clients paying £15. The extra £100 income would not be worth the resulting stress on the counsellor.

It is strange that a counsellor in employment may happily accept the value which an employer puts on the counsellor's services in terms of salary, pension contributions, national insurance, sick-leave, paid holidays, training, accommodation costs, equipment costs, telephone calls, stationery, postage, etc., and yet be reticent about charging the equivalent value in fees. Moreover, an employer who overworks a counsellor to the extent of inducing a breakdown could be sued for damages (Palmer 1995a). The private practitioner has no such redress.

The majority of private practitioners work in isolation for most of the working week and it is easy to allow a client caseload to dominate one's life or even to forget to 'switch out' of counsellor mode when dealing with friends and in social situations. In employment, contacts with fellow employees can help to relieve the pressures induced by difficult clients or intense counselling sessions. In private practice such relief is not so readily available. As a result, supervision assumes a greater importance and time needs to be put aside to develop professional contacts and support.

Many private practitioners make the effort to join local professional groups for networking, personal development, mutual assistance and support and, perhaps, peer-group supervision. As Ellis (1983) has said, a counsellor's most difficult client is often him or herself. Irrational beliefs can develop leading to intrapsychic stress and loss of counsellor effectiveness (Palmer 1995). Self-care, regular supervision and a balance of work and leisure activities help to prevent burn-out or breakdown.

Future developments

Although counselling and psychotherapy are becoming increasingly accepted and recognized, particularly for those suffering as a result of traumatic incidents, the number of counsellors in paid employment appears to have stagnated and private or independent practice appears to be the only option for people wishing to pursue a counselling career. Unfortunately, the 'apprenticeship' period necessary to produce a competent, 'seasoned' professional counsellor extends well beyond the typical length of any Counselling Diploma course and certainly exceeds the minimum requirements for BAC accreditation or membership of the UKCP. At the same time, training courses are generating many hundreds of 'fledgling' counsellors each year in response to growing interest in counselling.

The temptation thus exists, and is likely to continue to exist for some time, for inexperienced counsellors to set up in private practice before they are ready for it. This does not bode well for them, their clients, or the public image of counselling. These reservations, though, may not apply to those who may have spent many years deploying counselling skills in the course of their work, for example field social workers, nurses, paramedics, welfare officers, police etc., provided they also have the necessary personal qualities to make a competent counsellor.

If the way forward involves more rigorous accreditation and statutory registration (which also allows 'grandparenting', ie. acceptance of those who may not have had the required training but qualify through many years of practice and experience, as happened for the dental profession around the turn of the century), then as Dryden (1994) has pointed out, agreed national standards for training need to be established.

There are signs that this is likely to come about through the development of National Vocational Qualifications in Advice, Guidance, Counselling and Psychotherapy (Jolley and Spargo 1995).

References

Bond, T. (1993) *Standards and Ethics for Counselling in Action*, London: Sage, pp. 46–55.

Dryden, W. (1994) 'Possible Future Trends in Counselling and Counsellor Training: A Personal View', *Counselling*, 5(3): 194–7.

Ellis, A. (1983) 'How to deal with your most difficult client: you', *Journal of Rational-Emotive Therapy* (1): 3–8.

Feltham, C. (1995a) *What is Counselling?*, London: Sage.

——(1995b) 'The Stresses of Counselling in Private Practice' in W. Dryden (ed.) *The Stresses of Counselling in Action*, London: Sage.

Inskipp, F. (1993) 'Beyond Egan' in W. Dryden (ed.) *Questions and Answers on Counselling in Action*, London: Sage.

Jolley, R. and Spargo, V. (1995) *Guidance, Counselling and NVQs*, Cambridge: NEC.

Lazarus, A. (1989) *The Practice of Multimodal Therapy*, USA: Johns Hopkins University Press.

McMahon, G. (1994) *Setting up Your Own Private Practice in Counselling and Psychotherapy*, Cambridge: NEC.

Palmer, S. (1995) 'The Stresses of Running a Stress Management Centre' in W. Dryden (ed.) *The Stresses of Counselling in Action*, London: Sage.

——(1995a) 'Occupational Stress: Legal Issues and Implications For Stress Management Practitioners', *Stress News*, 8(1): 8–11.

Palmer, S. and Dryden, W. (1995) *Counselling for Stress Problems*, London: Sage.

Pilgrim, D. (1993) *Objections to Private Practice* in W. Dryden (ed.) *Questions and Answers on Counselling in Action*, London: Sage.

Syme, G. (1994) *Counselling in Independent Practice*, Buckingham: Open University Press.

Chapter eight

Counselling in voluntary organizations

Susan Wallbank

Introduction

For many, their first experience of counselling will be with a voluntary
organization. A frightened or confused child will pick up the telephone
and call ChildLine. A teenager may turn to a local Youth Access[1] project
to talk out their problems, a young drug user seeks out the special
understanding needed to deal with their difficulties. A young couple
may track down the nearest Relate service when their marriage hits
problems. The Pregnancy Advisory Service is there for those confused
about a coming birth. A hospice may provide the essential physical care
and emotional support when a family member is dying and, if bereavement support becomes necessary, families may call on Cruse Bereavement Care. For the alcoholic there is Alcoholics Anonymous, and for their
relatives, Al Anon. For the mentally ill, there exists Mind or Saneline. For
nearly every life crisis there is a voluntary organization in Britain offering
support and information and also, perhaps, that hard to define activity
called counselling.

The British voluntary sector is unique in its size and diversity. Over
2,000 entries appeared in the National Council for Voluntary Organization's 1995 *Directory of Voluntary Organizations* and this details only a
percentage of the organizations, associations, and numerous small groups
of people joining together in a voluntary capacity to provide a specific local
service or promote and foster the aims of a particular ideal.

The Wolfenden Committee (1978) defined voluntary organizations as
falling into four main categories: those offering mutual aid where everyone
is unpaid; those providing a service through volunteer helpers; those with a
mixture of paid and voluntary workers; and, lastly, the private non-profit-
making organizations which employ professional staff backed by voluntary
helpers.

The help provided by the voluntary sector will not always be free at the
point of service. Some will ask for set fees, others work on a sliding scale,
many will ask for donations to support their work. There may be other,

non-monetary payments expected: perhaps help given in exchange for trainee experience or material requested towards a research project. The economic background to the provision of voluntary services is complex. Nothing is ever obtained for nothing. Someone, somewhere, is supporting the basic economic needs essential for the survival of any service. Money from government grants, fund-raising activities, sponsorship, or the National Lottery may lie behind the service provided by voluntary organizations. Today, the British voluntary sector is made up of organizations and associations representing differing religious faiths, the young, the elderly, the poor, the disadvantaged and the sick. From out of these many diverse systems flow equally diverse services ranging from information, welfare rights, training and educational programmes, through to opportunities for self and other forms of personal support. Some still offer relief from poverty as their major purpose, countering that old adage of 'all help bar aid'. The pioneering work begun by Shaftesbury and Barnardo in the nineteenth century has continued to expand and develop and is now flourishing in the twentieth century. The majority of British people will be connected, at one time or another in their life, to a voluntary organization.

It was within this rich and varied voluntary ethos that counselling developed in Britain. The concept of counselling arrived in Britain a few years after Carl Rogers first coined the term in the United States in 1942. Once here, it spread rapidly, fed and influenced by thinkers in the fields of psychotherapy, psychology, psychoanalysis, psychiatry, and social work.

The Marriage Guidance Council, the Family Welfare Association and the Catholic Marriage Advisory Council recognized the need for personal help and support for those facing marital problems and by 1946 had developed systems of training volunteers to offer counselling in this area. Mind[2], established in 1946, began encouraging the growth of community services in the late 1950s. The Samaritans created their own telephone system of support to the suicidal at approximately the same time. They chose to define their helpers as listeners, not counsellors but employed Rogers' core principal, offering 'unconditional acceptance and respect' to their callers. The 1950s and 1960s saw the formation of many of the now largest counselling and befriending voluntary organizations in Britain: Cruse Bereavement Care[3], the Compassionate Friends, Youth Access, Alcoholics Anonymous, all began during this period of unique development and growth.

The voluntary sector quickly perceived the worth of this new method of help and support called counselling. The innovative work done by the Marriage Guidance Council was watched closely by other organizations and service providers, voluntary and non-voluntary, as well as by professionals working in allied fields. Since that early period of development, an increasing number of voluntary organizations and services have chosen to include counselling as part of the service they offer. An informed guess for

1995 would indicate that perhaps as many as a thousand counselling services (large and small) within the UK voluntary sector offer support to over half a million people a year.

Some established organizations introduced counselling as just one strand of a multiple service, designed to exist alongside advice, self support, educational, awareness, or financial services. Others adopted it as their major purpose. However, all large voluntary organizations also pursued other aims and have other obligations. They will all be engaged to some degree in publicity drives, fund-raising, and many also have an educational brief as a part of their mission statement.

From the start voluntary organizations found they needed to clarify the boundaries between counselling, befriending, self support, and listening. Each had to find the service provision that best suited their needs and the needs of those they served. Having made that decision, it was important that those turning to them for support knew the nature of the help they would receive for, though there may be a core of similar qualities existing at the heart of all such support, there are also important differences.

Cruse was started by Margaret Torrie in 1959. Trained as a social worker and married to a psychiatrist, she perceived the need for an organization for widows and their children. That organization should be capable of offering multiple help if it was truly to act as a source of aid to those facing the practical and emotional difficulties of widowhood and single parenthood. It also had a brief to raise the profile of the needs of this group and act as an educator within British society via the media and through the dispersal of leaflets, talks etc. In order to fulfil this multiple purpose it was conceived as an organization which would draw upon the skills of people with professional experience to support and advise trained voluntary helpers.

The National Association of Widows, conceived in 1971, whilst adopting similar aims, made the decision to be a mutual support organization, run by widows for widows. Like many self-help organizations it preferred not to use counselling, seeing this as a potentially unhealthy role definition through the creation of a power imbalance that destroys the ethic of equality, imposing as they saw it, a middle-class concept on to ordinary people undergoing a life crisis. Philosophical differences still exist between the non-counselling, life-experience advocates and those who believe that, with careful selection and counselling training, valuable help can be provided by people with no direct experience in a specific area. This offers a potential for conflict between organizations (and within them for those, like Cruse Bereavement Care, who employ both bereavement-experienced and non-bereavement-experienced counsellors).

Charities in Britain have to comply with the Charities Commission in defining their specific aims and purpose. Not all voluntary organizations seek or achieve charity status. Most will define the service they offer, either in terms of the locality they focus on, the service they offer or the specific category of people they serve. Thus, organizations such as those affiliated to the Westminster Pastoral Foundation will offer generic counselling to all within a certain area, whilst Relate's service is open to all those with marital and relationship difficulties, and Cruse Bereavement Care now offers support to those who are bereaved regardless of the relationship between the deceased and the bereaved person. Like everything else in life, voluntary organizations are constantly in a state of change and development. Perhaps there is no area of greater potential change than in those organizations offering counselling support.

Principles

Voluntary organizations offering counselling vary greatly in size, structure, and the nature of the counselling they offer. They possess some common factors. They all make use of the skills of voluntary workers to some extent and their prime purpose is to meet the need of the service user rather than make a profit for shareholders, service providers, company managers, etc. Those offering counselling in a specific focus will require workers to have acquired expertise through training or life experience in that area. The service provided by voluntary organizations will be influenced by the restraints of the resources at their command.

Developing services to meet the need of the users

Although individual face-to-face counselling is now perceived as the norm in Britain, as counselling increasingly seeks to define itself in the mode set by psychotherapy, the emerging larger voluntary organizations, faced with the task of offering support on a national scale to a wide-ranging group of needy individuals, responded by developing services whose primary purpose was to meet need. If needs were to be met, services had to be accessible. Lack of money should not constitute a bar to support and physical barriers had to be addressed in the drive to link supporter and supported.

The lack of rules in the early days of counselling development encouraged experiment: group meetings, telephone and letter work were all explored and developed as methods of contact alongside individual face-to-face work. Individual sessions took place where they were of greatest convenience to the client, be that in the client's home, the local clubhouse, the church hall or at the client's bedside. Where the contracting was between organization and client rather than independent counsellor and client, it was not considered appropriate for counselling to take place in the home of the counsellor, and few voluntary organizations were, or are, fortunate enough to have office space. The larger voluntary organizations, through their pioneering work, set a pattern that was copied by many hundreds of smaller voluntary groups and associations across Britain.

The group

The focus on the development of professional face-to-face counselling over the past years has tended to overshadow some of the methods of counselling originally developed, and still used, by many large organizations. Mind offers access to social support, self-support, anxiety, bereavement, men-only and women-only groups via 185 affiliated local associations. Cruse began its work by holding regular groups of widowed mothers led by social-work-trained group leaders. These groups had multiple aims. Primarily they were designed to enable group members to share problems and difficulties with one another in a safe environment. They also had the secondary objective of enabling the group leaders to learn from the members and disseminate that experience through fact sheets to other widowed mothers, social workers, doctors and the media. Permission was sought and names withheld to preserve confidentiality.

The concept of groupwork was further developed by Cruse in its large London social meetings where groups were observed by D. W. Winnicott. In order for a specialist organization to build up a body of knowledge on which to base its future work, it is essential that it has as much contact as possible with its members, who, after all, contain that knowledge. Alongside this, it will need research and development projects. Thus the group acts as a rich gathering ground for those who run it; it is also experienced as helpful to those who attend, enabling them to share thoughts and feelings in a safe environment and, when the group ends, to continue the social links created in the group setting. Although the large London gatherings are no longer held by Cruse Bereavement Care, many specialist counselling groups are held for those bereaved by suicide, for widowed mothers and fathers, for younger bereaved people and the newly bereaved. These smaller, specialist groups are led by experienced counsellors, usually trained in an apprenticeship form through co-leading with a counsellor who has acquired group leadership skills in one way or another.

It is worth mentioning some of the unique features of the London meetings that Cruse ran for over thirty years. At their height they contained nearly 100 widows coming from all parts of London. They were staffed by a team from Cruse headquarters which included the director of the organization at that time, Derek Nuttall (who had worked as Pastor of the Church of God at Aberfan in the period following the mining disaster in 1966), plus a team of counsellors and two external group leaders. Most counselling took place around tables in the large meeting room. There was little privacy and often an individual session would evolve into a small group as other members joined in and contributed their thoughts and feelings. Those who needed to talk to a counsellor alone were taken to one side.

Although the majority of the 90,000 Cruse counselling sessions each year now take place in the privacy of the client's home, this pattern of social group/counselling support still exists in some of the Cruse branches across the country. In other areas it has been superseded by the drop-in centre which also provides an opportunity for social contact alongside a more structured counselling setting. This arena is particularly valuable for the trainee counsellor who is in a position to observe and learn both from the clients and from the work of the more experienced counsellors present. Their own interactions with clients can, in turn, be observed and monitored.

The letter

The development of the National Vocational Qualifications in Advice, Guidance, Counselling and Psychotherapy have quite properly concentrated on issues surrounding access. For large voluntary national organizations access has always been a priority issue. Any national organization has an obligation to reach out to those in need of its service but the development of a comprehensive local network takes many years.

Since the early 1970s a small number of paid counsellors have been selected and internally trained as letter and telephone counsellors working from the Cruse central office. A national membership scheme secures the contract between organization and client and the service is backed by monthly Cruse newsletters. As the number of established branches has increased so national membership has declined but letter counselling continues to thrive and flourish in sparsely populated parts of the British Isles. It can be a unique and inexpensive source of continuing long-term support to the housebound, the deaf, and those living far from local counselling services. Although an annual subscription fee is required to cover membership costs, free membership is always offered to children and anyone who feels they are unable to afford to pay.

Letter counselling allows the client an opportunity to express thoughts and feelings and explore issues at the time when these are uppermost in the mind. Letters can be written at night when the children are in bed and continued over a period of days or weeks. The client determines the timing of their side of the contact. Putting words down on paper often enables the writer to feel a sense of control over their situation and is often perceived as therapeutic in itself. Knowing someone is there to receive, acknowledge and respond to letters can provide those moving through the long, often painful process of grief with a sense of security and provides an tangible opportunity to chart personal progress. For client and counsellor alike, the history contained in the exchange of letters over a period of time is a valuable learning opportunity. Contracts do not have to be long term and short-term contracts covering a period of life change or crisis can also be offered.

The telephone

It is not the letter but the telephone that has done the most to change and develop the face of counselling in Britain. The Samaritans proved beyond any doubt that there was a need for the form of 'instant access' support provided only through the medium of telephone. The past decade has seen a veritable explosion in telephone helplines.

Helplines rarely have the luxury of a single purpose but may include information-giving, referral, befriending, self-support, advice, and possibly counselling as part of the service they offer callers. A survey conducted by the King's College School of Medicine and Dentistry for the Telephone Advice Project found that 60 per cent of helplines that returned question-naires (150 out of 210) offered either counselling or listening services; 95 per cent offered factual information over the telephone. The survey found that helplines tended to involve a large number of volunteers, each working relatively short shifts; 74 per cent of helplines stated that they had some training for their paid staff and volunteers.

The children's helpline ChildLine receives over 2,000 calls each day. They have 800 workers, most of them voluntary counsellors, working four-hour shifts throughout the day and night. Cruse launched a national bereavement line in 1992 which has tripled its counselling telephone contacts.

The Telephone Helplines Association is engaged in laying down guide-lines for helplines and has been instrumental in the setting of basic standards. However, organizations representing counselling have, until recently, largely ignored this group.

The Telephone Advice Project asked helplines to describe their strengths and weaknesses. The strengths of this method of working were seen as the ability to offer a free, confidential service to callers; the personal experi-ence of the workers on self-support lines allowed them to understand and empathize with the caller and helpline operators could be trained to offer specialist advice. Weaknesses described included disruption to volunteers lives when calls were taken at home, difficulty in recruiting volunteers and paid staff, and lack of funding, with all the implications that brings.

Individual face-to-face counselling

Many of the large national voluntary organizations establishing their ser-vices in the 1950s and 60s in Britain sought to create networks offering local access to individual face-to-face counselling. No small task! It raised issues concerning the recruitment, selection, training, supervision and ongoing support of counsellors. Developing local voluntary counselling services confronted similar issues.

The key question, what is a counsellor? was addressed at a time when it was still possible to work directly from the needs of the service user into the creation of the service. Rogers' essential ingredients of warmth, genuineness and empathy, combined with the previous good training practice of pastoral care organizations and social caseworkers, added to the codes of confidentiality and supervision derived from psychotherapy and psychoanalysis add up to a product that people actually want. People want to be accepted, listened to, to know that what they say will not be passed on or used against them. They need space for themselves and their issues clear of the wishes, cares, self-regarding reactions and needs of the person they are speaking to. Occasionally they want to talk to someone who is not a friend or a member of their family. Before they talk they need to feel reasonably clear about what is going on. Are they going to have another chance to talk? Having started to talk, how long can they go on for? And, very important for the majority of voluntary organizations, if people turn to a specific organization for a specific reason they expect that organization to carry a sound understanding and knowledge of that subject.

Training

In order to turn the normal act of friendly listening into this new activity called counselling it was recognized that some form of training was necessary and, once the trained counsellor emerged, a system of ongoing support would become essential.

Colin Murray Parkes was instrumental in overseeing the development of Cruse Bereavement Care's counselling training in the early 1960s. Some organizations, such as the Marriage Guidance Council (now Relate), created centralized training, which allowed control over standards and uniformity. Cruse Bereavement Care, ensuring safety and standardization through written guidelines, handed responsibility to its local branches to organize and develop their own counsellor training, backed by the support of paid head-office and regional staff and the goodwill of local professionals who were often prepared to offer their expertise free or very much below market cost. The advantages of localized training was seen in lower training costs, thus increasing trainee accessibility to the courses. Putting on an annual training course is a complex and time-consuming task; it also develops the management, publicity, group leadership and assessment skills of those working within the branches. Because Cruse has an educational aim, courses served a dual purpose: to offer a source of understanding of the bereavement process to professionals and the general public, through a series of lectures and small group work, and, for those interested in and assessed as suitable, the recruitment of new counsellors for the local branch. The effects of centralization or localization of training in national organizations will be reflected in the power structure between branch and head office.

What common ground might be found in the training required by a voluntary organization of its counsellors? Of the thirty-eight entries under National Organisations and Self-Help Groups listed in the 1995 BAC *Directory* there was a wide variety of descriptions under the heading of training. The counselling organizations and groups' definition of their training requirements included: various, in-house, ongoing, intensive-introductory, in-service, own and personal psychotherapy, minimum basic, four-years psychosynthesis, personal therapy, appropriate, initial and in-service, selection and training based on the telephone guidelines, none, trained volunteers, personal experience, trained, appoint accredited or eligible for accredited counsellors, local training ongoing, interview, pre- and in-service training, relevant qualifications, accredited by trust, basic weekend training course, qualified counsellors and those in training, basic counselling skills, some trained counsellors, local schemes run courses, selected and in-house trained, qualification plus in-house training, in-house local group training, degree standard and personal therapy, two-years basic training by organization, experiential preparation, in-service training, and professional counselling qualification and additional in-house skills. This diversity of response reflects the diversity of service offered by voluntary organizations involved with counselling.

The counsellor within a voluntary organization will usually work within the organizational system. Although the setting of the counselling session may be in the client's or counsellor's home, an office, at the end of a telephone line, at a hospital bed, or even in a group held in a church hall, the fact that the counsellor is part of an organization influences the nature of the work. As the organization holds responsibility for the service provided in its name, the contract between organization and client underpins any contract subsequently made between client and counsellor. It is in the voluntary organization's best interest to ensure that work done on its behalf is to a certain standard. Ensuring standardization is an ongoing challenge for any organization. The key lies, as in private counselling, in selection, initial and ongoing training, assessment, and support systems.

Initial selection

For voluntary organizations offering counselling it is important that those it selects to work in its name will have the ability to offer a secure service. If training is to be offered, then initial selection procedures must ensure that the majority of those taken into training have the capacity to complete it successfully. Unlike other forms of training, where the more trained the greater the profit, for voluntary organizations training inevitably competes for ever-limited resources of time and money. Voluntary organizations, unless they are also training institutions like, for instance, the Westminster Pastoral Foundation, cannot afford to train counsellors that are not suitable or have little long-term commitment to work within the organization.

What core qualities should the potential counsellor possess? Nicholas Tyndall says in *Counselling in the Voluntary Sector* (1993: 11): 'The main resource for counsellors lies in their own qualities of warmth, perception and intuition'. Truax and Carkhuff (1967) identified 'genuineness, accurate empathy and non-possessive warmth.'

Voluntary organizations operating a service in a specific area may also require potential counsellors to already have knowledge and experience in that area. In order to qualify, a counsellor may have to be a certain age, gender, sex, race, or religion or to have experienced a certain life event. Most specific services will presume a level of interest from a potential counsellor in the field of work. Regardless of previous experience, though, organizations will often require counsellors to undertake training in specific areas. Clients will come with an expectation that the counsellor they see at a drugs centre will have an in-depth knowledge of drug problems. The person approaching an alcohol project will expect expertise in working with drink-related problems from their counsellor. It is this specific knowledge base that often constitutes the main aim of training in such organizations.

As voluntary organizations are being increasingly approached by people on counselling courses requiring students to undertake a certain number of placement or client hours, the nature of the counsellor in the voluntary setting is changing. There is a potential for a clash between career and non-career counsellors within organizations, containable only by a sure knowledge of the particular organization, its policies, guidelines and codes of practice and ethics. The presumption that someone will be working for an organization because they have a personal interest in that work can no longer be assumed. Student counsellors often bring enthusiasm and valuable external training with them. The benefits of such input into the counselling force of a voluntary organization have to weighed against lack of long-term commitment and the difficulty of maintaining a uniform counselling approach, with student counsellors under external influence to use other models. Issues of confidentiality have also to be carefully worked out as many college courses require case examination and supervision to be undertaken at the college.

Training voluntary counsellors

'Ordinary members of the community have a great deal to offer people who are experiencing mental problems.' The philosophy of Mind local associations is echoed by many voluntary organizations. An essential component of training is the development of those essential qualities of warmth, perception, and intuition; a programme through which the core ingredients of human interaction: listening, thinking, speaking, response and counter-response (commonly called basic counselling skills), can be analysed and practised for use within the specific counselling setting. The length spent in the initial training of voluntary counsellors varies between organizations. Peter Jenkins (1995) states: 'At one level, it is suggested that 45 hours of training can be sufficient for mastery of key skills, using the Microskills model (Ivey and Galvin 1984).' Truax and Carkhuff (1967) suggested that 100 hours was enough to achieve core communication skills. Many voluntary organizations such as Cruse Bereavement Care offer initial training schemes somewhere between these two time scales.

Monitoring and maintaining counselling standards

For the independent, non-organizational counsellor monitoring and main-tenance of work standard is likely to be arranged through regular super-vision, personal therapy or counselling, and ongoing training. These methods of ensuring counsellor development and client safety have been the focus of organizations such as the BAC over the past years.

The final component of training the counsellor in a voluntary organiza-tion is likely to be in the form of work apprenticeship. This, and subsequent work, may be overseen by line managers, supervisors and perhaps also through peer-group monitoring. Some organizations are fortunate in having access to professional workers: psychologists, psychiatrists, child psychol-ogists etc., who offer advice and act as an additional safety net to the service. There is a clear difference between the counsellor who primarily works alone and needs to ensure that the service they offer clients is adequately overseen, and the counsellor who works within a voluntary organization which provides a visible containment of the service offered through their counsellors. Such organizations, through their public profile, offer clients the opportunity to address issues of concern and complaints to someone outside the counselling situation. Where supervision is seen to be only one part of the monitoring system, although important, it may not be accorded the importance given to it by the non-organizational counsellor.

Although some voluntary organizations working in highly specific fields or in rural areas are under used, many large organizations offering free counselling have waiting lists. The majority of voluntary counsellors work-ing for organizations such as Cruse offer a small percentage of their time, taking on perhaps one or two clients a week and taking some years to build up a range of experience. Skill is needed in placing counsellor and client together appropriately. An organization can use skilled counsellors, asses-sors and referral secretaries to act as 'brokers' in the match. The newly qualified independent counsellor may not have the benefit of such a system of client referral. However, they may well be seeing more clients each week; again this will influence their need for support.

To summarize, the format for the making of a voluntary organizational counsellor might be described as: character + knowledge base + counselling skills + counselling framework + organizational framework = voluntary counsellor.

Issues

If there is one common factor that unites all voluntary organizations and those who work in them, it is the never-ending pursuit of funds to secure the service they offer. Few organizations can now rely upon government or local authority grants to provide more than a minimum percentage of their running costs. Money is obtained from service fees, donations, sponsorship, contract work and, if fortunate, the National Lottery. The concentration on project funding means that money no longer automatically follows need, but may become tied to innovative or 'glamorous' projects whilst the core service starves. Contract work potentially puts organizations in competition with one another and may even change the nature of service provision in the struggle to ensure that the service fits the demands of the contractor.

One of the most important issue for voluntary counsellors and the organizations that employ their services concerns the relationship that exists between them and their non-voluntary brother/sister counsellors. The world of counselling is constantly changing. Voluntary organizations, large and small, are in a state of perpetual development: learning as new information flows in; adjusting to the requirements of new legislation; expanding to meet new demands or contracting in the face of decreasing resources. The counselling offered via the voluntary sector has had a profound effect on the concept of counselling in Britain over the past decades. Many people know someone who has been to Relate or Cruse Bereavement Care or seen a Mind counsellor. Many others will have called the Samaritans in despair, joined Alcoholics Anonymous or Al Anon. A child's first experience of being impartially listened to may be via Child-Line. Each will have engaged upon the task of talking out a problem or difficulty with another human being, someone who will listen, show care, and act within a certain ethical framework. It is perhaps the large scale of the support offered by the voluntary sector which has countered the concept that counselling is only for Americans, the middle classes or the mad, and allowed people to move from feeling that to turn to counselling for support was to admit failure, to the point where they are able to request, even demand, the help they feel they need.

In turn, the recognition of the worth of counselling by the general public has been influenced by the establishment of the concept of the 'professional'

counsellor. There is an expectation that the professional will receive financial reward for the service they offer, not necessarily from the client.
Professional counsellors may be accessed via a local health centre or
come as part of the support package provided by a firm or college. Counsellors operating within such systems will, to some extent, inherit the
system's credentials. Then there is the independent, individual counsellor
offering a direct service to a client in exchange for money. The potential
client surveys a complex scene. In front of them is ranged the unpaid
voluntary counsellor offering a free service; the partially paid voluntary
counsellor offering an affordable service; the paid-by-someone-else counsellor offering a free service; and the independent counsellor charging
anything from a few pounds to a great deal of money. Is it possible for
the term counselling to encompass all of these services? Can counsellors
offering services in differing contexts live alongside one another in relative
harmony?

Expectations and evaluation

Increasing emphasis is being placed on service evaluation. Before a service
can be evaluated it has to be defined. Both service giver and service
receiver have to have some idea of the expectations of both parties of
the service on offer. Not only does counselling take place in a wide range
of contexts, the many theoretical models of counselling remain a mystery
to most laypeople.

Clients may well evaluate their counsellor in terms of understanding/
non-understanding and warmth/coldness. Clients are usually aware when
the codes of counselling are broken even if they are never spelt out to them.
They make the assumption that things said in the counselling session are
private (the knowledge that counsellors talk about their cases to their
supervisor, even in guarded terms, can be disturbing to some potential
clients). Clients know that counsellors should not talk too much about
themselves – even if they try and make them do so. Clients do not really
like a counsellor telling them what to do – even if they ask repeatedly for
advice. Clients do not expect to be criticized and they do expect their
counsellor to keep appointments. Where these basic expectations of counselling fail to be met, clients of counsellors working with the large voluntary organizations usually have a system for expressing their concerns.

Unofficial service evaluation is ongoing inside a local community. The
service becomes part of the community referral system. Referrers such as
local doctors, health centres, hospitals and social service teams receive
feedback from those they refer, which then determines future referrals.
Service users will also influence friends and family. Such evaluation will
eventually be reflected in the service statistics.

However, informal service appreciation requires backing from professional research if it is to gain credence. A research project at the Family Service at St Christopher's Hospice in South-east London found that bereavement counselling by selected volunteers was effective, reducing the consumption of drugs, alcohol and tobacco and the number of symptoms attributable to anxiety and tension. Parkes reported: 'My own study suggests that a counsellor takes about a year to become proficient. Thereafter many volunteer counsellors come to rival professionals (who often have less experience in work with the bereaved) and may even be able to tackle some of the pathological forms of reaction to bereavement' (Parkes 1980).

In the present climate where funding is dependent on service evaluation the combination of past research and informal gathering of satisfaction levels is no longer enough. Voluntary organizations are increasingly being asked to provide proof, in terms of questionnaire feedback, of the effectiveness of their service.

Client expectation and service evaluation are inextricably linked. The mechanisms seemingly created to protect the client: mission statements, codes of practice, standards and qualifications can convey doubt and uncertainty. After all, why should such an apparently simple activity require so much safety packaging? Is counselling potentially dangerous? Am I in danger? Am I not getting the real thing? One method of service evaluation increasingly used is the complaints procedure. This useful tool for the gathering of information on service provision is shadowed by the fear of the litigious client or trainee or counsellor. The voluntary organization attempting to provide a free or low-cost counselling service is inheriting the problems associated with the increased expectations created by the independent counsellors' drive towards professionalism. On the outside, a watchful media, unsure whether to cast counselling as hero or villain, plays its part in the formation of what the public think of a service in the process of change. This contributes to a drive towards ever higher standards, which, create rising expectations, which, in their turn, lead to a rise in the number of complaints when those expectations remain unfulfilled.

The counselling industry

The acceptance of counselling within society has understandably led to the expansion of counselling as an industry. This is most obvious in the rapid expansion of counselling courses across the country. Courses are now on offer from universities, colleges and innumerable other course-provision agencies. Courses on counselling can range in length from the introductory two-day skills development course to full-time and part-time study lasting many years. At present there is nothing to stop anybody after minimum (or even no) training from setting up as a private counsellor. The BAC has sought to standardize courses by the introduction of its course accreditation scheme. It has also introduced an accreditation scheme for individual counsellors and is introducing an accreditation scheme for trainers. Such accreditation schemes are not designed to address the needs of the average counsellor working in the voluntary sector. The drive to protect the client from the abuses of the under-trained, rogue counsellor who brings disrepute on counselling as a whole, has contributed to the establishment of the 'professional', highly trained counsellor. Further standards on supervision and ongoing training seek to ensure that, once accredited, the counsellor's work will remain secured.

The highly competitive training industry is primarily concerned with training counsellors for the non-voluntary sector. Counselling is seen by many as a desirable occupation which, when the necessary skills have been acquired, can earn one an appreciable income for many years ahead. In an increasingly insecure job market, counselling appears to offer an opportunity to utilize a quality many people feel they naturally possess – an ability to relate to others. Counselling training courses also attract those who have a need to investigate themselves, who are looking for the development of their own selves and for a new identity. Little wonder that counselling courses are popular and that this fact has been recognized by course providers.

There is as yet no clear indication of the effect which the arrival of large numbers of new counsellors each year will have upon the market. Will the need for counselling continue to grow to absorb an ever-increasing counsellor force? Or will market forces have to be controlled and the interests of those working in it protected by the introduction of ever higher entry requirements? Some courses now require potential students to have a degree, others have an upper age limit. Clearly, if voluntary organizations were prevented from offering free or reduced-fee counselling because they failed to achieve the required standards, this would open up a huge new potential market to private counsellors. Is there also a danger that the counselling industry will be driven to set increasing standards in supervision and on-going training, not because there is proof that these are essential for the security of the client, but simply to absorb the needs of course providers hungry for course participants?

Future developments

The British Association for Counselling has played a major part in the development of counselling in Britain over the past years. A charity itself, it faces the unenviable task of trying to define standards in an increasingly varied and complex field of work. As a membership organization it includes voluntary and non-voluntary organizations offering counselling, private counsellors, and agencies offering training in a wide variety of different counselling methods. These differing groups make uneasy bed-fellows. Each have their own agenda and needs.

This drive towards the creation of standards has many implications for voluntary organizations offering counselling. Few voluntary counsellors are BAC or COSCA accredited. As yet this is not important as there are under 1,100 practising accredited counsellors in Britain. A drop in the ocean compared to the many thousands of volunteer counsellors working in Britain. However, the fear exists that standards may be set in the future which will preclude the voluntary counsellor from counselling.

The recently developed United Kingdom Register of Counsellors has attempted to find a way of servicing the needs of both the voluntary organizational counsellor and the individual counsellor by the development of a dual-access system on to the register with different criteria for each. It has recognized that the work of the counsellor working within an organiza-tion will be safeguarded to some extent by the rules, regulations and codes of practice of that organization. The context within which counselling takes place allows for different criteria in training and supervision to be set. Whether the majority of organizational counsellors will reach the present criteria remains to be seen. Whether voluntary counsellor and voluntary organization will feel that the benefits of registration outweigh the cost in terms of time and money is still undetermined. There is the potential for splits to emerge between organizational counsellor and individual coun-sellor, and between the voluntary organizations and organizations such as the BAC.

The development of National Vocational Qualifications in counselling have offered the possibility of an alternative route through to recognized standards in counselling. At the time of writing neither system is yet in operation and it is premature to guess how they will fulfil the needs of voluntary organizations and their counsellors.

Counselling stands at a crossroads in its development. The therapeutic counsellor stares longingly towards the land of professionalisation, a utopia where charters and registers and accreditation procedures reward the inter-ests of the competent and protect the vulnerability of the client. Behind the therapeutic counsellor lie the many thousands of counsellors working in voluntary organizations. Many of them too aspire to professional status; they would like proper recognition of the value of the work they do, paid or unpaid. Others simply want to be left alone to go on doing what they have been doing.

The emphasis on service evaluation by funding agencies places new demands on both voluntary organization, voluntary counsellor, and client. New training methods requiring the recording of counselling sessions also affect the client/counsellor contract. Both changes raise ethical issues concerning the use of clients in fulfilling the training and funding require-ments of the service provider.

It is an uncertain situation, full of fear and frustration. Will counselling in Britain forever be held back by the inability of the counsellor in the voluntary sector to achieve appropriate standards? Will the drive of an élite force towards professionalism leave some counsellors abandoned to the wilderness of befriending and mere counselling skills. If voluntary organizations improve their standards who pays the price? If they fail, what then? Over-professionalization may exclude the voluntary counsellor and thereby prevent access to a source of support valued by many thousands of people in Britain today.

It is impossible to predict what lies ahead, but there is hope in the attempts made both in the United Kingdom Register of Counsellors and in the National Vocational Qualifications in Counselling to give due recognition to high-quality counselling both outside and inside voluntary organizations, to note their differences and ensure that both have a part to play in the future.

Notes

1 Youth Access was formerly called the National Association of Young People's Counselling and Advisory Services.
2 Mind was formerly known as the National Association for Mental Health (NAMH). It was formed by the amalgamation of the three major mental health organizations: the Central Association for Mental Welfare, the Child Guidance Council and the National Council for Mental Hygiene.
3 Cruse Bereavement Care was formerly called Cruse, the National Organisation for Widows and their Children, changing in 1980 to the National Organisation for the Widowed and their Children. It became Cruse Bereavement Care in 1986.

References

Ivey, A. and Galvin, M. (1984) 'Microcounselling: A Metamodel for Counselling, Therapy, Business and Medical Interviews' in D. Larson (ed.) *Teaching Psychological Skills: Models for Giving Psychology Away*, California: Brooks-Cole.
Jenkins, P. (1995) 'Two Models of Counsellor Training: Becoming a Person or Learning to be a Skilled Helper?', *Counselling* (3): 205.
Parkes, C.M. (1980) 'Bereavement Counselling: Does it Work?', *British Medical Journal* 281: 3–6.
Torrie, M. (1987) 'My Years With Cruse', pamplet obtainable from Cruse Bereavement Care, 126 Sheen Road, Richmond, Surrey TW9 1UR.
Truax, C. and Carkhuff, R. (1967) *Toward Effective Counseling and Psychotherapy*, New York: Sage.
Tyndall, N. (1993) *Counselling in the Voluntary Sector*, Milton Keynes: Open University Press.

Chapter nine

Counselling in the personal social services

Carole Sutton

Introduction: aspects of the historical background

The development of ' social casework'

The origins of counselling are far older than those of the personal social services and are lost in the mists of time. They are grounded, as Halmos (1965) suggests, in the experiences of comforting the distressed, sharing the grief of the bereaved and offering a listening ear to the perplexed. Throughout recorded history and doubtless before, the 'wise men' and 'wise women', the 'elders' and 'spiritual leaders' of the community were, and to some extent still are, the counsellors.

The personal social services in Britain developed from the philanthropic and voluntary services for the poor, the weak and the vulnerable which were an extension of the work of the churches in nineteenth-century Britain. Gradually these responsibilities, especially for children, became too complex and too expensive for voluntary organizations, even well-developed ones like Dr Barnardo's, to carry out on a national scale, and the twentieth century saw the gradual passing of responsibility, via statute, from the voluntary to the local authority sector.

Alongside these developments, the fragmented efforts of the voluntary charitable and philanthropic groups of the nineteenth century were gradu-ally brought together and coordinated in the Charities Organisation Society, and many groups who came under this umbrella are still known as 'voluntary organizations'.

In due course, such work became governed by statute and became more complex and demanding. Hence, the demand of workers in those fields arose for 'training'. Workers were developing practice in the children's departments and in the probation service, and at the same time special practitioners were seeking to help people in the fields of physical and mental health. Inevitably those who sought to train workers for these complex areas looked to existing contemporary theorists and practitioners in, for example, the field of psychiatry.

Thus, two major strands which contributed to training for working with people in the early and middle years of this century were religious philanthropy and psychoanalysis. The former is illustrated by the contributions of the court missionaries towards the development of the probation service, and the latter by Freudian psychoanalytic theory which was adopted as a cornerstone of much work with people and families in difficulty. Both these influences are still clearly discernible within contemporary counselling in the personal social services.

Out of such complexity developed an activity called 'social casework'. This was unapologetically individualistic and tended to see individual or family difficulties in terms of underlying pathology. Concern for the client was undoubtedly central, however, despite these debatable theoretical underpinnings. An influential text which reflected elements of both Christian concern and psychoanalytic theory was *The Casework Relationship* by Felix Biestek, S.J., published in 1957.

Principles underpinning casework: precursors of counselling

Biestek's (1957) text set out a number of principles which caseworkers should observe. These were:

(1) *Individualization.* This principle highlighted the uniqueness of each person whom the worker encountered.
(2) *Purposeful expression of feelings.* This highlighted the value of allowing and enabling people to acknowledge in a supportive setting feelings of which they may or may not have been aware. These were often socially unacceptable feelings, anger, jealousy, hatred, but whose release *freed* the person to live in more constructive ways.
(3) *Controlled emotional involvement.* This principle reminded the caseworker that it is inappropriate to identify too strongly with one person at the expense of others, or to involve him or herself too closely with a single issue or perspective.
(4) *Acceptance.* This principle confirmed the importance of dealing with people seeking help exactly as they are, whatever their strengths and weaknesses, and of affirming their innate dignity and worth.
(5) *The non-judgemental attitude.* This is linked with acceptance; the worker does not seek to assign guilt or innocence, but recognizes that there may be limits to the extent to which *actions* are acceptable.
(6) *Client self-determination.* This principle reminded caseworkers that they should avoid giving advice, but should enable those with whom they were working to explore which decisions were right for them.
(7) *Confidentiality.* This principle enjoined caseworkers to raise the issue of confidentiality or, if need be, limitations thereto.

While there have been many developments in counselling since 1957 and some of the basic assumptions have been questioned, Biestek remains a founding father of social casework and a major contributor to modern counselling theory and practice.

The impact of humanistic psychology upon counselling in social work

Practice based upon such principles took place, however, within a Freudian theoretical framework. The study of child development and of family and marital relationships was located within a matrix of psychoanalytic theory, so that Freudian psychosexual developmental stages – oral, anal, Oedipal and so on – were invoked to try to understand difficulties which arose in, for example, fostering and adoption work. Similarly, great attention was directed to *feelings* within individual, marital, and family counselling; if only personal relationships could be sufficiently explored, and associated or suppressed feelings released, then the resulting insight would effect a 'cure'.

The influence of psychoanalysis declined, however, as humanistic psychology, arising largely from the work of Rogers (1951) and Maslow (1954) and strengthened by the 'personal growth' movement, redressed the emphasis upon pathology in social work and other fields. The major review of studies published by Truax and Carkhuff (1967), *Toward Effective Counseling and Psychotherapy*, added weight to this change of emphasis, as the evidence it provided indicated that people who were helpful counsellors were distinguished less by the theoretical approach which they espoused and more by certain personal characteristics, namely: 'genuineness, empathy and non-possessive warmth'.

While some have questioned the value of this 'therapeutic triad', there is no evidence known to me which has seriously undermined its vital contribution.

Principles of counselling in social work: the present position

A definition of 'counselling' within social work

To be clear about what is meant by the term 'counselling' in social work, it is necessary to turn to the Barclay Report (National Institute for Social Work, 1982). Despite its early date, it is still this document which refers most clearly to these roles and tasks, namely,

(1) 'To plan, establish, maintain and evaluate the provision of social care.'
(2) 'To provide face-to-face communication between clients and social workers: the generic name of this is counselling.'

The Report later spells out the meaning which the authors attach to the term 'counselling':

. . . we use the word to cover a range of activities in which an attempt is made to understand the meaning of some event or state of being to an individual, and to plan, with the person or people concerned, how to manage the emotional or practical realities which face them. Such work is always part of assessment and may be a large or small part of meetings between client and social worker.

There are clear similarities between this definition and that of the BAC.

The place of counselling within social work

Those social workers who are still in a position to practise counselling as a primary and distinct component of their work are almost certainly very few in number. The primary concerns for most social workers now are decision-making, safety and risk, the legislative framework, cost, and resources. There are still, however, a few fields of practice where counselling is still a strong feature: some voluntary organizations, such as family service units, many of which work with families and children in relationship difficulties; some centres employing social workers to support people with drug- and alcohol-related difficulties; and also a few settings such as the maternity departments of hospitals where social workers employed by the local authorities still have time to offer counselling and can spend substantial periods of time with women – sometimes very young women – who seek terminations of pregnancy. Many social workers practising in mental health settings however, who formerly offered a substantial counselling service to people coping with anxiety, depression, and other problems are now required to act as purchasers of services from other organizations, rather than as the providers of the services themselves. Nevertheless, because many field social workers recognize the value of counselling in their work and know how beneficial it can be to enable people to speak confidentially about their personal circumstances and to explore their own needs with a supportive listener, efforts are made to find time to meet these needs. Such occasions, however, are subsidiary to the main thrust of the work which, as already indicated, is concerned with meeting statutory requirements within a limited budget.

Reliance upon 'client-centred' counselling as a core skill

The case that social workers need counselling skills is broadly accepted. The nature of the changing tasks of social workers means, however, that these skills can seldom be practised in their 'pure' form; they are far more likely to constitute a way of working with people, an orientation of respect and empathy towards them, rather than an end in themselves; counselling skills are therefore likely to *underpin* practice in many social services departments.

The model of counselling taught to students is likely to be the client-centred or Rogerian one. Sutton and Davies (1986), in an investigation of the teaching of psychology on forty social work courses in Britain, found that the average number of hours allocated to the total psychology syllabus was sixty-four; of these 3.75 hours were devoted to the teaching of client-centred and non-directive approaches. The attractions of the client-centred approach are apparent: it has a sound empirical base, it is positive in orientation, and it stresses respect for the client and the potential for growth and development within people. Social workers are likely to draw upon the approach differentially, however. For some, it will be the main vehicle of work in, for instance, helping a client to decide whether or not to place a child for adoption; for others, it will underpin skills of family therapy; and yet others will practise it but simply call it 'good interviewing'. Experienced social workers readily recognize the need to draw upon different approaches within the same interview. For example, a worker discussing welfare rights entitlement who sees the distress on a client's face would swiftly move from 'interviewing mode' to 'counselling mode' and back again, as time and circumstances permitted.

Use of the ASPIRE process for practice

I have made the case elsewhere (Sutton 1994) that many professional groups having responsibility to others can usefully employ this process for practice. ASPIRE is a mnemonic, made up of the first letters of other words (Sutton and Herbert 1992). It serves to remind us of stages in working with people when we feel swamped with information or by events and can help us to get our bearings again.

> AS   Assessment
> P   Planning
> I   Implementation
> RE   Review and Evaluation

The process can be thought of as linear or, as is more likely to correspond with what actually happens, as cyclical.

(1) *Assessment.* This often takes place in the first, or first and second, meetings although further matters needing attention may well arise later. The worker attempts to gather and organize information and to make sense of the person or persons as part of many systems – family, school, friendship, cultural and many more. He or she is then likely to attempt to agree *with the people involved* the key areas of concern, and which are the priorities areas. If there are statutory considerations,

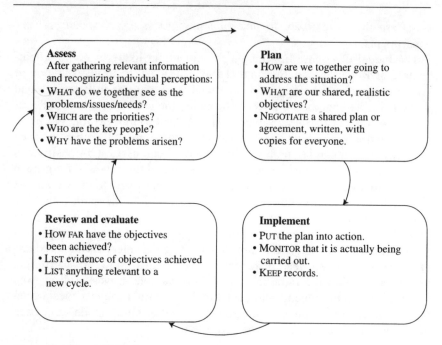

Figure 9.1 The ASPIRE process as a cycle

these will be of primary importance. An accepting and positive relationship is vital and so is establishing confidentiality and its limitations.

(2) *Planning.* Worker and client work out and agree how often they will meet and what will constitute the goals of their meetings. These may be put in the form of a 'contract' or agreement, which can also make explicit any statutory implications.

(3) *Implementation of plans.* At this stage the worker draws upon a wide repertoire of relationship and other skills, as well as the resources available from statutory and community agencies; he or she offers a structure so both worker and client can move towards attaining agreed goals, or renegotiating fresh ones.

(4) *Review and Evaluation.* The process of reviewing is essentially that of monitoring progress, or the lack of it, as client and social worker continue their work. This allows both parties to say how far they consider they are making progress towards the management or resolution of specified difficulties. Having clear and shared objectives permits client and worker to monitor work openly and explicitly.

Evaluation takes place right at the end of a piece of work. Client(s) and worker together make a final judgement as to how far agreed goals have been achieved and take steps accordingly. The approach emphasizes that clients have a clear voice in the evaluation and while this may be disconcerting for workers, it has the ethical advantage of empowering clients at a time when many of those who encounter social workers feel frustrated and powerless.

While to some this may seem an over-structured model of work, it is only a model, and can be adapted for use in different circumstances. Its strength is that it offers an *ethical* framework for monitoring the extent to which clients and workers are progressing towards agreed goals. It encourages workers to make explicit the statutory features of their work, and to think through with clients the specific goals of their efforts.

Greater understanding of the essentials of counselling

One of the grounds for concern which many people express about counselling is the proliferation of schools of thought, which train their students in their own theoretical ideas with specific terminology and concepts and which, far from showing how links may be made with other groups, emphasize their own distinctiveness and exclusivity. This can lead to great confusion amongst the public and to antagonism between people trained in different schools. Atkinson and his colleagues (1990) have made a major contribution towards establishing common ground between the various schools of counselling by distinguishing the crucial variables which appear to help people in distress and which are common to all schools.

(1) There is a relationship of warmth and trust in which the counsellor attempts to understand the person and to convey this understanding and respect for the person.
(2) The person is offered support by the counsellor; this may be support in coping with a distressing or crisis situation; support in terms of acceptance and respect as an individual; or support in facing past events or traumas.
(3) The person experiences a release of tension or reduction in anxiety which allows him or her to face or talk about a particular problem or problems.
(4) The adaptive responses of the person are reinforced. In learning to understand more about themselves and any self-defeating patterns of thought or behaviour, the person is given an opportunity of solving particular problems, improving relationships, etc. The counsellor shares any knowledge or skills which may be appropriate.

The concept of the worker/counsellor as having a repertoire

As we have seen above, however, it is likely that a social worker employed within the social services will be trained in, and expected to draw upon, an extensive repertoire of additional skills, knowledge and resources. These will include awareness of his or her statutory responsibilities, knowledge of voluntary means of help, such as specialist agencies for those with particular needs, as well as personal knowledge of community support groups. The wider the repertoire of knowledge of and contacts with well-tried resources, personal and financial, the better.

Different levels of counselling contributing to social-work practice

If skills of counselling underpin practice within social work, then it follows that there are a range of interactions in which social workers typically take part which contain a greater or lesser degree of traditional client-centred work. Figure 9.2 shows, in schematic form, the range of such interactions.

(1) *Counselling as empathic listening.* This is perhaps the form closest to what might be called 'classical or 'client-centred' counselling. The clearest example of this form is the work of the counsellor who supports those bereaved by death or other loss. As I have indicated above, however, such work would not routinely be accepted as a referral by over-stretched social services teams, although some hospital-based social workers are employed in frontline crisis work after road accidents and other major traumas.

(2) *Counselling as support in decision-making.* This again is near to traditional 'client-centred' work, in that the social worker seeks to support the person concerned in clarifying the implications of, and arriving at a decision in some important aspect of life. Examples are the elderly person who has to decide whether or not to give up his or her home; the adopted person who is wondering whether to try to trace his or her natural parents; and the pregnant woman who is undecided as to whether or not to seek an abortion. In each instance, the social worker will seek to clarify and discuss the issues, not to give advice.

(3) *Counselling as a component of family therapy.* Here counselling will form one important strand of the social worker's effort to enable a family to voice some of the tensions they are experiencing, and to communicate positively. There is good evidence, for instance Birchler (1979), that the very act of communicating feelings and fears is, of itself, therapeutic to families in distress. This can be enhanced by basic counselling skills : sensitive listening, the showing of respect, and empathy with each person in distress.

(4) *Counselling as a component of a task-centred approach.* Social workers are familiar with 'task-centred' work. This term, devised by Reid and Epstein (1972) refers to the breaking down of complex situations, such as the difficulties encountered by families with many disadvantages, into manageable tasks: for example, enabling a family to clear rent arrears, to apply for their financial entitlement, and to seek medical

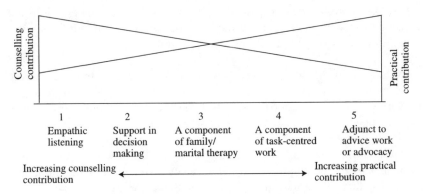

Figure 9.2 Differing levels of contribution of counselling to social work practice

or legal help. Such 'working agreements' are not achieved without relationship-making and trust-building skills which, in my view, are identical with those used by counsellors. That is, counselling skills underpin practice in task-centred work.

(5) *Counselling as an adjunct to advice or advocacy or statutory work.* Here too counselling skills underpin social-work practice, although some would claim that 'counselling' in these contexts is indistinguishable from 'skilled interviewing'. For example, social workers draw upon counselling skills when they are employed in welfare rights agencies; they know that some people, perhaps elderly, may have real difficulty in disclosing the extent of their need, and unless their trust can be gained, may never speak of this. Similarly, a parent who is seeking to place a child in, or to remove a child from, local authority care needs calm and respect, both verbal and non-verbal, from a social worker – all the more if the issue is contentious. To convey respect for, and a personal commitment to, people to whom one may have to say painful or unwelcome things can have an effect which, in the long term, may prove constructive; to convey disrespect will *certainly* be damaging. Thus in all these situations, from the 'purest' to the most complex, counselling skills have an integral role in social-work practice.

Issues: changes in legislation and social policy

The effects of changes in legislation

Through the 1970s, 1980s and early 1990s, five extremely important Acts of Parliament had direct effects upon social-work practice. The first two statutes were the Sex Discrimination Act 1975 and the Race Relations Act 1976. These together with the Disabled Persons (Employment) Acts 1944 and 1958 stipulated that each local authority has a statutory duty:

to make appropriate arrangements to ensure that its various functions are carried out with due regard to the need to eliminate unlawful discrimination and to promote equality of opportunity.

The impact of this legislation has been profound. It has drawn attention, for example, to the evidence that many black children do not have social workers or foster or adoptive parents from their own racial background; that the needs of gay and lesbian people are scarcely recognized, and, within social services departments themselves, that very small numbers of women hold positions of major responsibility. It has led to a developing awareness of the inadequacies of the services provided to disabled people and to the lack of choice in respect of day-care facilities. In the field of counselling, questions such as 'Is it possible for a black person to receive a satisfactory counselling service from a white social worker?' and 'Surely disabled people need counselling services from people with personal experience of disability?' have been hotly debated – and have not yet been resolved. Equal opportunities continue to be an extremely important issue in social work.

The third important piece of legislation was the Mental Health Act 1983 which brought order to and developed the law concerning the rights of people with mental-health difficulties. It set out requirements concerning the admission of people to psychiatric hospitals and clarified the circumstances under which they may be retained there compulsorily. Specially trained social workers, called approved social workers, have specific duties in relation to such admissions and need not only to be very knowledgeable about mental illness but also to be able to use informed listening and counselling skills so as to distinguish, say, cultural practices of talking to God in times of difficulty and distress from the generalized disorders of speech and behaviour which may be indicative of a schizophrenic episode (Westwood *et al.* 1989).

The fourth major statute was the Children Act 1989. This co-ordinated and developed the legislation setting out the duties of local authorities towards children in need which had formerly been located in a loose assembly of Acts. It contains three key principles: the first is that the child's welfare is paramount; the second is that children are best looked after within the family and the third is the affirmation of the concept of 'parental responsibility' which parents have towards their children. Local authorities are required to support parents in meeting these responsibilities, for example, by providing at least some day-nursery provision, and in circumstances where the local authority is required to intervene in order to protect or otherwise meet the needs of children, the wishes and feelings of the child must be ascertained and his or her racial origin. cultural, and linguistic background must be taken into account. The same considerations must apply to services and resources provided for those in need.

This legislation requires practitioners to work with children and young people in situations of extreme sensitivity and complexity: child abuse, neglect, injury, or sexual abuse. Unusually high levels of skill in communication are essential. The ability to listen, to discern the pain and distress behind anger and defensiveness, and to respond in ways which lay the foundations for constructive long-term outcomes are essentially the skills of experienced counsellors.

The fifth major piece of legislation was the National Health Service and Community Care Act 1990 which made social services departments responsible for developing and co-ordinating *in the community* services for people with disabilities, those with learning disabilities, and the elderly and infirm. This was a concerted effort to move the setting for the care and support of needy people from large, outmoded and expensive institutions into the context of ordinary, day-to-day life – and to maintain them, wherever possible, in their own homes. When elderly people or people with learning disabilities are faced with making major decisions it is essential that social workers are able to offer time, skilled listening and sensitive counselling; then anxieties can be voiced, feelings accepted and support given.

Despite all these new demands upon social workers, only the passing of the Children Act 1989 was accompanied by substantial central government funding to bring the knowledge and skills of practising social workers up to date with the requirements of the new legislation. Britain is still one of the few countries in Europe where a two-year training is considered adequate for social work. It is impossible to accommodate within two years the teaching and training necessary to bring students to the level of counselling skills necessary for them to practise effectively in the complex and demanding settings described above.

Changes in social policy

The Seebohm Report in 1968 led to the setting up of the 'generic' model of practice in the 1970s, whereby social workers were trained in, and expected to practise, skills needed by the many groups whom they were employed to serve: children and families, elderly people, young offenders, people with learning disabilities, and people who are mentally ill, whether in the residential sector or in the community. As the demands on social workers become more specialized, however, there has been a trend for training to focus more narrowly on particular groups in need so that generic models of training are tending to disappear in favour of the specialisms of work with children and families, in residential settings, and with adults needing services in the community rather than in institutions.

It is increasingly difficult for local authority social workers to engage in preventive work with those asking for help; instead there is an increasing trend towards 'gate-keeping'. This refers to the necessity, because of shortage of resources, of holding the gate against the large number of referrals which could be made, because of the impossibility of providing enough resources to meet demand. Moreover, it seems likely that it is the field social workers in the social services departments who will constitute the main thrust of the profession, because of their high-profile statutory responsibilities in the field of child protection. As child injury, child neglect and child sexual abuse become better recognized and so more frequently reported, so the demands upon social workers will continue to increase. The importance of skills of sensitive communication and counselling will increase commensurately.

As in other fields, turning over the practice of social work to market forces is seen by many practitioners as an overturning of values central to social work. There is preoccupation now, not with the importance and dignity of each person using the services, but with 'throughput' and 'unit cost'. Social workers are thus increasingly required to spend their time obtaining the 'best deal' for their department, rather than listening to the fears and distress of needy and distressed people and offering clients an individualized service, often the very reason they had entered social work in the first place.

The 'unitized' approach to education and training: the 'competency' model

Another major change which I wish to consider is the near universal move within higher education in Britain to compartmentalizing education and training. As the 'modular' system of teaching becomes increasingly common throughout the country, so students undergo shorter courses, and experience more 'packaged' learning. At the same time, in many practical settings, they are required not to demonstrate knowledge but 'competences', skill in practical tasks like interviewing and report writing. Programmes leading to the Diploma in Social Work are also likely to require that students are competent in certain specified skills of counselling. The major shortcoming of this approach, which otherwise has much to commend it, is the shortage of time allocated to teach these basic competences. In my own course the counselling component offered to all students was confined to one day's teaching in the academic year 1994–5 – although students receive further teaching while on placement.

The euro-centricity of counselling theory

It will be apparent from the above material that counselling, as a formal exchange between two or more people, governed by certain principles and guidelines, is a culture-specific phenomenon. In that it is an activity with a theoretical base which its practitioners learn in academic institutions and which they then practise in formal settings, it is unmistakably a product of Western culture – athough the same activities of sensitive listening and giving emotional support are certainly practised in other cultures but under different names and in different settings.

The question then arises as to whether counselling as formally practised is relevant to all cultures in Britain, including some indigenous Anglo-Saxon ones and some originating in Asia, Africa and Eastern Europe. To some communities the very idea of talking about one's intimate thoughts, feelings and actions may be entirely alien and wholly unacceptable. For some people their cultural frame of reference may mean that some assumptions of counselling, for example the 'self-determination' advocated by Biestek, conflict with deeply held principles about loyalty to one's family. For others, the notion of the expression of feelings, perhaps angry ones about one's parents, contravenes fundamental principles of honourable behaviour within a culture. Far from such expression bringing relief, it may in fact be followed by a deep sense of guilt.

Despite these extremely sensitive issues, which counsellors should be trained both to recognize and to handle, it is the case that leaders of many ethnic minority groups are calling for the provision of counselling and psychotherapy services for their members, particularly in respect of issues of mental health. They are asking, however, for services staffed by workers from their own communities who are both trained in the standards of professional counselling and who are also aware of the particular circumstances and needs of people from their own cultural or ethnic background. A substantial number of helpful books and articles (for example d'Ardennes and Mahtani 1989) is becoming available concerning the counselling needs of people from ethnic minority communities.

Possible future developments

We are in a situation of increasing demands upon social workers: different interest and pressure groups call for more attention to their particular needs; researchers in a range of disciplines call for more awareness of, and practice based upon, their findings; and the general public calls for greater openness and accountability.

In all this, social workers are under-resourced and under-trained. They are, in my experience, committed people, highly motivated and enthusiastic to learn, but so wide is the curriculum, so short the time available and so varied their roles in the field that it is extremely hard to educate and train them beyond a basic level of competence. That training for social work would be extended, a hope expressed in an earlier edition of this book (Dryden *et al.* 1989) has not been fulfilled; social workers in Britain still receive only two years education and training – by contrast with the three years of most of their European counterparts.

Increasing demands for specialist counselling but little time to practise it

Because social workers carry statutory responsibilities, it is virtually certain that in the future the tasks which will have first call upon their time will be the discharge of statutory duties. Many social workers regret this increasing 'social control' element of their work, and wish they could spend their time in, for example, preventive work, community social work and community development, and in combating the evils which contribute so much to the misery of their clients: unemployment, poverty, and discrimination.

Within their statutory roles, however, social workers are being called upon to deal in fields of practice which were scarcely recognized as little as ten years ago. Skills of intervening in situations where child abuse has been reported or is suspected are increasingly in demand, and these, as I have suggested above, are underpinned by communication and counselling skills. Similarly, the demand for training in counselling the victims of child abuse and child sexual abuse is growing, and is likely to grow further. As Brearley (1995) concludes in her review of counselling in social work:

> The irony is that skills in counselling are required in social work to a greater extent than ever before, and yet the means of developing them and using them has never been more threatened.

The increased use of 'agreements' within counselling

There is considerable evidence, from a range of settings, of the usefulness of 'agreements' within social work practice. For example, Hazel (1980) in a major study in Kent, found that it was possible to use agreements to place with foster parents almost 200 disturbed and delinquent adolescents who were unable to remain in their own homes. Written agreements devised between the foster parents, the social workers, and the young people concerned, set out very carefully the rights and responsibilities of all those involved. Seventy per cent of the placements which were supported by an agreement met the criteria for success. The evidence indicated that these agreements helped to clarify expectations and reduce misunderstandings and they contributed significantly to the success of this pioneering British study.

Workers in other fields advocate the introduction of the contract to clarify the aims of the work between client and helper. Rosenhan and Seligman (1984: 632–3), writing of research into the broad field of counselling and psychotherapy, noted:

> Many therapists arrive at an agreement with their client, not only regarding the goals of treatment, but also how long treatment will last.

That agreeement is put in the form of a contract and serves to remind each party of their aims and obligations.

The 'agreement' implies mutually binding responsibilities and can set out goals and commitments in a way which both increases clarity and also makes the counselling situation one of greater equality. The move is away from what might be called formal counselling, and towards the 'genuineness' found by Truax and Carkhuff (1967) to be such a beneficial feature of counselling. In such a setting two people meet as *people*, with different roles and tasks, it is true, but where status differences are recognized rather than emphasized. If this argument is correct, not only will social workers in a counselling role be trained in devising, and helping their clients to devise, agreements between say, teenager and parent, or between partners who are having relationship difficulties, but they will be encouraged to develop agreements between themselves and their clients. A notable feature of these is likely to be a statement of the goals which worker and client will seek to reach together. (Nelson Jones, 1982; Sutton 1987a).

The practice of writing a contract is increasingly used in research (Sutton 1987b) to good effect, and while there is only limited evidence of its effectiveness from well-designed research studies, it seems likely that the fact that lawyers now use it as an automatic accompaniment to a transaction, gives it considerable prima facie validity.

Increased readiness to evaluate their practice

A contractual approach to counselling and practice in general has many advantages: first, it is ethical, in that it engages the client from the beginning in clarifying expectations; second, it offers a structure so that both counsellor and client have a framework within which counselling can take place; and third, it allows evaluation by counsellor and client of the extent to which goals have been met.

Here is one way in which social workers can demonstrate that they recognize their accountability: *by, together with their clients, evaluating their work* using simple quantitative or qualitative means. I offer below a simple model of how this may be done. If a person comes to a social worker and tells her, for example, that she must put her children in care because she cannot cope, then the worker in his or her counselling capacity might seek to help the mother in several ways. By listening and counselling skills, the worker might put into words the mother's fear that she was going mad because of the throbbing in her head, the churning in her stomach and her feeling of tension. Drawing on his or her repertoire of knowledge, the worker would recognize these signs as the symptoms of anxiety. A second way of helping this mother might be to introduce her to a self-help group where she could learn relaxation skills. A third way might be to show her simple behavioural strategies of managing her children – if the assessment suggested that this was appropriate. Thus, one agreed goal for mother and social worker together might be 'that Mrs Andrews shall feel able to cope with her anxiety', and progress towards this could be monitored by the mother's reporting her anxiety symptoms week by week. Figure 9.3, which permits recordings of clients feeling that things are getting either better or worse, illustrates this schematically.

As I have emphasized above, at each stage the work of the counsellor will be informed by his or her knowledge and responsibilities. People do not come to social workers, even when the latter are acting most clearly in their counselling role, with neatly packaged difficulties, amenable to this or that package of responses. They come in distress, with complex personal problems, shortage of money and housing difficulties; they come with problems arising from mental illness compounded by alcohol difficulties; and they come with histories of involvement with the statutory services resulting in mistrust and active antagonism towards them. In such situations, the three qualities of effective counsellors pinpointed by Truax and Carkhuff (1967) (see p. 145) are likely to be essential prerequisites of constructive work but only part of the picture.

We have the responsibility to offer ethical and informed practice to our clients. Our statutory duties may mean that we cannot always meet their wishes, or even that we have to act entirely contrary to their wishes, but in

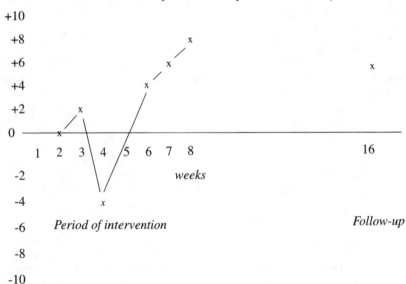

Goal: That Mrs Andrews shall feel able to cope with her anxiety

Figure 9.3 An example of goal-setting and evaluation by the client

all circumstances we owe them respecting, informed and accountable practice.

Reference

d'Ardennes, P. and Mahtani, A. (1989) *Transcultural Counselling in Action*, London: Sage.

Atkinson, R. L., Atkinson, R. C., Smith, E. E., Bern, D. J. and Hilgard, E. R. (1990) *Introduction to Psychology*, 10th edn, New York: Harcourt Brace Jovanovich.

Biestek, F. (1957) *The Casework Relationship*, London: Unwin University Books.

Birchler, G. R. (1979) 'Communication skills in married couples' in S. Bellack and M. Hersen (eds) *Research and Practice in Social Skills Training*, New York: Plenum.

Brearley, R. (1995) *Counselling and Social Work*, Milton Keynes: Open University.

Dryden, W., Charles-Edwards, D., Woolfe, R. (eds) (1989) *Handbook of Counselling in Britain*, London: Routledge.

Egan, G. (1982) *The Skilled Helper*, Monterey: Brooks/Cole.

Halmos, P. (1965) *The Faith of the Counsellors*, London: Constable.

Hazel, N. (1980) *A Bridge to Independence*, Oxford: Blackwell.

Maslow, A. H. (1954) *Motivation and Personality*. New York: Harper and Row.

National Institute for Social Work (1982) *Social Workers: Their Role and Tasks*, (The Barclay Report), London: Bedford Square Press.

Nelson Jones, R. (1982) *The Theory and Practice of Counselling Psychology*, New York: Holt, Rinehart and Winston.

Reid, W. and Epstein, L. (1972), *Task-Centred Casework*. New York: Columbia University Press.

Rogers, C. (1951) *Client-Centred Therapy*, Boston: Houghton Mifflin.

Rosenhan, J. and Seligman, M. E. P. (1984) *Abnormal Psychology*, London: W. W. Norton.

Report of the Committee on Local Authority and Allied Personal Social Services (1968) Seebohm Report, Cmnd 3703, London: HMSO.

Sutton, C. (1979) *Psychology for Social Workers and Counsellors*, London: Routledge and Kegan Paul.

——(1987a) 'The evaluation of counselling: a goal-attainment approach', *Counselling*, 60: 14–20.

——(1987b) *Handbook of Research for the Helping Professions*, London: Routledge and Kegan Paul.

Sutton, C. (1989) 'Counselling in the personal social services' in (eds) W. Dryden, D. Charles-Edwards, and R. Woolf, *Handbook of Counselling in Britain,* London: Routledge.

——(1994) *Social Work, Community Work and Psychology*, Leicester: British Psychological Society.

Sutton, C. and Davies, M. (1986) *The Teaching of Psychology on Social Work Courses*, Leicester: Leicester Polytechnic.

Sutton, C. and Herbert, M. (1992) *Mental Health. A Client Support Resource Pack*, Windsor: NFER/Nelson.

Truax, C. and Carkhuff, R. (1967) *Toward Effective Counseling and Psychotherapy*, Chicago: Aldine.

Westwood, S., Couloute, J., Desai, S., Matthew, P. and Piper, A. (1989) *Sadness in my Heart*, Leicester: University of Leicester.

Acknowledgement

I should like to thank Mrs Pat Osborne of the Central Council for Education and Training in Social Work for reading and commenting upon a draft of this chapter. Her suggestions were very helpful.

Chapter ten

Counselling in the medical context

Roslyn Corney

Introduction

The importance of psychological processes in the experience of health and illness has become increasingly recognized and acknowledged by the medical profession and the public. This is partly due to the changes in both health care and illness morbidity which have occurred in this country. While there has been a reduction in serious infectious disease, there has been an increase in chronic and degenerative problems, leading to more long-term treatments with an emphasis on control rather than cure. In addition, there has been an increasing emphasis on preventive medicine. In spite of the rapid expansion of sophisticated medical techniques for diagnosis and treatment, it is gradually being recognized that the patient's behaviour is vitally important and that both preventive medicine and the management of chronic illness need the active participation and involvement of the patient. As early as 1966, Mechanic, a leading medical sociologist, estimated that 95 per cent of all medical and surgical patients could profit from psychotherapy or behavioural medicine interventions (Mechanic 1966). Now, many practitioners are committed to the concept of holistic medicine, where attention is paid to the whole person, to psychological and social factors as well as physical illnesses and difficulties.

The use of counselling skills in secondary care and hospital settings

In medical settings, as elsewhere, there is much confusion relating to the distinction between counselling skills and counselling. All staff working in medical settings should be aware of the importance of listening attentively, responding appropriately, and giving feedback responsive to the individual's needs. If we consider that these represent the skills of counselling (in the broadest sense), they should be an essential part of the repertoire and training of all practitioners working in a medical context. This is perhaps becoming more important with the increasing emphasis on patient involvement in health care. Patients are increasingly being asked to make decisions on their treatment and to act as partners in treatment rather than passive recipients.

In 1987, the British Association for Counselling sponsored a survey conducted by Glenys Breakwell to map the extent of counselling provision in the National Health Service outside primary care. She conducted a postal survey of district health authorities, professional associations and training bodies and also interviewed a cross section of NHS staff. Breakwell found that within thirty-nine district health authorities, the job responsibilities of 32 per cent of staff in ten professional categories were considered by their managers to include counselling, although counselling was less likely to be included in their job descriptions. What was meant by the word counselling, however, tended to be interpreted differently by the various professions taking part. Nurses viewed counselling as primarily non-directive, whereas doctors interpreted counselling as either advice giving or problem solving.

Apart from health professionals whose many roles may include counselling, there are a number of individuals who would describe themselves as working predominantly as counsellors in a medical setting. Their training and theoretical orientation varies greatly and they include doctors, nurses, social workers, occupational therapists, psychiatrists, psychotherapists and chartered psychologists. In secondary health care and hospital medicine, in particular, there are also a number of individuals who work in a voluntary capacity. There are a great number of people in voluntary associations and self-help groups who befriend, offer advice and support, staff telephone lines as well as undertake counselling (Tyndall 1993).

The range of people who work as counsellors in secondary care settings was also investigated by a 1992 survey on oncology counselling. Obtaining information from a variety of sources, 267 oncology counsellors and specialist nurses working in the United Kingdom were identified (Fallowfield and Roberts 1992). More than half the sample were nurses, counsellors or specialist nurses. However, the remainder included social workers, chaplains and groups who worked in hospices, psychologists, psychiatrists and psychotherapists. Their training, orientation and caseload were highly variable. Only 19 per cent had any kind of formal counselling qualification such as a certificate, diploma or degree. Very few used any identifiable counselling model in their work. Most of the counsellors, especially the nurses, received no supervision and were tackling very large case loads.

Primary care settings and general practice

Working in general practice is one of the major growth areas in counselling at the present time. This has been reflected by the rapid increase in membership of the counselling in medical settings division of BAC over the last few years. This growth is not only due to the increasing recognition of the importance of counselling and psychotherapy in medical care but also because of recent legislative changes which make it easier for general practioners to employ counsellors. Since the new GP contract came into force in 1990, the range of staff eligible for reimbursement through the ancillary staff scheme was extended to include staff with a wider range of skills and training (including counsellors). Some Family Health Service Authorities have been willing to fund counsellors working in general practice using this scheme (the same scheme that funds practice nurses) and this has enabled some GPs to claim back the majority of monies spent. Other GPs have used money available for health promotion by getting counsellors to organize their sessions into clinics (often called stress clinics). This source of money came to an end in 1993, but many GPs found other ways of funding the counselling sessions once they had become used to having the service available and started to rely on it.

A survey of GPs in six health districts conducted in 1991, shortly after implementation of the new GP contract, indicated that 17 per cent of GPs had a link with a counsellor (in most cases, they were employed rather than voluntary). This compared with 48 per cent of GPs having some link with a community psychiatric nurse, 21 per cent with a social worker, 16 per cent with a psychiatrist and 15 per cent with a psychologist, although this varied considerably according to district and practice size (Thomas and Corney 1992). Another larger survey conducted by Sibbald and colleagues found that 31 per cent of practices had links with a counsellor of some kind but they included community psychiatric nurses, counsellors, and psychologists in this definition (Sibbald *et al.*, 1993).

The advent of GP fundholding has also meant that the number of counsellors working in general practice has increased with many fundholders paying for counselling sessions out of their budget. In a study conducted in January 1994 of 100 fundholding practices and 100 comparable non-fundholding practices, 53 per cent of the fundholding practices had a link with a counsellor as compared to 29 per cent of the non-fundholding practices (Corney 1996). The majority of these counsellors were employed directly by the practices. In addition, over one third of practices without a counsellor indicated that they would like increased links with a counsellor in the future. While these figures are overestimates of the national picture in 1994 (as the study only included larger practices who could take part in fundholding originally), they do suggest that in the next few years the majority of large practices, particularly fundholders, will have a counsellor attached.

Principles

Secondary care and hospital settings

Counselling can be seen to be valuable in all stages of medical treatment. In screening and prevention programmes, in assessment, diagnosis and treatment and also when no further active treatment is possible. Sometimes counselling may be helpful for patients with terminal conditions or long-term disability who have to accept that little can be done to alter their condition, apart from palliative care.

When individuals become ill, their concerns, preoccupations and worries have been shown to change dramatically, focusing around the illness and the effect it may have on their daily activities, their work and their family life. The most common reactions of patients to illness are distress and anxiety. Overall it has been estimated that between 30 and 60 per cent of general hospital patients experience psychological distress at the time of hospitalization and during the first year afterwards (Nichols 1984).

Distress is also common among relatives which in turn affects the patient. Recognizing the patient's feelings and concerns is important in medical terms as the presence of psychological distress has been found to have a negative effect on recovery from illness. In a large-scale survey, Querido studied 1,630 patients admitted to a hospital in Amsterdam. Six months after discharge, 70 per cent of patients who were classified as distressed whilst in hospital were in an unsatisfactory condition medically in comparison with only 30 per cent of those classified as non-distressed (cited in Nichols 1984).

Distress at all phases of an illness can usually be reduced by providing information about the illness and treatment. It is often the period of uncertainty, of not knowing, which patients claim as the most difficult to bear. Ley (1988), in his review of the literature, suggests that there is no evidence of increased anxiety or depression when patients are told of their diagnosis. Reviews of studies on a range of surgical patients show generally positive results on giving adequate information and preparation before surgery. Preparation has been shown to affect post-operative pain and symptoms, the time taken to recover as well as anxiety levels.

However, providing information is not always straightforward. It often needs to be given in a highly sensitive manner after first exploring what the individual already understands, wants to hear and can cope with at that particular time (Maguire 1991). It is for this reason that training in counselling skills is so important.

Other studies have also indicated that emotional distress can be reduced by actively involving the patient in treatment and in decisions regarding treatment. Thus patients regard themselves as being actively involved in treating or fighting the illness and exercising choice rather than feeling passive and helpless. This in turn will increase compliance with treatment and commitment. Patients who need to make a decision over treatment may find it helpful to discuss the alternatives with a counsellor who gives them all the relevant information about options.

In some hospital settings, every patient about to undergo a certain procedure or treatment (HIV screening, termination of pregnancy, mastectomy) is referred for counselling as a matter of course. In some situations, such as HIV testing or a termination, it is obligatory before the procedure is undertaken. Thus a number of hospital departments have a counsellor as part of their team, although in many cases, the 'counsellor' has few or no qualifications in counselling (Fallowfield and Roberts 1992). The counsellor is usually on hand to see patients at times of crisis (when an illness is diagnosed, for example) as well as seeing patients on an ongoing basis.

Little research has been conducted on the most appropriate time for a patient to be referred to a counsellor. A system which encourages self-referral may allow the individual to decide when counselling would be of most benefit to them. However, this can only be implemented when patients know what counselling can offer and when there is no stigma attached. Patients may still regard seeing a counsellor as an admission of personal weakness or failure. In the meantime, referral by other members of the medical team may still be the most effective way of ensuring that those who need the help receive it. The involvement of the counsellor as an integral member of the medical team may help reduce the stigma attached to seeing a counsellor as well as educate the medical team on the value of counselling and when best to refer.

Primary care and general practice

Epidemiological studies, in Britain and the United States, suggest that the rate of mental distress in the population is in the range of 10–15 per cent at any point in time (Goldberg and Huxley 1992). In the United Kingdom, the main point of medical contact for people with mental distress is not the psychiatric services but the general practitioner.

A high proportion of patients attending their GP or family doctor in both the United Kingdom and the United States are either depressed or anxious or both. It has been estimated that 60 per cent of visits to physicians in the United States are by patients who have nothing physically wrong with them. Follette and Cummings (1967) (cited in Cummings 1990) and Shapiro (1971) estimated that the number of stress-related visits to physicians ranged from 50 to 80 per cent of all consultations. People vary considerably in their help-seeking behaviour: some individuals will attend their doctor for minor ailments of recent origin while others delay even for serious problems. Attending a GP's surgery is likely to be influenced by a number of factors, including symptoms experienced, recognition of the problem and knowledge about the condition, presence or absence of psychosocial problems and social support, willingness to divulge personal information, accessibility to health-care facilities (both in time available, cost and travelling distance) and relevant health beliefs including perception of the effectiveness of medical care (Corney 1990).

Depression and anxiety and psychosocial problems are commonly inter-linked. Many people become depressed or anxious after some personal crisis such as a bereavement, increased marital stress or separation, or the discovery of a serious or chronic illness. The role of 'life events' and stressful situations has been investigated and discussed in a number of studies while growing interest has been shown in the effect on distress levels of the presence or absence of supportive relationships (Goldberg and Huxley 1992).

The results of these studies reinforce the argument that depression and anxiety should not only be treated by medication but also by some form of psychological help or social support and assistance. In addition, many patients are unhappy about taking psychotropic drugs and there is also a proportion of patients who do not respond to these drugs. Often patients seek the help and advice of their GP in the hope that the doctor, the 'expert', will be able to prescribe a solution. Others just want the oppor-tunity to talk through their problems with someone they know and trust. In many cases, the GP's ability to offer support or sympathy may be adequate or all that is needed. However, because of pressures of time, the GP is usually unable to offer much more than a brief chat and sometimes a prescription. In previous years, the only outside help available was referral to a psychiatrist or a clinical psychologist (usually with a long waiting list). In many cases, referral to a psychiatrist would not be appropriate as it is not the symptoms that need 'treatment' so much as the patient's personal and social situation. In addition, a psychiatric referral still carries the stigma of 'mental illness' and medicalizes what can be considered common life problems.

Another factor in favour of early psychological and social intervention is the relationship found between distress and physical health. Distress, espe-cially chronic distress, can bring about a variety of physical symptoms and illnesses. One study found that newly widowed men were 40 per cent more likely to die in the year following the death of their spouse than a control group of men matched for age and occupation. They died from a number of causes, but heart disease was the most common (Rees and Lutkins 1967). There is also evidence that depressed immune function is associated with lack of social support or chronic stress, and disruptive life events have been linked to a multitude of conditions from leukaemia to the common cold (Totman 1979).

Although studies of counsellor attachments (Corney and Jenkins 1993) indicate that the majority of their referrals are patients with depression, anxiety and/or psychosocial problems, there may still be an important role for the counsellor in primary care in terms of the management of patients with physical illness. Helping clients manage their chronic illness, discussing options for treatment, or being involved in health promotion are all important areas for the counsellor in primary care, although most studies indicate that at the present time, few patients are being referred with these problems.

In addition, there is the role of counselling in preventive medicine. A number of behavioural risk factors have been pinpointed as posing a threat to health, including smoking, diet, lack of exercise and drug taking. The aim of health promotion is to enable people to increase their control over and improve their health. Individual or group counselling can be an important adjunct to medical interventions. For example, many counsellors first became involved in general practice through the provision of stress management clinics. Counselling in this context may involve working with groups or individuals, using a variety of techniques including behavioural methods, offering support, discussing issues as well as more non-directive counselling.

It can be seen from the above account that counsellors may be referred a wide range of clientele when working in general practice, from adolescents with life crises, young people with financial difficulties, couples with marital difficulties, to problems of loneliness, bereavement and major physical illness in the elderly. This is in contrast with counsellors in hospital or secondary care settings, where the issues are inclined to be more specific and related directly to disease or surgery.

The value of counselling attachments to general practice is that those patients who need psychological help can be referred on without too much delay. Studies of successful counsellor attachments to general practice have found that they facilitate referral and feedback between the counsellor and the GP. Thus counselling may be offered and accepted by clients at an earlier stage of their problems (Corney and Jenkins 1993). With GP attachments, clients can see a counsellor in a familiar environment with no or little stigma attached. The fact that the doctor has suggested counselling may overcome the client's fear or initial scepticism of the value of counselling. Take-up of appointments for counselling in general practice is also higher than at a marriage guidance clinic or in a psychiatric outpatient clinic. One of the problems of referring patients to psychiatrists is that many patients fail to turn up for the first appointment (Illman 1983).

Thus one major advantage to attachments is that counsellors and health professionals can start to work in close conjunction. If good working relationships are developed between counsellors and the health professionals based in primary care, mutual learning and development of skills can occur. The supportive role of the counsellor may be particularly important in this context. In a survey of general practitioners working with marriage guidance counsellors (Corney 1986), respondents felt that the counsellors' main task was counselling referred clients, but a third of the doctors mentioned that the counsellor also provided support to practice members. GPs who work with counsellors appear to value their work with patients and appreciate the opportunity to share and discuss their own feelings about patients and their relationships with them (McLeod 1992).

Employing a counsellor in the practice team seems to heighten team members' awareness of their own reactions to patients and encourages them to improve their own counselling skills. Time needs to be invested by the counsellor in supporting and developing the skills of practice members who are interested in taking on a role in this area. McLeod points out that a counsellor who builds up a good relationship with a practice and who finds time for case discussion provides a new and useful resource in primary care. Very few team members have the luxury of time to reflect on their practice and yet offering such time could enable primary health care team members to function more effectively and feel more supported.

Although counsellors may see their role as enabling other staff to take on some of the emotional and psychological problems of their patients, it is also important that medical staff are aware that problems (and harm) can ensue when untrained staff attempt to counsel disturbed clients who need more experienced help. It can be dangerous when unsupported staff are left to deal with complex and difficult emotional problems on their own. A counsellor working closely with the team can advise staff on their management of patients as well as when to refer on.

Issues

Training and level of skills

Individuals trained to work as counsellors will not be able to perform all the counselling necessary in medical settings. There will always be a need for other professionals and volunteers to use counselling skills in their work. Evaluative studies are required to ascertain the training needs, levels of skills, competence and expertise required by other personnel who use counselling skills as part of their work. As part of a national initiative to improve the number and level of qualifications among the workforce, in 1986 the government established a new organization, the National Council for Vocational Qualifications (NCVQ), to oversee the development of qualifications linked to occupational standards. The Advice, Guidance and Counselling and Psychotherapy Lead Body was established in 1994 to set standards and qualifications for all those employed in advice, guidance, counselling and psychotherapy, irrespective of job or status. The new qualifications will be expressed in terms of the competencies required for working in these four areas at the various levels. The BAC and British

Psychological Society are likely to adapt their own procedures for accreditation to match the qualifications approved by the NCVQ.

There also needs to be a more unified and systematic training programme for individuals specifically working as counsellors in medical settings, with proper accreditation and registration procedures in place. The present system is inadequate and allows very little protection for the patient. Counselling does not have, as yet, a statutory body to direct its training, qualification and registration procedures. However, growing pressure from a number of sources both outside and within counselling and psychotherapy has meant that a register of counsellors and psychotherapists will soon be in place. Thus registered counsellors will belong to a national body which operates a complaints and disciplinary procedure. Counsellors would be barred from future practice if they contravened recognized codes of ethics and practice.

Counsellors working in medical settings also need to receive some form of specialized training, particularly in short-term work and being able to work as part of a multi-disciplinary team. The Counselling in Primary Care Trust is involved in sponsoring a number of postgraduate diplomas at masters level in counselling in primary care. The Trust is also cooperating in the development of a more rigorous classification of the competencies involved in counselling being undertaken by the National Council for Vocational Qualifications.

The training of counsellors currently in employment is highly variable. The BAC guidelines for the employment of counsellors in general practice made strong recommendations to GPs to employ counsellors who would fulfil the criteria for BAC accreditation (or equivalent) and to keep to timescales for the completion of training for those who have not (Ball 1993). However, studies indicate that counsellors working in general practice are very varied in the qualifications and experience they possess (Sibbald et al. 1993). Many GPs are unfamiliar with the qualifications that a counsellor may possess and may be more influenced by the counsellor's charges per hour. Fallowfield and Roberts' survey indicates that many counsellors in secondary care settings also have little training, with less than 20 per cent having a formal counselling qualification. This lack of training was acknowledged by respondents of the survey who in general felt that in-house training sessions were inadequate. This was also supported by Breakwell's study. She found that less than one-third of the district health authorities who completed her questionnaire were able to specify a budget for counselling training and the few who could give percentages indicated that it ranged from less than 1 per cent to 8 per cent of their total training budgets.

Collaboration and confidentiality

In medical settings, the doctor retains overall responsibility for the patient and this may lead to difficulties over confidentiality. Some counsellors feel strongly that all client information is confidential and therefore give little feedback on the client to other medical professionals. Other counsellors feel differently and make sure that clients are aware that any information divulged will be shared with the medical team responsible for their care.

There can be difficulties when counsellors work alone and do not give feedback to the doctors and others. One of the main reasons for locating counsellors in medical settings is the sharing of information with health professionals and the educational processes that occur in conjunction with this process of sharing. In addition, the counsellor may become isolated and weighed down by the distress of their clients. It then becomes even more important that regular supervision is available for counsellors.

An investigation by Tyndall on an interdisciplinary study programme found that counsellors were often less able to form collaborative relationships than other health workers or social service personnel (Tyndall 1993). In order to work effectively as a member of the medical team, the counsellor needs to have a clear understanding of the roles of others in the hospital or general practice as well as the wider community. Counsellors need to be aware of provision in the community which may also help their clients, such as social services personnel, community mental-health teams, voluntary and self-help groups. They should have an understanding of the medical model and the side effects of the drugs that their clients are receiving, even if they do not use the model themselves (East 1995). They need to collaborate with others and seek an understanding of the value of other team members. In this way, they will encourage their colleagues to understand the counsellor's role and contribution to overall patient care.

It is therefore crucial that the counsellor does not work in isolation from the rest of the medical team. Isolated counsellors may find themselves being referred the most challenging of clients or the most disturbed and distressed. They need to constantly monitor their own practice and give feedback on the suitability of clients referred and how their role fits into the team. Medical care is now constantly audited and counsellors should be willing to fit into this framework, monitoring contacts with clients, the nature of their referrals, those who drop out of treatment and those whom they consider benefit most. It is only by a serious consideration of the counselling process that the best use can be made of a limited resource. Being involved as a team member enables a counsellor to contribute to the care of many more people than the small number actually seen. The counsellor should consider that their responsibility is to the whole patient group and to developing a patient-centred approach to treatment and care in either the team or the practice.

Effectiveness of counselling

An increase in the use of counsellors in medical settings has resource and cost implications. There are many demands on the NHS budget and the efficacy of each new service needs to be considered and costed carefully. It is necessary to show that the increased use of counsellors will bring about an improved outcome in patients or that it reduces other medical costs (or both).

Investigating effectiveness is a complex issue. We need first to find out who will benefit most from counselling, and second what level of skill in the counsellor is necessary for benefit to occur. It is likely that these two issues are interlinked: some patients may benefit from less skilled help while others may need a counsellor with much training and experience and may be harmed by someone without this.

There is also the issue of the type of therapy given. At the present time, most research suggests that it is not the methodology that is important but the qualities of the counsellor; those who offer warmth, genuineness and empathy have been shown to be consistently effective (Corney 1993).

Apart from client outcome, other costs must be considered. Clients attending their GP with psychological distress and psychosocial problems often present somatic symptoms but when they are referred to a specialist, no organic problems are found. Referrals to secondary care may be reduced if counsellors are involved at an early stage. Many GPs find that the attachment of a counsellor to their practice reduces their stress levels. They may find distressed patients difficult to treat and welcome the involvement of another practitioner with this patient group. The costs of GP stress are difficult to quantify but it is an element that should not be ignored in any measurement of costs.

Some studies have indicated that psychotropic medication is reduced when a counsellor is involved. However, evidence suggests that there has been a recent increase in the costs of psychotropic drugs prescribed by most practices (Maxwell *et al.* 1993). This has been due to the increased prescribing of the new types of antidepressants (SSRIs) which are expensive but considered by many doctors to be much better tolerated by patients and more cost effective in the long term. Many studies suggest that improved outcome is more likely to occur if patients receive both medication and psychological help, so it may not be in the best interests of patients to receive only one form of treatment (Klerman *et al.* 1994).

In hospital settings, other factors need to be taken into account. Counselling may be found not only to improve patient well-being but also improve compliance with treatment and recovery from surgery or other medical treatments.

Subjective accounts

Subjective accounts suggest that the attachments of counsellors in medical settings work well, with much consumer, counsellor and GP or doctor satisfaction. One study conducted in 1980 by the Waydenfelds (cited by Corney 1993) found that forty-four out of the forty-seven clients who completed a client questionnaire indicated that help was received. Another study by Anderson and Hasler (1979, cited in Corney 1993) sent questionnaires to the first eighty patients referred to the counsellor. Fifty-five patients returned them (69 per cent). Of this group, forty-seven agreed that counselling should be available in general practice, forty-three said they would use the counselling service again and forty-six would recommend it to their relatives or friends. Numerous subsequent studies have yielded similar results.

Subjective accounts are valuable, but need to be treated with caution. It may be very difficult to criticize a service, especially when arranged by the general practice or medical team upon which one relies. It is also possible that similar favourable reports would be obtained if clients were given the same amount of time by an untrained, warm and caring befriender or by a self-help group which could also offer practical assistance on a longer-term basis.

Clinical trials of counselling

The results of clinical trials are more mixed and negative than subjective reports. Also, difficulties abound in conducting these studies. For example, the sample sizes may be too small to show an effect (often because the doctors find it difficult to refer patients to a clinical trial), the motivation of patients to receive counselling is often variable and patients may either refuse counselling or refuse to take part in the follow-up assessments. Thus subject attrition is often a considerable problem. In addition, in many trials there is a lack of any clear counselling model employed, the counsellors involved are often inadequately trained, the outcome measures used are inappropriate or the follow-up period too short.

In general practice, there is the additional difficulty that high proportions of patients with depression and/or anxiety improve over time, regardless of treatment received, although many will become ill again at a later date (Goldberg and Huxley 1992). It is the group of clients who will only improve with additional psychological help that need to be identified. More studies are needed on specific patient groups with specific therapies, particularly those measuring long-term effects.

Future developments

Developing the skills of other health professionals

Although a number of studies have amply demonstrated the importance of good communication skills, it is only relatively recently that attention has been paid to developing interviewing and communication skills in medical education. It has perhaps been assumed that these skills will come with practice and by observing the interactions of experienced doctors and health professionals. However, studies have found that medical students became less interested in their patients as people over time. Senior students were less likely than junior students to question patients on psychological or social dimensions. Students therefore become more doctor-centred as they progress through medical school (Nichols 1984).

Thus much more emphasis is necessary on training nurses and doctors in communication and counselling skills. This is starting to happen. In Project 2000, the new nurse-training scheme, a module on counselling skills is included within the course curriculum and opportunities for further counselling training are available within the more specialized vocational areas. There has also been much more emphasis on the training of doctors, particularly in the general practitioner training scheme.

Emotional support for health workers

Absence through staff sickness is estimated to cost the NHS as much as £200 million a year (HEA 1992). Much of this is linked to staff stress. While there is a widely expressed concern about stress and burnout in health professionals, many doctors and nurses still find it difficult to admit to stress believing it to be a sign of weakness.

Thus the emotional needs of the health professionals themselves must also be considered. While workers in other caring professions, such as counselling and social work, have supervision sessions built into their work, few health professionals have these opportunities. There may be no forum where they can be given support and help to disentangle their own feelings, avoidances, prejudices and emotional responses.

Professional groups are increasingly aware of the need to provide help for their members. In 1984, the Royal College of Nursing advocated the appointment of a counsellor in every district, and started a counselling service for nurses. In addition, a similar scheme with a telephone helpline has been recently set up for doctors and their families.

Conditions of service for counsellors in medical settings

Studies have indicated that counsellors in general practice are employed under a range of conditions. Some counsellors are only paid for patients who turn up while others are paid at an agreed rate which includes time for administration, meetings and supervision.

A multi-agency working group was set up to formulate and agree on national guidelines on counselling in general practice and these were launched in 1993 (Ball 1993). The document gave guidelines for the employment of counsellors, their roles in general practice, the minimum qualifications necessary, and their conditions of work. This included the need for regular supervision and payment for activities apart from those spent in direct client contact. The guidelines suggested that two-thirds of the counsellor's hours of employment be spent seeing clients, with a maximum of twenty hours of client contact per week. The need for professional indemnity insurance was also stressed. Future work is necessary, however, to increase general practitioner and other medical staff's understanding of the importance of these factors in order to achieve optimal counsellor effectiveness.

Counsellors in hospital settings have also been found to be working in difficult situations. Many have large caseloads, are often unsupervised and unsupported, with few opportunities for training. A similar set of guidelines has also been published by the BAC giving examples of a job description and conditions of employment.

Thus while patients need protection from poor counselling, counsellors, in turn, need protection from the stress and emotional burnout from doing a job without adequate training, supervision, backup or facilities.

References

Ball, V. (1993) *Guidelines for the employment of counsellors in general practice*, Rugby: BAC.

Breakwell, C. (1987) *Mapping counselling in the non-primary care sector of the NHS*, report for the British Association for Counselling, Rugby: BAC.

Corney, R. (1986) 'Marriage guidance counselling in general practice', *Journal of the Royal College of General Practitioners* 36: 424–6.

——(1990) 'Sex differences in general practice: attendance and helpseeking for minor illness', *Journal of Psychosomatic Research* 34 (5): 525–34.

——(1993) 'Studies of the effectiveness of counselling in general practice' in R. Corney and R. Jenkins (eds) *Counselling in General Practice*, London: Routledge.

——(1996) 'Links between mental health professionals and general practices in England and Wales: the impact of GP fundholding', *British Journal of General Practice* 46, 221–4.

Corney, R. and Jenkins, R. (1993) *Counselling in General Practice*, London: Routledge.

Cummings, N. (1990) 'Arguments for the financial efficacy of psychological services in health care settings' in J. Sweet (ed.) *Handbook of Clinical Psychology in Medical Settings*, New York: Plenum.

East, P. (1995) *Counselling in medical settings*, Buckingham: Open University Press.

Fallowfield, L. and Roberts, R. (1992) 'Cancer counselling in the United Kingdom', *Psychological Health* 6: 107–17.

Goldberg, D. and Huxley, P. (1992) *Common Mental Disorders*, London: Routledge.

Health Education Authority (1992) *Health at work in the NHS* (action pack), London: Health Education Authority.

Illman, J. (1983) 'Is psychiatric referral good value for money?' *BMA News Review* 9: 41–2.

Klerman, G., Weissman, M., Markowitz, J., Glick, I., Wilner, P., Mason, B. and Shear, M. (1994) 'Medication and psychotherapy' in S. Garfield and A. Bergin (eds) *Handbook of Psychotherapy and Behavioral Change*, New York: Wiley.

Ley, P. (1988) *Communicating with Patients*, London: Croom Helm.

Maxwell, M., Heaney, D., Howie, J. and Noble, S. (1993) 'General practice fundholding: observations of prescribing patterns and costs using the defined daily dose method', *British Medical Journal* 307: 1190–4.

McLeod, J. (1992) 'Counselling in primary health care, the GP's perspective' in M. Sheldon (ed.) *Royal College of General Practitioners Clinical Series on Counselling in General Practice*, London: RCGP Enterprises.

Maguire, P. (1991) 'Managing difficult communication tasks' in R. Corney (ed.) *Developing Communication and Counselling Skills in Medicine*, London: Routledge.

Mechanic, D. (1966) 'Response factors in illness: the study of illness behaviour', *Social Psychiatry* 1: 106–15.

Nichols, K. A. (1984) *Psychological Care in Physical Illness*, London: Croom Helm.

Rees, W. and Lutkins, S. (1967) 'Mortality and bereavement', *British Medical Journal* 4: 13–16.

Shapiro, A. (1971) 'Placebo effects in medicine, psychotherapy and psychoanalysis' in S. Garfield and A. Bergin (eds) *Handbook of Psychotherapy and Behavioral Change: an Empirical Analysis*, New York: Wiley.

Sibbald, B., Addington-Hall, J., Brenneman, D. and Freeling, P. (1993) 'Counsellors in English and Welsh general practices: their nature and distribution', *British Medical Journal* 306: 29–33.

Thomas, R. and Corney, R. (1992) 'A survey of schemes linking mental health professionals to general practice in six district health authorities', *British Journal of General Practice* 42: 358–61.

Totman, R. (1979) *The Social Causes of Illness*, London: Souvenir Press.

Tyndall, N. (1993) *Counselling in the voluntary sector*, Buckingham: Open University Press.

Chapter eleven

Counselling in education (primary and secondary)

Patrick Hughes

Beginnings

Guidance

Though a counselling movement can be said to have begun in Britain in the mid-1960s, the role and status of counselling in British schools cannot be understood except in relation to a longer-established tradition directed at meeting the vocational and personal as well as the more specific scholastic needs of pupils. The word which came to identify enlightened educational thinking and practice in this respect was 'guidance', and its principles and progress in the first half of this century are admirably summarized in the 1955 *Yearbook of Education*. In addition to providing a comprehensive account of the scope of guidance and of the meaning of the word in Britain, this symposium of views also re-emphasized the need for a more broadly based view of guidance than had existed in practice until then. In essence this conceived of the provision of professional psychological help and support as the prerogative of every child rather than as a service mainly reserved for children with special needs.

Counselling

The objectives of the attempt to introduce counselling into schools in Britain did not differ essentially from this earlier tradition, and in broader terms represented the continuation of long-standing attempts to democratize and humanize the school. This venture, partly because of its emphasis on the work of Carl Rogers and the active collaboration of eminent figures in the counselling movement from the USA in its initial stages, was popularly construed to be North American in origin. The philosophy of client-centred counselling, however, fitted in well with the existent pupil-centred tradition and with the aspirations of teachers and other educationists in Britain committed to the personal and social development of young people. The enterprise, which introduced training in counselling methods and theory for the first time in Britain, has been seen as the first major attempt in British schools since the establishment of the child study movement to bridge the gap between the ideals then expressed and actual practice in schools (Hughes 1971). It offered concepts and methods of working with others which were to enrich the role of the teacher and expand the range of strategies available to schools in furthering the personal and social development of their pupils.

The school counsellor

At an organizational level, this new development differed in at least one important respect from what had gone before in Britain. It inaugurated a new role of school counsellor for the secondary school, where increased attention to the psychological well-being and healthy development of young people in an age of rapid change and heightened stress was seen as an urgent need. Primary education was not directly included, as primary schools in Britain had a much better record in caring for the whole child and in maintaining relationships with home and community. In the long term, however, the more radical departure was the *de facto* acceptance that school personnel trained under educational auspices (and not, for example, under medical supervision) were capable of coping with emotional and motivational aspects of pupils' lives in ways which resembled methods common to well-established types of psychotherapy.

Wider implications

The implications of these enterprising innovations were far-reaching. Counselling was introduced as an acceptable and respectable activity for school personnel. Potentially, this represented an extension of responsibility and work methods well beyond the traditional role of the school teacher, and presaged the arrival of a more broadly based use of counselling skills. In essence, of course, this applied to the primary as much as to the secondary school, though it was not until later that the literature made reference to counselling in primary education (Sisterson 1983) and included discussion of the actual use of basic counselling skills to promote aspects of children's personal and social well-being (David and Charlton 1988).

Contrary views

In practice, the attempt to introduce full-time counsellors into secondary schools had limited success. At the beginning, LEAs with few exceptions were not enthusiastic about the experiment; many teachers were distrustful and sometimes openly hostile; universities and other institutions were slow to follow the lead of Reading and Keele, the universities which set up the first training courses; and the Department of Education and Science, while in general sympathetic to promising experiments, did not actively promote the idea in schools. Even when, eventually, a number of other institutions of higher education had introduced extended programmes of training, only a small number of schools actually appointed counsellors to their staffs. In some cases, heads of schools approved of the role but appointed candidates without training.

The responsibilities of the role were not always clearly defined and the types of activities which came to occupy the working life of those appointed as school counsellors tended to develop with the job. In the very early days, some counsellors for example attempted to work in a manner similar to that of a therapist in private practice, centring exclusively on counselling sessions with individuals and maintaining a distance between themselves and other staff and activities in the school. This mode of working did not survive for long. It tended to exacerbate suspicion and misunderstanding in other members of staff, isolate the counsellor from recognition and support, and heighten counsellor stress related to such issues as timetabling and confidentiality. Other tasks also came to be seen by both counsellors and schools as both an important and appropriate part of a counsellor's responsibilities. The role, then, fairly soon became a diversified one, including, in addition to individual counselling with self-referred and teacher-referred pupils, such activities as liaison with outside agencies and with personnel in the school's pastoral care system, home–school liaison and liaison with feeder primary schools, agent-of-change functions including training in guidance and counselling skills and objectives (Daws 1976).

Developments in pastoral care

While some of the negative attitudes towards counselling in schools ameliorated as the concept of counselling became better understood and more accepted, the progress of the counsellor model was overshadowed by the beginnings of a transformation within pastoral care. In the 1960s this was still an amateur and relatively underdeveloped system within British schools purporting to address the personal, as distinct from the scholastic, needs of pupils. The skeletal structure was already present in the form of house systems established in the 1960s on public-school lines in many of the new comprehensive schools. As the challenges and stresses of reorganization and social and economic change increased, pastoral-care posts over and above subject-department posts were created and pastoral-care structures of some kind were established in virtually all comprehensive schools.

A period of rethinking and experimentation in the 1970s ushered in important changes in attitudes and practice, examining the form tutor's caring role and offering a variety of strategies which teachers could adopt to meet the pastoral needs of their pupils (Best *et al.* 1980). This was followed by increasing attention on the part of practitioners, researchers and academics to the place of pastoral-care systems and, in particular, their relationship to the academic structures of the school. The inauguration of the National Association for Pastoral Care in Education at the beginning of the 1980s was an important step in this process. Its journal, *Pastoral Care*, continues to be the leading publication on theory and developing practice related to the welfare and personal development of school children in Britain. As can readily be seen from the contents since its inception and from a recent definitive text (Best *et al.* 1995), the last ten years have been a period of consolidation and further development.

Though the phrase 'pastoral care' is used rather than the term 'guidance', the values and aims of these contemporary writings can be seen as a continuation in more modern form of those attitudes and principles which came to characterize enlightened educational thinking in the second quarter of this century and are enshrined in the 1955 *Yearbook of Education*. What distinguishes current thinking and practice is a wider recognition of the importance of attention to affective factors in learning and to the development of a curriculum and a methodology sophisticated enough to meet these needs.

Summary

After a period, therefore, of some thirty years of review and innovation aimed at finding viable ways of meeting the welfare needs of pupils, pastoral care has come to be seen as the official repository of the secondary school's role in the promotion and delivery of services and programmes concerned with social and personal development. This defines the context in which those committed to the advancement of counselling, a key way of facilitating such development, need to operate in working with schools at the secondary level. In primary schools, the term 'pastoral care' was not in common use, as the practice of care had been seen as inseparable from child-centred education and it was easier to see counselling as a natural extension of the caring school.

Principles

Pastoral care, teaching, and counselling

More recently, attention has been drawn to the shared content and aims of school programmes and approaches in countries throughout the world to which the terms 'counselling', 'pastoral care' and 'guidance' have been attached. Lang, in a most helpful comparative analysis, suggests that all these current approaches can be subsumed under the term 'affective education', assuming that this is taken to include 'all work (individual, group and programmes) that is concerned with the student's feelings, emotions and personal and social development, the positive encouragement offered by schools and the support they provide when difficulties are encountered in these areas' (Lang 1995: 271). Given the clarity and emphasis with which these values have now come to be espoused by those committed to pastoral care, it is not surprising that the role of counselling in schools in Britain seems better understood and accepted than was the case over a decade ago. Three recent developments, however, have been particularly influential in bringing this about.

The advent of a new focus on social skills led in this country to the application of very effective training programmes in a variety of contexts (Argyle 1981). Earlier, a similar analysis (Carkhuff 1969) had been applied to counselling interviews in an extension of Carl Rogers' approach. The training programmes emanating from this work were incorporated into training courses (both extended and short-term) in this country in the early 1970s and continue as a most important feature in training, Egan's text (Egan 1986) being perhaps the most popular choice among those used in current courses. These systematic approaches with their instructional emphasis, have helped reduce the caution with which counselling was approached in the 1960s and 1970s.

At the beginning of the 1980s, the British Association for Counselling introduced a scheme for accrediting counsellors. In 1988, in consultation with its members and drawing on the accumulated experience of established courses in universities and other institutions of higher education, it launched a scheme for the formal recognition of in-depth (one year full-time or two to three years part-time) training courses. The number of courses which have successfully met the rigorous standards for recognition (BAC 1990) and those which have reached application stage has risen considerably since the scheme was introduced. During the last decade there has also been a growth in the availability of shorter-term training courses in counselling skills. There are many more opportunities for training, therefore, and more people with training than ever before.

Within the school, the Technical and Vocational Educational Initiative (TVEI), and, more recently, GCSE and such developments as, for example, profiling and helping students towards self-responsibility, demanded skills from teachers which had traditionally not been included in their training. In addition, other changes were initiated by these developments, so that tutoring and guidance, in one form or another, inside the classroom and out, became the responsibility of the majority of staff and not just of those in pastoral positions. 'Listening skills' (essential, of course for counsellors) as well as skills of discussion, negotiation, supervision, etc. are now spread among all staff, and tutoring and guidance have become 'not an "academic" or a "pastoral" task but a "teacher's" task' (Griffiths 1995: 77).

It would appear that at this stage in the history of its development in Britain, counselling can no longer be referred to as a movement. It has, rather, come to be recognized and accepted as a valuable human resource in many if not most areas of public life – not excluding education. The net result of such changes is that counselling in schools is no longer seen as a remote and esoteric practice, but one which overlaps with teaching and particularly with that aspect of the school's task concerned with the personal and social education of its pupils.

Counselling

Where situations arise in which counselling in more depth seems appropriate, extra training and experience on the part of the member of staff who assumes the counsellor role may be desirable and in some cases clearly essential (BAC 1990). Specialist activities of this kind, however, need not and should not, pre-empt the commitment of other members of staff involved with a child in need. Many of the problems which arise are not likely to be 'cured' or happily resolved, but counselling may help bring about changes in, for example, knowledge of self and others and lead to improvements in ability to cope.

Those points in the day-to-day life of schools where problems, needs, and conflicts of a personal kind appear or threaten to emerge are wide-ranging and varied, as a list of more common problem areas reported by teachers working as counsellors over a period of years will show:

> Bullying, friendship fractures, relationships with parents, discipline/disruption problems in lessons, identity crises, attendance problems, relationships with staff, difficulty in coping with expectations of parents/teachers/peers, victims of aggressive behaviour, social isolation, underfunctioning, school refusal, family breakdown, low self-esteem, social deprivation, sexual problems, overdoses, suicidal feelings, being in the wrong group for a subject, help in making decisions, self-image, learning difficulties, depression, future unemployment worries, anxiety, coping with work, dealing with their own aggression, study skills, examination anxiety, feelings of alienation with their school programmes, difficulty in adapting to a new school, boredom, sense of rejection, child abuse.
>
> (James 1983: 3)

Each particular situation is never quite the same as the last one of its kind, and it is impossible to predict what type of problem will next face a counsellor or other member of staff committed to the personal and social welfare of the pupil as an individual human being. It is also more difficult to translate values and intentions (for example, to be accepting and genuine) into practice in the mêlée of school life than in the relative isolation of a consulting room. It is not surprising that responses to such problems can also be varied and sometimes confused.

In spite of these difficulties, some general working principles might be suggested on the basis of the practical experience of pastoral-care staff, in particular those who have engaged in counselling in a more focused way. Examples may also help illustrate the way in which these developing principles have come to inform good practice.

Working principles

The first principle is a simple one, hardly one might think worthy of mention: always respond. It has a particular meaning for counsellors in that the importance of a statement or action by a client is determined not only by its apparent gravity or triviality in the circumstances in which it occurs but by what it means for him or her. Until you begin to interact with the other person, therefore, you are not in a position to evaluate its significance.

A second principle is communication. Highly desirable in many settings, it is a vital necessity in this one. From a counselling point of view, communication is a shared activity involving both helper and client, and a counselling approach in schools can often be distinguished from other types of approach by this characteristic. In broader terms, however, a teacher-counsellor's success and continued credibility in a school context is critically dependent on the way in which he or she communicates with others during, after, and before direct interventions in, for example, presenting problems of the kind referred to above. 'Others' include pupils, the head, staff in general and pastoral staff in particular, and, in the community, workers in key helping agencies. Again, in these cases, the kind of communication required is open dialogue without recourse to dissimulation or hidden agendas.

The next general principle concerns the maintenance of confidentiality, where disclosures are made on the understanding that they will not be divulged wihout permission. At first sight, this might seem contrary to the principle of communication. Effective counsellors, while generally resolute on the issue of confidentiality, are equally convinced that bringing hidden material into the open is in most cases beneficial, provided those they wish to help agree to do so. It is in these latter respects that those with training as counsellors might find themselves at odds with other members of staff.

Though these three principles are fairly broad in scope, adherence to them is seen as indispensable for credibility and success in occupying a counselling role in a school.

Other principles of working are more directly related to the counselling process itself. Respect or regard for the pupil as a person in his or her own right is perhaps the most fundamental of these. It is characterized by an unconditional acceptance of the individual, free from patronizing or paternalistic attitudes and from the sentimental do-gooding with which pastoral care has sometimes been identified. In practice, counsellors have found this an essential prerequisite for the kind of relationship they wish to establish with young people. It is notable, however, that experienced counsellors, while accepting and trying to understand the pupil in this way, maintain at the same time a degree of personal detachment. She or he does not get emotionally entangled in either the problem presented or in the feelings accompanying it. Taking these two together, one might say that the counsellor is seen and needs to be seen as someone who stands outside the argument while standing firmly at the side of the young person.

A further principle of critical importance to the conduct of real dialogues is listening, an inherent aspect of two-way communication. It is a principle of overriding importance in any counselling exchange as, without it, it is not possible to register, much less respond to what a client feels and thinks. In a school context, counsellors find it also both desirable and necessary to extend its application to important others who may be involved.

Examples

> Mandy, a year-eight pupil, in one of her good phases, in which she is pleasant, helpful, and working well, suddenly tells her form teacher that all is well at home and that her mother and her little brother are coming back home. The following week, she is uncooperative and bad-tempered again, in tears, slamming doors, throwing books on the floor. Mum apparently is not returning after all and Dad has brought in a new 'Auntie'.

This example draws attention to the caring role of the teacher, in this case clearly a key figure whose support and influence may be of very great significance in Mandy's development. It underlines the importance of two of the broad aims of pastoral care, prevention and support, and also indicates that the teacher in this case is making use of some basic characteristics of a counselling approach – listening and accepting. It is also noteworthy that a counselling approach may be conveyed to a pupil in other ways than face-to-face conversation. By paying attention to what Mandy told her in the first place, by responding later to Mandy's angry outbursts and misdemeanours with firmness, detachment, and patience, and by continuing to show uncompromising acceptance of her as a person, the teacher is in practice subscribing to the basic principles which have been applied to the process of conducting a counselling dialogue. Maintaining an approach of this kind, however, can be very demanding, and genuine communication with other members of staff, in particular pastoral-care staff and management, and, if and where appropriate, with outside agency staff, is highly desirable.

> David, a bright year-ten pupil, has a good relationship with his mother with whom he lives in a council flat. His parents separated when he was seven. Mother is still young, in her mid-30s. Father, who lives in the neighbourhood, is finding it hard to cope with life so David sees him rarely. During an interview in school in which the careers teacher allows the discussion to develop at a personal level, David reveals that when he goes into the sixth form he intends to make arrangements to live on his own so that he can allow his mother to live her own life without interference from him. He has not mentioned this to his mother. The possible difficulties in carrying out his intention worry him, but he intends to think them through for himself.

This example underlines the importance of having personnel in schools who can appreciate the value of counselling and when it should be used. A counsellor with appropriate training and experience should be able to enter into a counselling dialogue with David and enable him to explore the situation and his feelings about it more fully. If presented with this problem, s/he would not hesitate to allocate one or more sessions for this purpose, possibly a joint session for both David and his mother, and, if necessary, a follow-up visit at some time during the year. Whether David could be helped or not in the absence of such 'specialist' resources will depend on (1) the recognition accorded in the school to counselling, in particular to the principles specifically relating to the conduct of a counselling interview, and (2) the availability of the time and competence among existing pastoral-care staff to engage in a type of dialogue which depends for its success on counselling skills.

> In a small group run by a teacher-counsellor, five 'difficult' year-ten pupils are encouraged to express themselves openly and come to terms with their own feelings. Afterwards, one class teacher quizzes two of them about what is happening in the group and another teacher addresses the counsellor in an aggressive manner, demanding to know what this is all about, and threatening to report the matter to the Head.

While this example illustrates the degree of anxiety and antagonism sometimes engendered among teachers by those who take on a counselling role, it also stresses the importance of communication before and during as well as after an event. An incident of the kind reported above took place in a school where a genuine dialogue between the teacher-counsellor and other school staff had not yet been formed. It would be unlikely to occur in a school where good lines of communication had been established and where staff closely involved with the pupils concerned were consulted

beforehand and made aware of the counsellor's intentions. Had this been
done in the case of our example, suspicion and lack of trust might not have
assumed such proportions. It is much less likely that a reaction of this kind
would be met nowadays. The example has been included, however, to
stress the importance of the total school context in which conselling is to
take place. The principle of confidentiality, in particular, often the focus of
conflict between those who teach and those who counsel, would already
have been put in perspective. The pupils would understand the meaning of
confidentiality and its limits, and other staff members would know beforehand what the counsellor was or was not prepared to discuss with them.

> Karen's mother telephones the school counsellor to complain that her
> daughter has been unjustly treated by one of the teachers. No food is to
> be eaten in classrooms. Towards the end of break, Karen has just arrived
> in the room and started talking to two other girls already there when the
> Head of the Year enters, sees several empty crisp packets and other
> evidence of food consumption on the floor. He reprimands Karen and the
> others and orders them to clear up the mess. They refuse, saying that
> they didn't create the mess in the first place. The teacher gets very angry
> and tells them to report for detention until they decide to apologize.
> Karen's tutor, after receiving a note of complaint from the mother, has a
> talk with Karen, then arranges a meeting with her mother to talk it over.
> In a lengthy interview, Karen's mother begins by complaining about the
> Year Head's behaviour but continues by talking about Karen's anxious
> behaviour at home and how she is now saying she hates school and is
> frightened of the Year Head. At the end of the conversation, she dis-
> closes to the tutor that Karen had been sexually abused and has been
> seeing a social worker for some time for counselling to help her over her
> mistrust of men in positions of authority. With the mother's permission,
> the Year Head and the Head are told about the abuse. The former refuses
> to budge from the stand he has taken, but the latter, having investigated
> the situation further, dismisses detention and need for apology, and
> involves the tutor in discussing the position and the possible role of
> the school in this matter. The Head of Year felt his authority had been
> undermined, but remained on good terms with the tutor.

That this tricky (and time-consuming) incident was handled reasonably
well was not fortuitous, but depended to a considerable extent on the
establishment by the tutor over a long period of a reputation for being
able to cope with school situations in general as well as counselling-type
ones in particular. The psychological climate of communication as well as
the ability to conduct interviews according to counselling principles also
played an important part later in helping Karen's mother and Karen to work
through confused ideas and feelings about authority and the role of the

school, and in enabling a healthier and more realistic relationship to develop between home and school.

School-based situations in which counselling can make an important contribution are legion and may, of course, be more complex and difficult than those just illustrated. Even from these examples, however, it should be evident that living by principles of this kind demands a high level of personal competence and resilience in coping with the anxiety, anger, compassion, and many other powerful feelings frequently engendered on these occasions. It is not surprising, then, that sound training and the provision of support are likely to be of vital importance in determining the provision and quality of this work.

Issues

How is counselling to be distinguished from other types of intervention? What knowledge and skills are involved? How can people best be trained for a counselling role? These are only some of the many and varied questions that arise wherever counselling is undertaken. While some of these questions are shared across settings, particular issues become of special importance where counselling takes place within an institutional context. Issues which seem of particular importance for counselling in schools in Britain today may be considered under three broad headings: attitudes and values, identity, status and influence.

Attitudes and values

One of the most difficult issues from the point of view of practice centres round the conflicts which can arise or seem to arise between the authority of the teacher and the psychological welfare of the pupil. Pastoral care developed within a tradition of authority and control. The expansion of its organization and staffing from the 1960s onward was closely linked with stressful changes in schools during this period – comprehensive reorganization, the creation of new posts of responsibility, and other major developments such as mixed-ability teaching and the raising of the school-leaving age. As some of the foremost writers on pastoral care have argued, its rapid development was primarily 'a consciously evolved device for managing a potentially explosive situation which enables the teacher to remain in control' (Best *et al.* 1977: 131). This primacy of a social-control function and the tradition of paternalism which a number of contemporary writers have seen as inhering in pastoral-care practices (Best *et al.* 1977; Follet 1986) would inevitably lead to a different type of response from that developed within counselling, and to a quite different view of a helping relationship. Some examples of the 'pastoral curriculum' have indeed been identified by those committed to a counselling philosophy as being 'more about expropriating counselling for the purposes of minimizing personal growth than they are about self-actualization' (Murgatroyd 1983: 6).

While such attitudes would seem to have altered in the last decade, as awareness of the nature of counselling has increased, the distinction between a controlling aim and an enabling one is a critical one, not only from the standpoint of values and goals, but also from that of practice. Counselling is basically concerned with enabling clients to take control of their own lives. In what manner, therefore, should one approach the task of talking with a pupil about those forms of behaviour or experiences of events which deviate from institutional or social norms and expectations? How can it be certain that in opting for a counselling position one is acting in a way which is truly client-centred, nonjudgemental, accepting? In practical terms this divergence often gives rise to situations in which the adoption of a counselling stance is perceived as a threat to school discipline, to the authority of senior pastoral-care staff, or to the academic aims of the school. In a similar manner, neutral, nonjudgemental acceptance may appear as weakness, and the observance of confidentiality as the withholding of information of a possibly subversive or potentially damaging kind. Such perceptions are, if anything, encouraged by the re-emergence of competitive élitist attitudes, simplistic beliefs in the value of 'traditional' methods of teaching, and tough-minded, no-nonsense approaches to the problems and needs of young people.

Identity

Role diffusion

In the 1960s counselling was clearly differentiated from teaching. In the intervening years this distinction has been gradually eroded so that the term 'counsellor' no longer needs 'to be restricted to those who see their main role as counselling' (Bolger 1982: 14). On the whole, as indicated earlier in this chapter, the developments which have brought this change about have been healthy ones. They have, also, helped ameliorate the antagonism with which counselling was viewed in British schools some time ago. Difficulties, however, remain.

Conflicting philosophies and concepts

Though counselling as a concept and as an activity is better understood and accepted, the role difficulties associated with its practice in a school context can hardly be said to have diminished.

Commitment to the principle of self-direction and to the pre-eminent importance of interpersonal relationships may easily come into conflict with the organizational emphasis and controlling element in education. Conceptual confusion between teaching and counselling may exacerbate identity problems for counsellor-teachers, who occupy a 'teacher' role in the classroom and elsewhere but also need to switch between teacher–pupil and counsellor–client types of relationship. Increasing demands for achievement, evaluation and accountability and pressures on teachers for action rather than insight and for instruction rather than self-directed learning, also represent potential areas of friction and uncertainty for those committed to a counselling approach. In addition, as institutions go, the school is a most complex setting, and a large number of factors such as age, parental involvement, religion, and ethnic origin can be associated with ambivalent if not negative attitudes towards, for example, self-exploration and self-empowerment.

There are differences of emphasis, also, within counselling itself. Some important differentiations, of relevance to points made earlier in this chapter, might be summarized by distinguishing between experiential and skills-based approaches. Models of the latter kind, though sometimes presented as eclectic systems, rely heavily on principles derived from the experimental analysis of individual and social behaviour. Their emphasis on logical and systematic routines which make complex processes seem easy to understand and handle, and on performance-based criteria which are clearly describable and measurable, make them attractive in today's educational climate. They have been widely applied in a variety of forms in many kinds of human training and treatment situations as well as counselling (Hollin and Trower 1986), and have been particularly popular in careers education and counselling where many excellent skills-training programmes suitable for use in schools have been produced by, for example, the National Institute for Careers Education and Counselling (NICEC), the Counselling and Careers Development Unit (CCDU), or the Careers Research and Advisory Centre (CRAC).

Models, however, which rely heavily on behavioural analysis and structure are not so readily applicable in human situations of an irrational or contradictory kind, situations which, like those described earlier in this chapter, do not fit neatly into predetermined behaviours or categories. Feelings, intentions, and conflict are very much part of everyday life in schools, and those actively engaged in this area of work draw heavily on humanistic and psychodynamic sources. Within all three of these broad traditions, however, many derivative counselling practice theories have been developed. Those working as counsellors in schools today, therefore, have to deal with not only a vast and ever-expanding range of concepts and strategies but with contradictory philosophies and methods. Such apparent contradictions and competing sources can give rise to major issues of identity at both a theoretical and applied level, including that of training. In daily practice therefore, counsellors are required to cope with a diverse and divided knowledge-base at the same time as they seek to establish a secure self-image and a reputation for common sense and consistency.

Status and influence

Following on from changes in school practice referred to earlier in this chapter, the processes of listening, patiently talking things through, and paying attention to personal meanings as well as overt behaviour are in general better understood than they were even ten years ago. One of the results is that counselling, in which such skills and attitudes are of primary importance, is more widely recognized and accepted. Significantly, this is also reflected at government level, for example in the Children Act 1989, where counselling is specifically acknowledged and local education authorities required to make provision for counselling as well as advice and guidance. Particularly as a result of the growth and consolidation which have taken place in the last decade (Best *et al*. 1995: 288), pastoral care in practice now provides a more congenial milieu for counselling values and aims. The contribution from counselling tends to be accepted as complementing pastoral-care systems, and special areas of intervention – such as child protection, separation and loss, drug usage – are more readily seen as requiring skilled counselling help.

Current and future developments

In the early 1980s, there were signs that counselling was becoming more acceptable among school heads and staffs (Best *et al*. 1981; Rees 1982, 1983). This process has been advanced very considerably in the last decade, since counselling achieved respectability in the world outside the school and opportunities opened up for teachers to make use of counselling skills in their own work. Counselling is now recognized at all levels in education as a legitimate and relevant activity.

Need for understanding

School counselling does not take place in a vacuum. School staffs need to know something of the nature of the processes and skills involved in counselling and of how different levels of knowledge and skills may be required according to the nature and demands of the helping task at any particular time. Hamblin's analysis of different levels – immediate, intermediate, intensive – helps underline the complexities of such work (Hamblin 1993). While the diffusion of counselling skills has brought many benefits, it can also mask differences in levels of knowledge and competence which may make important differences to the quality and integrity of the help being offered. The use of counselling skills in some contexts may resemble a counselling interview but have very different parameters.

Discipline and confidentiality are two dimensions in particular which may be seen and handled very differently according to the level of competence in counselling of the person undertaking the task. Members of staff involved in counselling, therefore, whether conducting interviews or making use of counselling skills in the course of other duties, must be able to notice when counselling is or is not appropriate and to distinguish between counselling work at different levels. Such an understanding faces workers in pastoral care with 'the possibility that there may be special skills and experience that can help children directly but which require a level of work which cannot be expected as part of the general professional training of the teacher' (Nicol 1987: 660). Teachers without extra training beyond the level of basic skills are less likely to move beyond instinctive reaction to informed response. It is also true that an understanding of the influence and attitude of the pupil's teacher on the part of the specially trained person may make a difference to the success of such help.

It should be clear from this brief discussion that both training and understanding are essential, if such work is to be undertaken successfully.

Training and resources

Considerable progress has been made in the last ten years in filling the major gaps in the skills possessed by pastoral-care workers referred to by Lang and Marland in the mid-1980s (Lang and Marland 1985). No parallel focus for counselling has yet emerged at secondary or primary level, and training continues to be dealt with on an *ad hoc* basis. In the world outside the school, on the other hand, as a result of developments in BAC and in response to increasing demand for courses of training, there are now many more opportunities available for the study of counselling, ranging from short skills-based courses to full-length diploma or degree courses of the kind mentioned earlier. Teachers, however, represent a very small percentage of the students on such courses, and recent estimates suggest that less than 1.5 per cent of teachers now have a qualification of any kind in counselling (HMI 1992).

At the same time, increasing incidence of social and emotional problems among children, increasing pressures on social services and child guidance, and legislative changes – the Children Act in particular – are obliging local authorities and schools to provide counselling. Who will do this work and what their training will be are important questions.

Current position

The experiences of members of the BAC division concerned with primary and secondary education currently employed in school counselling (see for example their newsletter, *Counselling in Education*) suggest that a new trend may be apparent in local *ad hoc* solutions to these obligations.

Counsellors may be peripatetic; they may be located inside or outside the school (mainly secondary, but now occasionally primary); they may be working with the school but employed by the National Health Service; the majority will be part-time, and on a lower pay scale than that of qualified teachers; many will be graduates, and many will have trained or worked as teachers; and, finally, they will be referred to as 'school counsellors'.

Assuming that this is the likely pattern for the immediate future, it would appear that what has *de facto* been abandoned in education is the concept of the qualified-teacher-with-substantial-training-in-counselling, not that of the school-counsellor. The basic problems remain, however, of what levels of knowledge, skills and experience are necessary and of how maximum use can be made of these in meeting the needs of children and young persons during the course of their education.

While the context has changed, some of the issues raised by contemporary counsellors on the current and future role of counselling in schools (McLaughlin 1995; CIE Newsletters 1992 on) are very similar to those addressed on the early training courses of the 1960s and 1970s. A renewed confidence, however, and a determination to make it work seem much in evidence (for example, Klinefelter 1995).

The future

With hindsight, the creation of the school counsellor in Britain in the mid-1960s might be seen as an attempt to combine the counsellor (specialist) with the teacher (generalist). In recent years, a more searching analysis of welfare needs and the care of children in school (Best 1989; Best *et al.* 1995) and a widespread familiarization with the basic skills of counselling have increased the effectiveness of pastoral care. While the British tradition of the teacher as the key resource 'generalist' (Lang 1995) has been maintained in meeting those needs of children identified under the headings of development and prevention, it would now appear to have been conceded in practice that recourse to non-teaching 'specialists' in counselling is essential if needs under the heading of 'responsive' (and some of those under 'preventive') are to receive suitable attention. What is not clear at present is how such matters as location, funding, terms of employment, responsibilities, accountability, and level of training of this newly developing school-counsellor will be determined.

Finally, now more than ever there is an urgent need to 'explore in a realistic fashion the complexities of counselling in schools' (McLaughlin 1995: 63). The acknowledgement of counselling in public life and its recognition as a valid and important area of research and training by universities and other institutions with research interests (the British Psychological Society, in particular) suggest that the resources are now available for a comprehensive analysis of practice and possibilities in this important area of education. Such an undertaking could be an invaluable aid to the enterprise of counselling in education as it enters the twenty-first century.

References

Argyle, M. (1981) *Social Skills and Work*, London: Methuen.
BAC (1990) 2nd edn *The Recognition of Counselling Courses*, Rugby: BAC.
——(1996) *Code of Ethics and Practice for Counsellors*, Rugby: BAC.
Best, R. (1989) 'Pastoral care: some reflections and a restatement', *Pastoral Care in Education* 7(4): 7–14.
Best, R., Jarvis, C., and Ribbins, P. (1977) 'Pastoral care: concept and process', *British Journal of Educational Studies* 25(2): 124–35.
——(1980) *Perspectives on Pastoral Care*, London: Heinemann.
Best, R., Jarvis, C., Oddy, D., and Ribbins, P. (1981) 'Teacher attitudes to the school counsellor: a reappraisal', *British Journal of Guidance and Counselling* 9(2): 159–71.
Best, R., Ribbins, P., Jarvis, C., with Oddy, D. (1983) *Education and Care*, London: Heinemann.
Best, R., Lang, P., Lodge, C., and Watkins, C. (eds) (1995) *Pastoral Care and Social-Personal Education*, London: Cassell.
Bolger, A. W. (ed.) (1982) *Counselling in Britain*, London: Batsford Academic and Educational Ltd.
Button, L. (1975) *Developmental Group Work with Adolescents*, London: Hodder & Stoughton.
Carkhuff, R. R. (1969) *Helping and Human Relations*, Vols. 1 and 2, New York: Holt, Rhinehart and Wilson.
David, K. and Charlton, A. (1988) *The Caring Role of the Primary School*, London: Macmillan.
Daws, P. (1976) *Early Days*, Cambridge: Hobsons Press.
Egan, G. (1986) *The Skilled Helper*, Monterey: Brooks/Cole.
Follet, J. (1986) 'The concept of pastoral care: a genealogical analysis', *Pastoral Care* 4(1): 3–11.
Galloway, D. (1981) *Teaching and Counselling Pastoral Care in Primary and Secondary Schools*, London: Longman.
Griffiths, P. (1995) 'Guidance and Tutoring' in Best *et al.* (eds) *Pastoral Care and Social-Personal Education*, London: Cassell.
Hamblin, D. H. (1993) *The Teacher and Counselling*, 2nd edn, Oxford: Simon and Schuster.
Her Majesty's Inspectorate (HMI) (1992) *Survey of Guidance 13–19 in Schools and Sixth Form Colleges*, Stanimore: DES.
Hollin, C. R. and Trower, P. (1986) *Handbook of Social Skills Training*, Vol. 1, Oxford: Pergamon.
Hughes, P. M. (1971) *Guidance and Counselling in Schools*, Oxford: Pergamon.

James, J. (1983) 'School counselling in Devon 1983', *Counselling in Education Newsletter* August: 24.

Klinefelter, P. (1995) 'A School Counselling Service', *Counselling, Journal of the British Association for Counselling*, Vol. 5, No. 3, August.

Lang, P. (1995) 'International Perspectives in Pastoral Care' in Best *et al.* (eds) *Pastoral Care and Social-Personal Education*, London: Cassell.

Lang, P. and Marland, M. (1985) *New Directions in Pastoral Care*, Oxford: Blackwell.

McLaughlin, C. (1995) 'Counselling in Schools: its place and purpose' in Best *et al.* (eds) *Pastoral Care and Social-Personal Education*, London: Cassell.

Murgatroyd, S. J. (1983) 'Counselling at a time of change and development', *Journal of the Education Section of the British Psychological Society* 7(2): 5–9.

Nelson Jones, R. (1986) 'Relationship Skills training in school: some fieldwork observations', *British Journal of Guidance and Counselling* 14(3): 292–305.

Nicol, A. R. (1987) 'Psychotherapy and the school: an update', *Journal of Child Psychology and Psychiatry* 28(5): 657–65.

Rees, B. (1982) 'Teachers' attitudes to guidance and counselling', *The Counsellor* 3(5): 2–12.

——(1983) 'Heads' attitudes to school counsellors and careers teachers', *The Counsellor* 3(7): 13–23.

Sisterson, D. (1983) 'Counselling in the primary school', *Journal of the Education Section of the British Psychological Society* 7(2): 10–15.

Chapter twelve

Counselling in higher education

Elsa Bell

Introduction

The context in which student counselling takes place is both exciting and, at times, alarming. It is exciting because students of all ages have consciously chosen a journey of discovery. They see education as a way towards personal as well as professional development and their hope is that there will be evidence of change, in themselves and their circumstances, when they reach the point in their journey when the course has finished. This underpinning desire for change can be a powerful tool in counselling work.

The potential for alarm is rooted in the changing nature of the student population, with a noted increase in the level of disturbance (ASC 1995), and the rapid move towards expansion and structural change within the organization of higher education. These two matters may be linked. For some the rate of change, even when change is desired, can be a source of distress and alarm.

History and development

Student counselling in Britain began in the 1950s with individuals who had seen the need for dedicated services through their work as teachers, administrators, doctors and psychotherapists within universities (Bell 1996). By the mid-1960s a small number of formally established services were in evidence and with the advent of the Association for Student Counselling (ASC) in 1970 a framework for this new profession began to emerge. This development was within the context of political and economic change where there was investment in new universities and polytechnics and where there was a commitment in both schools and universities to a more student-centred approach to learning. Traditional universities had always offered intensive tutorial support and were justifiably proud of the quality of the educational experience their students enjoyed. The newer universities, polytechnics, and colleges of higher education were not structured to provide this explicitly personalized approach, but they were convinced of the value of, in the fashionable phrase of the day, 'education of the whole person'. This belief led to the setting up of personal tutoring systems and student services departments within which formal counselling services were established.

The next two decades saw much painstaking work by individual counsellers and by ASC to establish the identity and value of counselling as an integral part of higher education. ASC developed its accreditation scheme in order to ensure that its members were appropriately trained and experienced and worked to make sure that this standard would be accepted. In pioneering this work on counsellor accreditation ASC laid the foundations for the future of counselling as a whole, as well as ensuring that its own counsellors gained credibility within higher education communities. Parallel to the accreditation scheme ASC developed a document entitled *Advisory Service to Institutions* (undated). In this the framework for counselling was set out. ASC stressed that counsellors should be paid a salary equivalent to jobs of similar responsibility in the institution (indeed many of the posts created in the polytechnic sector were at a senior or principal lecturer level); that external supervision was essential; that counsellors needed time for administration and to think about their work with students, and that the number of client-contact hours should reflect this; that counsellors had a developmental and preventative role within the institution as well as one of offering individual counselling. A later document, *A Guide to Recognizing Best Practice in Counselling* (Bell *et al.* undated), was written especially for managers in education who were not themselves counsellors. It described what might be expected in terms of accountability from a good counselling service, the questions that could legitimately be asked of counsellors in order to assess the quality of their work, and suggested a possible tool for evaluation. These initiatives, alongside the development of other ASC committees on subjects such as research, showed that student counsellors accepted the need to monitor their work and that it was available for scrutiny.

The need to define and evaluate counselling became even more apparent in the early 1990s. Ratigan (1989), in the first edition of the *Handbook of Counselling*, drew attention to the increased call for value for money in education, and, as he suggested, counsellors found they could not escape the need to provide performance indicators for their work. This preoccupation with cost-effectiveness and outcomes was anathema to many counsellors and yet they found that, in order for services to survive, a way of describing, monitoring and evaluating their work had to be found. The constant struggle was to find a language that would be congruent with counselling values, and yet would be accessible and acceptable to managers and accountants. At the same time as polytechnics were re-named universities, government policy encouraged an expansion in student numbers (but without extra resources).

Thus restructuring, expansion and a change in the definition of university education added to the pressure for institutions to be competitive 'in the market-place'. Within this ethos, that education is a business, each department in the institution, including counselling services, was expected to compete for resources and to make an unequivocal case for their existence.

Despite these changing, and at times threatening, circumstances in higher education, in 1996 all universities, apart from one, had a counselling service. The level of provision was varied and failed to reach the recommendation of the National Association of Teachers in Further and Higher Education (1979) that there should be one counsellor for every seven hundred students. Nor has it even reached the ASC (undated) recommended ratio of 1 : 2,500. Nevertheless, there were clear indications that most universities recognized the value of having a counselling service within their repertoire of pastoral support.

Principles

From its inception ASC stated that student counsellors have a tripartite responsibility: to the student; to the institution; and to themselves.

Responsibility to the student

The first question to be answered is 'who and what is a student?' Until not very long ago it could be safely assumed that most students in higher education were between the ages of 18 and 21; that they had come to university straight from school; that they were high academic achievers and that they were in full-time education. Today, in some universities, over a third of students are over 25 at the start of their undergraduate studies. Many are involved in part-time courses and a wider access policy has meant that some students have to be taught the skills of academic study at the same time as they are expected to engage with a course. Universities have been happy, in the main, to recruit students from non-traditional routes and have welcomed the process of opening up higher education to more than a privileged élite. This means that student counsellors deal with students from a broad spectrum of society. If counsellors wish to act in a responsible way towards these students, they need a framework that allows an understanding of, and an ability to work with, a wide variety of issues.

A thorough knowledge of adolescent development underpins work with students. The struggle for autonomy and the drive to find a separate and defined place in the world is common to all students, whether they are eighteen or forty-eight. In fact for mature students who are thrown back into dependency needs by the process of being a student, this re-awakening of adolescent strivings can be a shock, and deeply disturbing. This is the core of student counselling work. And yet counsellors in higher education find themselves also dealing with, for example, marital difficulties, bereavement, unemployment or anxieties about future careers, family breakdown and illness, substance abuse, eating disorders, sexual and relationship difficulties, cultural shock. As well as these specific problems, identifiable in any population of around 15,000 people, students bring to counselling more diffuse and less accessible issues that have their roots in each student's individual psychological history. Thus student counsellors need a thorough training that allows them to understand the internal world of the student, considerable experience and skill to use this understanding in a way that is appropriate to the student's experience, and a theoretical framework that is not limited to problem solving in the external world.

The two major theories that predominate in student counselling are psychodynamic, based on the work of Freud, Klein and Winnicott (Noonan 1983) and person-centred therapy (Rogers 1969). There are few student counsellors who are trained in the cognitive or behavioural mode but these theories have a considerable influence in work on study skills, examination anxiety and stress management. The Association for Student Counselling in the first edition of its *Guide to Training Courses* (undated), which set out the essential and desirable features of a training for student counselling, stressed the necessity of an in-depth knowledge of one theoretical model and a familiarity with others. This recognized the fact that counsellors in this setting need a thorough framework on which to base their thinking about, and work with, students, but that they also need a flexibility that allows them to match their response to student need. This comes as much from the fact that there are few alternative services to which students can be referred, as from a deeply held conviction that counsellors should, *per se*, be proficient in a variety of modalities.

Whatever the theory on which student counsellors base their work there is a common requirement that the theory is adapted to the particular setting. Some of the dilemmas in this requirement will be considered further in the section on Issues. However, in relation to their responsibility to the student, counsellors have to use their preferred theoretical model to understand what it means to be a student. Understanding the impact of the setting is common to all counselling activity but in student counselling it is particularly focused. This setting makes powerful demands. There is the academic year with which to contend; beginnings and endings are always around. Examinations and continual assessment have a particular significance both in reality and within the internal world of students. There are always deadlines to be met and failure to do so can mean exclusion from a course and from the process of being a student. The constructs within which a student identity is defined can have both positive and negative impact on the development of the student's sense of self. The ambiguity of semi-dependence or independence can be confusing; at one moment the student is expected to be fully adult, engaging in self-directed learning and sophisticated time and resource management; at another, he or she is expected to be dependent on the expert teacher – to take in, to digest, to feed on the knowledge of the teacher/parent. All of these issues have an impact on the student and on the therapeutic experience in the counselling room.

Many practitioners who come into student counselling from other settings find the impact of the academic year, and the external tasks that each student must complete, an intrusion on their concept of therapeutic work. The constant breaks, the need to change appointments because tutorials have been re-arranged, the way students choose to pace their counselling so that they either finish before examinations or make sure that they are not dealing with too much disturbing material at that time, can be seen by the inexperienced student counsellor as an avoidance or a defence. The more experienced counsellor recognizes that all these external issues have a real meaning and that this must be valued. For some students, achieving academic goals, with its significance of developmental progress, can be as therapeutic as any encounter inside the counselling room. However, experienced student counsellors know, also, that the symbolic nature of these events (i.e. what the external event might represent in the student's internal world and psychological development) can be used therapeutically as each student attempts to understand what is his or her own specific experience of being a student. For example, a student who has examination anxiety may be facing not only the reality of the testing time ahead, but may also discover through counselling that the examinations represent unresolved rivalrous conflicts that have been out of his or her awareness. They have been an unconscious, but powerful, influence.

Most work with students is carried out in one-to-one, weekly sessions lasting fifty minutes, with the average number of sessions being between four and five. This means that the work is necessarily brief, but it does not mean that it is simple or easy. The complicated issues surrounding brief counselling will be looked at later in the chapter, but here it is important to note that for many, particularly those students who would be termed as within the late adolescent developmental stage, short-term work is appropriate. The psychological drive at this time is towards independence and autonomy and it is rare that a long-term therapeutic relationship is required, or is desirable. The process of long-term work allows a regression to an earlier developmental stage that for some may be necessary, but for most young people is counter-productive and, indeed, may be damaging. However, it does not come as a surprise that mature and graduate students are generally over-represented in the statistics of those requiring longer-term counselling.

As well as individual counselling most counselling services in higher education offer students some form of groupwork. This can be in the form of long-term therapeutic groups that are often geared towards graduate and mature students who tend to be resident in the area during vacation periods. This continuity in residence allows the group to function with few breaks and within the tradition of group therapy. A more radical use of group theory is in the short-term therapeutic groups offered to undergraduates. These tend to be of one or two terms' duration. Groups with a specific focus, and often with a more cognitive-behavioural flavour, are frequently offered. Examples of these are stress management, social skills training, dealing with study skills and/or examination anxiety, and assertiveness skills.

Another important area is the responsibility that counselling services feel towards students who take on a helping role in the organization. For some students this is within a clearly defined role such as welfare officers in the student union or as members of Nightline, the student telephone befriending service. Others find themselves helping students in less formal ways, as supportive colleagues. We know that students will naturally turn to their peers before they resort to help from tutors or a counselling service and that because of this a number of students attempt to help friends and colleagues with serious difficulties. Those who run training courses in basic helping skills for these students are always impressed by the quality of concern and, indeed, the sophisticated understanding that they demonstrate. But these students also need to learn when and how to draw boundaries, when to say 'no'. Although the groups offered to address these needs are training groups, they often have a therapeutic by-product as students are encouraged to examine their motivation and the consequences of taking on a helping role.

The work with this last group of students shifts the counsellor from the traditional work with individual students who present themselves to counselling services, towards his or her role in relation to the institution.

Responsibility to the institution

Counsellors who work in an organizational setting have to bear in mind their responsibility to the employing institution. In higher education this is less clearly defined than in some other settings where there is, for example, a statutory responsibility, and this can lead to ambiguity in the relationship.

Counsellors feel comfortable with the familiar role of having a responsibility to the client, but many are less at ease with the notion of responsibility to an institution. Acknowledging this responsibility demands that counsellors have an understanding of the organization's ethos and that they are prepared to work within it, and the various parts of the structure that characterize the ethos in practice. In the mid-1990s this has been a problem for some counsellors who see education moving away from a reflective and discursive mode of learning to one that is more goal and vocation oriented. There seems much less time to 'be' and to explore. You either have 'it', or you don't. With this emphasis on what seems simply survival, some counsellors have felt themselves to be out of tune with the organizations within which they work, and far from feeling a sense of responsibility to it have focused on what they feel to be a responsibility to remind the institution of individual student need. Whilst this latter role is an important function for counselling services it can also be a retreat and a defence against dealing with the complicated and dynamic force that is the organization within which they work. Smith (1996) has outlined the complexities and tensions for counsellors who try to work with integrity within changing institutions.

Most importantly counsellors need to ask themselves, and the institution, 'What does the counselling service represent in this particular organization?' The various answers produced by this question inevitably demonstrate both a conscious and an unconscious response to the presence of a counselling service. Noonan (1983) comments that counselling services can be vehicles for powerful organizational projections. At one moment they can be idealized and the next denigrated. They may be expected to contain all the disturbed people and the disturbing elements of the organization, and they are expected to do this silently. Then the problematic aspects of institutional life are out of sight and out of mind. If this is so, then for both the organization and the counsellor to remain healthy, it is the counsellor's responsibility to hand back these projections in a sensitive and appropriate way.

Some of the ways that student counsellors do this is to produce carefully written and widely distributed annual reports. This describes the reality of the work and details what a service can and cannot do. Services also run workshops and seminars for teaching and administrative staff, thus demystifying counselling whilst at the same time disseminating skills to people who have daily responsibility for students. Additionally, counsellors act as consultants to, for example, tutors who are in the process of helping distressed students. Not all students need to be referred for counselling but frequently tutors who feel inexperienced are grateful for the support a counselling service gives that allows them to continue helping the student with increased confidence. Sometimes a counselling service, in conjunction with medical services, can help a tutor to understand that a student would be helped most by being allowed to leave, or take time off, with dignity. Conversely they can help a department cope with students who are disturbed, or who are disturbing, but for whom there is no clear diagnosis of mental illness. At this time, when departments often feel helpless and powerless, clear information about what can be done, and what might be the signs of deterioration in the student, can help the department to contain its anxiety and thus the student. These are all ways in which a counselling service can contribute obviously and appropriately to the life of the institution.

More complicated is the issue of how counsellors can alert institutions to the way in which the structure of the organization and courses exacerbate student difficulty, or more optimistically, how these structures can help students to achieve their own and the organization's aims. Most academic communities have complicated and, at times, archaic structures for course and faculty review, and it is rare that those who have responsibility for change would think of including a counsellor or a counselling perspective in their deliberations. This is where student counsellors need a sophisticated understanding of organizational politics. They need to understand how to get their view heard, even if they are not able to make their comments in person. Who are the influential people and how can they be lobbied? Who will be prepared to lobby on behalf of a counselling service perspective and not feel threatened by the unconscious dynamics that will, without doubt, be engendered? What, and how much, will the committee be able to hear before the anxiety level rises to a point where nothing can be heard at all?

Despite all these, and many more, difficulties that make up institutional life student counsellors do find ways of bringing their perspective to the content of courses, the development of programmes to help students make transition to higher education, and to the process of learning itself. This is perhaps the most complicated and perplexing part of a student counsellor's role, and whilst not unique to student counselling, it is certainly one of the distinguishing features of working in higher education.

Responsibility to the counsellor

Hope (1985) in the first study on burnout and stress in student counsellors found that of the 185 counsellors in the sample, 14 per cent felt overworked all the time and a further 25 per cent felt overworked often. Ross (1995) examines the nature of stress in the role of directing a university counselling service and notes particularly the potential for conflict within the various functions of the role. The pressure of high demand on services, the immediacy of many of the problems presented, the prevalence of short-term work and therefore the high turnover of clients combined with the demands of the institution mean that student counsellors have to take great care that they do not lose themselves, and their own needs, as they respond daily to the needs of others.

Although personal therapy is not a prerequisite in the accreditation process of ASC, applicants are expected to show that they have attended to both their personal and professional development in a regular and thoughtful way. This is seen as one of the most important vehicles for addressing the inherent stresses of the job, as well as a way of making sure that counsellors are open to new ideas. The formal discussions of clinical work with colleagues and regular staff meetings where the process of working in a service is examined are additional ways of making the work more manageable. The emphasis on external clinical consultancy (supervision), away from the immediate demands of the service, gives counsellors an opportunity to be more reflective about the students they see and the impact of the counselling process on themselves. The formal structure of ASC, with its very real demonstration of peer support alongside its many pioneering activities, allows counsellors to develop a sense of professional identity which is of particular importance to those who feel that their identity and purpose is questioned by the employing institution. Perhaps just as importantly, the informal contacts developed through the student counselling network often provide a trusted voice at the end of a telephone at moments of anxiety or pressure.

All counsellors must use themselves in the process of counselling if the therapeutic relationship is to remain alive and relevant and this calls for great emotional energy and resilience. They must be able to tune into their feelings of, for example, frustration, anger or sorrow and then work to differentiate what might be their own feelings, founded in significant personal development, from those felt on behalf of the client who is conveying them in a powerful and dynamic way in an attempt to be understood. In student counselling there is the additional dimension that all counsellors, at some time, will have been students. Whilst this can be a valuable aid to understanding it can also be potentially dangerous if counsellors become over-identified with the students and their needs. In many ways student counsellors face the same dilemmas as mature students. The process of being in an educational institution and in the presence of a predominantly adolescent population can throw them back into earlier developmental struggles. Thus every client seen and every narrative heard has the possibility of placing the counsellor, psychologically speaking, in the position of being a perpetual student. This is why student counsellors have a specific responsibility to themselves (and thus to their students) to be in touch with both their past and present experience of being in an educational setting.

One particular example of the power of the educational setting serves as an illustration of the tensions that all counsellors share as they attempt to be in touch with students' and their own subjective experience of student life. Higher education, despite the move towards more open access, is still highly selective and constantly competitive. This is what students always bring to counselling alongside the various specific and personal difficulties that have prompted them to seek help, and this theme is paralleled every time counsellors discuss their work with other colleagues. Indeed, if case discussions in staff meetings do not have some degree of competition and rivalry within them, then an essential element of the impact of the organization on the student's internal world has been missed. A 'here-and-now' demonstration of the theme, perceivable in counsellors' responses to each other, allows the student to be more fully understood. However it is singularly unhelpful if counsellors merely act out their students' experience of needing to be constantly competitive since this is destructive to the individual counsellor and to the team as a whole. Responsibility to the student requires that competition is demonstrated. Responsibility to the counsellor requires that a high degree of objectivity is active whilst the subjective is experienced. Without this capacity to monitor and be responsible for oneself in the dynamic process, counsellors can become overly rivalrous, and thus distressed and damaged. Like their students they can feel that they have failed in an important examination of their work.

Issues

The preceding paragraphs indicate how underpinning principles are inextricably tied to specific practice issues and that issues are influenced by the context. So whilst counsellors, in general, must take responsibility for monitoring themselves in the counselling process, they must be aware of the specific contextual issues that influence them and their work. Similarly, the issues identified in this section are shared with many counsellors, but the context of counselling in higher education shapes the response.

Confidentiality

All institutions of education have sophisticated structures for monitoring students' work and progress. A central tenet is that this information is shared, between academic colleagues and with the students themselves. The existence of a counselling service that holds firmly to the principle of confidentiality can be both a relief and a threat. Students can be relieved that there is a private place away from the assessment process where they can explore their difficulties; academics can be relieved that they do not have to engage with deeply personal aspects of their students' lives. The threat is that there appears to be a place within the organization where the worst secrets of individuals, and of the organization itself, are stored. The challenge to student counsellors is to hold to the fundamental need for confidential counselling whilst at the same time making the work of counselling accessible and known.

Most student counsellors recognize that there is a need to liaise with tutors and others in the institution who have responsibility for the daily care of students. This is done with students' permission and can be beneficial to the student who recognizes the ethos of shared care in the process, to the tutor who is genuinely trying to be helpful, and to the counselling service as it attempts to dispel fantasies and encourage a realistic understanding of its work. However, Warburton (1995) demonstrates that this principle is not universally accepted. She argues that any deviation from the firm boundaries of a traditional therapeutic frame has a seriously damaging effect on the process and that students are ill-served if the counsellor is seduced into diluting the strict boundaries of therapeutic work. The notion of a fixed, and therefore safe, therapeutic space is well documented in the literature (Milner 1977; Langs 1982; Siegelman 1990), but in education it may be important to ask what actually constitutes the therapeutic space. It is clear that the purpose of education is not primarily therapeutic but it is also clear that the process of education has a deeply symbolic meaning for those who engage with it. Thus a student can have an unconscious relationship with the institution, its members (particularly with tutors), and even with the subject studied. For example, a very clever student was unable to write essays. He had grown up in a home with a father who may well have been psychotic and he was consciously aware of the many effects this had had on his own development. The counsellor working with him on his difficulties with essay writing began to wonder whether some of the student's fear of his father was being unconsciously transferred into the relationship with his tutor – it seemed that the tutor was felt to make unreasonable demands. However it became clear that it was not the tutor, but the subject, that had taken on the tyrannical overtones of the psychotic father. The student unconsciously perceived the subject as a source of persecution. It would never go away, and it could never be fully understood.

It can be argued, therefore, that the therapeutic space is the entire process of being a student. If this is understood by the counsellor then any communication, whether inside or outside the counselling room, can be part of the therapeutic process. Put simply, if a tutor needs information (and in reality this is sometimes essential), the process of deciding within the safety of the counselling room who conveys that information, what is contained within it, and the consequences of it being conveyed can all provide powerful therapeutic material. This radical notion of the boundaries of the therapeutic relationship with its respect for confidentiality within the counselling room, but with a recognition that there are others who may be involved in therapeutic change, has some of its basis in the more systemic approaches to therapy. However the particular context brings specific issues that have to be faced and Warburton rightly challenges those who favour the more radical approach to examine, carefully, the ethical consequences of such a stance.

The greatest challenge to confidentiality in student counselling comes not from the issue outlined above, where there is time to think through the consequences of a particular model of confidentiality, but from the very fact that counsellors are part of everyday, institutional life. If they are acting responsibly towards the institution they will meet academic colleagues and students at committee meetings, in corridors, and in informal conversations in senior common rooms and student bars. It is well known that it is in these informal settings that the 'maintenance' of the organization goes on – in the shared confidences, the gossip, the relaxation of formal roles. Here it is not unusual for someone to say in the middle of a crowded room, 'Oh, by the way, I sent student X to make an appointment with you yesterday. Did he turn up?' Then the counsellor has to find a way of gently reminding the inquirer of the boundaries of the counselling relationship, without destroying the friendly atmosphere of the moment, which may have taken some months to develop.

This casual comment also demonstrates another frequent problem in the area of confidentiality. The tutor who has taken the time to refer a student to the counsellor may be more sensitive than the previous inquirer in that he or she does not make a casual inquiry, but will nevertheless contact the counsellor because there is a strongly held belief that the tutor has a right to know what is happening to the student. Or a telephone call will come from an anxious parent who wants to know how best to help a son or daughter who is distressed. It is rare that a week passes without a seemingly benevolent request for information challenging the basis of a confidential counselling service. It is for this reason that counsellors and their services need a clear policy, so that counsellors and receptionists are not caught offguard, and tempted to cross the boundaries which results in destroying the therapeutic space, however that is defined.

Assumptions about the nature of counselling

One of the reasons for the inappropriate inquiry is that often those who make them do not understand the nature of counselling. This is partly because there are many variations of the counselling process that the public hears about through the press and media, and relatively few have experienced the intensity of a helpful counselling relationship. It is also because it is more comfortable for members of an institution to deny the serious nature of counselling in order for them to believe that there are few serious problems to be dealt with. When counsellors through legitimate routes describe the nature of their work, academic colleagues are often surprised, even shocked, at the weight of the problems presented and the complexities of the counselling relationship.

This also highlights the issue that institutions and counsellors do not always share the same assumptions about the purpose of a counselling service. The previous paragraphs describe the therapeutic nature of counselling as practised by most student counsellors. And yet the institution probably believes that most students arrive with circumscribed problems for which advice can be given and a resolution found. This belief may also illustrate the assumption that a university counselling service should not be providing 'therapy' but should focus its work on helping students to study effectively and pass examinations. Student counsellors have an important role in helping their colleagues understand what must go on in counselling if students are to be helped to function well, and indeed study effectively and pass examinations. This is important, not just for individual students, but for the future of student counselling as whole, an aspect that will be explored further in the section on Future Developments.

Short-term vs. long-term counselling

The heading of this section gives some indication of the unnecessarily polarized argument that has sometimes taken place in student counselling in the 1990s. The debate is influenced by increased demand for counselling, with no commensurate increase in resources, and by the assumptions about the nature of counselling outlined in the previous paragraphs. It is unfortunate that for many, 'therapeutic' has been equated with 'long-term', since this plays into counsellors sense that they are doing 'real' counselling only when they have sufficient longer-term cases. For administrators, the equation fuels fears that they are funding therapy for students who are ill, and who should more properly be referred to health services.

In reality long-term work in student counselling is, by comparison with other counselling and psychotherapy settings, quite short. ASC in its annual survey of student counselling uses the figure of sixteen or more sessions as an indicator of longer-term work but, in contrast, in British psychotherapy literature (Malan 1982) around thirty sessions is considered to be brief work. Whatever the definition used, it is clear from ASC statistics that a small percentage of students, nationally, is engaged in work of more than sixteen sessions, and anecdotal evidence suggests that it has been vital that this extended work has been offered.

At the other end of the spectrum a number of students use a few sessions to focus on a particular problem and to make decisions. Those who require, or have available to them, between four and, for example, twelve sessions present an interesting challenge to student counsellors in terms of the application of their theory and training. In an earlier paragraph it was stated that there is a sense that short-term work is appropriate to the developmental needs of the student population and yet those who are engaged in this work know how profound this short-term work can be. Coren (1996) and Thorne (1994), from a psychodynamic and person-centred perspective respectively, each demonstrate the deep and long-held difficulties that can be addressed in short-term work with students. Rather than continuing to polarize the debate, that one method is better than another, it would seem much more profitable for student counsellors to acknowledge that longer-term and short-term work are different, but that each has its appropriate place.

The dilemma for student counsellors in facing this debate is not just in giving value to both short- and long-term counselling, but in recognizing that few counsellors have been trained to work therapeutically in a brief, or time-limited way. This has practical implications, but also presents ethical issues. All who subscribe to BAC's *Code of Ethics and Practice for Counsellors* agree not to work outside their competence. The demand for short-term work means that student counsellors will, in turn, need to demand training in order to respond in an ethical way to both their clients and their institutions.

Future developments

In early 1996 the goverment decided to set up a review of higher education. The cynical view is that this review was introduced in order to avoid the necessity for immediate decisions about funding at a time when a general election was imminent. Whatever the reason, the result of the review will have major implications for the future of higher education towards the end of the century and well into the next. It is clear that during this comprehensive review, every aspect of higher education will be scrutinized and it is unlikely that student support, and thus counselling, will escape the process.

The Chair of the review committee made it clear within days of his appointment that he intends to look towards Australia and North America for models of good practice. This has implications for counselling services where the structures of services in those countries share similarities with the British model, but have significant differences. A current Vice-Chancellor, when asked to declare hopes for the review, headed the list with the need for a 'one-stop student support and guidance provision' – no mention of personal and therapeutic counselling in this view of the future. If counsellors have believed themselves to be part of extraordinary changes in education in recent times, it would seem that this has been merely a preparation for the fundamental changes to come.

In order to prepare for these changes and to ensure the future of counselling services within it counsellors will need to pay speedy attention to a number of issues.

Research

Research gives credibility within academic communities. A number of counsellors have engaged in modest research through masters programmes but little is published on student counselling in Britain. The kind of research that will engender credibility will not be on some esoteric aspect of the counselling relationship but of a calibre that shows that counselling contributes to the central aims of an educational institution. Rickinson and Rutherford (1995), in their study which shows how a counselling service can contribute to an increase in undergraduate retention rates, demonstrate the kind of research that will show the value of a counselling service to an institution.

The purpose and quality of a counselling service in higher education

Much that ASC has already written has been used to influence institutions in the provision of counselling. The challenge for the future is to expand on this and to be unequivocal in describing how therapeutic counselling contributes to the educational process. In this there will also be a need to be more explicit about what constitutes a good counselling *service*, as well as a good counselling relationship. Although the basics of this have been outlined in the ASC's *Advisory Service to Institutions*, the Association may have to make judgements about the standards of existing counselling services, an activity that it has so far eschewed in favour of drawing broad templates to which services and counsellors can aspire.

The development of an enhanced professional identity

The advent of a UK Register of Counsellors will challenge individual counsellors to meet agreed standards. So far, in BAC and ASC, accreditation has been a desirable option for members, but as the Register gains credibility with the public counsellors will find this to be no longer an option but a necessity. ASC, and individual counsellors, will have a specific task in persuading institutions that the Register has significance for them. The assurance of accountability and safety inherent in the Register may be attractive to institutions, but they may find it more difficult to accept the expense of appropriately trained and experienced staff, and the consequence of counsellors being formally accountable to an organization outside the employing institution's jurisdiction.

Counselling for staff

For many years a small number of university and college counselling services have been available to staff as well as students. More frequently student counselling services offered one consultation session to staff in order to help them find alternative sources of help. Where there was this limited service it was not simply a matter of resources that had governed the decision but also an understanding that counsellors have to work in other areas of the institution with academic colleagues. Counselling someone with whom, later, there might need to be a discussion about a student referral, can lead to very blurred boundaries. However in mid-1995, at a meeting of the Heads of University Counselling Services, it was noted that many Heads had been involved in discussions within their institutions about a formal conselling service for staff. A year later, most services were involved with staff counselling. This development mirrors the increase in the number of in-house counselling services in large commercial organizations and may be seen as a reflection of greater public awareness of the benefits of counselling. It may also be a response to a well publicized case where a social worker in the north of England was awarded a large sum in compensation when his employers were found to have failed to monitor his level of work stress, and thus to have contributed to a breakdown in his emotional and physical health. Whatever the reason for the increased interest in staff counselling, it is clear that a number of services will need to address the issue of resources, both financial and in terms of the expertise within the counselling team. They will also need to be clear about the ethical implications of counselling colleagues. But, equally importantly, the development of a counselling service for staff will bring them into a subtly different relationship with the institution, its managers and its employees and the nature of this change will have to be carefully explored and understood.

Conclusion

Student counselling has become one of the most well-established forms within the counselling field. The number of full-time permanent posts within universities and colleges of higher education has frequently been the subject of envy from counsellors in other, less established, sectors. However, alongside the envy there has also been a recognition of the contribution that individual counsellors and the Association for Student Counselling have made to the development of counselling as a whole. Whilst this does not seem likely to diminish in the immediate future, the long-term future holds many uncertainties. Whatever the uncertainties, it is clear that all student counsellors will have to continue to work to explain the relevance of counselling to institutions of higher education. The founding members of ASC faced this challenge. The present and future members of the Association will need the courage and stamina of its founder members to ensure that student counselling maintains its important contribution to education, and to counselling in Britain, into the twenty-first century.

References

Association for Student Counselling (undated) *Advisory Service to Institutions*, Rugby: ASC/BAC.
——(undated) *Guide to Training Courses*, Rugby: ASC/BAC.
Association for Student Counselling Research (1995), Rugby: ASC/BAC.
Bell, E. (1996) *Counselling in Higher and Further Education*, Buckingham: Open University Press.
Bell, E., Dryden, W., Noonan, E. and Thorne, B. (undated) *A Guide to Recognizing Best Practice in Counselling*, Rugby: ASC/BAC.

Coren, A. (1996) 'Brief Therapy – base metal or pure gold', *Psychodynamic Counselling* 1(2): 22–38.

Hope, D. (1985) *Counselling Stress and Burnout*, MA thesis, University of Reading.

Langs, R. (1982) *Psychotherapy: A Basic Text*, New York: Jason Aronson.

Malan, D. (1982) *Individual Psychotherapy and the Science of Psychodynamics*, Sevenoaks: Butterworth.

Milner, M. (1977) *On not being able to paint*, London: Heinemann Educational Books.

National Association of Teachers in Further and Higher Education (1979) *Student Counselling*, London: NATFHE.

Noonan, E. (1983) *Counselling Young People*, London: Methuen.

Ratigan, B. (1969) 'Counselling in Higher Education' in W. Dryden, D. Charles Edwards and R. Woolfe (eds) *Handbook of Counselling in Britain*, London: Routledge.

Rickinson, B. and Rutherford, D. (1995) 'Increasing undergraduate student retention rates', *British Journal of Guidance and Counselling* 28(2): 161–72.

Rogers, C. R. (1969) *Freedom to Learn; A View of What Education Might Become*, Columbus Ohio: Charles E. Merrill.

Ross, P. (1995) 'The Stresses of Directing a University Counselling Service' in W. Dryden (ed.) *The Stresses of Counselling in Action*, London: Sage.

Siegelman, E. (1990) 'Metaphors of the Therapeutic Encounter', *Journal of Analytic Psychotherapy* 35: 175–91.

Smith, E. (ed.) (1996) *Integrity and Change: Mental Health in the Market Place*, London: Routledge.

Thorne, B. (1994) 'Brief Companionship' in D. Mearns (ed.) *Developing Person-centred Counselling*, London: Sage.

Warburton, K. (1995) 'Student Counselling: a consideration of ethical and framework issues', *Psychodynamic Counselling* 1(3): 421–35.

Chapter thirteen

Counselling in the workplace

Michael Megranahan

Introduction

The earliest example of helping services in the workplace is the welfare department. The welfare department can be traced back to the early 1900s, where employers encouraged mature employees (often managers) to 'look after' the welfare of their employees. Whilst welfare departments continue to exist, mainly in larger organizations, they tend to be seen as a legacy of an earlier time. The actual term 'welfare' has been described as having connotations of charity, something which can be regarded as a handicap (Orlans and Shipley 1983).

It was from the welfare department that the personnel department evolved and employees still tend to regard the personnel department as the place where help for problems can be found. However, fewer and fewer personnel specialists today see welfare as part of their role. Personnel has assumed more of a management function in recent years and the people in this role, whilst sympathetic to employee problems, tend to regard these as secondary to business issues. Indeed a study in 1991 showed that there was no clear definition among the 100 companies surveyed, of what modern welfare provisions entailed nor where responsibility for developing or providing these services lay. (Edmonds 1991).

The occupational health department within organizations has often indirectly provided a form of counselling service. Ask any occupational health nurse about the mental health of the organization's employees and you will receive a comprehensive picture. However, as Orlans (1986) has reported, occupational health nurses are rarely trained in counselling. In her survey of thirty-five large UK organizations, thirty-two with occupational health departments, none of the nurses had undergone extensive counselling training and only a few had been on short counselling-skills training courses. This area has begun to see some changes in recent times, most noticeably in large organizations like the Post Office and Scottish & Newcastle where the medical departments have moved toward being proactive and now encompass counselling training as one of the key skills for nurses.

This works very well provided the limitations of this type of approach are observed.

Where employees identify a specific in-house resource to be an appropriate place to discuss problems, they will use such a resource. This clearly leaves the untrained recipient in a difficult position.

Other examples of counselling services within the workplace have been identified by earlier studies. In 1971 the British Institute of Management conducted a survey of 200 firms in the UK enquiring about their provisions for health care. Some 62 per cent offered regular medical checks for some of their managers at set intervals, and 5 per cent offered personal counselling services. The survey did not enlarge on what personal counselling entailed but is indicative of some early initiatives in this area. Industrial chaplains may also fulfil a counselling role and in the mid-1970s, Prentice (1976) reported there to be 150 full-time and 450 part-time chaplains.

In 1974 Shell Chemicals introduced an in-company counselling service for 3,000 employees in Cheshire. The year 1975 saw liaison between Mind and Plessey, and the subsequent provision of an external counselling service. This later became known as 'Stress at Work', a group of people who continue to provide external counselling services to businesses in the Northampton area. Other examples of companies employing a full-time counsellor include Shell International, some hospitals and police forces, and a number of trade unions such as the Royal College of Nurses. The first employee assistance programmes (one type of counselling service for employees: see p. 218) in the UK were established in 1981 in Control Data's EAP and SingerLink-Miles. EAPs are rapidly becoming the most common form of workplace counselling service due to the development of consultancy in this area and pre-existing welfare services of thirty or more years changing their names to EAP, possibly in an attempt to overcome the stigma identified by Orlans. A notable recent example of this switch is the Inland Revenue welfare service (*People Management*, September 1995).

Additional *ad hoc* external counselling services are provided by a variety of consultancies and academic institutions such as Sheffield University.

In 1977 the Standing Conference for the Advancement of Counselling, the forerunner of the British Association for Counselling (BAC), published the first book that discussed the need for and application of counselling at work (Watts 1977). From that time until the 1990s counselling found very few openings in the workplace. In the last five years however there has seen an increasing interest in the use and application of counselling at work. A number of reasons exist for this and include the acceptance of the term counselling as a valid support mechanism for issues like critical incident debriefing. The spate of bombings in London led to many financial institutions introducing trauma counselling services. It will be interesting to see whether these services have any kind of longevity.

Another factor has been the success of some employees in suing their employer for stress, in particular the Walker case (Palmer 1995). This has generated a renewed interest and concern among employers about the cause and effect of stress and the belief that counselling can play a mitigating role in reducing actions against them for stress. This belief is somewhat misguided but will nonetheless be a factor in the increase in counselling in the workplace.

Although many more examples of the use of counselling in the workplace exist than those given above, the main influences for introducing and keeping services of this kind appear to be (a) historical, i.e. we have had this service for some time so let's retain it; (b) head-office directives, i.e. we have the service in the States so why not in the UK; or (c) someone in a senior position within a company believes in the value of counselling and is prepared to push for it, perhaps influenced by new initiatives such as Health of the Nation (1995) or the trend of European Community legislation toward greater responsibility for employee well-being. It is only slowly that organizations are recognizing the need for and benefits of counselling, and subsequently meeting this need.

Principles

Introducing the service to employees

The problems that employees either bring to the workplace or experience within it are many and varied. It is not possible for an individual to remain unaffected at work by problems based in the home or vice versa. This invasion will and does occur, no matter how great the effort by the individual to prevent it taking place or being detected.

Just as the problems each person is likely to experience are varied, so are the associated emotional responses and visible manifestations which alert others to the existence of a problem:

- depression may occur some months after an employee has experienced a bereavement of someone close to him or her;
- anxiety may pervade all aspects of a person's life on hearing that redundancies are to be made;
- anger may be evident in an employee who has received a poor performance appraisal;
- an employee who exhibits a pattern of Monday and Friday absences may be exhibiting signs of an alcohol problem;
- a person who is irritable and moody with colleagues may be experiencing relationship difficulties at home;
- periods of sickness which fall into a regular pattern may be associated with specific and recurring aspects in the employee's job which are

stressful and with which he or she cannot cope, for example, depart-
mental meetings, presentations, deadlines.

The response to an employee experiencing problems of any kind can be
made at two distinct levels: first, by someone within the workplace trained
in counselling skills, for example, a line or personnel manager; and second,
by a designated and trained counsellor. Ideally, both levels should exist and
this is the case in some organizations. The employee may seek out help or
help may be offered and/or extended. Where an employee's job performance begins to be affected, it falls within the scope of the organization to
intervene and offer help and assistance to the employee. If this is not done
or the help is rejected, then the organization needs to make a decision
concerning the acceptability of the specific circumstances and look at other
options such as discipline, time off, reduced duties, and so on.
    There are a number of general principles which apply to any workplace
counselling system:

(1) Any counselling service needs to have the support of top management
     in order to be accepted and survive.
(2) A written policy statement of overall philosophy concerning the
     health and well-being of employees or which addresses specific fea-
     tures, for example alcohol, should be available. This creates a positive
     climate in which employees can seek help.
(3) Managers and supervisors should be trained to identify employees
     with problems at an early stage and know how to confront them and
     make referral to the counsellor.
(4) Access to the counselling service should be available to all staff at all
     locations.
(5) The service should be credible in the eyes of the employer, managers,
     trade unions, and employees.
(6) Confidentiality should be explicity stated, accepted, and understood
     by everyone.
(7) A continuation of care should be available, which includes referral
     and follow-up.
(8) The emphasis should be on self-referral.
(9) The counselling service should be independent of any specific or
     single treatment centre.
(10) A system should exist for evaluating and auditing the counselling
     service.

The counsellor needs to find a way of communicating the service to all
employees on an ongoing basis, otherwise it will be forgotten. Although the
number of self-referrals received is often the best way to assess whether the
service is being accepted by employees, the counsellor needs to think of

marketing the service in ways that will increase its accessibility for all employees.

Publicizing the service can be done in an number of ways, for example company newsletters. Although word-of-mouth recommendations are perhaps the favoured growth method of counselling services in organizations where this type of service is new and unusual, this cannot be relied upon. Counselling still carries a stigma associated with not being able to cope, and this needs to be reduced, particularly in organizations where the community is very close and the grapevine 'well oiled'. If the service is openly supported by the organization and access is freely available for all types of problems, then this will help. The counsellor also needs to be seen, since employees are more likely to contact someone they have met, even if only fleetingly.

Briefings of small groups of employees covering the scope and nature of the service are useful. Travelling to all company sites demonstrates that it is not just a head-office service. Visiting a night shift serves a similar purpose. It is not enough to have a title and office and wait for people to use the service. People need to be encouraged to do so and communication of the service and its personnel is vital to this. The aim is to give permission for the use of the service not to ferret out problems and lead to staff feeling that they must have problems.

The counsellor in the workplace

Many counsellors will not have worked in an employment context and should be aware that every counsellor–client contact is likely to have organizational implications. If this is lost sight of, the counsellor will find the service alienated by both management and unions.

The counsellor who is accustomed to seeing a client on a one-to-one basis needs to see the client in an organizational context and anticipate any problems others may have with the counsellor's assessment and recommendations for treatment. Recommending a course of counselling of once a week for ten weeks in office hours to a production manager who has self-referred, during a peak production time when the concern was not interfering with his or her work and therefore not visible to the management, would not be understood. An alternative would be to refer to an external resource that could see him in the evenings.

The counsellor needs to keep up to date with available resources and assess their quality since it is impossible to attempt to see everyone and deal with everything. This is what is expected of the counsellor, however, and to meet this expectation the counsellor needs to draw on other resources. The counsellor also needs to be familiar with organizational structures and channels of communication if he or she is to be able to influence management to make changes.

Most counsellors in companies will work alone and will therefore need to look carefully at their own support, environmental as well as professional. Negotiations at the beginning of the introduction of a counselling service should include accommodation, its location, clerical and technological support, and so on.

Employers often find these criteria difficult to understand and accept. To provide a counsellor with an office – a basic tool of the trade – is often resisted by an employer who does not appreciate the need for privacy. Internal politics can easily get in the way of providing an effective service and reflect a lack of commitment to the service by the organization. Lastly, a careful balance needs to be kept between personal and professional life, with counsellors taking some of the direction they provide to their clients.

Specific applications of counselling in the workplace

Redundancy counselling

The introduction of redundancy counselling is seen by some, for example Novarra (1986), as the single most significant area of activity contributing to the acceptance of counselling in the workplace. As a term this is certainly true. As a way of increasing the acceptance of specialists this is true. As a way of helping some line and personnel managers recognize that the impact and repercussions of redundancy cannot be alleviated by severance payments used in isolation this is true. Whether or not counselling takes place as opposed to the use of counselling skills and coaching is less clear. And it is this last aspect which has potentially given rise to most problems.

For many in the work context, counselling is synonymous with redundancy, an aspect which counsellors should work hard to dispel or else be tarnished with this until the demand for these services declines, at which time people working in this area are likely to find themselves redundant with few transferable skills relevant to counselling.

Redundancy counselling has shown how the use of specialist resources can assist organizations deal with discarded employees. It encompasses advice, information, and guidance. This type of service is also supported and complemented by the organization's existing management and personnel. Counselling should, however, be extended to the remaining or stable employee population. Real progress in the workplace will only be made once counsellors are invited through the front door to meet people whilst they are experiencing the stresses and strains, challenges, and opportunities of their chosen work organization. This whole area has a new term attached to it called 'survivor syndrome'. Progress in this area is slow but there have been some advances (see Chapter 21).

Alcohol counselling

The UK has seen agencies such as Alcohol Concern establish a government-funded workplace unit to promote the adoption of educative programmes and policies in the workplace. The Confederation of British Industry has produced a booklet in conjunction with Turning Point on the misuse of drugs, and the Industrial Society and the Institute of Personnel and Development also have a booklet concerned with alcohol policies. There is an ever-increasing number of documents being produced by industrially recognized bodies, something which would have been unheard of ten years ago.

Policy and education initiatives have been followed closely by the growth of private treatment centres. The value of these *vis-à-vis* NHS or voluntary units is debatable and an area that cannot be entered into here. Suffice it to say that, generally, private facilities are not available unless the employee has private medical insurance or the company is prepared to pay for treatment. Private medical insurers also give generous discounts to exclude psychiatric conditions under which alcohol misuse is included. As a consequence the option for support in this area is one of the most difficult to meet satisfactorily.

A number of companies do have their own in-house counselling services which can help employees cope with alcohol or drug abuse. However, where they rely on self-referral only, they are less likely to be successful than if training is provided to first-line supervisors. Training should encompass identifying employees whose job performance has been noted as poor or irregular, approaching the employee on this basis only, and using counselling skills within a disciplinary framework to motivate the employee to request or seek help.

An approach of this kind should be applied to all employees where poor job performance has been recorded and not only where an alcohol or drug problem is suspected. Where this is applied consistently (supported by policy) it will be seen to be fair, consistent and objective. As mentioned, actions of this kind are necessary to help the employee seek help and the supervisor is therefore actively involved in the intervention process and supporting the specialist counselling agency or counsellor.

The actual help the employee receives is itself an area of contention between different schools of thought. The majority of drug/alcohol counsellors subscribe to the disease model, while others regard controlled drinking to be a realistic objective. For the former counsellors any other problems the person may present are seen as deflecting from the main and only problem of alcohol or drug abuse. These counsellors tend to regard the abuse as the cause of all the other problems. The latter school of thought, however, will tend to start with the 'other' problems – for example, marital problems, financial difficulties, job stress, and so on – advocating that once these are resolved the reason for the alcohol or drug abuse will be removed.

There is insufficient space to enter into this debate fully and the above is a very simple statement of the differences (see Chapter 26 for a fuller discussion of this debate). Counsellors and employers should be aware of the differences and consequent forms of treatment. This is particularly important if the existing trend develops further and alcohol and drug abuse is the key to unlock the organization's door to counselling as has been the case in North America.

The area of alcohol and drug abuse is likely to be an important area for counselling in the workplace in the future. This is particularly true if the UK follows the American pattern of the development of employee assistance programmes, an area examined next.

Employee assistance programmes

Employee assistance programmes (EAPs) were developed in North America in the early 1960s as a response to the adverse effects of alcohol in the workplace. A number of companies providing an EAP found that employees had other personal issues which needed help, counselling and support and which also affected work performance. Consequently what has been termed 'broad-brush' EAPs were established in the early 1970s.

An EAP is essentially a short-term counselling and referral agency available to employees and their families. They are usually structured to provide an immediate 24–hour response to any personal concern or crisis, and are supported by a comprehensive referral network of community and private counselling resources.

EAPs were first introduced into Britain in 1981 through the influence of American parent companies and copying the structures already established. This structure includes, for some EAP services, autonomy from other in-company functions such as personnel, an advantage over functions like welfare. Outside provision of this service is also a cost-effective way for employers to extend counselling to employees.

The essential features of an EAP consist of the following:

(1) immediate access to trained professional counsellors;
(2) total confidentiality;
(3) training by EAP counsellors of line managers and supervisors in confronting and referring employees where job performance is affected due to personal problems;
(4) support to line managers and supervisors in dealing with troubled employees;
(5) efficient and professional referral capability;

(6) autonomy from the organization, i.e. not part of personnel department;
(7) evaluation processes to enable the organization to assess the value of
     the service provided.

The EAP introduces counselling 'up front' to employees with a well-proven structure for providing the service. It is therefore one example of how counselling is being accepted in the workplace as a preventive and responsive service. EAPs have expanded significantly in the 1990s and as mentioned many pre-existing services are changing their names to join the EAP trend. The challenge for employers is how to assess one EAP against another, ascertaining the value they get for investing in an EAP, understanding the true benefit of having an EAP in place, and most significantly, understanding the type and quality of counselling that is actually provided by the EAP. This last area is neglected by organizations since there is no precise body available to give guidance on good and bad practice or even appropriate and inappropriate models of counselling for the workplace environment.

Some of these issues have begun to be addressed by the establishment of an extension of the American body the Employee Assistance Professionals Association (EAPA). This body has published an anglicized version of the American standards for EAP practice but it carries no sanctions for poor practice nor does it deal with the difficulty of assessing whether the counselling resources used by an EAP are credible.

Issues

There are a number of issues that concern counselling in the workplace. These relate to (a) the counsellor's ability to be effective; (b) confusion as to what constitutes counselling; and (c) factors that prohibit the potential for the progress of counselling in the workplace. The following discussion covers the traditional concerns associated with counselling in organizations, for example, confidentiality; and examines the reasons and issues surrounding the limited use of counselling within organizations.

The use of counselling skills in the workplace

Whilst the development of workplace counselling services has been slow there has been a growth in counselling-skills training, primarily for managers and supervisors. This activity has greatly increased the acceptance of the term counselling in the workplace, but at the same time has led to confusion and controversy as to where counselling skills stop and counselling begins. Where counselling skills are being acquired for a specific purpose, such as general communication skills, interviewing skills, performance-appraisal interviews and so on, then counselling-skills courses should enhance the manager's skills.

However, where managers' expectations on completion of a short-skills training course lead them to regard themselves as counsellors, consequently equipped to deal with employees' personal concerns, problems are likely to emerge. The manager may fail to recognize the point at which referral of an employee is necessary, and the potential damage that can be done to both the manager and employee if the discussion begins to get out of the manager's depth. This failure may be attributed to two sources: first, the manager wanting or believing that he or she should personally help the employee resolve the problem, thereby disregarding any guidance given on the training course; and/or second, the training course failing to provide any guidance in this area and subsequent support.

If these two factors are adequately dealt with, the manager should also have the skills and knowledge to make an effective referral. Training should have helped the manager to know how to identify and assess the appropriate resource for his referral. The consideration of ways in which a referral network can be established and validated is also important and an area that is very neglected.

Managers who are properly trained and clear about their objectives in the training should be clear about the limitations of their ability to counsel within their role. Counselling skills training can be beneficial to the employee and organization where managers recognize (or are confronted with) an employee with a problem, talk constructively and sensitively to the employee, and either help the employee manage his or her problem or are able to make an effective referral to a trained counsellor.

A relationship of this kind, between the manager (or any other employee – it should not be regarded exclusively as a managerial role) with counselling skills and counselling resources, keeps the boundaries between the two areas distinct, and enables good practice to take place. To achieve this the quality of counselling skills training courses needs to be high, added to which they need to recognize the environment within which the manager is required to work. For instance, the course should deal with issues of confidentiality, contracting, and record-keeping, what to do if the working environment is open plan, and how to recognize problems before they become unmanageable.

Counselling-skills courses can provide an excellent skills base for people but they often fail to consider the person's work environment and the need for consistency in applying counselling skills. Also, counselling skills should be moulded into the person's existing style. If these issues are not considered on the course and the manager's style or behaviour changes as a result of the course, employees may be suspicious and the counselling skills undermined.

Another major issue that needs to be addressed is how to help employers determine which counselling skills courses are appropriate for their needs. Employers need to be clear about their own objectives and the context in which the person they send on the course is required to use the skills. Trainers who do not help an employer in this way are failing in their responsibility to the employer, the participant, and the employee who will be at the receiving end. Guidance is needed to provide employers with the confidence to train staff in the use of counselling skills, understand how and where the skills may be best used, and be prepared to support the use of these skills in the workplace.

The IPD *Statement on Counselling in the Workplace*, published in October 1992, attempted to provide guidelines for managers who find themselves in counselling situations. The statement was said to recognize the universality of counselling needs in the workplace and the positive contribution it can make to management problem solving (IPD 1992).

Confidentiality

Where a person is in the role of counsellor, whether it be the employee's manager, or a professional counsellor working within the organization or providing external resources, the issue of confidentiality needs to be looked at from two perspectives: first, as a manager (or person fulfilling a counselling role) and, second, as a counsellor.

Some organizations and managers find it difficult to accept that an employee would want to speak to someone in confidence. This may suggest an insecurity on the part of the third party (i.e. manager or organization) or a mistrust of how the content of interviews will be used. It is up to the person in the role of counsellor to reassure and educate the third party of the nature of this confidence. Reassurance will also be needed for employees who are also likely to be suspicious. Such a process will need to be ongoing for all parties as different issues arise. Without the principle of confidentiality and reassurance of it, a counselling service is not likely to succeed or be respected.

Differences are likely to exist in the extent to which confidentiality will apply. A manager in the counselling role, for instance, has a responsibility to the organization as well as to the employee, and the boundary between the two needs to be clear. Consequently, if a manager is told in an interview by an employee that the latter has been stealing from the company and the employee feels unable to disclose the matter personally, the manager is likely to feel that it is necessary to take some kind of action. The employee should be informed what this action will be and the reasons why it is being taken. If at all possible the manager should let the employee know that action will be necessary before the employee informs him or her of this type of problem, thereby preventing the need for a trust to be seen to be betrayed, the employee feeling cheated and the manager feeling guilty.

However, an employee who discusses with a manager his marital problems (before referral, if appropriate) and whose job performance is unaffected should expect this to go no further than the interview. No one else needs to know.

The counsellor, on the other hand, either working within the organization or a resource to it, may adopt a different approach, recognizing the employee's need to tell someone and desire to resolve the problem. This should involve discussing the employee's options. The counsellor may either not inform the organization, choosing to work with the employee to deal with the problem, or adopt a similar position to that described for a manager. This does not make the counsellor's responsibility to the organization any less than the manager's. The way of dealing with the issue is different, a difference consistent with the bounds of confidentiality within which each should be expected to work. The only time when confidentiality will be broken by a counsellor is when clients are a potential danger to themselves or others (consistent with the BAC's Code of Ethics), or where written permission has been given by the client. This type of informed consent can be very valuable in the workplace, enabling the counsellor to influence organizational behaviour. However, certain other codes of ethics may prevent a counsellor from taking this type of action.

Conflict of interests (individual versus employer) and hence confidentiality are often put forward as reasons why counselling cannot function effectively within an organization. These aspects are put forward by both counsellors and organizations. Conflicts will occur and pressure will be put on counsellors to breach confidentiality, but only where the boundaries have not been clearly drawn or where misunderstanding exists. There is a responsibility on both parties (employer and counsellor) to negotiate where this boundary should exist, and if this is unacceptable to either party, one of them is not ready to provide or receive counselling services in the workplace. In addition, once established, the boundary needs to be communicated to the potential clients. A written policy document would be ideal.

Evaluation

This single phrase has been for a long time the stumbling block for progress of counselling services in the workplace. Organizations want to see a quantifiable return for their investment and counselling is no different. Evaluation is easier when a valued employee has a problem which is affecting work performance and the situation has become 'public'. If counselling is able to help such employees and restore them to their former health, then there may be public acknowledgement of the benefits provided by counselling. Examples of this kind are insufficient to make a lasting impact and suggest a crisis perspective of counselling. This detracts from the preventive role that counselling can and does play where help can be accessed early.

Data are available to demonstrate the need for preventive counselling, including, for example, Goldsmith (1982), who suggested the cost to the UK of stress-related absence from work to be approximately £3,000 million per annum. The number of divorces and the extent of alcohol abuse in Britain also add up to a significant cost to industry. Employers do not appreciate that employees are a frail resource whose mental health can affect the organization's productivity and morale. Communicating this message is both difficult and frustrating. Many employers still do not recognize that their employees work within a stressful environment and therefore need support, and many managers still adhere to the attitude of 'if the weak can't make it, then we don't want them'. Indeed there is now a new business emerging which specializes in preselection screening of employees to assess how susceptible to stress they may be. The considerable research evidence demonstrating the adverse effects of stress for the organization as well as for individuals (for example, Cooper 1983; Aroba and James 1987) is being used to protect rather than improve organizations.

Attitudes are changing but it will be a lengthy process. Some organizations may have a culture or a senior employee who is more receptive to the introduction of counselling, and here the issue of evaluation is secondary to the values associated with helping employees. Where this ethos is not present the counsellor is likely to be hitting his or her head against a brick wall and should perhaps direct his or her energies elsewhere. For these organizations, even a neat and valid equation (which does not exist despite years of research in the USA) demonstrating the value of investment in counselling would not be persuasive enough.

Counselling does help an organization by protecting and maintaining what should be its most valuable resource, its employees. This can be seen in areas of reduced absenteeism and staff turnover, improved morale and communications, fewer accidents and insurance claims.The University of Manchester Institute of Science and Technology (UMIST) is currently finalizing a research project examining these very issues. Early results show that the quality of the counselling provided needs to be carefully assessed and that employers are poorly placed to achieve this goal. In terms of organizational value the picture remains vague, with internal counselling services appearing to have greater effect organizationally since they are often more able to effect change (see also Tehrani 1995). Until this and other work is complete, counsellors must work hard to convince others of their effectiveness through practical demonstrations of their worth which will lay them open to greater scrutiny and assessment. In the workplace this will increasingly mean having their work audited.

Introducing counselling services: anticipating and dealing with the responses of management and trade unions

In addition to the need for counselling to demonstrate through evaluation that it is an effective resource that organizations should actively consider, counsellors need to be proactive in promoting and consolidating their services. To achieve this there are potentially three groups within any organization that the counsellor needs to focus on: managers, trades unions, and employees. Each group will have its own perspective of a counselling service that includes both positive and negative elements. The section below will focus on managers and trade unions.

Counsellors often fail to recognize the unique viewpoint of each group and fail to anticipate the problems put forward by each, consequently finding it difficult to overcome them. It is useful to look at their needs seperately since they illustrate many of the issues that counselling in the workplace raises and which need to be addressed and overcome for counselling to be effective and successful in this context.

Working with managers

Managers and supervisors react to the introduction of a counsellor in different ways. A few may respond positively, seeing the counsellor as an ally in helping employees, some of whom may have had long-standing problems which have remained out of the reach of management. However, the general response is usually one of hostility or suspicion. Managers often see the counsellor as a soft option for employees and a threat to the manager's disciplinary control over the workforce.

Managers may for instance suspect that employees will use the counsellor as a protection against action for poor performance, claiming that this is due to emotional or alcohol problems and that disciplinary action should be excused. Other managers will deny the existence of problems; they regard the counsellor's remit as dealing only with people who have serious emotional problems, and therefore refuse to admit that employees with such problems could be working for them successfully.

Some managers will consider the care of their employees to be their sole responsibility and see the introduction of a counsellor as an indication of failure. Still other managers will regard themselves as counsellors or amateur psychologists who have been 'counselling' for years and are therefore providing all the help the employees require.

The counsellor needs to show that he or she is not, nor likely to be, working against management. The counsellor has a separate and distinct area of responsibility and authority that does not infringe upon the manager's area. Counsellors who fail to recognize and observe boundaries of this type will quickly find their role untenable. The counsellor may make recommendations to management about work practices or policies but the final decision about what actually happens in the workplace stays with the manager.

A counsellor can enhance the manager's role and this needs to be highlighted. A counsellor can increase the manager's time and free emotional energy by dealing with employees' personal problems. The manager's responsibility is to make sure that employees work to their fullest ability in order to increase productivity and reduce costs. Managers' commitment both to their staff as people and to their effectiveness in their work will, if they are enlightened, mean that they will be concerned that the staff are adequately supported if, for example, they are struggling to come to terms with a bereavement or a broken marriage. However, they may not have the time or skills to become their counsellors, nor will it be appropriate in role terms. The counsellor can relieve the manager of this task and enable the latter to focus on job performance, instituting disciplinary action where required, uncomplicated by having delved into personal problem areas.

Managers may be reluctant to take disciplinary action where it is known that an employee has a personal problem, perferring merely to refer the employee to the counsellor. It is important that in-company counsellors and managers understand the neutral role of the counsellor in this context and the beneficial outcome of a manager drawing a firm line when an employee's job performance is unsatisfactory. Motivation for change often follows clear limit-setting by managers. Counsellors for their part should recognize this need and that effective integration and the parallel use of disciplinary action and counselling is possible and beneficial.

The counsellor also needs to help the manager recognize that the counsellor is there as a resource for themselves. Counsellors need to remember that their role is neutral and that managers also have problems. Indeed, their stress levels are often especially acute. However, a manager may need additional encouragement to seek help, and to see such a request in terms of strength and not weakness.

Gaining support from management   If the structure of the counselling service within an organization allows, self-referrals are likely to be the most frequent type of contact a counsellor will have with employees. These will increase with time. The help and trust of management also needs to be enlisted in order to ensure that the service is used effectively for the good of the individual and organization. This can be done by making training available to managers and supervisors. The counsellor is able to involve the manager in the process of getting an employee appropriate help. Formal training sessions that advise the manager of the counsellor's role, types of indicators that suggest that an employee has a problem linked to documentation of any poor job performance, ways in which managers can approach employees without causing them to become defensive, and methods of referral to the counsellor – all are crucial to a successful and supported counselling service.

No referrals should be mandatory from management, but the manager is in a position, if job performance is suffering, to continue normal disciplinary actions if the employee does not seek help and job performance does not improve. Managers should be encouraged to consider that the option of counselling intervention may pay dividends, before disciplinary action is instigated, although this may not always be possible, especially in cases of what is classified as gross misconduct. Equally, if the manager knows that the employee is experiencing personal problems that do not affect job performance, the manager may recommend seeing the counsellor but would have no recourse to disciplinary action. The counsellor should also make it clear that feedback following management referrals is likely to be limited at best. The employee can, however, be encouraged to inform his or her manager, without revealing details, that support has been requested.

Informal contacts between the counsellor and employees at all levels are also important. Being visible in a low-key way that does not distract people from their tasks or lead them to feel that they have been singled out is helpful in reducing stigma and increasing confidence in a counselling service.

The counsellor should also endeavour to keep in touch with upper management. This serves two purposes. First, it enables the counsellor to inform management, whilst maintaining confidentiality, of his or her activities. This is an important and ongoing educative role. Managers change and if the counsellor does not work to inform new people of the value of the counsellor's role, then it is likely that the role will lose visibility and credibility. Counsellors also have a unique opportunity to assess information from all levels of the organization and feed back appropriate strategies and ideas for constructive change. Managers are only likely to be receptive to this type of input concerning organizational change when the service has shown that it is organizationally effective, for instance in reducing absenteeism and labour turnover.

Second, the counsellor, in turn, should also be prepared to answer questions from senior management concerning the service (whilst maintaining confidentiality) and respond to particular requests for help and assistance with specific employees or organizational problems. An employee may, for instance, refuse to see a counsellor and consequently the manager will need help and guidance on the best way to help the employee; or a group of employees may, for operational reasons, need to be retrained and resistance to these changes is envisaged. The counsellor may be asked to play a facilitating role to enabling the change to take place more smoothly.

The counsellor must also, where an employee has given permission, be prepared to advise management of that employee's progress towards resolving a problem.

Working with trades unions

The response of union representatives to the introduction of a counsellor is likely to be the same as that of managers: some will be receptive; others suspicious and hostile. Perhaps the single most crucial issue that the counsellor will need to overcome with the trades union is one of trust.

Where a counsellor is employed by the company he or she needs to demonstrate loyalty to employees' interests and needs as well as to the company's need to maintain productivity. Where a counsellor's role over-laps with existing in-company functions such as personnel, occupational health, or trades union, the union may be particularly suspicious of the company's motives. This is especially true in the case of broad-brush employee assistance programmes (see p. 218). Questions may be asked about the recording and storing of information and whether it is being transferred on to personnel files. As there should be no occasion when a counsellor would transfer any information, this should be made clear.

Another concern is where the trades union sees the counselling service as another fad, or an attempt to erode union power, especially where there is a history of management trying to introduce different schemes for employ-ees. Such suspicions are likely to be reinforced if the union has not been involved in introducing the service.

To help overcome some of the possible problems, trades union repre-sentatives should be invited to the same training sessions that the managers are attending. This enables each group to see that neither is being told something the other is not. Discussion at the end of these types of training sessions also encourages co-operation for the good of the employee who subsequently seeks help once the service is up and running.

The counsellor should also work with any services offered by the trades union and not attempt to circumvent union policies and procedures. Employees may prefer to consult with a counsellor rather than the union but employees should always be encouraged to explore this route first where it is appropriate to do so. In much the same way the counsellor needs to work to foster understanding from management so the counsellor should do the same with union leaders. Doing this reduces the opportunity for misunderstanding and the counselling service being caught in the middle of management–union disagreements. The counselling service must be seen to be neutral.

Future developments

Counselling in the workplace continues to gain a solid and consistent foothold. The 1990s have seen an increasing interest by employers in the use of counselling skills as a valuable managerial skill. Provided managers do not abuse these skills and acknowledge their limitations, then counsellors will be increasingly recognized for their contribution to employees' well-being.

Real progress will only be made when it is possible to demonstrate that an investment in an in-company counselling resource provides a return to the employer. Research aimed at giving valid evaluation of this area is inconclusive although a number of universities and management colleges in Britain continue to focus their efforts in this direction. Current results of these initatives are highlighting that workplace counselling is raising more questions than it is answering.

Employers who have decided to introduce counselling are often confused by the type of services available. There is a real need for a neutral professional body which can both advise organizations in this area and lay down agreed standards of good practice. The BAC continues to fail to grasp the nettle and is likely to be eclipsed by the British Psychological Society in the provision of clear and enforceable standards. Organizations will seek greater and greater clarity over the standards and controls applied to counselling particularly with the threat of litigation in the background (see Palmer 1995). Simply providing access to a counsellor will be insufficient, the calibre and qualifications of the counsellor will need to be checked and understood. As this requirement takes off, organizations like the BAC will need to keep pace.

In addition counsellors will need to be able to follow and demonstrate valid, professional, and recognized qualifications. General training courses, particularly those that promote longer-term counselling, will not be relevant in the workplace context (see initiatives in primary care settings toward short-term counselling). This also applies to all the different specialisms, for example, careers counselling, redundancy counselling, and so on. If this is not achieved then industry will reject counselling as being too vague a discipline. Initiatives to move for greater acceptance of counselling in the workplace need therefore to be accompanied by changes in training and accreditation.

References

Aroba, T. and James, K. (1987) *Pressure of Work – A Survival Guide*, New York: McGraw-Hill.

Cooper, C.L. (ed.) (1983) *Stress Research: Issues for the Eighties*, Chichester: Wiley.

Edmonds, M. (1991) 'Exploring company welfare', *Employee Counselling Today* 3: 26–31.

Goldsmith, W. (1982) 'Introduction to 1981 Stress Conference Proceedings' in L Booth (ed.) *Stress: Source of Positive Human Performance? or Human and Economic Disaster?*, Yelding, Kent: the Stress Syndrome Foundation.

Institute of Personnel and Development (IPD) (1992) *Statement on Counselling in the Workplace*, London: IPD.

Novarra, V. (1986) 'Can a manager be a counsellor?', *Personnel Management,* June: 48–50.

Orlans, V. (1986) 'Counselling services', *Organisation Personnel Review* 15(5): 19–23.

Orlans, V. and Shipley, P. (1983) 'A survey of stress management and prevention facilities in a sample of UK organisations', unpublished report of Stress Research and Control Centre, Department of Occupational Psychology, Birkbeck College, University of London.

Palmer, S. (1995) 'Occupational Stress and the Law', *Journal of the Institute of Health Education,* 33(2): 55–6.

Prentice, G. (1976) 'Faith at work. The message is the mission', *Personnel Management* 8(3): 33–6.

Tehrani, N. (1995) 'The development of employee support: an evaluation', *Counselling Psychology Review* 10(3): 2–7.

Watts, A.G. (ed.) (1977) *Counselling at Work: Standing Conference for the Advancement of Counselling,* London: Bedford Square Press.

Chapter fourteen

Counselling skills in the context of professional and organizational growth

Barbara Pearce

Introduction

This chapter presents a case for broadening counselling training through demystifying and disseminating the use of counselling skills to a much wider group of people than has previously been envisaged by those involved in the professional practice of counselling. The use of counselling skills is seen as both a generic helping skill and as a means of assisting professional and organizational growth. It will be argued that this is an inevitable development and that major changes have already taken place within certain sectors, in particular within the field of education. This chapter will compare counselling with other professions and their clients. It will also seek to demonstrate the fundamental changes which are taking place in vocational training in Britain and the growing demand for counselling in industry and commerce. Finally, it will consider the next stages in the development of counselling skills.

Background to counselling skills development

A growing number of people are undertaking counselling skills training and it is of value to consider reasons for this growth. Perhaps the most significant is that of social change, which is producing an inevitable increase in recognition of, and demand for, counselling. This change can be demonstrated in a number of ways. A glance at popular contemporary literature of the last one hundred years shows us that, compared with the population a century ago, individuals today face a world in which relationships are more transient, mobility has increased, and change at all levels is a much more dominating influence on our lives.

Futurist writers such as Toffler (1970) and Stonier (1978) have described the likely consequences of the enormous revolution that is occurring in terms of personal, psychological, social, and technological change. Toffler talks of 'the roaring current of change, a current so powerful today that it overturns institutions, shifts our values and shrivels our roots' (Toffler 1970: 11). Hopson and Scally (1981a: 6) state, 'we are living through a period of transition – and the demands on young people and adults will be similar. People will need to be adaptable, flexible and more personally competent than at any other time in our history.' Most poignant of all, Freire (1976: preface) writes:

> The time of epochal transition constitutes an historical 'tidal wave.' Contradictions increase between the ways of being, understanding, behaving and valuing which belong to yesterday and other ways of perceiving and valuing which announce the future. As the contradictions deepen, the 'tidal wave' becomes stronger and its climate increasingly emotional.

It is probable, however, that we are best able to register the acceleration of change, and its impact on our lives, through our own experience. Professionally and socially we are meeting new people all the time. This is very different from the experience of our grandparents, whose lives as they describe them are like the still shots from a static camera rather than the fast-forward video lives which we all lead. Our parents have faced the transition to a faster and increasingly changing lifestyle and we are the product of that transition. Our own children are growing up and adjusting to a very different life. The world has shrunk, thanks to mass and immediate communication and easily accessible travel; education is rapidly changing to accommodate new technology, unemployment, and changing circumstances; and the young now contemplate problems such as AIDS, eating disorders, substance abuse, unemployment, and crime which would have been unimaginable to the young of earlier decades, as would also the bewildering array of opportunities and choices.

Is it surprising, therefore, that help of various kinds is necessary at many different points in people's lives? At one time, such help as was required would be supplied by the extended family. With the breakdown of this unit after the Second World War and more recently with the increasing incidence of marital breakdown, a helping vacuum has been created. Society has become responsible, under the welfare system, for providing material assistance to those in need, but has singularly failed to provide, within its limited resources, for the psychological needs of those at risk. Social workers, educational and clinical psychologists, and psychiatrists have done all that is possible, given their heavy caseloads, but have been forced to work at crisis level rather than providing at a development level for those who have become the victims of the increasing pace of change.

It is this vacuum in the helping arena which the counselling skills movement is able to address. There will never be unlimited resources for the provision of the level of professional counselling which the changes in society are likely to require, and professional counsellors will therefore continue to be preoccupied with crisis demands. Although there has been some resistance to, and suspicion of, the growth of the counselling skills movement, it is in fact a natural response to growing demand and has frequently been triggered by those professionals who recognize that by imparting some of their skills to lay people, their own work can more realistically be focused upon those most in need. In addition, as access to and understanding of counselling skills increase within the population, those skills can begin to have a supportive, preventive, and developmental influence within the wider community.

During the last few decades there has been a growth in the scope of the helping agencies, mostly working at a voluntary level. These include, among many, Relate, Shelter, the Samaritans, Gingerbread, BACUP and local law centres. They serve different purposes but share the common theme of providing assistance that is not part of state provision. They arise in response to a specific need emerging over a period of time and are themselves reflections of the transition through which we are all passing. Some, for example law centres or Citizens Advice Bureaux, will be concerned with providing advice or information; others, like Homestart, are concerned with befriending and supporting; whilst yet others will help meet client or member needs through allowing individuals to explore the meaning of their situation and then to develop the skills and strategies for managing it.

There is a greater acceptance of both the need for help and support in general, and for counselling in particular. This is evident in many radio and television news broadcasts on sensitive issues where a counselling hotline number is provided. Indeed, there was much criticism when the popular soap opera *Brookside* ran a storyline on domestic violence without providing counselling support for viewers. It has become the norm to provide counselling support for victims, onlookers and for those helping at the scenes of disasters. A recent example is the help given to pupils whose headteacher, Philip Lawrence, was fatally stabbed; and to the bomb victims in London's Docklands.

Definitions

Before embarking on a discussion of the principles involved in counselling skills it is important to the understanding of this chapter within the context of this book that differences between my uses of the word counselling and counselling skills are made clear. There are basically five definitions which are relevant.

Counselling as a generic helping strategy

In this context counselling is one of a number of helping strategies which individuals use throughout their lives. Everyone has some of the skills required for each strategy but will become more skilful if they are aware of the different skills involved and are able consciously to use each strategy at appropriate times. These skills and strategies will be further explored later in this chapter.

Counselling as a professional practice

Those who are involved in the professional practice of counselling use the basic skills of counselling alongside a range of specific therapeutic approaches. Their work involves working with individuals, couples or families at a deeper level and is often carried out over a longer period of time. The counsellors concerned may work in a voluntary or paid capacity and on a full- or part-time basis.

Counselling as advice

In historic terms the word counselling is associated with giving expert advice or recommendations, most often in relation to the legal profession. This creates confusion to many newly involved in the field of personal responsibility counselling, in which a major aim is to encourage indivi- duals to take responsibility for their own actions and to help themselves. This confusion is further exacerbated by the media and by government agencies such as Training and Enterprise Councils who use the term in both senses. Thus, for example, they will recommend individual counselling and guidance in the sense used in this book for those about to leave school or who are on government employment schemes and yet also speak of coun- selling people *into* jobs.

Counselling skills

Wherever this term is used within this chapter it refers to the basic skills which are common to both counselling as a *generic helping skill* and to *professional counselling*. It is not concerned with the more specific ther- apeutic skills involved in the latter.

Counselling skills movement

This phrase refers to those people who use counselling skills consciously and who have had some training but who are not professional counsellors. They would not regard themselves as part of a recognized movement but are distinguishable from those who have undertaken much more rigorous training and supervision in order to practise counselling in a more professional capacity. It is in this sense that those involved are referred to as a movement in this chapter.

Principles

Counselling skills development

The counselling skills movement owes most to the work of Carl Rogers (1951, 1957), who describes the qualities of empathy, genuineness, and warmth as essential to the client-centred counselling relationship and which enhance all forms of helping. These qualities were later confirmed by Truax and Carkhuff (1967). Whilst it was stated above that the counselling skills movement is neither recognizable nor homogeneous, thanks to the work of Rogers, who could rightly be called father of the movement, there is sufficient common ground for those who use counselling skills to communicate effectively with each other. Sutton writes 'these principles are, up to a point, the very ones that common sense might have guided us to select as important' (Sutton 1979: 208). She then shows how the teachers, social workers, and health workers whom we most value demonstrate these qualities, and adds:

> if we meet with kindness, compassion, respect and consideration, and continue to meet with those attitudes, we lose our sense of vulnerability, our anxiety diminishes and we are able to perceive events and situations with a vision less clouded by self-protective emotion.

Counselling and helping

It was suggested that counselling is one of a number of generic helping strategies, and an exploration of counselling skills leads to an exploration of those helping strategies. Many writers, probably with a professional counselling audience in mind, turn immediately to the different helping strategies, techniques, and theories within counselling. Okun (1982: 132) summarizes these in tabular form under the headings psychodynamic, phenomenological-client centred, Gestalt, behavioural, cognitive-behavioural, and Transactional Analysis. Most people involved in using counselling skills at a basic level are unlikely to require such sophistication at the time of their initial interest, but may graduate to one or more such strategies at a later stage of development or as interest in the possibilities offered by counselling become clearer.

If individuals are asked to discuss the ways in which they have most recently helped other people they will identify very different circumstances, but most of the strategies can be categorized as giving information, giving advice, teaching, counselling, or taking direct action on behalf of another person. Occasionally someone will also identify working to 'change the system' as a helping strategy. These are among the strategies used by the Counselling and Career Development Unit (CCDU) in counselling skills training since 1976 and discussed by Hopson and Scally (1981b) and Murgatroyd (1985).

More recently, a further helping strategy has been identified by CCDU, namely that of 'reviewing' (Pearce 1987). The use of this strategy is emphasized in Profiling and Record of Achievement schemes in schools and colleges of further education and in the various youth training schemes developed by the Manpower Services Commission (Pearce *et al.* 1981). In this context, 'reviewing' is defined as a process which enables people to say things about themselves relating to past experience, present situations and feelings, and future potential and need.

A first step in developing an understanding of counselling skills is therefore to help individuals recognize the ways in which they already help others and to explore the skills common and unique to each strategy. A further step in this development might then be to examine the advantages and disadvantages of each strategy for different helping circumstances. In this way it becomes possible to become a skilled helper, using specific strategies with awareness and appropriately instead of intuitively. During this process, for example, a given individual may for the first time become aware that what he or she had previously defined as counselling was, in fact, more related to giving advice.

Such a process of learning through understanding more clearly a wide range of everyday helping strategies can also lead naturally to an understanding of the importance of encouraging persons in need of help to take responsibility for making their own decisions, so that all helping strategies are employed in a more sensitive way.

Relationship-building skills

A first step in assisting the understanding of helping strategies is through the exploration of relationship-building skills, which are fundamental to effective helping and provide the route through which sensitive helping decisions can be made. Use of these skills, which are derived from the essential qualities of warmth, empathy, and genuineness as defined by Carl Rogers (Rogers 1951, 1957), respects the autonomy of the individual and is an enabling process. As a key to understanding the skills inherent within these essential qualities, they can be translated to respect, understanding, and being yourself.

Respect

Through exploring the skills of listening for non-verbal as well as verbal signals and recognizing that this is one way of showing respect for another human being, trainees quickly graduate to recognizing the many other concrete ways in which they can demonstrate this: for example, through giving time or displaying common courtesy to any individual. A teacher might identify ways of showing respect for pupils in the classroom and a manager can similarly recognize the means of conveying respect to colleagues and customers. The skills involved in demonstrating respect for another person are the foundation for the unconditional regard and warmth defined by Rogers.

Understanding

It is often easier for trainees to grasp the notion of understanding than it is to convey empathy especially as empathy is frequently confused with sympathy. Empathy is concerned with recognizing and understanding the feelings of another *as if* they were being experienced by oneself, whereas sympathy involves being emotionally affected by the feelings of another. In a workshop it is possible to provide structured exercises which help trainees recognize and practise the skills of identifying the feelings of others and to understand the effect which it has when someone is empathetic in relation to themselves. The feeling of being unconditionally valued at the same time as identifying the elements which give rise to this feeling is a very powerful learning process.

Being yourself

The most important aspect of being yourself is the recognition that there is no single model of helping or being that is the right one. It is liberating to know that, coupled with the other two essential qualities, comes permission to be genuine and, with that, to convey all the sincerity which this implies. The major skill involved in being yourself is that of self-disclosure. It often requires practice for an individual to learn to be vulnerable enough to risk disclosing experiences or feelings, and to do this in a way which is appropriate to the helping relationship.

Helping and basic counselling skills

Although relationship-building skills enhance the helping strategies of giving information, giving advice, teaching, reviewing, taking direct action, changing the system, and are essential to counselling, each strategy also has specific skills related to it. Some of these are common to basic

Table 14.1 Helping skills

Informing	Advising	Teaching	Counselling	Reviewing
Interpreting	**Listening**	Designing	**Contracting**	**Contracting**
	Interpreting	**Listening**	**Listening**	**Listening**
	Analysing	Planning	Concreteness	**Questioning**
	Clarifying	**Questioning**	Immediacy	**Summarizing**
		Summarizing	**Questioning**	**Clarifying**
		Challenging	**Summarizing**	Giving feedback
			Clarifying	Asking for feedback
			Focusing	
			Confronting	

counselling, others quite distinct. As a starting point, consider Table 14.1, which lists some of the key skills specific to each helping strategy. The lists are neither prescriptive nor exhaustive and there will no doubt be other skills that readers will be able to identify. The skill of 'changing systems' has not been included as it requires a complex set of organizational and political skills not relevant to this book. The skills of 'taking direct action' on behalf of another person are also omitted as this chapter is concerned with strategies which leave the client rather than the helper in control. Those skills featured in bold type are those which are common to counselling and other helping strategies. It can be seen quite clearly that strengths in a range of helping strategies provide a basis for the development of basic counselling skills.

Focusing more specifically upon those skills which are specific to counselling, the following brief definitions may be useful to those who are less familiar with the counselling process:

Contracting: This is the process which would normally take place at the beginning of a counselling session and which serves to clarify the purpose, duration, and structure of the session. It may be necessary to return to this process at later stages of the session if a new direction seems to be valuable for the client. Contracting is an important means by which the client is seen to be a partner rather than the subject of the counselling session.

Concreteness: Often a client will be vague about feelings and concerns and the skill of helping the individual concerned to be more concrete may be used to overcome this. The counsellor may ask the client to give examples of occasions on which a particular feeling has been experienced or to be more specific about a situation.

Immediacy: This is the skill of enabling the client to focus on the 'here-and-now'. It may involve asking for present feelings or, more often, discussing the relationship as it exists at that moment between the counsellor and client.

Questioning: It is normal to ask 'open' as opposed to 'closed' or 'leading' questions: that is, questions which require answers which are more than one word and which provide scope for the client to determine the direction of the answer.

Summarizing: The counsellor may at times find it useful to summarize all or part of what has passed during the session or to ask the client to do this. This is a clarifying procedure for both parties and is particularly valuable at the end of the session.

Clarifying: As different opinions are held about the exact meaning of different words and phrases it is important to clarify that the counsellor and client share the same understanding. It is even more vital to ensure that the counsellor has correctly identified the client's feelings.

Focusing: In covering a wide range of concerns the counsellor may find it useful to ask the client to focus upon a specific aspect of concern and to explore this in more detail.

Confronting: Within the trust that has been established in the counselling relationship the counsellor will be able to confront contradictions which occur between words and behaviour in the client or sensitively to challenge uncomfortable aspects in the life of the client.

Action skills

The final phase of any helping strategy is that of taking action, although the emphasis on action to be taken will vary for different helping strategies and for different contexts. Ideally, in all situations the decision about the action to be taken will rest with the individual concerned, but the level of support required will vary; and in the case of both counselling and reviewing the action may be broken into a series of smaller actions taken after each session rather than one single action. In counselling, although it is not always necessary for action to take place, it is important to consider with the client whether any action is required at the end of a session.

To summarize, counselling is one of a range of helping strategies, all of which require an ability to build effective relationships. In addition, each strategy has its own unique set of skills as well as some which it shares with other strategies, and each strategy has an action phase, i.e.

Phase 1. Relationship building
Phase 2. Skills specific to a given strategy
Phase 3. Action

An individual who is able to use different strategies skilfully and with awareness is likely to be a more valued and skilled helper. There will be times when it is appropriate for a counsellor to turn to advising and there will be times when someone who is reviewing will need to counsel. The professional counsellor will need to develop a set of strategies and skills beyond those described above, not normally part of the 'tool kit' of the person using basic counselling skills, and he or she will have taken part in a much more rigorous programme of training and supervision. The essential skill of the counsellor, however extensively trained, rests in the ability to use these skills at appropriate times and with great sensitivity. Listening with every sense and with the whole of oneself is the key to achieving this. The basic skills of counselling are summed up in the counselling process as defined on courses run by the Counselling and Career Development Unit (CCDU) at Leeds University (Figure 14.1).

Mapping the field

If, as suggested, the growth of the counselling skills movement is both an inevitable and necessary response to social change, it may be useful to consider the circumstances in which individuals choose to explore counselling as a means of helping others, particularly as in many cases their counselling work is voluntary, or at best peripheral to the main categories and tasks as defined in their job description. Many, it would seem, are

---

THE COUNSELLOR

uses		*helps the client*
RELATIONSHIP-BUILDING SKILLS	Respect Empathy	to feel understood to understand more how s/he feels and why
EXPLORING AND CLARIFYING SKILLS	Contracting Concreteness Immediacy Summarizing Questioning Focusing Confronting	to explore understanding to explore feelings to consider options to examine alternatives to choose an alternative
ACTION SKILLS	Objective Setting Action Planning Problem Solving	to form action plans to do, with support, what needs to be done

Figure 14.1 The basic skills of counselling, as defined by CCDU, Leeds University.

people already involved in people-orientated, helping professions such as education and health or social services. They are people who recognize their own helping limitations and who turn to counselling skills training as an additional means of providing help.

Others, who perhaps have successfully faced a difficult situation in their own lives, turn later to help others facing similar situations; for example, women who have suffered the loss of a breast, might, through the Mastectomy Association, begin to counsel other women and assist them in coming to terms with their loss; men who have lost custody of their children through marriage break-up may join Families Need Fathers, both to help campaign and to provide mutual support. Given some guidance and training they can play a particularly important function since they act as a role model for their clients, as well as having the skills to help support them.

Lay helpers who may initially have been nominated to act in a befriending capacity must also be included. The Homestart scheme, for example, uses housewives who, after a short training period, provide a wide variety of support for families in temporary need. Their tasks could include looking after children, cooking the occasional meal, or just acting as a friend and providing a 'listening ear' for a lonely mother. The women in this group do not usually see the need for counselling or necessarily know about counselling skills, but recognize that they will need to respond to those they are helping in a sensitive and caring way. Their route through to counselling is via learning about active listening.

Finally, there are many hundreds of people who have volunteered to train to join one of the voluntary services such as Relate or the Samaritans. These agencies are growing in number and cover an ever-increasing spectrum of need. Most notable are those provided directly for children such as ChildLine, set up to provide a telephone link to children who are being abused physically, mentally, or sexually and the many set up to provide particular support for the victims of disease such as the Terrence Higgins Trust for those wanting help and advice about AIDS.

More recently, a new category of people recognizing and using counselling skills has become evident, namely industrial and other managers. Peters and Austin (1985) and de Board (1983) have written of counselling as a management skill and strategy. This will be returned to later in this chapter as it underlines the organizational thrust which the movement may need to take.

To summarize, I have defined a wide range of people concerned with helping others; some may formally recognize what they provide as counselling, while others may not recognize the label, but understand many of the skills. Some have received little or no training, while others have been rigorously trained and supervised. They are united only by the desire to be effective in the way they help. Those involved in the counselling skills movement range across a very wide spectrum of helpers from those concerned with more effective listening through to those who will use counselling strategies at something approaching a professional level. It is essential for the community that a wide range of people are ready and willing to become helpers either in a professional capacity, as para-professional, or as community helpers. It is only through this process that we will at least be able to withstand and at best creatively manage the trauma of 'Future Shock' (Toffler 1970).

Figure 14.2 illustrates two axes which may be helpful for mapping the field of the counselling skills movement. It does not suggest that any given individual member of society is placed as shown on the diagram, for, after all, a solicitor may also be a Samaritan, a teacher, or a marriage guidance counsellor. It is however likely that many social workers, whilst not formally trained as counsellors, will have an appreciation and some understanding of counselling, whilst teachers through their classroom training will have some training appropriate to counselling without necessarily recognizing its relation to the practice of counselling. The progression is likely to be around the diagonal line from the bottom left-hand corner of the figure to the top right-hand corner: that is, the higher the level of training, the greater the amount of counselling practice which is undertaken. This is not however always the case; for example, a teacher may have a recognized counselling diploma and yet have little opportunity to undertake counselling in its formal sense. There are many omissions from the figure but I hope readers will be able to add those which have most relevance for them.

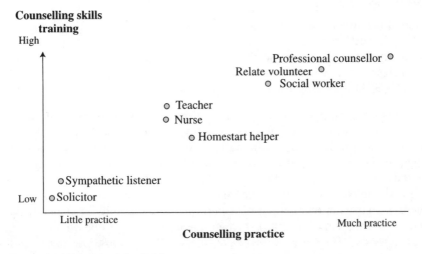

Figure 14.2 Mapping the field

Demystification of counselling

For more than a decade there has been a growth in the use of counselling skills as part of the process of organizational development. This has stemmed particularly from the field of education but is now spreading more widely through both the public and private sector. In order to understand the reasons for this growth it is first necessary to explore the premiss upon which much of the educational growth has rested – the demystification of counselling.

The need for extending an understanding of the counselling process has been recognized by a number of writers. Indeed, Murgatroyd (1985: 5) writes:

> I cannot agree that only certain kinds of people (for example, professional counsellors with specified academic qualifications) should be allowed to provide particular forms of help . . . helping is a process that can be and is widely used and available within a community and is not the sole prerogative of professionalised helpers and counsellors.

Hopson and Scally (1981b: 1) state that: 'It is vital that we "demystify" counselling', and that: 'There is nothing inherently mysterious about counselling. It is merely a set of beliefs, values and behaviours to be found in the community at large.' (1981b: 8)

If this is indeed the case, the question arises as to how far it is useful or necessary to distinguish between professional counsellors and those who use counselling skills. Nelson-Jones (1984) makes the distinction between counselling interviews and helping contacts. He states (1984: 99) that 'Counselling interviews involve counsellors and clients in formal settings', whereas

> Helping contacts may be made by people who use counselling skills as part of different or complex roles. For example, teachers, preachers, doctors, nurses, social workers and a host of others in the helping professions may each have opportunities to exhibit the skills of personal responsibility counselling.

Using this distinction some lay counsellors would be perceived as undertaking counselling interviews whilst many people in the helping professions, who may have had considerable training but be forced to practice in anything but ideal formal conditions, would be regarded as making helping contacts.

In Britain there are still comparatively few full-time counsellors and yet there is a growing recognition of counselling as an activity. Teachers who have a counselling diploma, for example, are unlikely to be employed in this capacity. They are more likely to use their counselling skills and knowledge within their teaching positions as part of the pastoral care offered by the school. Even those local education authorities which did employ school counsellors at one time have for the most part ceased to do so. This practice is reinforced by teachers themselves, who respect most those who continue to prove their ability to perform well in the classroom. It is these teachers who will have the credibility to add counselling to their other skills. In doing this they enhance their normal classroom practice as well as having additional skills when working with individual students. Indeed, Aspy and Roebuck (1977) have demonstrated that the best teachers already possess a high level of interpersonal skills. Similar views prevail throughout the people profession, ensuring that, for a while at least, counselling will most credibly be extended through encouraging a more universal understanding of the skills involved and their impact upon the present work of the professional person.

The work of CCDU

It was the belief in this process of demystifying counselling which in 1976 led the CCDU at Leeds University to launch a short but intensive counselling skills course intended for teachers and other education authority employees. The objectives of the course were to:

(1) identify the skills of counselling;
(2) compare counselling with other strategies;
(3) enable participants to identify their own skills to build upon these;
(4) explore the application of the course content to individual work situations.

The course was not intended to develop counsellors but to empower individuals to use counselling skills within their normal teaching practice, in order to help them deal more sensitively with pupil and staff problems, and to recognize when referral was necessary. The course used participative methods and gave all participants the opportunity to use closed-circuit television. Self-awareness exercises were also part of the course. Course members were explicitly discouraged from using role play because this was an opportunity not only to learn to use counselling skills but also to recognize the value of being counselled by another person and the vulnerability involved in being a client.

This course, with minor modifications, is still running and has been experienced by nearly 20,000 people since it was launched. It has only been possible to provide courses for such a large number of people because the underlying empowerment message contained within counselling became part of the organizational philosophy and practice of the CCDU.

A belief in demystifying counselling led to a process of demystifying training. Through the development of a training programme for potential volunteer trainers, large numbers of teachers from individual or groups of local education authorities were trained, further increasing the number of counselling skills courses which could be run. As a result networks of trainers began to develop. These trainers not only took part in running the CCDU course but also frequently became involved in training within their own institutions, and, through their influence and enthusiasm, a demand for counselling training among their fellow teachers increased.

As for the teachers who have attended the courses, some, as described above, have become trainers; some have sought opportunities for further counselling training; some have become volunteers for helping agencies; and very many have reported that the course has been of benefit to their work in the classroom, in working with individual staff and pupils and with parents. Some staff and trainers have left the field of education and are now working as trainers and managers in industry and the public sector and are influencing the system through their use of counselling skills.

The CCDU had started out with the intention of running short counselling skills courses which would themselves reflect the central values of counselling. Through this process organizational decisions were taken by staff concerned with helping individuals and organizations to help themselves. All other courses run by the CCDU were also influenced by this organizational perspective and the potential benefits of counselling skills and the counselling process to organizational growth began to be realized. Just as a counsellor may evaluate the effectiveness of a counselling session by considering how far the client has been able to take responsibility for themselves, so too does the CCDU evaluate its effectiveness by how far the organizations for which it has worked are able to continue that particular aspect of their work on their own.

There have been many counselling skills courses designed with similar objectives to those of the CCDU, which makes no claim to being the first in this field. The aim in describing a small element of its work (Pearce 1986) has been to explore the opportunity afforded by taking an organizational, as opposed to an individual view of counselling, for raising awareness of counselling to a much wider audience. Staff, voluntary trainers, and course members have continued to seek connections between different aspects of their work through counselling skills and it is this which has led to involvement in Record of Achievement courses, appraisal courses and management courses.

The organizational approach

The task of disseminating counselling skills has, as described above, already begun and is particularly evident in the field of education and training. Guidance and counselling is now part of the responsibility of the Training and Enterprise Councils and, although this is in its infancy, a start has been made which will bear fruit in years to come, as staff expertise increases. In the education service, there has been a minor revolution in the last decade with the development of a large number of short counselling skills courses. Perhaps of even greater importance is the recognition that counselling and reviewing have prospered within many of the newer initiatives in education. An increasing number of teachers accept the role of counselling within the pastoral care system; and reviewing as part of the process involved in tutoring a group of students in the development of the National Record of Achievement and Action Plan for year 11 pupils. Most important of all is the provision of skill development for students through personal and social development programmes. At their best, these courses are building a foundation for a generation of self-powered individuals who may come closer to building a more caring society. This view of the growth of counselling is supported by the initial findings of a questionnaire on counselling provision in education conducted by the University of Warwick. This has shown that: 'Whilst few Authorities now have a policy for employing full-time counsellors in schools, most felt they were providing some sort of alternative counselling support if only through their tutorial system.' (Hooper and Laing 1987) The survey which was sent to all 113 education authorities in England, Scotland and Wales had a 73 per cent response rate. The interim report goes on to illustrate the movement towards counselling skills through quoting some of the observations made by the advisors who replied to the questionnaire. The development of counselling skills is being further underlined by government demands for appraisal for teachers. The teaching profession is anxious that this should be developmental and empowering rather than controlling and oppressive, and may recognize that training in counselling and reviewing skills could be helpful in ensuring this approach.

Similar movement, although not as yet so dramatic, is also apparent in other public services and in industry and commerce. Peters and Waterman (1982) demonstrate that one of the factors which help companies to be successful in the commercial world is trust in employees and a constant attention to the needs of the individual in relation to the needs of the company. Peters and Austin (1985) go further and talk about the need for love which they relate to a range of practical helping strategies, including counselling, not dissimilar to those described earlier. They, like Rogers, have an optimistic view of the individual. This view is beginning to be an increasing part of the value system of organizations which are aware of how this liberates their own creative potential. Their approach and that of many modern management consultants is that people are the most important resource within an organization whether as customers, clients, or employees and that there must be constant attention to their needs. They reject the idea that this person-centred approach is a 'soft' option and suggest that true excellence can only be achieved by this means. It involves respect, trust, tolerance of mistakes and encouragement to take risks. This is perhaps the most heartening aspect of sharing the principles of counselling. Inevitably the practice does not yet match the rhetoric but the 'window of opportunity' exists if we are prepared to recognize it.

Issues

There are a number of issues relating to the use of counselling skills within the wider community. Many of these are interrelated and are concerned particularly with the perception which counsellors have of themselves, their clients and perhaps most importantly of each other.

Counselling as a profession

If we genuinely believe that counselling is about helping people to help themselves, then we must believe that they can take responsibility for the skills which some people in the professional field of counselling believe should remain exclusive to them. As Illich states: 'Professionals assert secret knowledge about human nature, knowledge which only they have the right to dispense.' (Illich *et al.* 1977: 19). In the same book McKnight (1977: 89) goes further and writes: 'We have reached the apogee of the modernised service society when the professional can say to the citizen:

We are the solution to your problem.
We know the problem you have.
You can't understand the problem or the solution.
Only we can decide whether the solution has dealt with your problem.'

I do not believe this to be true at the present time in the counselling profession, but there is a danger that such a view could be legitimized if counsellors claim 'legitimacy as the interpreter, protector and supplier of a special, this-worldly interest of the public at large' (Illich *et al.* 1977: 17). We must constantly question how far the systems and organizations which we have designed and supported are merely to protect the role of counsellors rather than to support the central ideas of counselling practice. It is important for members of BAC, for example, to question how far it is concerned with accrediting professionals and protecting their rights and how far it is an organization committed to helping individuals and organizations to help themselves.

The role of the counsellor

It is often difficult for those who are struggling to preserve a counselling service within schools and other institutions to come to terms with those, similarly trained, who would prefer to work in a different way; in particular, to recognize that a counsellor who chooses to work within the system

as a trainer or manager might be contributing to the eventual wider acceptance of counselling. This is perhaps an inevitable and potentially creative
tension. It is important for all those involved in counselling to support the
provision of counselling services. Those who at present operate as counsellors can best serve this through being concerned with their provision in
the present, whilst those working for system change have a long-term role
to play. This will involve modelling the values central to counselling in the
way they operate as trainers, teachers, nurses, social workers, managers
and so on. It will also involve setting up structures which encourage self-
empowerment and which are concerned with people working and living
together in a more sensitive and caring way.

It is this process which will cut through some of the apparent paradoxes
which exist. Many counsellors, for example, may find the idea of appraisal
counselling a contradiction in terms and yet at its best appraisal involves
the right of an individual to know how to improve working effectiveness.
Those who see appraisal as a developmental process are designing and
running systems which are staff-centred, based on evidence, and are often
peer-led.

Future developments

This chapter has been based largely upon the assumption that the counselling process, and in particular the skills of counselling, should be made
available to a wide community of individuals – indeed that some aspects of
counselling should be readily accessible to everyone. This notion of counselling skills training for all might at first seem provocative. If broken
down further, what is being suggested is the following:

- Counselling skills training should be a normal and necessary part of the
  training for all professionals. The depth of training in those skills is
  likely to be greater for those engaged in the helping professions such as
  nursing, teaching and social work than for lawyers, dentists, estate agents
  and so on.
- At a lower level the foundation for counselling skills training should be
  laid down in schools with an increasing emphasis on providing training
  for students in active listening and on helping them to understand and
  practice the concepts of respect, empathy and genuineness which contribute towards building effective relationships.
- Managers in industry and elsewhere need counselling skills training in
  order to understand how counselling integrates with their other functions
  in working with people.

By adopting such a broad vision of demystification there is the opportunity to raise considerably the level of understanding and acceptance of
the concept of counselling. It recognizes that the world is not divided into

'helpers' and those needing 'help' and that we can all assume some responsibility for responding to the needs of fellow human beings. At the same time it ensures that each individual understands more clearly the limitations of the help which they can personally provide and the necessity of turning to those with greater expertise at appropriate times.

By inviting an ever-increasing number of people to share an understanding of counselling we may begin to develop the notion of a truly caring society – not just through the provision of institutions such as the National Health Service or social services but also in the sensitivity of day-to-day contact between individuals.

Counselling skills training

Not everyone agrees that the essential qualities described by Rogers can be acquired, or practised, by everyone who seeks to use counselling skills. Hamblin (1974: 11) writes:

> It is at this point that we begin to see that not all teachers can be counsellors. The personality of the counsellor will influence the transaction which occurs between him and the pupil, and not every teacher can create the conditions necessary for honest self-exploration and helpful communication.

The viewpoint adopted by Rogers for client-centred therapy is essentially optimistic about human nature and is based upon the belief that individuals can take responsibility for their own actions. This optimism can and should be extended to the potential of every individual to understand and practice the essential qualities described by Rogers. If they are willing to confront the personal growth this requires, then those qualities can be learned. Figure 14.3 shows the map of the field described in figure 14.2, alongside a further development of the model which shows the relationship between counselling skills training and counselling practice necessary for professional counsellors, those who use counselling skills in a less formal capacity, and the community at large. There are of course overlaps: there will be many people within the community who will wish to extend their understanding further, just as there will be some teachers, social workers and so on who will operate at the same level as a professional counsellor. The model is meant to describe the minimum levels for which we should be aiming.

In Figure 14.4 each sector of the model is considered separately. In the bottom left-hand corner it is argued that there should be a greater effort to disseminate the basic skills of relationship building throughout the community, in particular by providing young people with opportunities to learn and understand them and by ensuring that all those who work in the public arena are aware of the part these skills play in making them more effective.

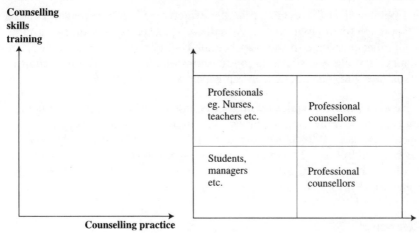

Figure 14.3 A model for counselling skills training

		Basic counselling skills		Basic counselling skills	Advanced counselling skills
Relationship-building skills		Relationship-building skills		Relationship-building skills	Advanced counselling practice

Students, managers, doctors etc.	**Teachers, nurses, social workers etc.**	**Professional counsellors**

Figure 14.4 Sectors of the model for counselling skill training

Those in the counselling skills movement will need to undertake basic counselling skills training though their understanding at this level may well graduate to gaining a greater understanding of counselling. It is only at this point that the more rigorous training and supervision necessary for professional counselling will be undertaken, as indicated in the right-hand box in Figure 14.4. It is beyond the scope of this chapter to discuss what is involved at this point.

Conclusion

Rogers (1978), who finally came to accept the political nature of the work in which he had been engaged throughout his life, summed up the challenge which faces counsellors in the following way:

I believe it is the evidence of the effectiveness of the person centred approach that may turn a very small and quiet revolution into a far more significant change in the way human kind perceives the possible. I am much too close to the situation to know whether this will be a minor or major event, but I believe it represents a radical change.

He also wrote: 'A quiet revolution is underway in almost every field. It holds promise of moving us forward to a more human, more person centred world.' (Rogers 1978: 290). It is this quiet revolution which this chapter has been addressing. I have demonstrated that it has already begun and our challenge is now to allow it to continue by recognizing, with Rogers, that our work is also essentially political in nature.

References

Aspy, D. N, and Roebuck, F. N. (1977) *Kids Don't Learn From People They Don't Like*, Amherst, Massachusetts: Human Resources Development Press.
de Board, R. (1983) *Counselling Skills*, Aldershot: Gower.
Freire, P. (1976) *Education: The Practice of Freedom*, London: Writers and Readers Publishing Co-operative.
Hamblin, D. H. (1974) *The Teacher and Counselling*, Oxford: Basil Blackwell.
Hooper, R. and Laing, P. (1987) *Questionnaire on Counselling Provision in England, Wales and Scotland* (initial findings), Warwick: School of Education, Warwick University.
Hopson, B. and Scally, M. (1981a) *Lifeskills Teaching*, London: McGraw-Hill.
——(1981b) *A Model for Helping and Counselling: Implications for Training*, Leeds: Counselling and Career Development Unit, Leeds University.
Illich, I., Zola, I. K., McKnight, J., Kaplan, J. and Shaiken, H. (1977) *The Disabling Professions*, Boston: Marion Boyars.
McKnight, J. (1977) 'Professionalized, service and disabling help' in Illich *et al.* (eds) *The Disabling Professions*, Boston: Marion Boyars.
Murgatroyd, S. J. (1985) *Counselling and Helping*, London: Methuen.
Nelson-Jones, R. (1984) *Personal Responsibility Counselling and Therapy – An Integrative Approach*, London: Harper and Row.
Okun, B. (1982) *Effective Helping – Interviewing and Counselling Techniques*, Belmont, California: Wadsworth.
Pearce, B. (1986) *CCDU – A Living Philosophy*, Leeds: Counselling and Career Development Unit, Leeds University.
——(1987) *Reviewing Skills*, Leeds: Counselling and Career Development Unit, Leeds University.
Pearce, B., Flegg, D., Varney, E. and Waldman, P. (1981) *Trainee Centred Reviewing*, London: Manpower Services Commission, Research & Development Series No. 2.
Peters, T. and Austin, N. (1985) *A Passion for Excellence – The Leadership Difference*, New York: Random House.
Peters, T., and Waterman, R. (1982) *In Search of Excellence*, New York: Harper and Row.
Rogers, C. R. (1951) *Client-centred Therapy*, Boston: Houghton-Mifflin.
——(1957) 'The necessary and sufficient conditions of therapeutic personality change', *Journal of Consulting Psychology* 21: 95–103.

——(1978) *Carl Rogers on Personal Power – Inner Strength and its Revolutionary Impact*, London: Constable and Co.

Stonier, T. (1978) *Education in a Post-industrial Society: Exchange 3*, Leeds: Counselling and Career Development Unit, Leeds University.

Sutton, C. (1979) *Psychology for Social Workers and Counsellors*, London: Routledge & Kegan Paul.

Toffler, A. (1970) *Future Shock*, London: Bodley Head.

Truax, C. and Carkuff, R. (1967) *Toward Effective Counseling and Psychotherapy*, Chicago: Aldine.

Chapter fifteen

Brief and time-limited counselling

Sue Culley and James Wright

Introduction

Currently, there is an enormous range of counselling help available to individuals, couples and families in Britain. Financial constraints notwithstanding, what most people are offered and seem to want, is short-term support. Brief and time-limited counselling presents a challenge to practitioners, inviting them to refine, capture and offer what is at the core of this complex activity.

There is no single model of brief counselling, although the concept of brief work will be familiar to most counsellors. The major approaches have been classified broadly into psychodynamic, cognitive-behavioural and tactical (Steenbarger 1992), the last derived primarily from systems-based family therapies. Probably the best known of the tactical models is solution-focused brief therapy (de Shazer 1985), an approach developed by de Shazer and Berg from their work as family therapists (de Shazer *et al.* 1986). There are also approaches which integrate concepts and techniques from different orientations within a guiding framework; for example, cognitive analytic therapy (Ryle 1990).

Although the intended goals for change, the techniques, the strategies and the processes of the various orientations may differ, we attempt in this chapter to discuss some particular and distinguishing features of brief and time-limited counselling.

Background

While there has been a growing interest in brief approaches to counselling and psychotherapy in the past decade, the quest for models that are both brief and effective has a longer history. Ferenczi and Rank attempted to reduce the length of psychoanalysis, the latter emphasizing the importance of setting time limits and mobilizing the client's 'will'. Ferenczi proposed a more 'active' involvement for the therapist, rather than relying on interpretation (Horner 1994). The pioneering work of Davanloo, Sifneos and

Malan has profoundly influenced the development and use of brief analytic therapy (Gustafson 1986). In the early 1950s, Ellis began to tailor his approach to clients unable to finance classical analytic therapy (Yankura and Dryden 1994). He introduced more active and direct methods than the relatively passive analytic procedures. He discovered that when practising this supposedly more 'superficial approach', clients fared as well or better than those receiving classical analysis. He began to formulate the theoretical principles and techniques of what he would later call 'rational therapy'.

While the initial impetus for offering brief counselling may have come from an economic rationale and a desire to maximize the use of scarce resources, the spur to develop elegant models which capture the essence of efficient psychotherapy should not be discounted. The work of de Shazer and Berg, for example, has been important in attempting to produce a 'clear and concise . . . specification of what brief therapy is about and the steps involved in doing it' (de Shazer 1988: v).

For the purposes of this chapter we will neither differentiate between counselling and psychotherapy, nor debate the distinction. The term brief counselling will also be used to encompass both *time-limited* and *short-term* work. We appreciate that distinctions may be made between a *time-limited* approach, which has explicit limits on the number of sessions available; and a *short-term* approach which also intentionally considers time limits but remains more open-ended about both number of sessions and duration.

Where is brief counselling offered?

The rationale for offering brief counselling has been and continues to be primarily an economic one. Organizations in both the statutory and voluntary sectors are faced with resource allocation and pressure to reduce waiting lists. Relate National Marriage Guidance, for example, has been encouraging short-term contract work over the past decade in order both to reduce the length of time perspective clients spend waiting to commence appointments and to allow a greater spread of scarce resources. Another growth area in brief counselling is in the surgeries of general practitioners. Clients are typically offered a limited number of sessions after referral by their doctor, social services and psychiatric outpatient departments are also offering brief counselling both to individuals and families (George, Iveson and Ratner 1990). Brief work is furthermore a continuing and important aspect of the support offered by student counselling departments in colleges and universities.

Working to brief contracts has additionally found major support within industrial and commercial settings. There has been an expansion in employee assistance programmes which offer external help on a limited basis to any employee experiencing either work-related or personal problems. Brief counselling therefore would seem to be in tune with the realities of providing counselling support in the commercial, statutory and voluntary sectors.

Defining brief counselling

Brief counselling is *time conscious*, and has typically been defined by time. While such a definition offers a convenient rule of thumb, the averages quoted demonstrate that there is a wide variation between what practitioners consider to be brief. Barkham and Rowan (1993) describe brief counselling as lasting from one to twenty sessions. Ryle (1992) advocates a norm of sixteen sessions for his cognitive-analytic approach; while Malan (1979) indicates brief therapy ranging from between four to sixty sessions. For de Shazer (1991a), brief therapy means therapy that necessitates as few sessions as possible, and no more, for clients to achieve a satisfactory solution. He has quoted the time which clients stay in therapy as being between one and twelve sessions, the average being three and a half. Dryden (1995) gives an account of brief rational emotive behaviour therapy of eleven sessions. What, therefore, is considered brief by one counselling approach may be considered a luxurious amount of time by another.

However, what seems to be important is to distinguish between, on the one hand, work that is brief because of arbitrary time limitations and, on the other hand, developing brief counselling as a distinct approach. Defining brief counselling by time neither assists us with identifying its essential and distinguishing features nor helps us to understand what practitioners do differently in brief work in terms of structure and process. Brief counselling is neither synonymous with hurrying or 'short-changing' clients nor is it doing less of the same (de Shazer 1988). In essence, it is a pragmatic approach which focuses on problem solution or management by the most efficient route. Brief counselling does not espouse the notion of 'cure' or have character change as one of its goals (Budman and Gurman 1988). It also questions the assumption that counselling, particularly for those with common psychiatric diagnoses, is invariably a long-term commitment.

Advantages and disadvantages of brief counselling

The advantages and disadvantages of brief work have been well documented (Barkham and Rowan 1993; Steenbarger 1992). The main advantage seems to be in terms of outcome. The majority of studies point to little difference between brief interventions and those of time-unlimited therapies. A survey of the relevant literature suggests that offering long-term counselling does not necessarily produce greater gains for clients, since most change appears to occur within the first eight sessions with correspondingly diminishing returns thereafter. However, most counsellors are alert to the notion of 'flight into health'. They are also aware – and may have had similar experiences themselves in their own counselling – that clients often experience surges of enthusiasm, hope and well-being during the initial stages as they confront the possibility of resolving their concerns. This 'growth spurt' (Gelso 1992) does not mean that more profound and equally important changes may not occur more gradually in later work. To conclude that, because change may be of the more gradual and difficult-to-measure variety, further sessions are not cost effective may be highly damaging to some clients. Research into employee assistance programmes, however, has clearly suggested that employees who receive brief counselling take sick leave less often and report feeling more healthy (Highley and Cooper 1995).

Brief intervention seems to match what users both want and expect. There appears to be a discrepancy between what counsellors view as an adequate number of sessions and the generally lesser number of sessions expected by clients. Counsellors appear to be biased toward longer-term work, whilst clients assume that change can happen over a comparably short time span. However, this apparent discrepancy should not lead us to discount the views of either group or assume that counsellor reservations about the value of brief work is a defensive reaction. Counsellors skilled in providing long-term support are able to observe the subtle developments that take place over time with their clients. They witness how slowly certain changes can occur and what struggles clients have to maintain these changes. While counsellors may underestimate the value of brief interventions for these reasons, they are also trained to make clinical assessments and judgements about client progress (Gelso and Johnson 1983). Any misgivings about the value of brief counselling need to be acknowledged and incorporated into the development of the approach.

The main disadvantage to brief and time-limited work is that clients may simply not be afforded the opportunity to do the work they need to do. The issues they bring and their state of preparedness may make brief counselling inappropriate or harmful to them. For some clients, to disturb their fragile equilibria under the pretext that some help, however short, is better than none may be doing them a gross disservice. However, comments from counsellors we approached suggested that, for clients with chronic concerns or disorders of the self, brief work could assume a kind of 'introduction' to counselling. The task for the counsellor would be to assist the client to achieve limited goals and provide a positive experience of counselling. Clients may then be motivated to commit themselves to longer-term work at some point. Brief contracts may also be used as a 'holding operation' for some clients. For example, they may be on waiting lists for particular agencies and want support until they are offered an appointment. This is occasionally a feature of workplace counselling and employee assistance programmes. While the type of contract negotiated is a key issue for any counsellor, not just practitioners of brief counselling, it assumes a greater salience if there is limited flexibility to re-negotiate further sessions.

Principles of brief counselling

We are considering here brief counselling that is *conceptually planned* as distinct from counselling where a time limit is imposed because of resource implications or clients ending prematurely.

Style of the counsellor

Working to brief or time-limited contracts demands that the practitioner adopt a typically more interactive and proactive style. Counsellors engaging in brief counselling report acting as 'encouragers' or 'galvanizers' to clients. Brief counselling requires that counsellors engage in an active way, be it to coach, confront, question, hypothesize, rehearse or teach (Cooper 1995).

Counselling relationship

The ability to form a vibrant relationship speedily and to sustain it, is clearly crucial. Kaplan (1992) stresses the importance of the relationship as the vehicle for change in brief work. Discussions with practitioners suggest that the quality of the relationship, one that is high in emotional involvement, is more important to a positive outcome than the techniques and strategies employed by any particular approach.

Cooper (1995) provides suggestions for achieving a positive alliance, a distinguishing characteristic of which is the expectation and encouragement of high, active client participation. He cites utilizing 'active listening', empathic understanding, showing respect for clients' frame of reference, introducing counselling and discussing mutual expectations. He further refers to the importance of practitioners remaining positive and confident in their expectations that clients will achieve reasonable goals.

Developing the capacity for empathic understanding, establishing a shared responsibility for the direction and flow of the work, and mobilizing clients' will are core components in brief or any counselling. Paradoxically, the fact that brief counselling has time constraints seems to make these qualities and aims for the relationship even more critical.

The 'core' or 'essential' qualities for building a containing space for the counselling work is very well documented and will not be discussed further here (Rogers 1951, 1961). Suffice it to say that it would be unhelpful to polarize outcome and relationship issues. They are not mutually exclusive, as every counsellor will recognize. Too much focus on what is to be achieved or what would be a desirable outcome may lead to an agenda which is unhelpfully rigid; while an over-emphasis on relationship issues may lead to unfocused work. The balance between the support of an energetic, respectful and understanding relationship and the challenge of keeping the focus of the work in view is a tough one to maintain and never more so than in brief work.

Client selection

While there may be differences in the claims made for the appropriateness of brief work for particular clients or variations in what might constitute a contra-indication, assessment of client suitability is certainly an important consideration for some, if not all, practitioners.

Malan (1979) for example, has indicated four conditions that clients must fulfil in order for brief work to be deemed appropriate. These are concerned with identifying a focus for the work, client motivation and ability to respond to interpretations, and finally the possible dangers to clients of being involved in brief therapy. De Shazer (1988) has used the terms 'customers', 'complainants' and 'visitors' to distinguish between potential clients and 'non-clients'.

While Dryden and Feltham (1992) consider brief counselling unsuitable for people with chronic disturbances, personality disorders and serious mental-health problems, Ryle (1990) regards cognitive-analytic therapy to be suitable for clients with personality disorders or other serious disturbances to the self. As a rule, brief work is not considered suitable for those clients who are seriously psychiatrically disturbed, on some forms of medication or who want to examine their lives and their internal worlds at their own pace.

Having drug or alcohol problems is not necessarily a contra-indication for brief counselling (Berg and Miller 1992b). Much will, of course, depend on the severity of the problem and the willingness of individuals to involve themselves in the process. However, comparative studies in the United States have pointed to the effectiveness of brief interventions in altering the problem drinkers' behaviour. While brief counselling showed a better outcome than no intervention, there was little or no difference in drinking outcomes whether the individual received brief counselling or more extensive help (Miller *et al.* 1994).

However, experience of practice suggests that counsellors operate with varying degrees of strictness when applying suitability criteria for brief work.

A working map

The major approaches to brief counselling provide the practitioner with the theoretical concepts both for understanding the nature of client concerns and for identifying particular targets for the counselling, for example, rational emotive brief counselling would typically be concerned with self-defeating patterns of behaviour and the irrational beliefs which sustain them. A cognitive-analytic approach uses the procedural sequence model which integrates the core of cognitive-behavioural therapy with concepts from psychoanalytic theory. Defences are understood as 'cognitive editing'.

However, it seems that whatever theoretical stance the practitioner espouses, whatever concepts they find useful to aid both their own and client understanding, a structure or *meta-model* for the counselling process can be identified. The structure is phase-based and provides a template for the integration of theory and process. Steenbarger (1992) has outlined three stages: engagement, discrepancy and consolidation. These stages have many similarities with the models developed by other important process theorists such as Egan (1990), Nelson-Jones (1988) and Ivey *et al.* (1987). While they have not specifically labelled their work as brief-intervention models, the frameworks they have developed and the values and assumptions they espouse bear all the hallmarks of brief counselling. Undoubtedly, the thinking and writing of Gerard Egan (1990) has had a most profound impact on counsellor training in the United Kingdom (see p. 32f). Egan considers helping, in most cases, to be a short-term proposition. The principles underpinning brief work are not foreign to the spirit of his model.

Cooper (1995) has outlined a procedure for brief therapy. He identifies relevant tasks for pre-intake, first and subsequent sessions, moving on to maintaining gains, ending counselling, and evaluation. This procedure is both relevant and appropriate to counselling which lasts for a single session. For the purposes of this chapter, we will simply use the terms opening sessions, subsequent sessions and ending.

Opening sessions

These sessions are typically concerned with assessing both clients' level of motivation and their suitability for brief work. Establishing a positive working relationship, gaining relevant information of present stresses and difficulties, plus establishing a working plan or agenda would also feature strongly. Successful work is seen as being dependent on knowing where clients want to go and finding the quickest way to get there. A characteristic of brief counselling is both rapid and continuous assessment which is integrated at the outset with finding solutions. This process of refining hypotheses about problems through trial action and feedback is referred to as 'ready, fire, aim' (O'Hanlon and Weiner-Davis 1989).

The number of sessions allocated to assessment and counselling planning will obviously vary. Cognitive-analytic therapy typically devotes sessions one to four to assessment of clients' concerns, working towards a clarification or reformulation and an agenda for the therapy (Ryle and Cowmeadow 1992). The first session of solution-focused therapy is concerned with listening to clients and to what they are complaining about in their lives. De Shazer (1988, 1991b) and colleagues routinely ask the 'miracle' question. This goes as follows: 'Suppose that one night while you were asleep a miracle occurred and your problem was solved. How would you know?'. The counsellor generally goes on to ask further exploratory questions such as: 'What would be different?'; 'How would your children know without you saying anything to them about it?'; 'How would your partner know?'. They also ask questions which invite clients to self-assess and consider times when their situation has improved. The purpose is to empower clients by searching for the positive, to start the reframing process and develop goals. Counsellors involved in brief work are usually concerned less with problems and their aetiology than the potential solution contained within the thoughts and actions of clients.

Dryden (1995) has argued that one or two sessions should be adequate to gain a clear description of clients' problems and an understanding of their frames of reference. The inexperience of the therapist notwithstanding, if more than three sessions need to be devoted to problem definition and goal-setting, Dryden considers that this could indicate that brief rational emotive behaviour therapy is unsuitable for the client.

The differences between the opening sessions of time-unlimited and brief work, in addition to clear contracts and agendas, are negotiating criteria for a successful outcome, and parsimony in the amount and type of information sought. Within a brief contract, taking a full history is generally deemed inappropriate and information gathering is confined to a definition of difficulties, patterns and themes, support networks and resources, and what outcomes clients want. Some practitioners also encourage clients to undertake *homework* or *between-session tasks* from the outset. The value and role of assignments are discussed with clients, in relation to both the outcomes they want and what they are willing to do.

Subsequent sessions

These sessions are concerned with treatment (Ryle 1992), new perspectives (Egan 1990), generating alternative solutions (Ivey *et al.* 1987) and discrepancy (Steenbarger 1992). What all these various labels have in common is the focus on further activity directed towards providing clients with experiences which assist in either the management or the resolution of the presenting problems.

The techiques and interventions used here will vary considerably and depend for the most part on client need, but also on counsellor orientation. Counsellors may, for example, employ active interventions such as two-chair work, role playing, imagery and rehearsal techniques. The skills of feedback, immediacy and confrontation are important in helping clients to remain present-focused and positive, and to review the outcome of homework.

Reviewing homework tasks against agreed goals would form an important part of this stage. While practitioners are not unanimous in either their use or approval of assignments, appropriate and agreed tasks can be immensely valuable for maintaining motivation and involvement by providing a 'bridge' between sessions. Clearly between-session tasks should neither be imposed upon clients nor present an additional burden. They should be relevant, capable of being achieved, and provide clients with both incentives and reward. Some practitioners would argue that in addition to being more active in sessions, employing tasks between sessions is one of the distinguishing features of brief counselling. Assignments are a practical way of keeping the counselling work, the goals and the progress in mind and maintaining the client as an active partner in the process.

Ending

Brief counselling perhaps more than any other has closure and ending in view. While counsellors offering brief work consider it important to remind clients from the outset of the number of sessions they have available, de Shazer considers it may prolong counselling unnecessarily. Malan (1976), on the other hand, has indicated the importance of working within a time limit from the outset. Ending typically deals with consolidation, evaluation of progress against goals, and agreeing coping strategies for the future. Clients are typically invited to anticipate obstacles and do some forward planning. The techniques of this phase may include: ending letters, reviewing journals, or 'writing a history'. The last method can be powerful in helping clients to construct new and more promising futures.

Timing of sessions

Following a conventional pattern of weekly contact may not be the most appropriate for brief work. Change is not a linear process for clients. It is typically accelerated at the outset and invariably continues beyond the counselling contract. Rather than concentrating sessions into a short time span, there would seem to be a case for both greater spacing between initial sessions and providing follow-up. Follow-up sessions can be important for reinforcing and rewarding new behaviours. Egan describes inertia and entropy as part of being human; for those clients who want support to maintain their gains or who experience a lack of energy for achieving their goals, reviewing is a way of providing an important 'dose' of encouragement. Providers of employee assistance programmes report that clients often build in their own safety net by keeping a session 'in reserve'.

Building in follow-up and review sessions also counters the 'termination myth' (Steenbarger 1992). The assumption that clients are or should be 'cured' and not need to return for further counselling is wishful-thinking (Budman 1990). Clients often seek help at different stages in their lives, as they confront new dilemmas and tasks (Cummings 1990). Offering review sessions as required is in tune with the view of change as a continuous, unfolding and variable process.

Working with present difficulties

Practitioners of brief and time-limited counselling are orientated to the present – the presenting difficulties and stresses of clients. This is not to imply that clients' histories are either deemed irrelevant or that practitioners avoid working with those who wish to examine and make sense of their past. However, the effort is directed to making rapid connections between clients' past and their present difficulties in order to discover how changes can be facilitated or symptoms relieved.

There will inevitably be clients whose presenting concerns cover deeper issues which are revealed some way into the counselling. Similarly, good initial and ongoing assessment may not necessarily prompt clients to disclose what is at the core of their concerns. Some clients may consciously decide not to bring in certain material, for a variety of reasons; for example, the counselling relationship may not have 'stood the test of time'.

The response to disclosures of more complex concerns is usually to negotiate additional time. This might be either with the current counsellor or by referral to a counsellor more experienced in the particular issue which the client has revealed. Usually, the amount of additional time will be agreed and kept under review.

Identifying a counselling focus

This is both an essential precursor to defining outcomes and a distinguishing aspect of brief work. Focusing involves discovering with clients what specifically they want to do something about. It involves finding the most direct route to managing difficulties and not getting side-tracked by discussing peripheral or unrelated issues.

The assessment and diagnostic frameworks which counsellors use will depend upon their orientation and training. Cooper (1995) suggests an initial strategy of reviewing cognitive, behavioural and affective coping patterns with clients. Hoyt et al. (1992: 62) suggest three metatheoretical questions both to establish a focus and to decide how to intervene. They are:

- how is the client 'stuck'; that is, what is maintaining the problem?
- what does the client need to do to get 'unstuck'?
- how can the counsellor facilitate or provide what is needed?

A focus might also be developed by discussing the following with clients:

- how their presenting concerns are a problem for them. For example, a fifty-year-old male client was asked how losing his job was a problem for him. He replied that it wasn't a problem for him, but his wife was extremely distressed at the thought of him not working!
- what has encouraged them to seek counselling now.
- what has improved since they made their appointment. Clients often report pre-session change. Discovering what they did to improve their situations and encouraging them to continue provides an initial focus.

Goal orientated

Identifying the problem or complaint provides the agreed focus for the work. The goals are the translation of what clients would consider to be satisfactory outcomes, into specific, achievable and positive terms. Brief work is essentially outcome orientated and with usually more limited goals than for longer-term involvement. The task for the practitioner is to help clients to decide outcomes which are both reasonable and within their control. The positive aspect to determining outcomes is important. Clients can usually describe what they want to avoid or stop doing, but that does not generally help them to discover what they need to do to make the changes they want. Outcomes are negotiated, kept under review and used to evaluate changes made by clients.

Issues

Approaches to brief and time-limited counselling

Brief counselling is in a kind of transitional state. What is evident from the literature is that there are *models of process* which provide clear guidance to practitioners in managing the first through to the final session. These models have a strong cognitive and behavioural orientation; and they seem to place equal, if not greater, emphasis on what happens in clients' lives outside the counselling room. Given that there are differences among the varous approaches to counselling and therapy in Britain, what seems to be important is consideration of how brief counselling models can be further developed to encourage integration of divergent theoretical perspectives.

Referral

Agencies and other counselling organizations are currently under pressure. It seems that they are being contacted by a growing number of clients with severe or chronic concerns – clients who five or ten years ago would have been under the care of a psychiatric hospital, the social services or a community psychiatric provision. Assessing whether the issue presented by the client can be substantially addressed by a short contract is crucial and so is the opportunity for referral for longer-term support. This is a safety net which has been radically reduced for all but those who can afford to pay.

Offering 'trial' counselling

Offering clients the option of a brief contract in order that they experience counselling as a way of resolving their concerns must be handled sensitively and ethically. The wish to encourage clients to become involved in longer-term work may come from a genuinely held view that little can be achieved with a brief contact. However, it is important that practitioners continue to challenge their beliefs about the relative merits of brief and time-unlimited work. While practitioners need to guard against encouraging clients into longer involvement than is appropriate, it seems equally important to disabuse clients of the belief that every issue or problem can be resolved by short-term intervention.

Training in brief counselling

Brief and short-term counselling forms the bulk of the counselling provision available to all but relatively few clients. However, not all counsellors have received specific training in the techniques, intervention strategies and management of brief contracts. This would seem to be important if counsellors are to work flexibly and competently with limited contracts.

Conclusion

There seems little doubt that brief counselling is effective in providing clients with the assistance they need to resolve their concerns. Whether brief counselling is more or less effective than time-unlimited work in producing durable changes, we do not know. Perhaps it is a contest that should not be joined. What is needed is not further demonstration of the efficacy of brief work but rather a clearer understanding of:

- which client groups are best served;
- the impact of time as a variable;

- what constitutes a 'catalytic' relationship and what goes into making one;
- what conditions serve to sustain change and inhibit relapse in particular client groups;

together with further exploration of systematic models which would serve practitioners as integrating frameworks.

References

Barkham, M. and Rowan, J. 'Counselling for a Brief Period' (1993) in W. Dryden (ed.) *Questions and Answers on Counselling in Action*, London: Newbury Park: New Delhi: Sage.

Berg, I. K. and Miller, S. D. (1992) *Working with the Problem Drinker: A Solution Focussed Approach*, New York: Norton.

Budman, S. H. (1990) 'The Myth of Termination in Brief Therapy' in J. K. Zeig and S. G. Gilligan (eds) *Brief Therapy: Myths, Methods and Metaphors*, New York: Brunner/Mazel.

Budman, S. H. and Gurman, A. S. (1988) *Theory and Practice of Brief Therapy*, New York: Guilford.

Cooper, J. F. (1995) *A Primer of Brief Psychotherapy*, New York: London: Norton.

Cummings, N. (1990) 'Brief Intermittent Psychotherapy Through the Life Cycle' in J. K. Zeig and S. G. Gilligan (eds) *Brief Therapy: Myths, Methods and Metaphors*, New York: Brunner/Mazel.

Dryden, W. (1995) *Brief Rational Emotive Behaviour Therapy*, Chichester: Wiley.

Dryden, W. and Feltham, C. (1992) *Brief Counselling*, Buckingham: Philadelphia: Open University Press.

Egan, G. (1990) *The Skilled Helper*, 4th edn, Pacific Grove, California: Brooks/Cole.

Gelso, C. J. (1992) 'Realities and Emerging Myths about Brief Therapy', *The Counselling Psychologist* 20(3): 464–71.

Gelso, C. J. and Johnson, D. H. (1983) *Explorations in Time-Limited Counselling and Psychotherapy*, New York: Columbia University, Teachers College Press.

George, E., Iveson, C. and Ratner, H. (1990) *Problems to Solutions: Brief Therapy with Individuals and Families*, Brief Therapy Press.

Gustafson, J. P. (1986) *The Complex Secret of Brief Psychotherapy*, New York: Norton.

Highley, C. and Cooper, C. L. (1995) *An Evaluation of British Employee Assistance Programmes and Workplace Counselling Programmes*, Manchester: School of Management, University of Manchester Institute of Science and Technology.

Horner, J. A. (ed.) (1994) *Treating the Neurotic Patient in Brief Psychotherapy*, Northvale, New Jersey: London: Jason Aronson Inc.

Hoyt, M. F., Rosenbaum, R. and Talmon, M. (1992) 'Planned Single Session Psychotherapy' in S. H. Budman, M. F. Hoyt and S. Friedman (eds) *The First Session in Brief Therapy*, New York: Guilford.

Ivey, A. E., Ivey, M. B. and Simek-Downing, L. (1987) *Counselling and Psychotherapy: Integrating Skills, Theory and Practice*, 2nd edn, Englewood Cliffs, NJ: Prentice Hall.

Kaplan, A. G. (1992) 'When All Is Said and Done, What Is the Core of Brief Therapy?' *The Counselling Psychologist* 20(3): 460–3.

Malan, D. H. (1979) *Individual Psychotherapy and the Science of Psychodynamics*, London: Boston: Durban: Singapore: Sydney: Toronto: Wellington: Butterworths.

Miller, W. R., Jackson, K. A. and Ward Karr, K. (1994) 'Alcohol Problems: There's a Lot You Can Do in Two or Three Sessions', *EAP Digest* January/February, pp. 18–35.

Nelson-Jones, R. (1988) *Practical Counselling and Helping Skills*, 2nd edn, London: Cassell.

O'Hanlon, W. H. and Weiner-Davis, M. (1989) *In Search of Solutions: New Directions in Psychotherapy*, New York: Norton.

Rogers, C. (1951) *Client Centred Therapy: Its Current Practice, Implications and Theory*, Boston: Houghton Mifflin.

——(1961) *On Becoming a Person*, London: Constable.

Ryle, A. (1992) *Cognitive-Analytic Therapy: Active Participation in Change: A New Integration in Brief Psycotherapy*, Chichester and New York: Wiley.

Ryle, A. and Cowmeadow, P. (1992) 'Cognitive Analytic Therapy (CAT)' in W. Dryden (ed.) *Integrative and Eclectic Therapy, A Handbook*, Buckingham: Philadelphia: Open University Press.

de Shazer, S. (1985) *Keys to Solutions*, New York: Norton.

——(1988) *Clues – Investigating Solutions in Brief Therapy*, New York: Norton.

——(1991a) Foreword in Y. M. Dolan, *Resolving Sexual Abuse*, New York: Norton.

——(1991b) *Putting Difference to Work*, New York: Norton.

de Shazer, S., Berg, I., Lipchick, E., Nunnally, E., Molnar, A., Gingrich, W. and Weiner-Davis, M. (1986) 'Brief Therapy: Focussed Solution Development', *Family Process*, 25: 207–2.

Steenbarger, B. N. (1992) 'Toward Science–Practice Integration in Brief Counselling and Therapy', *The Counselling Psychologist* 20(3): 403–50.

Yankura, J. and Dryden, W. (1994) *Key Figures in Counselling and Psychotherapy – Albert Ellis*, London: Sage Publications.

Part four

Themes

Chapter sixteen

Counselling and gender

Jocelyn Chaplin

Why is gender important?

Gender is still one of the main ways in which we differentiate between human beings, in spite of its deconstruction by feminists and others over the years. Yet it is not only about noticing those differences and trying to explain them. It is not only about having a womb or having a penis or about socially constructed expectations that women should be caring and passive and men active and aggressive. It is *also* about inequality. Gender differences, whether physical or social, are not equally valued differences. Gender is about power and inequality, hierarchy and oppression, because one gender, the male gender, and all the values and attributes associated with it, is deemed superior in most cultures of the world today.

In any unequal power relationship, those on the 'bottom' are far more limited by the differences than those on the 'top'. It is easier for men to argue that gender is not an issue, whereas for me as a woman, it is extremely important. The very way that I write this chapter, in a language and form that has developed in a male-dominated culture, makes me continually aware that I am a second-class citizen writing in terms laid down by my oppressor. I am living and working in a culture that was designed by the other gender, using values such as competition and linear thinking, that have been associated with that other gender. It often feels like an alien world for me in my female gender.

Yet I do not feel biologically determined by my gender. I feel fully capable of, for example, being assertive and thinking in a linear way. It is the other side of me, that which thinks in a more cyclical way and sees connections between everything, that is not equally respected in our culture. As a woman I am not treated by society as different but equal. I am reacted to as different and inferior, as marginal to mainstream society, as object rather than active subject.

At times I have felt that the world of counselling is one of the few areas of modern culture in which the values and ways of thinking associated with the female gender are genuinely respected. Even here, however, there seems to be an increasing male orientation.

However there *is* a level on which gender is not important. In a spiritual sense we are all part of the same universal energy patterns. Energy has no gender, only electrical poles; but once this energy starts to take animal and human form, gender becomes important. Most known human societies have some form of gender division, yet this division has not always been hierarchical. There have been societies, such as Minoan Crete, in which women and female-orientated values were respected as much as men and male-orientated values.

Today there is a great cultural variation in the expression of gender difference within Britain. I cannot possibly do justice to all these variations in one chapter. Also I am myself the product of a particular middle-class, white, post-colonial background that I have rebelled against as a woman, but am still affected by. I am at present a heterosexual. All these factors limit my perspective, yet I hope that many of the issues raised in the following pages will have meaning for people involved in a wide range of counselling activities.

On the social level in which most of us live most of the time gender is intimately connected with our identity and being. The first question asked when a baby is born is, 'Is it a boy or a girl?' Questions about its health or its weight usually come afterwards. Gender is seen as of supreme importance and defines the child in its social context long before it has any say in the matter. From the moment of birth the baby is reacted to according to that gender: little girls are often held more protectively than boys, for example. If we see counselling as being concerned with a person's own self-definition and conscious development, then gender can be seen as an obstacle to self-fulfilment. The complex person trapped inside the box of limited social gender expectations is often screaming to get out. The woman who wants to drive a truck or the man who wants to care for children are only slowly being given social approval to 'be themselves'.

Many people who come for counselling have a wide gap in their perceptions of how they 'ought' to be and how they feel they actually are. Many of these 'oughts' are connected with gender. The man who feels deeply inadequate because he does not feel comfortable with the 'macho' expectations of his male friends is a familiar figure. So is the woman who feels that she ought to be the 'perfect mother'. As she cannot be, the result is often self-hatred and depression. In our male-orientated thinking we have to be successful or we are losers. Success is often defined according to gender: for the man it is success at work, while even today for most women success means catching a good man and/or being a good mother. Women's status is still determined largely through male partners. On our own we still often think we are just not good enough.

Many psychological problems, from depression to low self-esteem, can

be traced back to gender issues (Nairne and Smith 1984). For women the
reality of second-class status leads very directly to low self-esteem. For
men it is more likely to be a mismatch between how they feel and how they
think men should be and feel. Much of counselling is about getting underneath the 'shoulds' and discovering and then accepting what is *really* being
felt. It is helping people to trust their guts. This includes getting to know
and respect our bodies that in a male-orientated culture have been so
devalued and split off from our minds, with which we are supposed to
control everything.

Social gender expectations tend to be largely mental constructs that are
deeply ingrained even before we learn to speak. Yet on another level we all
inhabit gender-defined bodies. While in counselling we help people to
question the social constructions of gender that they have learnt, we also
need to help people feel comfortable in and accepting of their bodies, male
or female. When we are grounded in our bodies then we tend to feel safer to
question and make choices about social roles.

Indeed, there are today far more choices available to both women and
men in terms of social roles. In some circles the 'new man' who shares
fully in child care is the new hero. In fact, new and equally limiting role
expectations can arise in subcultures which aim to reduce sexism. The need
to belong is one of the deepest human needs; and as soon as we make a
choice to belong to a particular group, certain role expectations connected
with gender arise. Even in all-female groups, there may be expectations
that all women should agree, for example. The idea of disagreements,
conflict and competition can be especially threatening for women's groups
which may still have gender expectations concerning how women 'should'
be.

At times the sheer range of possible roles can feel quite overwhelming.
There is so much choice, in social terms. Yet because we have connected
social role with personal identity we can feel split and torn apart by
wondering whether we should be a career woman *or* a mother, a poet *or*
a nurse. Yet all of us have many sides, some that are more associated with
males at present and some that are more associated with females. In
counselling we encourage people to explore these different sides, perhaps
play-act them, try them out. After all they are just roles. The drag queen is
often far better at playing the stereotyped *'femme fatale'* than the female
person who actually tries to be one. The drag queen knows that he is play-
acting. Seeing female and male roles as games, separate from our 'real
selves', can help distance ourselves from them, thereby reducing their
power over us. We are not our roles. Rather we are the process of change
itself that can pass through numerous different roles. We are not the
fantasies but we are the observers of our own fantasies. We are not the
many costumes that we dress up in, but we are the bodies underneath.

The love of our own bodies in all their gender-specified glory seems paradoxically vital to our escaping the limitations of social gender expectations. Many people come into counselling hating their own bodies yet trying to live up to very rigid social gender expectations. The large woman who hates her figure because she wants more than anything to be slim is a familiar example. There is also the man who cannot even feel his own body yet desperately seeks to be the 'perfect' macho male.

To summarize, gender is important for counselling on four main levels. First, it is important because counsellors are working in a society in which male-related values dominate the culture and women are still basically treated as second-class citizens. Power structures in the society affect people psychologically in numerous subtle ways. Second, gender can be seen as limiting role expectations that can be obstacles to full self-development and the expression of all sides of the self. Third, gender can be seen as a relatively superficial role, separate from individual personal identity, to be played like a game and not taken too seriously. We can *all* act many parts of ourselves, and some of these parts will be 'female' and some 'male'. Fourth, gender is simply one of the many forms into which universal energies take human shape.

Principles

Process

Counselling is a face-to-face relationship between two or more human beings in which one or more of them are the centre of focus and the other one plays a helping role. Quite apart from the content of counselling, the *process* brings gender immediately into the foreground. The gender of the people in these face-to-face contacts is probably the first aspect of them that is noticed.

The client coming for the first time might already know that she or he will be seeing a man or a woman. She might have certain expectations as a result of this knowledge, for example she might expect a woman to be gentle and supportive and a man to be more judgemental and confrontational. She might even be taken aback if they do not fit her role expectations.

On the other hand she may not know which gender they will be. A client going to see a psychiatrist, for example, might expect 'him' to be a man, and be surprised and even suspicious if 'he' turns out to be a woman. A female client may react with immediate submissiveness, perhaps combined with flirtatiousness, to a male counsellor, just because he is male, regardless of any more complex psychological considerations.

Strategies for 'gender-aware' counselling

Awareness of gender-related reactions to the counsellor

It is very important that the counsellor be aware of gender-specific reactions which may be superimposed on the client's 'deeper' problems. It is vital to keep a look-out for the kinds of learned reactions, especially to the opposite sex, that do not necessarily reveal the client's 'normal' behaviour patterns. A male counsellor, for example, might assume that a woman's submissive behaviour towards him is the way she behaves with everyone and is not mainly a learned response to male authority figures. At home she might be a little tyrant! If he did not recognize the importance of the particular male–female context of the counselling he could limit himself to working with only one side of her. He might fail to recognize her strengths or her temper, for example. He might even continue to treat her as the victim that she presents to him in her 'feminine' role of wanting the big strong man to help.

Awareness of power relationships in counselling

The power relationship is often the hidden agenda. In our male-orientated culture anybody in a 'helping' role tends to be seen as having power over the person being helped. Co-counselling, self-help groups, and notions of self-healing are all more connected with female-orientated ways of 'helping' and try to minimize unequal power relationships. Yet because our whole society is so permeated by concepts of competition and control, these issues still emerge in most helping relationships.

Female client/male counsellor   For most women growing up in a patriarchal society, men are still seen as the experts, the all-knowing ones. And men seem to collude very effectively in this myth. Thus for a woman going to see a male counsellor there can be particular difficulties concerning her wanting to give him great authority but also resenting it and him rejecting but still enjoying that authority. Most clients feel the contradictions of wanting an authority to tell them what to do and yet resenting that authority and basically wanting equality.

   Both female and male counsellors need to be aware of the power that is being projected on to them, but male counsellors need to be especially careful. They need to examine honestly their own feelings about being in such a powerful role. They need to find ways of minimizing the inequality in the counselling situation. Thus, for example, the arrangement of chairs or couches needs to be taken seriously and they need to be placed in a way that does not make the counsellor seem 'higher' or more important as when he sits behind a desk. For men, power is perceived as sexually attractive, so the male counsellor needs to underplay his sexual charms and be careful not to sit in a way that might be experienced as sexually threatening to the woman, nor should he touch her unless convinced that it feels appropriate for both parties and it has been agreed to by the client.

However, there are also many subtle messages that a male counsellor might give out unintentionally to retain control of the session, for example by interrupting his client or asking too many questions. Clearly, this depends on the style of counselling, but generally in the more directive counselling approaches there is a danger that the counsellor may exert too much control over the client. If the counsellor is a man and the client a woman, such control may serve to reinforce the pattern of dependency and low self-esteem that she has experienced every day of her life in patriarchal society. Men have a greater tendency to interrupt women than vice versa; so a male counsellor needs to pay particular attention to his listening skills and his ability to respect and take seriously whatever the female client brings. Women's reality has long been invalidated by men and counsellors should not therefore collude with society by disbelieving clients or invading them with their own views of the world (for example, through their interpretations).

Underlying many of the problems mentioned above is the prevailing social stereotype of the strong male doctor curing the weak female patient. Although most counsellors do not see themselves in this way, many clients still have this model deeply embedded in their unconscious. Indeed, it is possible that some male counsellors are themselves still unconsciously affected by this image. Such images need to be examined with great honesty by counsellors. At times it might be appropriate to bring attention to such stereotypes if they are referred to by the client: for example, 'You seem to think that all men are strong.' A male counsellor could even disclose something about his vulnerable side at this point.

Male client/female counsellor A male client with a female counsellor might be particularly prone to power struggles as he may be used to the idea that men should always be in the controlling position in relation to women. He might try to invade her boundaries, for example by staying late. It is especially important for female counsellors to be firm about their boundaries, stopping at the time given and not talking about themselves unless it is absolutely necessary. She may need to protect herself, for example by having other people on hand if she is working alone at home. She may have to avoid encouraging her client to talk at length about his sexual fantasies as many of these may include degrading women and no woman, in whatever role, should be forced to submit herself to male violence, even at a mental or fantasy level.

Male client/male counsellor   Male clients with male counsellors may get into the stereotypical male competition for supremacy that still lurks underneath so many supposedly helping male relationships. The male counsellor needs to monitor his own feelings about competition and control even as the sessions are taking place. The client may just say something that triggers off the counsellor's old feelings of needing to be in control, on top, or even just right about something. In fact the counsellor is not always right and needs to be aware that there are many paths to truth, many realities and ways of seeing. Counselling is not about winning arguments or proving to clients that you are right.

Female client/female counsellor   Woman-to-woman counselling can sometimes seem almost too cosy and similar to talking things over with friends, as women do 'counsel' each other in their everyday lives more than men. Yet counselling as described in this book is of a more formal kind in which there are two very different roles. The counsellor does not generally talk about herself, nor does she rescue the client as she would want to do with a friend.

There might also be a danger of over-empathizing with the female client and losing a clear sense of being separate people. Women are more used to connecting with each other and sharing what they have in common than sitting back and being different. Female counsellors need to keep reminding themselves that they are in the role of counsellor.

Content

In terms of the content of counselling, there is a need for the counsellor constantly to look out for the influence of gender-specific expectations. Many clients reveal beliefs such as women should not be angry or men should not cry. As counselling is partly about helping people to own and express all the feelings that they actually have, such gender-specific beliefs play a major role in preventing people from developing their full selves.

The counsellor's self-awareness

Counsellors need to question all their own assumptions about gender through reading, consciousness-raising, and thorough self-examination. This requires a ruthless honesty that can be painful as well as exhilarating. Only when counsellors have gone through this process themselves can they genuinely help their clients to question their own gender expectations and discover what they really feel and want. These expectations can be seen as obstacles to self-fulfilment rather than as goals to be achieved through counselling. Many counsellors may still think that a 'mentally healthy' woman ought to be more giving than her 'mentally healthy' husband, for example (Broverman *et al*. 1970). Some may still think that marriage, or at least a close heterosexual relationship, is a mark of mental health in women, while many women say that they feel 'healthier' outside such relationships with men. There can also be an assumption that women must be neurotic if they do not want children.

Exploring different gender roles

The counsellor can help the client to explore images and roles relating to gender without judgement. Clients can be encouraged to see their lives like plays in which they play many parts including those of the opposite gender. Some of these roles might feel comfortable while others can feel strange at first. A Gestalt-orientated counsellor might get the client to put two different sides of themselves on two different chairs. One might be male and the other female. One woman client had a female queen side and a naughty little boy side. She was encouraged to act out these two parts.

Painting or cutting out images from magazines can also help a client to explore the roles and images that they relate to, including images that fascinate but seem unacceptable. Thus, for example, a shy person might have a strong warrior image in the unconscious that represents the other side. A man might have a strong mother earth image or a prostitute image that represents hidden sides of the self, often of the opposite gender. Astrology or tarot cards can help supply us with gender-specific images that make up the complex and varied beings that we all are.

Beyond gender

Ultimately it is important that counsellors work with and acknowledge the aspects of their clients and of themselves that are not gender-specific, that are beneath (or above) the form visible to our eyes. Counsellors need to be able to tune into the level on which they can 'see' the human soul in front of them. The soul is neither male nor female. It is a person's being, his or her essence, a point of connection with all the other energies that dance around the universe. To be able to connect with and love this aspect of the person, whatever is brought to the counselling session in terms of problems, is a vital part of the healing process.

Being here in our bodies

On another level it is also important to keep the focus actually on the person in front of us. Women in particular often talk more about partners, children, or friends than about themselves. This is a result of the gender expectation that women *should* care more for others than themselves. To be able to bring them back repeatedly to themselves and how *they* are feeling is an invaluable technique in counselling. It also brings them back to their bodies and grounds them in the here-and-now. Their bodies need to be fully accepted in whatever shape or form. Dissatisfaction with our bodies can keep us operating solely on a mental level: we believe that everything can be controlled through our heads and we ignore our feelings. The counsellor needs to help provide a safe setting in which there is a sense of two human bodies here in this room together at this moment.

Sexuality in counselling

Sexual energy may be present in counselling between people of the same or different gender, as it is so intimate. This energy *can* be transformed into healing, loving energy without threatening the client (or the counsellor). In our male-dominated culture we are so used to associating intimacy with genital sex that it may be hard at first to accept and use the sexual energy that may be present in the counselling relationship. This is especially true for men in either the client or counsellor role as they generally have less experience of intimate friendships and talking out feelings outside their sexual relationships.

Clearly, however, there do have to be rules about not having physical/ genital sexual relations while in a counselling relationship (see Chapter 30). In the past some well-known male therapists have had sexual relations with female clients. This would be unacceptable today. We would see the male counsellor as exploiting his power. It is well known that for many women in our male-orientated culture, power itself is the 'greatest aphro- disiac'. Female clients with male counsellors are especially vulnerable, although clients often 'fall in love' with their counsellors regardless of gender. However, the counselling sessions need to be seen as quite outside the everyday world in which sexual attraction may actually lead to affairs.

It may also be important, nonetheless, for the client to feel that he or she can express sexual and other fantasies without fear of being judged. This may include fantasies about the counsellor. It may also include ones of which the counsellor does not approve, such as violence towards women. These will be much less dangerous if openly expressed, without fear that the person him- or herself will be rejected. The fantasy is not the person. However a female counsellor needs to feel able to stop a male client whose fantasies make her feel uncomfortable. She could share with him her feelings and stress that she is not rejecting him as a person. She might even talk about the influence of society on male sexual fantasies. He could be advised to talk to a man about them or join a men's group; but the female counsellor has a right to refuse to listen. We already live in a culture in which male violence has caused women untold psychological and phy- sical misery. For men, such violence is often a symptom of their own insecurity, inferiority, or humiliation. However, as women have been used as scapegoats for so much male pain, it may sometimes be more appropriate for male clients to see male counsellors when they are uncovering some of these very deep pains and resulting rage.

Not all counsellors go deeply into the client's childhood experiences; but even when working in a short-term way with immediate problems, gender issues are likely to be very important. Below are two examples of counselling situations in which gender plays a major role.

Sue came to counselling for depression. She had not asked to see a woman counsellor but was in fact allocated a woman to work with. At first she had seemed disappointed, but, after counselling, admitted that she could never have opened up so well with a man. By the end of counselling she had also stopped looking up to men so much.

Sue was married with two teenage sons, and before marriage had been a science teacher. At first she told her counsellor she had everything one could want – a nice house, plenty of money, a good husband – and yet she could not understand why she was depressed. When questioned more deeply about her life, it was clear that she played a fairly stereotyped housewife role, with which she claimed to be happy. She talked a lot about her sons and husband. The counsellor had to keep asking her about herself, for example, 'But how did you feel when your son called you a silly cow?' Gradually her anger was expressed.

It eventually emerged that she was depressed because she was so put down and taken for granted at home. She believed she was not so important as the others. The counsellor pointed this out to her and spent many of the early sessions helping her to feel more important and to find out what *she* really felt and wanted. Sue's denial of her feelings and desires was directly linked to her beliefs about a wife's and mother's role. She would say things like, 'But I have to be home to cook dinner.' The counsellor would say, 'Who tells you that you must?' and 'What would happen if you weren't there?'

Later in the sessions it turned out that a whole side of her was being ignored too. Her mind had stagnated, she said. Her confidence to go out and work was very limited. The counsellor helped her to list her skills and abilities, including the devalued one of managing a home.

She was also encouraged to write down her feelings in a diary to get to know herself better. Eventually her image of herself began to change. She drew on paper and acted out a variety of images of herself. These included the 'clever scientist', the 'career woman', the 'earth mother' and the 'shy little girl'. They *all* turned out to be parts of her. She did not have to stay stuck in the 'earth mother' and now obsolete 'perfect wife' image with which she had so totally identified. Her counsellor also did some assertion training with her to help her stand up for her rights at home.

Tom was a very shy, tall man who came to counselling because of anxiety attacks. He worked with a male counsellor. Tom had great difficulties making relationships with women. He could only approach them when drunk, yet he had lots of fantasies about women that at times became obsessive. The counsellor used relaxation techniques with him a lot at first to help him get to know his body and to allow him to express his fantasies without too much fear. He then encouraged him to imagine that he was some of the female characters in his fantasies. He had one image of a female warrior. By putting himself in that role he began to feel more confident about himself. His mother had been a rather dominating woman. but now he was able to incorporate that aspect into himself. The counsellor also encouraged him to walk around the room feeling his fully male body, to move his pelvis, swing his shoulders and to feel okay about being male. He role-played encounters with 'real life' women, and then acted out the women themselves. So while on the one hand he became more comfortable about his own male body, on the other hand he could recognize and use the 'female' aspects of himself.

Issues

The gender of the counsellor

One of the most important issues is the gender of the counsellor *vis-à-vis* the client. Many female counsellors will not take on male clients for the reasons mentioned above such as the fear of male mental (or even physical) violence, but also because they feel that women have been doing men's emotional 'work' for them for centuries and they would rather concentrate their energies on women who have usually been giving rather than getting emotional support.

Many female clients choose to have a female counsellor who will also have grown up as a female in a male-orientated society with whom they would feel more comfortable in opening up. The wish of a client to see a counsellor of a particular gender should, I believe, always be respected. I have often heard counsellors say that clients may not know what is good for them and perhaps if they ask for a woman, what they need is a man! There are many situations, such as counselling after a rape (of a woman by a man), where it would be totally inappropriate for a woman to see a male counsellor at first. Yet many women feel metaphorically raped by men every day of their lives.

Clients do project on to counsellors feelings that they had towards parents or siblings of both sexes. A male counsellor can sometimes have feelings about mother projected on to him. However, it is more likely that issues connected with the client's father arise when working with a male counsellor. Even women who need to work with women counsellors at first may later choose to work with a male in order to look at specific 'father' issues; but it must be the client's choice.

A male client may choose to work with a woman because he might feel safer and less threatened. However, a time might come when he feels that he wants to 'face up' to his fear of confrontation with men and work with a man. It depends very much on the stage of her or his personal journey as well as on the individual's background, as to the appropriate choice of a female or male counsellor. Availability may sometimes limit choices too.

Differing values

Another issue for counsellors is how to remain true to themselves and their values while working with clients with very different beliefs. Clients may come into counselling full of stereotyped notions of gender roles. Men may come describing ways in which they put down their wives. Women may come hoping that counselling will make them into better wives. The counsellor needs to respect the client and his or her values without having to agree with those values. The counsellor does not judge the client as a person but may judge the ideas she or he has. This can be a difficult contradiction.

The counsellor is there to help clients question their assumptions about all aspects of their lives, all their 'shoulds'; and gender expectations create a lot of 'shoulds'. Any sexist assumptions such as '*All* men are strong', 'But I'm *only* a woman (housewife)' can be questioned, gently. The counsellor could ask 'Who says all men are strong'? or 'I noticed that you said "only" a woman; that implies to me that you don't think much of being a woman.' Often just pointing out the revealing word like 'only' will be enough. Sometimes, as a woman counsellor working with women, I say, 'A lot of women feel that way', or 'We women often fall into that trap, don't we?' or even 'There is a lot of pressure from society to make women feel that they should be slim/want children and so on'. The counsellor is not going to deliver long lectures about sexism in society, but there are many subtle ways of exploring gender issues. In the early stages of counselling it is vital for counsellors to have some sense of how clients view the world, and then to start exploring these from where the clients are. Many clients will have already questioned many gender-defined role expectations; others will be starting from a less conscious position. Indeed, there are so many different ideas and attitudes towards gender that the counsellor cannot make any assumptions about her or his client's beliefs before getting to know her or him.

Nature versus nurture

Another important issue is the question about how much people can actually change through counselling and how much of the way we are is biologically determined? Does the mere possession of a womb, for example, lead to a natural maternal instinct? For academics these questions are still unresolved. For counsellors the issue relates to the range of choices actually available to our clients (and ourselves). A woman in counselling who clearly does not want to have children needs to be encouraged to explore all her feelings about her choice, including any losses or pain that may be involved, but it cannot be assumed by the counsellor that she is going against any 'natural' instinct. She is not mentally 'unhealthy' because she does not want children.

On the other hand, we are all born with certain potentials and biological characteristics such as colour and gender. Some of these cannot be changed, so a counsellor needs to help people accept their limitations as well as their choices. Indeed, what may be perceived as a limitation may also be a strength. People often come into counselling wanting to get rid of what they see as a vulnerable, unacceptable side of themselves. In modern society vulnerability and sensitivity, dependence and gentleness are generally associated with the female gender. Such characteristics are often especially unacceptable in men. Yet there is great strength in them too. Creativity often comes from this side of the self. Counselling helps people to accept and then perhaps transform and express these devalued sides. It may even help to talk to clients about the way that any characteristics associated with women are looked down on in our society. The counsellor needs to show that she respects these sides as much as the more acceptable ones by giving them her full attention, getting clients to draw or act them out, and by sharing feelings she might have about those vulnerable sides, such as relief or increased affection for the client. Or she may simply say 'It's OK to cry.'

It is equally important to stress the enormous range of choices that clients actually do have once they have begun to question gender-role expectations. Gender is often far less limiting than people believe. There seem to be far more variations of abilities, personality characteristics, and so on within each gender than between them. The limits are more likely to come from the way we think about gender than from our actual bodies.

Counsellors can use images of famous or ordinary, modern or ancient people to help clients recognize the range of characteristics available to their gender. Many Jungian-influenced counsellors today use myths and stories of ancient goddesses such as Artemis and Innana (Perera 1981) to help women empower themselves both by re-enacting the myths, visualizing or painting them, or simply learning about times when the female gender had more respect and value than it does today. And for men, there are increasing numbers of films and television programmes showing men who express the so-called 'feminine' side of themselves. Counsellors can refer to these images and they can also be models themselves of people who can express both 'masculine' and 'feminine' characteristics. Most male counsellors do seem to have accepted their own 'feminine' side to some extent or they would not be engaged in such a caring, so-called 'female' profession. Most female counsellors are fairly firm and assertive, which could be seen as an expression of their 'masculine' side. I use inverted commas with the words 'feminine' and 'masculine' because the socially constructed meanings around them are limiting when we try to talk about groups of characteristics that do not need to be gender-defined at all.

Future developments

Where is this field going in the future?

The whole field of counselling seems increasingly to be taking gender issues more seriously. There is more and more encouragement of the client's expression of the side of themselves previously associated with the opposite gender. The mushrooming number of assertiveness training courses reveals one way in which women are exploring their 'masculine' side. It is often harder for men to develop the 'feminine' because it is still relatively devalued in our society. However, there are now men's groups, books and courses to explore feelings about 'being a man'. In the past twenty years there has been an increase in the number of opportunities for men and women to do counselling in groups or with individuals separately and away from the opposite gender. Many women still feel intimidated in mixed groups and men still have a tendency to take over in these groups.

Places like the Women's Therapy Centre in London were set up to provide a safe place for women to explore their feelings honestly with other women. Women connected with the centre like Orbach and Eichenbaum (1983) have written about ways in which gender affects women at deep psychological levels. Factors such as lack of funding and the present 'conservative' climate, however, make the increase of such facilities seem unlikely in the near future. However, the range of women coming to the few women-only facilities that do exist is increasing, for example to include more black and working-class women.

Another trend is the increase of problems associated with questioning stereotyped gender roles and the need for counselling to help people come to terms with these changes. Thus, for example, many men are having sexual problems such as erectile dysfunction partly because the old gender roles are changing. Their sense of being a 'man' may be undermined through unemployment or even the increased assertiveness of their wives or girlfriends. Women, on the other hand, are suffering from feeling that they have to be superwomen and always play every role available to them, from mother to career woman, and so on. The stress involved can be enormous. Many counsellors are beginning to use stress management and relaxation techniques more and more in their work. They are having to look at the whole person, body and mind, within society. Counselling cannot be seen as separate from the society of which it is a part, and changes in social attitudes and behaviour affect both the process and content of counselling. Further, gender roles are changing quickly in society as a whole.

Gender issues are also related to sexual orientation and one direction for the future is an increase in counselling and self-help groups for gay and lesbian people, in which their orientation is *not* seen as a 'problem'. This issue is explored further in Chapter 18. It is important to be aware here that increasing numbers of people are taking gender explorations down deeper and wider routes than those familiar to the mainstream. They include trans-sexuals and cross-dressers as well as those beginning to talk of a third gender which is neither male nor female. The binary view of gender can itself be questioned. The third gender could be seen as androgynous or perhaps simply as a space into which people can project whoever they wish to be in that moment. In many senses gender is a performance, a construction, an imaginary concept. Counsellors need to be aware of these developments, value them, and work positively with clients who are brave enough to be exploring the outer limits of gender questioning.

Where should this field be going?

Both women and men need to love and express the power, joy, and sexuality of their own bodies, of whichever gender and of whatever shape, age, or colour. This can be through just fully being and living, or through relationships with people of the same or another gender. Counselling can play a vital role in this process. Feminism does not imply that men should start hating their own bodies and genuine undistorted sexuality, in the same way that women in the past were taught to hate theirs (Rowan 1987). We all need to explore ways of expressing our sexuality in non-oppressive, creative ways.

At the same time as loving and accepting our sex defined bodies we need to open up the choices in terms of roles and gender-associated characteristics. In other words we need to move towards psychological androgyny (Singer 1976). People who have available to them abilities and characteristics associated with both sexes do seem better able to cope with the modern changing world (Bem 1977): they are more flexible, adaptable, and are psychologically 'healthier'. Counselling can help people to become more psychologically androgynous. We all still have to survive in existing society, however, and until much deeper changes are made within that society, many people are likely to remain in 'unhealthy' gender-split ways of being, even after counselling.

References

Broverman, I. K., Broverman D. M., Clarkson, F. E., Rosenkrantz, P. S. and Vogel, S. (1970) 'Sex role stereotypes and clinical judgments of mental health', *Journal of Consulting and Clinical Psychology* 34: 1–7.
Bem, S. (1977) 'The measurement of psychological androgyny', *Journal of Consulting and Clinical Psychology* 44: 155–62.
Nairne, K. and Smith, G. (1984) *Dealing with Depression*, London: The Women's Press.
Orbach, S. and Eichenbaum, L. (1983) *Understanding Women*, Harmondsworth: Penguin.
Perera, S. (1981) *Descent to the Goddess*, Toronto: Inner City Books.
Rowan, J. (1987) *The Horned God*, London: Routledge & Kegan Paul.
Singer, J. (1976) *Androgyny*, New York: Doubleday.

Further reading

Chaplin, Jocelyn, (1989) *Feminist Counselling in Action*, Newbury Park: Sage.
Erickson, Beth M. (1993) *Helping men change: The role of the female therapist*, Newbury Park: Sage.
Ganley, Anne L. (1988) 'Feminist therapy with male clients' in M. A. Dutton-Douglas and L. E. A. Walker (eds) *Feminist psychotherapies: Integration of therapeutic and feminist systems*, Norwood: Ablex.
Goodrich, T., Rampage, C., Ellman, B. and Halstead, K. (1988) *Feminist family therapy: A casebook*, New York: Norton.
Hargreaves, David J. and Colley, Ann M. (1986) *The psychology of sex roles*, London: Harper & Row.
Keller, Catherine (1986) *From a broken web: Separation, sexism and self*, Boston: Beacon.
Lorber, Judith (1994) *Paradoxes of gender*, New Haven: Yale University Press.
Olivier, Christiane (1989) *Jocasta's children*, London: Routledge.
Pitcher, Evelyn Goodenough and Schultz, Lynn Hickey (1983) *Boys and girls at play: The development of sex roles*, New York: Praeger.

Chapter seventeen

Counselling and race

Colin Lago and Joyce Thompson

Issues

The subject of counselling and race is difficult to address in a clear manner, because as Jones (1985: 173) has put it, 'among other complexities, it is embedded in the fluctuating nature of race relations in our society and hence in a continually evolving sociocultural context.' At the heart of the subject there are several major debates that in part reflect contemporary views of 'race' in British society. The term 'race' used here is a broad one. We recognize that residing in Britain today are people from many races and racial origins. Many of these groups are likely to be disadvantaged, oppressed, or discriminated against by the dominant society (for example, the Irish, Jewish, Eastern Europeans, and so on). The specific focus, in this chapter, however, is concentrated upon the complex relationship between black and white people in Britain generally, and within counselling specifically. Nevertheless, in focusing on one specific set of relationships between black and white, it is hoped that more understandings might emerge implicitly for these other groups.

A major area of contention has centred around the extent to which counsellors require specialist knowledge of and sensitivity to race relations in Britain in order to counsel. One view holds that the knowledge and skills of counselling are all that is required with any client. The opposing view contains several major themes that may be summed up as follows:

(a) In order to understand relationships between black and white people today, a knowledge of the history between differing racial groups is required.
(b) Counsellors will also require an understanding of how contemporary society works in relation to race, the exercise of power, the effects of discrimination, stereotyping, how ideologies sabotage policies, and so on. In short, counsellors require a 'structural' awareness of society.
(c) Counsellors require a personal awareness of where they stand in relation to these issues

From this debate a key question emerges that has sometimes keenly split different groups. Can or should white people counsel black people? In doing so, it is argued, they are substantiating, symbolically, the erroneous and pejorative view that black people are inferior, that black people require help, and worst of all that black people do not have, within their midst, their own capacity to resolve difficulties.

White people are already, self-evidently, rooted in white culture. Also, as counsellors they will have been trained in bodies of theory and practice that have either central European or US origins and emphases. Certainly, white American counsellors have often asserted that black people do not respond well to traditional methods of psychotherapy (Jones 1985). Some black people within Britain assert that such methods are also culturally encapsulated within a white western view of the world and are consequently insensitive and totally inappropriate in their unthinking application to all counselling situations.

So far, we have concentrated on the white counsellor/black client counselling relationship. We do not wish this early focus to blind us to the black counsellor/white client relationship. Increasingly, black people are training in counselling and indeed some have already formed an Association of Black Counsellors (ABC).

The issues of race and racism exist, potentially, if not explicitly, within the above pairings as well as in the same-race counselling dyads (black–black or white–white). Whether covert or overt, very real dilemmas confront counsellors in terms of how subjects related to racism are managed in the process of counselling.

Further questions also exist for counsellor trainers. What is the knowledge base required in preparing trainees to work with clients of different racial origins? In doing so, are there specific individual skills that need to be disseminated? Many other questions arise out of the initial complexities already presented here. At the core of this maelstrom of debate, some of which has been painful and bitter, there exists a deep underlying question that goes something like this. Given that relations between black and white groups over several centuries have been typified by oppression, exploitation, and discrimination, how might contemporary relationships within counselling be transformed into creative (rather than further damaging) experiences?

Racism – the major issue

It is our contention that the issue of racism has to be addressed and worked with by counsellors in training who plan to work in today's multiracial society. This view is not held by all counsellors and counsellor trainers in the field. Similar to earlier sentiments expressed by US psychiatrists (Thomas and Sillen 1972), many white counsellors see themselves as caring, sensitive people who have chosen counselling precisely because they are concerned about other people. Therefore, they ask, how could they be racist in their practice? This genuinely held view does not take into account, however, a whole range of mechanisms, perceptions and experiences to which white people have been exposed throughout their lives. Such phenomena, if they remain unconscious, may affect the counsellor's behaviour and responses in ways that prove negative in cross-race counselling.

Notwithstanding the importance of this dimension, we are sensitive to the fact that any journey of exploration into the issues of racism will be, for many people, an intensely painful experience. White groups, after training, may experience vast realms of guilt and impotence. Black people, similarly exposed, may get in touch with powerful emotions such as depression and anger. Despite these apparently negative effects, our belief is that counsellors need to operate from a position of maximum awareness of self and of society.

Racism – the evidence

An abundance of research material clearly demonstrates that the black members of this society do not have equal access to the opportunities and provisions that exist within Britain (Coard 1971; Hartmann *et al.* 1974; Smith 1977; Dummett 1980; Jowell *et al.* 1984; Skellington and Morris 1992; Jumaa 1993). As far back as 1971 the Census suggested that the unemployment rate among young people of Afro-Caribbean origin was twice as high as among white teenagers. In addition, Little *et al.* (1978) asserted that the incidence of young people going to an interview and not getting a job was four times as great for black teenagers compared with white teenagers. Smith (1977) also indicated that as total unemployment rose, the minority groups tended to make up a greater proportion of the total: in other words, unemployment rates for minority groups rose more steeply than rates of total unemployment (*Guardian* 1994).

In the educational arena, Coard (1971) produced some frightening figures concerning the disproportionate incidence of black children in what were then termed 'educationally subnormal' schools. One race-relations selected bibliography confirmed that a considerable amount of research had emerged indicating that the average teacher had differential perceptions and expectations of poor and minority-group children; that these differential perceptions were associated with differential treatment and teaching techniques; and that these in turn could lead to a depressed performance on the part of the children treated thus (Skellington and Morris 1992).

The media also helps to perpetuate a view of black people that is pejorative. Research has revealed that a biased selection of issues concerning race is presented in the newspapers. Troyna (1981) reports that in a survey of major national and local newspapers, 47 per cent of all material on race issues were confined to the following themes; the National Front, crime, immigration, human interest, and 'normal'. Conversely, less than 10 per cent of items were devoted to housing, education, health, and employment. Some 25 per cent of all items in which West Indians were highlighted related to crime stories. Immigration was not dealt with as an issue of black people entering Britain but with seeking to keep them out. Perversely, 'white' hostility existed outside the framework of 'race' news; such discussions focused on issues such as democracy, the erosion of freedom, and so on. Conversely, black hostility was firmly placed within the framework of race-related material within Britain. Unfortunately, space does not allow other examples to be quoted, though there do exist substantial negative findings in other socio-economic areas (for example, housing, health, street arrests, and so on).

This consistent pattern of disadvantage and discrimination is so widespread and uniform across institutions in our society that the underlying issues of racism and racist attitudes are self-revealing and self-evident. Running parallel to this assertion and, indeed, extending it is the statement in the United States Mental Health Commission Report in 1965, which cited racism as the number one health problem in the USA. Within Britain in recent years violence has erupted in several cities and racism has been cited as one of the major reasons for these occurrences.

Consequently, in any counselling relationship between counsellor and client where there is racial difference, aspects of racism must be assumed to exist and might also require focused attention. One immediate area for concern, then, within counselling is that of the relationship between client and counsellor. This is explored in more detail in the next section.

The cross-racial counselling partnership – issues in practice

The following considerations have been devised by the authors in order to demonstrate the range of issues potentially present in various cross-race pairings of counsellor and client. Some generalized views and attitudes have been included in order to aid the visibility of such issues. However, we acknowledge that they are somewhat simplified and are themselves in danger of serving to confirm stereotypes. We apologize if this occurs: it is not intended.

Let us imagine four scenarios featuring different racial pairings of counsellor and client, as illustrated in Figure 17.1.

Scenario 1: Black counsellor / white client

The black counsellor   It is most likely that the counselling training a black person would have received would have been, first, in a white, middle-class organization or institute, and, second, theoretically and culturally

SCENARIO 1 White client Black counsellor	SCENARIO 2 White counsellor Black client
SCENARIO 3 White client White counsellor	SCENARIO 4 Black counsellor Black client

Figure 17.1 Possible scenarios of counsellor–client racial pairings

Eurocentric and American (i.e. US) in origin. Additionally, they are also likely to have been taught by white, middle-class trainers. Consequently, and quite contrary to a simplistic view of the situation, black counsellors, by virtue of their training and backgrounds, will have been predominantly geared to working with white people, not black people.

The aforementioned aspects of a black counsellor's training will hopefully constitute positive qualities towards working with white clients. However, in their lives as black people in white society, some will have experienced negative incidents and consequently feelings in relation to white people. For black counsellors, then, a serious element of their work with their white clients will be the nature of the countertransference that develops as the counselling unfolds (i.e. black counsellors' feelings and reactions to their white clients that occur during the counselling process). One might predict, therefore, that one element for discussion and exploration between black counsellors and their supervisors/consultants will be this very aspect, in order that the negative elements of the countertransference can be dealt with professionally, rather than being expressed inappropriately within the counselling encounter.

The white client   Obviously, it is difficult to predict accurately the nature of a white client's response to working with a black counsellor. However, the range of responses is likely to be stimulated by the following questions: what is the white client's perception of a black counsellor?; does this change over time?; would the white client be reluctant to expose his or her difficulty to a black person because of his or her own (erroneous) sense of superiority?; and to what extent would the white client presume that the black counsellor will not understand his or her predicament? In sum, what effects do the race, class, and culture of the counsellor have upon the client?

Questions in this section and the next have been deliberately employed to demonstrate the extent to which a multiplicity of responses might exist for each counsellor and each client. Unfortunately, space does not allow an expansion of these areas. Suffice it to say that it is hoped that the questions themselves may stimulate counsellors' reflections upon their own position.

Scenario 2: White counsellor / black client

The white counsellor   Again, a series of questions can assist us in addressing, briefly, the issues for a white counsellor with a black client: how structurally aware of society is the counsellor?; do they have an understanding of the myriad disadvantaging mechanisms that exist in contemporary society in relation to black people?; what class background are they from?; what experiences of black people have they had?; and what effects, perceptions, and attitudes have these left upon the counsellor?

From experiences gained by the authors whilst involved in training groups, it seems reasonable to state that many white people are quite unable to cope with radical black perspectives and black people's pain and anger, specifically in relation to racism. Rogers (1978) has noted this phenomenon and suggests that white people who are effective in responding to oppressed groups seem to learn two attitudes. One is the realization and ownership of the fact that 'I think white'. The other is the ability to respond empathically, to be able to enter into the black person's world of hate, bitterness, and resentment, and to know that world as an understandable, acceptable part of reality. To achieve this ability Rogers (1978) suggests that the white persons themselves need to listen to their own feelings of anger at unjust situations. This is clearly something that could most usefully be done in training and therapy, in order that the fullest opportunities for personal learning may be gained.

From the perspective of power, this combination of white counsellor with black client has a potential danger, namely a perpetuation of the notion of white superiority. The white person, as the counsellor in this situation, has the power. The sensitive handling of that power is absolutely crucial. White counsellors have to work out ways of enhancing their own sensitivity and knowledge beyond the counselling framework. To pursue their curiosity, however justified they might feel within the counselling process, would be an unethical abuse of their power. Black clients so used would have every right to experience further anger and a sense of injustice.

The black client   One aspect of colonial conditioning that many black people have experienced is that of viewing white people as positive, powerful, knowledgeable, intelligent, and so on. Consequently, such clients might have more confidence in a white counsellor. By contrast, black clients who are aware of the historical inequalities of the relationship between black and white people might be mistrustful of any meaningful interaction with a white counsellor. Indeed, it is unlikely that they would, knowingly, expose themselves to a white helper.

Some black clients might expect white counsellors not only to know their way around the British bureaucratic system but also to be able to influence that system on their behalf. The latter perspective raises further complexities as to the philosophical and theoretical nature of 'counselling' and how that equates with the reality of dealing with disadvantaged clients who are rendered less able, because of discrimination, to be effective in their world.

Suffice it to say, at least three different emphases have emerged in various counselling practices in relation to this quandary. One response has been for the counsellor to maintain the 'purist' perspective of engaging in therapeutic dialogue with the client, trusting that the client will learn sufficiently from this process to become able to deal with difficulties in their lives. An extension of this has been for some counsellors to offer educational teaching assistance to clients in areas such as assertion training. The third model has been the counsellor's adoption of an advocacy role on the client's behalf. Thus, based on the initial therapeutic work, the counsellor then moves towards negotiating with external agencies or persons on the client's behalf.

Scenario 3: White counsellor / white client

The white counsellor   This is the commonly assumed combination of counsellor and client whenever counselling is discussed. Though race is not often an issue within such alliances, nevertheless it does from time to time figure within the dialogue. Indeed, when this occurs the counsellor may well be challenged in terms of his or her responses to the client. Thus, for example, what is the counsellor to do if the client uses racist language and conveys stereotyped views throughout the counselling? – confront these attitudes?; accept them?; ignore them?; continue to work with the client in order (hopefully) to gain an understanding of the significance of such utterances and views?; refer them to someone else?

Each of these questions contains significant quandaries for every white counsellor concerned with racial justice. Clearly, from the above questions dealing with a 'whites only' counselling situation, it seems self-evident to note the crucial importance of introducing issues of race into all counselling training courses. Race is still an issue even in apparently non-racial situations. This question, which can have real consequences for the counsellor–client relationship, needs considerable thought by counsellors.

The white client   From the client's perspective, of course, they have a right to their views and to express them within counselling, even though they may be experienced as negative or objectionable to the counsellor. Indeed, these sentiments will also exist for many subjects that clients may bring to counselling. Self-evidently, the activity of counselling exists precisely to facilitate the expression and exploration of problems perceived by the client.

The white client might also assume that the counsellor will agree with his or her sentiments. Further, some clients might attempt to coerce their counsellors into colluding with their views on issues of racism, in the knowledge that they are both white.

Scenario 4: Black counsellor / black client

The black counsellor   The actual content and direction of the therapeutic interview between black counsellor and black client might well depend upon the counsellor's perception of the client's problems. The counsellor might for example be tempted to deal with the issue of racism and to explore this at the expense of other issues or problems which the client is having to deal and cope with. Of course, the opposite tendency is also a possibility: that is, the counsellor may concentrate, perhaps in-appropriately, on other issues at the expense of acknowledging the issue of racism as raised by the client. From the perspective of professional development it would be most important for black counsellors to check themselves for either tendency in order to further explore their own perspective on the subject. Also, black counsellors working with black clients are likely to find themselves caught up in ethical dilemmas stimulated by the client's own community. One such dilemma occurs when the counsellor supports the self-development of a client when that development is in conflict with the mores of the client's cultural group. Such dilemmas, if handled inappropriately or insensitively, could well create considerable difficulties, not only for the counsellor and client but also within the client's family, the local community, and the counsellor's agency.

In summary, the task of the black counsellor can be seen to have considerable consequences and is certainly beset with professional demands that would appear to exceeed those of white practitioners. Blend-ing British training with alternative traditional approaches and then having to cope with external consequences as well as with the client's internal world are formidable extra dimensions to the black counsellor's load.

The black client   Some black people, because of their own upbringing, find it difficult to perceive other black people who themselves enjoy equal status to their white counterparts, as equally knowledgeable and skilful. Such people, as clients, might end up feeling that they have only received second best. Inevitably, this sense of disappointment could lead to a deterioriation or withdrawal from the therapeutic process or a projection of inappropriate anger on to the counsellor. Conversely, there are black people who would welcome the opportunity of being counselled by a black counsellor by virtue of a perceived positive identification of the same values and belief systems as themselves, for example, 'I find it easier to talk to you, you remind me of my grandmother.' Such intial positive feelings of transference are likely to be a foundation for a good working relationship.

Further developments

Some of the responses outlined above, of both white and black participants, are more succinctly described within an emerging series of racial and ethnic identity development models developed in the United States (Helms 1984; Atkinson *et al.* 1989).

These models have been hailed as the 'most important development in cross-cultural counselling research' (Lee 1994) and are now being used on American counsellor training courses as a guide towards counsellor understanding of both where they and their client are in relation to their differential stages of racial identity development. These models support our views, detailed above, that indicate that there will be some cross-race counselling pairings that achieve appropriate therapeutic development and there will be others that never manage to establish a minimum level working relationship. The identity development models admirably explain these difficult and complex dynamics and thus will be helpful to counsellors in their pursuit of appropriate therapeutic effectiveness. Pontoretto and Pedersen (1993) provide an excellent review of an increasing number of these models that have been researched and constructed in relation to different majority and ethnic communities in the United States. Equivalent research work and the construction of currently relevant models has still to be carried out in the UK. Nevertheless the above American models are a most useful general guide to any counsellors working in a cross-racial structure.

Principles

Tentative guidelines for counsellor practice

Although the previous section on cross-race counselling relationships concentrated on complex issues, it also introduced some ideas in relation to what we consider to be good practice. The following guidelines constitute a development of such principles of practice.

(1) Attempt to gain an awareness and knowledge of your own culture and cultural style, race, and racial origins.

This apparently simple statement represents a considerably complex task for anyone to embark upon, certainly in relation to cultural 'style' (perceptions, behaviours, beliefs, and so on). As Hall (1976) has noted, 'Honest and sincere people in the field continue to fail to grasp the deep and pointing ways in which culture determines behaviour, many of which are outside awareness and beyond conscious control.'

It is our contention that it is crucial that counsellors know where they are coming from, culturally, historically, and behaviourally. Only through having such knowledge and awareness will they be able to have a sense of their effect upon others as well as access to an understanding of the dynamic process that unfolds between them and their clients.

(2) Specifically, attempt to gain more understanding of the historical and contemporary relationship that has existed and presently exists between your own race and that of your clients.

Such knowledge may be of enormous value in understanding your clients' present perspective. Historically, most relationships between black and white races have been based upon traditions of conquest, colonialism, exploitation, oppression, and so on. Further, the evidence cited earlier stresses the contemporary existence of racism in Britain.

Both perspectives might yield insights for the counsellor into how they may be perceived by the racially different client. Such knowledge will, one hopes, contribute to the sensitivity and awareness that the counsellor brings to the encounter.

(3) Develop a 'structural awareness' of society.

This should include the effects of history, as well as an understanding of the myriad mechanisms of oppression and systems of discrimination that operate in society. Judy Katz's book *White Awareness* (1978) is an excellent reference work for training ideas and exercises. Indeed several trainees with whom we have worked have written essays and articles that have been stimulated by the impact of such exercises upon them. The importance of this guideline lies in its potential to demonstrate to each white counsellor how they, however unwittingly, can contribute to discriminatory procedures in society.

(4) Attempt to gain knowledge of the client's culture, cultural style, race, and racial origins.

Thus is similar and complementary to our first guideline. One of the dangers of trying to learn about others is that of being tempted into simplistic beliefs and views of them based on inadequate, biased, or limited accounts. Such knowledge, therefore, has to be acknowledged as useful but limited. Indeed, willingness to change or modify one's views in the light of fresh experience is crucial.

In short, gain as much knowledge as is possible but also retain the ability to suspend that knowledge when working with a client. Extended awareness of how others live and view their lives will contribute to the extent to which counsellors may fully understand their clients.

(5) Hold in mind that any breakdown in communication may be attributable to the dynamic process between you.

You are not 'neutral' in your communication form and the client is certainly not deficient, just different. Breakdowns in communication can be most disturbing to both participants in counselling. At worst, negative stereotypes may be reinforced on both sides. The following pointers might be helpful in this regard:

(a) attempt to be clear and concise;
(b) avoid use of jargon and colloquialisms;
(c) check out the accuracy of your understanding of what is being said;
(d) be clear about what help it is that you are offering;
(e) possibly allow more time for the interview.

(6) Be aware of (and beware) your assumptions, stereotypes, and immediate judgements.

Some of these may be based on personal experience. Others may be gained from very old incidents, folk tales, parental influence, and so on. At worst, your assumptions and prejudices are likely to come between you and the client and operate as a barrier to real communication.

(7) Remember that many concepts like truth, honesty, intent, politeness, self-disclosure, and so on are culturally bound.

This may affect what the clients feel they can or cannot say and to what degree they can expose their feelings in relation to the issues they are bringing. Also, by holding this guideline in mind, counsellors may be further assisted in suspending initial judgemental attitudes.

(8) The dominant manner through which all counsellors operate is one that is underpinned by attention-giving and active listening to the client.

(9) Be alert to your usage of language.

Words and phrases can be loaded with connotative and ideological meanings. Gaining an awareness of the effect of the language we use is a very difficult process as we are so used to the words we utilize. Specific efforts have to be made to 'decode' and understand the implication of our utterances. Thus, for example, there are many expressions that have racist undertones. To use them not only abuses the victim of them and, by association, your client, but also affects and reflects the speaker. At one level you become the abuser and, as such, consequently no longer the helper.

Another aspect of language usage is contained in the following anecdote. This concerns a West Indian woman who arrived in Britain during the 1960s. She kept going to the labour exchange looking for a job. On her second or third visit, the woman behind the desk said 'I'm afraid we still haven't found a job for you.' The West Indian woman replied strongly, 'I don't want you to be afraid of me, I want you to help me find a job.'

It is virtually impossible to avoid such expressions as language is structured by them and is beset by them. However, what we can do, in addition to developing an awareness of them, is to broaden our range of vocabulary and expression in order that statements may be rephrased more appropriately or meaningfully. Sensitivity to clients' responses to your usage of language will also enable you to monitor the effect of what you are saying upon them.

(10) Pay attention also to paralinguistic phenomena for they also can ensure that real communication does not occur.

Paralinguistic phenomena such as sighs, grunts, intonation, expression, silences, the structure of who says what and when, are determined by cultural and linguistic backgrounds. Research has revealed how powerful these phenomena can be upon the deterioration of the relationship between two people in communication.

This tenth guideline is intended specifically to complement the fifth, seventh, and ninth outlined above. Each, in their various ways, encourage counsellors to suspend initial negative judgements in response to their clients. Cultural and linguistic phenomena can have such profound negative effects on people who are culturally different. It is as if all the standard cues for understanding someone else have been removed. Yet the listener is not necessarily aware of this. They continue to hear the same language being used and fall into the trap of assessing the other person based upon their own regular criteria. Unfortunately, even these criteria are seldom conscious.

This general point is a most complex one and deserves considerable thought on the part of counsellors.

(11) A more open and accepting approach to many models of counselling and helping is required within this sphere. (Remember also that this statement implicitly incorporates non-Eurocentric models of helping.)

At the moment in Britain there is available a whole variety of theoretically different courses of counselling training. Consequently, practitioners may become informed and skilled within a range of approaches to therapy. However, the vast majority of these have emerged from western societies.

What is more difficult to acquire are insights into non-western, traditional therapies that are based upon dialogue. Paradoxically, an insight into these therapeutic styes might greatly assist white western counsellors with black clients whose cultural origins are outside Europe. Thus, for example, one form of problem resolution in the Middle East is for the troubled person to consult various elders in the community. After gaining their views he or she then chooses a course of action based on the information gathered.

(12) Monitor your own attitudes during the interview, especially in relation to feelings of superiority or power over the client.

This point has been addressed briefly, earlier in the chapter. It relates specifically to the areas of oppression and racism. As elements of counter-transference it seems crucial that the counsellor reflects on the case with his or her supervisor or consultant.

(13) There are circumstances in which it will be appropriate for white and black counsellors, in being sensitive to the issues of racism, to explicitly acknowledge and explore this topic within the counselling process.

The precise details of how, why, or when to do this can clearly not be predetermined by the guidelines here. It is however crucial that counsellors are knowledgeable and sufficiently comfortable with the subject that they can acknowledge its existence and facilitate the exploration.

(14) We would encourage counsellors to proceed cautiously and be in favour of minimum contact rather than long-term work.

The former will hopefully be helpful, and the latter may become intensely complex and have a poor prospective outcome. In these circumstances, appropriate referral arrangements might prove more satisfactory.

(15) Generate possible sources of referral to helpers or counsellors of the same race/culture as the client.

(16) Similarly, try to locate a suitable consultant who has experience of or is of the same race as the client, if the client becomes a medium- to long-term one.

(17) Explore the experience of consulting racially different people with your own personal difficulties or for therapy in order to gain an insight into what it is you are attempting with your racially different clients.

Space does not allow any further exploration of the ideas contained in the above section. We offer these tentative guidelines as a basis for good counselling practice in the present. Hopefully, as interest develops in this aspect of counselling, the research might guide the development of future practice in more defined ways. Many of the above issues are considerably expanded in recent books written on both sides of the Atlantic (Lago and Thompson 1996; Lee and Richardson 1991).

Future developments

Implications for counselling education and training

Counselling and race, as a topic, is still not dealt with on many existing counselling courses. Historically, also, such courses have not concentrated upon the society and the social milieux within which counselling takes place. Rather, there has been an emphasis on the development of self-awareness, the enhancement of existing skills and theoretical knowledge, and a concentration upon micro-skills. We are fully in accord with such emphases in training. However, the perplexities we can now appreciate through counselling in a multicultural and multiracial community make it crucial that future training courses also make efforts to adopt a wider 'sociological' approach. Here, the term 'sociological' is used within the definition of 'structural awareness' as described earlier. It serves to imply the following:

(a) an increased understanding of today's multiracial society and the historical pre-conditions that contributed to its formation;
(b) the provision of experiential training in the areas of racism and cultural awareness and the development of anti-racist strategies;
(c) simulated exposure of skills practice with racially and culturally different clients; and
(d) the opportunity for case discussion and analysis to highlight the complex range of data generated when counselling within this milieu.

Such a combination of approaches would help individual trainees to develop a connectedness between their knowledge base, their attitudes and preconceptions, and their ability to practise.

Sue (1981) links five characteristics of culturally effective counsellors: (1) having self-knowledge; (2) possessing an awareness of generic counselling characteristics and their relation to culture and class; (3) having an understanding of socio-political forces affecting clients, especially racism and oppression; (4) having the ability to share world views of clients, without being culturally encapsulated; and (5) having mastery of an eclectic variety of skills and theories and an ability to choose which are appropriate for a particular client. To this list we would add having (6) self-knowledge of our own cultural origins and one's present (culturally determined) style, and (7) an awareness of one's own perceptions of people who are racially different.

If a white person in counselling training pursues these general suggestions laid out above, then several implications are likely to emerge for their personal life as well as their professional one. These include:

(a) a development of an attitude of concern for the creation of a racially just society and the elimination of racist practices;

(b) a development of personal apprehension or fear that they will become 'marginalized' within their own groups (friends, work, family) and become the subject of conflict or ridicule for holding such views;

(c) a need to acknowledge that combating racism is a long and painful process and consequently they will require stamina of purpose and motivation;

(d) the exploration of personal attitudes and the development of a knowledge base of how society operates discriminatory practices and implicitly invites individuals to make political, professional, and personal choices in the present and the future;

(e) firmly held beliefs about the theory and practice of counselling might have to give way to a more open appreciation of other models;

(f) the possibility of adding a 'preventive' educative function to their work in addition to the existing one of counselling individuals through disseminating such awareness (via workshops, community activities, and so on).

At the present time. unfortunately, there seems to be a shortage of informed and skilled trainers within this specific area. Further, it would seem important and necessary for counsellors involved in mixed-race settings to avail themselves of supervisors who have the necessary width and breadth of knowledge required. Again, such consultants are rare.

The above elements reflect a somewhat 'chicken and egg' situation. Clearly this scenario constitutes a frustrating predicament. Viewed from a slightly less pessimistic perspective, there exists a variety of short courses available (one-day, weekends) dealing with these phenomena. Indeed, increased demands have been made on members of RACE (Race and Cultural Education in Counselling, a division of the BAC) and the BAC to provide such facilities over recent years.

We can appreciate in the near future that, as a result of an increasing incidence of mixed-race counselling partnerships occurring, appropriate training methods and consultative support mechanisms will develop. Beyond that, issues such as specialist accreditation of counsellors, supervisors, and trainers for this specific element of counselling might have to be considered by organizations such as the BAC and the British Psychological Society. However, the labelling of certain individuals in this way might carry the unfortunate implication that most of us do not need to address the issues and problems of race in counselling.

The path towards increased training opportunities for black counsellors will also not be an easy one. The authors are already aware of situations in some allied 'helping professions' where white trainers have been accused of racism for failing black students. The overriding concern of and challenge to training agencies is that of maintaining 'academic' standards whilst encouraging black students from a range of backgrounds, some of whom may lack prior qualifications. Unfortunately such predicaments may well cause many agencies to avoid offering training that is sensitive to the subject of this chapter.

We have begun to map out above a potential area of development for counselling courses and individual counsellors. Our own experience contributes to a view that these initiatives are long overdue and require immediate attention. However, in reality, we fear that some of the challenges presented by this arena might prove too formidable to engage with directly. A shortage of existing trainers and supervisors (Thompson 1991) has already been acknowledged, and so too has the difficulty of encouraging black students, lacking traditional prior qualifications. A further barrier to comprehensive development is the lack of systematic research in two crucial areas, training and counselling practice. Such research might guide the formulation of sensitive and effective training programmes. It is our experience that some programmes in anti-racism education have had contradictory effects: that is, some participants have been further consolidated in their prejudicial attitudes. Trainers and researchers must therefore develop approaches to training that enable participants to explore these very difficult issues, without producing the contrary effects alluded to above.

Given the above apprehensions we predict that developments in training in this field are likely to be slow and *ad hoc*. It seems reasonable to suspect that some counselling courses, whilst not fully incorporating major new modules on counselling and race, will offer short introductory seminars on the subject. A rather more modest expansion of general awareness might thus be created over time which might then act as a catalyst for the development of substantial initiatives at a later date. It is perhaps only in this way that enough experience might be generated for a coherent development of 'good' training to occur.

One example of a substantial initiative would be the development of a specific postgraduate counselling course focusing on this area. Certainly there is no shortage of theoretical or experiential training material to fill such a course. Trainees could be drawn from the various professions which already use counselling methods. The course would offer a specific body of knowledge and skill to equip participants, first, more ably to counsel those who are culturally or racially different, and, second, to counsel members of ethnic minority groups

Other considerations for organizations offering counselling

Counselling is often seen as a middle-class activity, and thus as élitist, or certainly distant from the experience of working-class people, white and black. We believe that more effort needs investing in education, health, and public-relations programmes to counter this view and to increase general counselling provision. Counselling needs to be seen as a legitimate process for problem resolution.

Recent developments in training, in education, social services, and the National Health Service have seen an increase in the spread of counselling skills generally. However, this has not yet been accompanied by a visible expansion of counselling facilities, especially in areas having a higher incidence of ethnic minority peoples. With specific reference to counselling racially different clients there are very few specialist organizations offering help. Our view is that greater co-operation needs to take place between local authority and voluntary organizations and the different ethnic communities to stimulate the joint formation of projects that might be seen as directly relevant to the needs of those communities.

Much of this chapter has dealt with counselling as an activity that takes place between two people. There are other models of helping from around the world that are based on different assumptions, for example, working with families, working with community groups, using a series of counsellors in turn, and so on. Co-operation and consultation between various elements of local communities might lead to the establishment of counselling agencies that are more sensitively and appropriately equipped to help specific local communities. If counselling providers work only on a one-to-one model they might not only be guilty of cultural domination but will fail to provide the most relevant forms of help.

Given the present nature of Britain's multiracial society, it seems incumbent upon those whose concern is for the quality of people's lives generally to imaginatively expand that concern to all groups resident within Britain.

It is not enough to assume that there already exists an adequate network of informed agencies and counsellors. Developments in training, provision, research, and public information are all required so that any client, be they black or white, may have access to helpful counselling.

References

Atkinson, D., Morten, G. and Sue, D. W. (1989) *Counselling American Minorities: A Cross-Cultural Perspective*, Dubuque: William, C. Brown.

Coard, B. (1971) *How the West Indian Child is made Educationally Subnormal in the British School System*, London: New Beacon Books.

Dummett, A. (1980) 'Nationality and citizenship', in *Conference in Support of Further Education in Ethnic Minorities*, London: National Association for Teachers in Higher Education.

Guardian (1994) 'Labour figures show rise in reported race attacks in London', 18 March.

Hall, E. T. (1976) *Beyond Culture*, New York: Doubleday.

Hartman, P., Husband, C. and Clark, J. (1974) *Races as News*, Paris: UNESCO Press.

Helms, J. E. (1984) 'Toward a Theoretical Model of the Effects of Race on Counselling: A Black and White Model', *The Counselling Psychologist* 12: 153–65.

Jones, E. E. (1985) 'Psychotherapy and counseling with black clients' in P. Pedersen (ed.) *Handbook of Cross-cultural Counseling and Therapy*, London: Praeger.

Jowell, R., Witherspoon, S. and Brook, L. (1984) British Social Attitudes: the 1984 Report, Aldershot: Gower/Social and Community Planning Research.

Jumaa, M. (1993) 'From the Chair' *Race Newsletter*, December, No. 3, Rugby: BAC.

Katz, J. H. (1978) *White Awareness: Handbook for Anti-racism Training*, Norman: University of Oklahoma Press.

Lago, C. O. in collaboration with Thompson, J. (1996) *Race, Culture and Counselling*, Buckingham: Open University Press.

Lee, C. C. (1994) An Introductory Lecture given at a conference entitled 'Race, Culture and Counselling', Sheffield University, U.K. (July).

Lee, C. C. and Richardson, B. L. (1991) *Multicultural Issues in Counselling: New Approaches to Diversity*, Alexandria: American Association for Counselling and Development.

Little, A., Day, M., and Marshland, D. (1978) *Black Kids, White Kids, What Hope?*, Leicester: National Youth Bureau.

Pontoretto, J. G. and Pedersen, P. B. (1993) *Preventing Prejudice: A Guide for Counselors and Educators*, London: Sage.

Rogers, C. R. (1978) *Carl Rogers on Personal Power*, London: Constable.

Skellington, R. and Morris, P. (1992) *Race in Britain Today*, London: Sage/OUP.

Smith, D. J. (1977) *Racial Disadvantage in Britain*, Harmondsworth: Penguin.

Sue, D. W. (1981) *Counseling the Culturally Different*, New York: John Wiley.

Thomas, A. and Sillen, S. (1972) *Racism and Psychiatry*, New York: Brunner/Mazel.

Thompson, J. (1991) Issues of Race and Culture in Counselling Supervision Training Courses. Unpublished M.Sc. thesis, London: Polytechnic of East London.

Troyna, B. (1981) *Public Awareness and the Media*, London: Commission for Racial Equality.

Chapter eighteen

Counselling and sexual orientation

Paul Hitchings

Introduction

This chapter focuses on some of the variety of particular issues that a lesbian, gay, or bisexual client may bring into the counselling arena as well as the potential relevance that such sexual orientations might have for concerns that are more obviously universal. An example of the former category might well be a young person seeking help to come to terms with a homosexual/bisexual orientation, and an example of the latter category might be a lesbian couple in their early sixties having differences in choosing where to live in retirement.

What defines sexual orientation? The answer to this seemingly obvious question is in fact quite complex. Behaviour itself is of course only one of many factors to be considered and consequently authors such as Coleman (1985) suggest categories that take into account not only behaviour but also fantasy and emotional attachments. Garnets and Kimmel (1991) suggest individuals may be presumed to be lesbian or gay if their primary affectional/erotic attraction are to people of the same gender, bisexual if their affectional/erotic attachments are to both men and women, and hetrosexual when their primary affectional/erotic attachments are to members of the opposite gender.

The terms lesbian, gay, bisexual, and heterosexual are best considered as abstractions. Each person has a unique sexuality that is lost in categorization. In many ways such labels are meaningless and we need to constantly bear in mind the uniqueness and fluidity of each person over time. However I believe that in our current time such a simplification is both necessary and useful since naming helps to symbolize experience and allows the outlining of issues that are relevant to those clients who experience their sexuality as different from the prescribed norm of 100 per cent heterosexuality.

This chapter will address some of the issues that are likely to be presented by this grouping of clients, underlying dynamics, models of gay and lesbian development, and issues that counsellors will need to address carefully in themselves if they are to equip themselves effectively to work with this group without creating further damage.

Principles

Toxic shame

In working with clients who identify as or who are struggling to come to terms with a lesbian, gay, or bisexual identity the major underlying dynamic that the counsellor needs to maintain an awareness of, is what Bradshaw (1988) calls 'Toxic Shame'.

Having grown up in an essentially homophobic society it is fairly certain that the individual will have internalized the constructs offered. This is likely to have happened before the young person develops any sense of their own sexuality. This considerably hinders the development of a healthy self-concept and sometimes results in the development of a fragile, false self-concept which is often shored up through constant conscious or unconscious denial, usually accompanied by the terror of discovery.

Some of this shoring up takes the form of heterosexual marriage ('it's just a phase I'm going through – this will cure me'); overachievement ('so my parents will love me'); underachievement ('to prove I'm worthless'); casual sex with later denigration of the sexual partner ('homosexuals are bad/dirty'); rigid boundaries between work and personal life; distancing from others, secrecy, loneliness ('if they knew who I really was they'd be right to think I'm bad'); alcoholism (to anaesthetize the pain); and a higher than usual instance of suicide attempts ('I'm better off dead because I hurt too much'). All of these defences serve both at one and the same time to avoid the experience of 'Toxic Shame' and yet to perpetuate it.

Overcoming this experience of toxic shame and replacing it with pride is a lifetime's work. In order to undo the ongoing damage caused by a still hostile society, the remnants of internalized homophobia, and to remain healthy, an individual needs to gain positive affirmation from self, colleagues and friends on an almost daily basis. The beginning of this process has been referred to as 'coming out'.

Coming out

Cohen and Stein (1986), quoted by Hanley-Hackenbruck (1989: 21), define the term as follows:

> Coming out refers to a complicated developmental process which involves at a psychological level a person's awareness and acknowledgement of homosexual thoughts and feelings. For some persons, coming out ultimately leads to public identification as a gay man or lesbian.

Are there discernible stages in such a process? A number of authors have offered models of this process based upon their clinical experience (Cass 1979; Coleman 1985; Dank 1971; Grace 1979; Henken and O'Dowd 1977; Lee 1977). A brief account of these models is provided by Hanley-Hackenbruck (1989).

These models suggest that individuals who are homosexual need to negotiate certain stages in the formation of their identity development. However, the use of such a model does not assume that a person follows through each stage in a progressive, linear manner. A person may work at a number of stages concurrently and may need to recycle previous stages at particular points in their development. The five stages of Coleman's (1985) model are described below, together with some of the associated relevant counselling considerations.

1 Pre-coming out

Of this stage, Coleman (1985: 33) states:

> Because individuals at the pre-coming out stage are not consciously aware of same-sex feelings, they cannot describe what is wrong. They can only communicate their conflict through behavioural problems, psychosomatic illnesses, suicidal attempts, or various other symptoms. It is conceivable that some suicidal attempts by children and adolescents are due to this conflict.

At this stage a person is aware that there is something different about themselves but cannot conceptualize this difference and/or admit this difference to themselves. This task is filled with confusion. Cass (1979) refers to it as the stage of 'identity confusion'. This task is completed when an individual acknowledges to themselves their same-sex feelings.

Counselling considerations: In the early part of this stage the client is not aware of homosexual impulses as being the conflict that underlies the presenting problem. This possibility is then a loose counselling hypothesis. In both the early and latter parts of this stage the client is likely to be experiencing a high degree of conflict. The significant task at this stage is to allow the client to explore their sexuality without any prejudice on the part of the counsellor as to which orientation they should further explore and develop. This will eventually allow the client to make a genuine choice, at a pace that is in keeping with their own readiness. Whilst the counsellor needs to guard against pushing the client in one direction or another the counsellor needs nevertheless to provide accurate information including correcting common misconceptions about homosexuality. This requries a fine balance of judgement, since too frequent correction of misconceptions or, on the other hand, ignoring misconceptions, could be misinterpreted by the client as pushing towards one or other orientation. Of particular value at the latter part of this stage is for the counsellor to inform the client about potentially useful texts such as Hart (1984). Coleman (1985) states that a healthy resolution to this stage is to face the existential crisis of being different.

2 Coming out

Coleman (1985: 34) writes of this task:

> Once their same-sex feelings have been identified and acknowledged, individuals face the next developmental task of the coming out stage: telling others. The function of this task is to begin self-acceptance.

At the beginning of this task it is important that the person chooses to tell people who are relatively 'safe', that is, those who almost certainly will be validating of their sexuality. The counsellor is obviously within this category. When sufficient positive experiences have been accrued by the person, they are in a better position to tell people whose response is less predictable. On this point Coleman (1985: 34) comments:

> This is a very critical point, for the confidants' reaction can have a powerful impact. If negative, it can confirm all the old negative impressions and can put a seal on a previous low self-concept. If positive . . . The existential crisis begins to resolve in a positive direction.

At this stage it is of particular value for the client to begin to develop a friendship circle that can offer support and guidance, since social isolation can be especially damaging. Many lesbian and gay organizations run social groups specifically for people engaged in the process of coming out.

In the latter stages of this task, telling significant people in their lives who are heterosexual is an important step. Particularly painful can be negative responses from family members, and the person might find it helpful to remind themselves that such reactions can move in a more positive direction given time.

Counselling considerations: Here the counsellor needs to praise new behaviour, from the initial statements the client makes that they are lesbian/gay, to finding information about homosexuality and to telling significant others. The issue of telling significant others such as family members needs to be carefully dealt with by the counsellor. The client could possibly at this stage either approach the situation in a provocative manner or in an ill-thought-through way, motivated by euphoria at embracing their new-found self-concept. The possibility of delaying this self-disclosure until the client is more psychologically ready needs to be explored.

3 Exploration

This period is the equivalent of the adolescent period of learning through exploring and experimenting with relationships. A particular cluster of issues is often of relevance at this stage. These are: development of inter-personal skills for meeting others, the development of skills of sexual competence, setting appropriate boundaries for self, recognizing interna-lized self-oppression, and an awareness of the potential use of intoxicants to anaesthetize the pain and shore up a weak self-concept.

Perhaps for gay men there is also the issue of the separation of self-esteem from sexual conquest. Additionally, they must be aware of the danger of obtaining casual sex apparently for pleasure but in effect to reinforce a negative view of the self.

Cass (1979) describes this phase as the time when identity tolerance can lead to identity acceptance. This is a particularly intense phase of learning since the social rules and norms of lesbian/gay culture need to be learned. In addition, this is a phase like adolescence but without the usual parental and economic constraints which would normally operate to provide safe boundaries for the person. Grace (1979) has suggested the concept of 'developmental lag' to describe the process.

Counselling considerations: Many of the tasks of the counsellor will be more clearly educative than at other periods in the coming out process. Frequently the counsellor will need to teach certain social skills and/or encourage the client in order to overcome possible shyness and awkwardness. Additionally, the counsellor is well placed to help the client acquire the relevant information about health issues and/or to employ bibliotherapy.

The possibility of the client being stuck at this stage needs to be borne in mind by the counsellor. In the author's experience clients often present for counselling as a result of having been stuck at this stage for many years. This may well be indicative of internalized homophobia expressed in beliefs such as 'homosexual relationships will never last', which is then lived out as a self-fulfilling prophecy. The counsellor needs to be alert to subtle as well as more obvious manifestations of such belief systems and confront them as appropriate.

Towards the end of this phase clients frequently need to experience and express their feelings of anger and sadness at not having had permission from their parents and the wider culture to live their sexuality properly. There is often a period of mourning for the decades of their life that cannot now be lived in a way that would have been healthy and satisfying.

4 First relationships

First relationships, irrespective of sexual orientation, are frequently over-romanticized and essentially function as learning grounds for relationship skill-building. However, for homosexual clients who are chronologically older than is usual for this task, first relationships can often take on an intensity and optimism that is unrelated to the reality of the two people involved. Also, such relationships are often entered into before the previous tasks have been completed and consolidated. Frequently the individual attempts to use the relationship as a protection against dealing with a still delicate self-concept. A further factor here is the lack of homosexual role models or cultural support offered. When such a relationship ends there is the possibility that it will not be used as a learning experience but that the ending is bitter or traumatic. Such as situation can lead to depression, recreational drug abuse and, particularly for gay men, the use of casual sex to feel guilty and reinforce negative beliefs about homosexuality. In this way, then, the individual may return to the previous developmental phase and becomes stuck to it.

Counselling considerations: The counsellor needs to help the client think through the expectations made of the relationship and explore internalized homophobia which often is given expression in very subtle forms. when such a relationship ends the counsellor needs to encourage the client to appreciate what they have learned and to separate in as healthy a way as possible.

5 Integration

Cass (1979) refers to individuals at this stage as having moved from identity confusion through identity comparison, tolerance, acceptance, and pride, to identity synthesis. Here, then, is the task of fully 'choosing' to be gay in an existential sense. Being homosexual at this stage becomes at one and the same time central to the individual's identity and paradoxically totally irrelevant. Against such a background the individual is then free to negotiate the tasks of the various stages of adult life that we all face irrespective of our sexual orientation.

During this stage, which is essentially an ongoing process of growth, the client is likely to be involved with choosing a lifestyle that fits with their own temperament and with the phase they are in, in their life journey. Frequently, clients will put some energy into the creation of 'families' of their own making and choice, which may or may not include their biological family. For some gay clients this may involve lifestyles that are not modelled on the heterosexual norms and might involve more than one ongoing committed relationship, none at all, or an exploration of the variety of realtionships that are possible (see Kitzinger and Coyle 1995).

Counselling considerations: This is essentially the phase of existential work when homosexual clients, who are less likely to be distracted by the prescribed meanings offered by the majority heterosexual culture, engage with the existential task of choosing a meaning for their lives. Typically this is an issue that comes to the fore in the forties and fifties, and can be all the more clearly highlighted as the result of living a life that does not conform to the usual traditions.

Should lesbian, gay or bisexual clients always reveal their sexuality? There are instance when individuals whose sexuality is well integrated nevertheless choose not to reveal their sexuality or actively hide it. In a society where prejudice remains a real fact of life this 'passing' can be a sensible coping strategy. such prejudice covers issues from career disadvantage to the risk of begin beaten to death. Herek (1989) reports that 92 per cent of lesbians and gay men have experienced verbal abuse and 24 per cent experienced physical attack of which some result in death. Turque (1992) reports that 53 per cent of Americans in a Gallup poll believed that a homosexual lifestyle was unacceptable. Homosexual people need to learn to find a delicate balance between integrating their identities and maintaining an appropriate degree of caution.

Where such caution is unnecessary, or results in long-term loss of freedom then it is likely that internalized homophobia is operating which may well require gentle confrontation by the therapist.

Issues

Young people

There is clear evidence that young people who are grappling with the issue of coming to terms with a homosexual orientation have a much higher than average level of suicidal ideation. Remafedi *et al.* (1991) in a sample of gay and bisexual youth found that as many as one-third of the sample had attempted suicide at least once. This level of distress probably stems from the difficulties of the coming out process. High levels of distress are also known to reduce compliance to risk-reduction strategies within the context of HIV infection (Schneider *et al.* 1989). This presumably also holds for other behaviours such as the use of recreational drugs. Counsellors then need to pay particular attention to the assessment of these issues when working with lesbian and gay youth.

Couples

Whilst it is generally true that homosexual couples face fairly similar issues as do heterosexual couples, some of the important differences are all too easily missed. Differences in the overall place in the 'coming out' process between individuals in the couple can be a cause of friction. One may be more 'obvious' than the other which may raise internalized homophobic beliefs.

Also, because of the lack of given societal roles, such couples have to find their own. This process can be painful and difficult, although, if persevered with, can be liberating and psychologically very healthy. This is often essentially a negotiation about power in the relationship and consequently is likely to involve any issues concerning inequality between the two people, for example, age, education, income and the allocation of everyday tasks.

Being a couple also means that the homosexuality of the two people is more public. This can aid integration of identity but it also brings with it the potential experience of prejudice. Consider the seemingly ordinary issue of viewing one-bedroom flats to rent or going on a package holiday. Prejudice also clearly operates within the health-care system where the partner is all too frequently ignored by the staff and/or the relatives. These issues bring with them levels of stress that would not occur were the couple heterosexual. Being homosexual also becomes much more difficult to hide from work colleagues and family. Such issues also take on a particularly painful profile for those relationships which have been established in mid or later life, after a change in sexual identity. A further complicating factor here can be the issue of gaining legal custody of children.

Perhaps for some of the above reasons and perhaps from autonomous choice a far smaller percentage of homosexual couples choose to cohabit than heterosexual couples. Harry (1983) estimates that only 75 per cent of lesbian and 50 per cent of gay male couples cohabit, whereas this is much closer to 100 per cent for heterosexual couples.

Are levels of sexual satisfaction different in homosexual relationships? From our current understanding there does not seem to be any difference in this regard between heterosexual and homosexual couples. Blumstein and Schwartz (1983) found approximately 70 per cent of their sample of lesbians, gay men and heterosexuals were happy with their sexual activity with their partner.

A particular difference however is in sexual exclusivity. This is less common amongst lesbian and gay couples than heterosexual couples. Kitzinger and Coyle (1995) cite research that does show a significantly higher incidence of open relationships amongst gay men and to a lesser extent amongst lesbians. They note however that this is usually in the context of agreement and not secretive infidelity. They conclude: 'the more 'open' couple relationships sustained by gay men and (to a lesser extent) by lesbians, and their (apparently) differing levels of sexual activity are entirely compatible with mental health and fulfilling relationships.'

For the reader interested in a fuller discussion of the differences between heterosexual/lesbian/gay couples Kitzinger and Coyle (1995) offer an informative article.

Older lesbians and gays

What particular issues are there for counselling with this particular grouping? Because lesbian and gay people do not have as many 'natural' meeting places as their heterosexual counterparts it is all too easy for individuals (or couples) to limit themselves to the more easily accessible 'scene'. Typically (as in the heterosexual world) this revolves around the sexualized meeting places of bars and clubs. This can all too easily for the older person appear discouraging and be a reminder of the loss of youth. The well-informed counsellor can point to the numerous social groupings and alternatives that now exist. Gay Switchboard is an excellent resource.

The other major issue for older lesbians and gay men is that of giving meaning to their lives. As described earlier in the 'integration phase' of the coming-out process, meaning is not so obviously prescribed by society as it is for their heterosexual counterparts. This can easily lead to a level of depression and clearly the concepts of existential counselling are invaluable here.

Counsellor issues

Most counsellors working with lesbian, gay and bisexual clients genuinely ascribe to liberal beliefs that are supportive and that are anti-discriminatory. The days of gross prejudice are now almost over. The work that remains to be done is that of helping one another recognize the subtler and in many ways more insidious forms of prejudice that we all (probably) still harbour. To provide an example of this latter kind of prejudice I have detailed a personal experience below which makes the point extremely clearly.

At a conference of mental health professionals a colleague enquired of another whether he had a partner. The colleague reported that he did, at which point the inquiring colleague then asked in a neutral tone whether this partner was male or female. The look of horror on the face of the colleague being questioned would have been humorous to watch were the issue not so serious.

On this issue Greene (1994) states: 'Therapists must begin to assess the impact of a legacy of negative sterotypes about gay men and lesbians on their own thinking and they must do so before a gay or lesbian client ever appears before them.' Similarly Markowitz (1991) notes that it is not sufficient simply not to believe the stereotypes without an inquiry into their personal effects on deeper levels.

I assume that having grown up and living in our society we all have a certain degree of prejudice within us and that to remain aware requires ongoing active efforts. This I believe holds true of all types of prejudice in our society. As an aid to surfacing homophobic prejudice it can be useful to ask (especially if you identify as heterosexual) some self-searching questions such as:

Are you able to consider the possibility that you might one day find someone of the same sex attractive to you sexually?

Can you openly admire the beauty of another person of the same sex?

What reactions would you have if your son/daughter brought home from school a student of the same age and sex who was openly homosexual?

Would you let yourself ask a colleague if their partner was male or female?

Do you openly confront homophobia?

Sexual orientation of the counsellor

Are lesbian/gay clients more likely to be helped by working with a counsellor of the same sex and orientation? The answer to this question is complex, and to a considerable extent depends on what the client hopes to gain from counselling. The crucial variable is the ability of the counsellor to recognize fully and believe in the equal validity of a homosexual lifestyle and not so much the sexual orientation of the counsellor *per se*. This of course also applies to counsellors who have chosen a homosexual lifestyle since they are equally vulnerable to harbouring and communicating anti-homosexual prejudice. There are, however, arguments that a lesbian or gay psychotherapist can provide a client with certain dimensions that a non-homophobic heterosexual counsellor would be unable to offer. Rochlin (1982) argues that three particular dimensions are of significance: first, the enhanced degree of empathy that can be communicated from having personally shared the experiences of growing up gay in a heterosexual culture; secondly, the provision of a role model for clients who are unlikely to have been exposed to any positive role models in their childhood or their adult life; thirdly, the personal knowledge and experience of gay culture and lifestyles, which allows the client to further their work without having to educate the counsellor along the way.

Counsellor self-disclosure

Should the counsellor disclose their sexual orientation to clients? Almost all schools of counselling caution on the use of self-disclosure by the counsellor, from those that prohibit any information being proffered, to those which believe that appropriate self-disclosure is essential in maintaining the relationship as an authentic encounter. The question then becomes, when is it appropriate and when inappropriate for the counsellor in working with gay and lesbian clients to withhold information regarding their sexuality? Malyon (1985: 63–4) argues as follows:

> If the clinician is gay, it is often of therapeutic value to reveal this early in the treatment process in order to help assure the client that the details of his homosexual feelings will be understood and accepted by the therapist.

Leitman (1995) similarly argues the benefits of increased and realistic empathy if the counsellor is also gay and discloses this. In practice, where the counsellor is gay the client has often contacted them because they specifically want a gay counsellor and have gained this information form one of the various gay referral sources or via word or mouth within the gay community. Where the counsellor is not gay and the client clearly identifies as being gay, there is some benefit in the counsellor sharing explicitly with the client their value system with respect to a homosexul lifestyle.

Malyon (1985: 64) follows his position on self-disclosure with a caution:

> There are instances where early therapist disclosure would be counter-therapeutic, particularly where the client has not yet come out and is deeply conflicted over his homo-erotic promptings. In this instance therapist disclosure might be too threatening to the client and result in a premature termination of treatment.

Those clients who have not yet come out and might find such a counsellor disclosure too threatening are not likely to have been referred by such sources.

A related issue for homosexual counsellors working with a same-sex client is the possibility of finding oneself in the same gay/lesbian social venue as your client. The lesbian/gay community, even in a very large city, approximates to life lived in a small town. This has implications for those counsellors who have chosen not to reveal their identity to clients as well as those who have. For the latter group the maintainance of appropriate boundaries is an important issue. To do this whilst not at the same time being so distant as to give the non-verbal message of being ashamed to have been seen there requires fine judgement. Some counsellors choose to discuss in the early sessions of counselling how they are likely to behave in such a situation should it occur.

Future developments

The societal context within which different generations of lesbians and gay men have grown up has changed enormously over the last few decades. Just over thirty years ago male homosexual acts carried the possiblity of a prison sentence, were often accompanied by deep shame, and were usually enveloped in secrecy. In contrast homosexual people today have a multitude of meeting places, role models, lesbian and gay literature, radio stations, specific homosexual holiday destinations, in short a culture to which they can belong. This is not an argument for complacency. There is still much that militates against healthy development for lesbians and gay men. However, an important issue for counsellors is to bear in mind the different quality and nature of environment that lesbians and gay men of differing generations have experienced. This is likely to have a considerable bearing on the issues brought to counselling by lesbians and gay men of different generations.

An issue related to the above is the continuing validity of models of the coming-out process. It is likely that as the culture changes such models as discussed in this chapter will require amendment and refinement. Milton (1996) questions the validity of the first phase of Coleman's model ('pre-coming out') both from clinical experience and from a research account (Coyle 1991), arguing that there is usually some awareness of same-sex attraction from an early age. It may well be that the mechanisms of repression that played a part in the psychological makeup of homosexual people are now not as severe as they were some decades ago. Further research will allow more accurate maps to guide the counsellor over future decades.

Counsellor resources

There is now an Association for Lesbian, Gay and Bisexual Psychologies within Britain (ALGBP–UK), founded in 1993 and affiliated to the European Association. Membership is open to heterosexual as well as bisexual and homosexual colleagues with an interest in counselling or in the wider field of psychology. The UK Association holds an annual conference, one-day training events, publishes a regular newsletter, provides a referral list of practitioners and leaflets for the public, including one on guidelines to finding a non-homophobic counsellor. The Association may be contacted by writing to: ALGBP–UK, PO Box 7534, London NW1 0ZA.

Recommended reading

Davies, D. and Neal, C. (eds) (1996) *Pink therapy: A Guide for Counsellors Working with Lesbian, Gay and Bisexual Clients*, Buckingham: Oxford University Press.

References

Blumstein, P. and Schwartz, P. (1983) *American Couples: Money, work, sex*, New York: William Morrow.

Bradshaw, J. (1988) *Healing the Shame that Binds You*, Florida: Health Communications, Inc.

Cass, V. C. (1979) 'Homosexual identity formation: a theoretical model', *Journal of Homosexuality* 4: 219–35.

Cohen, C. and Stein, T. (1986) 'Reconceptualising individual psychotherapy with gay men and lesbians, *Psychotherapy with lesbians and gay men*. New York: Plenum Publishing Corp.

Coleman, E. (1978) 'Towards a new treatment model of homosexuality: a review', *Journal of Homosexuality* 3(4): 345–59.

——(1985) 'Developmental stages of the coming out process' in J. C. Gonsoriek (ed.) *A Guide to Psychotherapy with Gay and Lesbian Clients*, New York/London: Harrington Park (first published 1982).

Coyle, A. (1991) 'The Construction of Gay Identity' Vol. 1 and 2, unpublished Doctoral Dissertation, University of Surrey.

Dank, B. M. (1971) 'Coming out in the gay world', *Psychiatry* 34: 180–97.

Erikson, E. (1946) 'Ego development and historical change', *The Psychoanalytic Study of the Child* 2: 356–9.

Garnets, L. and Kimmel, D. (1991) 'Lesbian and Gay Male dimensions in the psychological study of human diversity' in J. Goodchilds (ed.) *Psychological Perspectives in Human Diversity in America: Masters Lectures* Washington DC: American Psychological Association.

Grace, J. (1979) 'Coming out Alive', paper presented at the Sixth Biennial Professional Symposium of the National Association of Social Workers, San Antonio. Quoted by E. Coleman in J. C. Gonsoriek (ed.) (1985) *A Guide to Psychotherapy with Gay and Lesbian Clients*, New York/London: Harrington Park (first published 1982).

Greene, B. (1994) 'Ethnic minority lesbian and gay men: Mental health and treatment issues', *Journal of Consulting and Clinical Psychology* (April).

Hanley-Hackenbruck, P. (1989) 'Psychothcrapy and the "Coming out process"', *Journal of Gay and Lesbian Psychotherapy* 1: 1.

Harry, J. (1983) 'Gay male and lesbian realtionships' in Macklin E. and Rubin R. (eds) *Contemporary Families and Alternative lifestyles: Handbook on research and theory*, London: Sage.

Hart, J. (1984) *So You Think You're Attracted to the Same Sex?*, Harmondsworth: Penguin.

Hart, L. E. (1981) 'An investigation of male therapists' views of women on the process and outcome of therapy with women', *Dissertation Abstracts International* 42: 2529B.

Henken, J. D. and O'Dowd, W. T. (1977) 'Coming out as an aspect of identity formation', *Gai Saber* pp. 18–22.

Herek, G. M. (1989) 'Hate crimes against lesbians and gay men', *American Psychologist* (44): 948–55.

Kitzinger, C. and Coyle, A. (1995) 'Lesbian and gay couples: speaking of difference', *The Psychologist* 8(2): 64–9.

Lee, J. D. (1977) 'Going public: a study in the sociology of homosexual liberation', *Journal of Homosexuality* 7(2/3): 59–70.

Leitman, N. (1995) 'To the Point', *Counselling News* 20 (December).

Malyon, A. K. (1985) 'Psychotherapeutic implications of internalised homophobia in gay men' in J. C. Gonsoriek (ed.) *A Guide to Psychotherapy with Gay and Lesbian Clients*, NewYork/London: Harrington Park (first published 1982).

Markowitz, L. M. (1991) 'Homosexuality: Are we still in the dark?', *The Family Therapy Networker*, pp. 26–9, 31–5 (Jan–Feb).

Milton, M. (1996) '"Coming Out" In Therapy', *Counselling Psychology Review*, 11(3): 26–32.

Remafedi, G. *et al.* (1991) 'Risk Factors for Attempted Suicide in Gay and Bisexual Youth, *Paediatrics* 87: 869–75.

Rochlin, M. (1982) 'Sexual orientation of the therapist and therapeutic effectiveness with gay clients' in J. C. Gonsoriek (ed.) *A Guide to Psychotherapy with Gay and Lesbian Clients*, New York: Harrington Park (first published 1982).

Schneider, S. G. *et al.* (1989) 'Suicidal Behaviour in Adolescent and Young Gay Men' *Suicide and Life-threatening Behaviour* 19(4): 281–394.

Turque, B. (1992) 'Gays under fire' *Newsweek* (14 September) pp. 35–40.

Chapter nineteen

Pastoral counselling

John Foskett and Michael Jacobs

Principles

Defining pastoral counselling

'Pastoral' can be used in different senses. It applies equally to the caring function of teachers, particularly in primary and secondary schools, as well as to the major part of the ministry of clergy and religious leaders. In this chapter our concern is to describe the counselling which takes place within and around the religious context, although too precise a definition of the nature and aims of pastoral counselling would limit the variety of its expression.

We use the term 'religious' because the interest in pastoral counselling not only brings together those of different Christian traditions but also provides common ground with members of the Jewish faith, as well as with those who belong to no church but who consider matters of faith and ultimate concern as of relevance to themselves and their clients. Pastoral counselling is not yet practised amongst those of other faith traditions, but as transcultural counselling develops (see Chapter 17), the exploration of believers' religious needs and aspirations will surely find its place amongst all faith groups, including the growing number of people involved in new-age spirituality.

In part pastoral counselling and its corollary, psychologically informed generic pastoral care, continues the ministerial tradition of 'the cure of souls', healing, spiritual direction and the confessional. However a distinctive feature of pastoral counselling is that it is practised by as many (if not more) 'lay' people as it is by ordained ministers, in the context of church-affiliated counselling centres, as well as in private work.

Nor can pastoral counselling be limited either to a religious setting or affiliation. It also refers to counselling which takes religious and spiritual problems seriously, and which is informed by the counsellor's concern for ultimate values and meaning – religion in its widest sense. This does not mean that the pastoral counsellor is only interested in religious problems, nor that matters of faith will automatically find their way on to the agenda. As we illustrate below, apparently 'religious' problems often disguise common issues such as personality and relationship problems, which are typical of many clients in other counselling settings. On the other hand long-term counselling and psychotherapy can give rise to deeper questions of meaning, which may also form part of the content of pastoral counselling.

The ambience of pastoral counselling

Given the similarity between the types of problem, and indeed the variety of therapeutic approaches used both in counselling generally and in pastoral counselling, it is not easy to identify the distinctive emphasis of the term 'pastoral'. Following in a long tradition of spiritual guidance and pastoral care, pastoral counsellors see themselves as working in a framework which includes other dimensions than the psychological, and more than concern for the individual client(s).

A well-tried definition of pastoral care is that it consists of 'helping acts, done by representative religious persons, directed towards the healing, sustaining, guiding and reconciling of troubled persons, whose troubles rise in the context of ultimate meanings and concerns' (Clebsch and Jaekle 1964: 4). Developed to apply to pastoral counselling, the *healing* function is seen in long-term counselling and pastoral psychotherapy, although the latter term is not widely used in Britain. It has much in common with what other counsellors offer to people with major personal and relationship difficulties. The *sustaining* function is more typically seen in supportive counselling, as in the long-term care of those with chronic problems and disabilities, or in crisis intervention with the bereaved. The *guiding* function is expressed in the counselling offered to those seeking direction in their lives, vocation or work, such as preparation for marriage, or career moves, or for retirement. Such guidance does not imply advice-giving, but involves helping the client to make her or his own decisions. The *reconciling* function is most often expressed in work with couples, families, or groups, although we could also emphasize the importance of reconciliation within individuals. Here, the traditional religious language of atonement between persons and God helpfully reflects the need for inner reconciliation or at-one-ment of persons to themselves, which is cherished by modern psychodynamic practice. This is especially true for those who understand God as being within the depths of themselves. Finally, in addition to the four functions in the definition, some writers add a fifth, *nurturing*, as seen in work with individuals and groups which encourages personal growth and development (Clinebell 1987).

An alternative definition of pastoral counselling, which expresses the philosophy and, in religious terms, the theology behind a counsellor's work, is that it is for the whole person as an individual, as well as part of a family and social unit; and as a whole person, body, mind, and spirit but with particular reference to the person's psychological, ethical, and theological frames of reference (Schlauch 1985). In this description, the inclusion of the term 'spirit' raises complicated issues with which religion has had to grapple since the advent of separate psychological understanding of persons. Yet there is more to people than body and mind. Whether spirit is a separate entity, or is a description of the whole body–mind unity is a difficult question, on a par with definitions of the 'self' in psychodynamic psychology. What is more obvious is that the term 'psyche', which lies at the root of different terms such as psychology and psychoanalysis, is the same as the more traditional religious concept of 'soul'. Pastoral counselling, therefore, is especially concerned with the whole person, and, when appropriate, with helping people find their own meanings for, and relationship to, the transcendent. In this respect the pastoral approach has something in common with the fourth of the major divisions of therapy and counselling, transpersonal psychology. (The other major divisions are behavioural, psychodynamic, and humanistic psychology.)

Pastoral counselling itself does not espouse one particular counselling orientation; pastoral counsellors differ to the degree in which they draw upon the techniques and theories of humanistic, analytic and behavioural psychologies. Nevertheless Freud and Jung and their modern counterparts have had a major influence upon many pastoral counsellors. Freud's criticism of religion has proved invaluable in helping pastors understand the neurotic aspects of religious belief, while Jung's frequent use of the symbols and imagery of world religions, and his apparent endorsement of a religious outlook on life as being central to the recovery of people in the second half of life, makes his thinking especially attractive to some pastoral counsellors. 'God' in Jungian terms is an 'archetype', and there is as much debate about the existence of archetypes as there is about the existence of a deity.

Nevertheless, the psychodynamic schools are concerned to understand the nature of persons, and tend to be less optimistic about people's capacity to change through their own efforts alone. Many of the issues which are tackled by psychodynamic theory therefore find parallels in the debates that have taken place in traditional theology: whether, for instance, the deterministic, and often unconscious, influences of infancy and childhood allow any place for the exercise of free will; whether persons are by nature good or bad, angelic or devilish; how the past influences the present, and the present influences the future. Similarly, pastoral counsellors find parallels between existential issues in therapy and theology. Anxieties about death, about meaninglessness, and about guilt constitute religious as well as therapeutic problems.

Pastoral counselling is not easily separated from pastoral care, so that while there has been the development of a specialized ministry of pastoral counsellors, this is a small, albeit influential, group in Britain. The majority of pastors have many duties in the course of their oversight and care of congregations. They are often sought out at crucial times in people's lives, such as the birth of a child, the blessing of a marriage, the advent of illness or tragedy, coping with death, and coming through bereavement. Faced with these expectations upon them, pastors have turned increasingly to the insights of pastoral counsellors, who themselves have tried to integrate the social and behavioural sciences with their religious and theological studies. Clergy and laity are increasingly benefiting from training in counselling skills and personal awareness, and from a grasp of sociological and psychological perspectives. This is leading them to offer a less directive, less authoritarian, and less moralistic ministry. In its place has emerged a greater capacity to help individuals and groups explore their own needs and aspirations, to resolve their own problems, and to seek their own direction. Indeed, pastors seek to be alongside people as, in biblical terms, they 'work out their own salvation with fear and trembling' (Philippians 2: 12), helping them to acknowledge that their God is as much within them as within any particular religious tradition.

From 1960 onwards a number of major pastoral counselling organizations have developed, some of which have had as much impact outside religious circles as within them. These include the Clinical Theology Association, the Richmond Fellowship, the Westminster Pastoral Foundation, the Raphael Counselling Centre (one of the specifically Jewish organizations), the Dympna Centre (primarily for the counselling of clergy, priests, and those in religious orders), and the Salvation Army Counselling Service. These and others came together to form the Association for Pastoral Care and Counselling, which is also the pastoral division of the British Association for Counselling (Foskett 1985). Furthermore, locally based groups have formed their own training and counselling services, sometimes linked to one of the major national organizations.

There is also a rather different type of religious counselling, mainly stemming from the evangelical churches. This is more explicitly Christian, and may involve the use of prayer and other more traditional pastoral practices such as the laying on of hands and the use of scriptural texts to guide and support the client. The Association of Christian Counsellors organizes its own training programme and accreditation scheme, both of which aim to support Christian counsellors in their use of secular psychologies, and the integration of these with Christian doctrines and traditions. As yet this latter type of religious counselling has not fully entered into dialogue with the pastoral counselling described in this chapter. In the authors' opinion, a pastoral counsellor needs to use her or his religious base sparingly and implicitly, and only to address religious issues explicitly if and when these are introduced by the client.

In his book *Counselling in the Pastoral and Spiritual Context*, David

Lyall (1995) explores the development of pastoral counselling in its many forms, both in the United Kingdom and in America, where the relationship between religion and psychology has a longer history.

Two examples of pastoral counselling

Most of the pastoral work which pastors undertake, whether using counselling skills in pastoral care or working as counsellors, has much in common with the problems presented to counsellors and carers working in other settings. Pastors, like other helpers, are confronted with problems of all kinds, only some of which have any clear religious component. However, the initial presentation of a person to a pastor may take a specifically religious form, such as a question about belief or moral attitudes, just as the presentation to a doctor usually takes the form of a physical illness. Clients expect pastors to be interested in religion, and therefore only to be interested in them if they present in religious terms. Yet the training and practice of pastors and pastoral counsellors has made them more aware of the deeper issues which underlie the initial presentation. In the following example, we show how the client presented a religious problem, but that in the course of counselling there turned out to be significant personal and relationship aspects.

> Jean had become increasingly depressed, and was treated first by her general practitioner and then by a psychiatrist, before being admitted to a hospital. She did not, however, respond to treatment, and became more and more obsessed with her badness. At one point she decided that she was possessed by the devil, and that only an exorcism could help her. She insisted on seeing the chaplain of the hospital, and then a priest who was responsible for handling such requests. Both chaplain and priest agreed that in their opinion there were no grounds for thinking that Jean was 'possessed'. The chaplain therefore offered her the opportunity of counselling, to explore what it was that made her so sure that she was in the grip of the devil.
>
> Jean was reluctant to accept this offer, and did so only on the understanding that she could tell the pastoral counsellor all about the devil inside her. She found this very difficult to describe at first, but gradually she painted a picture of herself as someone who was utterly revolting, and to whom something unspeakable had been done. She was now contaminated and a threat, especially to her husband and children. For a long time she could not bring herself to describe what it was that had happened to her, but eventually she related that she had visited a faith healer, because she had been suffering from recurrent back trouble. Only afterwards did she think this was wrong, because the healer was not a Christian.

The counsellor encouraged Jean to describe what precisely had happened when she had visited the healer. She explained that the man had put his hands on her back, and she had felt a strange sensation run all through her body. Jean then refused to discuss the matter further, and returned to the belief that it was only an exorcism that would save her. Re-telling the initial experience had clearly strengthened her anxiety.

Firmly but patiently the chaplain refused to act on her request for exorcism. Counselling continued, and Jean came back to the original incident, and to recognition of the strong sexual feelings aroused in her by the healer. That the chaplain could accept such feelings amazed and relieved her, and Jean slowly began to countenance the idea that her feelings, even if they had been disturbing, were not evil; and that because she had not acted upon them, there was no need to continue to feel such strong guilt. She was not wholly able to give up the idea of a devil within her, but the idea featured less and less in her counselling with the chaplain; and, bit by bit, Jean was able to discuss with her husband some of the things that had happened.

The second example demonstrates the close connection between a person's religious feelings and behaviour, and other dimensions of their past and present relationships. It confirms the view of some theologians, philosophers, and psychologists that many of the images that people have of God are projections; and that by working through the negative projections in particular, religious belief can contribute to more positive views of self and others.

George and his wife approached a counsellor for help with problems in their marriage. After they had seen the counsellor for a short time together, George elected to go on seeing her on his own, because counselling had already uncovered his deprived and traumatic childhood. With the help of the counsellor, George was able to face his sense of rejection, and get in touch with the enormous anger he felt towards his parents, and in particular towards his father. As counselling progressed he began to drift away from his church, realizing that when he worshipped he felt similar explosive feelings towards the church and especially towards the minister. The counsellor suggested that George could approach the minister to discuss his feelings, but he was afraid of offending the minister, whom he felt was too much like his father.

As an alternative he agreed to go and see a pastoral counsellor, and with her help he was able to explore the way in which his religious belief system had been retarded in the same way as his emotional development. The pastoral counsellor was able to show him the selective way he drew upon religious resources to reinforce his retardation and sense of oppression, and she gradually helped him to accept the idea of being angry with his God. In time this helped George to return to his church with much greater satisfaction and enjoyment.

This example demonstrates one of the particular advantages of working with a pastoral counsellor when it comes to matters of faith and 'religious' practice. While counsellors with no particular faith are often able to respect a client's own religious views, many of them are too respectful, and unsure of challenging false assumptions and distorted beliefs. Perhaps they are hesitant about entering the potential minefield of theological speculation; or see faith as primarily an intellectual position which has little to do with feeling. Some counsellors also fear that questioning a client's faith could lead to the collapse of an important belief system, leaving the client devoid of its comfort. They fail to appreciate that confrontation and analysis of unhelpful beliefs and practices often lead to more healthy religious attitudes, which in turn free the person to grow emotionally as well as spiritually.

Issues

Faith and psychology

In a pluralistic and largely secular society religious belief often seems an outmoded way of viewing life. Those who retain faith in the transcendent can easily be confused with those who use religious belief as a defence against taking more responsibility for themselves. Jean, in the example above, believed that she was possessed by the devil, rather than accept her own sexual excitement, and the anxiety that accompanied it. Yet the chaplain, and other people who were consulted, could see no evidence of possession. As her counsellor, the chaplain was faced with the question of how literally to respond to her conviction. He did not challenge her devil, but began to explore around it.

Carried to its logical conclusion, such an approach leads to dilemmas for many pastors, since the psychological tools which a pastor brings to her or his work tend to question the meaning and validity of many expressions of religious belief. Psychological explanations have a way of casting doubt upon more transcendent understanding of religious experience. There are tensions here for pastors, drawing them in different directions. Some are bewitched by the new and apparently liberating ideas emerging in the counselling movement, and find in it greater affirmation than religion gives them. For others, counselling's relativism and non-judgemental approach appears to undermine the centrality of their faith. Pastoral counsellors have tried to hold on to both sides of the tension: the work of Frank Lake and the Clinical Theology Association provides a good example of this (Yeomans 1986). Christian counsellors offer a more traditional solution to the tension, combining counselling methods with practices like prayer therapy and healing of memories. There is, however, a danger in using such methods lest they encourage a magical idea of religion, which fails to recognize the significance of the unconscious. For the majority of pastors, counselling has helped them recognize the importance, for good and for ill, that they themselves have for their clients. As good objects they represent much which can help their clients attain the health and understanding they seek. However, the same attachment can foster an unhealthy dependence upon the counsellor and the counsellor's abilities, and this can have a disabling effect upon the client. Much of the training of pastoral counsellors in self-understanding, together with their subsequent supervision, is to help them manage the transference relationship with their clients, whether or not they explicitly draw attention to it.

Another development which has been of indirect importance to pastoral counsellors has been the attempt to understand the nature and development of religious belief, in the same way that intellectual, moral, and emotional development has been studied by psychologists and psychoanalysts. Winnicott (1958) was one psychoanalyst who recognized the value of illusion, and so of the way in which not only religion, but equally art and science, enables people to contain the tension that exists between inner and outer realities. The research by James Fowler (1981, 1984, 1987; Jacobs 1993) led to his proposal of six stages of religious development, from mythical and literal views of faith to its highest expression in the lives of people like Gandhi or Mother Teresa. Fowler uses the term 'faith' to denote belief and value systems which are not necessarily theist. Faith is common to all humanity. The first part of his somewhat wordy definition of faith describes it as: 'People's evolved and evolving ways of experiencing self, others and world (as they construct them) as related to and affected by the ultimate conditions of existence (as they construct them)' (Fowler 1981: 92–3).

Paul Tillich is an example of an important theologian whose work combines theology and psychology, and which usefully informs a pastoral counsellor's thinking about faith and meaning. He suggested three different religious world views, starting with unconscious literalism in the person of simple and unquestioning faith; proceeding to conscious literalism in the person whose intellectual integrity has been challenged by other disciplines, and who has to find some way of reconciling literal faith with modern thought; and reaching the stage of broken myth. where a person treats religious ideas as essentially symbolic and metaphorical, to be believed only in so far as they have the power to express the ultimate when the symbols are broken, and to be used as pointers to ultimate concerns (Jacobs 1987: 114–18; Baldridge and Gleason 1978).

Such views of religious faith and development underline the subjectivity of the beliefs and practices seen in clients and congregations alike. Pastoral counsellors often find hope in the more radical theological positions espoused by people like Tillich or Don Cupitt. This kind of thinking has sometimes led traditional religious institutions and the more conservative-minded clergy and laity to dismiss the insights of pastoral counselling as doctrinally unsound. Pastoral counsellors' willingness to work with those aspects of persons which some religious people define as 'sinful', 'bad', and 'immoral' has in some cases prompted outright rejection of their ministry.

The understanding which pastoral counselling has brought to some of the major ethical debates amongst religious groups (Foskett 1992) also contributes to a certain amount of tension. Issues like the role of women in the church, attitudes to gays, lesbians, second marriages, and AIDS have been liberalized in the churches, partly through the work of pastoral counsellors. At the same time, those churches that espouse more dogmatic and moralistic attitudes, and offer their adherents a greater sense of certainty about faith and morals, are flourishing. Although pastoral counselling, with its more questioning outlook, helps balance this drift to the right, and heads off the return to the security blanket of religious certainty, inevitably these quite different approaches to religion and faith lead to conflicts between radicals and conservatives.

The relationship of pastoral counselling to pastoral care

The fact that counselling can often carry greater status and value than general pastoral care has also created some tensions within the movement itself, particularly with pastoral and practical theologians. These latter point to the danger of pastoral counselling becoming an egocentric preoccupation of the somewhat neurotic and narcissistic middle classes (Jacobs 1987: 130–6, 144–9). The criticism goes further, suggesting that counselling, like institutionalized religion, is in danger of making 'misfits' conform to society's expectations. Pastoral counselling may neglect the more prophetic aspects of pastoral care, where criticism of society and concern for the corporate and the social is as important as concentration upon the individual and the personal (Pattison 1988, 1994). Although it is not in practice easy to integrate the pastoral and the prophetic aspects of a pastor's work, we believe that to separate them is to make a false dichotomy, and that the conflicts between pastoral counsellors and pastoral theologians are potentially very creative. These issues are being addressed more squarely, as those who teach pastoral studies and those who train pastoral counsellors bring their respective insights to bear on common issues. Some pastoral counsellors are also beginning to address issues like the effect of the threat of nuclear conflict upon individuals and society, and forming their own subgoupings, linking in this case with the peace movement.

The international community

The wider awareness of pastoral counsellors has been helped through membership of international conferences and congresses on various themes related to pastoral care and counselling. These have brought British pastoral counsellors face to face with the application of counselling in other political regimes, such as the former Eastern bloc, and in cultures and amongst peoples of other faiths, in the countries of Africa, Asia, and South America. Pastoral counselling can easily become another means of trying to westernize and colonize, and pastoral counsellors can lead the way in accepting the essential need to listen, observe, and learn from others, rather than impose one's own views upon them. In Africa and Asia counselling is having to learn to take its place alongside equally effective folk myth and medicine (Dumalagan *et al.* 1983; Chanona and Sharif 1987; ma Mpolo and Nwachuku 1991).

The development of training

The training of pastors in counselling skills has developed rapidly from 1975 onwards and, increasingly, Anglican dioceses have been appointing Advisers in Pastoral Care and Counselling, with responsibilities for training and supporting clergy and laity. Theological colleges and seminaries offer more practical training in pastoral care than once they did, with placements in health, community, and social-service agencies. Lay training is much more common in all the major denominations. Such exciting developments nevertheless raise a number of issues and tensions, such as those between clergy of different generations; and between clergy, the traditional custodians of pastoral care, and the laity, who are often more open to training, and who become more skilled practitioners than many of the ordained.

There are also questions about the accreditation and monitoring of pastoral counsellors and, what is more difficult, of those involved in general pastoral care. The British Association for Counselling accreditation procedures, to which the Association for Pastoral Care and Counselling subscribes, often fail to attract those clergy and laity whose principal loyalty is to their work within the church, rather than to the wider but more specialized field of counselling. While monitoring and supervision is vitally important as pastoral care and counselling mushroom, there are problems with accreditation, lest by implication it deskills the effectiveness that the majority of pastors bring to their ministry, by creating a minority élite who simply practise as professional pastoral counsellors. There are also signs that the latter can grow to work more and more independently of any ecclesiastical organization or group, and that this in turn can heighten the sense of alienation between the theological and therapeutic aspects of pastoral care.

Future developments

Living in a multifaith society

Although pastoral counselling has been one of those arenas of joint action and concern that has helped co-operation across the divisions between churches, and has gone further by drawing Christians and Jews together, pastoral counselling has not yet addressed the multicultural and multifaith realities of the society in which it is practised. This is probably due to a number of different factors.

First, pastoral counselling, like most other kinds of counselling in Britain, is an activity predominantly involving the white middle classes, both as counsellors and as clients. It is therefore inclined to be racially and culturally exclusive (see Chapter 17). Second, pastoral counselling is a relatively small movement, which has been preoccupied with establishing its own position and credibility within Jewish and Christian traditions. As we have already shown, it appeals to those who seek in their faith an integration of the secular and the sacred; conversely it tends to be avoided by those who wish to preserve the unchanging traditions of their church or synagogue, or those who are attracted by the new spirit of their born-again beliefs. Adherents of other major faiths, like the many practising Jews and Christians, tend to fall into either of these two latter categories, and are therefore unlikely to be attracted to the pastoral care and counselling movement. The answers to their questions are found in their scriptures and tradition, or through their belief in divine inspiration, and they have little understanding of or sympathy for a non-directive approach.

Third, as yet there are few comparable developments within Buddhism, Hinduism, Islam, Sikhism, or other religious groups (de Silva 1990; Rothwell 1996; Weller 1993; APCC working party). The priests, imams, or other spiritual leaders, do not have an explicitly pastoral function, and pastoral care is practised informally within the extended family and kinship groupings. So while there are natural pastors and wise and understanding people within these traditions, no one would think of them specifically as being pastoral carers and counsellors; nor at first glance see what they have in common with Jewish or Christian pastors. In fact, we sense that they have much in common and much to share with one another if an appropriate medium can be found; but as yet this does not exist in Britain. There is evidence, however, from Africa and Asia that indigenous and western forms of ministry can complement one another, provided there is a context of mutual respect and understanding (Dumalagan *et al.* 1983; Lartey 1987; ma Mpolo and Sweemer 1987). To some extent the conditions which may provide this context are beginning to appear in this country, in the following ways.

There are similarities in the different faiths and traditions in patterns and methods of spirituality. Meditation is an obvious example. There are also communities and groups of different religions such as Interfaith Network UK (see Reference Addresses) who meet to share some of their practices with each other. There are also a small but significant number of counselling and caring agencies provided by and for ethnic minorities. Some have explicit religious connections, and all aim to help their clients with cultural and religious issues as well as other problems. The differing attitudes towards religion espoused by different generations are often a focus for their work, for example at NAFSIYAT (see Reference addresses).

Christian and Jewish pastors working in areas with many minority groups are being encouraged to develop patterns of care to which members of those groups can contribute. Religious groups have appointed race relations advisers from amongst the members of minority and ethnic groups, and guidance is now available to all pastors working in multicultural areas (Hooker and Lamb 1986). In some institutions too, particularly in the health service, chaplaincy teams have been extended to include pastors of other faiths. As pastoral counselling is a major part of a chaplain's work, this means that there are beginning to be opportunities for pastoral counsellors of different faiths to share and compare their work with one another.

The significance of story

The therapeutic model which dominated pastoral care and counselling from the 1960s to the 1980s has been complemented by a new model, which aims to integrate the theological and the therapeutic, through the common element of story and narrative. In different generations and amongst those of various religious traditions, one story tends to dominate: for instance, amongst counsellors it can be the client's story, whilst amongst pastors it can be the religious story. In fact three stories can be identified – the client's, the counsellor's, and the religious story – and in pastoral counselling all three have to find their place and interaction with each other for the ultimate benefit of client, counsellor, and the religious vision (Foskett and Lyall 1988: Chapter 5; Bohler 1987).

Counselling which is practised as an integral part of the life and activities of members of a church, congregation, or other religious group, is most likely to provide the context in which all the stories can be given equal weight, and their integration actively sought. This is much more difficult if pastoral counselling is practised in isolation from the rest of pastoral care. The same is true of two other possible developments: the contemporary interest in holistic approaches to health, and the rediscovering of the prophetic aspects of pastoral care. These too require an environment which encourages the containment of different approaches and perspectives, rather than an atmosphere which divides them into specialties.

The holistic approach

The contemporary interest in holistic and non-medical approaches to health has met with a ready response in some religious groups; pastoral counselling is often included amongst the resources offered within church health and healing centres and services, as a means of initial interview and assessment, and then as one amongst a number of other therapies and treatments, such as the Churches Council for Health and Healing (see Reference Addresses). Similar connections are beginning to be made with those involved in spiritual direction. Until recently, questions about spirituality have remained largely unexamined by pastoral counsellors. Given the essential body–mind–spirit unity which underlies theological ideas about the nature of person, current thinking about spirituality, and the concerns of holistic healing, there are grounds for a greater *rapprochement* between these different activities. There is evidence that those who guide the spiritual development of others are finding parallels between their own discipline and Jungian thought in particular. As pastoral counsellors begin to realize this interest, it is to be hoped that they will in turn explore the benefits of closer links with spirituality (Lyall 1995).

Rediscovering the prophetic role

Pastoral counselling is part of more general pastoral care, but pastoral care has other areas of specialized interest, such as the sociological and the political. Pastoral counsellors, like the counsellors in other settings, are faced with issues about the use of knowledge gained in private and in confidence (suitably disguised to preserve anonymity) to inform public decisions and policies. The growing divide between those who have and those who go without, and issues about caring for one another, are essential areas of interest to many pastoral counsellors who realize that major social problems and international concerns cannot be tackled simply by counselling individuals and families. As churches attempt to address the major problems of both inner urban areas (*Faith in the City* 1985; Pattison 1994) and poor rural areas, and focus their attention upon issues of social responsibility and cultural and racial justice, pastoral counselling will need to play its part in underlining the significance of external deprivation upon emotional, relationship, and spiritual problems. Since political pressure often gains from the weight of numbers as well as the force of argument, this is one field in which pastoral counsellors need to organize, on the one hand with other counsellors generally, and on the other, with the churches' social responsibility officers and boards.

Returning to roots

As pastoral counselling finds its identity, and shows the significance of its contribution to the counselling milieu generally, the time will come when many of those who found new insights in psychology and counselling methods will feel more confident about revisiting their original disciplines and training. They will want to look afresh at theology, in order to see in what ways theological reflection might enhance pastoral counselling (Foskett 1993). Furthermore, since religion has in the past provided one of the principal ways of trying to understand, explain, and come to terms with the mysteries of life and death, the needs and problems of persons, and the interrelationship between people and the world in which they live, the religious tradition has the potentiality for providing an even richer perspective on the issues with which pastoral counsellors are daily involved.

Reference addresses

Association of Pastoral Care and Counselling, 1 Regent Place, Rugby CV21 2PJ. APCC has an inter-faith working party exploring the place of counselling among major faith communities.

Churches' Council for Health and Healing, St Marylebone Parish Church. Marylebone Road, London NW1 5LT.

Interfaith Network UK, 5–7 Tavistock Place, London WC1H 9SS.

NAFSIYAT, Inter-Cultural Therapy Centre, 278 Seven Sisters Road, London N4 2HY.

References

Baldridge, W. E. and Gleason, J. J. (1978) 'A theological framework for pastoral care', *Journal of Pastoral Care* 32 (4): 232–8.

Bohler, J. (1987) 'The use of storytelling in the practice of pastoral counselling', *Journal of Pastoral Care* 41(1): 63–71.

Chanona, C. and Sharif, S. K. (1987) 'Pastoral response to the oppressed and the oppressor' in *Pastoral Ministry in a Fractured World*, Third International Congress of Pastoral Care and Counselling, Melbourne, Australia, pp. 92–106.

Clebsch, W. and Jaekle, C. (1964) *Pastoral Care in Historical Perspective*, New Jersey: Prentice-Hall.

Clinebell, H. (1987) 'Pastoral counselling' in A. Campbell (ed.) *A Dictionary of Pastoral Care*, London: SPCK.

Dumalagan, N. C., Becher, W. and Taniguehi, T. (1983) *Pastoral Care and Counselling in Asia*, Makati Medical Centre, Metro Manila, Philippines: Clinical Pastoral Care Association of the Philippines.

Faith in the City (1985) report of the Archbishop of Canterbury's Commission on Urban Priority Areas, London: Church House Publishing.

Foskett, J. (1985) 'Pastoral counselling', *British Journal of Guidance and Counselling* 13(1): 98–111.

——(1992) 'Ethical issues in counselling and pastoral care', *British Journal of Guidance and Counselling* 20(1): 39–50.

——(1993) 'Theology and counselling' in B. Thorne and W. Dryden (eds) *Counselling: Interdisciplinary Perspectives*, Buckingham: Open University Press.

Foskett, J. and Lyall, D. (1988) *Helping the Helpers*, London: SPCK.

Fowler, J. W. (1981) *Stages of Faith: The Psychology of Human Development and the Quest for Meaning*, San Francisco: Harper & Row.

——(1984) *Becoming Adult, Becoming Christian*, San Francisco: Harper & Row.

——(1987) *Faith Development and Pastoral Care*, Philadelphia: Fortress Press.

Hooker, R. and Lamb, C. (1986) *Love the Stranger*, London: SPCK.

Jacobs, M. (ed.) (1987) *Faith or Fear?: A Reader in Pastoral Care and Counselling*, London: Darton, Longman and Todd.

——(1993) *Living Illusions*, London: SPCK.

Lartey, E. Y. (1987) 'Intercultural pastoral care and counselling in Africa' in *Pastoral Ministry in a Fractured World*, Third International Congress of Pastoral Care and Counselling, Melbourne, Australia, p. 124.

Lyall, D. (1995) *Counselling in the Pastoral and Spiritual Context*, Buckingham: Open University Press.

ma Mpolo, M. and Sweemer, C. D. (1987) *Families in Transition, The Case for Counselling in Context*, Geneva: World Council of Churches Publications.

ma Mpolo, M. and Nwachuku, D. (1991) (eds) *Pastoral Care and Counselling in Africa Today*, Frankfurt: Peter Long.

Pattison, S. (1988) *A Critique of Pastoral Care* London: SCM.

——(1994) *Pastoral Care and Liberation Theology*, Cambridge: Cambridge University Press.

Rothwell, N. (1996) 'Therapy from a Buddhist perspective' in M. Jacobs (ed.) *Jitendra – Lost Connections*, Buckingham: Open University Press.

Schlauch C. R. (1985) 'Defining pastoral psychotherapy', *Journal of Pastoral Care* 39(3): 219–28.

de Silva, P. (1990) 'Buddhist psychology', *Current Psychology, Research and Reviews*, 9(3): 236–54.

Weller, P. (1993) (ed.) *Religions in the UK: a Multifaith Directory*, Derby: University of Derby.

Winnicott, D. W. (1958) 'Transitional Objects and Transitional Phenomena' in *Collected Papers: Through Paediatrics to Psychoanalysis*, London: Hogarth Press.

Yeomans, M. (ed.) (1986) *Frank Lake: Clinical Theology*, London: Darton, Longman and Todd.

Chapter twenty

Careers counselling and guidance

Diane Bailey

Introduction

Work is a major source of identity and status in our society. Changes in work patterns and practices have strong repercussions in individual lives and experiences. Over the last decade such changes have included relatively high levels of unemployment; a continuing shift away from manufacturing industry and towards the service economy: and a significant increase in part-time, often low-paid, work and in fixed-term and temporary contracts. At the same time there is evidence of skills shortages and of the inadequate training of the workforce. In addition many organizations, in both private and public sectors, have undergone radical restructuring to become slimmer and flatter, with fewer tiers of management, fewer core staff and more contractual staff. Political responses to these conditions have included more emphasis on vocational elements in the curriculum, such as the Technical and Vocational Educational Initiative (TVEI), National Vocational Qualifications, and the creation of the Training and Enterprise Councils (TECs), independent companies led by local business people to tackle training needs and improve business performance.

These changes have had implications for all those involved in careers counselling and guidance. Practically, there are problems in maintaining a current information base of labour-market and of training-scheme information. Operationally, there are difficulties in liaising with the numerous education, training, and employment agencies relevant to helping clients make decisions about work. Furthermore, counsellors and helpers are being challenged by wider conceptions of work, paid and unpaid, and by increasing awareness of how social factors, such as class, gender, age, and ethnic group, affect work opportunities.

'Guidance' is used in this chapter as an umbrella term encompassing the helping activities of informing, advising, counselling, coaching in appropriate skills (for example, decision-making), assessment, and providing advocacy and feedback to agencies (see Watts 1980). 'Careers counselling' here means, more specifically, offering the client a non-directive relationship in which to explore issues and carry through decisions about work. Guidance and counselling may involve both face-to-face help or may be mediated by telephone, letter, text, computer program or possibly even the Internet.

Principles

The relationship of theory and practice

Far-reaching changes in patterns of employment and in our conceptions of work have led to shifts in the models and forms of careers guidance which individuals need in order to cope with change. Theory and practice exist in a two-way relationship here. All practitioners work from sets of assumptions that inform their working styles and relationships. Careers workers express their theoretical perspective every time they conduct an interview or run a group session. It is the role of theory to challenge and develop these assumptions and to give practitioners tools to improve their grip on working issues. Likewise, models and principles need constant testing in the field to ensure their relevance and utility. Theory and practice are interlinked and both are embedded in social, economic, and political structures. In response to the changes in employment and work, there has been a broad shift from models of career development, which explain how people come to do the jobs they do, towards theories of guidance which provides a basis for action (Watts 1981).

A developmental model of careers guidance

One broad model of careers guidance with a wide currency is a three-stage process model adaptable to many contexts. The interactions are essentially developmental, based on a dynamic view of the person, and drawing on a range of helping processes. The three stages are:

(1) *Reviewing*: in which the helper explores with the client her or his needs in relation to work and ways in which available options might meet these.
(2) *Goal-setting*: in which the client is helped to clarify and set achievable goals.
(3) *Action planning*: in which an action plan is agreed, undertaken, and evaluated.

The key helping process here is probably counselling which may be provided in an interview or may be facilitated through self-exploration or through group discussions. However, other processes may be of considerable importance. Giving clients accurate, current, and relevant information is crucial to careers guidance, in order to help them realistically to assess options and make choices. This might include occupational information, up-to-date labour-market information, and information about relevant training and education or voluntary work. To give the information in a form and with the reinforcement which the client can use is a skilled business: a simple information sheet may be more helpful than a complete courses guide or direct access to a training database. Assessment, broadly defined to include structured self-assessment as well as external assessment and to cover values, interests, work experience, skills and aptitudes as well as achievements and qualifications, is also important. Information and assessment both feed into the reviewing and goal-setting stages of careers guidance.

In moving forward and in translating goals into action plans, clients may need forms of help which are less obviously person-centred and are more concerned with active interventions in the worlds of work and training: advising, coaching, and advocacy. However, it is important to conceive of these processes within a model of careers guidance aimed at promoting the individual's control and independence. Advising, the making of knowledge-based suggestions, can give the client access to other people's experience, expertise, or 'inside' information. Thus, for example, Careers Service staff may advise on which occupations are resistant to women's advancement; a co-ordinator of an education/business links scheme may advise on which employers are sensitive to issues of race. Coaching involves providing structured learning experiences for clients to gain the necessary competence in, for example, self-presentation at interviews, writing job applications, or job-searching skills. Advocacy involves taking action on behalf of and with the agreement of the client. One underlying assumption in advocacy is that the clients see the appropriate action or behaviour modelled by the helper and are thus able to act for themselves next time. Thus, for example, (in the early stages of job-seeking) a Job Centre adviser may phone on behalf of a client to make an appointment with an employer, but may suggest that the client subsequently does this for her- or himself.

The existing provision of services

This comprehensive developmental model of careers guidance. drawing on plural interrelated forms of helping, is useful for practitioners who deal with clients from various age-groups and categories. However, the reality is that constraints often prevent agencies from providing this level of comprehensive, client-centred, and developmental guidance. Students in schools, further and higher education, planning entry to work and adults planning mid-career changes, re-entry to work, or retirement may find it difficult to get the kind of careers guidance they need. Expansion in places and uncertainty about employment mean that about one-third of young people now enter higher education.

There is a very wide array of agencies, services, and individuals with a remit for some aspect of careers guidance or counselling. This provision for the pre-18 age group, involving careers teachers, college counselling, and Careers Services, with community and employer links is relatively coherent. However, provision for the post-18 group, especially the majority of adults not in higher education or training, is uncoordinated, under-resourced, and involves agencies with widely differing purposes. A gap often exists between the models of effective guidance to which practitioners subscribe and what is possible in day-to-day practice. Any survey of which helping activities are undertaken by particular agencies reveals gaps.

Job Centres and placement agencies offer mainly information on vacancies, job types, and training opportunities, with possibly some advice and advocacy. Private vocational guidance services charge their clients fees for assessment (usually by psychometric tests) and for advice on occupational suitability, with relatively little counselling or advocacy. Employer-based services might include programmes for career development, pre-retirement, or redundancy, with built-in counselling, assessment, and coaching in the appropriate skills (for example, decision-making, assertiveness, or working in teams). Some organizations buy in outplacement counselling or development programmes for their staff to increase their skills in managing change. The assumption is that the individual is responsible for managing her or his own career, including periods of unemployment. At the other end of the scale, services may be confined entirely to information on training. The Careers Service offers counselling as the core of its guidance provision and aims at a comprehensive model of helping. Nevertheless, most services can provide this level of help only for younger clients, and offer adults only the use of their information base. This overview shows that relatively few agencies offer objective client-centred careers counselling as a primary service.

In addition to this comprehensive model of careers guidance, a variety of more specific concepts and principles has been developed in relation to particular client groups (for example, pupils, students, and adults; employed, non-employed, and unemployed groups; mid-career changers and women returners) and also in relation to particular helping agencies (for example, placement services which match job seekers to employment opportunities). A review of some of these concepts and contexts, with examples of good practice, shows the range – and perhaps the limits – of careers guidance at present.

Careers education

The concept of careers education has been very influential. It refers to a structured approach towards teaching individuals the skills and knowledge needed to manage their future work-roles. Its aim is educational, to foster learning relevant to transitions from one life stage to another. Usually, the transitions are from education into employment or unemployment and it is most developed in the context of school–work transitions. Its principles would however be transferable from, say, employment to retirement or from unpaid work in the home to paid employment. The four main objectives of careers education have been identified (Law and Watts 1977) as the promotion of the following: opportunity awareness; self-awareness; decision learning; and transition learning. The first two objectives are relevant to the reviewing stage of careers guidance; decision learning relates to goal-setting; and transition learning relates to action planning.

Developing an awareness of opportunities is probably still the core of much careers education undertaken in schools. Increasingly, this includes opportunities in further education, leisure, the community, and the family, as well as in paid employment. Not only the formal economy, but also informal, alternative economies figure in the experience of many individuals, young and adult. Careers education needs to recognize this wide spectrum of opportunities if it is to be effective. A survey, *Careers Education in the Secondary School* (DES 1973), identified two possible approaches: the infusion approach in which the syllabuses of many subjects included learning about work; and the separate approach in which careers education was timetabled as a distinctive element. The survey noted that neither approach was then widespread, though more recently both have been extended throughout secondary education. Table 20.1 sets out what could be included in specific tasks and activities to enhance opportunity awareness.

Developing self-awareness involves helping individuals to evaluate their strengths and weaknesses, including abilities, aptitudes, practical and interpersonal skills, personal qualities, and physical attibutes. For adults this could mean a reappraisal of work experience to include domestic and parenting roles, voluntary work, and skills not accredited by exam. Of equal importance is the exploration of how individuals feel about work and themselves as workers. Young people and women may have underdeveloped or fragmented self-images because their work experience has been limited, interrupted, or in low-status and undervalued areas. Disabled people may become frustrated by lack of practical support or prejudice amongst employers. Many clients have blocks or anxieties about their own potential in the job market and about their saleable skills and competencies.

Counselling is the appropriate response to unblocking development and to strengthening self-images. Careers Service staff are trained and supported

Table 20.1 Tasks and activities for enhancing opportunity awareness

Opportunity awareness: Tasks	*Activities*
• Reviewing curriculum options at school or college	Group discussions, individual interviews
• Gaining information on further education and training	Talks, visits, careers conventions
• Increasing job knowledge (entry requirements, occupational styles, rewards)	Job-knowledge indices, Modern Apprenticeships
• Widening knowledge of occupational fields and families	Games, visits, occupational interest checklists
• Building a base of sources of occupational information	Careers library work
• Gaining knowledge of local employment	Work experience, placements
• Increasing perceptions of all kinds of work, paid and unpaid	Work shadowing, community and voluntary work

to offer such counselling. Many careers teachers may, however, feel uncomfortable in such a role. Although developing vocational self-awareness may be seen as a general objective of the curriculum in most educational settings, this is difficult to translate into successful programmes. The emphasis remains on subject-related assessments rather than on helping students towards an integrated self-assessment. However, for younger students NVQs and the identification of core skills is gradually changing this. For adults, broader formats of assessment are being tried, with greater client involvement and ownership: profiles, portfolios, self-assessment programmes, and the accreditation of experimental learning are all moves in this direction, albeit small-scale developments.

Table 20.2 sets out some specific tasks and activities in developing self-awareness.

Decision learning and transition learning are akin. The first concerns both raising the individual's awareness of how decisions are made and helping her or him to make decision wisely. This might include reviewing particular decision styles (for example, quick and intuitive, slow and deliberate) and practising strategies for actually making decisions (collecting and collating information, ranking needs, and evaluating outcomes). Transition learning is active preparation for coping with changes. This could involve searching out information about work organization, tax rates,

Table 20.2 Tasks and activities for developing self-awareness

Self-awareness: Tasks	Activities
• Reviewing qualifications and attainments	Profiles, Records of Achievement
• Reviewing interests and hobbies	Interest inventories
• Self-assessment of aptitudes, competencies, and attributes (intellectual, social, practical, physical)	Self-diagnostic tests
• Eliciting likes, dislikes, and values	Checklists of likes/dislikes, self-portrayals
• Examining perceptions of sex roles	Role-plays, paired interviews
• Exploring ideal lifestyles and occupational preferences	Guided fantasies, questionnaires

or retirement benefits, and practising the skills appropriate to managing change (for example, writing a curriculum vitae). Providing opportunities for an individual's decision and transition learning, structuring the practice, and giving feedback on progress could be undertaken for clients of all ages by a range of helpers: careers counsellors and teachers, personnel or training managers, and educational guidance service workers.

The concrete tasks and activities involved are set out in Table 20.3.

Further and higher education

In further and higher education the emphasis is still largely on placement into employment and on general guidance. Increasingly, however, careers counsellors are rethinking their services, despite financial constraints, to prepare clients more adequately for frequent job changes, 'serial' careers, possible unemployment, and plural work-roles. Group explorations and decision learning programmes are being provided, in addition to standard interviews. In some places the whole curriculum is infused with careers education (Ball 1984) and, increasingly, courses are designed in terms of higher-level NVQs. The government has set National Targets for Education and Training (NETS), to be achieved by 2000. These include, for example: 75 per cent of young people to achieve level 2 competence in communication, numeracy and IT by age 19 and 35 per cent to achieve level 3 in these skills by age 21; and 30 percent of the workforce to have a qualification at

Table 20.3 Tasks and activities for developing decision and transition learning

Decision learning: Tasks	Activities
• Raising awareness of personal decision-making styles and evaluating those of others	Video, simulations, games, role-plays
• Seeking and using feedback	Small group or paired work
• Outlining strategies for logical review of options	Career-decision programmes
• Identifying priorities	Critical-incident reflection
• Crystallizing work choices	Career-decision programmes

Transition learning: Tasks	Activities
• Acquiring study skills	Learning management programmes
• Acquiring coping skills (stress management)	Peer counselling, groupwork
• Knowledge of un/employment rights and benefits	Talks, visits, information sheets
• Practising applications and interviews	Role-plays, groupwork
• Gaining job-search and job-retention skills	Role-plays, work shadowing
• Induction to the workplace (structures, time-keeping, relationships, finance)	Mentoring, Modern Apprenticeships

NVQ level 4 or above. Achieving these will depend on the provision of good quality guidance, as well as good quality teaching.

Adults

Adults now make at least five significant occupational changes during their working lives. This suggests a large-scale need for both careers and educational guidance. Furthermore, since work affects other major aspects of people's lives – their economic and socal status, their self-image and confidence, their intellectual and emotional states – this has implications for other kinds of counselling. However, since the closure of the Occupational Guidance Units in 1980, the provision of work-related guidance has been inadequate and uneven. A pilot study undertaken in one town found a substantial demand for vocational guidance amongst particular groups: the unemployed, women returners, recent job-changers (two-thirds of whom see themselves as future clients for guidance), and the uncommitted (half the economically active sample were 'open to occupational change') (Killeen 1986). The specific forms of guidance they asked for (unprompted) were:

(a) testing and advice to enable them to identify jobs which match their existing abilites, skills, and training;
(b) information on vacancies, training, salary scales, and companies;
(c) counselling for goal-setting and decision-making;
(d) direct assistance in job-getting, or in getting particular types of work.

Existing services certainly do not provide this range or scale of help, but areas of good practice exist. A voucher system, funded via the TECs, allows unemployed clients to purchase guidance from local providers.

For a small proportion of clients courses are available with emphasis on confidence-building, self-evaluation, and decision-making. Access courses offer re-appraisal and bridges to further training or employment, with the additional benefits of peer-group support. Career-development courses help redundant professional staff to rethink their vocational profile and to practise career planning. Counselling supports participants in coping with the stress of change.

Educational Guidance Services for Adults (EGSAS), although concerned primarily with continuing education, also recognize the vital links between adults' roles as learners and workers. Service standards define them as: client-centred, confidential, open and accessible to all, free, independent, widely publicized and able to contribute to the development of education and training (UDACE 1986). As well as being client-centred, with all that implies for staff training, services are also extremely local in character and responsive to specific target groups.

Workplace services

Some level of career development and guidance is available to staff in some organizations, though it is not independent in nature. Developing a closer correspondence between organizational and employee goals can have benefits for both. One National Target is to have 70 per cent of organizations employing over 200 people recognized as Investors in People by the year 2000. This standard requires the organization to develop its workforce through training on a continuous basis. Three kinds of workplace services can be identified.

First, some companies provide guidance linked to particular stages: mid-career appraisal, resettlement services for employees who leave early, and redundancy and pre-retirement courses. Employers and unions both have a role in helping employees cope practically and psychologically with these watersheds in employment.

Second, career-development programmes are now widely undertaken by major employers and professional associations. Ideally, the employer develops a more flexible and motivated workforce and employees gain in skills and job satisfaction. Some large companies adopt a plural approach including peer counselling by volunteers, career- and life-planning workshops, and training for senior managers in careers-counselling approaches (Hopson 1985). Many organizations now develop the basic counselling skills of managers and encourage mentoring or co-counselling arrangements (de Board 1983).

Finally, some workplace training includes careers-education elements and transferable skills such as stress and conflict management, assertiveness, and group working. Training needs analysis itself can prompt individuals to review their existing roles and skills. This kind of work-related learning, although not systematic or accompanied by counselling, can increase participants' self-awareness and adaptability. It may, in fact, be the only careers guidance which some employees get.

Issues

Distinctively, careers counselling spans both the internal psychology of the preson and the external contexts of education and employment. Indeed, part of any practitioner's training is to develop a rationale for the inter-relation of the two, so as to help clients as effectively as possible. Most of the current issues in careers guidance and counselling revolve around divergent or even conflicting accounts of this relationship between the individual's requirements in relation to work and the social and economic structuring of work opportunities. All guidance agencies have to formulate their objectives in terms of this relationship – and moreover, as employers themselves, to ensure that their own employment practices match their principles for dealing with clients. The Lead Body for Advice, Guidance, Counselling and Psychotherapy has integrated equal opportunities perspectives and ethics into all its standards for professional practice and the requirements set out for awarding bodies. Such an approach is vital to improving both the quality and the accessibility of training.

Three areas currently reflect the divergence of views on how individuals and occupations relate and, as a result, what are the proper roles for careers guidance and counselling: changing patterns of employment: the long-running debate on whether people choose or are selected for particular occupations; and the rise of 'vocationalism'.

Changing patterns of employment

There are widely differing views of what constitutes a 'career'. Narrowly, a career has been seen as a succession of jobs, often of increasing status, which people move through in a more or less planned sequence. This view remains entrenched in the perceptions of some employers, as well as of the general public, despite its divergence from the work experience of large numbers of people, including women and the unemployed. More comprehensive theoretical definitions emphasize that career development, like other human development, covers the life-span and includes *all* a person's learning, decision making, and adjustments in relation to paid and unpaid work, 'beginning early in life and proceeding along a curve until late in life' (Super 1957).

One result of these wider definitions is that practitioners who have 'careers' in their job or agency title often wish to clarify with clients what this means. Clients with narrow conceptions of careers can have unrealistic expectations of what careers services can deliver. Their role is not that of helping clients match themselves to an occupation which they then climb like a ladder until their particular ceiling is reached. The emphasis may be rather on helping job seekers to assess their work-related skills on the basis of voluntary or domestic work; or on exploring with clients what kinds of rewards they need from paid employment (for example, status, money, flexibility, no travel, job satisfaction) and what compromises will best meet their particular priorities. Two major reports, *Better Choices*, outlining principles and practice for improving careers guidance in a period of radically changing employment patterns, stress the need for multi-agency partnerships to help clients cope (Education and Employment Departments 1994, 1995).

The psychology of occupational choice versus the sociology of opportunities

One of the most significant debates in careers guidance over the past decade is that between the psychologists of occupational choice (Daws 1981) and the sociologists of 'opportunity structure' (Roberts 1981). Basically, the debate is about how people come to do their jobs: do they 'choose' them, in any meaningful sense; or are they selected for them by combinations of labour-market forces and class stratifications? Psychological explanations stress personality differences, individual aspirations and striving, and the personal meanings which people give to their work-related behaviour. Sociological accounts, by contrast, stress the social and economic structures which shape people's life chances in education and in employment and the social and family groups which shape their work attitudes and values.

In general, counselling theory, especially person-centred, Rogerian models, draws more heavily on psychological than on sociological perspectives. Psychological accounts have more immediate appeal to practitioners, and theories of occupational choice are useful training for career workers (Dryden and Watts, 1993). Two theories have been particularly influential in careers guidance: 'matching' and 'developmental accounts'.

The first involves evaluating individual differences in abilities, aptitudes, values, or personality types and matching these to existing occupations. Private vocational guidance services and labour market policies often assume 'matching' models with a resulting emphasis on assessment. In fact, a range of assessment tools and resources has proved useful to practitioners who would not necessarily subscribe to matching theories of how people choose their occupations.

Developmental theories have had a much more powerful effect on careers counselling practice. They stress occupational choice as an evolutionary process, encompassing the person's life-span, rather than as a few, isolated decisions. The most comprehensive model is that of Donald Super, based on five life stages: Growth (birth–14), Exploration (15–24), Establishment (25–44), Maintenance (45–64) and Decline (65 onwards). Through these stages, the individual develops her or his self-concept, including core constructs about work and oneself as a worker, by making occupational choices. Super proposes a model of a life-career rainbow of nine major roles (child, student, 'leisurite', citizen, worker, spouse, homemaker, parent, and pensioner), played out in four 'theatres' (home, community, education, and work) (Super 1981). Developmental models provide a useful framework for practitioners to support clients in implementing their self-concept. The notion of multiple life-roles is also a useful one for helping clients to map their lives and to work on potential role conflicts.

Sociological explanations of occupational choice and of related areas such as social mobility, work entry, gender, and class have proved far less usable and comfortable for careers practitioners, although of evident relevance to their work. The 'opportunity structure thesis' explains occupational entry in terms of selection and employers' recruitment practices, rather than of individual choice (Roberts 1981). People do not choose their jobs; they take what is available. Furthermore, access to different levels of employment depends on educational attainments and, to some extent, on family and social group. Even people's expectations are formed by 'anticipatory socialization' in family and community.

These sociological perspectives represent a major challenge for careers workers. Roberts identifies two possible positions for guidance agencies: an acceptance of placement as their primary function, as part of the social-control apparatus; or an emphasis on clients' self-development, possibly leading them to unrealistic aims that are discordant with the opportunities available. Careers work is either aligned with 'realistic influences' or it is counter-cultural. It cannot be neutral and it is, in any event, marginal.

Rather than confronting these challenges head on and seeing psychological and sociological accounts as mutually exclusive, careers practitioners may prefer to see them as complementary. Many careers workers are fully alive to the contradictions in their work and the real options available to people of all ages. Ball (1984: 15) argues that many 'would be happy to admit that one of their major roles was helping young workers to adjust to work as much as it was to help them choose between work alternatives'. Individuals are still rational and purposive in their work-related behaviour. However problematic, practitioners may develop a framework that draws on both the psychology of choice and the sociology of opportunity.

Vocationalism versus education

Related to this issue is that of vocationalism and its relationship to careers education. The national curriculum GNVQs and the introduction of Modern Apprenticeships (the current government youth training scheme, whereby a young person learns on the job, with some part-time/day release attendance at college) emphasize vocational elements in the 14–19 curriculum. This has implications for careers, education, and training agencies. The Careers Service has a key role in curriculum development and in fostering education–business links. Programmes for all age-groups have been developed with social- and life-skills components and strategies for coping with periods of unemployment. The arguments for such elements are based on 'realism' about the probable life chances of participants. Critics argue, however, that such vocationalism, by being directed at supposedly non-academic groups, functions divisively and actually restricts opportunities and self-awareness. Vocational elements are not available equally across the ability range, but introduce a segregated curriculum at an early stage. As a result, some participants adjust their occupational goals downwards and psychological deskilling is subtly reinforced.

These issues affect not only the way all careers guidance activities are constituted and funded, at the level of policy, but also the daily relationship of helpers and clients. Overarching questions of how society structures and rewards different kinds of work and how work opportunities are allocated or chosen are constantly translated into daily decisions about resources, priorities, and counselling styles. For this reason practitioners need to engage with them as actively as possible.

Future developments

It seems unlikely that further resources for careers guidance and counselling will be available on a scale indicated by current trends. These trends include the growing proportion of women in the workforce; greater job mobility and more career changes amongst all adults; and an emphasis on adult retraining and continuing education, often in part-time, flexible, or open and distance learning forms which require learners to be clearly motivated and independent. Many practitioners in the field are wryly aware of the gaps between policy and experience, between, say, the rhetoric of lifelong learning and actual participation rates in adult learning or between fluctuations in unemployment figures and the hopes and frustrations experienced by many of their clients in relation to work.

Future developments are likely to consist of small steps in the directions already apparent, rather than in any radical reformation of services or new commitment of resources. The most likely areas for development are in the technologies for delivering services, in the more plural and flexible models of careers guidance and counselling, and in the training which underpins both these changes.

Self-help resources

One route for achieving more accessible and, possibly, more economical guidance is in the extended use of self-help resources and technology-assisted systems. There is now a wide range of aids and programmes which, either mediated by careers workers or acting as 'stand alone' facilities, meet some needs for information, assessment, and counselling. Popular examples are *Build Your Own Rainbow: A Workbook for Careers and Life Management* (Hopson and Scally 1984) designed to help users' career decision-making, and *What Color is Your Parachute?* (Nelson Bolles 1993) designed to help users review their work options and locate sources of help. Such publications are helpful in several ways. If used alone, they can prompt structured self-exploration, for example in eliciting what priorities the user has for employment. If used by a group, they can stimulate support and peer counselling. If used before a counselling interview, they can clarify issues and prompt more focused and purposeful questions by the client.

Computer-assisted services

Computerized guidance resources are of two kinds. There are database systems for information retrieval and processing which are becoming increasingly comprehensive and efficient. Second, there are programs for self-exploration, assessment, and decision learning which have been developed for specific user-groups (school students, higher education students, job changers, and so on).

In the first group are databases of national and, increasingly, local information which underpin much careers and educational guidance.

ECCTIS (Educational Counselling and Credit Transfer Information Service) is the best known of these, providing records of all further and higher education in the UK of more than 6 weeks and leading to a qualification. On-line access is available in many Careers Offices, colleges and guidance agencies.

Such computerized systems have obvious advantages over paper-based systems. There are, however, important questions about who should bear their considerable updating costs: providers of information, such as employers and colleges; guidance agencies and intermediaries; end users, either individuals or organizations; or government? Moreover, should such systems be developed as tools for guidance workers or as direct, hands-on information sources for clients?

Computerized systems for helping users to clarify options or to develop vocational learning are also quite widely available. Some require users to feed in information, either directly or in questionnaires, about their work preferences, aptitudes, and interests so that job suggestions, with relevant entry information, can be generated. MICRODOORS, JIIG/CAL (Job Ideas and Information Generator Computer-Assisted Learning) and CASCAID (Careers Advisory Service Computer Aid) have been widely used with school students and versions of the latter two are available for adults and higher education students. Besides these matching systems, there are more interactive programs. Here the emphasis is on reviewing preferences rather than on generating job suggestions. Prospect HE, developed as part of the DFEE's Computer-Assisted Guidance Project, helps users to understand career planning and decision-making; to assess their own current career development; to evaluate information about careers; and to formulate goals and action plans.

The potential of such systems is hardly glimpsed as yet. Evaluation shows some success in both raising self-awareness and developing vocational learning. Furthermore, people enjoy using them. As one element in a guidance process they can open up issues for counselling very creatively. As 'stand alone' systems their potential remains to be tested. They can offer complete privacy and limited structures for exploration; but they are costly to develop and need expensive refinement for various client groups and purposes. With the inevitable growth of information technology, the availability of all these systems will increase. How far development will be towards more truly accessible and client-owned guidance systems depends more on political and economic factors than on technological innovation.

More integrated services?

In the wider context the most significant improvement in guidance provision might be in the better integration of agencies. This would mean a rationalization of services for all ages and client groups. It is, for example, inequitable that higher-education students, already privileged, have provided for them a level and quality of careers counselling not available to other groups with equally distinct needs. The integration of educational and vocational guidance, if not well developed in conceptual models and theories, is slowly happening on the ground through regional networks and referral procedures. Education and work links are improving through work experience schemes and community interaction projects. Field research is important to evaluate the outcomes of specific schemes and to contribute to developmental models of guidance and counselling.

In a different dimension, more integrated services would also provide stronger links between careers counselling and personal or psychotherapeutic support. Choices about work frequently involve people's core identities, arousing powerful feelings about self-worth and self-image, which guidance workers may feel ill-equipped to acknowledge and cope with. In extreme cases, such as long-term unemployment, mid-career frustration, and changing relationship and family structures, the client's affective state may prevent any very constructive careers guidance. To discuss work preferences with clients who are suffering from chronic indecisiveness or acute anxiety caused by repeated rejections in the job market or who are experiencing paralyzing guilt over leaving their children, albeit temporarily, is unlikely to be productive. Guidance workers need to know when and where to refer their clients for personal counselling that responds to their pressing needs. Only after coping with these blocks can clients benefit from specific careers counselling.

In more general terms, it is arguable that existing models of careers counselling pay insufficient attention to the affective dimensions of decision making and to the profound repercussions that work roles have on clients' personal lives, including their marriages, parenting, and psychological well-being.

Since any significant increase in resources in unlikely, the better integration of servcies depends not only on improved networking but also on improved training. The Lead Body aims to make training and accreditation available at all levels of services. In addition, career specialists would benefit from knowledge of personal or psychotherapeutic strategies. Those who include careers guidance amongst other roles would gain from specific training in careers work. Managers, trainers, union and association representatives, tutors and teachers, broadcasters, and advisory-service staff all deal on a daily basis with clients experiencing work-related problems or considering career opportunities. Counsellors in medical or personal contexts often encounter career conflicts which have a sharp relevance to their client's well-being, although they are not the presenting issue. Providing training in careers guidance and counselling for a wide range of people in managerial or advisory roles is likely to prove both satisfying for them and cost-effective for organizations. Modularized programmes, open learning, and computer-aided learning on, say, careers-counselling interviewing would allow participants to select the level of training that matched their needs. Modules on both the practical and theoretical approaches to careers guidance, as well as awareness training on gender, culture, and class in relation to careers structures and opportunities, might be appropriate.

All these developments are towards the wider, if gradual, dissemination and co-ordination of careers guidance as a range of helping processes. It is not simply that more means better. More information, on occupations, relevant training, prospects, vacancies, and so on is not enough, unless ordinary people can locate it, relate to it, and use it. Information is a commodity which is unequally available, resulting in the 'information rich' and the 'information poor'. It is important to develop systems which are not only comprehensive, but fully accessible. This means that alongside information systems should be other forms of help – advice, counselling, assessment, and advocacy – if careers guidance is to be both effective and equitable.

References

Ball, B. (1984) *Careers Counselling in Practice*, London and Philadelphia: Falmer Press.

Daws, P. P. (1981) 'The socialisation/opportunity-structure theory of the occupational location of school leavers: a critical appraisal', in A. G. Watts, D. Super, and J. Kidd (eds) *Career Development in Britain*, Cambridge: CRAC/Hobsons.

de Board, R. (1983) *Counselling People at Work*, Aldershot, Hants: Gower.

Department of Education and Science (1973) *Careers Education in the Secondary School*, London: DES.

Dryden W. and Watts, A. G. (1993) *Guidance and Counselling in Britain: a 20-year Perspective*, Cambridge: CRAC.

Education and Employment Departments (1994) *Better Choices: The Principles*, London: Dept. for Education and Employment.

——(1995) *Better Choices: Putting Principles into Practice. Working Together to Improve Careers Education and Guidance*, London: Dept. for Education and Employment.

Hopson, B. (1985) 'Adult life and career counselling', *British Journal of Guidance and Counselling* 13(1): 45–59.

Hopson, B. and Scally, M. (1984) *Build Your Own Rainbow: A Workbook for Career and Life Management*, Leeds: Lifeskills Associates.

Killeen, J. (1986) *Vocational Guidance: A Study of the Demand in One Town*, Hertford: National Institute for Careers Education and Counselling.

Law, B. and Watts, A. G. (1977) *Schools, Careers and Community*, London: Church Information Office.

Nelson Bolles, R. (1993) *What Color is Your Parachute? A Practical Manual for Job-Hunters and Career Changers*, Berkeley: Ten Speed Press.

Roberts, K. (1981) 'The sociology of work entry and occupational choice', in A. G. Watts, D. Super, and J. Kidd (eds) *Career Development in Britain*, Cambridge: CRAC/Hobsons.

Super, D. E. (1957) *The Psychology of Careers*, New York: Harper & Row.

——(1981) 'Approaches to occupational choice and career development' in A. G. Watts, D. Super, and J. Kidd (eds) *Career Development in Britain*, Cambridge: CRAC/Hobsons.

Watts, A. G. (1980) 'Educational and careers guidance services for adults: 1. A rationale and conceptual framework', *British Journal of Guidance and Counselling* 8(1): 11–22.

——(1981) 'Career patterns', in A. G. Watts, D. Super, and J. Kidd (eds) *Career Development in Britain*, Cambridge: CRAC/Hobsons.

Unit for the Development of Adult Continuing Education (1986) *The Challenge of Change: Developing Educational Guidance for Adults*, Leicester: UDACE.

Chapter twenty-one

Counselling in the context of redundancy and unemployment

Jennifer M. Kidd

Introduction

Over the last decade or so, corporate 'downsizing', coupled with changes in the nature and structure of job opportunities have produced redundancies on a scale which the current working population could never have envisaged when they embarked on their working lives. Whole occupations have disappeared, as have assurances of a 'career for life' in organizations which previously offered long-term security and upward progression along well-trodden career pathways. As a consequence, more and more individuals are experiencing the trauma of redundancy, while many of those fortunate enough to keep their jobs appear to be suffering feelings of insecurity and guilt as they see their colleagues laid off.

Many organizations now offer outplacement services to redundant workers, particularly senior managers. A comprehensive service will offer personal counselling and support, possibly including group work; career counselling and career information; advice on job search; training in presentation and interview skills; and the use of office facilities for preparing curricula vitae and job applications. There are good business reasons for providing this service, since those remaining in the organization are more likely to retain their commitment to the company if they perceive the situation to have been managed fairly. However, few organizations have developed initiatives to support the 'survivors' directly. Through a review of the literature on job loss and unemployment, this chapter discusses some of the common reactions to redundancy experienced by those directly affected and by the survivors of redundancy programmes. It also identifies some implications for the provision of outplacement counselling to redundant workers and for providing counselling and support to those remaining in the organization.

Principles

The experience of redundancy and unemployment

For many, the experience of redundancy is devastating. Responses to losing a job have commonly been compared to the grief of bereavement, and there is considerable agreement among writers in the area that those remaining unemployed are likely to experience reduced levels of mental and physical health and that their families are also likely to be affected in harmful ways (see Warr (1987) and Winefield (1995) for comprehensive reviews of the literature).

There is less consensus, however, about how and why job loss and unemployment affect well-being. This is a serious problem for those with the task of designing effective programmes to help people cope with job loss, since any intervention is likely to founder in the absence of adequate theory and research which describes and explains the mechanisms leading to psychological distress and physical ill-health. Reactions to job loss, for example, are often described in terms of a sequence of stages in some ways similar to the states of the grieving process, for example, shock, anger, active job search, pessimism, then resignation. Eisenberg and Lazarsfeld (1938) were among the first to suggest this sort of pattern. These stages, if they could be demonstrated, would have clear implications for the counselling process. Unfortunately, however, although there is some long-itudinal evidence that psychological distress lessens with unemployment duration, presumably as individuals adapt to the unemployed role (Warr and Jackson 1987), there is little empirical support for a stages account. Although a grief-like reaction is commonplace, this seems to depend on the degree of attachment to the former occupation (Archer and Rhodes 1987). Yet much outplacement counselling seems to be predicated on the assumption that the stage model is a valid description of individuals' reactions to redundancy (see, for example, Pickman 1994).

Similarly, there is disagreement as to *why* unemployment has adverse effects. One of the most influential theories is Jahoda's 'deprivation theory' (Jahoda 1981). She suggests that, in addition to its function of providing income, work has five 'latent' functions which are psychologically beneficial in that they keep us in touch with reality. These are: the imposition of a time structure; the provision of social contacts; the provision of goals and purposes; the definition of status and identity; and the enforcement of activity. The theory assumes that all jobs have these latent functions, irrespective of whether workers seek such functions in their jobs, and that unemployment affects well-being because it deprives individuals of these experiences. Jahoda also implies that any job is preferable to unemployment. This model is persuasive, but evidence supporting the importance of the five latent functions is scarce, and several studies have shown that employed people in unsatisfactory jobs were no better off than the unemployed (see, for example, Wanberg 1995). Also, an unfortunate consequence of the attention given to this model is that the financial consequences of unemployment have been viewed as relatively insignificant, yet we now know that both financial responsibilities and financial distress have significant impacts on coping (Jacobson 1987).

Another problem with deprivation theory is its assumption that people are simply passive respondents to their employment situation. As an alternative, Fryer (1986) developed 'agency restriction theory', which suggests that unemployment has negative consequences because it restricts personal agency. Unemployment stops people doing what they want to do, largely because it deprives them of a regular income. This makes it difficult for people to plan and to organize satisfactory lifestyles. Also, the symbolic value of consumer spending and choice, which, in our culture, defines individuals as members of society, is lost. And since many people do not know how long unemployment will last, the ability to set goals is limited by uncertainty about the future. Again, however, although the theory is appealing, empirical support is limited.

Warr's (1987) 'vitamin model' draws no rigid distinction between employment and unemployment. Instead, the model proposes that it is the overall quality of the environment which is important for well-being. He suggests that nine features of the environment affect mental health in a manner similar to the ways in which vitamins affect physical health. These are: opportunity for control; opportunity for skill use; externally-generated goals; variety; environmental clarity; availability of money; physical security; opportunity for interpersonal contact; and valued social position. Warr suggests that some environmental features have an effect similar to vitamins A and D in that very high levels are harmful rather than beneficial. Others resemble vitamins C and E in that beyond a certain point, high levels have no further effect on mental health. Three features fall into the latter category – availability of money, physical security, and valued social position – while the remainder fall into the former group. The theory in some ways extends agency restriction theory in specifying which features of the environment are important. Some significant relationships between certain of these environmental features and indices of mental health have been established but, as Warr argues, the patterns of causal relationships are likely to be complex and reciprocal with the psychological effects of certain features of the environment affecting others.

Although evidence in support of these theoretical models explaining the psychological distress of unemployment is scarce, therefore, it seems clear from the research that the impact of unemployment varies substantially between individuals. In his review of the findings, Winefield (1995) shows that, not surprisingly, financial security enables people to cope better with unemployment, the middle-aged seem to cope less well than younger or older people, probably because of their greater financial responsibilities, and those with access to social support from family, friends and other people cope better. Also, unemployed people who become involved in constructive activities involving other people manage better. So far as attitudes are concerned, those who attribute their unemployment to internal factors, such as lack of ability or lack of effort, seem to be more likely to suffer from low self-esteem and hopelessness as a result than those who see the cause as due to external factors.

It is also becoming clear that some individuals, over time, are able to see job loss as a positive learning experience, and come to see the long-term gains as outweighing the losses. This may happen because of the opportunity to leave a dissatisfying job, to develop new skills or to redirect career aspirations. For example, in a study which has direct implications for counselling, Eby and Buch (1995) found that men who were more satisfied with their new job and thought that on balance they had gained from losing their job had certain features in common. They showed more emotional acceptance of the job loss, had a high activity level during the period of unemployment, were more dissatisfied with their previous job, had a shorter duration of unemployment and were supported by friends and co-workers. The variables predicting 'career growth' for women were different. Family flexibility seemed to be the most important, but the small female sample did not permit any firm conclusions. The cross-sectional design of this study does not of course rule out a dispositional explanation for the findings (those having a tendency to view the world more optimistically may experience higher levels of career growth, for example), but nevertheless it offers some indications of the kinds of counselling interventions that may be beneficial.

Implications for counselling redundant workers

This review of the literature has a number of implications for those designing and providing counselling interventions for redundant workers, as follows:

- People will differ in their reactions to redundancy, but most will experience psychological distress.
- It should not be assumed that everyone goes through a sequence of identifiable stages of grief and coping, but many will need help in coming to terms with the loss.
- Since gaining re-employment in an unsatisfactory job is unlikely to promote well-being, individuals may benefit from career counselling. Also, changes in employment structures will mean that increasingly individuals will need opportunities to reassess their skills and to consider the need for retraining.

- Because the individual's financial situation is likely to have a substantial impact on reactions to redundancy this will often need to be explored.
- For many, access to social support and encouragement to use time productively will be a helpful feature of the intervention.
- Exploring the individual's attributional style and, if necessary, intervening to change inappropriate internal causal attributions for job loss may promote increased self-esteem and optimism.
- It may be necessary to focus interventions differently for men and women. In particular, working with the families of women who have been made redundant to foster role-sharing and communication may be needed.

Recent surveys suggest that UK companies are making widespread use of outplacement services for departing employees. Doherty and Tyson (1993), for example, in a survey of 614 organizations ranging in size from 200 to 50,000 employees, found that 75 per cent of those involved in redundancy programmes offered employees outplacement. Assessing how far current practice attends to the above features is difficult, however, since little information is currently available about the nature of the services offered. One survey of 201 clients (or 'candidates' as they are often called) suggested that there was some dissatisfaction with the personal counselling received and the assistance provided for financial planning (Boynton and Thomas 1991).

The impact of redundancy programmes on survivors

We turn now to examine the effect of redundancies on those remaining in the organization. Following American research showing the dramatic impact of lay-offs on subsequent productivity of survivors of a redundancy programme (for example, Brockner 1988), the term 'survivors' syndrome' has come to be used to describe the reactions and behaviours of those who remain. These include shock, betrayal, animosity towards management, concern about their colleagues who have departed, guilt that they still have a job, and fear and uncertainty about the future. This may result in low morale and organizational commitment, and decreased trust in and loyalty to the organization. These reactions frequently undermine the goals of increasing output and competitive advantage which prompted the downsizing programme.

Recent research confirms the existence of this pattern of reactions in the British context. Doherty et al. (1995), for example, in a study of the survivors of a large-scale programme of downsizing in British Telecom, suggested that these employees had to recover from a triple blow. First, there was the sudden loss of valued colleagues and friends. Second, there was the threat of future job loss, which meant that the crisis was never fully over, since their jobs were seen to continue to be threatened. And third, as a result of job redesign they often had a substantially increased workload and were feeling increased stress as a result. Interestingly, the work group became a focus for these survivors. Friendships with colleagues and support from their line manager became their means of survival. Also, the role of the line manager was seen to be particularly difficult. They not only had their own worries about their jobs, but they were often blamed by their subordinates as the source of their distress.

These findings will be helpful to counsellors in suggesting the kinds of responses experienced by those affected by redundancy programmes but, as suggested earlier, interventions are more likely to succeed if they are informed by theories and models which help to describe and explain individuals' reactions and behaviour. Because outplacement counsellors most commonly work with individuals rather than with systems, the most useful theories tend to be those that attempt to describe and explain reactions to unemployment at the individual level of analysis. Those working with survivors, however, may have a potentially more wide-ranging role, since they could be working at the system level as well as with individual employees. As Orlans (1996) has argued, integrating a counselling initiative within broad aspects of organizational functioning highlights the importance of 'systemic thinking', and this may enable the counsellor to distinguish between pathological individual conditions and environmentally induced reactions.

So what kinds of theories might explain survivor syndrome and be helpful in guiding counselling interventions? Whilst its existence is well documented (although one might question the usefulness of lumping together this range of disparate reactions and behaviours), there have been few explicit attempts at theoretical explanations.

At the individual level of analysis aspects of 'learned helplessness' theory may apply. Seligman (1975), for example, proposes that when exposed to uncontrollable situations individuals' performance will be impaired in later tasks because of the following deficits: motivational – resulting in a reduced desire to control outcomes; cognitive – a belief that the outcomes are not controllable; and emotional – anxiety and depression. Also at the individual level, theories of stress may have something to offer, particularly in relation to the impact of increased job demands within a context of low control over task allocation and job design. Karasek (1979), for example, suggests that high workload has negative effects on well-being when workers have little control over how the work is done. Other theories of stress may help in understanding the potential impact of interventions because they suggest the moderating or mediating role of social support in coping with stress. Writers on social support suggest that it either acts as a buffer to the impact of stress, or that it has direct effects on well-being (see, for example, Ganster *et al.* 1986).

Some analyses of the antecedents of well-being examine the impact of role conflict and role ambiguity (see, for example, Fisher and Gitelson 1983). Notions of role conflict may be useful in understanding survivors' reactions to lay-offs, for example, by helping employees make sense of the tensions and dissonance generated by having to carry on working for the organization and the commitment to the company that is implied by this, and the desire to maintain social relationships with ex-colleagues. Similarly, taking a role perspective may help personnel practitioners understand better how to deal with conflicts they experience between the controlling and supportive aspects of their role, for example, administering a redundancy programme and supporting employees affected by it. In general. though. the explanatory power of these models is limited, since they merely offer a list of the sorts of variables that appear to produce manifestations of stress.

Warr's (1987) vitamin model of well-being, described earlier, is also relevant to an understanding of survivors' reactions. In particular, opportunities for control, environmental clarity and for interpersonal contact may be lessened after a redundancy programme. Significantly, this model suggests that opportunities for interpersonal contact may become particularly important in the absence of environmental clarity. This may help to explain the increased attachment to the work group found in the British Telecom case study noted above.

A major limitation of most of the theories described so far, however, is their view of individuals as more or less passive reactors to environments. Certain features of the work environment – conflicting demands, for example – are seen as leading inevitably to dysfunctional reactions. As a consequence, counsellors may be able to use this knowledge in helping individuals cope with change, but as Warr (1987) argues, we also need to attend to the impact of the individual on the environment. Someone experiencing distress, for example, may become less attractive to their work group, and so opportunities for social contact may be reduced. So it might be argued that more interactive theories are needed to understand and explain survivor syndrome.

Brockner and Lee (1995) offer an explanation based on 'self-affirmation' theory (Steele 1988). Steele argues that individuals strive to see themselves as 'adaptively and morally adequate': they need to feel confident, coherent, stable and capable of controlling important outcomes. He groups self-conceptions into three categories: esteem (competent, good); identity (coherent, unitary, stable); and control (capable of free choice, capable of controlling important outcomes). When people are faced with information which contradicts one or more of these self-conceptions they suffer a threat to their self-integrity, and this leads them to change their beliefs or behaviour until the threat has been reduced. Brockner and Lee cite research that shows that the more strongly survivors identify with those who have been laid-off the more likely they are to show reduced morale and performance (Brockner *et al.* 1987) and they use Steele's theory to argue that explanations of survivors' reactions based on threats to self-integrity may have some validity. Steele's theory also postulates that individuals' attempts to reaffirm their identity do not have to be in the same domain that originally posed the threat. Opportunities to restore self-integrity can be found in situations which may be unrelated to the original threatening context. It follows then that survivors who see a redundancy programme as posing a threat to their self-integrity should improve their morale when they have been given an opportunity to reaffirm themselves. Some evidence showing that this may be the case is provided by the findings of a study that asked one group of survivors to write an essay describing an event at work which had enabled them to feel good about themselves. Those who had written the essay and who were most affected by the lay-offs reacted less negatively than those not given the opportunity for self-affirmation (summarized in Brockner and Lee 1995). There are important implications for counselling here. Giving individuals the opportunity to reflect on their strengths and skills (in the context of career counselling, for example) could be a particularly valuable component of the process.

Another more interactive and dynamic interpretation of the reactions of survivors is Herriot and Pemberton's (1995) explanation, which is based on violations of the 'psychological contract' between individuals and their employers. They suggest that the old psychological contract – defined as the exchange deal which each party has with the other – of employee loyalty for employment security has all but disappeared and a much less favourable deal has been imposed in its place. The original contract may be seen to have been violated unilaterally by the employer and this is frequently seen as unfair, either because of the outcomes (for example, requiring survivors to take on more work or selecting some people for redundancy rather than others) or because the process was managed badly (for example, lack of consultation in redesigning survivors' jobs or insensitivity in the way employees were told about an impending downsizing). As a result of perceptions of inequity and unfairness, employees lose trust in their employers. Also, if the new contract is seen to be imposed without adequate consultation, individuals begin to feel powerless to affect what happens to them.

This model, then, emphasizes the importance of understanding survivors' reactions in terms of social exchange. Perceptions of unfairness and lack of communication and consultation will result in anger, distress and attempts to remove the inequity by reducing the effort and commitment that employees put in to the input side of the input–output ratio. Some evidence exists to support the model. McFarlin and Sweeney (1992), for example, showed that perceptions of fairness of human resource practices predicted organizational commitment, and Guest and Peccei (1992) found that survivors were more likely to retain their goodwill to their employer if they felt that the redundancies had been managed fairly.

Implications for counselling survivors and for facilitating the redundancy process

It was suggested earlier that counsellors working in the context of employee redundancy may have opportunities to work at the organizational level as well as with individuals. As we have seen, theory and research into survivor syndrome spans both levels of analysis. Significantly, much of the literature points to the importance of communication, consultation and opportunities for regaining self-esteem and control. Some implications for practice which follow from these analyses are as follows:

• Survivors may experience feelings of distress similar to those felt by redundant employees.
• They may benefit from opportunities to become more aware of their strengths and skills. Career-counselling and career-planning activities may help in this respect. These initiatives may also help to demonstrate that remaining employees are still valued by the organization.
• Interventions at the work group level may be beneficial in increasing social support and group cohesiveness after a period of restructuring.
• Individuals may need support to renegotiate their psychological contract. Assertiveness training may be helpful, for example.
• Those whose work involves directly administering the redundancy pro- gramme may need support, for example in coping with the role conflict that may ensue.
• Management may need to be helped to consider how best to commu- nicate the necessity for redundancies, emphasizing the way in which particular positions have been selected for cuts.
• Since survivors may cope better if they are offered opportunities to participate in decisions about the downsizing process, and about how their own jobs are redesigned, management may need to be helped to find ways of increasing employee involvement in these processes.

Although there has been some debate amongst legislators and managers about how best to handle redundancies, there have been few studies about how the survivors are treated. A recent survey of organizations in the financial services sector, however, showed that although 79 per cent of respondents used outplacement for departing employees only 45 per cent provided structured support for the survivors. Furthermore, those organiza- tions offering help rarely offered personal or career counselling on a one- to-one basis and the information provided focused largely on short-term issues concerning changes in reporting relationships and responsibilities, with little attention being given to the information needs of employees (Doherty *et al*. 1995).

Issues and future developments

Outplacement provision is of two types: *sponsored*, where clients are organizations paying for services provided to 'candidates' who are ex-employees or employees shortly to be made redundant; and *private*, where a service is provided to individuals who themselves pay for the counselling they receive. There are potential tensions and conflicts within both types of provision, not least because of marketplace pressures and differences in expectations between providers, sponsoring organizations, and individuals. But the dual-client relationship that exists in the case of sponsored services highlights most clearly some of the conflicts of interest arising from pressures to meet both organizational and individual needs.

One area where there is obvious potential for conflict is in perceptions of the goals of counselling. From the sponsoring organization's perspective, a likely primary goal is that redundant employees will obtain new employment as quickly as possible. Indeed, Boynton and Thomas (1991) found that 57 per cent of a sample of 196 employers saw this as the main objective.This goal may or may not be in line with the goals of outplacement firms, who will vary in the emphasis given to counselling as compared with placement. It seems clear, though, that many see their competitive edge in the marketplace as depending on having candidates on their books for as little time as possible. Individual candidates, for their part, will also have different needs and goals. Some will undoubtedly hope for fast re-employment above all else, while others are likely to value more the opportunity for personal counselling and re-evaluation of career goals.

A further problem with the dual counselling and placement function is that if the individual sees the counsellor's function primarily as placement, this can change the nature of the relationship with the counsellor. The individual may, for example, be more concerned with 'selling' him or herself to the counsellor, and so be tempted to engage in calculated 'self-presentation' rather than honest self-disclosure.

More seriously, avoiding retaliation and legal action will be at the top of the agenda for some employers. Knowingly or otherwise, outplacement counsellors may collude with this goal. Miller and Robinson (1994) take an extreme view on this issue, arguing that much of the crisis counselling carried out by outplacement counsellors in the United States is deliberately aimed at minimizing the potential for retaliation by 'neutralizing affect' and 'minimizing blame-placing behaviour'. This process is analogous, they argue, to the strategies used by confidence game operators in 'cooling-out' those they defraud. Practice in the United Kingdom may be beyond reproach in this respect, but the dual allegiance of counsellors working in sponsored services to their corporate clients on the one hand and to their candidates on the other can lead to serious professional dilemmas.

As we have seen, organizations are less willing to provide help to the survivors of downsizing programmes than to those actually made redundant. Furthermore, any support that is provided may be limited in its effectiveness because of the difficulties of meeting both individual and organizational needs. Employers will want survivors to remain committed to the organization, but employees will need to retain their self-esteem and integrity, and this may mean distancing themselves from organizational goals and values. More specifically, those surviving a redundancy programme will need accurate information about their future with the company, which an organization coping with rapid change may be unable to give. And if there are few opportunities for career development, commitment may be even more difficult to sustain.

As outplacement counselling expands and organizations begin to pay more attention to the survivors of downsizing, ways of resolving the issues outlined above will be needed. In particular, consideration should be given by the professional bodies concerned with the regulation of outplacement services as to how the work of outplacement agencies might be organized to minimize conflicts of interest between the various parties. Also, more clarity is needed as to the balance between the counselling and placement functions of outplacement. In addition, it would seem that outplacement counsellors may also have an increasing role in providing counselling and support to the survivors of redundancy programmes and as consultants to those managing redundancy programmes in their organizations.

References

Archer, J. and Rhodes, V. (1987) 'Bereavement and reactions to job loss: a comparative review', *British Journal of Social Psychology* 26: 211–24.

Boynton, J. W. and Thomas, R. (1991) *The UK Outplacement Report*, London: Kingsland James/BSL.

Brockner, J., Grover, S., Reed, T. G., De Witt, R. L. and O'Malley, M. (1987) 'Survivors' reactions to lay-offs: we get by with a little help from our friends', *Administrative Science Quarterly* 32: 526–41.

Brockner, J. (1988) 'The effects of work layoffs on survivors: research, theory and practice' in B. M. Staw and L. L. Cummings (eds) *Research in Organizational Behavior*, vol. 10, Greenwich, CT: JAI Press.

Brockner, J. and Lee, R. J. (1995) 'Career development in downsizing organizations: a self-affirmation analysis' in M. London (ed.) *Employees, Careers, and Job Creation*, San Francisco: Jossey-Bass.

Doherty, N. and Tyson, S. (1993) *Executive Redundancy and Outplacement*, London: Kogan Page.

Doherty, N., Bank, J. and Vinnicombe, S. (1995) 'Managing survivors: the experience of survivors in BT and the British financial sector', paper presented at New Deals Conference, City University.

Eby, L. T. and Buch, K. (1995) 'Job loss as career growth: responses to involuntary career transitions', *The Career Development Quarterly* 44: 26–42.

Eisenberg, P. and Lazarsfeld, P. F. (1938) 'The psychological effects of unemployment', *Psychological Bulletin* 35: 358–90.

Fisher, C. D. and Gitelson, R. (1983) 'A meta-analysis of the correlates of role conflict and ambiguity', *Journal of Applied Psychology* 68: 320–33.

Fryer, D. M. (1986) 'Employment deprivation and personal agency during unemployment: a critical discussion of Jahoda's explanation of the psychological effects of unemployment', *Social Behaviour* 1: 3–23.

Ganster, D. C., Fusilier, M. R. and Mayes, B. T. (1986) 'Role of social support in the experience of stress at work', *Journal of Applied Psychology* 71: 102–10.

Guest, D. and Peccei, R. (1992) 'Employee involvement: redundancy as a critical case', *Human Resource Management Journal* 2: 34–59.

Herriot, P. and Pemberton, C. (1995) *New Deals: The Revolution in Managerial Careers*, Chichester: Wiley.

Jacobson, D. (1987) 'Models of stress and meanings of unemployment: reactions to job loss among technical professions', *Social Science and Medicine* 24: 13–21.

Jahoda, M. (1981) 'Work, employment and unemployment: values, theories and approaches in social research', *American Psychologist* 36: 184–91.

Karasek, R. A. (1979) 'Job demands, job decision latitude and mental strain: implications for job redesign', *Administrative Science Quarterly* 24: 285–308.

McFarlin, D. B. and Sweeney, P. D. (1992) 'Distributive and procedural justice as predictors of satisfaction with personal and organizational outcomes', *Academy of Management Journal* 35: 626–37.

Miller, M. V. and Robinson, C. (1994) 'Managing the disappointment of job termination: outplacement as a cooling-out device', *Journal of Applied Behavioural Science* 30: 5–21.

Orlans, V. (1996) 'Counselling psychology in the workplace' in R. Woolfe and W. Dryden (eds) *Handbook of Counselling Psychology*, London: Sage.

Pickman, A. (1994) *The Complete Guide to Outplacement Counselling*, Hillsdale, NJ: Erlbaum.

Seligman, M. E. P. (1975) *Helplessness*, San Francisco: Freeman.

Steele, C. M. (1988) 'The psychology of self-affirmation: sustaining the integrity of the self' in L. Berkowitz (ed.) *Advances in Experimental Social Psychology*, San Diego, CA: Academic Press.

Wanberg, C. R. (1995) 'A longitudinal study of the effects of unemployment and quality of reemployment', *Journal of Vocational Behavior* 46: 50–4.

Warr, P. B. (1987) *Work, Unemployment, and Mental Health*, Oxford: Clarendon Press.

Warr, P. B. and Jackson, P. R. (1987) 'Adapting to the unemployed role: a longitudinal investigation', *Social Science and Medicine* 24: 1–6.

Winefield, A. H. (1995) 'Unemployment: its psychological costs' in C. L. Cooper and I. T. Robertson (eds) *International Review of Industrial and Organizational Psychology*, vol. 10, Chichester: Wiley.

Chapter twenty-two

Counselling, death, and bereavement

Pittu Laungani and Fred Roach

I don't mind dying, but I don't want to be there when it happens: Woody Allen

Introduction

The two most significant events in our lives are our birth and our death. Paradoxically, we experience neither of these events. We have no known way of experiencing our own birth – regardless of the fantastic claims of the 'birth trauma' made by a few psychoanalysts of the past, notably, Otto Rank. Nor can we take seriously the claims made by astrologers, palmists, and other soothsayers, who speak glibly of one's experiences of past births! This is not to deny that such experiences might not be true. Given the present state of scientific knowledge, all we can say is that *we have no way of establishing the validity of such claims*. It is perhaps reasonable to claim that one acquires an awareness of one's birth with time.

However, this chapter is concerned with the other side of the equation: death. To experience one's own death is not possible. It is a contradiction in terms. One cannot be dead and alive at the same time. Although this sounds like a truism, it should be pointed out that serious – and in some instances, acrimonious and esoteric – debates have been raised over this notion of death and life being an either/or, or a dichotomy. Modern science, aided by medical research, has raised serious questions concerning when it is legitimate to define death. Should one look upon a patient on a life-support machine in a state of protracted coma as being alive or dead? Should one wait and live in hope that one day perhaps, one's loved one, either as a result of scientific advances, or by an unexplained miracle, will recover, or should one accept the finality of death, and request the life-support machines be turned off? The answer to this question, as one can see, is not clear cut. It raises a series of moral, financial, social, psychological, and practical conundrums, to which clear answers are not available.

Death is best seen as being irreversible. Given our present state of knowledge, the dead do not and cannot be made to come to life. But this grim fact has not deterred a few enterprising scientists, referred to as cryonicists, from planning for the future. They are convinced that, one day, scientific advances will make it possible to revive the dead, who will then live forever. The lure of immortality has persuaded several persons to volunteer their bodies – at a steep price of course – to the cryonicists. Upon the death of the volunteer, the cryonicists take possession of the corpse, which is rushed to their laboratory and frozen in hermetically sealed concrete vats of liquid nitrogen at temperatures of minus 196°C. The body will then remain frozen for an indefinite period. Whether the scientists who have arranged to freeze the bodies will one day be able to revive the bodies and offer the resurrected immortal life, remains a futuristic issue.

However, leaving this aside, it needs to be stressed that from a clinical point of view, the organism, upon death, ceases to function; that is, the person who has died has lost the capacity to breathe and to sustain a spontaneous heartbeat. Death, as Lamb (1985) points out, marks the cessation of integrative action between all organ systems of the body. The established medico-legal system demands that one's death be documented in terms of time, place, and cause. For the purposes of this chapter, we shall accept the biological conceptualization of death stated above, viz. looking upon life and death in dichotomous terms, instead of it extending along a continuum.

While birth in principle leads to a celebration of a life to be lived, mountains to be climbed, death marks the completion, the end, the finality of a life that has ceased to be. Death is a universal phenomenon. It comes to us all. When it comes, it is final. As stated above, we would also like to assume that death is irreversible. Whether the dead, on the Day of Judgement, shall rise from their graves; or whether death, according to Hindu religious philosophy, marks the end of one life and the beginning of another, thus forming part of a series of lives and deaths, births and rebirths, are extremely profound issues. Answers to those questions doubtless play an important part in understanding the manner in which people all over the world conceptualize their own death and cope with the death of their loved ones. Although detailed analyses of these philosophical arguments lie beyond the boundaries of the present chapter, we shall refer to them as and when we discuss cultural issues related to counselling, death, and bereavement.

Our main concern here is to understand the nature and type of counselling which a trained, experienced counsellor ought to, or should be able to provide to a) a client who is dying; and b) to the person or persons who mourn the loss of their significant others.

One of the strangest aspects about death is the fact that none of us can ever experience our own. We can visualize it in our minds in its meticulous detail, we can imagine it, we can even role-play it, we can phantasize the effects of our death on those we leave behind, but we cannot experience it. To experience an event it is necessary for the person to be conscious and, therefore, alive. Yet although we shall never experience this final event, many of us are nonetheless terrified of its occurrence.

Although the fear of death is widespread, it would seem, according to Kubler Ross (1969), that the fear of death is universal 'even if we think we have mastered it on many levels' (1969). Why the idea of one's death should strike such universal terror in us all remains an unanswered question. Speculations abound. Whether the dread of death, or something after death, is due to the 'undiscovered country from whose bourn no traveller returns,' or whether it is due to other unexplained factors, which include ideas of hell and damnation, extinction and annihilation, permanent severence of oneself from one's loved ones and from the material world in which one has lived one cannot say with any degree of certainty.

In the West the fear of death can be attributed to several factors. Most Western societies have witnessed a decline in the status of established religion. At a psychological level this has resulted in diminishing belief in an afterlife, rebirth, and heaven and hell. This, along with the gradual dissolution of the extended family and community networks, has meant that the beliefs and practices, as well as the institutional structures which used to support the bereaved are now often unavailable or inadequate. In addition the socio-political processes of humanization and secularization, have shifted our attention away from the destiny of the deceased toward the fate of the bereft. Sadly, the individual is left largely on his or her own to cope and come to terms with this fundamental human problem.

However, each of us may have our own *private* reasons for fearing death, reasons which often remain unvoiced. There are some, like Walter (1996), who argue that the acceptance of a humanist philosophy prepares its adherents to face death without fear. He argues that death equals extinction and therefore it is not to be feared. Because we can never know of any life beyond the grave there is no point in worrying about it now. Therefore one learns to accept the inevitable with a sense of equanimity. What matters is not one's death, for that is inevitable and unavoidable, nor what lies beyond death (which of course one does not know), but *how one lives one's life*. A humanist is more concerned with living and life than with death and dying. It should be pointed out that a humanist view is a *rationalist* view of life and death, to which only a small minority is likely to be attracted. The majority of people – not just in Western societies, but all over the world – are unlikely to acquire an immunity from all the primeval dreads and terrors associated with death and extinction.

The acknowledged fear of death has led several commentators on the subject to speak more in terms of ways of coping with death and bereavement; and a great deal of energy is expended in an effort to help the dying person, the family, relatives, partners, and friends to cope and move beyond the emotional trauma that can engulf the bereaved for several months and, in some instances, for years. Life is seen as having a beginning, followed by growth and development, and it has an ending; the end state as we know it is called death. This life-span perspective dates back to the eighteenth century. It was offered by Johann Nicolaus Tetens (1736–1807), Friedrich August Carus (1770–1808); Adolphe Quetelet (1796–1874). They offered it as an initial step forward in the attempt to help the dying and the bereaved understanding what is going on. The ideas of Tetens, Carus and Quetelet suggest that development be treated as a continuous process from birth to death.

Briefly, the life-span theory of growth and development suggests that human development involves simultaneous growth and decline throughout life, that is from conception to death. Changes in different aspects of biological, psychological, and social function may have different starting points, end points and developmental trajectories (Clarke-Stewart *et al.* 1988). Change is constant and the death of various parts of the organism is constantly occuring throughout life. Thus when the entire organism ceases to function that change is called death – that is, the cessation of function or integrated function in all component systems of the organism as a whole.

Before examining the unique counselling problems which may arise when assisting a dying person, let us briefly turn to the general attitudes, beliefs, and values which people across cultures have towards death and bereavement.

Attitudes towards death and bereavement

For counselling to be relevant, meaningful, and effective it is essential that counsellors have a clear and objective understanding of the beliefs, attitudes, and values of their clients towards death and bereavement The counsellor needs to have an insight into the manner in which the client perceives his or her own impending mortality and the importance placed on the rites and rituals which precede death and those which follow death. A failure to perceive accurately the client's beliefs and attitudes may have an adverse effect on the counselling process. Although death is universal, attitudes to death vary enormously across cultures.

To many people death is seen as a period of transition. There is a widely held belief that upon death, although the human body if left unattended will decompose, the spirit or the soul remains free, unfettered, and unaffected. The soul goes either to heaven, to an everlasting afterlife, or – heaven forbid – to hell. It is imperative that the counsellor be aware of such beliefs in a dying client.

Some theorists, notably Morison (1977), offer the view that death is no more a single, clearly delimited, momentary phenomena than is infancy, adolescence, or middle-age. Others such as Veith *et al.* (1977) put forward the view that death is not a continuous event but an event that takes place at a precise time. It seems that in an age of increased medical, technological advancement this ongoing academic debate between death as an event and death as a process is set to continue for some time. The emphasis on death as a process stems from the use of machines which may be used to prolong death through life-sustaining functions (Ladd 1979). These 'death-as-process' views have so far remained vague. However, despite the differing opinions, the concept of 'death-as-event' has a pragmatic value for the counsellor. Irrespective of perspective, the fact remains that the person is dead and there is a need to cope with the various expressions of significant others who are concerned with that death.

One's attitudes to death are moulded not only by the culture in which one lives (this permits the acquisition of related cultural norms) but to a certain extent by the frequency with which a person comes into contact with the dying and the dead. In Western cultures, attempts are made to distance people from death. The spectacular advances in the medical sciences have raised hopes in people of longevity and even immortality. Such advances have given rise to the belief that death can be postponed, held in check, or even conquered permanently. Modern medicine, by regarding death as a medical failure, may have unwittingly perpetuated this image. The belief in longevity allows one to distance oneself from one's own death and those of one's loved ones. It is an event about which one does not have to concern oneself unduly. Yet people die every day, everywhere. And not all people die of old age. No society has discovered the elixir of life.

It is not surprising therefore that the distancing of oneself from death is carried to extreme lengths in the West. People in general, and children in particular, are often shielded from the 'trauma' of beholding a dead body. This is a result of the *medicalization* of death in Western countries. Most people in the West die in hospitals or hospices. The dead are seldom or hardly ever brought home. They are attended to by professional funeral directors who remove the corpse to their own premises, and who on the day of the funeral bring the coffin to the crematorium or cemetery for the performance of the last rites. In keeping death away from the home, in absolving ourselves from all the rituals related to the handling, laying out, and dressing of the body, Western society to a large extent has succeeded in distancing itself from death.

One might go so far as to suggest that in the West, one learns of death in the abstract. One acquires a cognitive awareness of death. One learns that it is the final event in every individual's life. But the knowledge of death is in the head: neither the heart nor the eye experiences it directly. Thus when death is about to occur (and as is inevitable, does eventually occur) the Westerner is unprepared to face it and come to terms with it. Such beliefs and attitudes place further demands on the role of bereavement counsellors, whose role it is to ensure that the dying and the bereaved come to terms with their own death and the death of their loved ones.

When one turns to non-Western cultures one learns that neither children nor adults are prevented from witnessing a dead body. First, in third world countries, most people die at home, not in hospitals. All the funeral arrangements are undertaken by members of the family and not by professional undertakers. Second, death is a freely talked about subject. The theme of death occurs in daily conversation, among friends, among relatives, within families, and between strangers. Death is around one, it is part of the human condition, and there is a tacit acceptance of its eventuality. Finally, death in non-Western countries is not *medicalized*. As a result, death is seen as a common, everyday occurrence, and although it may hold the same private terrors as it does for people in the West, the close proximity with death makes its denial a virtual impossibility (Laungani 1996).

It is obvious therefore that people across the world adopt different ways of viewing death and expressing their sorrow, loss, shame, guilt, and all the subjective responses that the universality of death promotes. Given that there are significant differences both within and between cultures in the manner in which death is conceptualized, the performance of the rites and rituals related to death, including the final disposal of the body, the pattern, period, and process of bereavement, how does the effective counsellor deal a) with the client who is dying; and b) the person or persons who are mourning the loss of their significant others. We will examine each of these in turn, but first let us examine the main theoretical approaches to death and bereavement counselling.

Principles

Theoretical approaches to counselling in death and bereavement work

Do the bereaved need professional help? Schiff (1979) puts forward the view that the bereaved can best gain comfort, understanding, and hope from others who have been through the despair and recovery that follows loss. Although Schiff recognizes that professional intervention might sometimes be helpful, he places a great deal of emphasis on experience. Such a view is limited in its usefulness. It is not clear what would happen in those situations where the loss experienced by the bereaved is due to circumstances which are unique and are unlikely to be experienced by others, for instance where death is due to genocide. Professional help, it might be argued, is never totally devoid of experience.

There are several theoretical approaches which are available to counsellors (see Chapter 1). The one which seems to focus its principles firmly in the area of experience is the *cognitive approach*. Cognitive theory is an insight therapy that emphasizes recognizing and changing negative thoughts and maladaptive beliefs (Corey 1991). Developed by Beck (1987), it argues that in order to understand the nature of an emotional episode or disturbance, it is essential to focus on the cognitive content of an individual's reaction to the upsetting event or stream of thoughts (DeRubels and Beck 1988). The goal is to change the way the person thinks.

Cognitive therapy is based on the belief that cognitions are the major determinants of how we feel and act (Corey 1991). Beck (1976) states that in the broadest sense cognitive therapy consists of all the approaches that alleviate psychological distress through the medium of correcting faulty information processing and dysfunctional assumptions. When a person is facing a stressor such as death (or is bereaved) there is a greater awareness of the presence of dysfunctional assumptions (schemata) such as, 'I am vulnerable'. The task of the counsellor involved in cognitive therapy would be to help the person modify inaccurate and dysfunctional thinking and therefore become less emotionally disturbed.

It should be pointed out that there are some limitations with such an approach. It assumes that there is a corresponding one-to-one relationship between cognitive processes and behaviour. Forty years of research, starting with Festinger's pioneering work on cognitive dissonance (1957), has demonstrated quite clearly that it is unwise to assume a direct, one-to-one relationship between the cognitive components and the behavioural components of attitudes. People do not always translate their cognitions (or intentions) into corresponding actions. Nor do they, conversely, always change their cognitions to fit in with any behavioural changes. A direct correlation between the two does exist, but it is by no means a one-to-one relationship.

In addition to the cognitive approach, counsellors can opt for a variety of other approaches such as the person-centred or the psychodynamic approaches to bereavement counselling.

The person-centred approach arises out of the theoretical formulations of Carl Rogers (1961, 1970, 1972) which are rooted in humanist philosophy. To help the client Rogers believed that it was important for the therapist to concentrate on the present experience of the client, adopt a more active and self-disclosing role for the counsellor, for group as well as individual counselling (Ivy *et al.* 1993). This approach is characterized by an increased personal involvement, with greater emphasis being placed on relational issues. The counsellor needs to be warm, open, and empathetic in order to help the client articulate, understand, and reappraise the present situation. This form of counselling calls for high-level cognitive and verbal skills on the part of the client. It may not be suitable for those who do not possess such skills.

The psychodynamic approach owes its origins to Freudian theory. The emphasis is on the client to uncover and bring to consciousness material which he or she may have repressed. This is in keeping with the underlying developmental assumption that experiences and events in one's past have a strong bearing on the understanding of one's present problems. In the process of uncovering the past, the client gains insight into his or her present innermost unconscious problems and, over time, may achieve a positive reintegration of his or her personality. There are several variants of the psychodynamic approach, ranging from classical Freudian psycho-analysis to group family therapy. The counsellor may also rely on a variety of techniques, such as free association, analyses of the transference situations, dream interpretation, etc.

Pyschodynamic approaches have not been without their critics (Eysenck 1985; Sloane *et al*. 1975; Williams and Spitzer 1984). Not only has the validity of such approaches been questioned, so have their usefulness. Despite these criticisms, the psychodynamic approach appears to have found favour among counsellors of different persuasions.

Counselling the dying person

Although death is universal, the manner in which each individual breathes his or her last varies considerably. It might sound a truism to maintain that there are different types of death, with suicide at one extreme and murder at the other. Between these two tragic extremes are deaths which result from accidents, natural calamities and disasters, sudden unpredictable cardiac seizures, protracted illnesses, infectious diseases, malnutrition and extreme poverty, infirmity, and the scourges of old age. Cutting across this dimension of types of deaths lies an *age-related dimension*, starting with miscarriages and termination of pregnancies, still-births, infant death, death in adolescence, to death due to old age. Thus not only are there different types of dying and different types of death, but there are different ages at which people die.

The counsellor, it need hardly be emphasized, needs to be aware that not all persons who are dying might wish to be counselled. Persons who commit suicide, or are killed at the hands of others, or persons who meet with sudden tragic deaths, by the very nature of the event, cannot be counselled. Nor can those who remain in a coma until death, or until a decision is taken to turn off the life support-machines. It is extremely unlikely that infants, young children, persons with severe mental disabilities, etc., will benefit from any form of counselling.

Even if one wanted to, logistically, it would not be possible to offer counselling to every dying person, for there are more people dying every day than there are counsellors available. In any event, a great majority of individuals, it should be realized, do not need counselling. They have either their own inner resources and/or a network of social, cultural, religious, and familial support systems, which enable them to come to terms with their impending death. And most individuals learn, in their own way, to make their own peace with themselves, with others, and with their God. It is therefore important for the counsellor to take the above factors into serious consideration when planning appropriate counselling strategies for the dying.

Given the variations in cultural, social, familial, religious, illness-related and age-related factors affecting the dying person, how would one expect a counsellor to function effectively under those circumstances? Let us offer some tentative answers. At a general level, the counsellor would need to be in tune with and accommodate an understanding of multi-culturalism in general. and the client's (the dying person's, that is) culture in particular. After all, it is not a simple business of merely disposing of a dead body: there is within the human psyche a powerful recognition and acceptance of dignity in the human corpse, and, as a result, there are important rites and rituals (hallowed by tradition) to be observed, ceremonies to be performed; and, above all, the dying person may ardently desire the perpetuation of all the rituals preceding and following his or her death. It is important that the counsellor is aware (or made aware) of such customs, is sympathetic to them and is familiar with the means by which they might be observed and perpetuated.

Each counsellor knowingly (or, in some instances, unknowingly) operates from within his or her theoretical framework. The paradigm sets out the parameters, defines the nature, the techniques, the strategies of counselling, the adoption of which will lead to, what the counsellor believes, effective counselling. Although it is difficult to define effective counselling – let alone measure it – effective counselling, in this instance, would mean allowing the dying individuals to articulate their fears and anxieties, genuinely accept their imminent mortality, make their peace with those whom they must inevitably leave behind, and with themselves and their Gods, if any. It is possible that the theoretical framework within which the counsellor 'plies his or her trade' may be in sharp conflict with the striking cultural differences between the client and the counsellor. The counsellor must not let theoretical frameworks and notions of psychological intervention over-ride cultural or ethnic determinants. In death, as in life, the person has needs and this means that, whenever possible, the rights and customs of the dying person need to be respected.

The counsellor's approach should reflect a positive attitude and understanding which is wide and broad enough, notwithstanding theoretical adherence, to exclude prejudices in their own attitude to death and how to help the bereaved in a multi-cultural society. In the case of the terminally ill when the person can no longer deny the imminent circumstances, a positive attitude might be hard to engineer. Painful treatments, hospitalization, worries about money or financial settlements may also be a hindrance. The person might be preoccupied with sadness, guilt, or depression.

Occasionally, a dying person might desire that upon his or her death, their body be transported to their native land, to be among their own people, where all the rites and rituals, codes and customs, including the bereavement processes, can be observed in the traditional manner. The counsellor will need to take account of the preparatory grief a person will have to undergo in order to prepare for the final separation from the world (Kubler-Ross 1985). The counsellor's understanding of the life-span perspective may offer some solutions here in utilizing the principles associated with helping the person who is facing death, irrespective of personal philosophy and setting. The overall aim must be to help the dying to deal with unfinished business and to say an appropriate goodbye to the loved ones that will be left behind. As Worden (1987) points out, the counsellor should therefore have a set of objectives, such as:

(a) helping the dying person to deal with his/her underlying feelings;
(b) increasing the reality of loss;
(c) helping the dying person to come to terms with impending death;
(d) helping the person to say final goodbyes.

Helping the dying person deal with feelings

Dead people do not talk. The counsellor ought to be able to reach the person concerned *before* he or she dies. It is important to talk to them and to capture their wishes and desires. The dying person's needs and responses need to be understood, respected, and, in so far as is possible, fulfilled while there is time to do so. This would help to evaluate the nature of the service that is provided to them and to the people around them. It must be remembered that the dying person is still alive and will require things for their living as well as things for their dying. Stedeford (1989) reflects that many dying persons have rich inner resources to draw on; there is also strong support from relatives and friends. Professional intervention must take account of what the dying persons have to offer at their moment of dying. People who are dying are often sad as they come to realize that they are about to reach the end of their life's journey and soon will lose much, if not all, that they have valued in their lives. It is too late to take account of this when the person has died. The counsellor should offer such care, understanding, and comfort as would enable the client to face his or her impending death with courage and equanimity.

Counselling the bereaved

Responding to the reality of the loss

There is a sense of shock and the feeling of being shaken up that is experienced by persons who learn of the death of someone close to them. The counsellor needs to be aware of sudden, sharp changes that may occur in the bereaved person: personality changes, mood swings, symptoms of physical illness and, in extreme cases, suicidal tendencies. These might become most apparent in the single bereaved who might manifest more physical distress and who are likely to take more alcohol and drugs for symptom relief than do their married, non-bereaved counterparts (Clayton 1974). Heymon and Gianturco (1973) showed that there are few changes among older men and women with regard to physical health, visits to doctors and number of hospitalizations. It has been shown that the bereaved suffer from more depressive symptoms during the first year after the loss than non-bereaved controls (Parkes and Brown 1972). Following the death of a spouse there is an increase of symptoms such as headaches, trembling, dizziness, heart palpitations and various gastro-intestinal symptoms (Worden 1991). There is also a sense of disruption of normal activities. There is a protective emotional numbness which prevents the person from becoming totally overwhelmed with sadness. There is denial, i.e. the person may try to deny what has happened. What becomes important is the need to accept what has occurred and it is at this stage that the questioning begins. It is the need for the person to question themselves and to question others. There is a feeling of guilt and blame and an apportioning of responsibility and looking for fault. Grief then emerges as the dominant emotional force. The person returns to the loss and considers what has been lost. There is a search for meaning to what has happened and the need to deal with the emptiness around them. The bereaved may develop symptoms like those experienced by the loved one or significant other before the death. Zisook and Devaul (1976) refers to this as facsimile illness or masked grief.

The counsellor must allow the person to talk about the dead person's symptoms and ascertain if the person is adopting any such features. The aim should be to avoid despair taking over the person. The person needs to develop the capacity to deal with these negative emotions and learn new ways of coping. If the reaction becomes chronic more psychological-psychiatric intervention may become necessary (Parkes 1964, 1965). Recovery involves learning to return to life without the person who has died.

The counsellor's task is to help the person understand that when a loved one dies there is always a feeling of unreality about the occurrence of death. Therefore it is necessary to confirm that death has occurred and to encourage the person to talk about it. The counsellor can ask a number of questions which help the person to engage in this 'talking out' process. It is often helpful if the questions are geared towards helping the person talk about the circumstances surrounding the death. Some people need to repeat the circumstances over and over again until actualization of the loss is achieved. The counsellor can help the person review the event of the loss and the circumstances surrounding it in their mind. The counsellor needs to be a patient listener and encourage the bereaved person to verbalize the poignant memories of the dead person.

Grief reactions

The bereaved person may show a range of reactions, some of which may be complicated. Lindermann (1944) suggested a number of characteristics to look for in normal grief: bodily distress; preoccupation with the image of the dead person; guilt related to the person or to their death; hostility or anger; difficulty in functioning as one did before the death; and behavioural manifestation of traits associated with the dead person. The relative frequency of these features from person to person remains unclear (Parkes 1972). However, it is the task of the counsellor to identify what is happening to the bereaved and to help them make sense of the changes that they are experiencing.

Anger directed at loss

Krupp *et al.* (1986) note that the bereaved may show anger toward the loss of the love object, toward the self, and toward those who may, in some sense, have 'caused' the loss. Anger may also be directed at benevolent well-wishers who remind the mourner of the reality of the loss. The anger may be displaced and may arise because the bereaved cannot yet accept the reality of the death of their loved one. They may therefore blame others for their plight and become very critical of their treatment or of the efforts being made by others to help them (Stedeford 1989). Professional carers need to deal with these hostile feelings with great skill and sensitivity. The use of good listening may help the person come to terms with the fact that their anger is displaced. Relationships may improve if the bereaved are allowed to redirect their anger toward the actual cause of the death rather than toward any one individual who they may feel is responsible for the death. The person may refuse to accept the change and may regress to childish behaviour. Telling the counsellor about their feelings may help to resolve some of the underlying anger and conflicting emotions. Thoughts like 'I don't need to grieve' (Pincus 1976) may become apparent.

Bowlby (1980) observed that those who avoid grieving run the risk of breaking down and developing some form of depression. Euphoric responses are extremely fragile and short-lived (Parkes 1972). The counsellor will need to help the person acknowledge his or her anger and to put it into context. The bereaved will need to look at their frustration at not being able to do anything to prevent the death; and see their behaviours as those that are quite normal to experience at the loss of someone close. The counsellor needs to help the person to understand that there is a tendency to regress, to feel helpless, to feel unable to exist without the person and then to experience the anger that goes along with these feelings of anxiety (Worden 1991). This anger needs to be identified and properly focused so that the bereaved can feel comfortable with the changed situation with which they now have to cope.

The counsellor needs to help the person accept their own feelings, bring about an effective resolution, and then help understand that immediate relief is not possible.

Helping with denial

It is necessary for the bereaved to face the fact that the person is dead. The counsellor will become aware that denial may be reflected in different ways. The person therefore needs some time to come to terms with the change that has taken place in their life. They may not want to believe that the loss has occurred, nor in its irreversibility (Dorpat 1973). It may be necessary to help the person obtain some relief from current responsibilities in order to help them get to grips with what has happened. Denial of the loss may vary in degree and intensity from slight distortion to delusion, or the person may even deny the meaning of the loss (Worden 1991). Thus active intervention may become necessary especially in more extreme cases of denial where the person may be manifestedly psychotic, eccentric, or reclusive (Gardiner and Pritchard 1977). There is a need to let the person know that there is nothing wrong with feeling shame. Engaging the bereaved in some traditional or spiritual rituals may help the person through the denial phase towards acceptance of the death.

The counsellor needs to help the person accommodate the loss by looking at new ways of living without the dead person. The counsellor may engage a problem-solving approach and help the bereaved learn new coping skills and decision-making skills and how to establish and build new relationships. Although the bereaved may want to make quick decisions to reduce their pain they may well be encouraged to wait until they are less vulnerable and feel more capable of making important decisions which have a longer-term effect.

Resignation, acceptance, and saying goodbye

The dead person is seldom forgotten by those most bereaved. The survivor's readiness to enter new relationships depends on finding a suitable place for the spouse in the psychological life of the bereaved (Shucher and Zisook 1986). The counsellor needs to help the person find a new place in their life for the lost loved one. The person may wish to reminisce and every encouragement to do so might prove beneficial. This will help the person to relocate their emotions about the deceased and move forward in building new relationships.

The dying person, family, relatives, partners, and close friends

The counsellor needs to allow time for clients to grieve. Williams (1976) states that the family will go through stages of grief: denial, anger, bargaining, depression and acceptance. It is necessary to learn how to recognize these stages and help the family through them without rushing from one stage to another. Williams also reminds us that we must not fall prey to them in the process. It is also important to follow up the bereaved family. This may help the healing process and prevent some problems which may arise, especially with the younger members of the family. Strong support may become necessary. The family member who has died is no longer there to provide or do those things which were done in the past. Resentment, pessimism, denial, and communication problems between family members may have to be resolved. There is a need to avoid being hurt. The counselllor needs to identify what the family want and some bargaining may be necessary and rituals might help where children are involved. The counsellor may need to supervise care and from an early stage give the family an active role in the provision of care of their relative. The counsellor must understand and help the bereaved to interpret normal grief behaviours, allowing for individual differences, so that they may feel reassured that their own behaviour is not out of the ordinary and is what one would expect under the circumstances.

Counselling exercises

The following techniques may be used on their own or in conjunction with each other to facilitate relief for the bereaved.

Letters, poetry or story writing: The bereaved might benefit from writing to the dead person. The counsellor may give them a choice of writing a letter, poem, or story. This may help the person to cope with their own grief experience at a personal level and give personal meaning to their loss.

The use of art, drawing and design: The creation of art might provide some therapy for the individual. This could be expressed in drawings or designs. If the person is computer literate the counsellor might encourage them to use the computer to help them express their feelings.

Role-play and drama: The counsellor can help the person to acquire new skills and find new ways of coping through the use of role-play and drama. The bereaved can act out feelings and review their reactions to the loss.

Diaries and albums: The bereaved might find a return to the good memories of the person useful. This may be located in looking back at diaries of events that were attended together and photographs taken while the person was alive. A 'walk down memory lane' might provide an opportunity to come to terms with the loss and the need for emotional readjustment.

The use of imagery: The person may benefit from creating a situation in which presence of the dead person is felt. Here the counsellor has the opportunity to help the person express how they feel toward the person in a very direct way.

Language styles: Words that evoke feelings may help people with reality issues concerning the loss of the loved one and may motivate the person to talk about some of the painful feelings and experiences. The use of the past tense rather than the present tense may prove useful in helping the person come to grips with the reality of the death.

Symbolization: The use of symbols help the counsellor get a clear sense of the intensity of the loss and what the bereaved is experiencing. These symbols might include photographs of the dead person, letters, books, diaries, drawings, sketches, tapes, articles of clothing, and any item which brings the bereaved person emotionally and spiritually closer to the deceased.

Cognitive restructuring: The counsellor can help the person modify faulty thoughts surrounding the dead person. The person is helped to recognize these thoughts and to test them for accuracy against reality. The counsellor can help the person over feeling bad about things or self by helping the person come to terms with the irrationality of their thinking about things or self.

Terminating the counselling

It is important to know when to end counselling (Stedeford 1989). The counsellor will have to be aware when the bereaved is once again feeling comfortable. Slipping into the background is a necessary step that the counsellor has to take when it is judged right to do so. Follow up sessions may be offered and this will provide the continuing support that the bereaved person may be looking for. The counsellor needs to provide hope over the long term and referral to a support group might be a help. The counsellor should also identify pathological problems if they exist and refer the person to other specialist(s) who might be better able to help the bereaved person.

Issues

All counsellors should be trained

Counselling should be based on a sound theoretical knowledge and understanding of human behaviour and personality (Worden 1991). It is not enough to be aware of techniques. The main purpose of techniques should be to encourage expression of thoughts and feelings surrounding the dead person. Organizations such as BACUP, Cruse, and many hospices provide trained volunteers specializing in either counselling the dying or the bereaved.

Who should be offered counselling?

Common sense suggests that it would be impractical to counsel all who are facing death or are bereaved (Stedeford 1989). Those who ask for help or who are identified as requiring help ought to be offered counselling, although these may not be the most in need. Stedeford (1989) puts forward the view that whether counselling is offered to the dying is determined more by the sensitivity, knowledge, and resources of those close to them. The need to counsel everybody facing death has remained generally unaccepted. There is every reason to believe however that counselling should not be left to the ill-equipped sympathizer. The characteristics which may define the counsellor tend to depend on the nature of the counsellor's theoretical position and general frame of reference.

Noom (1992) discusses the difficulties in GPs providing counselling to their patients. The GP's role is already defined in terms of a doctor–patient relationship. If the GP takes on a counselling role it might present some ambiguity *vis-à-vis* the sick role (Parsons 1951). Patients consulting their GPs may have a set opinion of their expectations from the GP whereas in the case of counselling the patient's opinion of what is expected from the counsellor may not be in keeping with what is necessary to help the person feel better and improve their condition. This might be determined by the counselling relationship which corresponds to the eclecticism in psychological therapy.

Dealing with unexpected and sudden death

Societies are faced with changes which affect people from all walks of life. From day to day there are reports of traumatic deaths including murder, suicide, accidents, strokes, heart attacks, miscarriages, and still-births. Harrison (1987) argues the need for supportive structures within the community if long-term emotional and psychological disturbances are to be averted. Erikson (1976) found that people from among a community who escaped an horrific accident had made little progress after two years.

HIV and AIDS

The counsellor should be aware that the person affected by HIV and AIDS would probably have had some previous involvement with counselling services offering pre- and post-test counselling related to the condition. The person will have to deal with the same reactions in addition to others, such as stigma, disbelief, illness, fear of death, confidentiality, suicidal ideation, and sexuality issues (see Chapter 25). The counsellor will need to give the person time to feel wanted and understood in the face of the difficulties, and the bereaved will need time also to come to terms with the shame they may feel and the longer-term aspects of stigma which they may attach to themselves. The need to feel that confidentiality will be respected is very high for the dying and the bereaved in these cases.

Dealing with the counsellor's own grief

Worden (1991) points out that the experience of grief and bereavement in the client may affect the counsellor personally in at least three ways. First, working with the bereaved may bring about an awareness in the counsellor of his or her own painful losses. If the loss has not been adequately resolved, it may create some difficulty in helping the client. Second, grief may occur in terms of the counsellor's *feared* losses, for instance aged parents. Third, grief in the client may bring to the surface of the counsellor's mind, his or her own existential anxiety, and the fears associated with his or her own death. It is therefore important for counsellors to explore these profound issues both in their training programmes and in the course of their subsequent work if they are to be effective.

Future Developments

Counselling in community care settings

Under the recent Care in the Community proposals, more and more people see their GP as the person to whom they can turn in a state of crisis. Death is no exception. The problem arises when GPs are not equipped to deal with delicate emotional problems such as bereavement. The GP has the option to refer the person to an expert, usually a clinical psychologist or in some cases to a counsellor who may be attached to their surgery. Pringle and Lavity (1993) observed that it would be wise for GPs to guard against appointing unqualified people. Sibbald *et al.* (1993) have shown that less than half of all practising counsellors in Britain have received specialist training in counselling. To engage seriously in counselling it is necessary to have undertaken a recognized course of training. The idea of exposing the bereaved person to a naïve but well-meaning helper is unlikely to serve any useful purpose.

The characteristics of the counsellor may be defined in terms of their therapeutic approach(es) to helping the bereaved person. Many therapeutic approaches are available to a client. The counsellors 'feel psychologically comfortable' in adopting a specific approach which is in keeping with their own philosophy and ideology concerning the nature and process of counselling in general, and bereavement counselling in particular. From a clinical point of view, counsellors may be keen to recommend their own approach because they feel that the approach works, in the sense that it helps the bereaved to accept the reality and the permanence of their loss and, over time, make the necessary readjustments to lead a positive life. *These recommendations, although based on sound clinical experience, arise out of counsellors' subjective evaluations of the process and outcome of counselling.*

From a scientific point of view, the recommendation of any therapeutic proposal ought not to be based on subjective evaluations of the clinicians and counsellors. Regardless of how many – or indeed all – counsellors recommend and extol the virtues of a given therapeutic approach, it does not follow that the recommended approach is valid. All we have here is a measure of reliabilty, not validity. As has been pointed out elsewhere (Laungani 1995), if a thousand million people tell you the earth is flat it does not make it so. Reliability ought not to be conflated with validity.

Although attempts have been made to test the efficacy of diverse therapeutic approaches, in some instances it will be necessary to undertake rigorous, carefully controlled cross-over studies, involving the use of control groups, a clear deliniation of outcome criteria, etc. Such studies, given the nature of the trauma and crises being experienced by the client, who is in desperate need of help, are extremely difficult to undertake. The practical and moral problems involved in the design and execution of such studies act as a strong deterent, which only the 'brave' would attempt to overcome. But unless such studies are undertaken, and the superiority of one therapeutic technique over the others is unequivocally established, one is left with subjective evaluations, which, in some instances, at best might turn out to be platitudes, and at worst, counter-productive.

Given this caveat, any recommendations as to the choice of a given therapeutic approach must be made with conservative caution – and with the proviso that it might not prove to be effective in certain cases. Its lack of effectiveness may quite easily apply to cross-cultural counselling encounters, for example a Western (male) counsellor dealing with an Asian (female) client from the Indian sub-continent. The counsellor to his dismay may find that there is a lack of congruence of mutually shared assumptions, which forms the the preliminary basis of meaningful social encounters. This may be due to several factors, including linguistic differences, differences in value-orientations, beliefs, attitudes, and a lack of awareness of rites and rituals (see Chapter 17).

References

Beck, A. T. (1976) *Cognitive Therapy and Emotional Disorders*, New York: New American Library.

Bowlby, J. (1980) *Attachment and Loss* Vol. 3, London: Hogarth Press.

Clarke-Stewart, K. A., Perlmutter, M. and Friedman, S. (1988) *Lifelong Human Development*, Chichester: Wiley.

Corey, G. (1991) *Case Approach to Counselling and Psychotherapy*, 3rd edn, Pacific Grove, CA: Brooks/Cole.

Clayton, P. J. (1974) 'Mortality and Morbidity in the First Year of Widowhood', *Archives of General Psychiatry* 30: 747–50.

DeRubels, R. J. and Beck, A. T. (1988) 'Cognitive Therapy' in K. S. Dobson (ed.) *Handbook of Cognitive-behavioral Therapies*, New York: Guilford Press.

Dorpat, T. L. (1973) *Suicide, Loss and Mourning, Life Threatening Behaviour* 3: 213–24.

Erikson, K. T. (1976) *In the wake of the flood*, London: George Allen & Unwin.

Eysenck, H. J. (1985) *Decline and Fall of the Freudian Empire*, Aylesbury: Viking.

Festinger, L. (1957) *A Theory of Cognitive Dissonance*, Evanston Ill.: Row, Peterson.

Gardiner, A. and Pritchard, M. (1977) 'Mourning, Mummification and Living with Death', *British Journal of Psychiatry* 130: 23–8.

Harrison, W. (1987) *After the Bradford fire, Bereavement Care*, 6, 1, 6–8.

Heymon, D. and Gianturco, D. (1973) 'Long Term Adaptation by the Elderly to Bereavement', *Journal of Gerontology* 28: 359–62.

Ivey, A. E., Ivey, M. B. and Simek-Morgan, L. (1993) *Counselling and Psychotherapy: A Multicultural Perspective*, 3rd edn, Boston: Allyn & Bacon.

Krupp, G., Genovese, F. and Krupp, T. (1986) 'To have and have not: Multiple identification in Pathological Bereavement', *Journal of the American Academy of Psychoanalysis* 14: 337–49.

Kubler-Ross, E. (1969) *On Death and Dying*, London: Tavistock.

——(1985) *Questions and Answers on Death and Dying*, London: Macmillan.

Ladd, J. (1979) 'The Definition of Death and the Right to Die' in J. Ladd (ed.) *Issues Relating to Life and Death*, Oxford: Oxford University Press.

Lamb, D. (1985) *Death, Brain-Death and Ethics*, London: Croom Helm.

Laungani, P. (1995) 'Can Psychotherapies Seriously Damage Your Health?' *Counselling, Journal of the British Association for Counselling* 6(2): 110–15.

——(1996) 'Implications for Practice and Policy' in C. M. Parkes, P. Laungani and B. Young (eds) *Death and Bereavement Across Cultures*, London: Routledge.

Lindermann, E. (1944) 'Symptomatology and Management of Acute Grief', *American Journal of Psychiatry* 101: 141–5.

Morison, R. S. (1971) 'Death: Process or Event?', *Science* 173: 694–8; also in R. E.

Weir (ed.) *Ethical Issues in Death and Dying*, New York: Columbia University Press.

Noom, J. M. (1992) 'Counselling GPs for scope limitations of the Medical Role in Counselling', *Journal of the Royal Society of Medicine* 85: 126–8.

Parkes, C. M. (1964) 'Grief as an Illness', *New Society* Vol. IX, April 9.

——(1965) 'Bereavement and Mental Illness, part ii: A Classification of Bereavement Reactions', *British Journal of Medical Psychology* 38: 13–26.

——(1972) *Bereavement: Studies of Grief in Adult Life*, London: Tavistock.

Parkes, C. M. and Brown, R. J. (1972) 'Health and Bereavement: A Controlled Study of Young Boston Widows and Widowers', *Psychosomatic Medicine* 34: 449–61.

Pincus, L. (1976) *Death in the family: The importance of mourning*, London: Faber and Faber.

Parsons, T. (1951) *The Social System*, Glencoe, Ill.: Free Press.

Pringle, M. and Lavity, J. (1993) 'A Counsellor in Every Practice', *British Medical Journal* 306: 2–3.

Rogers, C. (1961) *On Becoming a Person*, Boston: Houghton Mifflin.

——(1970) *On Encounter Groups*, New York: HarperCollins.

——(1972) *Becoming Partners*, New York: Delta.

Schiff, H. (1979) *The Bereaved Parent*, London: Souvenir Press.

Shucher, S. R. and Zisook, S. (1986) 'Treatment of Spousal Bereavement: A Multidimensional Approach, Psychiatric Stages in Bereavement' in P. Chancy, *Dealing with Death and Bereavement*, Jackson, pp. 73–6.

Sibbald, B., Addington-Hall, J., Brenneman, D. and Freeling, P. (1993) 'Counsellors in English and Welsh General Practices; their nature and distribution', *British Medical Journal* 306: 29–33.

Sloane, R., Staples, E., Cristol, A., Yorkston, N. and Whipple, K. (1975) *Psychotherapy versus behavior therapy*, Cambridge, MA: Harvard University Press.

Stedeford, A. (1989) 'Counselling, Death and Bereavement' in W. Dryden, D. Charles-Edwards and R. Woolfe (eds) *Handbook of Counselling in Britain*, London: Routledge.

Veith, F. J., Fein, J. M., Tendler M. D., Veatch, R. M. Kleimon, M. A. and Kalkines, G. (1977) 'Brain Death: A Status Report', *JAMA* 238: 1744–8.

Walter, T. (1996) 'Secularization' in C. M. Parkes, P. Laungani and B. Young (eds) *Death and Bereavement Across Cultures*, London: Routledge.

Williams, J. (1976) 'Stages in Bereavement' in P. Chancy, *Dealing with Death and Bereavement*, Jackson.

Williams, J. and Spitzer, R. (eds) (1984) *Psychotherapy research: Where are we and where should we go?* New York: Guilford Press.

Worden, J. W. (1987) *Grief Counselling and Grief Therapy – A Handbook for the Mental Health Practitioner*, 2nd edn, London: Tavistock/Routledge.

Zisook, S. and Devaul, R. A. (1976) 'Grief related facsimile illness', *International Journal of Psychiatric Medicine* 7: 329–36.

Chapter twenty-three

Counselling and sexual dysfunctions

Grahame F. Cooper and Jane Read

Sexuality is ever-present in human life, and sexual dysfunctions have plagued humankind for a long time. Although the treatment of sexual dysfunctions is often considered to be a recent phenomenon, Bancroft (1989) has reminded us that some 180 years before Masters and Johnson started the 'new sex therapies', John Hunter, of surgical fame, used similar psychological methods to cure a man with erectile dysfunction. Most people do not seek or obtain help from a specialist in sexual dysfunctions, but many could be helped by those other professionals who, in addition to basic counselling skills, have an awareness of sexual functioning and dysfunctioning and a willingness to help by using well-established principles of sex counselling. In this way nurses, general practitioners, health visitors, occupational therapists, social workers, clergy, and others may (within their existing work contexts) be able to offer help which would otherwise be unobtainable or unacceptable.

The sexual dysfunctions

Sexual dysfunctions of psychological origin are a clear example of psychosomatic conversion, i.e. an alteration or disruption of a bodily function occurring as a result of emotional trauma such as anxiety, guilt, anger, or grief. In describing the sexual dysfunctions and their treatment through counselling, a four-phase model of human sexual response will be used here. Table 23.1 demonstrates the relationship between this model (Cooper 1988), the four-phase model of Masters and Johnson (1966), the three-phase model of Kaplan (1979) and the four-phase model from the American Psychiatric Association's (1994) *Diagnostic and Statistical Manual of Mental Disorders IV (DSM IV)*.

In planning treatment, some of the important factors are discussed below.

Occurrence

Any of the sexual dysfunctions may be of *general* or *specific* occurrence. These are referred to as Generalized and Situational Types respectively in

Table 23.1 The phases of human sexual functioning

Cooper (1988)	Masters and Johnson (1966)	Kaplan (1979)	DSM IV (1994)
		Desire	Desire
Desire			
Arousal	Arousal	Arousal	Excitement
	Plateau		
Orgasm	Orgasm	Orgasm	Orgasm
Resolution	Resolution		Resolution

the *DSM IV* (1994) classification. The sexual dysfunction is of general occurrence if it occurs with any partner and (in so far as it is applicable) when attempting to masturbate alone. If the dysfunction only occurs when with a particular partner and not in other situations, then it is said to be specific.

Origin

A sexual dysfunction is of *primary* origin if the person has always had it. When a previously satisfactory sexual function is lost or impaired, the dysfunction is of *secondary* origin. In *DSM IV* (1994) these are listed as Lifelong and Acquired Types respectively.

A dysfunction can be both secondary and specific – for example, a client who is sexually functional with one partner may be dysfunctional when with another partner.

Physical and psychological causes

The particular tasks of counselling people who have disabilities are discussed in Chapter 24 by Segal. Four relevant factors here are:

(1) Physical disabilities can cause sexual dysfunctioning either by directly affecting genital responses or by indirectly affecting the capacity for sexual acts and interactions.
(2) In some conditions there is no clear distinction between physical and psychological causes for sexual dysfunction: for example, in multiple sclerosis or diabetes intermittent dysfunctions caused by the disorder can set up anxieties which then disrupt sexual functions.
(3) Some people with physical disabilities have sexual dysfunctions of purely psychological origin, as able-bodied people do, for example due to the grief response to loss.
(4) Some malfunctions in the hormonal systems cause sexual dysfunctions.

The principles and practice of sex counselling will be described here in relation to heterosexual dysfunctions. Homosexual people suffer similar dysfunctions and the principles of treatment described here are equally valid for them.

Table 23.2 presents the psychogenic sexual dysfunctions, and shows that there are no distinctions between female and male dysfunctions within the desire and resolution phases.

Dysfunctions of the arousal phase

These are due, in both male and female, to a failure of the normal mechanisms which lead to increased blood flow and vaso-congestion in the genitals.

Dysfunctions of the orgasm phase

These show interesting and important differences between men and women. A comparison of the so-called orgasmic 'dysfunctions' of women with the orgasmic dysfunctions of men shows a gradation of degree of dysfunction in both sexes. However, experience suggests that women more commonly present with orgasmic dysfunctions than men. Both the nature and function of the orgasm differ between the sexes, despite the similar rhythmic contractions at 0.8 cps of comparable groups of muscles.

For the male, orgasm and ejaculation are often used synonymously and are assumed to be the same event, but under some circumstances these two functions can be separated – pre-pubescent boys, for example, often experience orgasm during masturbation before they are sufficiently developed for ejaculation to occur. Dysfunctions of this phase in the male are commonly described in terms of ejaculation – the outward and visible sign of the male orgasm. In the male, orgasm is the sensation experienced during ejaculation, a vital process in procreation. There is no such connection in women between orgasm and procreation and the biological function of the female orgasm is unclear.

Although some women are able to experience multiple orgasms, a significant proportion of women have difficulty in achieving orgasm during heterosexual intercourse and furthermore some women fail to achieve orgasm at all. It is possible that in some of these women, certain pelvic reflexes are absent or weak, thus raising the possibility that their orgasmic dysfunctions may be neurogenic rather than psychogenic. For some women the multiple orgasm has become the norm which they 'ought' to attain and failure to do so may lead to anxieties and to dissatisfaction with self or partner. It is generally held that the male orgasm differs in that it is followed by a refractory period, during which further stimulation is ineffective, rendering multiple orgasm impossible. Lowndes Sevely (1987), however, contends that the difference is only an ageing factor in men.

Treatment – counselling or therapy?

The terms counselling and therapy are, unfortunately, often used synonymously. Although the boundaries are not absolute, these authors find that a useful distinction can be drawn between counselling and therapy, both theoretically and practically.

Counselling

Counselling is a working process appropriate for helping people with difficulties of recent or immediate origin – that is, due to a recent traumatic event or conflicting feelings or beliefs associated with a recent event. In general, it is a process which helps people through those transitions of life that many people overcome simply with the help and support of relatives and friends. An example in sex counselling might be a person who fails to become sexually aroused whilst suffering stress or fatigue. This failure produces anxiety and on the next occasion that anxiety alone is sufficient to prevent sexual arousal from occurring and so a self-sustained condition is set up arising from recent causes.

Therapy

Therapy is a working process appropriate for helping a person with a problem which is of remote origins (Kaplan 1974, 1987), i.e. which has its roots in distant events of childhood and infancy that are deeply buried or in the unconscious. In general, psychotherapy may be appropriate where there is distress or behavioural disturbance which can be traced back to early experiences by utilizing the transference within the helping relationship. In sex therapy, resistances to the treatment programme may indicate such early traumatizing experiences.

These authors' usage of a clear distinction between counselling and therapy encompasses Kaplan's (1974) concepts of sexual dysfunctions of 'remote' or 'immediate' origins and is influenced by, amongst others, the concepts of Worden (1991).

Principles

The principles of the new sex therapies provide a means of understanding sexual dysfunctions. This understanding can be used by those helpers who are not specialist sex therapists to offer counselling and 'sexual first-aid' to people in need. These principles have already been presented in a form suitable for use by the public (Brown and Faulder 1979).

Table 23.2 Heterosexual dysfunctions of psychological origin

Female dysfunctions	Male dysfunctions
DESIRE PHASE	
Inhibition of sexual desire: Lack of interest in seeking or attaining sexual interaction. Not available to sexual arousal.	
AROUSAL PHASE	
Dyspareunia: insufficient vascular engorgement leads to lack of vaginal lubrication and relaxation, hence acceptance by the vagina of fingers or penis is painful. Erection of the clitoris will not occur and masturbation may also be difficult.	(a) *Partial erectile dysfunction:* insufficient vaso-congestion occurs to initiate and/or sustain full erection of the penis, hence masturbation or penetration may be difficult.
Vaginismus: pain and tightness make acceptance of penis or fingers impossible. In severe vaginismus, powerful reflex adduction of the thighs may occur.	(b) *total erectile dysfunction:* no significant enlargement or erection of the penis occurs.
ORGASM PHASE	
Orgasmic 'dysfunction': this occurs to varying degrees: (a) Orgasm not achieved by vaginal intercourse unless simultaneous direct stimulation of clitoris. (b) Orgasm not achieved by simultaneous intercourse and direct clitoral stimulation. It is achievable by masturbation when with a partner or when alone.	*Orgasmic/ejaculatory dysfunctions:* (a) *Premature ejaculation:* ejaculation occurs 'too quickly' for the man and/or his partner. (b) *Retarded ejaculation:* difficulty in achieving ejaculation 'within a reasonable time' (may be associated with partial erectile dysfunction).

Female dysfunctions	Male dysfunctions

ORGASM PHASE

(c) Orgasm not achieved by simultaneous intercourse and direct clitoral stimulation nor by masturbation when with a partner. Achievable by masturbation, but only when alone.

(d) *An-orgasmic*: orgasm not now achievable with any stimulus or

(e) *Pre-orgasmic*: orgasm has never been achieved.

(c) *Ejaculatory failure*: ejaculation retarded indefinitely. It cannot be achieved by intercourse, direct penile stimulation, or masturbation.

RESOLUTION PHASE

Dysphoria due to guilt, anxiety, or revulsive reactions.

New sex therapies

Masters and Johnson (1966, 1970) provided easily explicable models of human sexual functioning, dysfunctioning, and therapeutic principles. Their approach, which emphasized the active involvement of the client in the therapeutic process, had wide application and brought together existing concepts and developed new ones. Their methods have since been modified and developed by various practitioners (for example Kaplan 1974, 1979; Bancroft 1989; Fairburn *et al.* 1983; Hawton 1985) as part of the natural progression towards the development of an integrated approach.

Kaplan's contributions (1974, 1979) clarified the distinction between disorders of desire and disorders of arousal, and provided appropriate therapeutic strategies. She emphasized the psychodynamic aspects of this approach which Masters and Johnson did not address explicitly in their early writings (1966, 1970), although the important transference issues are mentioned in Kolodny, Masters and Johnson (1979).

The following principles can be clearly seen and are commonly, though not invariably, adhered to by current practitioners in Britain.

Working with the couple

Even though only one of the couple may present symptoms of sexual dysfunction, it is usually appropriate to work with them as a couple in sex counselling, since both will be affected and a positive outcome is more likely if both are actively involved in the counselling. The unconscious processes of the interactions between the couple should be observed and considered. If the partner is unable or unwilling to attend, then Bennun's (1985) unilateral marital therapy model might be applicable, but the limitations must be recognized.

Stress reduction

Anxiety is a major factor in causing or sustaining psychogenic sexual dysfunctions. Fear of failure and other performance anxieties are eliminated or reduced by asking the couple to agree to a total ban on sexual intercourse or other 'performance achievements' in the early stages of treatment.

Communication

Communication difficulties are important in precipitating and sustaining sexual problems, and work will focus on *verbal* communication, including sexual vocabulary and communication of feelings, both positive and negative; and *physical* communication, the giving and receiving of sensual and sexual pleasure. Mutually pleasurable sexual intercourse may be seen as the ultimate communication between the couple.

Motivation

The couple must be sufficiently committed to the treatment contract and programme to endure discomfort which may arise from exposing, and perhaps challenging, the nature and strength of the relationship. Many sexual problems are symptomatic of the state of the relationship and the level of communication, and high motivation is essential for a successful outcome.

Education

Sexual ignorance, misinformation, and myths (see Zilbergeld 1995 and Dickson 1985) contribute significantly to dysfunctioning, and hence education in sexual functioning and dysfunctions is important in the treatment. Useful resources for clients' use include Docherty (1986) and Ward (1976). A common example of an anxiety-creating myth is the belief that the vagina has to be *penetrated* (a forceful act requiring a stiff penis), part of the dominant male view of sexuality. This anxiety can be reduced by education about the positive female action of *accepting* (taking the penis into the fully aroused vagina) an act which does not require an erect penis.

Practical aspects of sex counselling – general

The general application of these principles in treatment programmes is given in brief outline here and illustrated by some specific case materials relating to erectile dysfunction.

Counselling

Couples often arrive with a double load of anxiety: they are anxious about their problem and anxious about coming into counselling. Helpers must therefore be able to offer the core conditions of acceptance, empathy, genuineness, and clear communication in order to establish a relationship (a therapeutic alliance) within which difficulties can be understood and help can be given and received.

Anxiety reduction

General anxiety is reduced by forming a good relationship, and problem-specific anxiety is reduced by (a) exploration of stress and negative feelings, thus improving communication between the couple; (b) educative work to increase understanding of sexual functioning and their specific dysfunction; (c) reducing sexual performance demands by banning sexual intercourse and encouraging sensual love-making which is not performance-orientated, through a sensate-focus programme.

Sensate focus

Using the sensate-focus programme modified from Masters and Johnson (1970) removes the anxiety of sexual intercourse and provides opportunities for non-demand sensual love-making. In the first stage the couple are asked to take turns in giving and receiving sensual pleasure in a warm and safe environment of their choice, by touching, stroking, kissing, caressing and so on, but avoiding stimulating the genitals, breasts, or other erogenous areas. Talking about it afterwards increases communication skills and in these ways they learn to give and receive sensual pleasuring and to share their emotional responses.

The second stage includes the specific sexual areas in the pleasuring, but continues the principle of non-demand. If arousal occurs, it may be enjoyed and allowed to come and go, but it is not an objective of the exercise and the absolute ban on intercourse remains.

Illustrative case note 1: Alan and Brenda

Alan's erection failed when attempting intercourse with Brenda. He was fatigued after a stressful week and had drunk some alcohol. Despite Brenda's understanding response, he became worried when on two further occasions he again failed. In the first counselling session, the mechanisms of sexual arousal and the causes of his dysfunction were explained. They accepted a total ban on sexual intercourse and a sensate-focus programme to provide non-sexual pleasuring, and increased mutual understanding and communication.

They were seen weekly; progress in the sensate-focus home assignments was monitored and any difficulties explored. In this non-demand experience Alan's confidence (and his erectile function) recovered. Intercourse was resumed in similar non-demand conditions, with Brenda on top lowering herself on to Alan so that her fully-aroused vagina *accepted* and contained his penis, without performance demands upon him.

By the time counselling ended after five sessions, they were able to have intercourse as before, and with a much greater sense of mutual understanding and security than ever before.

Applications of sensate focus

The change factors necessary in counselling to bring about transformation and the building of sound foundations for positive sexual functioning from the specific blocks which precipitate or sustain negative sexual functioning have been described elsewhere by this author (Cooper 1988). Sensate focus is an important component of these processes which offers a valuable double effect. First, by listening carefully to the clients' accounts of their usage, or avoidance, of sensate-focus exercises, the counsellor gleans valuable diagnostic information as to the causes and the effects of their sexual dysfunctions. Second, sensate-focus offers people immediate, active involvement in their own treatment by physical, verbal, and non-verbal communication exercises, thus overcoming one of the specific blocks.

Participation in the sensual, non-demand exercises of sensate focus may highlight beliefs about non-sexual love-making and about the participants' own bodies. Negative beliefs will need to be discussed in counselling to overcome blocks, whilst further individual physical assignments are appropriate where there is a negative body-image.

There are full accounts of sensate-focus work in Fairburn *et al* (1983), Hawton (1985), and Cooper (1988), and a well-illustrated massage sequence in Kitzinger (1985).

Sexual vocabulary

What are the right words to use? For many people there are no comfortable sexual words, only the awkward, clinical vocabulary of the professional (vagina, penis, coitus) or the unacceptable, derogatory vocabulary of the football ground (cunt, prick, fucking). This difficulty, arising from family and cultural influences, exacerbates sexual dysfunctions for the couple by making it impossible to discuss the problem either between themselves or with the therapist.

Every helper must ensure that he or she is familiar with the wide colloquial sexual vocabulary to ensure that inappropriate reactions are not shown. McConville and Shearlaw (1985) is a resource recommended for this purpose.

The word game

The following exercise enables clients lacking a sexual vocabulary to discover usable words for themselves. (A modified version is used for training sex counsellors and therapists.) Each partner writes down all the words he or she knows under headings such as female genitals, male genitals, sexual intercourse, masturbation, orgasm, and so on. The lists are then shared, one at a time with the partner and they then discuss their reactions. With which words do they feel uncomfortable? With which words do they feel comfortable? Which words would they like to use in their own discussions and with their sex counsellor? If they do not like any of the words listed they can invent their own. Through this exercise the couple establish a vocabulary so that the therapeutic work can proceed.

'Making friends with your body'

Many people suffering from sexual dysfunctions appear to be alienated from their own bodies. They lack a vocabulary with which to talk about their bodies, and are often ignorant of its basic structure and functioning. This difficulty is more commonly presented by women, although it also affects some men who have sexual dysfunctions. The negative self-images include adverse comparison with others. In sex counselling, individuals have the opportunity to effect important positive changes in their self-image and beliefs.

It is often difficult to love another unless one can love oneself. Specific individual work, as described below, will often help people to 'become friends' with their own bodies. Sensual bathing (purely for pleasure) is encouraged before visual and tactile exploration and appreciation of his or her own body. This is followed by self-massage with appropriate oils, lotions, or talcum powder, which leads to erotic appreciation and stimulation. Complete privacy in a warm, comfortable, and conducive environment is essential. Brown and Faulder (1979) and Zilbergeld (1995) give fuller descriptions.

Illustrative case note 2: Eric and Freda

Family attitudes and shyness had left both Eric and Freda ignorant about their own bodies and sexual functioning. They had not been able to consumate their marriage. Their shyness slowed the building of the counselling relationship, but they were well motivated and welcomed the learning opportunities, including the sensate-focus programme. They enjoyed the 'freeing up' which came from the word game; prior to that Freda's only words had been 'You know – round the tops of the stockings'. Her strong negative-feelings about her body initially made the 'making friends with my body' programme difficult for her. In the bath, she would only touch her vulva with a flannel 'because it's dirty down there'. Eventually, she felt comfortable about touching herself and partially inserting her own finger into her vagina.

Practical aspects of sex counselling – specific dysfunctions

Having described treatment concepts of general application above, additional techniques for other specific dysfunctions follow with illustrative case material.

Disorders of arousal

Dyspareunia

Dyspareunia means painful intercourse. It can be of physical or psychological origin, and is more common in women. In men it is mostly of physical origin – for example, inflammation (balanitis) or tight foreskin (phimosis). Some physical causes in women are infection (for example, thrush, genital warts, genital herpes), incomplete healing after childbirth, and oestrogen deficiency atrophy.

Psychological inhibition of arousal leaves the vagina dry and relatively tight instead of well lubricated, soft, and relaxed. When the vagina is dry and unready to accept penis or fingers, penetration will inevitably be painful. Arousal can be inhibited by anxiety, guilt embarrassment, grief or anger. Previous pain of physical origin can cause anxiety which prevents arousal and so causes pain of psychological origin.

The origins of dyspareunia may be immediate, easily recognizable, and treatable in counselling, or they may be due to remote, traumatizing past events which require therapy. Treatment of dyspareunia in women by counselling is based upon anxiety reduction and education through sensate-focus programmes and individual work on 'making friends with your body'. When full arousal is being achieved, genital intercourse may then be included in the pleasuring, but initially the woman controls the rate and depth of acceptance of the penis into her vagina by being on top of the man.

Vaginismus

In dyspareunia, intercourse is possible but painful, whilst in vaginismus the reflex reactions are so powerful that it is only possible to *penetrate* by force, since the positive female action of *accepting* the penis into the vagina does not occur. In severe cases, even touching the genital area or thighs will cause a powerful reflex adduction of the thighs. Treatment is similar to that for dyspareunia but the counsellor must be aware of resistances to psychological penetration which indicate underlying conflicts. Sometimes behavioural interventions are needed to overcome the conditioned reflex, in addition to counselling. This is illustrated by referring again to the case of Eric and Freda (see above).

After learning to accept her own finger in her vagina, Freda began using

Stanley Vaginal Trainers[1] (Stanley 1982). She inserted these size-graded smooth plastic rods for increasing periods of time, using a lubricant (KY jelly). In this way her vagina was trained to accept increasingly large objects without triggering the reflex and with greatly reduced discomfort. The principle here is of *training* the vagina to accept the object, *not* dilating the vagina. When accustomed to the largest trainer, she felt ready to accept her husband's penis. With Eric on his back Freda lowered herself down on to his penis, thus controlling the depth and speed of entry herself and so minimizing anxiety. After ten counselling sessions they were confidently enjoying sexual intercourse in various positions.

Disorders of female orgasm

Table 23.2 shows the range of these disorders. Treatment is usually based on the general techniques described above and sensate-focus programmes. The following describes the treatment of a woman with primary anorgasmia who was fully capable of sexual arousal, but had low sexual desire.

Illustrative case note 3: Gill and Harry

Gill loved her fiancé Harry, but her sex drive was low and although she became aroused when he initiated love-making, she was anorgasmic. Progress with sensate-focus was good although in Harry's keenness 'to get on' the intercourse ban was sometimes broken. Gill was delighted to discover, through pleasurable bathing, self-exploration, and eventually masturbation, that her vagina was not 'yukky' and that she was a fully sexual woman capable of orgasm. The use of literature (particularly Friday's *My Secret Garden* 1975) enabled her to accept sexual fantasies and to develop her own. After six counselling sessions Gill was regularly orgasmic and had a greater sexual appetitie than Harry, somewhat to his surprise!

Disorders of male orgasm

Premature or retarded ejaculation are defined by the clients' own words: 'He comes too quickly for me to be satisfied' or 'It takes me so long to ejaculate I feel like giving up.' In clinical practice, measurements of time to ejaculation from entry will not define these conditions adequately.

Premature ejaculation

Sensate focus forms the initial basis of counselling treatment but later, direct behavioural interventions, based on the concepts of Semans are indicated (see Bancroft 1989; Fairburn *et al* 1983; Cooper 1988).

Semans' treatment actively involves the partner in 'retraining' the man's response to intense sexual arousal. The man learns to recognize when ejaculation is about to become inevitable, so that stimulation can be reduced and hence ejaculation controlled. Once good recognition, and thus control, has been achieved, intercourse can be resumed but with the man underneath so that he can concentrate on recognizing the sensations and controlling his partner's movements on his penis. In this way gradually increasing periods of containment and then movement can be achieved by the man before choosing to ejaculate in the vagina. Zilbergeld (1995) gives useful modifications of this technique for the man to use alone.

Retarded ejaculation

In counselling, sensate focus is used and individual homework assignments may be devised for the male, similar in principle to those for female clients. This increases sensory awareness and implicitly 'gives permission' for masturbation and orgasm (see Brown and Faulder 1979; Zilbergeld 1995).

Illustrative case note 4: Ian and Janet

Ian's ejaculatory difficulties started after Janet had spontaneously aborted, and he had been totally unable to ejaculate in intercourse or by masturbation for the past four months.

During a lengthy treatment which included individual therapy for Ian, masturbation became enjoyable but ejaculation did not occur until, watching an erotic video alone, he masturbated and ejaculated. He then used this graded series of steps with Janet's willing approval and help:

(1) ejaculation when alone in the house,
(2) ejaculation with Janet in another room,
(3) ejaculation with Janet in the same room,
(4) ejaculation when in bed with Janet,
(5) ejaculation whilst cuddling with Janet,
(6) ejaculation onto her pubic area,
(7) ejaculation into her vulva,
(8) intercourse with ejaculation in her vagina.

This behavioural programme was successful after his individual therapy had dealt with his introjected beliefs and his hidden anxiety that he would be responsible for further painful suffering if he made her pregnant again. The roles of elective abortions and fertility problems as potential causes of sexual dysfunctions are further considered by Read (1995).

Janet's individual counselling and homework assignments had included the Kegel exercises which trained her to contract her pubococcygeal muscles. These muscles can constrict the vaginal cavity, thus gripping the inserted penis, enhancing the woman's sexual pleasure, and providing greater stimulus for her partner.

Gillan (1987) gives details of the Kegel exercises. The principles are: *identifying* the sensation of pubococcygeal muscle contraction by voluntarily stopping urine flow during micturition; *enhancing* awareness and contractions by practising contractions when not micturating; *strengthening* the muscles by contracting them frequently – as the muscle strength increases with regular training, a woman will be able to feel the contractions in the vagina with her finger.

Issues

Use of co-worker or single-worker models

Masters and Johnson (1970) considered it vital to use a man–woman co-therapy team in the treatment of couples, but treatment outcomes with single therapists are not significantly different (Kaplan 1974). The author's survey of sex therapists in the UK (Cooper 1988) found that only 14 per cent normally used a co-worker model, and some were all-female teams. Non-specialist workers wishing to use the single-worker model may do so without fear of it being significantly detrimental.

Clients as individuals or couples

Clients without a partner may request help for sexual problems such as disorder of arousal, anorgasmia, or premature ejaculation. The non-specialist worker should not be deterred from helping single clients with sex problems, provided that the worker can create a good counselling relationship, can discuss all aspects of sex and sexuality comfortably and knowledgeably, and has the skill to adapt techniques for use by single clients. Within a good counselling relationship, much relief can be provided by giving accurate information to counteract taboo and ignorance, by the implicit permission-giving which comes with the 'word game', and with 'making friends with your own body' for both men and women. The Kegel exercises can be taught and there is a description of the Semans technique suitable for the single male in Zilbergeld (1995). Much help and relief can be given to the individual with a sexual problem simply through acceptance and real understanding, both at the factual and the feeling levels, by an interested counsellor.

Groupwork

Group treatment for sexual dysfunctions has developed slowly, apparently due to participants' anxiety about confidentiality, and therapists' anxieties that people might change partners in a group for couples. The participants receive support from others with similar dysfunctions whilst for the administrator there is improved cost-effectiveness. Gillan (1987) has written about single-sex, mixed-sex, and couple groups. This interesting technique should only be used by counsellors experienced both in groupwork and in sexual dysfunction work.

Therapeutic approaches

The principles and practices of the 'new sex therapies' have been deliberately emphasized here because they are readily accessible to, and usable by, helpers who are not specialist sex counsellors. Other 'schools' of sex counselling and therapy, with differing beliefs about the nature and origin of sexual problems, are described elsewhere (Cooper 1988). These schools include psychoanalytic and psychodynamic therapies, behavioural sex counselling, cognitive therapy, and rational emotive behaviour therapy.

Sexual dysfunctions are seen as arising at different levels in the psyche by these different schools, with comparable differences in the level of the treatment intervention (Cooper 1988). The levels should not be considerd as 'watertight compartments'; there is dynamic interaction between the levels, and intervention at one level will also affect other levels. The authors of this chapter firmly believe that sex counsellors and sex therapists should always be aware of, and take appropriate account of the psychodynamic level of the clients' functioning.

Towards an integrated approach

Although some of the 'schools' mentioned above are seen as purist, there are historical connections between them and none of them were developed in isolation. This leads naturally to consideration of the concept of developing an integrated approach to sex counselling and sex therapy which crosses the boundaries of the 'schools'.

To develop the clarity and confidence necessary for effective functioning whilst relatively inexperienced, it may be necessary to train in a specific school. However, with experience, the practitioner will (unless completely rigid and closed) begin to explore the potential of other approaches, recognizing that certain clients may require variations of what has been learned in the primary training. Almost inevitably, then, there is a move towards an integrated approach. Within the coherent philosophy which is reflected in the formation of the therapeutic alliance, the experienced practitioner will select appropriate techniques and interventions which match client needs. Thus, micro-level events reiterate the macro-level development and interweaving of ideas through the history of sex counselling and sex therapy. The individual practitioner's philosophy and practice of working will necessarily be dependent upon his or her beliefs about the nature of human life, human psychological functioning and the meaning of sex and sexuality.

It is therefore unlikely that a single method or therapeutic approach can be found which will give the best results with *all* clients. The very nature of the sex-counselling relationship inevitably means that the practitioner's personality (influenced by his or her own sexual and psychological history) will always determine what can be available for the client. The individuality of self and other must be accepted and not denied. This individuality is determined by the imagery of the inner world within which the person lives, and effective therapy can only be offered or received, if the *meanings* are congruent with that inner world.

Future developments

Physical diagnosis

The increasing range of investigative techniques (Bancroft 1989; Kaplan 1983) may now detect physical causes for cases which previously would have been labelled as 'psychogenic' – an unfortunate mis-labelling, since 'not proven' would have been more accurate and helpful.

Hormonal disturbances cause sexual dysfunctions comparatively rarely, but continuing advances in theory and in assay methods should improve diagnosis and treatment.

Selective arteriography provides useful evidence for the state of the penile blood-supply. There appears to be a considerable lag in developing comparable techniques for investigating genital blood-flow in women with disorders of arousal.

The direct injection into the penis of vasoactive erection-producing substances, such as papaverine and prostaglandins, has become one of the main treatments now used for male erectile dysfunction. This technique has diagnostic as well as therapeutic uses and many men presenting with erectile problems may have an intra-cavernosal injection (ICI) as part of the diagnostic procedure. It is, however, becoming increasingly clear that using such injections as treatment without taking due account of the potential emotional impact on both the man and his partner, or of the deeper significance of their problems for them, can lead to further difficulties within the relationship (Wagner and Kaplan 1993).

Future treatments

Male erectile dysfunctions continue to attract more effort and attention than other aspects – perhaps an unfortunate reflection on the undue emphasis our society places on the importance of a stiff penis, whilst continuing to ignore the equivalent female dysfunction known as Clitoral Erectile Disorder. No doubt expensive penile implants of increasing sophistication will continue to be developed and used owing to the persistent misconception that erection is essential for genital intercourse.

Outcomes

Outcome research shows that in addition to couples who are cured, there is a significant percentage whose dysfunction persists but who are no longer troubled by it because of their increased understanding and communication.

In the urgent quest for a cure, it may be overlooked that counselling is often concerned with the 'inner world' rather than the 'outer world' i.e. with the client's ability to integrate and manage that which cannot be cured or changed, whatever its origins.

Whilst the purist schools, particularly perhaps the behavioural, will continue to produce new treatment procedures such as the 'negotiated timetable for sexual intercourse', these should be assimilated and used within an integrated approach. Treatment can then be based more on the accurately perceived needs of the clients, than on the practitioner's need to adhere rigidly to a particular school.

In addition, as research continues to clarify the essence of effective therapeutic relationships, sex counselling and sex therapy may become more effective in *brief* interventions.

Preventative measures

The wide adoption of the following educative measures could lead to a significant reduction in the prevalence and severity of sexual dysfunctions, thus reducing treatment needs.

The cases presented show how ignorance and poor communicaiton exacerbate and sustain psychogenic sexual dysfunctions. A plea is therefore made for a threefold change:

(1) a programme of *sensual* education from an early age to familiarize individuals with their bodies, thus leading to a higher level of self-acceptance and positive body-image;
(2) a *sexual* education programme which ensures that individuals have a comfortable sexual vocabulary and adequate information about psychological factors in sexual functioning and dysfunctioning, as well as basic anatomy and physiology; and
(3) positive efforts to prevent the perpetuation of damaging cultural myths about both male and female sexuality through the media, particularly by the advertising industry.

AIDS and sex counselling

AIDS has become a fact of life that we now live with, and whilst, in this country, it has not become the epidemic that was once feared, we cannot ignore its impact on our lives. The campaign for 'safer sex', whether heterosexual or homosexual, underlines the need for programmes of *sensual* education. It now seems that, amongst those who perceive themselves as at risk, there is an awareness of the need to take account of 'high risk' behaviours, and to modify their sexual practices. (Wellings *et al.* 1994). The risks of HIV infection and AIDS are factors causing anxiety amongst clients in general as well as in sexual counselling.

However, there may also be some positive effects because the publicity has led to sex becoming an acceptable topic of conversation to an extent previously unknown in our society. If this increased openness can be sustained, it will lead to more available sexual information and increased ease of discussion for couples with sexual difficulties, thus reducing the likelihood of exacerbation and the need for sex counselling.

Conclusion

Whither sex counselling?

The last four decades have seen powerful changes in public attitudes to sex and sexuality. After emerging from an earlier restrictive period, there was a liberal movement through the 'swinging 60s' and the 'permissive 70s', but in the late 1980s and the 1990s there has been a resurgence of a restrictive sexual morality.

The 90s have been a time of conflict between liberalism and fundamentalism and sexual expression is one of the battlegrounds for this conflict, which has its impact on sex-education programmes. This direct interference by the state, through its legal system, also imposes on the private behaviours of individuals and groups, restrictions that are unprecedented in recent times, as seen in R vs Brown (the 'Spanner' case) (Thompson 1994).

From facets of the work discussed in this chapter, it can be seen that these changes are both reflected in, and affected by, sex counselling and therapy. It will be interesting to observe the movement during the next decade and to see if the interactions between current attitudes and sex counselling result in a changing balance between counselling and other treatment approaches to sexual dysfunctions.

Note

1 Stanley Vaginal Trainers are supplied by Downs Surgical, Parkway Close, Parkway Industrial Estate, Sheffield S9 4WJ. Other vaginal trainers now available include Amielle supplied by Owen Mumford, Brookhill, Woodstock, Oxford OX20 1TU.

References

American Psychiatric Association (1994) *Diagnostic and Statistical Manual of Mental Disorders (DSM IV)*, Washington: APA.

Bancroft, J. (1989) *Human Sexuality and its Problems*, 2nd edn, Edinburgh: Churchill Livingstone.

Bennun. I. (1985) 'Unilateral Marital Therapy' in Windy Dryden (ed.) *Marital Therapy in Britain, Vol 2: Special Areas*, London: Harper & Row.

Brown, P. and Faulder, C. (1979) *Treat Yourself to Sex – A Guide to Good Loving*, Harmondsworth: Penguin.

Cooper, G. F. (1988) 'The psychological methods of sex therapy' in M. Cole and W. Dryden (eds) *Sex Therapy in Britain*, Milton Keynes: Open University Press.

Dickson, A. (1985) *The Mirror Within: A New Look at Sexuality*, London: Quartet.

Docherty, J. (1986) *Growing Up*, London: Modus.

Fairburn, C. G., Dickerson, M. G. and Greenwood, J. (1983) *Sexual Problems and their Management*, Edinburgh: Churchill Livingstone.

Friday, N. (1975) *My Secret Garden – Women's Sexual Fantasies*, London: Virago.

Gillan, P. (1987) *Sex Therapy Manual*, Oxford: Blackwell Scientific Publications.

Hawton, K. (1985) *Sex Therapy – A Practical Guide*, Oxford: Oxford University Press.

Kaplan, H. S. (1974) *The New Sex Therapy*, New York: Brunner Mazel.

——(1979) *Disorders of Sexual Desire*, London: Baillière Tindall.

——(1983) *The Evaluation of Sexual Disorders*, New York: Brunner Mazel.

——(1987) *Sexual Aversion, Sexual Phobias, and Panic Disorder*, New York: Brunner Mazel.

Kitzinger, S. (1985) *Woman's Experience of Sex*, Harmondsworth, Penguin.

Kolodny, R. C., Masters, W. H. and Johnson, V. E. (1979) *Textbook of Sexual Medicine*, Boston: Little Brown and Co.

Lowndes Sevely, J. (1987) *Eve's Secrets*, London: Bloomsbury.

McConville, B. and Shearlaw, J. (1985) *The Slanguage of Sex*, London: Futura.

Masters, W. H. and Johnson, V. E. (1996) *Human Sexual Response*, Boston: Little, Brown and Co.

——(1970) *Human Sexual Inadequacy*, London: Churchill.

Read, J. (1995) *Counselling for Fertility Problems*, London: Sage.

Stanley, E. (1982) 'Vaginismus' in S. Lock (ed.) *Sex Problems in Practice*, London: British Medical Association.

Thompson, B. (1994) *Sadomasochism*, London: Cassell.

Wagner, G. and Kaplan, H. S. (1993) *The New Injection Treatment for Impotence*, New York: Brunner Mazel.

Ward, B. (1976) *Sex and Life*, London: Macdonald Educational.

Wellings, K., Field, J., Johnson, A. and Wadsworth, J. (1994) *Sexual Behaviour in Britain (A National Survey of Sexual Attitudes and Lifestyles)*, London: Penguin.

Worden, J. W. (1991) *Grief Counselling and Grief Therapy, A Handbook for the Mental Health Practitioner*, 2nd edn, London: Routledge.

Zilbergeld, B. (1995) *Men and Sex*, 2nd edn, London: Harper Collins.

Chapter twenty-four

Counselling people with disabilities/ chronic illnesses

Julia Segal

Introduction

There are more than one million people registered as disabled in Great Britain today. Some have physical disabilities, some intellectual, and some emotional. Some were born with disabling conditions; some developed them later in life. Some know approximately how their condition will affect them throughout life; others suffer great uncertainty.

Many people with disabilities or disabling chronic illnesses are not registered as disabled, either because they do not want the label or because they do not qualify.

Principles

I have spent twelve years counselling people with disabilities, using an approach influenced mainly by Kleinian psychoanalysts but also by people with disabilites themselves and by others working in the field before me. The following are some principles I find useful.

General Principle: People will make efforts to distance themselves from a disability or illness in many different ways. Recognizing these is important.

Principle 1: Use of language should reflect the fact that people with disabilities or illnesses are first and foremost people.

Current opinion maintains that if I lose my hand I have an *impairment*. If as a result I cannot write, I have a *disability*. If as a result I cannot get a job, I have a *handicap*. The concept of 'the handicapped' is challenged on the grounds that a handicap depends on society as much as the individual; for instance, being unable to read is no handicap in a non-literate society.

Our difficulties with the language reflect the fact that, however hard we try, it *is* difficult to really see both 'the person' and 'the disability' (or illness) until both have become familiar.

Feelings and assumptions reflected in the words 'the handicapped', 'spastics', 'epileptics', for example, are still powerful determinants of social and emotional reactions in counsellors and clients and their families.

It is particularly when, without consciously recognizing it, we equate 'being disabled' with our incompetent, weak, ugly, envious or otherwise 'bad' self that we are most at risk of attributing these characteristics to a disabled person, whether this disabled person is ourselves, our clients or a member of our family.

Before working with people who are ill or disabled it is essential for counsellors to talk through their own fantasies around disabilities and illnesses. Sorting out what is your own fantasy, belief, assumption, experience or reaction, and what is or might be different for someone else cannot be done in isolation.

Principle 2: A disability, chronic illness or handicap affects whole families and social networks, not just the individual.

It can be very hard having a disability or illness; it can also be very hard living with or loving someone who has one. Many of the feelings and the losses involved are shared, though they affect each person differently. Part of the work in counselling may involve helping people to deal with the guilt, sorrow, anger, resentment and frustration of this. Many people, (adults and children) hate being dependent; they may also have difficulties with the fact that other people's comfort depends on their health and physical capacities. In particular it can be very painful knowing that children's lives are affected by what happens to their mother or father.

Principle 3: The meaning of the disability is as important as the disability itself.

It is useful to consider two aspects of the meaning of a disability or chronic illness: the practical and the emotional. Getting up and going to bed may take two or three hours because of a disability. Going to the shops may have to be organized weeks in advance and may break down because someone fails to arrive. Getting an alteration to the house paid for by some authority can take many months. All of this can give rise to perfectly understandable feelings which need to be acknowledged when counselling someone with a disability or their partner.

Of equal importance are questions such as 'Can anyone love me when I'm like this?', 'What have I done to deserve this?', 'Would the family be better off if I/they were dead?'. Sometimes discussion of practicalities can be a way of testing whether the counsellor can face these more disturbing issues. In counselling, people with disabilities and their families can examine and sometimes change the emotional meaning of a condition. Changing this may affect lives significantly even where the condition itself is unaltered. Some disabilities are in fact caused by the *reaction* to an impairment or illness.

For years Alice refused to go out because she did not want people to see her ungainly walk.

A man who suffered from painful spasms took care not to use his left arm for fear of precipitating a spasm by touch. He had not had a spasm for a long time. A physiotherapist was able to show him that his left arm had become considerably weaker than his right simply through disuse. When he began to strengthen this arm again his spasms did not return.

Valerie Sinason, in her pathbreaking book *Mental Handicap and the Human Condition* (1992) describes people who disabled their minds, becoming 'stupid' in order to defend themselves and others from knowledge and associated grief. The knowledge often concerned damage or a negative difference: such as brain damage at birth, the differences of Down's syndrome, or the damage of sexual abuse. In some patients, where 'stupidity' was exaggerated in this way, significant gains in IQ were made during psychoanalytical psychotherapy.

Principle 4: People with disabilities and handicaps should be offered counselling which is as near to 'normal' as possible.

Attempts to maintain normal rules of counselling (and of social behaviour) are important. One of the frustrations faced by people with disabilities is the difficulty in persuading others to treat them like anyone else. If the counsellor 'kindly' behaves in a different way with a disabled client, the client may feel the loss of the normal situation keenly. Most rules for counselling in any setting have developed for good reason; these reasons are likely to have just as much force for a client with a disability. Any deviation from the normal can usefully be discussed by a counsellor, preferably with their supervisor, but possibly with the client too. It may be necessary, but it may raise important issues within the relationship which should not be avoided.

Home visits are a particular case of this. A client who has the freedom to break appointments by not turning up is in a different situation from a client who can only refuse to open the door or arrange an interruption. Some people feel invaded when their condition seems to give others the right to intrude into their home and their body. The social status implications of being visited rather than visiting are also significant. Counselling at home is a skill in itself, requiring different techniques and different knowledge from counselling in a counselling room. Valerie Sinason discusses some of the issues involved in Chapter 4 of her book. Some occupational therapists and some older social workers are trained in these skills; most counsellors are not.

Principle 5: Confronting reality in a skilled way is an essential ingredient of counselling, whatever the problem involved.

People often seem to have difficulty sorting out what they have lost, what they have to give up, and what they may choose to keep if they pay a price.

> For twenty years a man refused to use a leg-bag for his urine in spite of his family's whole life being disrupted by the urgent need to get him to the toilet every hour. He was sure that his wife would stop being sexually attracted to him if he had one. In counselling he faced this and discovered it could not be true. The life of his whole family was subsequently changed.

People are sometimes afraid that their relationship would be damaged by acknowledging really upsetting fears or facts. They can also be afraid that their statements or questions would be self-fulfilling prophecies. This can apply to people with disabling conditions, to their families and to counsellors. Realities are often avoided because people are afraid of them; they feel that illusions are safer.

> 'I know he's being unrealistic but isn't it better to let him keep his illusions? What good would it do to face him with reality?'

Unfortunately, maintaining illusions takes a lot of energy. In fact, experience shows that denial and illusions are used as defences against fears which are far worse than reality. With the right person and in the right setting, facing up to fears and unpleasant beliefs, however painful, can be experienced as a relief. Sometimes it shows up frightening beliefs as unrealistic. At worst, it leads to sharing and acknowledgement of real cause for grief or mental pain.

> A young man with serious difficulty in social relationships and some physical disabilities kept insisting that his father was far less competent than he was. He changed considerably after work following on from the counsellor (against her own resistance) pointing out how much it must hurt him that his father had been able to have a wife and son, whereas he could not.

Counsellors as well as others can be caught by the assumption that illness, a distorted body, a difficulty speaking, or a slowness of intellectual grasp must all be accompanied by a lack of emotional strength. Work presented at an informal workshop at the Tavistock Clinic in London, run by Valerie Sinason and Jon Stokes, has repeatedly demonstrated that insight and understanding as well as the ability to experience grief, depression, or any other emotion in a realistic way – and to hide them – can be evident in people who are extremely impaired, both mentally and physically.

Perceiving others' disabilities is always in some way painful. Socially it is normal to cover up the discomfort rather than discuss it or the disability. This means that this area is generally left to fantasy and illusion for both parties. In counselling the rules are different and pretence is not an option. It can still be difficult for a counsellor or caring professional not to block the direct expression and sharing of painful beliefs connected with the condition, for example, by some spoken or unspoken encouragement to 'be positive'.

Issues

Professional health workers and counsellors can benefit from discussion of the issues which affect their clients, some of which I describe below. Preparation for facing such issues (particularly the 'tricky' ones, such as death, suicide, sex, and family violence) can make the difference between a counsellor who can 'contain' fears and anxieties, and a counsellor who by their behaviour confirms to the client that certain fears or anxieties are quite unthinkable.

These issues affect not only the client but also their families. Any issue which is of importance to a person with a handicap or illness or disability must affect their family, and vice versa. Other people's reactions, cares and fears affect all those around them and may need to be understood in counselling.

Grief

Grief arises with the *giving up* of some past reality, which may include ordinary hopes and expectations for the future. The development of new ways of thinking, behaving, and living cannot take place without grief for the old. The pain involved should not be underestimated. It often gives rise to anger. Sometimes this anger is not expressed directly but is evoked in someone else who responds either angrily or with rejection. People are often angry at having to feel a loss.

Growing older with a disability (particularly your own, your child's, or your parent's) gives rise continually to a new set of losses appropriate to the age and life stage. Each of these must be somehow acknowledged and incorporated into the automatic assumptions made by the individual and those around. The pain that accompanies each new awareness of a loss caused by the disability may be avoided at times; long-term avoidance causes social and emotional difficulties.

The ability of a counsellor to bear grief with a client without minimizing it, exaggerating it or denying it may be of enormous value. It seems that grief which is expressed can be better tested against reality and may be more easily worked through. Other opportunities for this may not be available to the client.

Grieving for real losses (such as the loss of a leg), may enable people to discover what they can salvage (such as the ability to socialize without playing tennis). Grieving in company may reduce the feeling of being alone and abandoned which often arises with any loss.

Earlier losses are evoked by new ones and may give rise to grief which seems unrealistic in the new context. (A common example of this is when the death of, say, a pet releases grief for a parent who died maybe years earlier.) Grief for the losses caused by a disability may be disentangled from grief for losses which have nothing to do with disability, yet which are themselves in some way crippling.

A woman came for counselling about her multiple sclerosis and spent her sessions grieving for the loss of three babies by miscarriage and abortion (unrelated in fact though not in fantasy to the multiple sclerosis), and talking about an incident when as a teenager she was sexually assaulted. Her relationships with her daughters and her husband improved, in particular in connection with the family's handling of her disabilities.

How each member of the family deals with their grief affects the others. The grief of losing one's own faculties and the grief of the watching partner are closely connected. The grief of being born deformed or imperfect is connected powerfully with the grief this brings to the mother. A mother's difficulty grieving about her child's physical impairment may cause the child as many problems as the condition itself, but it is very hard for a mother to find the space, time, and help to grieve for her lost imaginary 'normal' baby or child.

'Accepting the illness/disability'

This is a phrase often used, particularly by family members and professionals. Sometimes it seems to be used as an unrealistic accusation: 'I want you to help him to accept that he is really useless, that he can't do anything'. Sometimes it seems to be used more realistically, though impatiently: 'She hasn't accepted it; she won't use the wheelchair.'

Acceptance is clearly bound up with recognizing reality and grieving for what has to be given up. It seems to take in general about two years to accept any significant loss in the sense that nearly all the automatic assumptions made about the world will include the loss rather than deny it. This means that people with progressive illnesses or disabilities are often mentally about two years out of date in terms of their physical situation. Awareness of this can help people who would otherwise think that grieving was going to last for ever.

Exploring what 'accepting it' or 'fighting it' means to the people concerned is often valuable.

A young man felt that if he accepted that he had multiple sclerosis it would mean he would lose his only chance of getting rid of it, which was to bargain: 'If I don't ask too much, and don't accept it, I will be given back the use of my legs'. Once he realized this was how he thought, he could not maintain it.

Making sense of the situation

People often feel the unfairness of their fate. It is as if we all expect certain things: a reasonable lifetime of good health; work to be followed by retirement; that our children will outlast us. When these things do not happen, we feel something has gone wrong.

The need to make sense of the situation can throw people back on to very primitive beliefs, often superstitions (for instance, God is punishing us so we must suffer). These beliefs can sometimes be more disabling than the condition itself.

A young woman who was physically scarcely affected at all, felt that because she had multiple sclerosis she ought not to look for a husband; she should dress badly and stop going to parties in case someone was attracted to her.

I discuss the meaning people give to their condition in more detail in Segal (1991a).

'Being bad'

When people think of how they would feel if they were disabled, they probably think of their 'bad' self, angry, accusatory, guilty, or envious, represented by the multiple pejorative meanings of 'sick', 'bad', 'ill', or 'mad' rather than a more rounded and human self.

This can also be applied to the future self.

A woman in her twenties, diagnosed with multiple sclerosis twelve months previously, said she had suddenly 'seen' horrible fungus growing out of a filing cabinet at work. 'That's me,' she said. 'That's how I think of myself, full of fungus, vile, really yukky inside.'

Applied to others it may produce patronizing, over-protective or placatory behaviour as the self is idealized by attributing its own badness or incompetence to someone 'more unfortunate' who is not allowed truly 'good' characteristics.

Parents with handicapped children often unconsciously believe that the child is the result of 'bad' sex, or a consequence of their own inner badness. This can affect their treatment of the child.

People sometimes talk of 'wishing' their condition on to someone else.

This can make them feel wicked and bad. Mothers can also feel they are bad if they do *not* wish their children's disabilities or illnesses on to themselves.

The desire to make people better

This is terribly important to explore with family and friends. It can also help to discuss their frustrations with the person who has an incurable illness or disability themselves. Sometimes the people who are closest are the least able to show their concern, if they feel too guilty for not being able to make the person better. It can. for instance cause a husband to withdraw or attack whenever his wife tries to tell him she feels ill or in pain, but it can occur in any close relationship. Understanding when and why this is happening can uncover buried love between the people concerned.

Sometimes those around try to take control of the condition (illness/ disability) by controlling the person who has it, partly out of misguided attempts to *make* them get better. Children have their own ways of trying to make an ill or disabled parent better; when these fail they may despair and behave badly or withdraw into themselves (Segal and Simkins 1996).

Severely disabled or chronically ill children can also have strong desires to make their parents better, including making them happy when they are sad. Where their own condition brings grief to their parents, this can cause the child enormous distress which he/she may cover up in order to protect his/her parents.

Dying

Disabilities and chronic illnesses often face people with anxieties about dying. Parents worry about what will happen to their disabled children; people with a present or potential disability worry about being a burden or being abandoned. People have very mixed feelings about wanting to be dead themselves or wanting a member of the family to die, especially if severe pain is involved. Children are particularly prone to worries about losing either or both parents if one is ill, even if 'everyone' knows it is not a terminal illness. One parent dying can arouse serious anxieties about the other dying (Segal and Simkins 1996).

Since it is seldom a topic of social conversation, ideas about death and dying are often quite unrealisic. They may include the fear that if you talk about death, it will happen, or you will be wishing the person dead. Often these ideas seem to have been formed in childhood and not to have changed much since.

Sharing thoughts about dying and death often seems to help, particularly where they have not been clearly articulated. Realistic ideas about how, when, and where death is likely to happen may then replace more terrifying ones.

A bright, busy woman in her thirties 'never thought about dying', although she smoked thirty cigarettes a day and had a progressively disabling disease. On being pressed to think about it, she imagined herself in a large public ward. Asked where her husband would be, she was surprised to realize he was not there in the picture. She then described a quite different place she knew, where she felt she would be able to die with dignity and with her husband close by. At the end of five sessions of counselling she no longer had to keep doing things all the time and said she was much more relaxed. She also gave up smoking.

Counsellors and other health professionals who have never discussed their own feelings about death and dying may be unable to hear or to respond when clients or patients raise these issues or hint that they worry about them.

Suicide

People who hint or mention that they have considered suicide often find it a relief to speak of it openly. The desire to be rid of pain and the problems of life may need to be acknowledged, and the frustration and anger which may accompany the decision not to hurt the family and friends in this way.

It can be useful to look at hidden aggressiveness behind suicidal wishes; the question of who would suffer is often important. People who initially say simply that they want to relieve their family of a burden may on further discussion express their anger with these carers and their failings, and a desire to punish them and make them suffer: 'I'll kill myself and then they'll be sorry'. Uncovering the mixed feelings involved can be helpful.

Again, counsellors need to have discussed these issues *before* they arise in counselling.

Loss of role

There is a common idea that one should be relieved of other troubles and duties when ill and, by extension, when disabled. This however lays the basis for excluding disabled people from ordinary social roles, and can be examined and challenged.

A particular case of this involves the assumption that the sick or disabled person should not be worried or made angry. This can have the effect of seriously weakening their ability to take on normal roles such as that of parent, spouse or adult son or daughter.

An eight-year-old girl said she had not told her mother she had been homesick when she stayed at her friends' house for the night, because her grandmother had said she should not worry Mummy. Before her mother was ill (with multiple sclerosis) she had always told her things like that.

Not only the family but also the person with the disability or chronic illness themselves may encourage this behaviour.

A disabled mother spoke of herself as one of the children and persuaded several social workers to do so too.

The behaviour of the medical profession

This is an issue which often arises in counselling. Disappointment, resentment, and unrealistic expectations mingle with experience of unthinking or defensive behaviour or mistakes on the part of doctors. Both the reality and the exaggeration, and the guilt and upset they can arouse in the patient, may need to be understood and acknowledged. People often feel guilty if they catch someone else in the wrong, and they often desperately want to keep the doctor as a good, helpful figure who can do no wrong.

Counsellors may need to 'practise' their own neutrality in such situations, where they have to acknowledge the reality and the feelings involved, without being drawn into taking sides.

Social stigma

For many people their or their children's disabilities mean some kind of social stigma. People can and do make life difficult for those with disabilities. They can be positively unpleasant, patronizing, over-protective, unhelpful, and thoughtless.

The feelings aroused by such behaviour may need to be acknowledged. There is often a furious indignation and resentment:

'I have to cope with the illness/disabilities; why should I have to cope with other people's inability to handle it too?'

An assumption that somehow you have paid your debt to society if you or your child have a disability, and that everything else should be made easy, often gives rise to wry laughter when discovered, owned, and clarified.

There is a serious problem where the disability or illness arouses great anxieties in those around. The film *The Elephant Man* graphically illustrates the horrified and horrifying reactions of people viewing a severely disfigured face for the first time. Revulsion and disgust – and fascination too – may flicker across the most well-disciplined face in such circumstances. It is painful to empathize with someone who has to endure this with every new person they meet.

As with any kind of counselling, if a client is complaining about the attitude of 'society' or someone close to them it can be useful to ask '. . .

and is there a part of you that agrees with them?' The power to do something about it may be regained, or the grief for a real loss may be owned, without denying that the attitude of others may be a real problem. This can help to combat the temptation to see 'the disabled' as poor, helpless victims who bear no responsibility for the way they are treated.

> One woman felt that she could not talk to friends about her multiple sclerosis because everyone pitied the disabled. When asked about her own attitudes she said that she had had a boss who was in a wheelchair. It appeared that what she actually felt towards her boss was a mixture of envy and resentment: why should *a disabled woman* have a husband, children and a prestigious, well-paid job when she herself had none of them? After one session of counselling she was able to tell friends about her multiple sclerosis and it then took up less of her attention.

Control, dependence, and independence

Control of your own life often becomes more restricted if you have a disability or if you care for someone with one. This can be for practical reasons: it may be difficult to get up at a time you choose if you live in a residential institution or depend on someone else's help, or if someone else depends on you. Unrealistic assumptions can also be involved.

> A woman said she was afraid that if she went into a wheelchair it would be awful for her husband. Asked in what way precisely, she said, 'Well, you know, the *responsibility*.' The counsellor said it sounded as if she felt that the loss of her legs would mean she abdicated all responsibility for herself; she looked astonished, and then laughed.

Reactions to constraints on independence vary with individuals. Some people cannot imagine being happy without a caring and cared-for partner; others cannot imagine being happy without the option of living alone.

Reactions are also affected by the sensitivity of those in control. People pushing wheelchairs can do so making it clear that they are in the service of the person in the chair, or they can simply treat the occupant as if they were part of the chair itself, with no mind or opinion to be consulted. People being pushed too can treat the pusher with consideration or rudeness.

Fears of losing control of one's life often depend on unrealistic beliefs about how much life can ever be under control, and about how much independence of others is ever possible or desirable. Experiences of being unable to control nurses or other helpers – when needing bedpans or being fed, for example – also colour attitudes to dependence.

For some people being dependent means reverting to childhood; their experiences as children will affect how they feel about this.

> A disabled farmer refused to go out on his scooter since he had fallen off and been unable to get up. He was not found for several hours, but it was not this that worried him, he said. He could not bear to have to tell his wife where he went in the future; this to him meant being a child again, and he preferred to stay at home.

Counselling can sometimes help people discover a new concept of 'dependent mature adult', where previously they only recognized 'dependent child' and 'independent adult'. The dependence of others on the disabled person, for love and comfort, for example, may also be newly recognized and valued through counselling.

Some people fear that others will not love them if they do not keep control; loss of control then means loss of being loved and may be very frightening indeed. Unfortunately, people who are put in a position of power by someone else's disability may use it in ways which are not to the benefit of the person on the receiving end, either from ignorance or malice, or as a result of conflicting demands.

It is hard to make decisions on someone else's behalf. Often people seem to feel they must 'play safe' by keeping control, in spite of the fact that this control may disable. A child who is never given any responsibility does not grow up normally; but giving responsibility to a very disabled child may be extremely difficult.

> A woman on a ward for the terminally ill was told by the nurses she should not smoke. She asked a passer-by to get her a cigarette. The nurses felt this was manipulative behaviour. It had not occurred to them that she could be allowed to decide whether to end her life smoking or not.

Sometimes unreasonable attempts to control others can be ways of trying to get rid of feelings of powerlessness. These feelings can be brought about by a body which will not obey or by a social situation. Where someone feels they have no rights and respect themselves, they may treat others as if they have no rights and respect due to them. This can clearly apply both to people with disabilities and to those who care for them professionally or voluntarily.

Sex

The attitude that sex is inappropriate for 'the disabled' may still be detected in the general public, including people with disabilities themselves. There are many situations connected with disability where sex needs to be considered. Here I mention only a few.

(a) Teenage anxieties about sex (and aggression) may not be modified by normal private interactions with other teenagers if impairment brings too much adult supervision.

(b) Physically and mentally impaired children are particularly vulnerable to sexual abuse and incest. Adults who were sexually assaulted as children may blame the assault for later illnesses or disabilities in themselves or their children.

(c) Not everyone finds disabled or impaired or weak bodies unattractive: sexual attraction may be unaffected or increased by disabilities. People sometimes find this surprising or even shameful. People with severe disabilities do fall in love and do marry.

(d) People often find that they cannot combine the roles of sexual partner and nurse/carer. They may have to take this into account when deciding whether or not to allow someone else to take care of their partner's bodily needs.

Relationship difficulties connected with disabilities

I have grouped these into a separate section because there are particular issues which affect relationships between people with disabilities and others. The counselling relationship as well as other professional and non-professional relationships may be confused by them.

Those who have little experience of others' disabilities are often afraid: 'I won't know how to behave; I'll say the wrong thing; I'll make a fool of myself.' It can be difficult to know how to behave when first meeting someone with a gross deformity or odd social behaviour.

'Normal' social rules may also not apply easily, and it can be difficult to know what new rules to use in their place. It can seem rude to sit and watch someone struggling to put on their coat rather than helping them; deciding when and how to offer help and when to assume that the person can do what they are doing in their own time can be difficult. The individual concerned may have their own strong beliefs about when and how help should and should not be offered, and these may not be easily guessed.

Experience helps; so too can discussing the difficulty straightforwardly with the person concerned. They have probably been in the situation before, and in the right setting they may value insight into someone else's reactions to their condition. Local disability groups sometimes offer 'consciousness-raising' workshops.

Relationships can often be distorted in particular ways as a result of assumptions made about 'the disabled'.

Assumption 1: You have to be kind to the disabled and think nicely about them; they've got enough to put up with as it is.

> A psychologist rang to discuss counselling a woman who had multiple sclerosis. She said she felt so sorry for her. I asked if there was something in the client which gave rise to this feeling, or did it come from the psychologist herself? There was an embarrassed silence and the psychologist then said that actually the woman made her extremely irritated, but she felt she shouldn't feel like that about someone with an illness like multiple sclerosis.

The feeling that one should not experience irritation with 'the poor dears' can be a serious barrier both to real work (for professionals) and to close relationships (in the family and socially), and can maintain unnecessarily asocial behaviour.

> A deaf boy was being nasty to a small girl. His mother told him off. The girl's mother said, 'Oh, you can understand how he feels,' – meaning, don't be so hard on him, he's deaf. The boy's mother disagreed, saying he had to learn he could not treat other children like that or he would never have any friends.

Assumption 2: No-one can understand what it is like to have a disability unless they are disabled too.

People with similar disabilities can often help each other considerably in many ways, but they may not understand each other any more than any two people taken at random would understand each other. The problem is that no two disabilities are the same since the people who have them are different.

The effort, character, and skills people need to try to understand someone with a disability may be no different from those needed to understand anyone else whose outlook and situation differs from their own.

Assumption 3: It is not fair to be happy and satisfied yourself when others are disabled and suffering.'

> A counsellor working with disabled people said that at first she felt guilty about enjoying her work; it did not seem fair that she had the work satisfaction and they had the disabilities.

> A mother said she felt guilty every time she enjoyed the sun; how could she be happy when her son had multiple sclerosis?

These feelings have to be tolerated. Life and living are always at risk from envy. It can help to recognize that disabilities do not take away all pleasure and happiness, and that others' success or good fortune in life may always be potentially a source both of pain and of enjoyment. Even if people's pleasures are limited by their disabilities, they may still have satisfactions the counsellor or their mother do not have. Not everyone reacts with envy and jealousy at seeing others happy; people can enjoy others' happiness and can obtain pleasure from participating in a different way.

A blind woman enjoyed going to the cinema.

A man who used to go fell walking with his wife enjoyed hearing her describe walks she took without him.

A woman thought her newly disabled husband would be unhappy seeing his children playing on the beach as he would get upset that he could not now join in. He said he did want to watch them, and he liked seeing them enjoying themselves.

Future developments

There have been many changes in attitudes to disability in recent years, often brought about by the efforts of people with disabilities themselves. In journals for counsellors and psychoanalytical psychotherapists articles about work with physical illness and disability have appeared regularly in the literature over the last five years; work with people who are HIV postitive has contributed to this but not overwhelmingly.

I hope and expect to see a continual development and refinement of such work as counsellors in particular increase their exposure to working with people who are diagnosed with a physical illness or have a disability.

Both the demand for counselling and the attitudes of counsellors have also been changing as a result of general changes within society. People with disabilities are less likely to be seen as objects of pity or charity and more likely to be seen as active participants in society. One effect of this has been considerable effort within the British Association for Counselling towards making the training of counsellors as well as provision for coun-selling accessible for people with physical disabilities.

Availability of counselling

Counselling is slowly becoming recognized in this country as a practical and useful way of helping people to live better with their own or others' disabilities; however, there is still too often an assumption that anyone can offer counselling, and that it can be fitted in by social workers, teachers, psychologists, doctors or anyone else, whether or not they have the time, training, supervisory support, personality or inclination. Training in work-ing with people with disabilities is not included on all counselling courses, or is only cursory. The counselling world has not yet decided if this is a job for specialists or whether any counsellor should be able to do it (Segal 1995). At present there are very few specialists.

An important development has been the employment of counsellors in general practice surgeries where they are in a position to pick up people as they are diagnosed with disabling conditions. However, at a conference I attended in 1990 for counsellors in general practices, I was told that people with disabling conditions or life-threatening illnesses were *not* commonly referred for counselling. More recently (1995) a GP expressed doubt as to whether 'his' counsellor could be expected to work with a severely disabled man who was actively seeking counselling.

At present few counsellors are employed by hospitals; however, the new pressures on the National Health Service are in some places leading to innovation. At the Central Middlesex Hospital Trust in London the model of an MS unit for people with multiple sclerosis, providing multidisciplinary services including specialist, professional counselling, has been taken over from a self-help charity. Health authorities in other regions are considering following this model. This clinic also has a consultant in rehabilitation; such posts are almost as rare as counsellors in the field, but where they do exist the expertise provided should considerably improve the treatment of people with disabilities.

With the increase in self-confidence of those with disabilities, many self-help groups have developed. These offer practical help to those who are prepared to accept the necessary label, and also to those who wish to learn about and perhaps change their own attitudes. Often such groups offer helplines which provide information and perhaps some kind of basic listening. Sometimes the people on the helpline are trained; in other cases they are not. Some of these organizations offer counselling or put callers in touch with professional counsellors with relevant knowledge, skill, and interest. Most will provide relevant information to professionals with a client who has a particular disability.

Change in attitudes to disability

As disabled people gradually become more visible (via 'Equal Opportunity' employers, for example) and integrated into schools, disabilities become less unfamiliar and frightening. This is already influencing opinions and behaviour. So too are books written by people with disabilities, particularly those with an autobiographical component. Counsellors will be affected by these changes just as others are.

Counsellors' own attitudes and assumptions

Most counsellors wanting to work with people with disabilities will have to make some efforts to modify their expectations towards people who are overtly disabled or chronically sick. They may have to learn how to avoid patronizing or 'taking-over' approaches. They may have to work to uncover hidden prejudices in themselves, just as is necessary with racism and sexism. This applies whether they have an obvious disability themselves or not.

Within the general population, assumptions about the kinds of allowances which have to be made, and which should or need not be made are at present in a state of flux. Counsellors are in a position to influence the development and direction of such attitude changes by their willingness to look carefully at attitudes and beliefs with clients and to challenge assumptions. To do this best they need considerable awareness of their own attitudes and assumptions.

Discussion with colleagues and personal therapy for counsellors are both in my opinion essential for future developments in counselling in general. They are particularly important when counselling this particular client group. The ability to grieve with clients depends upon the counsellor's own experience of sharing grief and of being understood by somebody else. The experiences of being dependent on somebody else, of being offered something you do not have yourself, and of coping with the mixed feelings this engenders, are all experiences common to people with disabilities and people in therapy themselves. Counsellors who avoid this dependency relationship with a therapist cannot fully understand the difficulties their clients face. The counsellor's own mental and emotional disabilities need to be uncovered and worked with in a therapeutic context if clients are not to be used to cover up the counsellor's own difficulties.

One of the problems of being disabled is that you may become the butt of other people's projections: you may come to stand for parts of themselves which are disabled and perhaps pitied, despised or rejected. Counsellors need to work on their own mental state in order to do their best to avoid adding to the problems of their clients. I would like to see increasing recognition of this amongst all counsellors; I think it is particularly vital when working with people whose circumstances make them especially likely targets for emotional exploitation. People who have been ill-treated as children are also in my experience particularly vulnerable to arousing the counsellor's worst side; and where people with chronic illnesses or physical disabilities have also suffered violence as a child, the counsellor is likely to need considerable help.

Demand for counselling

New assumptions about the abilities of people with disabilities can create new pressures. For some, these pressures will be unwelcome and they will want to be left alone to do things their own way. For others there may be the thought that if they are not living to the full then they could ask for help or they could be offered it. Like anyone else, people with disabilities and those who live with them can sometimes feel extremely insulted at the idea that they might 'need' counselling, particularly if they see it as yet another way of distinguishing them from the rest of the population, imagined somehow not to 'need' counselling. Others have more of an idea that people can help each other handle difficult situations rather than simply mock their inabilities. For these, counselling may be seen as a possible aid to real self-determination.

Where people have chronic illnesses which lead to physical or mental deterioration there is an increased sense that people *should* be offered some kind of help with dealing with the emotions aroused. Beginning with AIDS and cancer, it is slowly becoming accepted that people with certain conditions should be offered counselling, not only for themselves but also for their families.

Demand for staff- or group-counselling

Although far more people with disabilities are now expected to live 'in the community' there are still many situations where people with disabilities gather together under the care of professionals, who may or may not be well-qualified and caring. Even where people are able to live at home supported by carers they may meet up in a day centre. Clients and staff involved at home, in a day centre, or any kind of residential setting have to negotiate their relationship. There have been recent changes, particularly in the climate of opinion, which affect the balance of power, but there are many issues which remain difficult to manage.

Once people are not patronized they may be treated with more dignity, but the same allowances may not be made for them. How much politeness and consideration is demanded and given by either party may be a tricky issue. So too may questions of sexuality and aggression. What does it mean to be 'understanding'?

What kinds of behaviour are to be tolerated and what can be rejected? Balancing the rights of the individual and the group, the 'cared for' and the 'carer', in a day centre, a nursing home or any kind of group living situation (including a family), is far from easy. Do staff or parents have the right to say 'I do not like to see this happening'? Do they have the right to enforce their likes and dislikes? Who has the power in fact: the helper or the helped, or how is it divided between the two? These issues are discussed in Segal (1991b).

Staff in some institutions are discovering the value of staff support groups. Consultants are sometimes brought in to help such groups look at their own feelings and behaviour and to find new ways of working which incorporate an increased respect for the client. Obholzer and Roberts (1994) describe such work, for example, in a school for physically handicapped children and in a ward for the elderly.

Need for counselling

The need for counselling for people with disabilities is considerable. It is difficult facing a disability, whether preventable or unpreventable; brought on by a chronic illness or by a traumatic event such as an accident; at birth or later on; in the self or in someone close. The way people face disabilities or try to avoid facing them affects the treatment expected and received by people who have them. Such treatment can range from extreme cruelty to considerable self-sacrifice with the whole gamut of normal human behaviours between. Counselling can help to reduce the cruelty and the damage, done to the self and to others, as a result of fears aroused by disabilities.

Conclusion

Counselling people with disabilities, their families, and professionals involved with them I personally find extremely rewarding. There is often much which can be achieved in a short time, simply because no one before has ever sat down with the people concerned and discussed openly and honestly the 'unspeakable' things they may have believed and feared. Even one or two counselling sessions can sometimes uncover and remove difficulties which have prevented normal social interaction from taking place. The changes brought about in people's feelings about themselves and their consequent behaviour can be dramatic. In the process, with good supervision, the counsellor too learns and changes – and perhaps prepares for his or her own future.

References

Segal, J. C. (1991a) 'Use of the concept of Unconscious Phantasy in understanding reactions to chronic illness', *Counselling* 2: 146–9. Also in S. Palmer, S. Dainow and P. Milner (eds) (1996) *Counselling: The BAC Counselling Reader*, London: Sage.

——(1991b) 'The Professional Perspective', S. Ramon (ed.) *Beyond Community Care: Normalisation and Integration Work* Part II, London: Macmillan Education.

——(1995) 'The Stresses of Working with Clients with Disabilities' in W. Dryden (ed.) *The Stresses of Counselling in Action*, London: Sage.

Segal, J. C. and Simkins, J. (1996) *Helping children with ill or disabled parents*, London: Jessica Kingsley.

Sinason, V. (1992) *Mental Handicap and the Human Condition: New Approaches from the Tavistock*, London: Free Association Books.

Obholzer, A. and Zagier Roberts, V. (1994) *The Unconscious at Work. Individual and Organisational Stress in the Human Services*, London and New York: Routledge.

Chapter twenty-five

Counselling people affected by HIV and AIDS

Bernard Ratigan

Introduction

Towards the end of the second decade of what we now understand as the Human-Immuno Deficiency Virus (HIV), the virus that can lead to the constellation of symptoms known as Acquired Immune Deficiency Syndrome (AIDS), there is still no clear evidence that a vaccine is even on the horizon despite all the basic scientific effort. Although survival rates continue to increase, most of those with the virus die prematurely, usually their life expectancy reduced by many decades. Many with the virus are young adults in their 20s, 30s and 40s who have grown up in a society where longevity is increasingly generally assumed and taken for granted. Death is not something that routinely happens to young people in our society unless it is by accident or self-harm. As a consequence of this, psychological, social, and spiritual interventions remain some of the most powerful ways of helping people with, and affected by, the virus. Because of the way the virus is often, but not always, acquired – through sexual contact or by intravenous drug use – it has, until now, attracted considerable social and moral interest if not opprobrium.

Those affected by HIV are a much greater number than those actually infected with the virus. HIV, as a bio-psycho-social phenomenon, penetrates social structures and personal existence. It cannot be ignored even though the early predictions by epidemiologists have not turned out to be as catastrophic as at first feared. The British experience needs contrasting with that of near neighbours in the European Union, like France, Italy and Spain, in which rates of infection are much higher. Some countries of Latin and South America, sub-Saharan Africa, the far East, North America and the countries of eastern Europe report incidence of HIV sero-positivity. HIV is a global phenomenon in that, at some level, it affects people everywhere yet some areas and some social groups are much more profoundly affected than others. For those who can afford it, the growth of mass and relatively cheap travel has also meant that international boundaries pose little or no problem for the spread of the virus. Large differentials in health care availability also means that those infected with the virus can sometimes be found a long way from home in the hunt for treatment or cure. Attitudes to health education programmes to warn people about HIV vary, often reflecting deeper cultural, legal, and religious attitudes towards sex and gender.

HIV has become *the* disease of the late twentieth century. In doing so it follows a catalogue of other physical illnesses and medical conditions which have, in the past, been seen in moral terms. Examples which spring to mind are leprosy, syphilis, tuberculosis, and cancer all of which in their turn have been seen as 'meaning' something about the moral status of those suffering them. Sontag (1989) has attempted to place HIV in this wider historical context, encouraging reflection on the deleterious impact of attributing meaning to a disease. Notwithstanding Sontag's analysis, HIV continues to have meaning attached to it and especially about the route of its acquisition. One of the tasks facing the HIV counsellor is to understand what, if any, meanings individuals attach to their condition. In work with families this can be an especially important, if painful, activity in that it is sometimes necessary to give voice to hitherto unvoiced feelings about the person who now has the virus and family attitudes towards her or him.

HIV is problematic because it links sex and death. Even with the many changes that have taken place in twentieth-century cultural and social attitudes, there remain areas of human existence which are mysterious, frightening, and the subject of powerful taboos. The social anthropologist, Mary Douglas, has explored some of the roots of notions such as contamination, pollution, dirt, and danger (Douglas 1966). The counsellor will often be aware that even with seemingly sophisticated clients, there can be unconscious layers of fear and dread which defy rational, cognitive, or reassuring interventions. Once counselling begins these unconscious fears may need to surface before a psychologically healthier equilibrium is achieved.

The existing literature on HIV counselling has reflected dominant models of practice derived from cognitive-behavioural, systemic, and humanistic paradigms. There is currently little agreement in the field about what psychological therapies are appropriate, for what clients, at what stage in their HIV careers. In this, HIV counselling is little different from other forms of counselling and psychotherapy at the moment. What is prescribed for clients is usually what is available rather than the result of a careful and detailed assessment of the clients' psychological functioning and needs.

There is currently a gap in the HIV counselling literature in that there is not a text that surveys, let alone evaluates, the range of psychological interventions. From the United States, amongst a field dominated by cognitive-behavioural approaches, there are contributions from Winiarski (1991), Dansky (1994) and Zegans et al. (1994). Systemic work in the US is reported in Walker (1991) and in Britain in Bor et al. (1992). Miller et al. (1986) is representative of British cognitive-behavioural interventions. A very thorough and evidence-based coverage can be found in Catalán *et al.* (1995). From the standpoint of Jungian analytical psychology Bosnak (1989) is notable. From psychoanalysis, Molnos (1990) has considered the role of group analysis, Burgner (1994) and Grosz (1993) have written about individual analytic psychotherapy and psychoanalysis proper as, more controversially, have Hildebrand (1992) and Limentani (1994). Odets (1995) has written magisterially on the impact of HIV on those who are affected but not infected.

Context

HIV counselling can occur at a number of points in the career of a person affected by HIV or AIDS. For the purposes of this chapter I will use HIV to include all stages of the infection from sero-conversion to death and I will include all forms of individual, couple, group, family, and systemic psychological interventions (including psychotherapy and psychoanalysis) under the rubric of counselling. In Britain, HIV counselling typically occurs in the following locations: departments of genito-urinary medicine (where the bulk of HIV testing occurs), in GP surgeries and other health facilities; in specialist HIV agencies staffed by both volunteer and paid counsellors; and, more generally, in other counselling and psychotherapy agencies.

Because of the relative infancy of counselling (and cognate disciplines) generally there are few, if any, objective, clear, and widely agreed principles to guide either the counsellor, referrer or would-be client. So it is in HIV counselling. There are dominant modes in the field such as cognitive-behavioural therapy and humanistic models as well as others which are less frequently encountered, especially those derived from psychoanalysis. It is unclear why some models are routinely thought appropriate. In general, it seems that cognitive-behavioural interventions are favoured in public-sector, and more humanistic models in voluntary-sector facilities. This chapter provides an overview of what is being practised in the field of HIV counselling and offers possible ways forward to bringing some rationality of service provision.

The last two decades of the twentieth century have seen in Britain a slight move away from a form of secular Calvinist ideology which declared, 'If you need a helping hand there are two at the ends of your arms!' A number of disasters occurred, leading to many deaths and injuries, which contributed to this sea-change but HIV has itself made a major contribution to a commonly held view that some form of counselling must be offered when any traumatic event happens either to an individual or a collection of people. This chapter has as a basic assumption that, logically, any psychological intervention that can help must also, in principle, be capable of doing harm. There is no such thing as an intervention that is benign and only does good. It has also to be said that some of what passes as 'counselling' in the area of HIV would hardly pass muster, certainly not be within a BAC definition of the activity. It can sometimes be of the most perfunctory kind and constitutes hardly more than giving sufficient information so that it can be claimed 'informed consent' has been given before an HIV test. Fortunately, it is now widely recognized that pre- and post-HIV test counselling, although sometimes extremely brief, is a skilled professional intervention and if done well can be of great benefit to the client. It can also act as an important screening mechanism for identifying where a client has pre-existing mental health or other problems, has an atypical adjustment reaction to a positive or negative test result, or is likely to have psycho-social problems during the course of the his or her HIV career (Perkins *et al.* 1993)

HIV counselling typically takes place at the following points:

- Before an HIV test is taken.
- Whilst, and after, an HIV result is given.
- Over adjustment reactions.
- During the pre-symptomatic phase.
- Once physical symptoms occur.
- Over relationship/family/disclosure/work issues.
- Over choices of physical treatment.
- At the onset of psychological, psychiatric, neurological symptoms.
- As an anticipation of, and coping with, terminal stage issues.
- As a preparation for death.

In addition, those affected by HIV may be involved in counselling because they

- are related to or in relationship with a person infected with HIV;
- are experiencing an adverse or atypical reaction to the death of someone from HIV;
- believe they have put themselves at risk of HIV infection;
- they fear they might put themselves at risk of HIV infection.

HIV is linked with homosexuality. Psychoanalysis and its derivatives have a big problem with homosexuality, being stuck in a position where it is seen as a perversion. Therefore there are considerable tensions. Denman (1993) has written acerbically of the prejudice surrounding homosexuality and has not spared the present author from her strictures (Ratigan 1991). This is not just an academic debate about the relationship between homosexuality and psychoanalysis. Many counsellors may claim that they have no interest in, or time for, psychoanalysis. This seems to fail to address important clinical issues about self-hatred, guilt and fear of discrimination, which are not infrequently brought up by clients. Psychoanalysis, like the major monotheistic religions of Judaism, Christianity, and Islam, has, at times, taken up negative positions with regard to homosexuality or same-sex relations. When clients are presenting material which indicates self-hatred, loathing, fear, and sometimes frank homophobia, they are expressing views already held in the wider community and can suffer much emotional pain as a consequence (Lima *et al.* 1993)

Principles

The first principle is that HIV is never just an individual problem. Because of the extreme societal, cultural, moral, and religious epiphenomena in which the virus is embedded, a diagnosis of HIV always has a larger context in which it must be understood. Because of the strong societal reactions to HIV, the work of the counsellor needs always to be even more respectful than usually of the need for confidentiality. Knowledge about a person's HIV status can have severe implications for areas such as housing, insurance, employment, and even medical treatment.

A further principle in undertaking HIV counselling is the need for adequate training and information. It is axiomatic that anyone undertaking this work is properly trained, supervised, supported, and working within a frame of professional and ethical practice. Because HIV can be such a problematic set of illnesses with powerful psychological, social, and moral dimensions, a secure counselling framework needs to be in place *before* the actual clinical work of the counsellor starts. It is almost as if the physical virus has a psychological equivalent which has the capacity to wreak considerable emotional damage both to clients and their familial networks as well as among voluntary and statutory workers (Ratigan 1991). There need to be clear boundaries, contracts, and responsibilities (Bond 1993).

HIV is a medical condition. Counsellors are, of course, concerned with the emotional life of their clients but it should be remembered that this is always in the context of a series of physical parameters. One of the distinguishing marks of those infected with HIV is, that to an extent not yet seen before, many in Britain have the opportunity to know more about their physical condition than people with other (non-HIV) illnesses. Knowledge about HIV and the various attempts to treat the way it presents is available perhaps more than many other conditions. Because of the history of HIV, knowledge about it has never been the preserve of the medical profession. There have been and continue to be great power struggles between AIDS activists and the medical/governmental establish-ments. In HIV counselling there is no such thing as a non-contentious 'fact' which is not the subject of debate, pain, and rage. Counsellors working in this area have a duty to both keep abreast of the burgeoning scientific, clinical, and political developments and to interpret the emotional reactions of their clients to these developments. It is not an easy task.

There are so many developments in the basic sciences underpinning HIV clinical research in such areas as pharmacology and neurology that a review chapter on counselling such as this is not the place to rehearse the current medical 'facts' about HIV. The reader is referred to the *National AIDS Manual* (1996).

People with HIV may develop neurological and/or psychiatric symptoms. The HIV counsellor needs to be aware of the growing literature in this field and develop the diagnostic skills which can lead to appropriate referral to medical colleagues. As physical treatment interventions become more effective, clients are living longer. This now means that, whereas in the past clients might have died relatively quickly, they are now more likely to develop cognitive and neurological problems as a result of the virus affecting their brain and central nervous system and psychiatric symptoms as a result of having the virus (Catalán *et al.* 1995; Selnes *et al.* 1995; Rosenberger *et al.* 1993; Williams, J.B.W. 1991; Fell *et al.*. 1993; Oechsner *et al.* 1993). Although there are considerable methodological problems in establishing the prevalence of suicide amongst people with HIV, it does appear likely that there is an increased risk (see Pugh *et al.* 1993 and Rabkin *et al.* 1993).

The psychodynamics of HIV

Thinking about HIV is not easy. Because it generates such powerful psychological reactions it has the capacity to make thinking rationally about it difficult. This can be seen both in the life of the individual client and in those attempting to help. There is often considerable mistrust and fear. The sources of these are not difficult to perceive in that they stem from social reactions to the moral status of those acquiring the virus. Hence there can be considerable public sympathy for 'innocent victims' such as babies and haemophiliacs but little for 'AIDS sufferers' who have acquired the virus through the pursuit of their assumed hedonistic (and sinful) 'lifestyle'. The psychological mechanisms of splitting and projection can be seen to be at work here. What is important to recognize is that these cosmic psychic battles can be, and often are, played out in the minds of people with HIV, in social groups involved in HIV work, and in the wider society. When a client says that, for her, HIV is a 'dirty secret' the counsellor is faced with a many-layered statement which will take considerable effort to understand. It can be very painful to work with clients who have become 'bad objects' to themselves. My understanding is that what is happening in circumstances like this is that earlier, usually child-hood, premorbid emotional, frequently traumatic, experiences in the life of the person meet the highly negative and stigmatizing projections held in the wider society. The intersection of these two vectors is in the mind of the client. The result can be catastrophic and lead to the development of extrapyramidal symptoms of depression, anxiety and possibly psychotic illness on top of the physical condition (Catalán 1995).

The defence mechanism of denial may be operative. Suspecting, or knowing, that a person has the virus can be kept out of mind; for example, where a client is terrified of telling his family that he has the virus or is living with someone who has it. People can go to extraordinary lengths to protect themselves and their families from what is perceived as dangerous knowledge. Bion, a psychoanalyst initially much influenced by Klein, has written about thinking and not thinking and attacks on thinking. Attacks on thinking can happen when the emotional risk of thinking something can be too great to carry (Ratigan 1995). What is also often clear is that whilst the individual can be busily not thinking, or repressing, painful material, others in the network who are being protected from the dangerous knowledge can often have more than an inkling of it anyway. Having to both come out as gay *and* as a person with HIV can be a very painful double process.

Skilled assessment can assist in evaluating the likely meanings and strengths of these defence mechanisms. What seems vital to stress is that ego defences, like all intrapsychic mechanisms are there for a purpose and have valuable functions. It can sometimes be tempting to meddle but in the context of HIV, where the stakes are very high for the individual, great caution should be exercised by the counsellor.

Issues

Training and counter-transference

This chapter has emphasized the distinctive nature of HIV counselling. It is an area in which there are often high anxiety levels, great fears, and where loss is a recurring and constant theme. In areas of high sero-prevalence, both clients and counsellors can be subjected to frequent, multiple losses. Because of the nature of the counselling process, it is inevitable that counsellors will be affected to what happens to their clients. Unlike professions such as medicine, with its long training and rituals to distance client and doctor, counsellors need to find different ways of being with those they try to help which allows for intimacy but also preserves some emotional distance. In the early years of HIV there was much talk of 'burn out' especially by those working in the voluntary sector. The chapter argues that effective counselling is best undertaken by someone who has completed, or is well on the way towards completing, a thorough training either in counselling, psychotherapy, or in counselling psychology. The training triad of theoretical instruction, well-supervised clinical practice, and the experience of personal therapy or counselling is necessary *before* beginning this demanding and stretching work. For those who are not used to working with the particular client groups often found in HIV work, such as gay men, drug users, women, children, people from very different cultural backgrounds, specialist supervision is essential.

Those selecting would-be counsellors for HIV work will also want to be aware of the need to screen out those who see this form of work as a way of 'saving souls' particularly those coming from fundamentalist religious backgrounds who, consciously or otherwise, see people with HIV as sinners in need of salvation.

A difficult question arises over the question of over-identification by the counsellor with the client population. A substantial number of those involved in HIV counselling are themselves gay and *ipso facto* affected by the virus in that it is the gay community which has, in this country, carried the brunt of its impact. A balance needs to be struck between the extra sensitivities given by sometimes a very close, indeed personal experience of having or being very closely affected by the virus, and the need to see the client as him- or her-self. A delicate path needs to be walked between solipsism – the notion that we cannot know another person's experience at all – and over-identification where merely because a counsellor knows about or has HIV they think they know about their client's inner world. Clearly this area needs continual surveillance in both training courses and in supervision. Following on from this there is the ever-present question of loss and multiple loss which, tragically, happens when working with people with late stage HIV. Supervision, support, and personal therapy are all indicated as essential for counsellors working with clients with HIV.

Service provision and levels of sero-positivity

Although absolute numbers of people in Britain identified as having the virus remain low when compared with, say, other EU countries, there are high concentrations in some cities. London, in particular, has a large number of gay men who are infected as well as nationals from other countries who, for a number of reasons both political and economic, have gone to live there. It is important to understand why, for example, so many gay men end up living in London. Britain remains a deeply homophobic society. Life for gay men and lesbians, especially for young people, in small towns and in rural areas can be particularly difficult. There has been for many centuries a thriving gay scene in London and it continues to attract people, as does the opportunity of living a life freer from effects of anti-gay prejudice. In terms of HIV, there has been a consequent concentrating together of large numbers of people with the virus. There are also numbers of people with HIV from other (mainly southern) European Union countries and from sub-Saharan Africa who have chosen or been forced to leave or flee their own countries and have come to the UK similarly seeking sanctuary, care, and treatment.

What unites all migrants, from wherever they have come, is that they have left a kinship network or family grouping which is not available to provide the support that might be expected of it in the face of a life-threatening illness. Because of the stigma that can be, and often is, attached to people with HIV they are often understandably wary of disclosing their HIV status to their families, fearing a hostile reaction. For gay men now in Britain there are psycho-social and counselling facilities which are at least in existence and usually gay affirmative. Others affected, for example women (often with children) living with the virus in non-metropolitan, especially rural localities, can experience multiple layers of isolation. Counsellors can find themselves working with women with the virus sometimes acquired from a partner who has himself had a secret life and partner(s). To the layers of isolation can be added multiple layers of loss: partner, children, and kinship and friendship networks (Cohen and Alfonso 1994). Service provision must recognize special needs.

What has happened in the large cities and towns of Britain during the last decade of HIV is the growth of numerous voluntary- and statutory-sector responses to HIV. There is currently imbalance between the high sero-prevalence areas which, although they can have a rich tapestry of counselling and psychosocial support facilities, are overwhelmed by the demand for services. This can contrast starkly with service provision in smaller communities which sometimes seems underused and may have consequent problems of motivating and retaining staff. Hard pressed, usually metropolitan, HIV counselling services have introduced maximum-contact parameters which have seen the development of focal and/or brief counselling modalities. A number of issues are raised by these new directions: for example, who decides, and on what assessment criteria, that any particular client is a suitable candidate for brief/focal interventions? Where do those not found suitable go for help? If clients are being referred out of the statutory and voluntary sectors what quality standards are in place to ensure adequate service delivery? A particular question arises over the issue of money. It is still usually the case that in the National Health Service and often in the voluntary sector counselling is provide free of charge to the user, but once the private sector is entered, who pays?

Religious and spiritual issues

In some ways HIV and religion are very closely linked. One of the reasons why HIV is such a problematic disease category is because the most frequent ways of acquiring it involve sex or drugs. Encounters between HIV and religious belief can be problematic and painful. HIV usually means taboos have been broken. The client can experience great conflict in his or her own mind between what were perhaps once strongly held moral beliefs emanating from religious faith and what they have come to believe is right for him or her as an individual. A commonly recognized example of this is the out gay man with HIV who can still experience considerable internal guilt at his lifestyle and feels a need to protect his family from his current living arrangements. The present writer encounters a number of gay men with HIV who are being referred for psychotherapy and who have come from strong religious backgrounds. Often these backgrounds are very condemning of any sexual expression save in marriage. Sometimes, such individuals have even gone to the extreme of actually getting married before the reality of the strength of their real sexual orientation was faced and they came out as gay. Gay but not unscarred. The scars can sometimes need considerable psychological attention when the body now has HIV in it.

If a deep split exists in a person between what they have been told they ought to be and the reality of what they are, a price will have to be paid. Is it possible that people with such deep fissures inside their mental apparatus can sometimes unconsciously be putting themselves at great risk? If people reject central aspects of their existence, such as their sexuality, hide it and only bring it out in secret and perhaps dangerous places and activities, it creates a potentially toxic cocktail. Many people with HIV feel themselves to have been deeply hurt and traumatized by their religious upbringing and by religion generally. Counsellors working with clients with HIV will serve them better if they themselves are able to allow religious material, however worded and coded, to be expressed and worked through.

The approach of death brings many questions that need the security of a safe counselling relationship. Counsellors working with people with HIV are in a privileged position to help to put into words often frightening and painful areas. Questions often arise which need revisiting: What will happen at the end? How will I die? Will I die alone? What will happen to me after I die? How will my partner/family cope? These universally important questions are both practical and spiritual. They can make all the difference between a death which is peaceful and one that is not (see also Chapter 22).

Prisoners

It is not known precisely what the incidence is of HIV in the current prison population in Britain. What is known for certain is that there are people in the prison system who have the virus. Some have tested sero-positive before they are incarcerated and others do so whilst they are serving their sentences. The problems that may be experienced by non-prisoners are often many times worse for prisoners. It is well known that it is very hard to keep secrets in any social situation and this is even more so in the penal context. Total institutions are really very leaky places, at least at the level of information.

Organizing counselling for HIV-infected and -affected prisoners is not easy. Prisoners have to identify themselves or be identified. As in any secure forensic setting issues of consent can be very fuzzy. Unlike in many other settings, the process by which a prisoner actually gets to see a counsellor is often problematic. Non-prisoners usually have the freedom to not attend sessions by simply not turning up. For a prisoner to do or not do this almost always leads to third parties being involved and usually wanting to know what is going on. Prisoners with HIV who need to talk about and therefore experience sometimes deeply buried emotions can be faced with leaving the counselling session upset, and having to return to their cells spending much of the day and night alone. Such prisoners can be experienced by staff as difficult to manage and counsellors find themselves drawn into discussions in which they are frequently invited to breach confidentiality. Counsellors can find themselves being blamed, consciously or otherwise, for 'upsetting' their prisoner–clients. Sometimes it also seems as if there is an organizational unconscious at work in penal (and other) institutions in which conspiracies exist to ensure that arrangements with regard to basic facilities such as room availability, the actual arrival of the prisoner, and not being interrupted can never be taken for granted. Prisoners, of course, get moved around the system to fit in with the needs of the system not the needs of the counsellor or client. As one prisoner with HIV, serving a life sentence for murder put it, 'I have a double life sentence. Will I get out before this thing kills me?' It is the experience of the present writer that many of those in prison for long sentences who also have HIV usually have had traumatized early lives, have often been physically and/or sexually abused, and quite often have long psychiatric histories (Allers *et al.* 1993). They pose a considerable challenge to any counsellor.

Counselling people with HIV in the prison system is a skilled and stressful activity and needs careful thought before it is begun. Again, careful assessment should precede it and specialist supervision should be in place alongside for it to have benefit for the client and not leave the situation worse than before. Some knowledge of the workings of the prison system and the responsibilities of the various professionals (especially medical, nursing, psychology, chaplains, probation officers as well as prison officers and governors) involved in caring for and managing prisoners is also necessary. Learning on the job whilst trying to undertake HIV counselling in prison settings is not recommended. To be effective it needs a thorough prior general training in counselling and ideally some orientation to the workings of the prison system.

Future developments

HIV in Britain has not become the dreaded epidemic that some in the 1980s feared it might. Because of a reasonably effective public health education programme and some other reasons the numbers infected have remained relatively small. However, for each person infected it is a major personal disaster and for some social groups, like gay men, it is nothing short of a collective catastrophe. Because of pressure from groups of gay men in the United States and in this country a change has occurred in medical practice – a move that could well do with spreading to other areas of the doctor–patient relationship.

HIV counselling has benefited from a growth in awareness of the need to have modes of practice which are sensitive to cultural, gender, ethnic, and sexual orientation differences.

In terms of the future of HIV counselling itself there are considerable developments to take place in the development of research and practice. Counselling itself is a very under-researched area and, being itself a new-comer, HIV counselling needs careful attention. Yet, although a newcomer, HIV counselling is a strong infant. It will continue to play a lead role in the total package of care and treatment that is offered to clients. Even when an effective vaccine is discovered, a benchmark for good practice has been established. Human beings are bio-psychosocial and spiritual entities: they are always more than a disease category or a diagnosis. HIV may be in many ways the prototypical disease of the twentieth century. The way HIV has involved individuals, social and community groups as well as profes-sional carers, now provides a model to take to other potentially or actually life-threatening conditions.

At a technical level, there is much work to do sharpening up counselling method. Psychoanalysis, the start of counselling, began about 100 years ago. We have moved some distance in that century but in many ways are still primitive in our theory and our methods. HIV has become the first modern disease to emerge since the development of the formal psycholo-gical therapies. Although part of the reason why HIV counselling has 'taken off' is because the scientists have not yet come up with an effective vaccine, it also needs to be emphasized that it is believed to be effective in helping clients. There is much work to be done in providing evidence for this assertion. Also, at the methodological level, there is room for much thought about which theoretical models work best for which clients. This work is for the future and may have to wait until the wider psychotherapy/counselling house goes some way to answering this question.

AFTERWORD

This chapter builds upon that by John Sketchley in the first edition of this *Handbook*. It is written from a different theoretical perspective by a psychoanalytic psychotherapist working in the National Health Service with people infected and affected by HIV. The chapter therefore picks out its own distinctive emphases. Nevertheless, the reader is referred to the original chapter (Sketchley 1989).

This chapter is dedicated to my many friends and patients who live with or have died from HIV related illnesses.

REFERENCES

Allers, C.T., Benjak, K.J., White, J. and Rousey, J.T. 91993) 'HIV vulnerability and the adult survivor of childhood sexual abuse', *Child Abuse and Neglect*, 17: 291–8.
Bond, T. (1993) *Standards and Ethics for Counselling in Action*, London: Sage.
Bor, R., Miller, R. and Goldman, E. (1992) *The Theory and Practice of HIV Counselling: A Systemic Approach*, London: Cassell.
Bosnak, R. (1989) *Dreaming with an AIDS Patient*, Boston: Shambhala.
Burgner, M. (1994) 'Working with the HIV patient: a psychoanalytic approach', *Psychoanalytic Psychotherapy* 8(3): 201–13.
Catalán, J. (1995) 'Psychological interventions in infection with the human im-munodeficiency virus', *British Journal of Psychiatry* 167: 104–11.
Catalán, J., Burgess, A. and Klimes, I. (1995) *Psychological Medicine of HIV Infection*, Oxford: Oxford Medical Publications.
Cohen, M. A. and Alfonso, C.A. (1994) 'Definition of HIV: How serious is it for women, medically and psychologically?' *Annals of the New York Academy of Sciences*, 736: 114–21.
Dansky, S. F. (1994) *Now Dare Everything: Tales of HIV-Related Psychotherapy*, Binghampton, New York: Harrington Park Press.
Denman, F. (1993) 'Prejudice and homosexuality', *British Journal of Psychother-apy* 9(3): 346–58.
Douglas, M. (1966) *Purity and Danger: An Analysis of Concepts of Pollution and Taboo*, Harmondsworth: Penguin.
Fell, M., Newman, S., Herns, M., Durrance, P., Manji, H., Connolly, S., McAll-ister, R., Weller, I. and Harrison, M. (1993) 'Mood and psychiatric disturbance in HIV and AIDS: changes over time', *British Journal of Psychiatry* 162: 604–10.
Grosz, S. (1993) 'A phantasy of infection', *International Journal of Psycho-Ana-lysis* 74: 965–974.
Hildebrand, H. P. (1992) 'A patient dying with AIDS', *International Review of Psycho-Analysis* 19(4): 457–69.
Lima, G., Lo Preston, C.T., Sherman, M.F. and Sobelman, S.A. (1993) 'The relationship between homophobia and self-esteem in gay males with AIDS', *Journal of Homosexuality* 25(4): 69–76.
Limentani, A. (1994) 'On the treatment of homosexuality', *Psychoanalytic Psy-chotherapy* 8(1): 49–62.
Miller, D., Weber, J. and Green, J. (1986) *The Management of AIDS Patients* London: Macmillan.
Molnos, A. (1990) *Our Response To A Deadly Virus: The Group-Analytic-Approach*, London: Karuck Books.
National Aids Manual (1996) London: NAM Publications.
Odets, W. (1995) *In The Shadow Of The Epidemic: Being HIV-Negative In The Age Of AIDS*, London: Cassell.
Oechsner, M., Möller, A.A. and Zaudig, M. (1993) 'Cognitive impairment, dementia

and psychosocial functioning in human immunodeficiency virus infection: a prospective study based on DSM-III-R and ICD-10', *Acta Psychiatria Scandinavia* 87: 13–17.

Perkins, D.O., Davidson, E.J., Laserman, J., Liao, D. and Evans, D.L. (1993) 'Personality disorder in patients infected with HIV: a controlled study with implications for clinical care', *American Journal of Psychiatry*, 150(2): 309–15.

Pugh, K., O'Donnell, I. and Catalán, J. (1993) 'Suicide and HIV disease', *AIDS Care* 5(4): 391–400.

Rabkin, J.G., Remien, R., Katoff, L. and Williams, J.B.W. (1993) 'Suicidality in AIDS long-term survivors: what is the evidence?' *AIDS Care* 5(4): 401–11.

Ratigan, B. (1991) 'On not traumatising the traumatised: the contribution of psychodynamic psychotherapy to work with people with HIV and AIDS', *British Journal of Psychotherapy* 8(1): 39–47.

—— (1995) 'Inner world, outer world: exploring the tension of race, sexual orientation and class and the inner world', *Psychodynamic Counselling* 1(2): 173–85.

Rosenberger, P.H., Bornstein, R.A., Nasrallah, H.A, *et al.* (1993) 'Psychopathology in human immunodeficiency virus infection: lifetime and current assessment', *Comprehensive Psychiatry* 34(3): 150–8.

Selnes, O.A., Galai, N., Bacellar, H. (1995) 'Cognitive performance after progression to AIDS: a longitudinal study from the multicenter AIDS cohort study', *Neurology* 45: 267–75.

Sketchley, J. (1989) 'Counselling people affected by HIV and AIDS', in W. Dryden, D. Charles-Edwards and R. Woolfe (eds) *Handbook of Counselling in Britain*, London: Routledge.

Sontag, S. (1989) *AIDS And Its Metaphors*, London: Allen Lane.

Walker, G. (1991) *In The Midst of Winter: Systemic Therapy With Families, Couples and Individuals with AIDS Infection*, New York: W. W. Norton.

Williams, J.B.W., Rabkin, J.G., Reimein, R.H., *et al.* (1991) 'Multidisciplinary baseline assessment of homosexual men with and without human immunodeficiency virus infection, II: standardised clinical assessment of current and lifetime psychopathology', *Archives of General Psychiatry* 48: 124–30.

Winiarski, M. G. *AIDS Related Psychotherapy*, New York: Pergamon.

Zegans, L. S., Gernard, A.L. and Coates, T.J. (1994) 'Psychotherapies for the person with HIV disease', *Psychiatric Clinics of North America* 17(1): 149–62.

Chapter twenty-six

Counselling people with alcohol and drug problems

Richard Velleman

This chapter will start by making some general points about the nature of work with people who experience drug- or alcohol-related problems. It will then examine some of the major issues which are current in this growing area of help before outlining some areas in which changes and growth may be predicted.

This chapter is about 'counselling'. Although there certainly are distinctions which can be drawn between counselling and other forms of help, none will be drawn here. Instead, the term 'counselling' will be used in a very broad way, and for the purposes of this chapter such terms as counselling, intervention, help, and so on, will be used interchangeably. Similarly, it is recognized that alcohol is a psychotropic drug, with effects comparable to a range of other drugs.

Principles

Alcohol- and drug-related problems are areas in which stereotypes abound. If members of the general public are asked about people with these problems, common views are of male alcoholics on park benches drinking cider, or of drug addicts injecting heroin in dingy squats in run-down urban areas. Yet, whereas there are individuals who conform to these stereotypes, the reality is that the range of people with drug- and alcohol-related problems is vast. This range and diversity is apparent in every area, be it client group, type of drug used, type of problem generated by the drug use, technique of intervention used, setting in which the intervention takes place, or aims of the counselling.

To take some examples, clients of agencies specializing in drug or alcohol problems vary along many dimensions:

(1) *age* (early teens or even younger to clients of pensionable age and considerably older);
(2) *sex* (with earlier figures of higher representation of men in both alcohol and drug agencies being superceded by far more equal representation);

(3) *who has the problem* (whether the problem is due to their own alcohol or drug use, or to someone else's – a spouse, a child, a parent, some other close relative or friend);

(4) *socio-economic status*;

(5) *type of social grouping* (glue-sniffing children, teenagers and young adults mixing amphetamines and alcohol, cannabis-smoking and LSD-using hippies, heavy-drinking middle-aged business people, tranquillizer-using or secretly drinking housewives, elderly people on cocktails of a wide variety of prescribed drugs. Clearly these examples utilize further familiar stereotypes which surround this area, although these stereotypes are in fact based largely in reality);

(6) *type of drug used* (alcohol, solvents, prescribed drugs, and a huge range of illicit drugs including cannabis, amphetamines, cocaine, heroin, hallucinogens, and prescribed drugs sold illicitly);

(7) *method of use of the drug* (drinking, smoking, sniffing, injecting, eating);

(8) *problem areas associated with the drug use* (problems with the law, the family, other relationships, with finances, job, physical health, mental health, housing, and of course problems of addiction and dependency as well);

(9) *seriousness of alcohol or drug problem* (from mild to serious, and occasional to constant).

Around 28 per cent of men and 11 per cent of women run the risk of developing an alcohol problem, in that they currently drink above the sensible limits for alcohol consumption. This is equivalent to around 7 million adults aged 18 plus in England alone. Estimates of alcohol-related deaths range from 5,000 to 40,000 per year, in England and Wales, depending on the calculations (Health Education Authority 1993). More than a million individuals have prescribed-drug-related problems (Cooper 1987). There are probably around 100,000 people (mainly young men and women) who have problems with their use of heroin, and there are large numbers of people who have problems with other drugs, especially amphetamines, cocaine and crack cocaine, with some users also having problems with hallucinogens and cannabis. Each year there are around 10,000 *new* notifications to the Home Office, and every 6 months there are over 20,000 *new* clients visiting drug agencies in Britain (ISDD 1994). Furthermore, each of these individuals with alcohol- or drug-related problems will have contact and will influence a wide range of others: family members, friends, workmates, members of the public (who for example share the same roads as intoxicated drinkers or drug-users). The number of people who may need information, advice, and counselling related to their own or someone else's alcohol or drug problems is immense. It is also the case that not all of these people will have very serious alcohol or drug problems. Instead they fall on a continuum from early and mild problems at one end to serious and life-threatening at the other.

Yet it is not only the clients who differ to such an extent. Agencies and individual helpers will also differ in terms of their:

(1) *philosophy and theory of the causation of problems* (alcohol or drugs – the addictive substance – is 'the problem', mentally ill people or people with inadequate or addictive personalities are 'the problem', society and its inequalities is 'the problem', the law is 'the problem', individuals' loss of religious beliefs is 'the problem');

(2) *definition of counselling* (including peer support, behavioural orientation, psychoanalytical orientation, Rogerian, eclectic);

(3) *techniques used to intervene* (maintenance doses of a drug to encourage stable rather than chaotic use, gradual planned reduction of drug or alcohol use, immediate or very speedy reduction of use, withdrawal relief, relapse prevention techniques, specific techniques such as social skills or assertion training and cue exposure methods, concentration on physical-health issues, counselling individually, in groups, using existing networks such as marriages or other relationships, or families);

(4) *setting in which the intervention takes place* (specialist drug- or alcohol-dependency treatment unit, detoxification unit, rehabilitation-house, -hostel or -community, in-patient psychiatric or general hospital unit, out-patient clinic, community-based alcohol or drug service, local voluntary information/advice/counselling agency, self-help group); and

(5) *aimed-for outcome of the intervention* (lifelong abstinence from alcohol or drugs, controlled or 'sensible' use, harm minimization, safer methods of ingestion, lifestyle changes, changes in social and relationship skills, increased life satisfaction).

This range and diverstiy means that, although there are important principles of practice which are shared by workers in this field, the first and possibly the most important point to make is that there can be no one set of key principles, methods, and techniques which will be the 'correct' one for every individual.

Nevertheless, from the examples above, three principles do emerge. The first is that the theory which a counsellor holds about the nature and cause of the problem will determine the nature of the intervention. If the counsellor believes that their clients are 'alcoholics' or 'addicts' who possess some chemical imbalance where a taste of alcohol or other drug of misuse will automatically lead to uncontrollable abuse, then their solution must be lifelong abstinence; whereas if the counsellor believes for example that the drink/drug problem is a result of prior learning experiences or inadequate coping strategies then the solution is to re-learn or to develop more appropriate coping mechanisms.

The second principle is that dealing with individuals with alcohol or drug problems will almost invariably involve dealing with two distinct but related areas. One will concern the individual's use of drugs or drink *per se*, and the second will concern other problems which connect in some (not necessarily causal) way with this problematic use. Within the specialist field of counselling concerning alcohol or drug problems, it is common to find helping agencies or individuals who argue that one or other of these areas is 'the important one' – that if one deals with the alcohol/drugs, then the other areas will fall into place; or that if one deals with the other problems (for example, housing, poverty, loneliness) the problematic alcohol/drug use will not be necessary and hence cease. In fact, both are important. In almost all cases, individuals who misuse alcohol or drugs do so for reasons which are not solely alcohol- or drug-related, and it is the task of the counsellor to explore these reasons with clients and to enable them to start to do something about them. Yet it must also be recognized that alcohol and other drugs are substances which can produce considerable dependency, and this will usually lead to difficulty in giving up or cutting down, even if the reasons for the abuse are examined and successfully tackled. Hence, it is important that both these areas are examined in counselling, and that arguments are dispensed with concerning which out of the alcohol/drug use or the other problems is 'the problem'.

The third principle is that counselling clients with alcohol or drug problems is no different to any other type of counselling. Any counsellor working in this area needs to have both good general counselling skills and specific knowledge about the area of drugs and alcohol. Clients will often present with a range of problems besides their alcohol or drug abuse, and any counsellor working in this field needs to be able to address these issues. This is no different to any other form of counselling. However, there are particular problems which the client will commonly experience which are connected with the drug/alcohol use *per se*, and concerning which a counsellor will find it useful to have some particular rather than general counselling knowledge. For example, how much alcohol or other drug is dangerous? What are the early signs of physical deterioration in a client who uses alcohol or drugs? How quickly should someone withdraw from tranquillizers? or from heroin? or from alcohol? What is the best method of preventing relapse? How does one get a client to report accurately his or her drug or alcohol use? All these and other questions will regularly confront a counsellor working in these areas; hence it is important that people who counsel clients with such problems are familiar with the information which they will need. Many of these issues are covered in more depth by this author in other publications (Velleman 1991, 1992a).

It is not necessary that every counsellor who works with a drug- or alcohol-related problem be a specialist counsellor: indeed the numbers referred to earlier would make that an impossibility. Rather, the idea is that counsellors in the many areas in which they will come into regular contact with these problems should undergo some basic informationally orientated training to enable them to work (and feel *confident* about working) with these problems when they arise. Alcohol and drug problems do arise in a variety of counselling settings: for example, many people attempt to cope with bereavement by drinking or taking drugs, and develop some sort of problem as a result. These people may make their first contact with a bereavement counsellor. Alcohol and drugs are closely connected with marital violence and arguments; relationship counsellors may be the first to see such clients. Young people are a target for much alcohol advertising and will often be introduced to drugs, and youth counsellors may see many early problem-drinkers or drug-takers. There are more examples, but the point is that many clients want to discuss their drinking or their drug use, and the related problems; but they need counsellors to have the confidence to tackle the issue.

The changing context

Since writing the first edition of this chapter, huge changes have occurred in national policy concerning health and social services provision. All of these changes have radically altered the context from within which statutory and non-statutory counselling services are offered, and some of them have directly affected services for alcohol and drug problems. Some of these changes are structural: the fourteen Regional Health Authorities first merged to make only eight, and from April 1996 no longer exist; and many District Health Authorities have merged (with other DHAs or with the Authorities responsible for providing GP services) to make Health Commissions. Other changes are even more substantial. The functions of Health Authorities have been split, and Health Authorities/Commissions are now only responsible for purchasing health care, not for providing it. This division between purchasing and providing has meant that all services, including drug and alcohol ones, need to be much more clearly specified than might previously have been the case. There is also a move in the ways that the usefulness of services is measured, towards examining outcomes and effectiveness, and away from simply measuring activity. Another change and division is between social care and health care. Especially in areas such as alcohol and drug services, the boundaries between these two components of care are very unclear; but central government policy has demanded that both resources and responsibility for social care aspects of dealing with problems be transferred from health to social services. This move has led to considerable uncertainty within the substance-misuse field, particularly with residential facilities, who now need to convince two sets of funders that parts of their service are 'social' and other parts are 'health'.

The government also decided to take a public health perspective on health problems, and issued *Health of the Nation* (1992), a document that set targets for preventative and harm-reducing behaviours for the whole population over the 1990s. These targets were grouped into five key areas (heart disease, cancer, accidents, mental health, and sexual health); unfortunately substance misuse was not selected as one of these. On the other hand, two of the specific targets subsumed within these key areas related to substance misuse, one aiming to reduce the percentage of the population drinking over the recommended maximum weekly sensible levels of alcohol, and other aiming to reduce the number of drug users who share injecting equipment. These targets relate to the issues of minimal intervention and harm minimization discussed later in this chapter.

Finally, there have been two major thrusts of government policy aimed specifically at substance misuse. First in the late 1980s an inter-ministerial group was set up with the Leader of the House of Commons as chair, to attempt to co-ordinate the widely differing policies towards alcohol pursued by the range of different government departments. Two offshoots of this were the appointment of Regional Alcohol Co-ordinators in each of the fourteen health regions in England, and the financing of the Alcohol Concern Grants Programme. Certainly the grant programme has contributed substantially to increasing the number and strength of agencies across the country attempting to deal with alcohol-related problems, but the Regional Co-ordinator scheme has been allowed largely to disappear as part of the structural reorganization mentioned previously, and as government focus has shifted from alcohol to drugs. The other major thrust concerns drugs, with the publication in 1995 of *Tackling Drugs Together*, the White Paper setting up Drug Action Teams across the country. The White Paper focused on three issues: crime and policing, education of young people, and helping people with drug-related problems, and required the teams to both take action, and to report this action to the Department of Health and the Central Drugs Co-ordination Unit. It remains to be seen whether this latest initiative marks a long-term commitment to dealing with substance misuse, or whether, as with the earlier focus on alcohol, it is just a passing political interest.

Issues

There are a number of current debates within the area of alcohol/drug counselling. These can be encapsulated within five main themes: aims and processes of counselling, who should do the counselling, where should counselling take place, training and skill development, and drugs and alcohol counselling and the criminal-justice system.

Aims and processes of counselling

There are a number of issues incorporated within this theme. The first relates to what is an ethically permissible aim of counselling, and as with so many ethical issues, the area is strongly bound up with philosophical stances.

Ethical aims

The field of alcohol and drug misuse has been under the influence of a medical model of addiction for a considerable period, and one of the concomitants of this model is the belief that certain people are addicts (or alcoholics) who are chemically different from 'normal' people and who must always and forever abstain from alcohol or any other drug of misuse. This has led to a very limited counselling approach: on the one hand counselling has focused very largely on alcohol/drug use *per se* as opposed to other problem areas connected with the use; on the other hand, within this focus on alcohol/drug use, this medical model has led to a total concentration on counselling aimed at abstinence.

Over the last twenty years this model has come to be increasingly questioned. A wide variety of different models explaining the taking up and development of problematic use of alcohol or other drugs has arisen (Orford 1985). Instead of viewing the population as either 'addicts' (who have a range of problems) or 'normal people' (who have none), a view has appeared suggesting that alcohol or drug problems occur along a variety of continua: where, for example, individuals could be more or less dependent on their drug, more or less in debt, or more or less violent.

These other views have brought with them a variety of alternative aims in counselling. Hence, a focus on alcohol/drug use is now not the only or even the major preoccupation of specialist agencies: a focus on other problem areas and on life-style changes is equally important. Furthermore, within the area of counselling about drug/alcohol use itself, the focus only on abstinence has come under increasing question. The idea of 'controlled drinking' has been increasingly developed in the alcohol field. In the drugs field, the idea of 'controlled drug-use' is not new (Velleman and Rigby 1990); there is a long history of intervention services providing users with drugs to help stabilize their use, and this notion has been given further impetus by the AIDS issue. Attention is being increasingly placed upon the means of taking the drug (injection or not) rather than focusing solely on the issue of helping clients to stop taking it. This has led to agencies being increasingly concerned with the supply of a safe means of injecting (the needle-supply or exchange schemes). It has also raised the profile of non-drug-related aims of counselling, with agencies becoming involved in promoting harm reduction – for example, 'safer sex' by supplying condoms and information.

These changes are not occurring without conflict (Sobell and Sobell 1984; Strang 1992). Many argue that 'allowing' clients to think that controlled use is a possibility is highly unethical. If the disease model is correct, it is not possible for an addict to control use: it is an incurable and progressive disease from this viewpoint. By mentioning controlled use a professional counsellor gives permission for the client to try it, and increases the likelihood of that client attempting control and hence relapsing.

This issue relates to that of relapse prevention (Gossop 1989; Saunders and Allsop 1991). It has long been recognized that problems of dependency and addiction are relapsing conditions, and indeed Prochaska and DiClemente (1986) have incorporated relapse as a clear component of their influential 'cycle of change' theory. The difficulty is not helping clients to stop using alcohol or drugs, it is to get them to stay stopped. The argument for training in relapse prevention is that if many clients are at risk of relapse, it makes sense to warn them of the risks, to identify possible problem situations, and to get the client to work out ways of coping with relapse if it does occur. This means that any relapse should be as minor and as short-lived as possible. Again, however, this can be attacked as 'unethical' on the grounds that telling clients that there is a strong risk of relapse will reduce motivation and give clients 'permission' to relapse.

Abstinence or controlled use is not only about individuals' *beliefs* as to what is ethical – evidence also exists! This evidence implies that there *are* indicators which suggest whether or not controlled use or abstinence is likely to prove more effective (Armor 1980). Hodgson *et al.* (1979), for example, show that severity of dependence is related to success in controlling alcohol use, with more severely dependent problem drinkers being more successful in abstaining and less severely dependent ones being more successful in controlling their drinking. They also show, however, that the most important concern is the clients' wishes on the matter.

Nevertheless, even the most enthusiastic proponents of 'controlled use' as an intervention aim usually accept that there is a large difference between 'controlled use' and 'normal or social use'. Someone with a serious alcohol or drugs problem will almost certainly never be able to become a 'normal', 'social' user again. Some individuals will certainly drink or take other drugs again, but drinking or other drug-taking has become, for them, a risky business, an area in which they have already experienced their behaviour getting out of control. The likelihood is that such individuals will always have to be aware of and wary about their drinking or other drug use in a way that individuals who have never developed this sort of problem do not have to be.

Success in counselling

The second issue relates to what constitutes a successful counselling intervention. First, this clearly relates to the issue previously discussed with respect to legitimate aims of counselling. A second question, however, concerns the relationship between aims and outcome. From the 1960s onwards there have been reports in the literature of individuals who have been engaged in abstinence-orientated programmes being found on follow-up to be currently controlling their drinking or drug-taking (Davies 1962). More recently there have been reports of the reverse as well: clients in controlled-use orientated programmes being found on follow-up to be abstinent (Sobell and Sobell 1984). These are cases in which the aims and the seemingly successful outcomes are different. Furthermore, what is to be concluded about success in cases where a client is still misusing alcohol or drugs, but who is managing better other aspects of his or her life such as health, employment, relationships? Do all these cases where clients change in positive directions (which may be different to or only part of the explicit aim of counselling) count as success? Furthermore, for how long does a client have to remain problem-free (or even problem-reduced) before counselling is counted as a success? This is an issue over which there is little consensus in the field.

The provision of services

A third issue relates to the process of providing, and the nature of, the intervention. There are a number of points here. The first is peculiar to the field of alcohol and drug problems. In other areas of counselling, counsellors expect clients to be currently experiencing the problem for which they are seeking help. Hence an agency which deals with depressed clients will expect clients to be depressed when they attend; an agency dealing with marital and sexual problems will expect clients to attend when they are currently experiencing marital and sexual problems. Yet agencies dealing with alcohol and drug problems often have a very different approach, only offering help if the client is no longer behaving in the way which is defining them as having a problem – i.e. no longer drinking or taking drugs. Hence, many agencies will only admit a client into their hostel, hospital ward, out-patient clinic, or counselling agency if they are currently abstaining, and will define a client's reported inability to do this as a sign of lack of motivation. Thus, for example, one local counselling agency dealing with alcohol problems which is extremely innovative in many ways still has a rule that clients who have had any alcohol at all during the day must not be seen, even if they are not at all intoxicated, and even if they are pursuing a controlled drinking goal! Although this attitude is starting to change, the majority of agencies will still only help if a client is abstinent, at least on the day of counselling. It must also be added that this issue is particularly true for alcohol-problem agencies. Many drug agencies follow a policy of insisting that clients' behaviour must be controlled when they attend, without insisting that their drug use must be controlled or absent.

The second point relates to the nature of the intervention. Over the past ten years the linked issues of early intervention, minimal rather than maximal intervention, and of information and advice rather than 'treatment' have all become important. This is for two reasons. The first of these relates to the previous discussion of the gradual replacement of the medical model (which divided people into addicts/alcoholics versus normals) with an approach which views the use and associated problems of alcohol/drugs as falling along a continuum. As outlined earlier, using this latter approach, individuals could have a range of problems which might stretch from relatively slight to severe problems and from temporary and transient to chronic and long-term ones. This continuum concept means that services only developed to serve the chronic and massive problems of confirmed 'alcoholics' or 'addicts' were inappropriate for the large number of clients with less severe drug- or alcohol-related problems.

Early interventions using less intensive methods have become more important for a second reason as well: the previously popular intensive treatments have not proved to be very successful, even when dealing with clients at the later, more difficult and more chronic end of the continuum. From the 1950s to the 1980s there was a steady increase in the development of specialist NHS in-patient treatment units catering for severe problem drinkers or drug-takers. Various evaluations of these services showed that success rates were low (Robinson and Ettorre 1980; Thorley 1981). Much of this low success rate was attributed to the very severe range of problems with which these specialists units had to deal. Yet at the same time as intensive interventions were shown not to be highly successful, other studies have shown that a single session of advice and counselling can produce success rates which are at least as high, even assessed on 1- and 2-year follow-ups (Orford and Edwards 1977). Hence, these and other studies have all implied that intensive treatment is not necessarily the most efficacious method of intervention even if a client does have a severe problem; and as already discussed the majority of clients do not have problems of a severity to warrant such intensive interventions (Effective Health Care 1993; Richmond and Anderson 1994).

A third point relates to the importance of engaging clients into counselling or other forms of therapy. Work in the alcohol-, drug-, and family-therapy fields (Carpenter and Treacher 1983; Velleman 1984, 1992a) has underlined the importance of engaging clients into counselling, and has reiterated the obvious point that this first step is the most important: unless clients can commit themselves to attending and staying in counselling, no work can be successfully performed, as the clients will not be there!

Who should do the counselling?

The second theme concerns who is the best person to do the counselling. People who counsel problem drinkers and drug-takers stand along a number of continua: those who have themselves had an alcohol/drug problem or not, those who work with this client group voluntarily or get paid for it, those who have some professional qualification or not, those who are specialist or generic workers. Hence, a counsellor of a problem drinker/ drug-taker may be an untrained volunteer working in a peer-support/self-help network who has had a similar problem, or a trained volunteer counsellor working in a local counselling agency, or a professionally qualified clinical psychologist, social worker, or psychiatrist working in his or her professional department or in a specialist alcohol or drugs treatment unit or service.

Which of these individuals is the best person to counsel a client with an alcohol- or drug-related problem? People can be found who will argue that one particular combination out of the range of combinations that can be created from the four continua outlined above is the best, but there exists little evidence to advance any one claim.

Sharing the problem

Whether someone who counsels problem drinkers or drug-takers needs to have had a similar problem in order to be able to help is another issue peculiar to this field. To take the same examples used previously, few authorities would argue that a counsellor need have experienced severe depression in order to be able to counsel depressed clients, or to have experienced marital or sexual dysfunction before being able to counsel about these problems. Yet is is commonplace to find both clients and counsellors arguing that a prerequisite of helping individuals with alcohol or other drug problems is to have had such a problem oneself. Clearly, having had a similar problem can be helpful: the growth of the self-help movement internationally implies that many people find the sharing of experiences with others a helpful phenomenon. Yet no evidence exists to suggest that counsellors who have not themselves experienced alcohol or drug problems cannot as effectively help clients with these problems.

The issue here is one of empathy: the ability of the counsellor to put him- or herself in the place of the client. Having 'been there' may be very helpful, if the counsellor is able to recognize that no two situations are ever exactly the same, and that what worked for the counsellor may not be appropriate for the client. It is the experience of many agencies that counsellors who have experienced similar problems make either the best or the worst counsellors: depending on whether or not they are able to use their experiences in non-dogmatic ways where they can both empathize and yet see the client as an individual with similar but different problems and possible solutions.

Voluntary versus paid work

This issue is heavily bound up with political philosophy (Velleman 1992b). On the one hand, it is argued that services which utilize volunteers (a) exploit peoples' willingness to help, (b) reduce the pressure on statutory agencies to provide paid counselling jobs which in turn both (c) deprive people of paid employment and (d) serve to reduce the professional status of counselling and counsellors. On the other hand, it is also argued that (a) using volunteer members of the general public is a way of mobilizing them, of utilizing members of the community to tackle community problems rather than simply getting outside paid helpers to do this; (b) this does not take away from the creation of paid jobs because these jobs will only be created if there is sufficient interest within the community to argue for their creation, and that using volunteers will speed up this process by augmenting that community interest; (c) there simply are not the resources to provide the number of counsellors needed in this area, so if volunteers do not perform this work no one will; and (d) the issue of *professional* status is dependent on quality of training rather than whether the job is paid or not. Certainly the issue of training and accreditation is an area over which both the national bodies in England and Wales responsible for alcohol and drug problems (Alcohol Concern and SCODA) are concerned. Both bodies are heavily involved in the development of relevant National Vocational Qualifications (NVQs) for the counselling field which will incorporate the work of alcohol- and drug-counselling agencies.

Professional qualification

The term 'professional' as used here refers mainly to the 'core' mental health professions – psychology, psychiatry, social work, psychiatric nursing, and occupational therapy – although it also includes those with helping qualifications granted by any nationally recognized body. The issue of professional qualification is very largely linked with the two previously discussed issues. Historically, in the alcohol field, professionally qualified help was almost impossible to obtain, and in the drugs field the only professional help available was for opiate addicts, and this was largely limited to the prescription of maintenance doses of morphine, heroin, or methadone. Counselling of problem drinkers and drug-takers was left almost entirely to the self-help/peer-support network of Alcoholics Anonymous and Narcotics Anonymous, or to various of the 'concept house' therapeutic community establishments based on the Minnesota Model (Cook 1988). Hence, counselling was largely offered by individuals who had themselves suffered from the problem and this counselling was largely offered voluntarily (except in the case of the private 'concept houses').

Over the years this has changed. Alcohol and drug misuse have become 'speciality' areas in their own right, with National Health Service alcoholism treatment units, drug-dependency clinics, community alcohol or drug teams, and detoxification wards, and so the issue of whether or not nonprofessionally qualified counsellors are competent to counsel has arisen. In some ways, of course, this is a clear case of professional imperialism, with professionals, once they have decided that the addictions are a definable speciality, attempting to annex and incorporate the area under their own professional umbrellas; yet, as will be discussed under the next theme, there are real issues of training and skill development here as well. There has been little research on the relative merits of volunteers versus professional counsellors in this field, but the weight of evidence in the counselling literature overall suggests that well-trained volunteers produce success rates which are at least equal to and often better than those produced by such professionally qualified mental health specialists as psychologists, psychiatrists, and social workers (Berman and Norton 1985).

Specialist versus generic

'Alcoholism' and 'addiction' are regarded as difficult areas in which to work by many generic professionally qualified workers. Indeed many of these workers hold negative stereotypes about these clients: addicts/alcoholics are liars, unmotivated, untrustworthy, unpredictable. This has led to a pattern of services in which clients with these problems tend to be seen by 'specialist' addiction services: self-help groups, voluntary, or statutory agencies. Yet as specialist services have become more involved in the areas of early intervention, prevention, advice, and information as well as counselling and therapeutic interventions, so the scale of the problems has become clearer. The figures provided at the start of this chapter show that there are millions of individuals who are affected by their own or someone else's alcohol or drug use – the number of people who may need information, advice, and counselling related to this is immense. This has led to a gradual realization that specialist or expert workers in this area will never be able to deal with more than a fraction of the total number of people needing help, leading to the conclusion that generic workers must be made interested and informed so that they too can work with those with alcohol- or drug-related problems.

The Health Education Authority has taken this issue seriously, and has developed 'Helping People Change' courses which run throughout the country. These courses train generic professionals in the elements of the Prochaska and DiClemente (eg. 1986) theory of the 'cycle of change', which suggests that people with addiction problems go through various stages in the process of change (of pre-contemplation, contemplation, action, and maintenance, with relapse commonly occurring at one or other of these stages), and with different interventions being used depending on what stage the client is at.

Where should counselling take place?

In the community or not?

Although the self-help/peer-support network was always primarily based within the wider community, other provision was until recently largely based outside this. Statutory provision for problem drinkers was largely linked to in-patient, psychiatric hospital bases. The drug rehabilitation centres (mainly private or charitable) were also often based outside the wider community because they were often sited in relatively isolated rural settings. This has meant that those requiring greater help than the peer-support network could provide needed to leave their communities in order to be helped. These individuals then usually had to return to these same communities after 'treatment' with little ongoing support. Over the last fifteen years this has gradually been changing, with the increasing development of both statutory and voluntary agencies committed to providing a service within the community where people with the problems live. Thus, for example, the statutory Community Alcohol or Drug Teams and grant-supported voluntary agencies such as Local Alcohol or Drugs Advisory Services which have grown up, all provide counselling from a community base and sometimes offer community groups, domiciliary visits, and family and marital counselling.

A linked issue is whether there are any interventions for alcohol and other drug problems which require hospital as opposed to community provision. One of the areas which had been presumed usually to require hospital care was that of detoxification, but even this is increasingly being viewed as a primarily community-based need, with hospital back-up being required only in an emergency (Stockwell *et al.* 1986). Nevertheless, it is still the case that even well-developed community services require some form of structured residential unit to provide a safety net for some very damaged clients (those with organic brain damage, for example).

Linked or separate services?

Another issue concerning where counselling should take place is whether alcohol and drug services should be integrated or separate. In many cases this is confounded by political power and financial concerns: if there are two agencies currently funded in any area, one offering services for drug misusers, the other for alcohol misusers, will a combined service retain the same level of resources? Who will direct the combined agency? The trend across Britain currently is for previously separate services to link up, at least informally, and many are attempting to integrate in all ways. This is often aided by existing agencies who cater for one client group expanding to cater for a second if services for this second group do not already exist. It is the case, however, that particular problems often arise when alcohol-problem agencies attempt to fit drug-users into existing routines which are inappropriate for them, such as the use of strict appointment systems. These issues are also tied in with requirements from health and social services purchasers for value for money and clearly defined outcomes.

A related issue is whether services for clients with illicit drug problems and those with prescribed drug problems should be offered from the same agency. With both this and the previous issue the concern is often that clients coming for one problem may be put off by meeting clients coming for another. In practice agencies which cater for more than one client group do not report this. Indeed the discussion in the first part of this chapter on the range of clients within any of these groups mediates against limiting access on the grounds of which drug is taken.

Counselling in the workplace

A final issue relates to the identification of and intervention with alcohol and drug abuse at work. The view is increasingly being taken that good industrial-relations practice requires employers to offer at least some assistance to employees with drink and drug problems. The provision of counselling in the workplace is a growing area of interest (Alcohol Concern 1995) – see Chapter 13.

Training and skill development

Specialist workers

This author does not subscribe to the view discussed above that all such workers should be trained professionals – which is fortunate, because few professional-qualification training courses currently pay more than a cursory glance at the area of alcohol and drug abuse. Most training courses allocate at best an afternoon to the topic and at worst an hour's talk from a visiting 'expert', which is potentially interesting but unintegrated into the course and hence soon forgotten. This is an area in which gradual change can be perceived. The Central Council on Education and Training in Social Work (CCETSW) has increased its emphasis on training in alcohol and drug work in basic social-work training (Harrison 1993). The Royal College of Physicians argued in its 1987 report that 'the first group who need education on alcohol problems are medical students and young doctors'. Psychologists have also argued for greater emphasis in basic training (Sutherland *et al.* 1992). In terms of more advanced training, a variety of institutions throughout the British Isles (such as the Leeds Addiction Unit, the University of Kent, Paisley College) have now developed a wide range of courses, ranging from day-release to year-long, and incorporating distance learning, on more advanced issues in working with clients with drug or alcohol problems (Kent 1993). The Institute for the Study of Drug Dependence (ISDD), a library and information service, is a national research and resource centre about drugs. Nevertheless, it is still the case that most professionally qualified staff are ill-trained in this area, and that often the best trained workers with individuals with alcohol and drug problems are trained voluntary counsellors (Velleman 1992b). It is to be hoped that the drugs field will soon develop an accreditation system for their counsellors alongside or incorporating that used in the alcohol field, and linked with the new NVQ awards currently being developed.

Generic workers

With the discovery that the number of people with alcohol- or other drug-related problems is large has come a growing realization of the need to inform, educate, train, and support a growing number of counsellors who may not be 'specialist' alcohol or drug workers, but who, in the nature of their jobs, will make contact with many people with these problems. This move towards training and skill development has been aided in both the alcohol and the drugs area. In the alcohol field the aid came in the guise of the publication in 1976 of *Responding to Drinking Problems* (Shaw *et al.* 1976). These authors argued that the only way that services could be organized to match the needs within the population would be for the bulk of the client work to be performed by primary-care workers within the community such as voluntary agencies, general practitioners, social workers, and probation workers. As a result of their own research, however, these authors also argued that most of these workers lacked the confidence to counsel these clients, who they perceived as being difficult and unrewarding to work with. The answer, suggested Shaw *et al.*, was for specialist workers to devote most of their time not to counselling clients with these problems, but to training and supporting primary-care workers who, if they had sufficient support, would deal with all but the most difficult cases themselves. This recommendation, coupled with the growth of interest in training following the development of the network of accredited volunteer counsellors specializing in working with alcohol problems, resulted in a growth in training for generic as opposed to specialist workers.

In the drugs field the creation of the Regional Drugs Training Units has greatly helped training and skills development. The brief of these units is to promote the transmission of knowledge and skills relating to drug use to a wide professional and general audience. Furthermore, many of the growing number of Drugs Advisory Services see training of generic workers as a major part of their brief.

The growth of training for generic workers has also been aided by the production of a number of books aimed at a more general audience (eg. Gossop 1993; Robertson and Heather 1986; Velleman 1992a). Training, developing the skills, and supporting generic workers is an important area which needs to be continued and extended.

Alcohol and drugs counselling and the criminal justice system

Drug and alcohol consumption often brings people into conflict with the law. Such conflict is a major life event which can lead to a number of effects. It can lead individuals to seek help with their previously unacknowledged problems. It can lead the criminal justice system to identify individuals as being in need of help, and so compel them to accept 'treatment'. It can lead people to be punished for their law-breaking, which can reinforce those individuals' negative self-images and so exacerbate the problem. And because of the stigmatizing aspect of criminal proceedings, it can lead to the loss of whatever gains may have been accrued through counselling, such as finding a job, improving family relationships, and finding a place to live.

This inescapable impact of the criminal justice system on the counselling of at least some clients with alcohol and drug problems also leads to a variety of issues arising for counsellors and agencies. Thus, for example, in order to increase the accessibility of the service, do agencies involve themselves with the criminal justice system? Alternatively, do they have little contact with clients from this source, because the issue of client 'motivation' has become obscured, due to either their compulsory treatment, or their belief that entering counselling will lead to a reduced or deferred sentence?

No counsellor working with alcohol or drug problems can consider him or herself uninfluenced by these issues. Unless the counsellor operates a very selective referral system, some clients will inevitably present themselves in conflict with the law, and this will have effects on both client and counsellor.

Future developments

In the first edition of this book, I suggested a number of areas of change and development which I thought would occur over the subsequent few years: these were the further integration of alcohol and drug services, the further development of community-based services, the development of greater services for family members, and more input and co-ordination into prevention. It is certainly the case that there has been movement on all of these fronts. Alcohol and drug services have continued to merge and integrate, although many workers still argue that services need to be provided in different ways to drug and alcohol problem clients, even if the management of the agencies is integrated. There has been a continued development away from hospital-based services into community ones, although this has been offset by the growth in private-sector treatment-centre provision. There has been an increased awareness of the impact that someone's alcohol or drug problem can have on other family members (Velleman *et al.* 1993; Velleman 1993), and there has been an upsurge in the area of prevention, with the development of both the National Drinkwise programme and Regional Drug Prevention teams, and the latest Tackling Drugs Together initiative outlined previously.

My predictions of future developments and changes over the next decade include the following:

Drugs

Two major concerns are the growth of drug use and the related younger starting of many young people; and the growing problems concerning drugs and crime and public safety. Both these issues have strong implications for a predicted rise in demand for drugs counselling. Another major issue for the drugs sector is the prescribing debate. The issue of whether it is effective to prescribe opiates at all, especially under a maintenance as opposed to a reducing regime, is once again highly controversial. At a time of increasing health-care rationing, the policy of giving drugs to drug users, especially over long periods, is an easy target. It is ironic that the drugs field might be moving away from prescribing maintenance doses to attempt to keep dependent users at a stable level, at the same time as the notion of controlled use as a viable alternative goal of counselling has been generally accepted for those with alcohol problems. An interesting difference between the two fields is that the clients for whom controlled drinking is recommended are the most stable ones; younger, married, with a stable job, and having a shorter excessive drinking history; whereas the clients for whom maintenance opiates are recommended are the opposite – the most chaotic users with the longest histories. The issues underlying this contrast deserve more discussion. However, even if prescribing is seen to be effective, there is still the issue of who funds this service: is it strictly 'health', or is it equally an issue for the police, probation, and social services in that its effects might be felt as greatly on reduced crime rates, drug-related prosecutions, and increased social stability, as on health.

Two other areas of change can be predicted. First, there needs to be an increased awareness and focus on Hepatitis C, as well as the current focus on HIV control and prevention. This is clearly a serious and growing problem. Second, there is likely to be an increase in attempts to examine alternatives to standard detoxification regimes. Home-based regimes are already being introduced, following the alcohol detoxification model, but it is likely that both rapid-detox models (involving detoxification under general anaesthetic followed by relapse-management training) and the use of alternative medicine such as acupuncture, will grow over the next decade.

Alcohol

Two main areas are likely to be important over the next few years. First, there is currently great controversy over the relationship between alcohol and health. It had previously been thought that low to moderate levels of consumption might have a neutral effect, with higher levels being increasingly harmful. Some evidence now seems to suggest that moderate drinking might have a *beneficial* effect on some health outcomes (especially leading to a reduction in coronary problems). Because of this, the combined Royal Medical Colleges asked a joint working group to report on whether the so-called 'sensible drinking limits' should be altered. In fact, they concluded (Joint Royal Colleges 1995) that the limits should be reaffirmed. In spite of this advice, the government shortly after produced new and higher 'sensible drinking limits' (Interdepartmental Government Report 1995), suggesting that men should not drink more than four units per day, and women should not drink more than three units per day. Over a seven-day period, therefore, the new limits suggest no more than 28 units for men (21 for women), as opposed to the old limits of 21 units for men (14 for women). It is likely that the issues of alcohol and health, and sensible drinking limits, will remain controversial.

The second area concerns Alcoholics Anonymous. Although AA used to work quite closely with the old Alcoholism Treatment Units, and its philosophy is an integral part of many current Minnesota Model establishments, most alcohol counselling agencies in Britain have a relatively distanced relationship with AA. This has always been very different in the United States, where there is a much closer *rapprochement* between agencies and AA, but the closeness has been based on ideological agreement, not research evidence of its effectiveness. This is currently changing in the US, where there is a significant move to demonstrate whether or not AA involvement is an effective addition to other forms of intervention (McCrady and Miller 1993). Given some findings suggesting that such a *rapprochement* is beneficial, it is likely that AA will become more widely used in Britain again, as an integral part of a counselling agency's approach, as well as in its current guise as an alternative to counselling intervention.

Other issues

Two other issues need a final mention. Over the past decade it has become increasingly obvious that more clients are experiencing difficulties with *both* alcohol *and* drugs. This cross-addiction is a source of great concern, and is an added argument for at the least greater co-ordination and co-operation between those drug and alcohol agencies which are still separate. The other issue relates to mental health and substance-misuse problems. One of the impacts of the general move to community care is the growing number of homeless people with both mental-health and substance-misuse problems. It is certainly the case that services over the next decade are going to see growing numbers of clients with such complex problems.

All the issues raised above have major implications for the development of alcohol-and drug-counselling agencies, and for staff training and recruitment.

While the field will change if these future developments come to fruition, will they be sufficient to turn the tide of the present degree of misuse in society, with all that this implies concerning the quality of life of misusers and those close to them such as family, friends, and colleagues? It is the impression of this author thay they will not. Reducing the impact of alcohol and drugs requires a sustained campaign on two fronts: a clear commitment from central government to use its powers (taxation, licensing outlets, policing) to reduce alcohol and drug consumption, or at least keep it stable; and a national campaign to alter public attitudes to the use of mind-altering drugs such as alcohol, tranquillizers, and illicit drugs. Both these elements have occurred concerning smoking over the last decade, and their effects are being seen in a reduction in cigarette use. Neither of these elements are apparent concerning alcohol consumption; and although both are overtly present concerning illicit drugs, on neither front is the action taken effective. Until these elements are present, it is likely that alcohol- and drug-related problems will continue to grow.

Acknowledgments

The author thanks Gill Velleman for her useful comments on an earlier draft of this chapter. He is also grateful to the editors of the first edition, Windy Dryden, David Charles-Edwards, and Ray Woolfe, as well as Gerald Conyngham, Gill Velleman, Helen Kendall, and Ian Sherwood for their useful comments on an earlier version of the chapter for the first edition.

References

Alcohol Concern (1995) 'Alcohol at work still a problem, but employers take a softer line', *Alcohol Concern Magazine* 10(2): 12–13.

Armor, D. (1980) 'The Rand Reports and the analysis of relapse' in G. Edwards and M. Grant (eds) *Alcoholism Treatment in Transition*, London: Croom Helm.

Berman, J. and Norton, N. (1985) 'Does professional training make a therapist more effective?' *Psychological Bulletin* 98: 401–6.

Carpenter, J. and Treacher, A. (1983) 'On the neglected but related arts of convening and engaging families and their wider systems', *Journal of Family Therapy* 5: 337–58.

Cook, C. (1988) 'The Minnesota Model in the management of drug and alcohol dependency: miracle, method or myth? I: philosophy and programme; II: evidence and conclusions', *Addiction* 83: 625–34 and 735–48.

Cooper, J. (1987) 'Benzodiazepine prescribing: the aftermath', *Druglink* 2(5): 8–10.

Davies, D. L. 'Normal drinking in recovered alcohol addicts', *Quarterly Journal of Studies on Alcohol* 23: 94–104.

Department of Health (1992) *Health of the Nation: A Strategy for Health in England*, London: HMSO.

Effective Health Care (1993) *Brief Interventions and Alcohol Use*, Leeds: University of Leeds.

Gossop, M. (1989) *Relapse and Addictive Behaviour*, London: Routledge.

——(1993) *Living With Drugs*, 3rd edn, Aldershot: Ashgate.

Harrison, L. (1993) *Substance Misuse: designing social work training*, London: CCETSW.

Health Education Authority (1993) *Health Update 3: Alcohol*, London: HEA.

Hodgson, R., Rankin, H. and Stockwell, T. (1979) 'Alcohol dependence and the priming effect', *Behaviour Research and Therapy* 17: 379–87.

Institute for the Study of Drug Dependence (1994) *Drug Misuse in Britain, 1994*, London: ISDD.

Interdepartmental Government Report (1995) *The Interdepartmental Government Report on the Sensible Drinking Message*, London: HSMO.

Joint Royal Colleges (1995) *Alcohol and the Heart in Perspective: sensible limits reaffirmed*, London: Royal Colleges of Physicians, Psychiatrists, and General Practitioners.

Kent, R. (1993) *Training For Alcohol Practitioners: a review and recommendations*, London: Alcohol Concern.

McCrady, B. and Miller, W. (1993) *Research on Alcoholics Anonymous*, New Jersey: Rutgers Centre of Alcohol Studies.

Orford, J. (1985) *Excessive Appetites*, Chichester: Wiley.

Orford, J. and Edwards, G. (1977) *Alcoholism: A Comparison of Treatment and Advice, with a Study of the Influence of Marriage*, Oxford: Oxford University Press.

Prochaska, J. and DiClemente, C. (1986) 'Towards a comprehensive model of change' in W. Miller and N. Heather (eds) *Treating Addictive Behaviour*, New York: Plenum.

Richmond, R. and Anderson, P. (1994) 'Research in general practice for smokers and excessive drinkers in Australia and the UK. I: interpretation of results; II: representativeness of the results; III: dissemination of interventions', *Addiction* 89: 35–62.

Robertson, I. and Heather, N. (1986) *Let's Drink To Your Health*, Leicester: British Psychological Society.

Robinson, D. and Ettorre, B. (1980) 'Special units for common problems: Alcoholism Treatment Units in England and Wales' in G. Edwards and M. Grant (eds) *Alcoholism Treatment in Transition*, London: Croom Helm.

Royal College of Physicians (1987) *A Great and Growing Evil*, London: Tavistock.

Saunders, W. and Allsop, S. (1991) 'Helping those who relapse', in R. Davidson *et al.* (eds) *Counselling Problem Drinkers*, London: Routledge.

Shaw, S., Cartwright, A., Spratley, T. and Harwin, J. (1976) *Responding to Drinking Problems*, London: Croom Helm.

Sobell, M. and Sobell, L. (1984) 'The aftermath of heresy: a response to Pendery *et al*'s (1982) critique of "Individualised Behaviour Therapy for Alcoholics"', *Behaviour Research and Therapy* 22: 413–40.

Stockwell, T., Bolt, E. and Hooper, J. (1986) 'Detoxification from alcohol at home managed by general practitioners', *British Medical Journal* 292: 733–5.

Strang, J. (1992) 'Harm reduction for drug users: exploring the dimensions of harm, their measurement, and strategies for reduction', *AIDS and Public Policy* 7: 145–52.

Sutherland, A. *et al* (1992) 'Do psychologists give a XXXX for alcohol?' *Clinical Psychology Forum* 41: 2–5.

Thorley, A. 'Longitudinal studies of drug dependence' in G. Edwards and C. Busch (eds) *Drug Problems in Britain: A Review of Ten Years*, London: Academic Press.

Velleman, R. (1984) 'The engagement of new residents: a missing dimension in the evaluation of hostels for problem drinkers', *Journal of Studies on Alcohol* 45: 251–9.

——(1991) 'Alcohol and drug problems', in W. Dryden and R. Rentoul (eds) *Adult Clinical Problems: A Cognitive-Behavioural Approach*, London: Routledge.

——(1992a) *Counselling For Alcohol Problems*, London: Sage (Counselling in Practice Series).

——(1992b) 'The use of volunteer counsellors in helping problem drinkers: community work in action?', *Journal of Mental Health* 1: 301–10.

——(1993) *Alcohol and the Family*, Institute of Alcohol Studies Occasional Paper, London: Institute of Alcohol Studies.

Velleman, R. and Rigby, J. (1990) 'Harm-Minimisation: Old Wine in New Bottles?', *International Journal on Drug Policy* 1: 24–7.

Velleman, R., Bennett, G., Miller, T., Orford, J., Rigby, K. and Tod, A. (1993) 'The families of problem drug users: the accounts of fifty close relatives', *Addiction* 88: 1275–83.

Chapter twenty-seven

Counselling adults who were abused as children

Peter Dale

Introduction

This chapter is based on a mixture of clinical and research experience. I have worked as an individual therapist with adults who were abused as children over the last fifteen years, and also supervise other practitioners. The research perspective involves a Ph.D. study (sponsored by the NSPCC) entitled *Clients' and therapists' perceptions of the psychotherapeutic process: a study of adults abused as children* (Dale 1996). This is a qualitative study involving fifty-three in-depth interviews with clients who were abused as children who had received therapy; therapists who provide such help; and therapists who were themselves abused as children. In this chapter I am drawing on both clinical and research perspectives.

It is customary to begin the introduction to a subject with a comment about definition and prevalence. The danger of doing so with the topic of child abuse is that this could easily consume all the space available by virtue of the complexities and controversies which surround theories of abuse, and questions in relation to how widespread in society child abuse actually is. Research into the prevalence of child abuse over recent decades has produced wildly different findings. One reason for this is that there are no commonly accepted definitions of abuse, and studies have used very different definitions in exploring the prevalence of abuse in various communities. Not surprisingly, studies based on different criteria produce large variations in reports of prevalence of abuse. Over recent years figures for sexual abuse of females have varied between 6–62 per cent; and for males between 3–31 per cent of the population (Taylor 1989). In Britain, the best known study reported prevalence rates of 12 per cent for females and 8 per cent for males (Baker and Duncan 1986).

Notwithstanding these discrepancies and the controversies they continue to generate, it is clear that many communities include large numbers of people who were abused as children. A great deal of research has been undertaken over the past twenty years exploring the consequences in adult life of childhood abuse, most of which has focused on females who were sexually abused as children by men. The role of women as sexual abusers of children has been a blind spot until very recently, a taboo area which represents the most recent manifestation of a long history of social denial of child abuse (Elliot 1993).

In recent years, a largely unquestioned assumption has been that all adults who were abused as children must have been significantly emotionally damaged by such experiences and therefore be in need of therapeutic help. A consistent finding however, from research on consequences of childhood abuse, is the significant proportions of people who do not consider that the abuse either had any long-term negative consequences, or that it was damaging at all. The ways in which people construe the impact of abuse upon themselves is complex and beyond the scope of this chapter. Nevertheless, the point is underlined that it is by no means automatic that lifelong emotional disability follows from early trauma, and counsellors should be wary of making such assumptions. Moreover, people who were abused as children may seek help for a range of problems which are not fundamentally associated with 'unresolved' abuse, and to associate every such problem in living and relating with abuse ignores the multiple causes of personal difficulties and distress.

However, the greater proportion of published material (both research and clinical) highlights the damaging consequences of abuse (Briere 1992; Feinauer 1989; Mendel 1995). Browne and Finklehor (1986) concluded that approximately 40 per cent of sexually abused children suffer consequences serious enough for them to need therapy in adult life. Damage is more likely for those who were chronically and multiply abused over an extended period of time, beginning at an early age, in the context of a significantly dysfunctional family, and who responded with dissociative defences. It should be noted that most of this research stems from a focus on sexual abuse, and there is much less knowledge about the long-term impact of physical and emotional abuse. Also, it is not clear in situations of multiple abuse which aspects of this are the most damaging. My clinical impression is that the insidious nature of emotional abuse, deprivation, or rejection which often underlies most other forms of abuse, is understated in the literature in terms of its detrimental impact on personality development and coping abilities.

One focus of published material relating to the long-term consequences of child abuse has been attempts to delineate a specific 'post-sexual abuse' syndrome whereby constellations of certain adult symptoms or problems could indicate childhood abuse, even if the adult had no conscious knowledge of this (Bass and Davis 1988; Blume 1990; Ellenson 1986). However, no such syndrome has been widely accepted which can reliably isolate child abuse as the specific cause of adult problems. Furthermore, attempts to do so have attracted fierce criticism of the all-encompassing nature of the problems claimed to be associated with child abuse (Lindsay and Read

1994). This argument, in turn, has been used by the current 'backlash' movement which argues strongly that the prevalence of sexual abuse in society is overstated (Goldstein and Farmer 1992).

Such disputes about the 'social construction' of child abuse can seem a very long way from the counselling room, and successions of clients who feel that their lives and relationships have been disturbed and sometimes devastated by the continuing effects of abuse they experienced as children. To witness directly the intense impact of memories of abuse alongside chronic depression, shame, loneliness, self-contempt, and fear leaves little doubt as to the clinical repercussions of abuse. Such consequences span the physical, emotional, cognitive, identity, existential, relational, sexual, and social domains. I have illustrated these in some detail elsewhere (Dale 1993). Other useful sources for review of consequences of abuse are Briere 1992; Cahill *et al.* 1991; Jehu 1988; Kendall-Tackett *et al.* 1993.

Principles

The activities of psychotherapy and counselling have existed for far longer than the current public recognition and concern about childhood abuse. Over the last decade therapists of all persuasions have been faced with the challenge of applying their skills to explicit abuse issues. Clients have increasingly sought help for abuse as a specific problem, and others have felt more able to reveal this in the course of counselling which may have begun in relation to other matters.

A central question arises as to whether or not there is anything specific or unique about effective therapy with this population of clients, and whether therapy that focuses on unique precipitating events is more effective than that which deals with presenting problems irrespective of causal factors (Beutler and Hill 1992). Moreover, there is a significant lack of research knowledge about processes and outcome of therapy of different orientations with adults who were abused as children. The major theoretical approaches described in the clinical literature can be conceptualized as: i) psychoanalytic/psychodynamic models; ii) trauma models; iii) 'survivor'/'recovery' models; and iv) eclectic/integrative models.

Psychoanalytic/psychodynamic models

These are less well represented in the recent literature and this may reflect the underlying historical lack of emphasis within this paradigm relating to the reality and impact of child abuse. This has received much criticism (Fortgang 1992; Masson 1990; Miller 1983; Webster 1995). However, the trend towards an object-relations focus has led to developments in the application of analytic and attachment theory specifically to abused clients (McElroy and McElroy 1991). An increasing tendency in abuse-related psychodynamic literature is the incorporation of features from models located in other paradigms such as feminism, self-psychology, and trauma theory (Davies and Frawley 1994; Haaken and Schlaps 1991; McCann and Pearlman 1990; Rose 1991).

One of the strengths of the psychodynamic paradigm is that it incorporates recognition of clients' feelings of attachment, ambivalence, and loss regarding relationships where one aspect of the relationship – but not necessarily all of it – was exploitative or abusive. Weaknesses of this approach are that the distant and abstinent stance within the therapeutic relationship can be experienced as cold and punishing, especially when clients are naïve about therapy and have histories of significant emotional deprivation. Also, because of the traditional inflexibility about 'boundaries', the approach is not generally effective in helping clients deal with crises.

Trauma models

The general failure of psychoanalysis to be effective with trauma patients led to trauma models of therapy being developed within the psychiatric tradition influenced by research on the psychological effects on combatants in wars and survivors of other catastrophes (Horowitz 1986). From such research the diagnostic category of post-traumatic stress disorder (PTSD) was established in 1980, which highlights the three symptomatic criteria of: persistent re-experiencing of the traumatic event; persistent avoidance of stimuli associated with the trauma; and persistent symptoms of increased arousal (APA 1994). A central constituent of trauma theory is the conceptualization of difficulties as being normal adaptive responses to abnormal events. It is the tendency for such reactions to persist for long periods subsequent to the traumatic events, when the person is again living in a non-traumatic environment, which constitutes the maladaptive element.

Post-traumatic stress disorder has some applicability to some adults who were abused as children, particularly in respect of the oscillations of intrusive recollections (flashbacks) and numbing phenomena. The emphasis on therapeutic stages of stabilization, desensitization, and cognitive restructuring/meaning attribution is of proven effectiveness for people in crisis. However the model has limitations in relation to childhood abuse, and may not be as widely applicable as 'treatment of choice' for such clients as is sometimes believed. The model does not accommodate the significance of pre-traumatic personality and relationship factors as affecting subsequent response to trauma, nor does it recognize that not all abuse occurs in situations or relationships which are experienced as traumatic. The PTSD formulation does not explicitly acknowledge that not all stresses promote disorder, and that stress, even traumatic stress, can be growth-inducing.

'Survivor'/'recovery' models

These have become highly influential over the last decade. A large number represent minor variations on a general theme, based on the belief that childhood abuse creates a particular constellation of adult problems which require specific abuse-focused therapy. Clients are seen as 'victims' whose recovery path involves the transformation into 'survivors'. The general principles upon which such models are based include conceptualization of 'recovery' as following a largely predetermined process which includes specific stages and actions. This principle stems from the established '12-step' recovery programme of Alcoholics Anonymous. Steps include: believing and accepting that one was abused; ventilation of cathartic anger; development of a 'survivor' identity; 'reclaiming' memories of abuse; therapist 'validation' of such memories; confronting the abuser; and 'reparenting' the 'inner child' (Bass and Davis 1988; Dinsmore 1991; Forward 1990; Frederickson 1992).

Although largely unevaluated by research, one of the reported strengths of 'recovery' models is the solidarity and support generated by associated 'survivor' peer groups illustrated by the testimonies of many people who report that such fellowship has had a profound impact upon their lives. The theory and practice of 'recovery' models, however, has recently become subject to increasingly vigorous criticism from several directions. For example, the 'false memory' pressure groups accuse such therapists and the associated literature of implanting false notions of childhood abuse into the minds of highly vulnerable and suggestible clients whose emotional and relationship problems are not connected with childhood abuse (Goldstein and Farmer 1992; Pendergrast 1995). Questions also stem from other theoretical perspectives in relation to the tendency for the 'recovery' movement to underestimate the significance of other events not directly related to abuse, and in taking a simplistic view of therapeutic complexities (Davies and Frawley 1994; Haaken and Schlaps 1991).

Recovery models are also limited in that they are less congruent for people who were abused as children in the context of affectionate caretaking relationships; for those who experienced pleasurable sexual arousal in response to the abuse; for those who feel a significant sense of loss in relation to the abuser; and for people who were sexually abused by women. Such clients can feel deviant or inadequate in response to the expectations explicit in recovery models as to how stereotypical 'victims' and 'survivors' are supposed to feel and behave.

Eclectic/integrative models

Notwithstanding the competing high public profiles of the 'recovery' and 'false memory' movements, most academically authoritative clinical publications are firmly orientated within an eclectic/integrative paradigm. Following from a recognition of the wide range of potential consequences of childhood abuse, emphasis in the eclectic/integrative paradigm has been placed on the importance of utilizing treatment approaches from across varying models to address specific issues. These involve, for example, a focus on therapeutic responses to combinations of trauma (Blake-White and Kline 1985; Ochberg 1991); loss (Courtois 1988); cognitions (Jehu 1988; Salter 1995); affect (Cornell and Olio 1991; Gil 1988); self-psychology (Briere 1992; McCann and Pearlman 1990); unconscious processes (Briere 1989; Haaken and Schlaps 1991); object-relations (Davies and Frawley 1994; Gardner 1990); family systems (Gelinas 1983; Giarretto 1982); sexual (Maltz and Holman 1987); and memory processes (Courtois 1992; Olio 1989; Sanderson 1990).

Issues

Despite the extent and breadth of the literature connected with these four theoretical perspectives, the question remains whether there is anything different about therapy with people who were abused as children in contrast to clients who are troubled by the effects of other unhappy circumstances. Having been immersed in this work clinically for a long time, and more recently through research, my considered view tends to be: 'No' – and 'Yes'.

This recognizes that in clinical practice a great deal of the process of counselling with adults who were abused as children is indistinguishable from that with clients experiencing distress in relation to a wide range of other problems, events and histories. The accumulation of counselling and psychotherapy research is clear that it is the provision of a safe context, as well as an understanding and accepting relationship in which clients feel able to talk honestly, feel understood, and create meaning for their experiences which are the factors clients consider to be the most helpful ingredients of effective therapy (Howe 1993).

In this context, abused clients – in the same way as a general range of clients – explore cognitively and emotionally the impact of various life events, losses, deprivation, moods, identity/existential concerns, relationship difficulties, and spiritual matters. However, at this point, some indications that adults who were abused as children may face special issues or challenges in therapy begin to become apparent. With all client groups, the formation of a working alliance is fundamental to progress. However, one major component of an effective working alliance is the ability to trust, and for many adults who were abused as children, inability to trust – or indiscriminate trusting – is one of the major disabling consequences of their childhood experiences. Therefore the establishment of this alliance can be particularly challenging for client and counsellor alike, and may require much more careful attention and exploration in the early stages of therapy than with those clients whose damage to trust is less pronounced.

In my research this factor was very evident in clients' stories where a hyper-alertness to the context of therapy and characteristics of therapists powerfully influenced their gut reactions as to whether the counsellor could be trusted. Of particular note is that much of this client experiencing remains private and uncommunicated. Clients experience on a multidimensional level in therapy, and abused clients may be more prone to conceal significant inner doubts, anxieties, and dissatisfaction about the therapeutic context, whilst at the same time complying with what they consider to be their therapist's expectations of them. As one client in the study remarked:

> Oh, I'd politely sit there and nod and agree and, you know – the way I was brought up to . . . (Emily)[1]

Emily's comment suggests that counsellors may be largely unaware of the amount of 'nodding and agreeing' that goes on in therapy. Therapists can be oblivious to such adaptive responses which convincingly cover up clients' deeper feelings of fear, distress, and anger. This illustrates a tendency that adults who were abused as children may be particularly prone to in therapy: to experience the therapist as a representation of a significant other (e.g. as an abusing, non-protecting, seductive, distant, preoccupied, critical, or powerful parent) and to behave in therapy in ways which are reminiscent of these earlier relationships. This potential for the context of therapy to invoke thoughts and feelings in relation to the abusing family environment is to be expected from a psychodynamic perspective, and can be a vital and helpful area of exploration in therapy, when open communication has been established and where the boundaries within the therapeutic relationship have been appropriately negotiated. Without such explicit communication some clients may be particularly prone to the combination of their vulnerability, and the intensity of their reactions to the therapeutic environment, combining in ways which render them highly susceptible to harm engendered by ill-considered or inappropriate therapeutic responses. At worst this can involve exploitation and abuse by therapists (see Chapter 30).

Increased attention has been given recently to instances of sexual abuse of female clients by male therapists, and the damage this creates through confirmation of clients' vulnerability, exploitation and betrayal (Jehu 1994; Russell 1993). What has received very little attention, however, is the phenomena of female therapists exploiting and abusing female clients in therapy. My study revealed surprising instances of quite bizarre situations in which clients felt dominated and manipulated by female therapists. Such therapists were largely perceived by these clients as being dependent on them for their own emotional satisfactions, and also to be working out their own emotional or abuse problems at the clients' expense:

> I said to my husband 'You know, she's an unhealed one – she's one that's working at it before she's healed herself' . . . I felt she wanted to control me – that was it – she wanted to be able to set a plan for me with what I should be doing with her and where she wanted me to go . . . it felt as though she was using me as a guinea pig . . . .Oh, I carried on, yes. I was back in the victim role, I suppose: 'this is the only person I've got to turn to, so this will work eventually . . .' She had got me and I hadn't the strength to say 'No, I'm not having any more of this' . . . I kept hoping for the miracle, I suppose, that we would get somewhere. We didn't. (Alice)

This is one area in which the study did not support the feminist/survivor theoretical view regarding suggested advantages of female therapists working with clients who were abused as children. Rather, it indicates that such a single-gender based analysis is limited and simplistic, in particular by underplaying the clinical reality of mother–daughter conflict, neglecting the role of mothers as active or passive abusers, and by adopting a generalized benign view of female therapists.

As has been noted, research highlights the significance of the therapeutic relationship in clients' evaluations of helpful and harmful factors in therapy. Many styles and orientations of therapeutic relating are possible; and each client's specific needs (which may change over time) must be taken into account as each unique relationship develops. Clarkson's (1993) model of five types of relationship is a very helpful way of conceptualizing and linking the various styles of relating which may occur in therapy. These involve attention to structure and task within the working alliance; the value of exploration of transference phenomena; opportunities for the relationship to provide a developmentally reparative component; the experience of intimacy within a real person-to-person 'I–Thou' contact; and the potential for transpersonal or spiritual exploration.

All of these styles have relevance for therapy with adults who were abused as children, although the unique needs of each client must determine in which sphere the relationship predominantly operates, and how it evolves. The significance of trust issues for adults abused as children in establishing an effective working alliance has already been emphasized. Exploration of transference issues, experiences of therapeutic reparation, and 'I–Thou' contact in various combinations, when handled well, can be profoundly helpful. When handled badly, either through inexperience, persistent misjudgement, or through the intrusions of therapists' personal emotional agendas, things can go badly wrong.

For some very emotionally deprived people unexpected intense needs can be provoked as an unintended negative consequence of a sudden high dosage of the 'core conditions' involving undiluted attention, acceptance, positive regard, and warmth. On occasions, especially for lonely clients with no previous experience of therapy and few support systems, this can become disorientating. This reaction may also develop more slowly in longer-term therapy as clients experience an unexpected level of dependency and intensity of yearning for recognition, acceptance, and love. Allowing the experience of neediness, dependence, and vulnerability within the therapeutic relationship can have profound positive impact on clients revising long-held impressions of themselves as being unworthy, unacceptable, and unlovable. Yet, within the same atmosphere, the potential for such dynamics to re-enact disappointing, rejecting, exploitative, or abusive experiences is great.

In addition to such therapeutic dilemmas, challenges and opportunities, communication issues are of particular importance for adults who were abused as children. A number of inherent factors significantly inhibit clients' abilities and willingness to talk about abuse:

> The hard thing about therapy is they want you to talk. And the problem with being an abused child is that you are told not to . . . (Esme)

Therapy involves, for many, the very difficult emotional challenge of speaking the unspeakable, facing embarrassment, guilt and nausea; as well as shameful expectations of therapists' disgust, excitement, disbelief, or rejection. A significant internal inhibitor for a number of clients involves disgust and shame regarding a degree of enjoyment of the erotic component of the abuse. The inhibiting aspect of erotic responses to abuse is particularly powerful in that this is an experience which is rarely talked about or discussed in detail in clinical or popular literature. Such silence can leave clients with feelings of being uniquely bad, perverse, responsible, complicit, and very alone. Similar inhibitions also occur regarding certain types of abuse – especially that which involves sexual abuse by mothers.

In addition to intrinsic blocks, therapist factors also inhibit clients' ability to talk about abuse. These include fears of not being believed; concerns that therapists could not cope with the material or did not have sufficient skills to handle the situation; or the belief that they had fixed ideas about what is thought to be helpful. For example, whilst some schools of abuse-related therapy suggest that therapists' modelling anger about the abuse and the abuser may be helpful, it is apparent from clients' experiences in my study that such angry responses most often served to further inhibit clients talking about abuse. Similarly, self-disclosure by therapists of their own abuse can act as a strong force in both directions by enhancing or diminishing clients' inhibitions in talking about their abuse. Whilst such self-disclosure can be helpful for clients in facilitating communication, this is by no means always so. This discrepancy conflicts with the theoretical assumption in 'survivor' models that hearing details of others' abuse is a helpful aspect of therapy.

Talking about abuse is a delicate aspect of the therapeutic process which should be motivated by the client's therapeutic needs (not the therapist's curiosity or theoretical assumptions), take place at the client's pace, to the extent that the client wishes, and not be forced in any way. Consequently, this focus needs to be carefully discussed and agreed with each client. A preliminary phase of 'talking about talking about' can in itself be very therapeutic. This focus enhances clients' abilities to gain a greater under-standing of inhibitions in their communication processes and to explore in what ways these remain appropriate, or are redundant and open to revision.

Another key aspect with regard to communication involves the extent to which clients – especially 'naïve' clients – can experience distress and dissatisfaction for long periods of time whilst feeling 'stuck' in relation-ships with therapists they are unable to discuss, alter, or leave. Getting away from such professionals has been a desperate challenge for some clients:

> I was with her in all about eighteen months, but it took me six months to get out of it. It took a lot of guts actually. I tell you it was one of the hardest things I ever did. For a long time I just used to go and I used to say 'Right, this week I'm going to say it' – and I'd rehearse it all week. And the amount of time I put into that is unbelievable. And I'd get there and I just couldn't do it. For months I did that . . . I knew that she was going to be angry – and I wasn't wrong. She wasn't going to like it one little bit. And what I had to do was to get into a position where I no longer cared enough about her anger, that she really couldn't touch me. So I had to really detach myself completely from her to be able to do it . . . And when I finally said 'I really don't want to come any more' – she went *nuts*. She screamed and yelled and yes – she went completely nuts . . . (Esme)

Being trapped in such ways can involve prolonged helplessness, hidden unhappiness, and adaptiveness resulting in the context of therapy subtly – and sometimes explicitly – becoming highly evocative of the childhood abuse environment.

Future developments

It would not be topical to conclude this chapter without reference to the current controversy relating to the veracity of 'recovered' memories of childhood abuse. Theoretical arguments revolve around cognitive psycho-logical models of memory versus the notion of 'repression', and disputes rage as to whether it can be empirically established that total memory for significant trauma can be 'repressed' to be 'recovered' many years later (Read and Lindsay 1997). The controversy has been heightened by pressure groups such as the false memory societies who allege that vulnerable and highly suggestible clients are being led by ill-informed or malicious therapists to falsely believe that childhood abuse is the cause of their adult difficulties. They argue that in the context of such influence and suggestion clients respond by 'remembering' incidents of abuse to satisfy therapists' expectations and are encouraged on that basis to go on to confront alleged family abusers.

Despite my initial resistance to this argument, in the course of my research I have spoken to some clients who describe this sort of experience with 'abuse-driven' therapists. However, to avoid this controversy continually being fuelled by anecdote it is vital to get into perspective the proportions of people who were abused as children who experience 'recovered' memories (as opposed to those who have always remembered), and also to gain knowledge about the numbers and characteristics of therapists who practise in such ways.

My own clinical experience as a therapist and supervisor over many years is that most clients have always had conscious awareness of their abuse. A smaller proportion have always had some knowledge of abuse, whilst also experiencing other memories 'returning'. Still others, but a much smaller category, have the experience of never having been consciously aware of childhood abuse until some precipitating event brings such memories into their awareness either in the form of a sudden crisis, or gradually. Such experiences of remembering often lead people to seek therapy, rather than existing therapy precipitating their 'memories'; although memories clearly do 'return' in the course of therapy. This impression is in accord with the small number of research studies which have been undertaken to investigate the base-rate ratio of 'recovered' memories of abuse in comparison to constant memories (e.g. Elliot and Briere 1995; Pope and Hudson 1995).

My research illustrated that the phenomena of memories in relation to abuse is much broader than that suggested by 'true–false' or 'constant–repressed' dichotomies. Categories of memories of abuse include:

(1) ever-present memories (with or without intrusion);
(2) ever-present but 'disavowed' memories (where memories are outside of daily awareness but remain accessible to motivated recall);
(3) 'recovered' memories from total amnesia for abuse;
(4) 'recovered' memories from partial amnesia for abuse;
(5) 'recovered' memories which were subsequently corroborated in some way;
(6) 'recovered' memories some of which were subsequently recognized as being inaccurate in significant ways;
(7) 'false' memories which were temporarily developed as a result of hypnotic or powerful suggestion (Dale 1996).

Clearly, therefore, some people do experience the return of 'memories' which are not strictly 'true'. This occurs outside of therapy; yet it also must be acknowledged that unacceptable therapeutic practice can influence the creation of such beliefs. The scale on which this has happened is not known, but a minority of therapists behaving in such ways with a large proportion of their clients could result in a problem on a non-trivial scale (Lindsay and Read 1994). Studies have begun to show that there is real cause for concern about the proportions of therapists who hold scientifically unjustified beliefs about memory (Yapko 1993); and who practice 'memory recovery' therapy or use 'memory recovery' techniques (BPS 1995; Poole *et al.* 1995). In contrast, the point can also be made that over-generalization from small numbers of cases of established dangerous practice can serve as further manifestation of denial of child abuse at both the personal and social levels.

If we are going to talk fruitfully about a 'false memory syndrome' (and hopefully avoid the degree of animosity which is occurring in the United States) then it seems important to develop this notion more systematically. Currently, the prominent aspect of 'false memory syndrome' relates to the alleged implantation of inaccurate memories in suggestible people (who had no prior knowledge that they were abused) by abuse-obsessed therapists. This is the 'false-positive' scenario, and is indisputably damaging. However, such a 'syndrome' also needs to take account of the 'false-negative' scenario: that is 'false memories' of not abusing. Anybody who has worked in child protection contexts will be familiar with the psychological processes of denial, involving lying, minimization, and counter-accusations, plausibly demonstrated by some abusers notwithstanding incontrovertible evidence (including criminal convictions) regarding their offences. Also, some 'false memories' of not abusing may derive from amnesia for abusing stemming from alcohol and drug use, or dissociative states. These are the so-called 'true liars' whose 'false memories' of not abusing are a genuine reflection of lack of conscious knowledge.

Memory processes in relation to being subject to child abuse, and child abusing, are in urgent need of further research. Unresolved questions about the reality and extent of 'repression' of childhood abuse memories are frequently ignited into controversy by the interaction of philosophical differences in relation to phenomenological, narrative, clinical, and legal concepts of 'truth'. Individuals and families are being significantly harmed by this dispute. In cases where the phenomena of 'false memories' appear to have some credence (for example where the client subsequently comes to realize that the 'memories' were not true), clients, parents, siblings, and often grandchildren have been devastated by the impact of such allegations. Other families remain polarized by an impasse which has little benefit or potential resolution for any of the family members.

High-profile texts are still prominent in bookshops and libraries containing assertions about abuse memories which do not withstand scientific scrutiny (e.g. Bass and Davis 1988; Blume 1990; Frederickson 1992). However, there are indications from recent research that therapists are revising their adherence to such theories and are increasingly better informed about the complexity of memory processes in relation to childhood abuse (BPS 1995; Polusny and Follette 1996; Yapko 1993).

The 'false memory' pressure groups have successfully forced professional and public attention on to concerns about specific forms of bad therapy practice. This has galvanized prominent therapists to revise and restate key ethical and practice guidelines for effective and non-harmful therapy with this client group (e.g. Briere 1997; Courtois 1997). Such material needs widespread dissemination and discussion within the therapeutic community including training courses and accreditation/registration processes.

However there are some potential dangers attached to the success of the 'false memory' campaign. The fact has sometimes become obscured that 'false memory' scenarios do not apply to the substantial proportion of adults who were abused as children who have always remembered their abuse. This causes offence to many people who feel that their experiences and struggles to develop satisfying lives are being undermined by an emerging doubting and dismissive social climate about child abuse. Also, there is a tendency for accusations of bad practice to be over-generalized against therapy as a whole. This fuels a developing over-scepticism regarding the usefulness of counselling and therapy, and may have an unintended consequence of deterring adults in distress from seeking appropriate help which many would find beneficial.

With regard to the nature of help, one of the strongest messages from my research was that clients have multidimensional, varied, and ambivalent experiences of abuse (and of therapy). On this basis it is inappropriate to conceptualize and stereotype adults who were abused as children as a unitary group, such as 'victims' or 'survivors'. Whatever the apparent similarities in their histories, each person is unique in their experiencing of events and the meanings they construct for themselves to make sense of those experiences. Effective counselling is ultimately far more likely to stem from a phenomenological exploration of this unique experiencing and ways of attributing meaning than from the application of a predetermined and formulaic therapeutic programme.

One final conclusion is that there remains a great need for the general community to remain aware of the reality and damaging impact of child abuse. However, there is also a need for the therapeutic community to be proactive with public education about good practice, bad practice, acceptable standards, and the importance of informed consent for those who seek and utilize counselling and therapy services.

Note

1 All quotes are from Dale (1996). All names are pseudonyms.

References

American Psychiatric Association (APA) (1994) *Diagnostic and Statistical Manual of Mental Disorders* (DSM IV) USA: APA.

Baker, A. and Duncan, S. (1986) 'Prevalence of CSA in Great Britain' *Child Abuse and Neglect* 9(4): 457–69.

Bass, E. and Davis, L. (1988) *The Courage to Heal: a Guide for Women Survivors of Child Sexual Abuse*, New York: Harper and Row.

Beutler, L. E. and Hill, C. E. (1992) 'Process and outcome research in the treatment of adult victims of childhood sexual abuse: methodological issues', *Journal of Consulting and Clinical Psychology* 60(2): 204–12.

Blake-White, J. and Kline, C. M. (1985) 'Treating the dissociative process in adult victims of childhood abuse', *Social Casework* 66: 394–402.

Blume, E. S. (1990) *Secret Survivors: Uncovering Incest and Its Aftereffects in Women*, New York: Ballantine.

Briere, J. (1989) *Therapy for Adults Molested as Children: Beyond Survival*, New York: Springer.

——(1992) *Child Abuse Trauma: A Theory and Treatment of the Lasting Effects*, London: Sage.

——(1997) 'An integrated clinical approach to self-reported recovered memories of abuse' in J. D. Read and D. S. Lindsay (eds) *Recollections of Trauma: Scientific Research and Clinical Practice*, New York: Plenum Press.

British Psychological Society (BPS) (1995) *Recovered Memories: The Report of the Working Party of the BPS*, London: BPS.

Browne, A. and Finklehor, D. (1986) 'Impact of child sexual abuse: a review of the research', *Psychological Bulletin* 99: 66–77.

Cahill, C., Llewelyn, S. P. and Pearson, C. (1991) 'Long-term effects of sexual abuse which occurred in childhood: a review', *British Journal of Clinical Psychology* 30: 117–30.

Courtois, C. (1988) 'The memory retrieval process in incest survivor therapy', *Journal of Child Sexual Abuse* 1(1): 15–31.

——(1997) 'Informed clinical practice and the standard of care: guidelines for treating adults who report delayed memory for past trauma' in J. D. Read and D. S. Lindsay (eds) *Recollections of Trauma: Scientific Research and Clinical Practice*, New York: Plenum Press.

Cornell, W. F. and Olio, M. A. (1991) 'Integrating affect in treatment with adult survivors of physical and sexual abuse', *American Journal of Orthopsychiatry* 61(1): 59–69.

Clarkson, P. (1993) *On Psychotherapy*, London: Whurr.

Dale, P. (1993) *Counselling Adults Who Were Abused As Children*, Rugby: BAC.

——(1996) 'Clients' and therapists' perceptions of the psychotherapeutic process: a study of adults abused as children' University of Brighton: unpublished Ph.D. thesis.

Davies, J. M. and Frawley, M. G. (1994) *Treating the Adult Survivor of Childhood Sexual Abuse: a Psychoanalytic Perspective*, New York: Basic Books.

Dinsmore, C. (1991) *From Surviving to Thriving: Incest, Feminism, and Recovery*, New York: Albany.

Ellenson, G. S. (1986) 'Disturbances of perception in adult female incest survivors', *Social Casework* 67: 149–59.

Elliot, D. M. and Briere, J. (1995) 'Posttraumatic stress associated with delayed recall of sexual abuse: a general population study', *Journal Of Traumatic Stress* 8(4): 629–47.

Elliot, M. (ed.) (1993) *Female Sexual Abuse of Children: The Ultimate Taboo*, London: Longman.

Feinauer, L. L. (1989) 'Relationship of treatment to adjustment in women sexually abused as children', *American Journal of Family Therapy* 17(4): 326–34.

Fortgang, S. (1992) 'An investigation into practice: adult incest victims and psychoanalytic psychotherapy', *Smith College Studies in Social Work* 62(3): 265–81.

Forward, S. (1990) *Toxic Parents: Overcoming the Legacy of Parental Abuse*, London: Bantam Press.

Frederickson, R. (1992) *Repressed Memories: A Journey to Recovery from Sexual Abuse*, New York: Simon and Schuster.

Gardner, F. (1990) 'Psychotherapy with adult survivors of child sexual abuse', *British Journal of Psychotherapy* 6(3): 285–94.

Gelinas, D. (1983) 'Family therapy: characteristic family constellation and basic therapeutic stance' in S. Sgroi, *Vulnerable Populations, Vol 1*, Lexington: Lexington Books.

Giarretto, H. (1982) 'A comprehensive child sexual abuse treatment programme', *Child Abuse and Neglect* 6(3): 263–78.

Gil, E. (1988) *Treatment of Adult Survivors of Childhood Abuse*, Walnut Creek: Launch Press.

Goldstein, E. and Farmer, K. (1992) *Confabulations: Creating False Memories; Destroying Families*, Boca Raton, FL: SIRS Books.

Haaken, J. and Schlaps, A. (1991) 'Incest resolution therapy and the objectification of sexual abuse', *Psychotherapy* 28(1): 39–47.

Horowitz, M. J. (1986) *Stress Response Syndromes (2nd edn)*, Northvale, NJ: Jason Aronson.

Howe, D. (1993) *On Being a Client: Understanding the Process of Counselling and Psychotherapy*, London: Sage.

Jehu, D. (1988) *Beyond Sexual Abuse: Therapy with Women who Were Childhood Victims*, Chichester: Wiley.

——(1994) *Patients As Victims: Sexual Abuse in Psychotherapy and Counselling*, Chichester: Wiley.

Kendall-Tackett, K. A., Williams, L. M. and Finklehor, D. (1993) 'Impact of sexual abuse on children: a review and synthesis of recent empirical studies', *Psychological Bulletin* 113(1): 164–80.

Lindsay, D. S. and Read, J. E. (1994) 'Psychotherapy and memories of childhood sexual abuse: a cognitive perspective' *Applied Cognitive Psychology* 8(4): 281–338.

McCann, I. L. and Pearlman, L. A. (1990) *Psychological Trauma and the Adult Survivor: Theory, Therapy, and Transformation*, New York: Brunner/Mazel.

McElroy, L. P. and McElroy, R. A. (1991) 'Countertransference issues in the treatment of incest families', *Psychotherapy* 28(1): 48–54.

Maltz, W. and Holman, B. (1987) *Incest and Sexuality: A Guide to Understanding and Healing*, Lexington: Lexington Books.

Masson, J. (1990) *Against Therapy: Emotional Tyranny and the Myth of Psychological Healing*, London: Fontana.

Mendel, M. P. (1995) *The Male Survivor: The Impact of Sexual Abuse*, Thousand Oaks: Sage.

Miller, A. (1983) *For Your Own Good: The Roots of Violence in Child Rearing*, London: Faber and Faber.

Ochberg, F. M. (1991) 'Post-traumatic therapy', *Psychotherapy* 28(1): 5–15.

Olio, K. A. (1989) 'Memory retrieval in the treatment of adult survivors of sexual abuse'. *Transactional Analysis Journal* 19(2): 93–100.

Pendergrast, M. (1995) *Victims of Memory: Sex Abuse Accusations and Shattered Lives*, Vermont: Upper Access, Inc.

Polusny, M. A. and Follette, V. M. (1996) 'Remembering childhood sexual abuse: A national survey of psychologists' clinical practices, beliefs, and personal experiences', *Professional Psychology: Research and Practice* 27(1): 41–52.

Poole, D. A., Lindsay, D. S., Memon, A. and Bull, R. (1995) 'Psychotherapy and the recovery of memories of childhood sexual abuse: U.S. and British practitioners' opinions, practices, and experiences', *Journal of Consulting and Clinical Psychology* 63(3): 426–37.

Pope, H. G. and Hudson, J. I. (1995) 'Can memories of childhood sexual abuse be repressed?' *Psychological Medicine* 25: 121–26.

Read, J. D. and Lindsay, D. S. (1997) *Recollections of Trauma: Scientific Research and Clinical Practice*, New York: Plenum Press.

Rose, D. S. (1991) 'A model for psychodynamic psychotherapy with the rape victim', *Psychotherapy* 28(1): 85–95.

Russell, J. (1993) *Out of Bounds: Sexual Exploitation in Counselling and Therapy*, London: Sage.

Salter, A. C. (1995) *Transforming Trauma: A Guide to Understanding and Treating Adult Survivors of Child Sexual Abuse*, Thousand Oaks: Sage.

Sanderson, C. (1990) *Counselling Adult Survivors of Child Sexual Abuse*, London: Jessica Kingsley.

Taylor, S. (1989) 'How prevalent is it?' in W. Stainton-Rogers, D. Hevey and E. Ash (eds) *Child Abuse and Neglect: Facing the Challenge (1st edn)*, London: B.T. Batsford.

Webster, R. (1995) *Why Freud Was Wrong*, London: HarperCollins.

Yapko, M. (1993) 'Suggestibility and repressed memories of abuse: a survey of psychotherapists' beliefs', *American Journal of Clinical Hypnosis* 36(3): 163–71.

Chapter twenty-eight

Counselling for trauma and post-traumatic stress disorder

Michael J. Scott

Introduction

Traumas as diverse as armed combat and road traffic accidents may produce an emotional destabilization of the individual. The duration of a person's destabilization can vary enormously from days. weeks. or months to a lifetime. Post-traumatic stress disorder (PTSD) is a particular manifestation of destabilization and the term can only be applied to a specific collection of symptoms that exist at least a month after the trauma. The diagnostic criteria for PTSD (American Psychiatric Association 1994) are shown below:

A The person has been exposed to a traumatic event in which both of the following were present:

(1) the person experienced, witnessed or was confronted with an event or events that involved actual or threatened death or serious injury, or a threat to the physical integrity of self or others;
(2) the person's response involved intense fear, helplessness, or horror. *Note*: In children this may be expressed instead by disorganized or agitated behaviour.

B The traumatic event is persistently re-experienced in one (or more) of the following ways:

(1) recurrent and intrusive distressing recollections of the event, including images, thoughts or perceptions. *Note*: In young children, repetitive play may occur in which themes or aspects of the trauma are expressed;
(2) recurrent distressing dreams of the event. *Note*: In children, there may be frightening dreams without recognizable content;
(3) acting or feeling as if the traumatic event were recurring (includes a sense of reliving the experience, illusions, hallucinations, and dissociative flashback episodes, including those that occur on awakening or intoxicated). *Note*: In young children trauma-specific re-enactment may occur;

(4) intense psychological distress at exposure to internal or external cues that symbolize an aspect of the traumatic event;
(5) physiological reactivity on exposure to internal or external cues that symbolize or resemble an aspect of the traumatic event.

C Persistent avoidance of stimuli associated with the trauma and numbing of general responsiveness (not present before the trauma), as indicated by three (or more) of the following:

(1) efforts to avoid thoughts, feelings or conversations associated with the trauma;
(2) efforts to avoid activities, places or people that arouse recollections of the trauma;
(3) inability to recall an important aspect of the trauma;
(4) markedly diminished interest or participation in significant activities;
(5) feeling of detachment or estrangement from others;
(6) restricted range of affect (e.g. unable to have loving feelings);
(7) sense of foreshortened future (e.g. does not expect to have a career, marriage, children or a normal life span).

D Persistent symptoms of increased arousal (not present before the trauma), as indicated by two (or more) of the following:

(1) difficulty falling or staying asleep;
(2) irritability or outbursts of anger;
(3) difficulty concentrating;
(4) hypervigilance;
(5) exaggerated startle response.

E Duration of the disturbance (symptoms in criteria B, C and D) is more than one month.

F The disturbance causes clinically significant distress or impairment in social, occupational or other important areas of functioning.

Specify if:
Acute: if duration of symptoms is less than three months.
Chronic: if duration of symptoms is three months or more.

Specify if:
With delayed onset: if onset of symptoms is at least six months after the stressor.

   If the person meets the above criteria but it is less than a month since the trauma the term acute stress disorder is used.
   The distinction between acute stress disorder and PTSD highlights the increasing concern over clients with symptoms after longer periods post trauma. For example for rape victims (Resick 1993) 94 per cent will show

acute stress disorder in the immediate aftermath but by three months 47 per cent are still suffering from PTSD. Similarly Blanchard *et al.* (1995) in a study of motor vehicle accident victims found of those suffering PTSD 25 per cent no longer met the criteria four months after the assessment and by six months 50 per cent no longer met the criteria.

With PTSD there is a window of opportunity so that most of any naturally occurring change occurs within the first six months post trauma. How clients are functioning eighteen months post trauma reflects how they are likely to be for many years to come. It is important to stress however that many people destabilized by a trauma eventually find a way of adaptively interacting with the memory of the trauma without debriefing or counselling. Nevertheless it has become the regular practice to conduct debriefings following trauma in the hope of ensuring effective adaptation. For those with long-term PTSD specific counselling strategies are recommended (see Scott and Stradling 1992). Before going on to detail the principles of counselling for PTSD, strategies for debriefing are described.

Debriefings are typically conducted in group format within days of the trauma. Participants are given the opportunity to express their feelings about the trauma and distress is acknowledged as a 'normal' response to an 'abnormal' situation. In this way the emotions of the traumatized individual are legitimized and this is particularly facilitated when other group members express similar distressed feelings. It is important that the leader of the debriefing generates hope by informing participants that probably most will become symptom free within six months. However if symptoms do not resolve, specific counselling may be necessary.

A particular focus in the debriefing will probably need to be on the 'safety' concerns of the victims, for example the staff of a bank subjected to an armed robbery are going to have very real concerns about whether the trauma will be repeated. The counsellor should help the victims determine the statistical likelihood of the trauma, based on the data available. Thus, for example, if the branch of the bank had never been robbed before then the likelihood of it recurring is going to be much less than for one robbed many times before. The likelihood should be expressed numerically and applied to say the next six months, for instance, one in a hundred chance of a further robbery in the next six months. Traumatic experiences by their very nature are very 'vivid' and this gives a mistaken impression about their likelihood, hence as an antidote to this the statistical argument is invoked. To help victims appreciate the wisdom of thinking statistically it is useful to use an example that is not as emotionally charged as their recent trauma. Thus in the case of the bank staff one might ask them to recall seeing a road traffic accident and ask them whether it had deterred them from driving and, probably, why it had not done so. It can then be suggested that implicitly they had calculated the odds, worked out that the chances of an accident were remote, and therefore continued driving.

The second string to the statistical argument is that even supposing the trauma were to be repeated, what are the chances of it being truly catastrophic, for instance resulting in someone dying. If the group were to say that the chance of a catastrophic outcome were, say, one in ten then the joint probability of it happening *and* being catastrophic would be one in a thousand. The discussion can then move on to whether they customarily take risks of that magnitude.

Pressure should not be put on the individual or group member to talk about their trauma if they do not want to do so. Some degree of mental avoidance of the trauma may be adaptive in the short term; in the longer term acknowledgement of the trauma and placing it in a wider context is necessary. In the author's view there is no merit in pressurizing a victim to relive their trauma, indeed it may constitute a secondary victimization. Clearly a debriefing alone is likely to be insufficient where victims have lost friends and/or relatives or where they are now forced to move their job or living arrangements. In these cases a broader psychosocial approach is called for.

Principles

In post-traumatic stress disorder the perceptual details of the trauma dominate the client's life. Working memory has visual, spatial, and auditory components, for instance: 'I saw him hanging there, his face was blue, eyes popping out of his head and people were screaming', as well as a verbal component: 'I brought back the wrong resuscitation equipment'. Normally these components of working memory are all subjected to the scrutiny of a central executive which decides on the action-implications of the various stores. In making its decision the central executive compares the newly formed memories with older memories i.e. it contextualizes them and the perceptual details are placed as it were in a conceptual envelope. It is suggested that in PTSD the central executive is rendered virtually inoperable and the normal hierarchy of central executive over the other components of working memory is reversed. In these circumstances working memory operates with the default option of hypervigilance; threat is assumed to be omnipresent. As a consequence of this all manner of situations are avoided. All energies are devoted to the survival of the organism, energy is conserved, with little or no energy spent on everyday interactions. Hence the depression which is the common concomitant of PTSD. However the PTSD victim is still conscious of his pre-trauma actions and goals even if the positive memories that were the raw material for them are no longer explicitly accessible. Because the system has shut down, the PTSD client, with his pre-trauma actions and goals, becomes uncharacteristically irritable, which in turn tends to sabotage close relationships. In PTSD it is primarily the perceptual details of the memory that are controlling the client. (There is always in fact an admixture of perceptual and conceptual processing; it is the relative weightings of these that it is suggested differs between non-PTSD survivors of trauma and PTSD victims of trauma).

The PTSD client usually makes great efforts to avoid thinking or having conversations about the trauma. In terms of the model described above, cognitive avoidance is likely to be a pointless endeavour, because only a conceptualization of the trauma will contain the trauma. In fact the client will exhaust himself with the cognitive avoidance. Any suggestion by the counsellor to the client that they deliberately re-live the trauma is met with disdain (see Scott and Stradling 1995a) because it is perceived as yet again making them a victim of the stores in the working memory. If then cognitive avoidance and re-living of the trauma are rejected as strategies, how does one progress with the PTSD client? Below is a list of guidelines for counselling the PTSD client followed by a short discussion of each point.

Guidelines for couselling the PTSD client

(1) Acknowledge the client's distress at the trauma.
(2) Coach better ways of handling intrusive memories by facilitating a switch from the perceptual details of the trauma to a conceptual level using 'yes . . . but'.
(3) Access the client's view of life the day before the trauma and have the client elaborate at length on the positive experiences that led to that view.
(4) Challenge the prototypicality of the trauma using 'yes . . . but . . . therefore'.
(5) Tackle the distal causes of irritability by first determining the action and goals of the client pre-trauma and then either reinstate the goals, provide alternative means to the goals, or distil alternative goals.
(6) Tackle the proximal causes of irritability by developing 'I-can't-stand-it-itis' antidotes and involving significant others.
(7) Tackle any co-morbid disorder, for example depression arising from trauma-related guilt or substance abuse arising as a means to avoid acknowledging the trauma.

(1) Acknowledging the client's distress.

The client's memory of the trauma will have cognitive, emotional and psychological components. It is a matter of respect for the client to enquire about each of these domains with questions such as: 'what went through your mind at the time? (and now?)', 'what was your worst feeling then? (and now?)', 'what physical reactions did you get then? (and now?)'. The particular cognitions, emotion, and physiology encoded in memory will likely be unique to the individual; it is important not to dismiss their response because others perhaps involved in the same trauma have reacted differently. Acknowledging the client's distress is primarily about accepting him/her without which there can be no further progress.

(2) Coaching better ways of dealing with intrusive memories – 'yes . . . but'.

Clients can be introduced to the notion of properly 'policing' the intrusive memories. They are like somewhat dubious characters on his patch which have to be handled with discretion and sensitivity; locking them up is not a viable option, they would be out in no time! In the style of the TV detective, Columbo, there is an acknowledgement of the person's report of their experience and then the hint of a possible alternative perspective with a 'but . . .' question. For example, in response to a nurse suffering PTSD following the hanging of a patient, the counsellor used the following 'yes . . . but':

> 'Yes that must have been awful to see him hanging there, especially when you had been having a friendly chat to him hours earlier. So when you saw him hanging there you ran as fast as you possibly could for a Brooks Airway [emergency breathing device] but brought back the wrong thing, is that right?'
> The client replied in the affirmative.
> 'But would you have thought it right to run any slower than you possibly could?'
> The client answered, 'No'.
> 'But if you go as fast as you can all the energy is pumped to the leg muscles, reducing oxygen to the brain, so that when you arrive you are probably a little light-headed and flustered and more likely to make a mistake'.
> At this juncture the client replied that he should not make a mistake, that he was a professional. The counsellor continued, 'But what alternative did you have to going as fast as you could? If you went slower and collected the Brooks Airway, that loss of time would have been crucial.'

Thus in the 'yes . . . but' technique the trauma is photographed from a slightly different angle. In order to do this it is first necessary to determine what angle the client is adopting with regard to the trauma. The client's perspective emerges to some degree from discussions with the counsellor. It is useful to ask the client to help you get a clear picture of how they look at the trauma, by either having them write about the trauma for a couple of minutes each day or talk about it into a tape for a period of about three to four weeks. Clients do typically find this a painful exercise, it should be stressed that this is not an attempt to get them to re-live the trauma, but simply a way of the counsellor coming to appreciate how they have come to be so distressed by the incident.

(3) Help the client access their view of life the day before the trauma.

Clients with post-traumatic stress disorder and particularly their relatives often report that they have undergone a 'personality change'; it is as if the person they were prior to the trauma no longer exists. Intellectually they are aware that, say, they engaged in activities that they no longer engage in and were happier, but the person they were feels very remote. Specific positive memories from the pre-trauma period are almost inaccessible (McNally 1995). Clients should be asked to write in the first person about how their pre-trauma view of life came about and what positive experiences they had, for example, 'I really enjoyed skiing. I would be exhausted at the end of the day; I can just feel the warmth of the log fire getting into me. I would sleep like a log at night. I remember one night I built a snowman immediately ouside Paul's door!' Even when clients have accessed these positive memories they are likely to dismiss them because their current lifestyle excludes such experiences, for instance they no longer go on holiday or they have a reduced capacity to derive enjoyment from such activities. However the important point is that their positive experiences led to a generally positive view of life and that it is only since a change of outlook that they have had problems.

Further, the generally positive view of life has greater credence because it is based on many more years and experiences than the trauma. A political analogy is sometimes useful here: one may have come to a certain political viewpoint because of a whole variety of experiences, then an event happens that causes you to change your political allegiance. However after a period of calm reflection you conclude some modification of your original position might be more consistent with the data of your whole life. One does not bemoan the fact that one changed sides (though some might), rather you would concentrate on being who you were before (engaging in the same behaviour and thoughts) albeit with some minor modifications.

Additionally clients can be advised to spend twenty minutes a day talking with a significant other about specific positive pre-trauma events. This is made easier if the other person shared these events. The client is given a rationale of 'really getting to know again the person I was'. As such it is inappropriate and self-defeating to spend any time bemoaning the deleterious changes post-trauma. Indeed if the counsellor has contact with the client's significant other the latter can be instructed to hold up, say, a red card when the client begins talking of the positives in terms of loss.

(4) Challenge the prototypicality of the trauma using 'yes . . . but . . . therefore'.

Encourage 'business as usual' i.e. teach the client how to overcome avoidance behaviour. The PTSD client behaves as if their trauma was likely to be an everyday experience. However if the counsellor has coached the client in accessing his/her positive view of the world and positive experiences this sets the scene for challenging whether the trauma is prototypical i.e. whether it is truly relevant to daily life. The counsellor can break the client's life down into, say, five-year blocks, and enquire whether the trauma was representative of events in that period, and what events more typified the various periods. However it should be remembered that as a consequence of the trauma the client has formed a new schema (template for processing information) about himself/herself and his/her relation to the world and he/she will in all probability selectively attend to information that confirms the new negative view. For example, a bus driver who suffered PTSD following an assault by a passenger replied to the counsellor's pointing out that he had not been previously assaulted in twenty years of driving, that: 'Last week I heard of another driver in another depot who had been badly assaulted'. In this instance one would ideally perhaps wish him to adopt his pre-trauma schema that for all practical purposes he was safe in work. However more usually the schema that one can actually coach the client to adopt is between these two extremes. In the bus driver's case he felt safe enough to go shopping in town by himself. Essentially the task is to enable the client to acknowledge the trauma (yes . . .); then to challenge its current representativeness or relevance (but . . .); and as a consequence begin to engage once again in many of the pre-trauma behaviours (therefore I . . .). It is not unusual for clients to reply: 'I know with my head there is really no reason why I shouldn't go and do X and Y as I used to but my guts say something else'. This is because the post-trauma contains not only trauma-related beliefs such as 'I am not safe anywhere', but there is an associated emotional and psychological tension. One way of getting the client to carry on despite the uncomfortable emotion and tension is to have him or her look at a card that has on it a written antidote to the trauma-related belief and to focus on this when they encounter post-trauma avoided situations.

(5) Tackle the distal causes of irritability by first determining the actions of the client pre-trauma.

It often appears that a PTSD client's irritability is about some event in the present, for instance the children being too noisy. Certainly this irritability impedes current relationships and some present-centred coping strategies are necessary for this. These are discussed in the next section. This irritability I would suggest is fuelled by a perceived inability to pursue pre-trauma goals; the individual first feels hurt by this – 'why should I be the victim?' – and then explodes in anger. The first step in dealing with this anger is to distil whether it is truly impossible to pursue the pre-trauma goals, or whether it would simply be difficult. If such goals are impossible it is then a question of generating as many possible options that might produce a similar sense of achievement or pleasure. The client is asked to consider the option for homework and discuss with others possible new options, and then to begin experimenting with an option. The counsellor insures in advance against the client becoming demoralized if his option does not work by saying that nobody has a crystal ball and can know for certain what is the best option; the counsellor might say for instance, 'Try it and see, if it does not work out try another option'.

Many PTSD clients are likely also to be depressed and tend to personalize any failure, seeing it as a sign of their own inadequacy. It is therefore very important to guard against this possibility. With some clients it is necessary to point out that if they are inactive on their own behalf that itself is a choice among many. Further they may want to consider the advantages and disadvantages of being inactive compared to other options. Part of the anger of the PTSD client is a result of seeing themselves as a victim. This is true in the sense that they were recipients of the trauma, but not in the sense of being specifically singled out for deliberate harm. For example, in the case of the bus driver assaulted by a passenger, the victim could have been any bus driver. If appropriate, challenging the 'victim' status of the PTSD client may help with the anger. Obviously this is much more difficult in some contexts, for instance that of a woman raped by her partner.

(6) Tackle the proximal causes of irritability, by using 'I-can't-stand-it-itis' and involving significant others.

There are two main beliefs that tend to trigger an angry response, the first is that another person has done something deliberately to cause upset. This belief can be challenged by asking the client how they can 'know' that the other person had deliberate harmful intent. Usually there is little evidence of such intent and the client has been engaging in 'mind reading' to reach his conclusion. The second belief is that the incident that has happened or might happen will be truly catastrophic. In fact the client is usually exaggerating the significance of the event. One way of drawing this to the client's attention is to draw a mountain at one end of a line and a molehill at the other. The mountain might represent their trauma and the molehill might represent a very minor irritation, for example, it started raining on their way to visit you. Then the client is asked to place another two or three hassles in their life along the line, the more serious the hassles the nearer the mountain end of the line they are located. When any further 'upset' occurs to them they are required to gauge where it should be placed along the molehill/mountain line, thereby putting the incident in its proper perspective.

A major difficulty for the angry client, however, is that they often feel their upset and anger sweeps over them in an instant. This can be dealt with by helping them to become aware of the first physiological signs of anger, perhaps butterflies in the stomach or a tightening of the jaw. At the onset of these signs they are then encouraged to imagine a set of traffic lights on red and instructed to shout STOP! to themselves. The next step is to watch the lights change to amber. As their lights are on amber they are asked to have an internal dialogue in which they ask themselves whether there is really any deliberate intent in the situation, or whether the situation is truly catastrophic. Finally they are asked to compare the current hassles with other events in their life. After answering these question they are asked to visualize the traffic lights changing to green. If they are still beside themselves with anger they are instructed to 'move off' to another room away from people to unwind; alternatively if they have become reasonably calm they can 'move off' and do something pleasant, for example listen to some favourite music. The 'traffic light' routine can be facilitated by having the client place sets of the three colours in strategic places to serve as reminders.

(7) Tackle any co-morbid disorder.

PTSD rarely occurs by itself and it is almost always accompanied by some degree of depression. Sometimes the depression improves simply as a spin-off from treating the PTSD but on other occasions it may need special focus. This is particularly the case where trauma-related guilt is a major component of the depression. Where this is the case it is often useful to point out to the client that there were at the time of the trauma only worse and less worse solutions available, there were no good solutions. For example, a client may have only had the physical energy to rescue one of two people from the sea, and he perhaps had to choose which of the two to swim towards. In these circumstances a client can be left with a feeling of guilt but it is important that the client does not take these feelings as evidence. To do so would be to engage in emotional reasoning. Guilt should instead be regarded as a moral matter rather than a question of feelings. The most ethical response in some situations is simply to perform the least worse act. Nevertheless clients can still be plagued with 'shoulds' about the incident, for instance, 'I should have pushed myself more to try and rescue the other person'. There are two possible lines of approach in such cases, the first is to suggest that it is meaningless to talk about a 'should' unless one has the capacity. 'I should feed everyone in the Third World' is clearly fatuous because one person simply does not have that capacity. With the passage of time clients often forget what capacity they had at the actual time of the trauma and it is necessary to get them to elaborate on what exactly were their capacities at the time. For example, could they remember spluttering with the amount of water they were swallowing, just how exhausted were they, what were the size of the waves? The second strategy focuses on the modification of a hindsight bias. For instance, a client became distressed when he remembered he 'could' have thrown a lifebelt from the boat to the second person, instead of which he focused on the well-being of the person he had rescued. With such clients it is necessary to point out that such situations are like being lost in a foreign town, all exits look equally perplexing and it is pure luck which one turns out to be the best, but that it is meaningless to assume responsibility for the consequences of the choice of exit. In short, guilt is only appropriate when the consequences could have been reasonably foreseen in the context in which the incident occurred.

Other disorders such as panic disorder and substance abuse may also co-exist with PTSD. Unfortunately space does not permit addressing these and other disorders in this chapter. For details of counselling clients with these difficulties see Scott and Stradling (1995b).

Issues

Debriefing

It has become commonplace to provide psychological debriefing after a trauma, indeed it seems a natural humanitarian response. There is a belief that early intervention in the first week or two after a major trauma may prevent the development of post-traumatic stress disorder. Unfortunately the jury is still out as to whether debriefing does prevent the development of long-term psychological problems. Whilst those who have undergone a debriefing typically rate the experience as helpful, in the long term they are usually no less symptomatic than trauma victims who have not been debriefed. Indeed some studies (for example Kenardy et al. 1995) found less improvement over time amongst those who had been debriefed.

In practice debriefing is almost certainly here to stay but the case for it has yet to be demonstrated. It may be that some forms of debriefing are actually harmful, some beneficial and others have no effect. There is a clear need for randomized controlled trials of the different forms of debriefing. In the meantime it is important not to exaggerate the importance of debriefing, certainly when compared to the counselling of those who develop PTSD. There is a suspicion that the 'hype' surrounding debriefing has more to do with the media coverage it has received than the needs of the victims themselves.

What form of debriefing might actually worsen recovery? It may well be that a debriefing in which an individual is put under pressure to disclose their feelings or to talk about the trauma is deleterious. In the wake of a trauma most individuals welcome the opportunity to talk about it but some do not. It should not be assumed that not wanting to talk about the trauma at this early stage is necessarily unhelpful to the individual. For this reason it is not recommended that participants in a debriefing are seated in a circle and each asked how they feel, a scenario which puts each individual on the spot. There is evidence that from about two weeks post trauma individuals begin to resent being asked about it (Kenardy *et al.* 1995) and that there is an inhibition period before an adaption phase in which they think much less about the trauma. Use of the debriefing strategies detailed above within the first two weeks post trauma, in a group context in which individuals are free to engage or disengage whenever they wish, would seem the best bet. Whether it is remains to be demonstrated. Ensuring that all individuals are given a contact number if they continue to be debilitated by symptoms is most important.

Evidence for the efficacy of treatments

Most of any naturally occurring improvement in PTSD symptoms takes place within the first six months or so post trauma, certainly how clients are eighteen months to two years post trauma reflects how they will probably be in the long term. The second major issue is what evidence there is for the efficacy of the various treatments for PTSD.

Penava *et al.* (1995) have conducted a review of the effects of different psychological and pharmacological treatments of PTSD. They identified three studies in which cognitive restructuring was evaluated. This form of intervention most closely approximates to the strategies described in this chapter. Cognitive restructuring by itself or in combination with exposure therapy proved to be more effective than hypnosis or brief psychodynamic therapy and much more effective than supportive counselling. Peneva *et al.* (1995) cite evidence for the efficacy of exposure therapy alone, in which the client is encouraged to re-live the trauma, both in the session and at home, to the point that they are no longer distressed by it, i.e. until there is a habituation response. However Scott and Stradling (1995b) have pointed out that this procedure is often unacceptable in routine counselling practice, particularly with the 50 per cent of PTSD clients who are severely depressed. Further they point out that the outcome studies have largely been confined to the mildly/moderately depressed.

Future developments

In *DSM IIIR* (APA 1987) the stressor criteria for PTSD required that an individual experience a 'psychologically distressing event that is outside the range of usual human experience'. In *DSM IV* (APA 1994) the stressor requirement is that the client 'has experienced or witnessed or was confronted with an unusually traumatic event that has both the following:

(1) the event involved actual or threatened death or serious physical injury
     to the patient or to others; and
(2) the patient felt intense fear, horror or helplessness.'

The stressor criteria are the gateway to PTSD in that clients may have the necessary intrusion, avoidance and disordered arousal symptoms but if they do not meet the stressor criteria they cannot be said to be suffering from PTSD. What then do we make of clients who have the requisite PTSD symptoms but do not meet the stressor criteria? Brewin *et al.* (1995) have found that PTSD-like symptoms are common in adult depressed clients. Memories of childhood abuse were found to be a considerable preoccupation amongst the depressed clients. He also found that they had average scores on the Impact of Events scale (reproduced in Scott and Stradling 1992), comparable to clients in PTSD studies. Scott and Stradling (1992, 1994) have argued for a definition of prolonged duress stress disorder in which clients fulfil the PTSD symptom criteria but do not meet the stressor criteria. They give examples such as the persistent maltreatment of an individual by his employer, a wife caring for her husband with a progressive neurological condition, and a scenes-of-crimes officer who had eventually 'seen too much'.

The links between depression and PTSD symptoms will likely be further elaborated in years to come. Certainly they have in common that sufferers of both conditions are particularly vague when it comes to memories of positive events. It remains to be seen whether making pre-trauma positive experiences explicit and detailed, both cognitively and emotionally, better enables the traumatic event to be contextualized resulting in a diminution of PTSD symptoms.

The enthusiasm for new techniques must be tempered by a sober appraisal of their efficacy. The counsellor can himself/herself determine the efficacy of interventions by first of all bearing in mind the stressor criteria in *DSM IV* and then using self-report measures of PTSD symptoms, both before and after intervention. The PENN Inventory and Impact of Events scale are both measures of the severity of PTSD (Scott and Stradling 1992). A score of over 35 on both almost certainly indicates a 'clinical 'case of PTSD. Scores of less then 25 on both following intervention probably indicate a clinically significant improvement.

References

American Psychiatric Association (1987) *Diagnostic and Statistical Manual of Mental Disorders*, 3rd edn, (*DSM IIIR*), Washington DC.: APA.
——(1994) *Diagnostic and Statistical Manual of Mental Disorders*, 4th edn, (*DSM IV*), Washington, DC.: APA.
Blanchard, E. B., Hickling, E. J., Vollmer, A. J., Loos, W. R., Buckley, T. C. and

Jaccard, J. (1995) 'Short-term follow up of post-traumatic stress symptoms in motor vehicle accident victims', *Behaviour Research and Therapy* 4: 369–78.

Brewin, C. R., Phillips, E., Carroll, F. and Tata, P. (1995) 'Intrusive Memories in Depression', paper presented at the World Congress of Behavioural and Cognitive Therapies, July, Copenhagen.

Kenardy, J., Webster, R., Carr, V. and Lewin, T. (1995) 'Stress Debriefing and Patterns of Recovery Following an Earthquake', paper presented at the World Congress of Behavioural and Cognitive Therapies, July, Copenhagen.

McNally, R. (1995) 'Autobiographical Memory Disturbance in Post-Traumatic Stress Disorder', paper presented at the World Congress of Behavioural and Cognitive Therapies, July, Copenhagen.

Penava, S. J., Otto, M. W. and Pollack, M. H. (1995) 'An Effect Size Analysis of Treatment Outcome Studies For Post-Traumatic Stress Disorder', paper presented at the World Congress of Behavioural and Cognitive Therapies, July, Copenhagen.

Resick, P. A. and Schnicke, M. K. (1993) *Cognitive Processing Therapy for Rape Victims: A Treatment Manual*, London: Sage.

Scott, M. J. and Stradling, S. G. (1992) *Counselling For Post-Traumatic Stress Disorder*, London: Sage.

——(1994) 'Post-Traumatic Stress Disorder Without The Trauma', *British Journal of Clinical Psychology* 33: 71–4.

——(1995a) 'Depression and The Viability of Exposure Based Treatments For Post-Traumatic Stress Disorder', paper presented at the World Congress of Behavioural and Cognitive Therapies, July, Copenhagen.

——(1995b) *Developing Cognitive-Behavioural Counselling*, London: Sage.

Part five

Issues

Chapter twenty-nine

Research and evaluation in counselling

John McLeod

Introduction

The aim of this chapter is to provide an overview of the type of counselling research that has been conducted in Britain in recent years, and to consider the place of research and evaluation within counselling as a whole. In the past, the counselling profession in Britain has been able to draw upon only a very restricted substantial research base. This situation is changing, as more counsellors and counselling educators become trained in research methods. Also, the last few years have seen the publication of several new books providing detailed information on how to design and implement research in counselling (Aveline and Shapiro 1995; Barker, Pistrang and Elliott 1994; Heppner, Kivlighan jr. and Wampold 1992; McLeod 1994b; Parry and Watts 1989; Watkins and Schneider 1991). However, counselling research remains under-funded and under-developed, and many counsellors are either unaware of the contribution that research knowledge can make to their practice, or are sceptical about the relevance of research for the kind of work they undertake. My hope is that this chapter will enable readers to gain a better understanding of what research can and cannot achieve, and will thereby help to de-mystify the research process. In this chapter, I will be referring as far as possible to research studies that are specifically in the area of *counselling*. There are, of course, many more studies in fields such as psychotherapy, social work, nursing, and clinical psychology that address similar topics and constitute a valuable resource for counsellors.

Approaches to research: some basic principles

There is no one way of carrying out research. Ultimately, counselling research relies on the sense of inquiry of the researcher, on his or her willingness to ask questions and challenge assumptions. The various methods described below should all be regarded as strategies for enabling questions to be explored and examined. It is important, too, to keep in mind that social and psychological research can never 'prove' anything to be 'true'. It is more appropriate to regard research as an ongoing debate or conversation, in which the emergence of a consensus over any issue inevitably leads to further questions and further research. For example, there is now overwhelming evidence on the association between a positive client–counsellor therapeutic alliance and good client outcomes (see Orlinsky, Grawe and Parkes 1994). This evidence has led some researchers to look more closely at the phenomenon of the therapeutic alliance, and to ask questions such as: How many sessions does it take to establish a good working alliance? How are 'ruptures' in the alliance repaired? Are there types of who clients resist forming an alliance with their counsellor? The study by Agnew et al. (1994) is an interesting example of this kind of 'second generation' research.

It is also important to keep in mind that a single piece of research, no matter how well thought-out, can in itself make any only a limited contribution to understanding. Research is like a huge jigsaw or mosaic, with individual studies serving to 'fill in' a bigger pattern. Each study must be read within the context of the global picture that is the research 'literature'. And it is essential for those carrying out research to familiarize themselves with previous research in their area, to be able to contextualize their investigation within that literature.

The central counselling research question that, historically, has captured most attention and has had most energy and effort devoted to it is the question of *outcome*: how effective is counselling (Barkham 1996)? Within the broader field of psychotherapy, there is now plentiful evidence that therapy is, in general, effective. However, there have been relatively few outcome studies conducted specifically relating to counselling in Britain (see McLeod 1995), or to specialist areas of counselling such as employee counselling, student counselling, or counselling in general practice. There is a need for further research to establish the effectiveness of counselling in different settings. Barkham and Barker (1996) offer some useful ideas about how this goal might be achieved.

There are, however, many other types of research question that can be asked. A sample of the potential range of counselling research topics, with examples of recent British research papers on these topics, is given in Table 29.1. It can be seen that there are many different research questions that may be asked, and many different ways of answering them. In recent years, there has been an increasing interest in research into the *process* of counselling. If counselling can be regarded as, on the whole, effective, then what are the components of effectiveness: *how* exactly does counselling work? The work of Carl Rogers and his colleagues in the 1950s into process factors such as counsellor empathy, acceptance and congruence, and client depth of experiencing, remains one of the most powerful examples of process research which has informed practice. Within psychodynamic approaches to counselling and psychotherapy, therapeutic processes

Table 29.1 Examples of recent counselling research carried out in Britain

Research question	Method	Author(s)
How effective is time-limited occupational counselling?	Post-counselling questionaires completed by 233 clients and counsellors	Rogers, McLeod and Sloboda (1995)
What are the effects on adult male survivors of sexual abuse in childhood?	In-depth qualititative interviews with twenty-five survivors	Etherington (1995)
To what extent do students undertaking counselling training in Higher Education institutions experience a gap between theory and practice?	Interviews with ten students	Scanlon and Baillie (1994)
What are the social, historical and political factors influencing the development of Relate Marriage Guidance?	Participant observation, interviews and documentary analysis	Lewis, Clark and Morgan (1992)
How many counsellors are there in general practice, and what kind of work do they do?	Large-scale questionnaire survey	Sibbald *et al.* (1993)

such as interpretation, transference, and resistance have been studied. Hill and Corbett (1993) provide an authoritative review of trends and issues in counselling process research. In addition to counselling outcome and process questions, there are also a wide range of important research topics within such areas as training, supervision, counsellor characteristics, and the dynamics and functioning of counselling agencies.

Research into counselling has mirrored research in psychology and the social sciences in being largely split into two distinctive research styles: *quantitative* and *qualitative*. As in the other social sciences, quantitative research in counselling has traditionally been given greater status and credibility. The strengths of quantitative approaches to research, such as surveys and experiments, are that they yield objective, 'robust' findings upon which generalizations can be made. The key characteristics of quantitative research are: accurate measurement of 'variables', statistical analysis, hypothesis-testing, and the role of researcher as detached observer. Qualitative research, by contrast, seeks to gather informants' personal accounts or stories, through techniques such as interviewing, participant observation, or personal documents such as diaries. The strength of the qualitative approach to research lies in its descriptive richness and sensitivity to meaning. Many counselling researchers are turning to qualitative methods in an effort to generate data and findings that are more relevant to practice (Rennie 1994). However, qualitative research is highly time-consuming, and personally demanding for the investigator. Also, there are some research questions, for example concerning outcomes of large numbers of clients, that are probably more appropriately addressed using quantitative techniques. Some researchers have advocated the adoption of a greater degree of methodological 'pluralism', through the combination of quantitative and qualitative approaches in the same studies (Howard 1983). This strategy is an attractive one, but there can be problems involved in integrating research methodologies each of which have their own unique 'logic of justification'. In other words, the criteria for a good quantitative study may be quite different from those for a good qualitative study (Brannen 1992; McLeod 1994b), and combining the two approaches may end with the researcher carrying out a piece of work that does not satisfy the standards associated with either perspective.

A final basic principle of counselling research concerns the requirement to conduct research in an ethical, morally-grounded fashion. The main ethical considerations arising in counselling research are the right of the person to decide whether or not to participate in a study (informed consent), the maintenance of confidentiality, and the necessity to intrude as little as possible on the counselling process itself (avoidance of harm) (see Meara and Schmidt 1991). Traditionally, counselling researchers have used the general ethical guidelines published by professional associations such as the British Association for Counselling (BAC) or the British Psychological Society (BPS). More recently, in recognition of the fact that counselling represents a particularly 'sensitive' (Lee 1993) area of inquiry, the Research and Evaluation Sub-Committee of the BAC has prepared a set of ethical guidelines for counselling researchers (BAC 1996) (see Appendix 5).

Issues in the development of counselling research

Although the trend over the last few years has been in the direction of an expansion of British research into counselling, this growth has brought with it a clearer focus on a number of key issues that counselling researchers need to face. The main issues are: the gap between research and practice, the development of an appropriate methodology for counselling research; and the provision of adequate resourcing to enable good-quality research to take place. In many ways all three of these issues centre on the question of *values*. Counselling in Britain is associated with a philosophical stance of respect and acceptance in relation to clients, reflective self-awareness on the part of the counsellor, and an overall commitment to empowerment. There are some respects in which these values are not wholly consistent with research, or at least with some varieties of mainstream experimental-empiricist research.

The gap between research and practice

The existence of a gap between research and practice was first identified in the psychotherapy community in the United States in the 1970s. It is important to note that in the USA the usual qualification for psychotherapy practitioners is a Doctorate. Thus, all therapists there have undergone research training and have completed a piece of research in the form of a research thesis. Nevertheless, in surveys carried out by Morrow-Bradley and Elliott (1986) and Cohen, Sargent and Sechrest (1986) of psychotherapist members of the American Psychological Association, it was found that very few therapists reported that research had any significant impact on their practice. When asked about the sources of information about therapy which they found most useful, they mentioned that they learned from on-going experience with clients, from their colleagues, and from being a client themselves. For the vast majority, research was the *least* useful source of new learning. When asked about their attitude toward therapy research, they complained that researchers tended to ignore the subtleties and complexities of the therapeutic relationship and concentrate instead on superficial generalizations across large samples of subjects. These findings have been confirmed in unpublished surveys of BAC members carried out by some of my own students.

The gap between counselling research and counselling practice is apparent on many occasions when researchers ask counselling agencies to collaborate in research. Typically, counsellors are anxious about what they perceive as a potential threat to their clients, and may often resist attempts to set up research projects (see Hardy 1995; Mellor-Clark and Shapiro 1995; Shipton 1994). The absence of research awareness is also evident in the small number of research inputs to the main BAC and BPS Division of Counselling Psychology annual conferences, and in the low proportion of research articles from British writers in the two main British counselling research journals, the *British Journal of Guidance and Counselling*, and the *Counselling Psychology Quarterly*. The lack of published counselling research by British authors under-represents the amount of research that is actually being carried out. At present, between 100 and 200 counsellors complete Masters dissertations each year in

British universities and colleges. Possibly around 10 per cent of these dissertations are of publishable standard, but very few are in fact submitted to journals. Clearly, there are substantial incentives attached to completing a Masters degree, but little perceived additional benefit to be gained from re-working and summarizing a dissertation to article length. Unfortunately, this means that many practically relevant pieces of research enjoy only a very restricted readership. These factors, taken together, have the consequence that professional discourse (defined as debate, discussion and dialogue in professional journals and conferences) about counselling in Britain is not, apparently, informed to any great extent by research findings.

The underlying issue here concerns the need to undertake research that makes a difference. There are two sides to this issue. The first is for research to be carried out and reported in a manner that is meaningful to practitioners. The second is for practitioners to have realistic expectations of what research can achieve, and to possess the skills to access research articles and to decode them once they have been tracked down.

Developing an appropriate methodology

The challenge of doing research that is meaningful for practitioners is linked to the second main issue facing counselling research in Britain in the latter half of the 1990s, that of developing an appropriate methodology. Virtually all the published North American and British counselling research is either conducted by psychologists, or by people using the methods of empirical-experimental psychology (i.e. measurement, control of variables, hypothesis-testing, etc.). In stark contrast, the majority of practitioners of counselling in Britain are people who are entering counselling after a previous career in fields such as social work, health care, education, management, religion or the humanities. Even those counsellors who have been trained in psychology are often the very ones who have been most critical of the positivistic bias of their psychology degree curriculum. Most counsellors know from their own initial, pre-counselling education that valid knowledge can be achieved through qualitative methods such as hermeneutic interpretation, participant observation fieldwork, and action research. What is perhaps needed, at this stage in the development of counselling research in Britain, is a set of exemplar studies demonstrating how these research techniques can be applied in studies of counselling (McLeod 1996).

However, even within the domain of more conventional mainstream quantitative approaches, counselling researchers are faced with the problem of how best to evaluate the outcomes of counselling in a manner consistent with the values and practice of counselling in Britain. There are four basic methodological issues that arise when attempting to assess outcome:

(1) selecting measures that will be sensitive to all the different dimensions of client change that may occur;

(2) not overburdening the client with a huge number of questionnaires to complete;

(3) assessing dimensions of potential change that are consistent with the aims of the counselling that is offered; and

(4) using assessment tools that are reliable and valid for the group of clients being studied.

These methodological difficulties represent a substantial challenge for counselling researchers. For example, if the effectiveness of counselling is only assessed in terms of a single factor, such as change in anxiety levels, then clients who significantly improve their social skills but remain on the whole fairly anxious could be wrongly classified as 'failure' cases. If the researcher attempts to overcompensate for this pitfall by measuring all the possible change variables he or she can think of (for example, anxiety, depression, self-esteem, work performance, alcohol use, etc.) then the client will be confronted by a battery of tests that they may well not be able to complete in any meaningful way, or will experience as overly intrusive. Moreover, many of the most widely used evaluation question-naires, such as the Beck Depression Inventory or the General Health Questionnaire (see Bowling, 1991 for further details), have been primarily developed for use in psychiatric settings, and essentially assess *psychiatric* concepts (such as anxiety, depression, and health status) rather than con-structs derived from counselling models. Finally, very few assessment instruments take into account cross-cultural differences in understanding about psychological well-being, and as a result cannot readily be employed in multi-cultural counselling situations.

The struggle to devise adequate means of assessing the outcomes of counselling and psychotherapy has preoccupied researchers since the ear-liest systematic outcome studies carried out in the 1940s. More recently, Lambert, Ogles and Masters (1992) have attempted to construct a scheme for the comprehensive evaluation of counselling outcomes. These research-ers suggest that, ideally, anyone evaluating the outcomes of counselling (or of training or supervision) should assess change in terms of three main domains: *intrapersonal* (which includes affect, behaviour, and cognition), *interpersonal relations*, and *social role* (contribution to society). Further, evaluation should encompass data from five sources: client self-reports; counsellor ratings; ratings from trained observers; ratings from relevant others; and institutional judgements. Methods of gathering data should include retrospective judgements (for instance, 'how satisfied are you with the counselling you received?'); before-treatment and after-treatment descriptions of key attributes; observations of behaviour, and changes in status (for example marital status). This somewhat simplified account of the Lambert, Ogles and Masters (1992) scheme serves to illustrate the inherent difficulty of assessing outcome. While other writers have debated the adequacy of this particular model (Elliott 1992; Schacht and Henry 1992; Lambert, Masters and Ogles 1992), there is little dissent from the claim that the benefits of counselling are complex, subtle and sometimes difficult to detect, and that the more holistic the assessment of the client, the more likely it is that any change that occurs will be picked up.

There are many other research questions and challenges contained within the overall question of 'does therapy work?' For example, the recent trend in psychotherapy research has been to argue that the effectiveness of an approach to therapy can only be accurately measured or known if the researcher has confidence in whether the therapists in the study are delivering a 'pure form' of the therapy being investigated. This dilemma has led researchers to design studies in which counsellors and therapists are trained to follow a strict therapy protocol or *manual*, with their work with clients being monitored to ensure that they adhere to the guidelines set out in the manual. Compared to the normal conditions under which most counsellors practice, this type of research design sets up a somewhat artificial and unusual clinical situation, in which one might argue that realism is being sacrificed in favour of scientific rigour. The use of 'manualized treatment' in research is discussed more fully in McLeod (1994b). Another intriguing outcome-related question focuses on the issue of whether more highly trained and experienced therapists and counsellors are more effective than those who are in training (for example, counsellors in some voluntary agencies). Surprisingly, perhaps, the evidence does *not* suggest that either training or experience makes much of a difference to effectiveness! Beutler, Machado and Neufeld (1994) review the literature on this topic, and point out how difficult it is to carry out research on therapist differences that is systematic and ethical, and yet also sensitive enough to all the potential factors involved.

Resourcing of counselling research

The above observations lead to the issue of the inadequacy of current *resourcing* of counselling research. In Britain, social research is funded through the government, mainly through the Economic and Social Research Council and the Medical Research Council, and through charitable trusts such as the Nuffield and Leverhulme Foundations. Over the past few years, the funds available from these agencies have been under extreme pressure. These agencies channel their research funds almost entirely through projects initiated by university departments and university-based research centres. Unfortunately, counselling in Britain does not yet enjoy a strong enough institutional base in the university sector to make effective use of these opportunities. While allied professions such as clinical psychology, psychiatric nursing, and psychotherapy have been successful in gaining some major research funding, counselling research remains significantly under-funded. Most of the research into counselling currently being carried out in Britain is self-resourced by people taking postgraduate degrees (Masters or Doctorates), with a limited amount of funding from the Counselling in Primary Care Trust and the Mental Health Foundation and from counselling providers such as Relate and Supportline. The largest piece of counselling research being undertaken at present, an evaluation of counselling in general practice, has been funded by the National Health Service Research and Development Executive, through the auspices of a university department of psychiatry.

Future directions

This brief review of the state of counselling research in Britain has offered an outline of some of the main themes and developments apparent in the current scene. It is always difficult to anticipate future directions. However, it does seem clear that there are good grounds for optimism that research in counselling will continue to expand and consolidate. There are now active, if small, counselling research groups at City University, London, at the Universities of Birmingham, Keele and Strathclyde, and at Roehampton Institute and Regent's College in London. The newly established Centre for Psychological Therapies, at the University of Leeds, directed by Professor David Shapiro, is an internationally recognized psychotherapy research unit which strongly supports counselling research. From 1995, the BAC has held annual research conferences, and is devoting more attention to research within the pages of its house journal, *Counselling*. The Society for Psychotherapy Research (UK) organizes an annual conference which includes much of interest to counselling researchers.

There are two quite distinct yet highly significant future developments in the area of research methodology that should come to fruition fairly soon. Dr Michael Barkham, at the University of Leeds, is directing a project funded by both the Mental Health Foundation and the Counselling in Primary Care Trust, which has the aim of constructing a short, practicable outcome-assessment battery that can be used by counsellors. Once available, this set of assessment instruments should make it much easier for counsellors to carry out outcome research within their own practice or the agencies within which they work. It should also make it easier to organize collaborative research involving different groups pooling data. The other methodological development is less concrete, but equally important. There appears to be an emerging movement among counselling researchers in Britain to create a qualitative approach to research that more fully reflects the values of counselling. The work of Dr Peter Reason and his group at the University of Bath (Reason and Rowan 1981; Reason 1986, 1988, 1994) has been influential in encouraging researchers to see inquiry as a process that can be collaborative, reflexive, and empowering.

In conclusion, it is necessary to temper optimism with caution and realism. Although there is an increasing understanding and awareness of the relevance of research for counselling, there is still only a limited amount of research being carried out. There are many items on the 'research agenda' for counselling (McLeod 1994a) that remain unexplored. There are many ways that well-designed research can help to enhance the accessibility and effectiveness of counselling. But more research needs to be done, and practitioners need to possess a more finely tuned critical appreciation of the strengths and weaknesses of research. Crucially, counselling must discover its voice in debates over what research should be done, and what the results of research might signify. Counsellors in settings such as voluntary agencies, colleges, and employee counselling schemes are increasingly required to be 'accountable' and subjected to 'audit' (Parry 1992). The current fashion in the NHS is to insist on 'evidence-based care', that is, to spend NHS resources only on treatments that have been shown to be effective. In the NHS, and elsewhere, the movement is toward carrying out 'economic' analyses of interventions such as counselling and psychotherapy; in other words to estimate the relationship between the cost of therapy and the economic benefits (for example lower drug bills, fewer episodes of hospitalization, etc.) accruing from it (Tolley and Rowland 1995). The mechanics of carrying out an audit or cost-benefit analysis are fundamentally the same as the procedures involved in any counselling outcome study, and are subject to the same methodological problems discussed above. In this case, the (undoubtedly flawed) 'accountability' research being carried out is designed to feed into very real policy decisions about numbers of counsellors employed, and the kinds of work counsellors will do. This is one of the reasons why counsellors might consider taking research seriously.

References

Agnew, R. M., Harper, H., Shapiro, D.A. and Barkham, M. (1994) 'Resolving a challenge to the therapeutic relationship: a single-case study', *British Journal of Medical Psychology* 67: 155–70.

Aveline, M. and Shapiro, D. A. (eds) (1995) *Research Foundations for Psychotherapy Practice*, Chichester: Wiley.

Barker, C., Pistrang, N. and Elliott, R. (1994) *Research Methods in Clinical and Counselling Psychology*, Chichester: Wiley.

Barkham, M. (1996) 'Quantitative research on psychotherapeutic interventions: methodological issues and substantive findings across three research generations' in R. Woolfe and W. Dryden (eds) *Handbook of Counselling Psychology*, London: Sage.

Barkham, M. and Barker, C. (1996) 'Evaluating counselling psychology practice' in R. Woolfe and W. Dryden (eds) *Handbook of Counselling Psychology*, London: Sage.

Beutler, L. E.. Machado, P. P. P. and Neufeldt, S. A. (1994) 'Therapist variables' in A. E. Bergin and S. L. Garfield (eds) *Handbook of Psychotherapy and Behavior Change*, 4th edn, Chichester: Wiley.

Bowling, A. (1991) *Measuring Health: A Review of Quality of Life Scales*, Buckingham: Open University Press.

Brannen, J. (ed.) (1992) *Mixing Methods: Qualitative and Quantitative Research*, Aldershot: Avebury.

British Association for Counselling (1996) *Ethical Guidelines for Counselling Research*, Rugby: BAC.

Cohen, L. H., Sargent, M. M. and Sechrest, L. B. (1986) 'Use of psychotherapy research by professional psychologists', *American Psychologist* 41: 198–206.

Elliott, R. (1992) 'A conceptual analysis of Lambert, Ogles and Masters's conceptual scheme for outcome assessment', *Journal of Counseling and Development* 70: 535–7.

——(1995) 'Therapy process research and clinical practice: practical strategies' in M. Aveline and D. A. Shapiro (eds) *Research Foundations for Psychotherapy Practice*, Chichester: Wiley.

Etherington, K. (1995) 'Adult male survivors of childhood sexual abuse', *Counselling Psychology Quarterly* 8: 233–41.

Hardy, G. (1995) 'Organizational issues: making research happen' in M. Aveline and D. A. Shapiro (eds) *Research Foundations for Psychotherapy Practice*, Chichester: Wiley.

Heppner, P. P., Kivlighan jr., D. M. and Wampold, B. E. (1992) *Research Design in Counseling*, Pacific Grove, CA: Brooks/Cole.

Hill, C. E. and Corbett, M. M. (1993) 'A perspective on the history of process and outcome research in counseling psychology', *Journal of Counseling Psychology* 40: 3–24.

Howard, G. S. (1983) 'Toward methodological pluralism', *Journal of Counseling Psychology* 30(1): 19–21.

Lambert, M. J., Masters, K. S. and Ogles, B. M. (1992) 'Measuring counseling outcome: a rejoinder', *Journal of Counseling and Development* 70: 538–9.

Lambert, M. J., Ogles, B. M. and Masters, K. S. (1992) 'Choosing outcome assessment devices: an organizational and conceptual scheme', *Journal of Counseling and Development* 70: 527–32.

Lee, R. M. (1993) *Doing Research on Sensitive Topics*, London: Sage.

Lewis, J., Clark, D. and Morgan, D. (1992) *Whom God Hath Joined Together: the Work of Marriage Guidance*, London: Routledge.

McLeod, J. (1994a) 'The research agenda for counselling', *Counselling* 5 (1): 41–3.

——(1994b) *Doing Counselling Research*, London: Sage.

——(1995) 'Evaluating the effectiveness of counselling: what we don't know', *Changes* 13: 192–200.

—— (1996) 'Qualitative approaches to research in counselling psychology' in R. Woolfe and W. Dryden (eds) *Handbook of Counselling Psychology*, London: Sage.

Meara, N.M. and Schmidt, L.D. (1991) 'The ethics of researching counselling/ therapy processes' in C. E. Watkins jr. and L. J. Schneider (eds) *Research in Counseling*, Hillsdale, NJ: Lawrence Erlbaum.

Mellor-Clark, J. and Shapiro, D. A. (1995) 'It's not what you do, it's the way that you do it: the inception of an evaluative research culture in Relate Marriage Guidance', *Changes* 13: 201–7.

Morrow-Bradley, C. and Elliott, R. (1986) 'Utilization of psychotherapy research by practicing psychotherapists', *American Psychologist* 41(2): 188–97.

Orlinsky, D. E., Grawe, K. and Parks, B. K. (1994) 'Process and outcome in psychotherapy: noch einmal' in A. E. Bergin and S. L. Garfield (eds) *Handbook of Psychotherapy and Behavior Change*, 4th edn, Chichester: Wiley.

Parry, G. (1992) 'Improving psychotherapy services: applications of research, audit and evaluation', *British Journal of Clinical Psychology* 31: 3–19.

Parry, G. and Watts, F. N. (eds) (1989) *Behavioural and Mental Health Research: A Handbook of Skills and Methods*, London: Lawrence Erlbaum.

Reason, P. (ed.) (1988) *Human Inquiry in Action: Developments in New Paradigm Research*, London: Sage.

——(1994) 'Three approaches to participative inquiry' in N. K. Denzin and Y. S. Lincoln (eds) *Handbook of Qualitative Research*, London: Sage.

Reason, P. and Heron, J. (1986) 'Research with people: the paradigm of cooperative experiential inquiry', *Person-Centered Review* 1(4): 456–76.

Reason, P. and Rowan, J. (eds) (1981) *Human Inquiry: A Sourcebook of New Paradigm Research*, Chichester: Wiley.

Reason, P. *et al.* (1992) 'Towards a clinical framework for collaboration between general and complementary practitioners: discussion paper', *Journal of the Royal Society of Medicine* 85: 161–4.

Rennie, D. L. (1994) 'Human science and counselling psychology: closing the gap between research and practice', *Counselling Psychology Quarterly* 7: 235–50.

Rogers, D., McLeod, J. and Sloboda, J. (1995) 'Counsellor and client perceptions of the effectiveness of time-limited counselling in an occupational counselling scheme', *Counselling Psychology Quarterly* 8: 221–31.

Scanlon, C. and Baillie, A. P. (1994) ' "A preparation for practice?" Students' experiences of counselling training within departments of higher education', *Counselling Psychology Quarterly* 7: 407–27.

Schacht, T. E. and Henry, W. P. (1992) 'Reaction to Lambert, Ogles and Masters: "Choosing outcome devices" ', *Journal of Counseling and Development* 70: 533–4.

Shipton, G. (1994) 'Swords into ploughshares: working with resistance to research', *Counselling* 5: 38–40.

Sibbald, B. (1993) 'Counsellors in English and Welsh general practices, their nature and distribution', *British Medical Journal* 306: 29–33.

Tolley, K. and Rowland, N. (1995) *Evaluating the Cost-Effectiveness of Counselling in Health Care*, London: Routledge.

Watkins jr., C.E. and Schneider, L.J. (eds) (1991) *Research in Counseling*, Hillsdale, NJ: Lawrence Erlbaum.

Chapter thirty

Counsellor–client exploitation

Kasia Szymanska and Stephen Palmer

Introduction

Counselling in Britain is now well established. This is reflected in the twofold increase in membership of the British Association for Counselling since 1991. At the time of writing this chapter, the association has over 14,000 individual and 822 organizational members. As with other professions, counselling is under increased public scrutiny and criticism. The need to maintain high standards is therefore essential and to this end the British Association for Counselling is involved in the development of the United Kingdom Register of Counsellors. The United Kingdom Council for Psychotherapy (UKCP) introduced a National Register of Psychotherapists in 1992. In addition the National Advice and Guidance, Counselling and Psychotherapy Lead Body is in the process of developing National Vocational Qualifications (NVQs) in counselling.

Specifically within this arena, one topic has emerged as the main focus of public scrutiny: the exploitation of clients by their counsellors. Unless addressed this could lead to public concern and damage the integrity of the profession. In the United States this issue has received attention since the early 1970s on account of four factors. First, the publication of *The Love Treatment* by Martin Shepard, a psychiatrist, in 1971. It was aimed at the general public and was accompanied by widespread media attention. One article in the magazine *Vogue* (Weber 1972) was entitled 'Should you sleep with your psychiatrist? The raging controversy in American psychiatry'. Second, the publication of *Women and Madness*, a widely read book by psychologist Phyllis Chesler in 1972. This described mistreatment of women in therapy, including their sexual exploitation. Third, the widely publicized case of Julie Roy vs. Renatus Hartogs, MD, which made headlines around North America, in which a patient sued her psychiatrist who was also a psychiatric columnist for the magazine *Cosmopolitan*. This gave rise to a book, *Betrayal*, (Freeman and Roy 1976), later made into a film, although neither had as much impact as the original headlines. The next sexual exploitation suit against a psychiatrist in New York led to a newspaper headline, 'Second Psychiatrist Sued'. Over the subsequent two decades sexual misconduct has been the leading cause of lawsuits against psychologists and accounted for about 50 per cent of all malpractice costs in the field of psychology. A number of these ended up as front-page stories. Fourth, a study published in 1973 by Kardner, Fuller and Mensh in the *American Journal of Psychiatry* found that about 10 per cent of physicians, including psychiatrists in the Los Angeles area, acknowledged having sex with at least one patient. This brought about considerable debate within the professions. At the 1976 meeting of the American Psychiatric Association the issue was hotly debated and the code of ethics was revised. A clause was inserted, declaring sexual activity unethical. The American Psychological Association followed suit in 1977. Concurrently research into the prevalence of exploitation increased (Holroyd and Brodsky 1977; Bouhoutsos *et al.* 1983). At present, empirical research and professional awareness of this issue is now firmly established in the USA.

In Britain exploitation has only come to the attention of the professions and public within the last decade (Chaitow 1994). However, The Prevention of Professional Abuse Network (POPAN) estimate that over 35,000 people in this country have been abused by health-care practitioners. There are reports of abuse dating back over fifty years. Forms of abuse referred to were: breach of confidentiality, financial exploitation, emotional, physical, and sexual abuse. Although research is very limited, an early small-scale study found that of twelve people who responded to a newspaper advertisement, nine reported sexual contact with their counsellors. Eight considered the behaviour 'role-inappropriate sexual behaviour' (Russell 1990). More recently the only national study conducted in the UK of clinical psychologists found that 3.4 per cent reported sexual contact with current or former clients (Garrett and Davis 1994).

The British Psychological Society (BPS) estimate that complaints about psychologists have increased at a rate of 38.9 per cent per year (Lindsay 1995). The nature of complaints vary from boundary violations to sexual contact with clients. Thus exploitation can be seen on a continuum, at one end can be excessive therapist self-disclosure, the other sexual contact or rape. Two initial boundary transgressions known to the authors involve a counsellor who brought his puppy into the sessions which later bit the client, and another therapist who tidied her consulting room during the session and referred to her sex life, in particular her inability to attain orgasm (Szymanska and Palmer 1995). On occasions such boundary violations precede client sexual abuse. This, depending on the literature definition of sexual contact adopted, can include kissing, fondling, masturbation, oral/anal sex, or vaginal intercourse.

In this chapter exploitation will be defined as behaviour on the part of the counsellor which due to its nature is intended to satisfy the counsellor's non-therapeutic intentions. Throughout this chapter the term 'counsellor' is used interchangeably with therapist and other psychotherapeutic professions in general. Additionally it is important to bear in mind that in the USA, Canada, and Britain counselling is carried out by a broad range of professionals, including physicians, pastoral counsellors and social workers.

Principles

The Oath of Hippocrates, authored between the third and second centuries BC, prohibited 'sexual' contact with patients or any other members of their household. However, subsequent codes of ethics for physicians did not refer to it, although there are periodic references to the issue in medical writings. In what may have been the first psychotherapeutic relationship, strong erotic feelings emerged in the relationship between Joseph Breuer and Anna O. in the 1880s. Freud later termed these transference and countertransference. The early analysts often struggled with feelings of attraction to their clients, sometimes quite unsuccessfully. In recent years the sexual transgressions of many early figures in the field have become apparent (for instance Carl Jung and Ernest Jones). Women analysts were not immune, with Karen Horney having multiple relationships with male patients, and Freida Fromm-Reichman becoming romantically involved with and later marrying her patient Erick Fromm.

Current codes of ethics for the British Association for Counselling and the United Kingdom Council for Psychotherapy state clearly that practitioners must not exploit their clients financially, emotionally, or sexually, such behaviour being construed as strictly unethical.

Epidemiology

Empirical research into the prevalence of counsellor–client abuse was initiated in the mid-1970s, while the majority of studies were conducted in the 1980s, largely in the form of self-report/subsequent counsellor surveys and case studies.

One of the first nationwide studies conducted by Holroyd and Brodsky in the United States (1977) surveyed 1,000 psychologists' attitudes and practices towards erotic and non-erotic contact. With a response rate of 70 per cent, over 25 per cent reported non-erotic contact such as kissing, hugging, or affectionate touching with clients of the opposite sex. Erotic contact, defined as 'that which is primarily intended to arouse or satisfy sexual desire', was reported by 10.9 per cent males and 1.9 per cent of females. Of these respondents, 5.5 per cent of male and 0.6 per cent of female psychologists admitted to sexual intercourse with clients. Three years later in a paper entitled 'Does touching patients lead to sexual intercourse?' the same authors found that psychologists who had sexual intercourse with opposite-sex clients were more likely to use non-erotic contact with their clients (Holroyd and Brodsky 1980).

Later surveys of psychotherapists and psychiatrists by Bouhoutsos *et al.* (1983), Gartrell *et al.* (1986) and Herman *et al.* (1987) confirmed incidence levels of between 0.8 per cent and 7.1 per cent. Positive responses to sexual contact were higher for males than for females. Reasons given for sexual involvement included love, enhancement of self-esteem, and helping the client to overcome sexual problems or sexual orientation. Another alarming aspect which came to light as a consequence of the research was the number of therapists who acknowledged sexual contact with more then one client. Specifically Gartrell *et al.* (1987) found that repeat and one-time offenders were more likely to know other therapists who had been sexually involved with their clients and have worked with clients who had been exploited sexually by previous therapists.

In the main, studies that examined different professional groups yielded similar results. However, Borys in a nationwide study (Borys and Pope 1989) surveyed psychologists, psychiatrists, and social workers as to their attitudes and practices on dual relationships. Their definition of 'dual relationships' encompassed incidental, social/financial involvements, and dual professional relationships. Results indicated that there was no difference between these professions as to dual relationships. Only 0.2 per cent of women and 0.9 per cent of men engaged in sexual contact (no strict definition of this term was provided). Other behaviours such as post-termination sexual contact, provision of therapy to an employee, and inviting a client to a social event were also considered and in general deemed unethical. The issue of post-termination sexual contact will be discussed in detail later in the chapter.

The only British survey of incidence (Garrett and Davis 1994) tends to support the American research. An anonymous questionnaire was sent to 1,000 clinical psychologists. All were members of the British Psychological Society, division of Clinical Psychology. The response rate was 58 per cent, with 581 questionnaires completed. The majority of respondents worked within the NHS with adults and used a cognitive-behavioural approach. Twenty psychologists reported having sexual contact with current or former clients. Sexual contact was defined as kissing, non-genital touching, hand genital/oral genital contact, vaginal/anal intercourse, and other.

A subsequent analysis of the data concerning the twenty who reported client sexual contact revealed the following:

(1) Twelve were male, seven were female, one did not reveal his/her gender.
(2) Fifteen of the psychologists reported heterosexual contact, two homosexual contact, three did not specify the nature of the sexual contact.

(3) Thirteen psychologists only had sexual contact with former clients, six with current clients, and one with both current and one former client(s).
(4) On average, sexual contact occurred with just one client, although two psychologists reported over 800 episodes of sexual contact with current and former clients.
(5) Reasons cited to sexual contact were client initiation, mutual attraction, and love.

Despite the need for other British empirical studies, this one piece of research illustrates an incidence level which raises cause for concern, particularly as Borys and Pope (1989) found no differences in behaviour among professions i.e. psychologists, psychiatrists and social workers. Given this information, are there characteristics which the abusers have in common? And are there any precipitating factors for this exploitation?

Issues

Characteristics of counsellors who exploit and precursors for abuse

Current surveys and case studies suggest that the majority of clients who become involved with their counsellors are female and the counsellors male (Gartrell *et al.* 1987). Although this is not to say that female counsellors do not exploit their male clients (Bouhoutsos *et al.* 1983). Likewise counsellors exploit clients of the same gender (Mogul 1992; Benowitz 1995) and one survey showed evidence of the abuse of children under the age of sixteen (Bajt and Pope 1989).

A short, early, and by no means definitive description of an exploiter suggests a middle-aged male counsellor about ten to twelve years older than his clients (Bouhoutsos *et al.* 1983; Gartrell *et al.* 1986). He compensates for personal problems by over-investing emotionally in clients. Folman (1991) has described such a counsellor as vulnerable, needy, lonely, and lacking in affection. More detailed models which shed light on the psychopathology of perpetrators are outlined by Jehu (1994) and Schoener and Gonsiorek (1989). Based on clinical observations of over one thousand cases of abuse, Schoener and Gonsiorek were able to classify the majority of exploitative counsellors into the following six categories:

(1) Uninformed or naïve counsellors who lack understanding of boundary violations.
(2) Healthy or mildly neurotic counsellors who tend to exhibit an understanding of their unethical behaviour and attempt to make amends.
(3) Severely neurotic and socially isolated counsellors with low self-esteem, who may involve clients in game-playing.
(4) Counsellors with impulsive character disorders and a history of abuse in other areas of their lives; some can be classed as 'sex offenders'.

(5) Counsellors who have sociopathic or narcissistic character disorders; they may be manipulative, detached, and adept at hiding their exploitation.
(6) Counsellors with psychotic or borderline character disorders; this group includes counsellors with serious psychological problems, for example thought disorders; a number may be members of psychotherapeutic cults.

Having examined possible shared characteristics, the next step is to address the boundary violations or precursors to sexual exploitation as a mechanism towards prevention. The literature in this area is growing. Psychiatrist Robert Simon (1995) has written extensively about this topic, referring to the 'slippery slope', and Richard Epstein (1994) has developed an 'exploitation index'. One precursor which has received some attention is excessive self-disclosure. Schoener asserts that, 'the most common precursor and the best predictor by far, present I would say in 95 to 98 per cent of cases, is something people don't think about, excessive self-disclosure by the therapist' (Szymanska and Schoener 1995). Legitimate self-disclosure has a therapeutic purpose and is brief. Benowitz (1995) found that discussion about personal problems was the most common precursor to sexual contact. Others included inappropriate body language, comments designed to make the client feel special, and social meetings with the clients outside the sessions.

Analysis of other mediating factors such the counsellor's personal counselling, status within the field, and prior training tends to be conflicting (Pope 1990). For example, Gartrell et al. (1986) found that psychiatrists who admitted sex with clients were more likely to have had personal therapy than those who did not, and also were more likely to have been in placement in an approved setting. In contrast, over half of the perpetrators in the British study (Garrett and Davis 1994) had not received therapy. Nor are offenders fringe practitioners or of low status in their fields. Sonne and Pope (1991) mention presidents of professional associations and professors who have been accused of exploiting their clients. While the research data has not suggested any association between therapeutic orientation and client exploitation, one survey by Pope et al. (1979) found that female psychologists who as students reported sexual contact with their educators were more likely to repeat this behaviour with their own clients. Equally Garrett and Davis (1994) found that some clinical psychologists had sexual contact at undergraduate level with tutors and with tutors/supervisors while in clinical training.

The consequences of client exploitation

The consensus in the literature is that the effects of sexual contact between counsellors and clients is harmful to clients. Only a very small percentage of clients have stated that they found it beneficial (Bouhoutsos *et al.* 1983). In these cases sexual contact was either mutually initiated or initiated by the client. The effects of exploitation have been compared to parent–child incest (Bates and Brodsky 1988) and some exploited clients have been diagnosed as suffering from post-traumatic stress disorder or PTSD (Benowitz 1995). Pope and Bouhoutsos (1986) have defined it as a distinct syndrome, the 'therapist–patient sex syndrome'. The features of this syndrome are: ambivalence, guilt, emptiness and isolation, sexual confusion, difficulty in maintaining trust, identity boundary and role confusion, emotional liability, suppressed rage, increased suicide risk, and cognitive dysfunctions (e.g. involuntary thoughts, nightmares, and flashbacks). Other reactions include grief, self-mutilation, substance abuse, and psychosomatic problems. It is also worth noting that while the majority of the feelings and behaviours experienced by clients are negative, therapists need to be aware of the positive feelings that some clients may have towards their previous therapists such as loyalty, love, and appreciation. Unless these feelings are acknowledged within the new therapeutic relationship clients are liable to feel misunderstood and to terminate treatment (Jehu 1994).

Treatment for exploited clients

Since the inception in 1976 of the first group (Milgrom 1989) for clients who had been sexually exploited by their counsellors, there has been an increase in the variety of treatment available. Depending on the individual needs of the person, the following treatment types are recommended: workshops, advocacy, family/relationship treatment, individual and group counselling (Schoener *et al.* 1989). According to client feedback the latter stands out. As Schoener states, 'support groups, consumer groups, and professionally led groups are worth their weight in gold' (Szymanska and Schoener 1995: 93). Therapeutic groups have the advantage of providing clients with a safe environment in which they can share their experiences and develop strategies to cope with the effects of the abuse. Some clients have also found that attending individual therapy was advantageous as an adjunct to the group. Based on her experience of running time-limited women's treatment groups for nine years, Luepker (1989) suggests that the themes central to each group include worries about confidentiality; feelings of countertransference experienced by the facilitators, such as the desire to be seen as more efficient than the previous therapist; dealing with a sense of betrayal; educating clients about the nature of therapy and maintenance of boundaries; exploring the next step, for example the possibility of lawsuits or complaints.

Individual therapy is often recommended for clients who are in crisis and/ or prefer working one-to-one. Schoener *et al.* (1989) provide a framework for working with clients on an individual basis; the issues discussed are also common to the group approach. A selection includes exploration of the client's feeling about entering therapy; clarification about the type of sexual contact which occurred; and discussion of the client's problems which can be unrelated to the exploitation. Nestingen (1995: 90) succinctly sums up the skills required to work effectively with these clients: 'a strong sense of self from the therapist as well as clear, solid boundaries, developed clinical skills, patience and maturity'. Although no single theoretical orientation has emerged as being more incisive in the treatment process, the authors recommend cognitive-behaviour therapy because it is a structured, didactic approach which emphasizes the use of assessment, provision of information, and goal setting. For clients who may have been involved in a therapeutic relationship in which boundaries have been blurred and the therapist regarded him/herself as omnipotent, these characteristics provide a framework from which techniques can be applied according to the identified client problems. A summary of interventions, including techniques for dealing with PTSD, is provided in Jehu (1994).

Rehabilitation: a viable option?

From a conceptual standpoint and in practice, the issue of rehabilitation of counsellors has led to much debate. In an early paper on prevention of sexual misconduct, Pope (1987) presented a hypothetical case of a therapist at risk of boundary violations and/or sexual misconduct which could be treated with a variety of therapeutic interventions. Three years on, he addressed the 'questionable nature and efficacy of rehabilitation' in terms of a lack of 'replicated research studies' (1990: 232), empirically validated procedures and the rights of clients to know they are receiving counselling from a perpetrator in the process of rehabilitation. Another argument presented against rehabilitation is the possibility of recidivism. As stated previously, some counsellors have repeated their exploitative behaviour. However, as Schoener points out, recidivism occurred only when rehabilitation or punishment were not implemented or the rehabilitation plan was not completed (Szymanska and Schoener 1995). The first three-step process model for assessment and rehabilitation known to the authors was devised by Schoener and Gonsiorek (1989). The stages are: assessment, rehabilitation, and re-assessment.

(1) Assessment: at this point, information is gathered about the perpetrator to deduce the reasons for abuse. Details about the person's life and professional history, supervision arrangements, and the sexual contact are established. When appropriate, psychological testing is also used to gather information about the perpetrator's psychopathology. The assessors also take into account the description of the abuse from the

victim's perspective, a unique feature of this model. A rehabilitation plan is only developed if the perpetrator admits the offence and a clear hypothesis of what occurred is reached. In some cases this is not possible and a contributing factor may be the counsellor's psycho-pathology. For example, due to the intrinsic and enduring character-istics pertaining to personality disorders, rehabilitation is contra-indicated for offenders with such disorders. Generally counsellors who have a tendency, for example, to get over-involved or are classed as neurotic can be rehabilitated.

(2) Rehabilitation: at this stage specific, time-limited, monitored strategies depending on the perpetrators needs are implemented. These include counselling, re-training, supervision, and practice restrictions.

(3) Re-assessment: finally, for counsellors who have successfully com-pleted the programme, their re-entry into the profession is evaluated and planned with stipulations for continuation of practice. Gonsiorek writes that this process has only one aim, '0 per cent incidence of repeated professional impropriety until death or retirement' (1995: 159). At this stage, due to the recency of this programme, it is difficult to assess the efficacy of rehabilitation. Additional consideration to this issue will be given later in the chapter.

Post-termination relationships: the debate continues

As sexual contact prior to termination is considered strictly unethical, the issue of post-termination relationships remains a grey area, subject to conflicting opinions within the professional arena. In particular, it is worth noting that post-termination sexual contact is difficult to separate from contact *in* therapy for the following reasons: many of the earlier studies did not differentiate between sexual contact during therapy and after the therapeutic contract had ended; many offenders rationalized that they terminated first; many who claim it was post-termination were not telling the truth. Taking these points into account, views about this problem can be grouped under three tentative headings: ethics and incidence; the nature of the post-termination relationship; and the time lapse between the onset of the relationship and termination.

Ethics and incidence

In a survey of members of the American Psychological Association (APA), Pope *et al.* (1987) found that 0.4 per cent of the respondents stated that post-termination sexual contact occurred at 'times' and 0.2 per cent stated 'often'. When asked whether the behaviour was ethical, the first group replied they were unsure and the second described their behaviour as ethical. One year later Akamastu (1988), in a survey of the same Division of Psychotherapy (APA) focusing specifically on attitudes and behaviours, found that 14.2 per cent of male respondents and 4.7 per cent of female respondents admitted to involvement with clients after termination. When all the survey respondents were asked the question, 'To what extent do you feel intimate relationships with former clients are unethical?', 22.9 per cent were uncertain about the ethical nature of the involvement, 3.7 per cent responded it was 'somewhat ethical', and 4.7 per cent considered it 'very ethical'. In the study reported by Borys and Pope (1989), 7 per cent of psychiatrists, 11.9 per cent of psychologists and 1.6 per cent of social workers engaged in sexual contact with clients after termination. In the British study previously discussed Garrett and Davis (1994), sexual intimacy occurred mainly with former clients.

Nature of the relationship

Beliefs about the nature or type of post-termination relationships also influenced opinions about ethical behaviour. Akamastu (1988) found that 87.5 per cent of the sample considered 'informal socialising, friendships and non-sexual relationships' as ethical. Attitudes about social encounters with former clients by lesbian, gay, and bisexual therapists were also surveyed by Lyn (1995). Social contact with former clients was considered 'ethical under rare conditions' by 28.6 per cent, 'ethical under some conditions' by 13.2 per cent and 'ethical under many conditions' by 1.7 per cent. In this case the results may have been correlated to the smaller size of the communities leading to a greater chance of encountering former clients. A survey by Conte *et al.* (1989) comprising psychologists, social workers, and psychiatrists highlighted several interesting points about post-termination contacts. Termination with a view to marriage was considered acceptable by 9.2 per cent of the sample. The percentage increased when 'proper termination' after short- and long-term therapy was cited as a reason for marriage (20.4 per cent and 29.6 per cent respectively). The second point of interest concerned long-term therapy and the existence of transference, which authors have argued continues long after termination, regardless of whether it is deemed 'proper'. Gabbard and Pope (1989: 117) conclude that 'there seem to be no research data to date to demonstrate that transference disappears or even begins to lessen in intensity upon termination'.

Time lapse between termination and behaviour

Current codes of ethics either make no reference to this 'interval' or, usually, specify a time limit. The British Association for Counselling states that 'counsellors remain accountable for relationships with former clients' and adds that 'any changes in relationships must be discussed in counselling supervision' (see Appendix 1). The British Psychological Society does not have a prohibition on post-termination relationships. American States and Associations vary in their responses. For psychologists in the state of Florida the prohibition is forever. The American Psychiatric Association has a lifelong ban, while the American Psychological Association advocates a two-year ban and also places limitations based on the client's life history and problems (for instance sexual abuse victims are excluded forever). Practitioners responses also vary. Akamastu (1988) found that 37.8 per cent of psychotherapists felt that post-termination relationships were unethical, with 16.3 per cent believing a one-year lapse to be appropriate. Some psychologists in the Garrett and Davis (1994) study described time limits between termination and contact of under one year and up to two years as ethical.

Regardless of the above post-termination guidelines, American State Association Ethics Committees have adopted a hard line towards psychologists who have had sexual relationships with former clients. The majority were found to be in breach of ethical standards (Gottlieb *et al.* 1988). This is contrary to the standpoint of some practitioners who suggest violation of personal choice is being questioned (Akamastu 1988). Bearing in mind the wealth of divergent beliefs and behaviours and the lack of agreed standards from Associations it is advisable to proceed cautiously. Further empirical research into practitioner post-termination attitudes and behaviours and the effects on former clients needs to be carried out.

Future developments

In this section recommendations for further British research and strategies for dealing with this issue will be outlined with the aim of engendering an educated and accurate viewpoint.

Research options

The American research provides a good starting place for British research which can seek to replicate or extend knowledge of this phenomenon. The Garrett and Davis (1994) survey set a precedent in British research, providing details about the topic and case examples, and should not be disregarded. Instead it should provide the basis for incidence surveys across the counselling. psychological. and psychotherapeutic professions. One problem with the American surveys is the lack of uniformity in terms of types and number of behaviours included and the wording of questions which can lead to misinterpretation. Thus standardization of questionnaires would be a good starting point. The consequences to clients of exploitation also need to be empirically validated in the form of questionnaires and case studies. The belief that sexual contact with current and former clients is not harmful, as stated by a proportion of British psychologists, also merits further investigation. This is in contrast with the negative effects described by clients (Jehu 1994; POPAN 1994). Different treatment approaches need to be formulated and then researched with the goal of matching the most appropriate treatment with the client's needs. Current British interventions focus on self-help groups (POPAN 1994) and individual therapy. It would be interesting to compare client outcomes for both approaches and to focus on any similarities or differences in terms of specific strategy and technique implementation. Finally the issue of rehabilitation requires further research. Psychologists expelled from the British Psychological Society are within their legal rights to continue practising as are counsellors whose membership with BAC has been terminated. If their expulsion was due to exploitation it is possible they will go on to re-offend. In these cases, for the protection of clients, rehabilitation would be the best option.

Counsellor training

Discussion of exploitation in training courses at all levels has a number of benefits: increased awareness of the phenomenon; opportunity for the trainer to identify trainee character traits which could lead to abuse; and a possible deterrent to counsellors. To this end Russell (1993) has outlined a number of exercises which focus on sexual attraction to clients and ways of dealing with it. Sexual attraction to clients is not uncommon and should not immediately be construed as harmful. Unless students are made aware of this and encouraged to discuss their feelings in a supportive setting (for example, in supervision), sexual attraction can be a precursor for actual behaviour. However education *per se* also has drawbacks. Students who were involved with their educators on an intimate level were more likely to repeat this behaviour with clients. The current BAC Code of Ethics and Practice for Trainers prohibits any sexual contact between trainers and trainees. Unless this code is adopted by all the therapeutic professional organizations, the possibility of students modelling themselves on their trainer's behaviour remains.

Supervisor training

Supervisors would also benefit from training in the arena of therapist–client exploitation. One issue in particular, relationships with former clients, requires further attention. The current BAC Code of Ethics and Practice for Counsellors states that counsellors 'must exercise caution over entering into friendships, business relationships, sexual relationships, training and other relationships. Any changes in relationships must be discussed in counselling supervision' (see Appendix 1). Thus the responsibility lies with the supervisor to provide the counsellor with appropriate guidance in the matter. Unless supervisors receive training on how to deal with this issue, complications may arise.

Organizational guidelines

A framework for the employment of counsellors has been documented by Schoener (1989). The individual's past employment is scrutinized for terminations of employment or resignations as they could be indicative of prior exploitation. Other boundary violations are also examined and applicants are asked to sign a statement which gives the organization permission to investigate professional competency, for instance in discussion with previous supervisors. On commencing employment counsellors are fully informed of ethical guidelines relating to boundary violations and the implications of unethical behaviour. The necessity for regular supervision and manageable caseloads is also addressed. Eilers (1985 in Rasmussen 1987: 32) writes: 'the greatest deterrent to sexual abuse in therapy . . . is strong clinical supervision, supervision that considers the process of therapy, transference and countertransference levels'. Rasmussen adds: 'that kind of supervision is found more often in the elementary levels of therapy than it is where experienced professionals practice'.

Public education

Potential clients need to be educated about therapy, what it involves, and how to recognize when exploitation has occurred, as research has indicated confusion and self-blame on the part of clients (Bates and Brodsky 1989; Jehu 1994). The issue of exploitation is seldom explicitly explained or raised in information sheets, especially in the United Kingdom. To counteract this a brief checklist has been developed by the authors (adapted, Palmer and Szymanska 1994, see Box 30.1). While already in use in various counselling centres, it is envisaged that this checklist will be available in a wider range of settings, for instance doctors' surgeries, and to all clients attending counselling sessions within professional organizations. One American study by Thorn *et al.* (1993) has suggested that both clients and psychologists responded positively to a brochure outlining information on the do's and don'ts of counselling which was given to clients either before the first session or during it. In fact the authors suggested that reading the brochure increased clients' trust in the therapist. Other media such as television, radio, and the press already distribute information on counselling. Often it is portrayed in a factual and informative light. However, reports of negative subject experiences are also common and, due to their emotive nature, can be interpreted as pervasive. Thus the need to provide clear, explicit, jargon-free information is very important.

Issues For The Client To Consider In Counselling Or Psychotherapy

1. Here is a list of topics or questions you may wish to raise when attending your first counselling (assessment) session:
   a. Check that your counsellor has relevant qualifications and experience in the field of counselling/ psychotherapy.
   b. Ask about the type of approach the counsellor uses, and how it relates to your problem.
   c. Ask if the counsellor is in supervision (most professional bodies consider supervision to be mandatory; see footnote).
   d. Ask whether the counsellor or the counselling agency is a member of a professional body and abides by a code of ethics. If possible obtain a copy of the code.
   e. Discuss your goals/expectations of counselling.
   f. Ask about the fees if any (if your income is low, check if the counsellor operates on a sliding scale) and discuss the frequency and estimated duration of counselling.
   g. Arrange regular review sessions with your counsellor to evaluate your progress.
   h. Do not enter into a long term counselling contract unless you are satisfied that this is necessary and beneficial to you.

If you do not have a chance to discuss the above points during your first session discuss them at the next possible opportunity.

General Issues

2. Counsellor self-disclosure can sometimes be therapeutically useful. However, if the sessions are dominated by the counsellor discussing his/her own problems at length, raise this issue in the counselling session.

3. If at any time you feel discounted, undermined or manipulated within the session, discuss this with the counsellor. It is easier to resolve issues as and when they arise.
4. Do not accept significant gifts from your counsellor. This does not apply to relevant therapeutic material.
5. Do not accept social invitations from your counsellor. For example dining in a restaurant or going for a drink. However, this does not apply to relevant therapeutic assignments such as being accompanied by your counsellor into a situation to help you overcome a phobia.
6. If your counsellor proposes a change in venue for the counselling sessions without good reason do not agree. For example, from a centre to the counsellor's own home.
7. Research has shown that it is not beneficial for clients to have sexual contact with their counsellor. Professional bodies in the field of counselling and psychotherapy consider that it is unethical for counsellors or therapists to engage in sexual activity with current clients.
8. If you have any doubts about the counselling you are receiving then discuss them with your counsellor. If you are still uncertain, seek advice, perhaps from a friend, your doctor, your local Citizens Advice Bureau, the professional body your counsellor belongs to or the counselling agency that may employ your counsellor.
9. You have the right to terminate counselling whenever you choose.

Footnote: Counselling supervision is a formal arrangement where counsellors discuss their counselling in a confidential setting on a regular basis with one or more professional counsellors.

Source: adapted Palmer and Szymanska 1994

Box 30.1 Issues for the client to consider in counselling or psychotherapy

Statutory registration

The BPS is currently pressing for a Parliamentary Bill to establish a statutory Register of Psychologists. If accepted, anyone setting out to offer 'psychological services' and claiming to be a psychologist would have, by law, to be on the Register. Those on the Register will have to abide by the Registration Council's Code of Conduct and to have reached a specific level of qualification to be deemed competent to practice. The BAC is also working towards a United Kingdom Register of Counsellors, due to be launched in 1997. Presently membership of the BAC for individuals and organizations is voluntary on the basis that all members abide by the codes of ethics. Complaints are dealt with by an adjudication panel who have the power to impose sanctions on the individual or organization or to retract membership. Likewise the United Kingdom Council for Psychotherapists, set up in 1989, is an umbrella organization for specific psychotherapeutic organizations listed by school of thought. The UKCP has a National Register of Psychotherapists which it publishes annually. All the psychotherapists listed on the register adhere to the code of ethics of their member organization. These in turn reflect a general code of ethics published by the UKCP, made available for organizational guidance. Complaints are dealt with by the member organization or, in the case of appeals, by the UKCP Governing Board.

Thus at present the BPS is aiming towards statutory registration as soon as possible with the UKCP attempting to follow suit. Conceptually the argument for statutory registration is simple: only practitioners who have attained a certain level of competence would be included in the register, consequently members of the public would be 'protected'. However in the USA psychologists, psychiatrists, and social workers all have to be licensed (the equivalent to statutory registration) and this did not preclude them from exploitation as the research verifies. Also, while expulsion from the register on grounds of unethical behaviour would prohibit the person from legally working as a psychologist it would not inhibit them from working under another title. Only if statutory registration was adopted by all the helping professions would the expelled practitioner find it very difficult to continue practising.

Criminalization of sexual contact

Criminalization is already in place in fifteen states of the USA and others are considering it. Wisconsin was the first state to pass this law in 1984. It is applicable to any practitioner, licensed or not, who is deemed to be practising psychotherapy. Sexual exploitation is defined along a continuum and refers to contact within the session and outside of it (Bisbing *et al.* 1996).

Conclusion

Against the backdrop of therapists' assertions that sexual contact had a place within the therapeutic relationship, media publicity and consumer concern over the phenomenon of counsellor–client exploitation began to take shape in the 1970s. As with rape and incest it was subject to denial and resistance to the issue was strong. A paper presented at the annual meeting of the American Psychiatric Association in 1977 by Davidson was entitled 'Psychiatry's problem with no name: therapist–patient sex'. However, due to increasing pressure and research, professional acknowledgement in the form of revisions of ethical guidelines occurred. Research took on the form of self-report and subsequent therapist surveys, client narratives, and clinical observations with emphasis on incidence and the consequences to clients (Bouhoutsos *et al.* 1983; Bates and Brodsky 1989; Sonne and Pope 1991). A prevalence level of sexual contact of 5 to 10 per cent was established with an overall higher incidence for male therapists. The effects on clients included guilt, depression, suicide, and post-traumatic stress disorder. The provision of subsequent treatment for clients has not emphasized theoretical approaches, rather arenas of counselling. Due to the recency of treatment no one arena has been empirically proven as effective but discussion with clients has pointed to the group approach as being beneficial.

Characteristics of perpetrators and the process of rehabilitation have also received attention. Jehu (1994) and Schoener and Gonsiorek (1989) have identified a number of traits which can be interpreted as antecedents to exploitation. Rehabilitation for therapists is already in place, but unless the perpetrators are willing to accept responsibility and, depending on psychopathology, rehabilitation is not always recommended. As to effectiveness, this can only be established once therapists have been rehabilitated and are practising again. Until then it is difficult to draw conclusions as to the level of recidivism.

Britain's position is comparable to that of the United States twenty years ago, but it has the added advantage of access to American data. Until recently this issue has remained behind closed doors. The reasons for this may be due to lack of professional interest, unwillingness to open the professions to investigation, and lack of funding for research (Szymanska and Palmer 1993).

Now, acknowledgement needs to pave the way for significant changes in professional attitude and practice. A proactive stance needs to be adopted in the form of further research in conjunction with the implementation of preventative strategies such as changes to ethical guidelines in the helping professions, increased counsellor training and supervision, review of counsellor employment procedures, regular supervision, and consumer education. Additionally, two other areas which to date seem to have been overlooked and need to be addressed are supervisor–supervisee and trainer–trainee sexual contact.

References

Akamastu, T. J. (1988) 'Intimate relationships with former clients: National survey of attitudes and behaviour among practitioners', *Professional Psychology: Research and Practice* 19: 454–8.
Bajt, T. R. and Pope, K. S. (1989) 'Therapist–patient sexual intimacy involving children and adolescents', *American Psychologist* 44: 455.
Bates, C. and Brodsky, A. M. (1989) *Sex in the Therapy Hour: A Case of Professional Incest,* London: Guilford Press.
Benowitz, M. (1995) 'Comparing the experiences of women clients sexually exploited by female versus male psychotherapists' in J. C. Gonsiorek (ed.) *Breach of Trust: Sexual Exploitation by Health Care Professionals and Clergy,* London: Sage.
Bisbing, S., Jorgenson, L. and Sutherland, P. (1996) *'Sexual Abuse by Professionals: A Legal Guide'*, Charlottesville, Virginia: Michie & Co.
Borys, D. S. and Pope, K. S. (1989) 'Dual relationships between therapist and client: A national study of psychologists, psychiatrists and social workers', *Professional Psychology: Research and Practice* 20: 283–93.
Bouhoutsos, J., Holroyd, J., Lerman, M., Forer, B. and Greenburg, M. (1983) 'Sexual intimacy between psychotherapists and patients', *Professional Psychology Research and Practice* 14: 185–96.
Chaitow, L. (1994) 'Editorial: Intolerable practices', *International Journal of Alternative and Complementary Medicine* 12 (3): 3.
Chesler, P. (1972) *' Women and Madness'*, New York: Avon Books.
Conte, H., Plutchik, R., Picard, S. and Karasu, T. (1989) 'Ethics in the practice of psychotherapy: A survey' in G. R. Schoener, J. H. Milgrom, J. C. Gonsiorek, E. T. Luepker, and R. M. Conroe (eds) *Psychotherapists' Sexual Involvement with Clients: Intervention and Prevention,* Minneapolis: Walk-In Counseling Center.
Davidson,V. (1977) 'Psychiatry's problem with no name: Therapist–patient sex' *American Journal of Psychoanalysis,* 37: 43–50.
Eilers, M. (1987) in J. Rasmussen (ed.) *'Couched in Silence: An Advocacy Handbook on Sexual Exploitation in Therapy'*, Milwaukee, WI.: author, p. 32.
Epstein, R. (1994) *'Keeping Boundaries: Maintaining Safety and Integrity in the Pschotherapeutic Process'*, Washington DC: American Psychiatric Press.
Folman, R. Z. (1991) 'Therapist–patient sex: Attraction and boundary problems', *Psychotherapy* 28: 168–73.
Freeman, L., and Roy, J. (1976) *Betrayal*, New York: Stein and Day.
Gabbard, O., and Pope, K. S. (1989) 'Sexual intimacies after termination: Clinical, ethical, and legal aspects' in G. O. Gabbard (ed.) *Sexual Exploitation in Professional Relationships*, Washington, DC: American Psychiatric Press.
Garrett, T., and Davis, J. (1994) 'Epidemiology in the UK' in D. Jehu (ed.) *Patients as Victims: Sexual Abuse in Psychotherapy and Counselling*, Chichester: John Wiley.
Gartrell, N., Herman, J., Olarte, S., Feldstein, M. and Localio, R. (1986) 'Psychiatrist–patient sexual contact: Results of a national survey, I: Prevalence', *American Journal of Psychiatry* 143: 1126–131.
——(1987) 'Reporting practices of psychiatrists who knew of sexual misconduct by colleagues', *American Journal of Orthopsychiatry* 57: 287–95.

Gonsiorek, J. C. (ed.) (1995) *Breach of Trust: Sexual Exploitation by Health Care Professionals and Clergy*, London: Sage.

Gottlieb, M. C., Sell, J. M. and Schoenfield, L. S. (1988) 'Sexual/romantic relationships with present and former clients: State licensing board actions', *Professional Psychology: Research and Practice* 19: 459–62.

Herman, J. L., Gartrell, N., Olarte, S., Feldstein, M. and Localio, R. (1987) 'Psychiatric–patient sexual contact: Results of a national survey, II: Psychiatrists' attitudes', *American Journal of Psychiatry* 144: 164–9.

Holroyd, J. C., and Brodsky, A. M. (1977) 'Psychologists' attitudes and practices regarding erotic and non-erotic physical contact with clients', *American Psychologist* 32: 843–9.

——(1980) 'Does touching patients lead to sexual intercourse?', *Professional Psychology* 11: 807–11.

Jehu, D. (ed.) (1994) '*Patients as Victims: Sexual Abuse in Psychotherapy and Counselling*', Chichester: John Wiley.

Kardner, S. H., Fuller, M. and Mensh, I. N. (1973) 'A survey of physicians' attitudes and practices regarding erotic and noerotic contact with patients', *American Journal of Psychiatry* 133: 1077–81.

Lindsay, G. (1995) 'Values, ethics and psychology', *The Psychologist: Bulletin of the British Psychological Society* 8: 493–8.

Luepker, E. T. (1989) 'Clinical assessment of clients who have been sexually exploited by their therapists and development of differential treatment plans' in G. R. Schoener, J. H. Milgrom, J. C. Gonsiorek, E. T. Luepker, and R. M. Conroe (eds) *Psychotherapists' Sexual Involvement with Clients: Intervention and Prevention,* Minneapolis: Walk-In Counseling Center.

Lyn, L. (1995) 'Lesbian, gay, and bisexual therapists' social and sexual interactions with clients' in J. C. Gonsiorek (ed.) *Breach of Trust: Sexual Exploitation by Health Care Professionals and Clergy*, London: Sage.

Milgrom, J. H. (1989) 'The first group for clients sexually exploited by their therapists: a twelve year perspective' in G. R. Schoener, J. H. Milgrom, J. C. Gonsiorek, E. T. Luepker, R. M. Conroe, (eds) *Psychotherapists' Sexual Involvement with Clients: Intervention and Prevention,* Minneapolis: Walk-In Counseling Center.

Mogul, K. M. (1992) 'Ethics complaints against female therapists', *American Journal of Psychiatry* 149: 651–3.

Nestingen, S. L. (1995) 'Transforming power: Women who have been exploited by a professional' in J. C. Gonsiorek (ed.) *Breach of Trust: Sexual Exploitation by Health Care Professionals and Clergy*, London: Sage.

Palmer, S. and Szymanska, K. (1994) 'How to avoid being exploited in counselling and psychotherapy', *Counselling, Journal of the British Association for Counselling* 5 (1): 24.

The Prevention of Professional Abuse Network (POPAN) (1994) *Development Plan 1994–1997*, presented at the October POPAN conference.

Pope, K. S. (1987) 'Preventing therapist–patient sexual intimacy: Therapy for a therapist at risk', *Professional Psychology: Research and Practice* 18: 624–8.

——(1990) 'Therapist–patient sex as sex abuse: Six scientific, professional, and practical dilemmas in addressing victimization and rehabilitation', *Professional Psychology: Research and Practice* 21: 227–39.

Pope, K. S. and Bouhoutsos, J. C. (1986) *Sexual Intimacy between Therapists and Patients*, New York: Praeger.

Pope, K. S., Levenson, H. and Schover, L. R. (1979) 'Sexual intimacy in psychology training: Results and implications of a national survey', *American Psychologist* 41: 147–58.

Pope, K. S., Tabachnik, B. G. and Keith-Spiegel, P. (1987) 'Ethics of practice: the beliefs and behaviours of psychologists as therapists', *American Psychologist* 42: 993–1006.

Russell, J. (1990) 'Breaking boundaries: A research note', *Counselling: The Journal of the British Association for Counselling* 1 (2): 47–50.

——(1993) *Out of Bounds: Sexual Exploitation in Counselling and Therapy*, London: Sage.

Schoener, G. R. (1989) 'Administrative safeguards' in G. R. Schoener, J. H. Milgrom, J. C. Gonsiorek, E. T. Luepker and R. M. Conroe (eds) *Psychotherapists' Sexual Involvement with Clients: Intervention and Prevention*, Minneapolis: Walk-in Counseling Center.

Schoener, G. R. and Gonsiorek, J. C. (1989) 'Assessment and development of rehabilitation plans for the therapist' in G. R. Schoener, H. H. Milgram, J. C. Gonsiorek, E. T. Luepker, R. M. Conroe (eds) *Psychotherapists' Sexual Involvement with Clients: Intervention and Prevention*, Minneapolis: Walk-in Counseling Center.

Schoener, G. R., Milgrom, J. H., Gonsiorek, J. C., Luepker, E. T., and Conroe, R. M. (1989) (eds) *Psychotherapists' Sexual Involvement with Clients: Intervention and Prevention*, Minneapolis: Walk-In Counseling Center.

Shepard, M. (1971) *'The Love Treatment: Sexual Intimacy between Patients and Psychotherapists'*, New York: Peter Wyden.

Simon, R. (1995) 'The natural history of therapist sexual misconduct: identification and prevention', *Psychiatric Annals* 25: 90–4.

Sonne, J. L. and Pope, K. S. (1991) 'Treating victims of therapist–patient sexual involvement', *Psychotherapy* 28: 174–87.

Stake, J. E. and Oliver, J. (1991) 'Sexual contact and touching between therapist and client: A survey of psychologists' attitudes and behaviour', *Professional Psychology Research and Practice* 22: 297–307.

Szymanska, K. and Palmer, S. (1993) 'Therapist–client sexual contact', *Counselling Psychology Review* 8 (4): 22–33.

——(1995) 'Beyond the boundaries', *Counselling News* 17: 26.

Szymanska, K. and Schoener, G. R. (1995) 'In the counsellor's chair: An American Perspective on therapist–client abuse', *Counselling, The Journal of the British Association for Counselling* 6 (2): 92–4.

Thorn, B. E., Clayton Shealy, R. and Briggs, S. D. (1993) 'Sexual misconduct in psychotherapy: Reactions to a consumer-orientated brochure', *Professional Psychology: Research and Practice* 24: 75–82.

Weber, M. (1972) 'The raging controversy in American psychiatry', *Vogue* January pp. 78–9.

Chapter thirty-one

Professional issues in counselling

Tim Bond and Catherine Shea

Introduction

From modest beginnings in the 1960s, counselling has expanded rapidly in Britain. The individual membership of the British Association for Counselling (BAC) has grown to over 13,000 individuals and almost 800 organizations in just under 20 years. This not only makes BAC the largest counselling organization nationally but also the largest outside the United States. With over two-thirds of the membership providing counselling as part of their employment, the association has been a major forum for considering professional issues. Such rapid growth requires an almost constant process of reassessment and adjustment which is not always tension free. The intimate friendliness of a small organization has been eroded by increased size. A degree of fragmentation into informal and formal divisions representing specific interests has been inevitable. Ray Woolfe, one of the authors of the first edition of this chapter (Dryden *et al.* 1989: 401), has likened the current state of counselling to a comet. The paid counsellors act as the nose cone, leading the way over professional issues because of their commitment to professionalization and access to resources. They merge into the voluntary counsellors who form the next stage of the comet. These maintain the vision of counselling as contributors to social change by a personal commitment which is independent of payment. There is a degree of interchange of people between the cone and this next stage as many volunteers have the opportunity for earning fees as the demand for counselling grows. Similarly, many paid workers also work voluntarily. The boundary between this stage and the comet's tail is similarly ill-defined. The tail consists of the enormous numbers of people who have been influenced by the values, theory and methods of counselling. These they apply to other caring roles as users of counselling skills in advisory and welfare services, health care, education, and many other roles. The metaphorical comet encompasses many more people than the membership of BAC. Dr Raj Persaud has stated that the Department of Employment estimates that over 2.5 million people use counselling (or counselling skills) as a major component of their jobs. It is estimated that over 270,000 people provide counselling in the voluntary sector with about 30,000 people earning a living from counselling (Persaud 1993: 8). Even when allowance is made for the estimated nature of these figures, the counselling movement is a substantial size with considerable potential for both social good and harm.

The large numbers of people involved as service providers or users has inevitably attracted media attention. Some of this has been positive with agony aunts, phone-ins and many features on personal or health problems recommending counselling and disseminating information about how to obtain it. Other coverage has been more critical reporting individual incidents of malpractice or raising more general issues. A recurrent concern has been the largely unregulated nature of counselling and therapy, which is now of sufficient size to be counted as an industry. The fact that anyone can simply set themselves up in private practice as a counsellor, without any training or professional regulation, is criticized by the media in the same terms used for 'cowboy' builders and fraudulent investment advisors. These stories are usually accompanied by arguments for legislative controls, which have become both more frequent and more forceful in recent years as the size of the counselling industry has become apparent to the media. However the pressure to professionalize counselling from both inside and outside the movement is problematic to significant aspects of counselling, although not all. This relates to the perceived nature of professions being seen as antagonistic to the 'spirit' or 'ethos' of counselling.

Professions

Traditional professions are exclusive in that members have to have completed one of a limited set of courses and have obtained qualifications of sufficient academic or financial difficulty to restrict the numbers of new entrants. The strict admission procedures, claims to a distinctive body of knowledge, the protection of economic and social status creates an élite which holds statutory powers to regulate itself and to protect itself from outsiders using the professional title. The existence of professions of this kind has been viewed positively by some as contributing to social stability; forming an essential link between government and the people; and, a way of maximizing a profession's credibility and competence. Others have concentrated on the negative aspects of these arrangements which can create a powerful élite more concerned to protect their income and professional autonomy than to provide an effective service and which becomes increasingly distanced from the people they claim to serve.

However professionals are not exempt from social change. International competitive pressures, the needs of organizations and changes in patterns of employment have and will continue to expand the range of professions

(Watkins *et al.* 1992). In pre-industrial society the traditional professions were lawyers, clergy, and doctors. With industrialization this expanded to include engineers, chemists, and accountants. More recently, new professions have become established in welfare (teachers and social workers), enterprise (business and management specialists), and in information technology. The proliferation of professions has diminished the status of being a professional, blurred the boundaries between professions, and created competition between them. Government has also intervened to erode restrictive practices. The combined effect of these trends has resulted in new professions becoming more egalitarian than some of the older professions by their openness to new members, recognition of the changing nature of their knowledge base, and accountability to users and the public. These changes in the nature of modern professions may ease some of the difficulties for counselling in joining their ranks but do not eliminate them altogether.

The counselling ethos

Historically, counselling has always much greater counter-establishment tendencies than its close 'cousins', counselling psychology and psychotherapy. When Carl Rogers was prevented from calling himself a psychotherapist, a term reserved for medical practitioners in the 1920s in the United States, he adopted the term 'counseling' from its originator, Frank Parsons, a social campaigner on behalf of the urban poor (Thorne 1984). The radical association may have suited Rogers because he was also challenging the established power relationship between the therapist and client, in that he came to trust the clients' wisdom about what is best for them. As a consequence he redefined the therapist as a facilitator who gives particular attention to the quality of the relationship. Over time, Rogers evolved a distinctive theory and method but his basic ideas have remained influential within British counselling as other models of therapy from the psychodynamic, behavioural, and other traditions have been incorporated within the scope of counselling. The emphasis on personal empowerment has encouraged the use of counselling within the voluntary sector as a method of offering assistance to others to counter social disadvantages or manage personal problems. Counselling has also been used extensively within the women's movement to support women seeking social change. The active use of counselling in these circumstances has helped to maintain a counter-cultural tendency even when counselling has been co-opted to work alongside more established professions.

The use of counselling within education and health care has highlighted a number of features of counselling which are potentially antagonistic to the ethos of the established professions. Firstly, the counsellor's commitment to respect for the autonomy of service users has tended to be more wholehearted and rigorous in comparison to other professions working in health care and education. School counsellors, student counsellors, and counsellors in GP surgeries have reported that ensuring the client's right to choose and to confidentiality has been problematic. There have also been some more profound differences. The philosophy which underpins counselling is more directly concerned with subjective experience, that is, someone's perceptions of events, rather than the 'objectivity' of the scientific discourse which is so dominant in society. This emphasis on subjectivity is reflected in debates about the best methods for researching counselling (McLeod 1994; Strong *et al.* 1995) and has also created problems for counsellors when asked to explain their work in medical and legal settings where the emphasis is usually on discovering 'facts' rather than on someone's 'perceptions'. Similarly, the relationship between counselling and social work has been problematic. The emphasis on an individual's capacity for personal change within counselling stands in contrast to the social-work theory which places greater emphasis on understanding society and social structures in order to counter the powerlessness of most of their clients and the forces which discriminate against them. These points of difference with other professions are not fixed and change over time as academic disciplines evolve; but, in its relatively short history, counselling has been characterized by a degree of conflict with the dominant discourses of the professions with whom counsellors have most contact.

The sense of being besieged, misunderstood, and having difficulty in finding a secure place within the existing professional networks has had a profound influence on the attitude to professionalization of counselling. Some want nothing to do with professionalization and see it as contradictory to the values and aspirations of counselling. No one knows the strength of this view outside BAC but within the association it is probably a significant minority view. The majority view within BAC appears to be in favour of increasing professionalization, with an expectation that it can achieve the following aims: it should provide real protection for clients against malpractice; the form of professionalization should be consistent with the egalitarian values of counselling and not transform counselling from skilled facilitation to authoritative expertise; professionalization of an appropriate kind might even be welcomed if it strengthened the ability of counselling to convey its distinctive message. These aims seem to be achievable within the greater flexibility of new-style professions. However, there is a further concern which is much more problematic. The counselling movement has been remarkable for including diversity and valuing difference within its membership, especially within BAC. Splinter movements have arisen over difficult issues but have frequently returned and been welcomed back. This desire for inclusivity is a distinctive feature of counselling in comparison to other talking therapies. Counselling psychology has entrance requirements which exclude all non-graduate psychologists. Psychotherapy, as represented by the United Kingdom Council for Psychotherapy, is a post-graduate activity and is characterized by much more divisiveness between different traditions and between national organizations. A commitment to inclusivity does not sit easily with professionalization, which could fracture the existing 'comet' formation of counselling. At some point a profession has to mark a boundary between those who are included and those who are excluded. The boundary can be marked by those who achieve certain standards in terms of practice. In the next sections we will explore some of the standards which are distinctive to counselling before we return to the way in which BAC has sought to maximize the inclusivity of counselling.

Codes of standards and ethics

One of the distinctive features of any organization committed to professional standards is the production of codes and guidelines. These serve several purposes simultaneously. They are a tangible commitment to providing a basic set of rules for the protection of service users. All professions are characterized by a concern with being trustworthy. The rules also declare a basic set of values and requirements which enable the profession to establish its identity, and thus mark out the territory of the profession and its relationship with other professions.

The first code produced by BAC in 1984 was contained on four pages. It was written in abstract and relatively open-ended terminology which established the spirit of counselling in terms of general principles but offered little specific guidance. Significantly, this code made no provision for breaking confidentiality to protect a client from serious self-harm or suicidal intent. The absence of these limitations on confidentiality and the desire to tighten up the restrictions on sexual relationships with clients led to a radical rewriting in the late 1980s. This produced a much longer code containing more detailed guidance (Bond 1991a). The structure of the revised code of practice indicated how much more complex the working environment of the counsellor had become. It distinguished between different areas of responsibility of which responsibility to the client was paramount but not to the exclusion of responsibility to self as counsellor, to other counsellors, to colleagues and members of the caring professions, and to the wider community. Detailed guidance on confidentiality, counselling supervision, and advertising was also included prior to a section on resolving conflict between ethical responsibilities. An additional section was added in 1993 to establish safeguards against the exploitation of former clients. As this version of the code is available in its entirety in Appendix 1, we will select a few key themes for comment as well as considering some of the potential challenges to current ethics and practice.

Client autonomy

Respect for client autonomy is the foundation stone upon which the professional ethic of counselling is constructed. Arguably, this is as much a
matter of necessity as an ethical virtue. By its very nature, counselling
requires the full engagement of the client and unlike many physical therapies cannot be undertaken on an anaesthetized or passive subject. Giving
priority to respect for the client's capacity for self-government is an
essential component in maximizing the client's active commitment to the
counselling. In actual practice, a counsellor's commitment to autonomy
entails:

(1) An emphasis on the voluntary nature of counselling being freely under-
    taken by a client. If someone has been 'sent' for counselling, the first
    task is to help the client explore whether he/she really wants counsel-
    ling and on what basis. Throughout the relationship there is an on-
    going emphasis on the client giving free and informed consent to
    important decisions about ethical and therapeutic issues.
(2) Clarity of contracting over the counsellor's and client's expectations of
    each other and the therapeutic goals are also required. In practice, this
    requirement has proved difficult to implement because many clients do
    not wish to engage in detailed discussions about contracts at the start of
    a counselling relationship, especially if they are seeking urgent relief
    from an emotional or personal crisis. As a result, increasing numbers of
    counsellors provide a brief leaflet of pre-counselling information which
    sets out a brief description of the counsellor, the methods used, ex-
    pectations over attendance, details of any fees, arrangements for can-
    cellation of sessions and a basic statement about confidentiality (see
    below). These formalities ensure that the client is empowered by
    knowledge and therefore best able to make an autonomous decision
    about the basis on which he/she wants to receive counselling.

The importance of confidentiality is a corollary of respect for client
autonomy. The counsellor's commitment to confidentiality ensures that
the client controls the outcome of counselling in other aspects of his/her
life without interference from the counsellor.

Confidentiality

The management of confidentiality is one of the most recurrent sources of
ethical difficulty for counsellors. Confidentiality is a high priority because
it is both essential to respect for client autonomy and because assurances of
confidentiality maximize personal frankness which is so essential to counselling. However, it cannot be an absolute priority in all circumstances.
Counsellors are sometimes faced with making difficult choices between

confidentiality and other legal or ethical imperatives. The safest way to resolve these dilemmas is to involve the client in the decision-making process and to obtain his/her consent to any disclosures. Seeking the client's consent can be frustrated because the client is uncontactable, too distressed to make autonomous decisions, or simply refuses consent. The counsellor is left with a considerable ethical dilemma.

The challenges of managing confidentiality vary according to the setting. Counsellors in independent private practice tend to be most troubled about when they are permitted to break confidentiality if there are good grounds for believing that clients will cause serious physical harm to others or themselves (BAC 1993:ss.B.4.4). Suicidal risk-assessment is becoming increasingly important in making the decision about how to respond to an adult client (Eldrid 1988; Hawton and Catalan 1987; Bond 1993). Without a prior agreement with a client either in the contract or by subsequent agreement, it may be an actionable legal breach of confidence to disclose the suicidal intent of a client because of the growing legal trend to permit adults to refuse treatment. On the other hand, there is a public policy commitment to reduce the suicide rate. Whether working in private practice or elsewhere, counsellors need to consider carefully obligations over confidentiality for suicidal clients. As in the United States, counsellors in Britain tread a tightrope with potential professional liability for over or under reacting. In contrast to the United States, the British counsellor cannot assume a legal or ethical right in all circumstances to breach confidentiality on behalf of a suicidal client without that client's consent (Austin *et al.* 1990; Bond 1994a).

The challenges for counsellors working within organizations are more complex because of the potential for conflicting obligations to the client and to the organization. For example, there may be a duty to make routine disclosures of confidential information to team members or elsewhere in the organization. There are differences of opinion within the talking therapies about how to respond. BAC ideally requires the client's consent or an explicit condition within the contract (BAC 1993:ss.B.4.3/4). The British Psychological Society requires that all psychologists shall 'endeavour' (an ambiguous requirement) to inform recipients of services about sharing information with colleagues (BPS 1993:ss.4.2). The guidelines specific to counselling psychologists require rigorous respect for matters of confidentiality and the identification in advance of circumstances in which confidentiality will be breached (BPS 1995:ss.1.5.1). In contrast, psychotherapists regard making the decision to inform colleagues a matter of professional judgement of the best interests of the client who should have been informed, although there is some ambiguity about the requirement to inform the client when GPs and relevant psychiatric services are being informed (UKCP 1995:ss.2.5). Some counsellors working in medical settings have been taxed by the expectation of referrers to receive some form of brief report on progress. Most counsellors resolve this issue by seeking the client's consent and many agree the content of the report with the client. When the counsellor is responsible for making the referral, it is considered essential to seek the informed consent of the client. In order to be considered 'informed', the client should know in advance the nature of the services on offer and the degree of confidentiality given to information which would be passed on by the counsellor. This may involve the counsellor in preliminary discussions with a potential service provider in which the identity of the client is protected until he/she has sufficient information to make an informed choice. A recent study (SCODA 1995) on confidentiality for alcohol and drug services contains examples of pre-counselling information for clients, an agency policy statement, complaints procedures, and recommends that confidentiality be included within the contract of employment of counsellors and their support staff. These are considered the basic ingredients of an effective agency policy on confidentiality. It is essential that it is supported by staff training.

Confidentiality is an aspect of counselling which can create legal liability, usually leading to awards of damages or injunctions against the counsellor. Fee-paying clients can seek redress in the local county court, a relatively cheap and simple action in which the court will assume a condition of confidentiality in the counsellor–client relationship unless there is clear evidence of a contrary agreement. There are also important ways in which the law will protect the confidentiality of counselling records during police searches. However, there are also exceptional circumstances in which counselling records may be required to be produced in court (Bond 1994a). This is one aspect of practice where counsellors need to keep abreast of the law as well as professional codes.

Prohibitions on exploitation

It is self-evident that counsellors should not exploit their clients. There has nonetheless been disagreement about what constitutes exploitation. In 1984, the prohibition on sexual relationships with current clients was disputed by a minority of counsellors as unnecessarily restrictive. However studies about the harm caused to most clients have ensured widespread support for this prohibition (Pope *et al.* 1993; Russell 1993). By the early 1990s, a number of cases had arisen where former clients appeared to have suffered harm from sexual relationships with people who had once been their counsellor. This resulted in a debate about whether the prohibition should be for the term of the client's life, or whether criteria could be agreed to ensure that the counselling relationship was sufficiently completed before the possibility of a sexual relationship was contemplated. After some heated debate (Bond 1994b) the latter course was chosen. A contemporary study produced independently of the debate within BAC reached similar conclusions (Jehu 1994). Typically, debates on exploitation focus on sex; but counsellors need to be equally vigilant in business relationships and emotional relationships which are not necessarily sexual, such as friendships with current and former clients.

Counselling supervision

The requirement of regular and ongoing supervision for counsellors throughout their time as counsellors is a distinctive feature of the counselling, counselling psychology, and humanistic psychotherapy traditions in Britain. Internationally, the practice of restricting supervision to trainees is widespread across all types of counselling fields, although the concept of ongoing supervision is gaining greater credence. The practice in Britain became established primarily because counsellors valued ongoing supervision and believed it benefited their clients. Early descriptions of the tasks of supervision recommended a balanced combination of monitoring standards, developing new insights and skills, and personal support for the counsellor (Proctor 1988; Inskipp and Proctor 1989). Increased experience in organizational settings suggests that there is an additional task of helping the counsellor to consider her/his work in the context of the organization and other sources of help for clients (Bond 1991b; Bond and Shea 1996). Other approaches to counselling supervision from a psychodynamic perspective have emphasized the development of the internal supervisor (Foskett and Lyall 1988) or a cyclical way of structuring the supervision session (Page and Wosket 1994).

The nature of supervision may also vary according to the counsellor's experience from dependence on an expert to a peer relationship in which the experienced counsellor is in the driving seat (Stoltenberg and Delworth 1987). However, in all its varieties, counselling supervision is not primarily directed towards line-management functions (BAC 1995:ss.3.2). The professional responsibility for the counselling rests with the counsellor and not the supervisor. The latter is a facilitator of the counsellor working with a joint aim of enhancing the work with clients. In this respect, it is different from the supervision arrangements traditionally used in social services or for clinical supervision in health care which often involves line-management accountability. Counsellors have rejected this arrangement because it would inhibit the frankness of the counsellor's personal self-examination, so important in counselling supervision. In this respect, counselling supervision has some similarities to mentoring as well as some unique features.

The parts that codes cannot reach

Codes are much better at addressing issues such as role definition, ethical principles, and the fundamentals of their application, but they have limitations. Issues which may be important to some counsellors, for instance a requirement to keep records, may be omitted because they are not universally applicable. Sometimes there may be internal conflicts of responsibility between ethical priorities or differences between codes of practice which apply to a particular situation, for example a nurse counsellor may find some differences of emphasis between BAC and the codes for her professional registration. These situations test the counsellor's ability to solve ethical problems with the support of supervision. However, there are more significant limitations to codes. Inevitably the values which inform codes are stated positively and unequivocally; but nonetheless they may be controversial. For example, any system of ethics based primarily on respect for individual autonomy has been questioned from a feminist perspective (Gatens 1995). Similarly, the concept of individual autonomy is culturally Western and may be inadequate in cultures where the family or community are the primary ethical point of reference rather than the individual. This means that current codes may be an inadequate support to counsellors primarily working with gender issues or cross-culturally. They may also be silent about the contextual issues faced by counsellors working in organizations dealing with ethical dilemmas arising from the ethos or unconscious within the organization (Bond and Shea 1996). These inadequacies in existing codes may be resolved in future revisions although it is inevitable they will never address all possible issues or exclude the necessity of exercising ethical discretion in specific circumstances.

Complaints procedures

An important part of a profession's responsibilities is to hear complaints. As a profession unregulated by statute, BAC and other counselling organizations can only hear complaints against their own members, as they agreed to observe the codes and be bound by complaints procedures at the point of seeking membership. However the outcome of these complaints procedures are limited. There can be no power to prevent someone counselling, only to expel them from membership as the ultimate sanction. Complainants may be deterred from pursuing a complaint through fear of a profession being partisan on behalf of its own members, even though every effort is made to act impartially between the parties concerned. The basis of a complaint within BAC is breach of a specific section of a code, which has the benefit of clarifying the decision-making process for complainant and complained-against. On the other hand, it excludes the possibility of serious issues of concern being considered if they are not included within the codes. In this respect, complaints about a counsellor's competence are particularly problematic unless the incompetence is such to involve other ethical principles. This dilemma is shared by all the caring professions.

Recognition and accreditation

Professions are characterized by a specific body of knowledge and range of skills which are exclusive to them. Often the curriculum and validation of courses is controlled centrally. The diversity of counselling and the desire to be inclusive has led to a more devolved system whereby, in order to be recognized, courses are required to meet partially self-defined criteria in ways appropriate to the course values. This allows for much more flexibility about the body of knowledge required for counselling than traditional professions, but it is much more labour-intensive in making the assessments. Another source of flexibility is the absence of any restriction on training having to be by a recognized route. Individual counsellors can compile their own portfolio of training for assessment against criteria which parallel those for recognized courses.

The development of National Vocational Qualifications in counselling is still in its infancy. However, it is anticipated that they will be available in the late 1990s. BAC is committed to including them as an additional way of satisfying the training component.

Training is only one aspect of accreditation as a counsellor. This also requires evidence of a defined length of supervised counselling practice. The length of practice varies in proportion to the training received. In spite of the considerable flexibility of this system of accreditation, it has not attracted sufficient applicants to meet the public demand for accredited counsellors. Currently, only 1,100 of the 14,000 members of BAC are accredited, although a recent review has suggested ways of increasing this proportion as a matter of urgency (Hooper 1996). The relative dearth of accredited counsellors has weakened counselling in comparison to counselling psychology and psychotherapy, so there is some urgency for counselling as a whole, as well as individual advantage, in increasing the number of accredited counsellors.

Voluntary and statutory registration

Plans for introducing a voluntary United Kingdom Register of Counsellors have now come to fruition. The register operates at two levels. Registration as an independent practitioner operates through the accreditation schemes of BAC and the Confederation of Scottish Counselling Organizations (COSCA). A separate route for counsellors working in agency settings was piloted in late 1996. The second route ensures that both the individual counsellor and the organization satisfy basic criteria appropriate to the service provided. This route allows for considerable flexibility in response to the diversity of counselling, but inevitably there will be counsellors in organizations who will not satisfy the criteria. This may be a source of regret for a voluntary registration scheme but takes on a particular significance if the scheme were ever to become statutory.

Statutory registration is the delegation of power by government to a profession to regulate itself and it is often seen as the hallmark of an established profession (McDonald 1995). The achievement of statutory registration is often considered to be the ultimate goal of professionalism but from the viewpoint of counselling there are consequences which might be considered strengths or weaknesses. One of the consequences of statutory registration is a prohibition on unregistered practitioners using the registered role title. Restrictions on the use of the titles 'psychologist' or 'psychotherapist' are controversial but less problematic than 'counsellor' which is used in many diverse ways. It may be that the registered professional title would have to be qualified in some way, perhaps 'therapeutic counsellor' or 'state-registered counsellor'. Regardless of the final wording of any title, statutory registration will create a more visible demarcation within counselling between those who are included and those who are excluded in a way which voluntary schemes do not. For those concerned about the protection of the public, or their capacity to maximize income and status, this may seem an attractive option. For others, this represents an unwelcome fracturing of the counselling movement and an erosion of valuing the diversity within it. It is not surprising that the most carefully argued case against statutory registration has been based on a humanistic orientation to therapy, the section of the counselling movement most concerned to protect inclusivity and creativity within counselling (Mowbray 1996). Other orientations appear to be more sanguine about the possibility of statutory registration, especially if it can be designed in ways which minimize the breaking-up of the existing counselling movement.

Conclusion

Compiling this chapter has drawn our attention to the extent to which counselling, as represented by BAC in particular, has sought to redefine the term 'professional'. The concern for standards and the protection of the public is shared with other professions. However the emphasis within counselling on a rigorous respect for client autonomy is at the expense of a degree of professional discretion which characterizes more traditional professions. Similarly, the requirement of ongoing supervision creates a network of accountability to peers and professional development within counselling which is almost unique. The complexity of the course recognition, individual accreditation, and forthcoming voluntary registration scheme is due to a concern to provide the maximum number of routes to attainment of the required standards. This desire to be as inclusive as possible of the diversity of the field of counselling pervades the way professional issues have been approached.

The next major issue on the horizon is the decision about whether to seek statutory registration. It is difficult to anticipate how counsellors will respond. Much will depend on the experience of the voluntary scheme. External forces will also have a considerable influence. A change of government policy from the deregulation favoured by the Conservatives towards encouraging regulation could be decisive, especially if backed by a media campaign. Some counsellors might be particularly vulnerable if counselling psychology and psychotherapy succeeded in obtaining statutory registration without a similar status for counselling. For example, counsellors in independent practice and in the health service might be disadvantaged in the competition for work and income. On the other hand, unless any statutory scheme is inclusive of the best of the voluntary sector, the counselling movement stands to lose its fundamental characteristics of inclusivity, service and vision. These are not easy issues to resolve.

In the past, it was acceptable to avoid debates about professionalization by reframing them as issues of professionalism or professional standards, a terminology considered more inclusive of the paid and unpaid sectors within counselling. We doubt that a serious debate about professionalization can be deferred any longer. This is *the* professional issue of the moment. By the decisions already made, counselling has taken a distinctive approach to what it means to be a profession. Should counselling go further and seek a distinctive way of professionalization which, as far as possible, incorporates into a statutory registration scheme the valued features of counselling? Are there better ways forward? These are the urgent questions of the moment which challenge everyone with an interest in counselling.

References

Austin, K. M., Moline, M. E. and Williams, G. T. (1990) *Confronting Malpractice: Legal and Ethical Dilemmas in Psychotherapy*, Newbury Park, CA: Sage.

BAC (1984, 1990, 1992, 1993 (amended version)) *Code of Ethics and Practice for Counsellors*, Rugby: British Association for Counselling.

——(1995) *Code of Ethics and Practice for Supervisors of Counsellors*, Rugby: British Association for Counselling.

Bond, T. (1991a) 'Suicide and Sex in the Development of Ethics for Counsellors', *Changes: International Journal of Psychology and Psychotherapy* 9(4): 284–93.

——(1991b) *HIV Counselling: Report on National Survey and Consultation*, Rugby: British Association for Counselling.

——(1993) *Standards and Ethics for Counselling in Action*, London: Sage.

——(1994a) *Counselling, Confidentiality and the Law*, Rugby: British Association for Counselling.

——(1994b) 'Ethical standards and the exploitation of clients' in *Counselling, Journal of the British Association for Counselling* 4(3): Stop press 2–3.

Bond, T. and Shea, C. (1996) 'Ethical Issues for Counselling in Organisations' in M. Carroll and M. Walton (eds) *The Handbook of Counselling in Organisations*, London: Sage.

BPS (1993) *Code of Conduct, Ethical Principles and Guidelines*, Leicester: British Psychological Society.

——(1995) *Guidelines for the Professional Practice of Counselling Psychology*, Leicester: British Psychological Society.

Dryden, W., Charles-Edwards, D. and Woolfe, R. (eds) (1989) *Handbook of Counselling in Britain*, 1st edn, London: Routledge.

Eldrid, J. (1988) *Caring for the Suicidal*, London: Constable.

Gatens, M. (1995) 'Between the sexes: care or justice' in B. Almond (ed.) *Introduction to Applied Ethics*, Oxford: Blackwell.

Foskett, J. and Lyall, D. (1988) *Helping the Helpers: Supervision and Pastoral Care*, London: SPCK.

Hawton, K. and Catalan, J. (1987) *Attempted Suicide: A Practical Guide to its Nature and Management*, Oxford: Oxford University Press.

Hooper, D. (1996) 'Accreditation Review' (unpublished paper), Rugby: British Association for Counselling.

Inskipp, F. and Proctor, B. (1989) *Skills for Supervising and Being Supervised*, St Leonards on Sea: Alexia Publications.

Jehu, D. (1994) *Patients as Victims: Sexual Abuse in Psychotherapy and Counselling*, Chichester: John Wiley.

McDonald, K. M. (1995) *The Sociology of the Professions*, London: Sage.

McLeod, J. (1994) *Doing Counselling Research*, London: Sage.

Mowbray, R. (1996) *The Case Against Psychotherapy Registration: A Conservation Issue for the Human Potential Movement*, London: Trans Marginal Press.

Page, S. and Wosket, V. (1994) *Supervising the Counsellor: A Cyclical Model*, London: Routledge.

Persaud, R. (1993) 'Talking your way out of trouble', *Sunday Times*, 26 September, Style and Travel Section: 8–9.

Pope, K. S., Sonne, J. L. and Holroyd, J. (1993) *Sexual Feelings in Psychotherapy: Explorations for Therapists and Therapists in Training*, Washington: American Psychological Association.

Proctor, B. (1988) 'Supervision: a co-operative exercise in accountability' in M. Marken and M. Payne (eds) *Enabling and Ensuring: Supervision in Practice*, Leicester: National Youth Bureau.

Russell, J. (1993) *Out of Bounds: Sexual Exploitation in Psychotherapy and Counselling*, London: Sage.

SCODA (1995) *Building Confidence and Advice for Alcohol and Drug Services on Confidentiality Policies*, London: Standing Conference on Drug Abuse/Alcohol Concern.

Stoltenberg, C. and Delworth, U. (1987) *Supervising Counsellors and Therapists: A Developmental Approach*, San Francisco: Jossey-Bass.

Strong, S., Yoder, B. and Corcoran, J. (1995) 'Counseling: A social process for constructing powers' in *The Counseling Psychologist* 23(2): 374–84.

Thorne, B. (1984) 'Person-centred Therapy' in W. Dryden (ed.) *Individual Therapy in Britain*, London: Harper and Row.

UKCP (1995) *Ethical Guidelines*, London: United Kingdom Council for Psychotherapy.

Watkins, J., Drury, L. and Preddy, D. (1992) *From Evolution to Revolution: The Pressures on Professional Life in the 1990s*, Bristol: University of Bristol.

The British Association for Counselling's Code of Ethics and Practice for Counsellors

1. Status of this code

In response to the experience of members of BAC, this code is a revision of the (1992) 1993 code, amended by the Management Committee (May 1996).

2. Introduction

2.1 The purpose of this code is to establish and maintain standards for counsellors who are members of BAC, and to inform and protect people who seek or use their services.

2.2 All members of this Association are required to abide by the current codes appropriate to them. Implicit in these codes is a common frame of reference within which members manage their responsibilities to clients, colleagues, members of BAC and the wider community. No code can resolve all issues relating to ethics and practice. In this code we aim to provide a framework for addressing ethical issues and encouraging best possible levels of practice. Members must determine which parts apply to particular settings, taking account of any conflicting responsibilities.

2.3 The Association has a Complaints Procedure which can lead to the expulsion of members for breaches of its Codes of Ethics and Practice.

3. The nature of counselling

3.1 The overall aim of counselling is to provide an opportunity for the client to work towards living in a way he or she experiences as more satisfying and resourceful. The term 'counselling' includes work with individuals, pairs or groups of people often, but not always, referred to as 'clients'. The objectives of particular counselling relationships will vary according to the client's needs.

Counselling may be concerned with developmental issues, addressing and resolving specific problems, making decisions, coping with crisis, developing personal insight and knowledge, working through feelings of inner conflict or improving relationships with others. The counsellor's role is to facilitate the client's work in ways which respect the client's values, personal resources and capacity for choice within his or her cultural context.

3.2   Counselling involves a deliberately undertaken contract with clearly agreed boundaries and commitment to privacy and confidentiality. It requires explicit and informed agreement. The use of counselling skills in other contexts, paid or voluntary, is subject to the Code of Ethics and Practice for Counselling Skills.

3.3   There is no generally accepted distinction between counselling and psychotherapy. There are well founded traditions which use the terms interchangeably and others which distinguish between them. Regardless of the theoretical approaches preferred by individual counsellors, there are ethical issues which are common to all counselling situations.

4. Equal opportunities policy statement

All BAC members abide by its Equal Opportunities Policy statement. The full statement can be found at the end of this Code.

5. The structure of this code

This code has been divided into two parts. The Code of Ethics outlines the fundamental values of counselling and a number of general principles arising from these. The Code of Practice applies these principles to the counselling situation.

A. CODE OF ETHICS

Values
Counsellors' basic values are integrity, impartiality and respect.

A.1   Responsibility
All reasonable steps should be taken to ensure the client's safety during counselling sessions. Counselling is a non-exploitative activity. Counsellors must take the same degree of care to work ethically whatever the setting or the financial basis of the counselling contract.

A.2   Anti-discriminatory practice
Counsellors must consider and address their own prejudices and

stereotyping and ensure that an anti-discriminatory approach is integral to their counselling practice.

A.3   Confidentiality

Counsellors offer the highest possible levels of confidentiality in order to respect the client's privacy and create the trust necessary for counselling.

A.4   Contracts

The terms and conditions on which counselling is offered shall be made clear to clients before counselling begins. Subsequent revision of these terms should be agreed in advance of any changes.

A.5   Boundaries

Counsellors must establish and maintain appropriate boundaries around the counselling relationship. Counsellors must take into account the effects of any overlapping or pre-existing relationships.

A.6   Competence

Counsellors shall take all reasonable steps to monitor and develop their own competence and to work within the limits of that competence. Counsellors must have appropriate, regular and ongoing counselling supervision.

B.   CODE OF PRACTICE

Introduction

This code applies these values and ethical principles outlined above to more specific situations which may arise in the practice of counselling. The sections and clauses are arranged in the order of the ethics section and under the same headings. No clause or section should be read in isolation from the rest of the Code.

B.1   Issues of responsibility

B.1.1   The counsellor–client relationship is the foremost ethical concern. However, counselling does not exist in social isolation. Counsellors may need to consider other sources of ethical responsibility. The headings in this section are intended to draw attention to some of these.

B.1.2   Counsellors take responsibility for clinical/therapeutic decisions in their work with clients.

B.1.3   **Responsibility to the client**
Client safety

B.1.3.1 Counsellors must take all reasonable steps to ensure that the client suffers neither physical nor psychological harm during counselling sessions.

B.1.3.2   Counsellors must not exploit their clients financially, sexually, emotionally, or in any other way. Suggesting or engaging in sexual activity with a client is unethical.

B.1.3.3   Counsellors must provide privacy for counselling sessions. The sessions should not be overheard, recorded or observed by anyone other than the counsellor without informed consent from the client. Normally any recording would be discussed as part of the contract. Care must be taken that sessions are not interrupted.

Client self-determination

B.1.3.4   In counselling the balance of power is unequal and counsellors must take care not to abuse their power.

B.1.3.5   Counsellors do not normally act on behalf of their clients. If they do, it will be only at the express request of the client, or else in exceptional circumstances.

B.1.3.6   Counsellors do not normally give advice.

B.1.3.7   Counsellors have a responsibility to establish with clients, at the outset of counselling, the existence of any other therapeutic or helping relationships in which the client is involved and to consider whether counselling is appropriate. Counsellors should gain the client's permission before conferring in any way with other professional workers.

Breaks and endings

B.1.3.8   Counsellors work with clients to reach a recognised ending when clients have received the help they sought or when it is apparent that counselling is no longer helping or when clients wish to end.

B.1.3.9   External circumstances may lead to endings for other reasons which are not therapeutic. Counsellors must make arrangements for care to be taken of the immediate needs of clients in the event of any sudden and unforeseen endings by the counsellor or breaks to the counselling relationship.

B.1.3.10 Counsellors should take care to prepare their clients appropriately for any planned breaks from counselling. They should take any necessary steps to ensure the well-being of their clients during such breaks.

B.1.4   **Responsibility to other counsellors**

B.1.4.1   Counsellors must not conduct themselves in their counselling-related activities in ways which undermine public confidence either in their role as a counsellor or in the work of other counsellors.

B.1.4.2   A counsellor who suspects misconduct by another counsellor, which cannot be resolved or remedied after discussion with the counsellor concerned, should implement the Complaints Procedure, doing so without breaches of confidentiality other than those necessary for investigating the complaint.

B.1.5 **Responsibility to colleagues and others**

B.1.5.1 Counsellors are accountable for their services to colleagues, employers and funding bodies as appropriate. At the same time they must respect the privacy, needs and autonomy of the client as well as the contract of confidentiality agreed with the client.

B.1.5.2 No-one should be led to believe that a service is being offered by the counsellor which is not in fact being offered as this may deprive the client of the offer of such a service from elsewhere.

B.1.5.3 Counsellors must play a demonstrable part in exploring and resolving conflicts of interest between themselves and their employers or agencies, especially where this affects the ethical delivery of counselling to clients.

B.1.6 **Responsibility to the wider community**
Law

B.1.6.1 Counsellors must take all reasonable steps to be aware of current law as it applies to their counselling practice. (See BAC Information Guide 1 'Counselling, Confidentiality and the Law'.)
Research

B.1.6.2 Counsellors must conduct any research in accordance with BAC guidelines. (See BAC Information Guide 4 'Ethical Guidelines for Monitoring, Evaluation and Research in Counselling'.)
Resolving conflicts between ethical priorities

B.1.6.3 Counsellors may find themselves caught between conflicting ethical principles, which could involve issues of public interest. In these circumstances, they are urged to consider the particular situation in which they find themselves and to discuss the situation with their counselling supervisor and/or other experienced counsellors. Even after conscientious consideration of the salient issues, some ethical dilemmas cannot be resolved easily or wholly satisfactorily.

B.2 **Anti-discriminatory practice**
Client respect

B.2.1 Counsellors work with clients in ways that affirm both the common humanity and the uniqueness of each individual.

They must be sensitive to the cultural context and world view of the client, for instance whether the individual, family or the community is taken as central.

Client autonomy

B.2.2 Counsellors are responsible for working in ways which respect and promote the client's ability to make decisions in the light of his/her own beliefs, values and context.

Counsellor awareness

B.2.3   Counsellors are responsible for ensuring that any problems with mutual comprehension due to language, cultural differences or for any other reason are addressed at an early stage. The use of an interpreter needs to be carefully considered at the outset of counselling.

B.2.4   Counsellors have a responsibility to consider and address their own prejudices and stereotyping attitudes and behaviour and particularly to consider ways in which these may be affecting the counselling relationship and influencing their responses.

B.3   Confidentiality

B.3.1   Confidentiality is a means of providing the client with safety and privacy and thus protects client autonomy. For this reason any limitation on the degree of confidentiality is likely to diminish the effectiveness of counselling.

B.3.2   The counselling contract will include an agreement about the level and limits of confidentiality offered. This agreement can be reviewed and changed by negotiation between counsellor and client. Agreements about confidentiality continue after the client's death unless there are overriding legal or ethical considerations.

B.3.3   **Settings**

B.3.3.1   Counsellors must ensure that they have taken all reasonable steps to inform the client of any limitations to confidentiality that arise within the setting of the counselling work e.g. updating doctors in primary care, team case discussion in agencies. These are made explicit through clear contracting.

B.3.3.2   Many settings place additional specific limitations on confidentiality. Counsellors considering working in these settings must think about the impact of such limitations on their practice and decide whether or not to work in such settings.

B.3.4   **Exceptional circumstances**

B.3.4.1   Exceptional circumstances may arise which give the counsellor good grounds for believing that serious harm may occur to the client or to other people. In such circumstances the client's consent to a change in the agreement about confidentiality should be sought whenever possible unless there are also good grounds for believing the client is no longer willing or able to take responsibility for his/her actions. Normally, the decision to break confidentiality should be discussed with the client and should be made only after consultation with the counselling supervisor or if he/she is not available, an experienced counsellor.

B.3.4.2 Any disclosure of confidential information should be restricted to relevant information, conveyed only to appropriate people and for appropriate reasons likely to alleviate the exceptional circumstances. The ethical considerations include achieving a balance between acting in the best interests of the client and the counsellor's responsibilities to the wider community.

B.3.4.3 Counsellors hold different views about the grounds for breaking confidentiality, such as potential self-harm, suicide and harm to others. Counsellors must consider their own views, as they will affect their practice and communicate them to clients and significant others e.g. supervisor, agency.

B.3.5 **Management of confidentiality**

B.3.5.1 Counsellors should ensure that records of the client's identity are kept separately from any case notes.

B.3.5.2 Arrangements must be made for the safe disposal of client records, especially in the event of the counsellor's incapacity or death.

B.3.5.3 Care must be taken to ensure that personally identifiable information is not transmitted through overlapping networks of confidential relationships.

B.3.5.4 When case material is used for case studies, reports or publications the client's informed consent must be obtained wherever possible and their identity must be effectively disguised.

B.3.5.5 Any discussion about their counselling work between the counsellor and others should be purposeful and not trivialising.

B.3.5.6 Counsellors must pay particular attention to protecting the identity of clients. This includes discussion of cases in counselling supervision.

B.4 **Contracts**

B.4.1 **Advertising and public statements**

B.4.1.1 Membership of BAC is not a qualification and it must not be used as if it were. In press advertisements and telephone directories, on business cards, letterheads, brass plates and plaques, etc. counsellors should limit the information to name, relevant qualifications, address, telephone number, hours available, a listing of the services offered and fees charged. They should not mention membership of BAC.

B.4.1.2 In oral statements, letters and pre-counselling leaflets to the public and potential clients, BAC membership may not be mentioned without a statement that it means that the individual, and where appropriate the organisation, abides by the Codes of Ethics and Practice and is subject to the Complaints Procedure of the British

Association for Counselling. Copies of these Codes and the Complaints Procedure are available from BAC.

B.4.1.3 Counsellors who are accredited and/or registered are encouraged to mention this.

B.4.1.4 All advertising and public statements should be accurate in every particular.

B.4.1.5 Counsellors should not display an affiliation with an organisation in a manner which falsely implies sponsorship or validation by that organisation.

B.4.2 Pre-counselling information

B.4.2.1 Any publicity material and all written and oral information should reflect accurately the nature of the service on offer, and the relevant counselling training, qualifications and experience of the counsellor.

B.4.2.2 Counsellors should take all reasonable steps to honour undertakings made in their pre-counselling information.

B.4.3 Contracting with clients

B.4.3.1 Counsellors are responsible for reaching agreement with their clients about the terms on which counselling is being offered, including availability, the degree of confidentiality offered, arrangements for the payment of any fees, cancelled appointments and other significant matters. The communication of essential terms and any negotiations should be concluded by having reached a clear agreement before the client incurs any commitment or liability of any kind.

B.4.3.2 The counsellor has a responsibility to ensure that the client is given a free choice whether or not to participate in counselling. Reasonable steps should be taken in the course of the counselling relationship to ensure that the client is given an opportunity to review the counselling.

B.4.3.3 Counsellors must avoid conflicts of interest wherever possible. Any conflicts of interest that do occur must be discussed in counselling supervision and where appropriate with the client.

B.4.3.4 Records of appointments should be kept and clients should be made aware of this. If records of counselling sessions are kept, clients should also be made aware of this. At the client's request information should be given about access to these records, their availability to other people, and the degree of security with which they are kept.

B.4.3.5 Counsellors must be aware that computer-based records are subject to statutory regulations. It is the counsellor's responsibility to be aware of any changes the government may introduce in the regulations concerning the client's right of access to his/her records.

B.4.3.6 Counsellors are responsible for addressing any client dissatisfaction with the counselling.

B.5   Boundaries
With clients
B.5.1   Counsellors are responsible for setting and monitoring boundaries throughout the counselling sessions and will make explicit to clients that counselling is a formal and contracted relationship and nothing else.

B.5.2   The counselling relationship must not be concurrent with a supervisory or training relationship.

With former clients
B.5.3   Counsellors remain accountable for relationships with former clients and must exercise caution over entering into friendships, business relationships, sexual relationships, training, supervising and other relationships. Any changes in relationship must be discussed in counselling supervision. The decision about any change(s) in relationship with former clients should take into account whether the issues and power dynamics present during the counselling relationship have been resolved.

B.5.4   Counsellors who belong to organisations which prohibit sexual activity with all former clients are bound by that commitment.

B.6   Competence
B.6.1   Counsellor competence
B.6.1.1 Counsellors must have achieved a level of competence before commencing counselling and must maintain continuing professional development as well as regular and ongoing supervision.

B.6.1.2 Counsellors must actively monitor their own competence through counselling supervision and be willing to consider any views expressed by their clients and by other counsellors.

B.6.1.3 Counsellors will monitor their functioning and will not counsel when their functioning is impaired by alcohol or drugs. In situations of personal or emotional difficulty, or illness, counsellors will monitor the point at which they are no longer competent to practise and take action accordingly.

B.6.1.4 Competence includes being able to recognise when it is appropriate to refer a client elsewhere.

B.6.1.5 Counsellors are responsible for ensuring that their relationships with clients are not unduly influenced by their own emotional needs.

B.6.1.6 Counsellors must consider the need for professional indemnity insurance and when appropriate take out and maintain adequate cover.

B.6.1.7 When uncertain as to whether a particular situation or course of action may be in violation of the Code of Ethics and Practice, counsellors must consult with their counselling supervisor and/or other experienced practitioners.

B.6.2 **Counsellor safety**

B.6.2.1 Counsellors should take all reasonable steps to ensure their own physical safety.

B.6.3 **Counselling supervision**

B.6.3.1 Counselling supervision refers to a formal arrangement which enables counsellors to discuss their counselling regularly with one or more people who are normally experienced as counselling practitioners and have an understanding of counselling supervision. Its purpose is to ensure the efficacy of the counsellor–client relationship. It is a confidential relationship.

B.6.3.2 The counselling supervisor role should wherever possible be independent of the line manager role. However, where the counselling supervisor is also the line manager, the counsellor must have additional regular access to independent counselling supervision.

B.6.3.3 Counselling supervision must be regular, consistent and appropriate to the counselling. The volume should reflect the volume of counselling work undertaken and the experience of the counsellor.

B.6.4 **Awareness of other codes**

Counsellors must take account of the following Codes and Procedures adopted by the Annual General Meetings of the British Association for Counselling:

Code of Ethics & Practice for Counselling Skills (1988) applies to members who would not regard themselves as counsellors, but who use counselling skills to support other roles.

Code of Ethics & Practice for Supervisors of Counsellors (1996) applies to members offering supervision to counsellors and also helps counsellors seeking supervision.

Code of Ethics & Practice for Trainers (1997) applies to members offering training to counsellors and also helps members of the public seeking counselling training.

Complaints Procedure (1997) applies to members of BAC in the event of complaints about breaches of the Codes of Ethics & Practice.

Copies and other guidelines and information sheets relevant to maintaining ethical standards of practice can be obtained from the BAC office, 1 Regent Place, Rugby CV21 2PJ.

Equal opportunities policy statement

The 'British Association for Counselling' (BAC) is committed to promoting Equality of Opportunity of access and participation for all its members in all of its structures and their workings. BAC has due regard for those groups of people with identifiable characteristics which can lead to visible and invisible barriers thus inhibiting their joining and full participation in BAC. Barriers can include age, colour, creed, culture, disability, education, 'ethnicity', gender, information, knowledge, mobility, money, nationality, race, religion, sexual orientation, social class and status.

The work of BAC aims to reflect this commitment in all areas including services to members, employer responsibilities, the recruitment of and working with volunteers, setting, assessing, monitoring and evaluating standards and the implementation of the complaints procedures. This is particularly important as BAC is the 'Voice of Counselling' in the wider world.

BAC will promote and encourage commitment to Equality of Opportunity by its members.

Effective from 1 January 1998

The British Association for Counselling's Code of Ethics and Practice for Counselling Skills

A. Introduction

The purpose of this Code is:

- to clarify the ethical issues for anyone using counselling skills;
- to establish standards of practice;
- to inform members of the public about their use.

One of the purposes of Codes of Practice is to clarify the expectations of both providers and users of services.

B. The meaning of counselling skills

1.1   The term 'counselling skills' does not have a single definition which is universally accepted. For the purpose of this code, 'counselling skills' are distinguished from 'listening skills' and from 'counselling'. Although the distinction is not always a clear one, because the term 'counselling skills' contains elements of these other two activities, it has its own place in the continuum between them. What distinguishes the use of counselling skills from these other two activities are the intentions of the user, which is to enhance the performance of their functional role, as line manager, nurse, tutor, social worker, personnel officer, voluntary worker, etc., the recipient will, in turn, perceive them in that role.

1.2   Ask yourself the following questions:

     a)   Are you using counselling skills to enhance your communication with someone but without taking on the role of their counsellor?

     b)   Does the recipient perceive you as acting within your professional/caring role (which is NOT that of being their counsellor)?

         i.   If the answer is YES to both these questions, you are using counselling skills in your functional role and should use this document.

ii.   If the answer is NO to both, you are counselling and
       should look to the Code of Ethics and Practice for Coun-
       sellors for guidance.
iii.   If the answer is YES to one and NO to the other, you
       have a conflict of expectations and should resolve it.

Only when both the user and the recipient explicitly contract to enter into a
counselling relationship does it cease to be 'using counselling skills' and
become 'counselling'. When this occurs, the Code of Ethics and Practice
for Counsellors should be referred to.

C.   THE CODE OF ETHICS

C.1   Issues of responsibility

1.1   The users of counselling skills are responsible for the appropriate
       use of those skills within any existing Code of Ethics and Practice
       governing their functional roles. If there is no existing Code of
       Ethics and Practice then the user's Agency or occupation may find
       it helpful to reflect on such issues.
1.2   It is desirable that anyone in receipt of services which include the
       use of counselling skills should have access to the Code of Ethics
       and Practice governing their use.

C.2   Issues of competence

2.1   The user of counselling skills should ensure that s/he has received
       sufficient training to be able to use them appropriately.
2.2   Training in counselling skills is not sufficient for users to consider
       themselves qualified counsellors.
2.3   The user of counselling skills should maintain his/her level of
       competence.

D.   THE CODE OF PRACTICE

D.1   Management of the work

1.1   The user of counselling skills is responsible for their use in a way
       which is consistent with good practice in the user's functional role.
1.2   The user should be clear whose interests s/he is serving. This may
       involve discussion of any conflict of interests.
1.3   Counselling skills should be used in accordance with the Codes of
       Ethics and Practice governing the user's functional role.

D.2   Confidentiality

2.1   While there may be no automatic presumption that the relationship

between the user and the recipient of counselling skills is confidential, nonetheless the user should work within D2.2 – D2.4.

2.2 The user of counselling skills should work within any agreement
made with the recipient about confidentiality.

2.3 Any agreement made between the user and the recipient should be
consistent with any written code(s) governing the functional role of
the user of counselling skills.

2.4 Exceptional circumstances in which the user of counselling skills
might break her/his agreement about confidentiality with the recipient should be indicated within any written code. The user should
indicate this at the time of making the agreement. The exact
circumstances in which any agreement about confidentiality may
be broken should be included within any written code.

D.3   Endorsements of codes of practice

3.1 Individual and organisational members of the British Association
for Counselling may submit Draft Codes of Ethics and Practice to:
>
> The Convenor,
> Standards & Ethics Sub-Committee,
> British Association for Counselling,
> 1 Regent Place,
> Rugby,
> Warwickshire CV21 2PJ

for constructive comments.

3.2 Codes which have been approved by the Standards & Ethics Sub-
Committee of this Association may contain a statement to this
effect.

Addendum

The following Codes of Practice may be useful.
Existing Codes of Ethics and Practice for:
> Counsellors
> Trainers in Counselling and Counselling Skills
> Supervisors of Counsellors

© BAC 1989   Amended AGM September 1989

British Association for Counselling's Code of Ethics and Practice for Supervisors of Counsellors

1. Status of the code

1.1   In response to the experience of members of BAC, this Code is a revision of the 1988 Code of Ethics and Practice for the Supervision of Counsellors.

2. Introduction

2.1   The purpose of the Code is to establish and maintain standards for supervisors who are members of BAC and to inform and protect counsellors seeking supervision. Throughout this Code the terms 'counsellor' and 'counselling' are used in accordance with the definition of counselling in the Code of Ethics and Practice for Counsellors.

2.2   All members of this Association are required to abide by existing codes appropriate to them. They thereby accept a common frame of reference within which to manage their responsibilities to supervisees and their clients, colleagues, members of this Association and the wider community. Whilst this Code cannot resolve all ethical and practice-related issues, it aims to provide a framework for addressing ethical issues and to encourage optimum levels of practice. Supervisors and supervisees (counsellors) will need to judge which parts of this Code apply to particular situations. They may have to decide between conflicting responsibilities.

2.3   Counselling supervision is a formal and mutually agreed arrangement for counsellors to discuss their work regularly with someone who is normally an experienced and competent counsellor and familiar with the process of counselling supervision. The task is to work together to ensure and develop the efficacy of the supervisee's counselling practice.

Counselling supervision is the term that will be used throughout this code. It is also known as supervision, consultative support, clinical supervision or non-managerial supervision. It is essential part of good practice for counselling. It is different from training, personal development and line-management accountability.

2.4   This Association has a Complaints Procedure which can lead to the expulsion of members for breaches of this Codes of Ethics and Practice.

3.   Nature of counselling supervision

3.1   Counselling supervision provides supervisees with the opportunity on a regular basis to discuss and monitor their work with clients. It should take account of the setting in which supervisees practise. Counselling supervision is intended to ensure that the needs of the clients are being addressed and to monitor the effectiveness of the therapeutic interventions.

3.2   Counselling supervision may contain some elements of training, personal development or line management, but counselling supervision is not primarily intended for these purposes and appropriate management of these issues should be observed.

3.3   Counselling supervision is a formal collaborative process intended to help supervisees maintain ethical and professional standards of practice and to enhance creativity.

3.4   It is essential that counsellor and supervisor are able to work together constructively as counselling supervision includes supportive and challenging elements.

3.5   There are several modes of counselling supervision (see section 5), which vary in appropriateness according to the needs of supervisees. More than one mode of counselling supervision may be used concurrently. This Code applies to all counselling supervision arrangements

3.6   The frequency of counselling supervision will vary according to the volume of counselling, the experience of supervisees and their work setting.

4.   Anti-discriminatory practice in counselling supervision

4.1   Anti-discriminatory practice underpins the basic values of counselling and counselling supervision as stated in this document and in the Code of Ethics and Practice for Counsellors. It also addresses the issue of the client's social context, B.2.7.3 of that Code (1993).

4.2   Supervisors have a responsibility to be aware of their own issues of prejudice and stereotyping, and particularly to consider ways in which this may be affecting the supervisory relationship. Discussion of this is part of the counselling supervision process.

4.3   Supervisors need to be alert to any prejudices and assumptions that counsellors reveal in their work with clients and to raise awareness of these so that the needs of clients may be met with more sensitivity. One purpose of counselling supervision is to enable supervisees to recognise and value difference. Supervisors have a responsibility to challenge the appropriatness of the work of a supervisee whose own belief system interferes with the acceptance of clients.

4.4   Attitudes, assumptions and prejudices can be identified by the language used, and by paying attention to the selectivity of material brought to counselling supervision.

5. Modes of counselling supervision

There are different modes of counselling supervision. The particular features of some of these modes are outlined below. Some counsellors use combinations of these for their counselling supervision.

5.1   **One-to-one, supervisor-supervisee**
This involves a supervisor providing counselling supervision on an individual basis for an individual counsellor who is usually less experienced than the supervisor. This is the most widely used mode of counselling supervision.

5.2   **Group counselling supervision with identified counselling supervisor(s)**
There are several ways of providing this form of counselling supervision. In one approach the supervisor acts as the leader, takes responsibility for organising the time equally between the supervisees, and concentrates on the work of each individual in turn. Using another approach the supervisees allocate counselling supervision time between themselves with the supervisor as a technical resource.

5.3   **One-to-one peer counselling supervision**
This involves two participants providing counselling supervision for each other by alternating the roles of supervisor and supervisee.

Typically, the time available for counselling supervision is divided equally between them. This mode on its own is not suitable for all practitioners.

5.4   **Peer group counselling supervision**
This takes place when three or more counsellors share the responsibility for providing each other's counselling supervision within the group. Typically they will consider themselves to be of broadly equal status, training and/or experience. This mode on its own is unsuitable for inexperienced practitioners.

5.5   Particular issues of competence for each mode are detailed in the Code of Practice B.2.6.

6.   The structure of this code

6.1   This code has two sections. Section A, the Code of Ethics, outlines the fundamental values of counselling supervision and a number of general principles arising from these. Section B, the Code of Practice, applies these principles to counselling supervision.

A.   CODE OF ETHICS

A.1   Counselling supervision is a non-exploitative activity. Its basic values are integrity, responsibility, impartiality and respect. Supervisors must take the same degree of care to work ethically whether they are paid or work voluntarily and irrespective of the mode of counselling supervision used.

A.2   **Confidentiality**
The content of counselling supervision is highly confidential. Supervisors must clarify their limits of confidentiality.

A.3   **Safety**
All reasonable steps must be taken to ensure the safety of supervisees and their clients during their work together.

A.4   **Effectiveness**
All reasonable steps must be taken by supervisors to encourage optimum levels of practice by supervisees.

A.5   **Contracts**
The terms and conditions on which counselling supervision is offered must be made clear to supervisees at the outset. Subsequent revisions of these terms must be agreed in advance of any change.

A.6   Competence

Supervisors must take all reasonable steps to monitor and develop their own competence and to work within the limits of that competence. This includes having supervision of their supervision work.

B.   CODE OF PRACTICE

B.1   Issues of responsibility

B.1.1   Supervisors are responsible for ensuring that an individual contract is worked out with their supervisees which will allow them to present and explore their work as honestly as possible.

B.1.2   Within this contract supervisors are responsible for helping supervisees to reflect critically upon their work, while at the same time acknowledging that clinical responsibility remains with the counsellor.

B.1.3   Supervisors are responsible, together with their supervisees, for ensuring that the best use is made of counselling supervision time, in order to address the needs of clients.

B.1.4   Supervisors are responsible for setting and maintaining the boundaries between the counselling supervision relationship and other professional relationships, e.g. training and management.

B.1.5   Supervisors and supervisees should take all reasonable steps to ensure that any personal or social contact between them does not adversely influence the effectiveness of the counselling supervision.

B.1.6   A supervisor must not have a counselling supervision and a personal counselling contract with the same supervisee over the same period of time.

B.1.7   Supervisors must not exploit their supervisees financially, sexually, emotionally or in any other way. It is unethical for supervisors to engage in sexual activity with their supervisee.

B.1.8   Supervisors have a responsibility to enquire about any other relationships which may exist between supervisees and their clients as these may impair the objectivity and professional judgement of supervisees.

B.1.9   Supervisors must recognise, and work in ways that respects the value and dignity of supervisees and their clients with due regard to issues such as origin, status, race, gender, age, beliefs, sexual orientation and disability. This must include raising awareness of any discriminatory practices that may exist between supervisees and their clients, or between supervisor and supervisee.

B.1.10 Supervisors must ensure that together with their supervisees they consider their respective legal liabilities to each other, to the employing or training organisation, if any, and to clients.

B.1.11 Supervisors are responsible for taking action if they are aware that their supervisees' practice is not in accordance with BAC's Codes of Ethics and Practice for Counsellors.

B.1.12 Supervisors are responsible for helping their supervisees recognise when their functioning as counsellors is impaired due to personal or emotional difficulties, any condition that affects judgement, illness, the influence of alcohol or drugs, or for any other reason, and for ensuring that appropriate action is taken.

B.1.13 Supervisors must conduct themselves in their supervision-related activities in ways which do not undermine public confidence in either their role as a supervisor or in the work of other supervisors.

B.1.14 If a supervisor is aware of possible misconduct by another supervisor which cannot be resolved or remedied after discussion with the supervisor concerned, they should implement the Complaints Procedure, doing so within the boundaries of confidentiality required by the Complaints Procedure.

B.1.15 Supervisors are responsible for ensuring that their emotional needs are met outside the counselling supervision work and are not solely dependent on their relationship with supervisees.

B.1.16 Supervisors are responsible for consulting with their own supervisor before former clients are taken on as supervisees or former supervisees are taken on as clients.

B.2   Issues of competence

B.2.1 Under all of the modes of counselling supervision listed above, supervisors should normally be practising and experienced counsellors.

B.2.2 Supervisors are responsible for seeking ways to further their own professional development.

B.2.3 Supervisors are responsible for making arrangements for their own supervision in order to support their counselling supervision work and to help them to evaluate their competence.

B.2.4   Supervisors are responsible for monitoring and working within the limits of their competence.

B.2.5   Supervisors are responsible for withdrawing from counselling supervision work either temporarily or permanently when their functioning is impaired due to personal or emotional difficulties, illness, the influence of alcohol or drugs, or for any other reason.

B.2.6   Some modes require extra consideration and these are detailed in this section.

	A	B	C	D	E	F	G	H
One-to-one supervisor–supervisee	X							
Group counselling supervision with identified and more experienced supervisor	X	X		X	X			
One-to-one peer counselling supervision	X	X	X	X			X	X
Peer group counselling supervision		X	X	X	X		X	X	X

A.   All points contained elsewhere within the Code of Practice should be considered.

B.   Sufficient time must be allocated to each counsellor to ensure adequate supervision of their counselling work.

C.   This method on its own is particularly unsuitable for trainees, recently trained or inexperienced counsellors.

D.   Care needs to be taken to develop an atmosphere conducive to sharing, questioning and challenging each others' practice in a constructive and supportive way.

E.   As well as having a background in counselling work, supervisors should have appropriate groupwork experience in order to facilitate this kind of group.

F.   All participants should have sufficient groupwork experience to be able to engage the group process in ways which facilitate effective counselling supervision.

G.   Explicit consideration should be given to deciding who is responsible for providing the counselling supervision, and how the task of counselling supervision will be carried out.

H.   It is good practice to have an independent consultant to visit
        regularly to observe and monitor the process and quality of the
        counselling supervision.

B.3   Management of work

B.3.1   *The counselling supervision contract*

3.1.1   Where supervisors and supervisees work for the same agency or
        organisation the supervisor is responsible for clarifying all con-
        tractual obligations.

3.1.2   Supervisors must inform their supervisee, as appropriate, about
        their own training, philosophy and theoretical position, qualifica-
        tions, approach to anti-discriminatory practice and the methods of
        counselling supervision they use.

3.1.3   Supervisors must be explicit regarding practical arrangements for
        counselling supervision, paying particular regard to the length of
        contact time, the frequency of contact, policy and practice regard-
        ing record keeping, and the privacy of the venue.

3.1.4   Fees and fee increases must be arranged and agreed in advance.

3.1.5   Supervisors and supervisees must make explicit the expectations
        and requirements they have of each other. This should include the
        manner in which any formal assessment of the supervisee's work
        will be conducted. Each party should assess the value of working
        with the other, and review this regularly.

3.1.6   Supervisors must discuss their policy regarding giving references
        and any fees that may be charged for this or for any other work
        done outside counselling supervision time.

3.1.7   Before formalising a counselling supervision contract supervisors
        must ascertain what personal counselling the supervisee has or has
        had. This is in order to take into account any effect this may have
        on the supervisee's counselling work.

3.1.8   Supervisors working with trainee counsellors must clarify the
        boundaries of their responsibility and their accountability to their
        supervisee and to the training course and any agency/placement
        involved. This should include any formal assessment required.

B.3.2   *Confidentiality*

3.2.1   As a general principle, supervisors must not reveal confidential
        material concerning the supervisee or their clients to any other
        person without the express consent of all parties concerned. Excep-
        tions to this general principal are contained within this Code.

3.2.2   When initial contracts are being made, agreements about the people to whom supervisors may speak about their supervisees work must include those on whom the supervisors rely for support, supervision or consultancy. There must also be clarity at this stage about the boundaries of confidentiality having regard for the supervisor's own framework of accountability. This is particularly relevant when providing counselling supervision to a trainee counsellor.

3.2.3   Supervisors should take all reasonable steps to encourage supervisees to present their work in ways which protect the personal identity of clients, or to get their client's informed consent to present information which could lead to personal identification.

3.2.4   Supervisors must not reveal confidential information concerning supervisees or their clients to any person or through any public medium except:

    a)   When it is clearly stated in the counselling supervision contract and it is in accordance will all BAC Codes of Ethics and Practice.

    b)   When the supervisor considers it necessary to prevent serious emotional or physical damage to the client, the supervisee or a third party. In such circumstances the supervisee's consent to a change in the agreement about confidentiality should be sought, unless there are good grounds for believing that the supervisee is no longer able to take responsibility for his/her own actions. Whenever possible, the decision to break confidentiality in any circumstances should be made after consultation with another experienced supervisor.

3.2.5   The disclosure of confidential information relating to supervisees is permissible when relevant to the following situations:

    a)   Recommendations concerning supervisees for professional purposes e.g. references and assessments.

    b)   Pursuit of disciplinary action involving supervisees in matters pertaining to standards of ethics and practice.

In the latter instance, any breaking of confidentiality should be minimised by conveying only information pertinent to the immediate situation on a need-to-know basis. The ethical considerations needing to be taken into account are:

    i.   Maintaining the best interests of the supervisee

    ii.   Enabling the supervisee to take responsibility for their actions

    iii. Taking full account of the supervisor's responsibility to the client and to the wider community

3.2.6   Information about work with a supervisee may be used for publication or in meetings only with the supervisee's permission and with anonymity preserved.

3.2.7   On occasions when it is necessary to consult with professional colleagues, supervisors ensure that their discussion is purposeful and not trivialising.

B.3.3   The management of counselling supervision

3.3.1   Supervisors must encourage the supervisee to belong to an association or organisation with a Code of Ethics & Practice and a Complaints Procedure. This provides additional safeguards for the supervisor, supervisee and client in the event of a complaint.

3.3.2   If, in the course of counselling supervision, it appears that personal counselling may be necessary for the supervisee to be able to continue working effectively, the supervisor should raise this issue with the supervisee.

3.3.3   Supervisors must monitor regularly how their supervisees engage in self-assessment and the self-evaluation of their work.

3.3.4   Supervisors must ensure that their supervisees acknowledge their individual responsibility for ongoing professional development and for participating in further training programmes.

3.3.5   Supervisors must ensure that their supervisees are aware of the distinction between counselling, accountability to management, counselling supervision and training.

3.3.6   Supervisors must ensure with a supervisee who works in an organisation or agency that the lines of accountability and responsibility are clearly defined: supervisee/client; supervisor/supervisee; supervisor/cleint; organisation/supervisor; organisation/supervisee; organisation/client. There is a distinction between line management supervision and counselling supervision.

3.3.7   Best practice is that the same person should not act as both line manager and counselling supervisor to the same supervisee. However, where the counselling supervisor is also the line manager, the supervisee should have access to independent counselling supervision.

3.3.8   Supervisors who become aware of a conflict between an obligation to a supervisee and an obligation to an employing agency must make explicit to the supervisee the nature of the loyalties and responsibilites involved.

3.3.9   Supervisors who have concerns about a supervisee's work with clients must be clear how they will pursue this if discussion in counselling supervision fails to resolve the situation.

3.3.10 Where disagreements cannot be resolved by discussions between supervisor and supervisee, the supervisor should consult with a fellow professional and, if appropriate, recommend that the supervisee be referred to another supervisor.

3.3.11 Supervisors must discuss with supervisees the need to have arrangements in place to take care of the immediate needs of clients in the event of a sudden and unplanned ending to the counselling relationship. It is good practice for the supervisor to be informed about these arrangements.

AGM Sept 1995 • Effective 1 Jan 1996

The British Association for Counselling's Code of Ethics and Practice for Trainers in Counselling and Counselling Skills

1. Status of this code

1.1   In response to the experience of members of BAC, this Code is a revision of the 1996 Code.

Structure of this Code

This code is in four sections:
A.   A Code of Ethics for all Trainers.
B.   A general Code of Practice for all Trainers.
C.   Additional clause for Trainers in Counselling.
D.   Additional clauses for Trainers in Counselling Skills

2. Introduction

2.1   The purpose of this Code of Ethics and Practice is to establish and maintain standards for trainers who are members of BAC and to inform and protect members of the public seeking training in counselling, counselling skills or counselling-related areas, whatever the level or length of the training programme. Training in counselling-related areas includes training in counselling supervision, group work, interpersonal skills and other topics involving counselling theory and practice.

     Sections A and B apply to all trainers. Section C contains an additional clause for trainers in counselling. Section D contains additional clauses for trainers in counselling skills.

2.2   The document must be seen in relation to all other BAC Codes of Ethics and Practice and BAC Course Recognition Procedures.

2.3   There is an important relationship between the agency employing the trainer and the trainee undertaking the training. This Code reinforces the principle that agencies which are organisational members of BAC abide by all BAC codes.

2.4　Ethical standards comprise such values as integrity, impartiality and respect. Anti-discriminatory practice reflects the basic values of counselling and training. Members of BAC, in assenting to this Code, accept their appropriate responsibilities as trainers, to trainees, trainees' clients, employing agencies, colleagues, this Association and to the wider community.

2.5　In the context of this Code, trainers are those who train people in counselling, in counselling skills or in counselling-related areas. They should be experienced and competent practitioners. Trainers have a responsibility to draw the attention of trainees to all BAC Codes of Ethics and Practice.

2.6　Trainers must be aware that there are differences between training in counselling, training in counselling skills and training in counselling-related areas. Trainees must be made aware of this and trainers should endeavour to ensure that their intending trainees join an appropriate training programme.

2.7　There should be consistency between the theoretical orientation of the programme and the training methods and, where they are used, methods of assessment and evaluation (e.g. client-centred courses would normally be trainee-centred).

2.8　Training is at its most effective when there are two or more trainers. Trainers and their employing agencies have a responsibility to ensure this wherever possible.

2.9　The size of the group must be congruent with the training objectives and the model of working. Decisions about staff: student ratios must take account of the learning objectives and methods of assessment and of the importance of being able to give individual attention and recognition to each course member. Where direct feedback between trainer and trainee is an important part of the course a maximum staff to student ratio of 1:12 is recommended best practice.

A. CODE OF ETHICS FOR ALL TRAINERS

A.1 Values

Training is a non-exploitative activity. Its basic values are integrity, impartiality and respect. Trainers must take the same degree of care to work ethically whether the training is paid or unpaid.

A.2 Anti-discrimination

Trainers must consider and address their own prejudices and stereotyping. They must also address the prejudices and stereotyping of their trainees. They must ensure that an anti-discriminatory approach is integral to all the training they provide.

A.3 Safety

All reasonable steps shall be taken by trainers to ensure the safety of trainees and clients during training.

A.4 Competence

Trainers must take all reasonable steps to monitor and develop their competence as trainers and work within the limits of that competence.

A.5 Confidentiality

Trainers must clarify the limits of confidentiality within the training process at the beginning of the training programme.

A.6 Contracts

The terms and conditions on which the training is offered must be made clear to trainees before the start of the training programme. Subsequent revision of these terms must be agreed in advance of any changes.

A.7 Boundaries

Trainers must maintain and establish appropriate boundaries between themselves and their trainees so that working relationships are not confused with friendship or other relationships.

B. GENERAL CODE OF PRACTICE FOR ALL TRAINERS

B.1 Responsibility

B.1.1   Trainers deliberately undertake the task of delivering training in counselling, counselling skills and counselling-related areas.

B.1.2   Trainers are responsible for observing the principles embodied in this Code of Ethics and Practice and all current BAC Codes and for introducing trainees to the BAC Codes of Ethics and Practice in the early stages of the training programme.

B.1.3 Trainers must recognise the value and dignity of trainees, with due regard to issues of origin, status, gender, age, beliefs, sexual preference or disability. Trainers have a responsibility to be aware of, and address their own issues of prejudice and stereotyping, and to give particular consideration to ways in which this may impact on the training.

B.1.4 Trainers have a responsibility to encourage and facilitate the self-development and self-awareness of trainees, so that trainees learn to integrate practice and personal insights.

B.1.5 Trainers are responsible for making explicit to trainees the boundaries between training, counselling supervision, consultancy, counselling and the use of counselling skills.

B.1.6 Trainers are responsible for modelling appropriate boundaries.

1.6.1 The roles of trainee and client must be kept separate during the training; where painful personal issues are revealed, trainers are responsible for suggesting and encouraging further in-depth work with a counsellor outside the training context.

1.6.2 The providers of counselling for trainees during the programme must be independent of the training context and any assessment procedures.

1.6.3 Trainers should take all reasonable steps to ensure that any personal and social contacts between them and their trainees do not adversely influence the effectiveness of the training.

B.1.7 Trainers must not accept current clients as trainees. Former trainees must not become clients, nor former clients become trainees, until a period of time has elapsed for reflection and after consultation with a counselling supervisor.

B.1.8 Trainers are responsible for ensuring that their emotional needs are met outside the training work and are not dependent on their relationships with trainees.

B.1.9 Trainers must not exploit their trainees financially, sexually, emotionally, or in any other way. Engaging in sexual activity with trainees is unethical.

B.1.10 Trainers must ensure that consideration is given to the appropriateness of the settings in which trainees propose to, or are expected to, work on completion of the training programme.

B.1.11 Trainers are expected, when appropriate, to prepare trainees to practice effectively within their work setting.

B.1.12 Trainers have a responsibility to ensure that appropriate counselling supervision arrangements are in place for trainees where working with clients is part of the course.

B.1.13 Visiting or occasional trainers on programmes must ensure that they take responsibility for any former or current pre-existing professional or personal relationship with any member of the training group.

B.1.14 Trainers must acknowledge the individual life experience and identity of trainees. Challenges to the views, attitudes and outlooks of trainees must be respectful, related to the stated objectives of the course, and model good practice.

B.1.15 Trainers are responsible for discussing with trainees any needs for personal counselling and the contribution it might make to the trainees' work both during and after the programme.

B.1.16 Trainers must at all times conduct themselves in their training activities in ways which will not undermine public confidence in their role as trainers, in the work of other trainers or in the role of BAC.

B.2 Competence

B.2.1 It is strongly recommended that trainers should have completed at least one year's post-training experience as practitioners in an appropriate field of work. They should commit themselves to continuing professional development as trainers.

B.2.2 Trainers must monitor their training work and be able and willing to account to trainees and colleagues for what they do and why.

B.2.3 Trainers must monitor and evaluate the limits of their competence as trainers by means of regular supervision or consultancy.

B.2.4 Trainers have a responsibility to themselves and to their trainees to maintain their own effectiveness, resilience and ability to work with trainees. They are expected to monitor their own personal functioning and to seek help and/or agree to withdraw from training, whether temporarily or permanently, when their personal resources are so depleted as to require this.

B.3 Confidentiality

B.3.1   Trainers are responsible for establishing a contract for confidential working which makes explicit the responsibilities of both trainer and trainees.

B.3.2   Trainers must inform trainees at the beginning of the training programme of all reasonably foreseeable circumstances under which confidentiality may be breached during the training programme.

B.3.3   Trainers must not reveal confidential information concerning trainees, or former trainees, without the permission of the trainee, except:
   a. in discussion with those on whom trainers rely for professional support and supervision. (These discussions will usually be anonymous and the supervisor is bound by confidentiality);
   b. in order to prevent serious harm to another or to the trainee;
   c. when legally required to break confidentiality;
   d. during selection, assessment, complaints and disciplinary procedures in order to prevent or investigate breaches of ethical standards by trainees;

If consent to the disclosure of confidential information has been withheld, trainees should normally be informed in advance that a trainer intends to disclose confidential information.

B.3.4   Detailed information about specific trainees, or former trainees, may be used for publication or in meetings only with the trainees' permission and with anonymity preserved. Where trainers need to use examples from previous work to illustrate a point to trainees, this must be done respectfully, briefly and anonymously.

B.3.5   If discussion by trainers of their trainees, or former trainees, with professional colleagues becomes necessary, it must be purposeful, not trivialising, and relevant to the training.

B.3.6   If trainers suspect misconduct by another trainer which cannot be resolved or remedied after discussion with the trainer concerned, they should implement any internal complaints procedures that may be available or the BAC Complaints Procedure. Any required breaches of confidentiality should be limited to those necessary for the investigation of the complaint.

B.4 Management of the training work

B.4.1   Trainers must make basic information available to potential trainees, in writing or by other appropriate means of communication, before the start of the programme. This should include:

a. the fees to be charged and any other expenses which may be incurred;

b. the dates and time commitments;

c. information on selection procedures, entry requirements and the process by which decisions are made;

d. basic information about the content of the programme, its philosophical and theoretical approach and the training methods to be used;

e. the relevant qualifications of the trainers;

f. any requirements for counselling supervision or personal counselling which trainees will be expected to comply with while training;

g. guidelines for work experience or placements to be undertaken as part of the training;

h. evaluation and assessment methods to be used during the programme and the implications of these;

i. if the programme carries a qualification, arrangements for appeals should a dispute arise.

B.4.2   Trainers must check whether training is being undertaken voluntarily or compulsorily and, if necessary, draw employers' attention to the fact that a voluntary commitment is the more appropriate.

B.4.3   Trainers should ensure that trainees receive regular feedback on their work and that self and peer assessment are encouraged at regular intervals.

B.4.4   Trainers must be alert to any prejudices and assumptions that trainees reveal and raise their awareness of these issues, so that trainees are encouraged to recognise and value difference.

B.4.5   Trainers should ensure that trainees are given the opportunity to discuss their experiences of the programme and are also invited to evaluate these individually, in groups, or both, at least once in a training programme.

B.4.6   Trainers who become aware of a conflict between their obligation to a trainee and their obligation to an agency or organisation employing them, must make explicit to both the trainee and the agency or organisation employing them the nature and existence of this conflict and seek to resolve it.

B.4.7   Where differences between trainer and trainee, or between trainers, cannot be resolved the trainer and, where appropriate the trainer's line manager, should consult with, and when necessary refer to, an independent expert.

C. ADDITIONAL CLAUSE FOR TRAINERS IN COUNSELLING

C.1   Trainers are encouraged to ensure that:

a. practical experience as a counsellor in an external setting is, where possible, part of the training programme;

b. the setting where trainees propose to practice as counsellors is appropriate, paying particular attention to the need for confidentiality, privacy and counselling supervision.

D. ADDITIONAL CLAUSES FOR TRAINERS IN COUNSELLING SKILLS

D.1   Trainers are responsible for ensuring that their trainees consider the appropriateness of the setting in which they use their counselling skills.

D.2   Trainers should ensure that trainees are clear that using counselling skills may lead to conflicting responsibilities. These should be discussed on the training course and in supervision.

Effective 1 January 1997

The British Association for Counselling's Ethical Guidelines for Monitoring, Evaluation and Research in Counselling

Introduction

These guidelines have been produced by the Research and Evaluation Committee of the British Association for Counselling in consultation with the Standards and Ethics Committee.

The need for a set of guidelines became clear as the result of a number of enquiries made to the Research and Evaluation Committee where counsellors were unhappy about the ethics of research in which they had been asked to take part or where investigators had ethical dilemmas.

It should be noted that these are guidelines and not a Code of Ethics and Practice. As such they are not mandatory, although the Research and Evaluation Committee strongly encourages their use and hopes they will be regarded as normative.

Basic principles

Counsellors owe a duty to their clients, to other counsellors and to society generally to measure and assess the effectiveness of what they do.

The duty to the client arises out of the nature of the counselling contract. The counsellor should work in ways which can reliably, and on objective grounds, be expected to be of benefit to the client.

The duty to society occurs, in part, because counsellors represent to society that counselling is a valuable and worthwhile activity. Counsellors should be ready to examine both the grounds for, and potential or actual argument against, that representation.

The duty to other counsellors arises from the professional obligation to maintain, and verify the maintenance of, high standards of practice.

The basic ethical principle to be observed is that the activity of investigating and measuring the effectiveness of counselling should be performed with the same values as underlie good counselling practice generally.

Section B7 of the BAC Code of Ethics and Practice for Counsellors must be complied with.

It is important to acknowledge that well-conducted investigations into the effectiveness of counselling can enhance the individual therapeutic relationship.

Research is a supervised activity. Investigators have a responsibility to ensure that they have adequate supervision or consultation arrangements in respect of the investigatory activity in addition to that required for counselling. The supervisor should be skilled in research issues and have suitable knowledge of counselling practice.

Definitions

'Monitoring' refers to the gathering, whether on a regular or occasional basis, of basic statistical information about counselling activity.

Examples of monitoring might include: the number of clients seen in a year; their gender and ages; sources of referral.

'Evaluation' refers to the making of informed judgements (including comparative judgements) about the effectiveness of particular counselling practice.

Examples of evaluation might include: a survey of how satisfied the clients of a particular agency are with the service they received; a counsellor looking at whether most of her/his clients feel that they have achieved what they hoped to achieve; comparing the experience of clients at one agency with those at another.

'Research' refers to the purposeful investigation of the effects of the counselling process.

Examples of research might include: examining whether counselling reduces the demand for medication; seeking to find out whether counselling can alleviate obsessions or phobias; determining whether employee assistance programmes are cost-effective.

These categories are not rigid, and particular investigations may involve more than one category (thus e.g. evaluating the effectiveness of counselling in a GP practice may yield information about the alleviation of depression).

Nonetheless, the basic distinctions are useful, since the ethical considerations applying to each of them are in practice somewhat different from each other.

The term 'investigation' is used to include all of the preceding activities.

General

All investigations should be carefully considered in advance, so that:

- the purpose of the investigation is clearly understood;
- the data required has been defined;
- the procedures for data analysis (e.g. statistics, phenomenological analysis, grounded theory analysis) to be used have been identified;
- the likely impact on the client has been thought through.

The statistical tests or methods to be used should be appropriate to the type of data being considered, the reliability of the results or conclusions, and the limits of its validity. Consideration of methods must include consideration of cultural issues as an integral part of the investigation design.

Cultural issues

The investigation should be considered from the standpoint of the diverse cultures and groups in our society. Examples are: age, gender, sexuality, race, ethnic origin, belief (religion), disability, lifestyle, responsibility for dependants.

Note: The question 'How well do you relate to the opposite sex?', for example, has been seen as excluding the experience of lesbians and gay men; the question 'Over the past two weeks have you been doing the housework well?', when addressed to women, has been felt to be sexist; the question 'Are you able to talk about your feelings openly with your friends?' has been said to make cultural, amongst other, assumptions; and the heading 'Marital status' on a section of a form has been criticised because it appears to say that marriage is the norm by which other relationships or a state of being single must be evaluated.

The investigator needs to be aware that they may not have adequate knowledge of what is or is not acceptable to, or is overtly or covertly judgemental of, others. Checking out the draft protocol of an investigation, the questions to be asked in questionnaires or other instruments, and other relevant matters, with members of relevant groups should be a standard part of the development process of all investigations.

For this purpose the relevant groups are all those whose members may become subjects of the investigation, even if the group itself is not being investigated. For example an investigation into the level of mental distress shown by patients attending a GP surgery may not itself differentiate between the ethnic origins or sexuality of the patients; but any GP practice can be expected to have patients from a range of ethnic backgrounds and of differing sexuality, and the investigation ought to be sensitive to this. No investigation should leave members of any group feeling that their welfare or dignity has not been respected.

Consent

Counselling is an activity that is freely entered into. To conduct any investigation that involves clients without their informed and free consent potentially devalues the activity of counselling and is destructive of the therapeutic relationship.

In order to be able to exercise free consent, the client needs to be told:

- the purpose of the investigation;
- what they will be asked to do (e.g. fill in a questionnaire, allow a session to be taped or videoed, be interviewed by a researcher);
- whether or not their identity will be known to anyone other than the counsellor, and, if so, by whom;
- whether or not any personal information will be known to anyone other than the counsellor, and, if so, what and to whom;
- what will happen to all records relating to them (e.g. 'Your data will be kept for three months and will then be securely disposed of.');
- the procedures for withdrawing consent or making complaints;
- any possible harm that may happen to them (e.g.: 'Talking to an interviewer about past traumas may be upsetting, and we can look at what you can do if it is.');
- any other information which might affect their decision.

The investigator needs to take into account that there is often an inequality in the counselling relationship, and that a client may feel an obligation to please the counsellor by giving consent to being involved in an investigation. The client should not be expected to make a decision without adequate time to consider the request.

Except in circumstances where persons are being specifically recruited for a project set up for the purposes of research, the client must be informed clearly and unequivocally that declining to give consent will not affect the counselling they receive.

The emotional state of the client should be considered; if the client is unlikely to be able to exercise free choice, then they should not be included in the investigation.

Where there is a possibility that the client may not fully understand the information given about the investigaion or the implications of giving consent, it is the responsibility of the investigator to ensure that the person does in fact have an adequate understanding of that information and/or implications before including the client in the investigation.

If an investigation involves detained persons, particular care should be taken to ensure that the circumstances are such that they can give real, free and informed consent. In the case of investigations involving children a judgement must be made about their ability to give consent. The investigator should familiarise themselves with any relevant law, e.g. The Children Act.

Where an investigation consists of several separate parts or will last for some time, it may be appropriate to re-obtain consent periodically.

Investigations without consent

There are differing views about the acceptability of investigations that do not involve the obtaining of the client's consent. The presumption should be in favour of gaining consent. Not obtaining consent requires particular justification for each separate investigation.

If it is thought that proceeding with an investigation without obtaining the client's consent may be justified, great care should be taken to ensure that the reasons for this are both cogent and compelling. The only likely justifications are that the investigation results would be affected by obtaining consent, in such a way that the outcome would be invalid, or that obtaining consent for the investigation would adversely affect the counselling relationship (though instances of this will be rare).

It is necessary to take into account that for a client to discover that they have been involved in an investigation without their knowledge or consent is likely to be destructive of the counselling relationship, and may, indeed, be considered abusive.

No counsellor should be obliged to be involved in such an investigation against their conscience.

When it is proposed to forego obtaining consent it is imperative that at least one external disinterested person with substantial knowledge and/or experience both of counselling and conducting research is consulted. Only if they are satisfied that there is no practical alternative should the investigation proceed.

In qualitative research, the writing of case studies without consent, even if the client's, or former client's, identity is fully disguised, should be regarded as being subject to these guidelines. Brief vignettes which are illustrative and contain no identifiable material may be written without consent, although it is good practice to obtain consent wherever possible.

In the case of a former client about whom it is desired to write such a case study, every reasonable effort should be made to contact the person to obtain consent. However, if it proves impossible to contact the former client, it is justifiable to write a study provided both that the identity of the client is adequately disguised and also that the study is integral to the work being done.

Adequately disguising a person's identity requires careful thought. Mere changes of name or gender are insufficient. The aim is both that the client should not recognise themselves and also that the features of the case study relevant to the research are not distorted.

The client should be informed about, and given adequate explanations of, their participation in the investigation at the conclusion of the investigation or of counselling, unless there are compelling reasons not to do so.

Withdrawal of consent

Clients should be informed at the outset of any investigation that they have an absolute right to withdraw their consent at any time.

When consent is withdrawn, the person should be informed that they have the right to require that data about them is destroyed.

Potential inconvenience to the investigator or the investigation is not a reason for failing to advise the client of this right.

Avoidance of the investigation should be acknowledged as a potential withdrawal of consent.

If consent is withdrawn during an investigation, it is unethical to apply pressure to persuade the person to change their mind. Giving additional information or explanation does not constitute pressure if done sensitively: the criterion to be applied is whether the person will *perceive* the investigator/counsellor as putting pressure on them.

The client has the right to withdraw consent retrospectively, as a result of an explanation given after an investigation, or for other reasons. The client should be informed of their right to require that data about them is destroyed.

Ownership of information

Irrespective of any legal considerations, the moral ownership of personal information about any person belongs with that person.

It should, in general, be normal practice for clients to be able to see research records pertaining to them.

Where questionnaires are used to provide scores, the client has a right to have the score(s) and the significance of the score(s) explained to them in an appropriate way.

The principles of confidentiality inherent in counselling apply to all investigations into the counselling process no matter who is doing the investigating. The investigator must not breach that confidentiality (see BAC Code of Ethics and Practice for Counsellors Sections B4 and B5 and Counselling, Confidentiality and the Law). It is particularly important that in multi-disciplinary investigations this principle is adhered to.

If confidentiality cannot be guaranteed, then the client must be fully informed of this in advance of being asked to give consent.

The counsellor also has a right to refuse to be involved in an investigation if they have reason to believe that confidentiality may not be respected.

The provisions of the Data Protection Act will apply to any information stored magnetically, i.e. on computer, audio tape and video tape.

Note: The Data Protection Registrar has stated that information stored on computer must not be used for any purpose other than that for which it was originally obtained. If the holder wishes to use it for anything else or impart it to another person, he or she must have the client's permission. This is a legal requirement, and the Registrar has taken action in cases where it has been infringed by researchers attempting to undertake research without obtaining consent.

Clients who have taken part in an investigation should be given the opportunity to be informed of the outcome of the investigation.

Case notes

When notes of the counselling process are kept by the counsellor the client is entitled to presume that those notes will be used only for the purposes of the counselling itself and for any necessary supervision, unless the client has freely entered into some other arrangement. It follows that the use of case notes for the purposes of research without the client's specific consent for that purpose is unethical, except in the circumstances outlined in section 7 of these guidelines.

Consent should be obtained following the same procedures as in any other investigation.

Explanations

All explanations of the nature of an investigation, of individual data and scores, and of results, along with other information, given to clients participating in an investigation should be straightforward, in plain language which avoids jargon, and should not assume particular levels of knowledge.

Simplicity of explanation must not lead to the person's understanding of the significance of the information given being distorted.

The giving of explanations after the event does not justify unethical aspects of any investigation.

Random allocation methods

Some medical and other investigations involve randomly assigning clients/patients to particular types of treatment.

Counsellors may vary in their willingness to be involved in investigations of this type. Their views should be respected.

An appropriate, disinterested and external advisor, with experience of both counselling and conducting investigations, should be consulted as to whether the use of such a method is justified.

Colleagues

Investigators and counsellors share in a general responsibility for the ethical conduct of research. An investigator or counsellor who believes that another investigator or counsellor or other relevant person is counselling or conducting investigations which are unethical should encourage that person to re-evaluate their investigation. Such re-evaluation should involve an appropriate, disinterested and external advisor.

Monitoring

Particular in agencies, it may happen that data about clients is used for the routine compilation of statistics about the service. Such routine monitoring is often not regarded as coming under the general heading of 'research'; however, inasmuch as information given by the client in connection with their counselling is being used for purposes outside that counselling, the client has the right to know that such statistics are compiled, and to know that in advance of entering into the counselling contract.

While some professionals, often though not exclusively in medical and social work settings, may be resistant to the idea of obtaining specific consent for the use of data about clients for routine monitoring purposes, it must nonetheless be understood that the client is normally entitled to determine what information about them shall be known, by whom, and for what purposes, and that obtaining consent is therefore good practice.

Nevertheless, the collection without consent, for monitoring puposes, of such basic data as numbers of referrals/cases, gender, ethnicity, and age-group is not objectionable unless the relevant individual data or data-entries may act so as to identify the client.

Reluctance on the part of a client to give information is not a ground for refusing a service.

Evaluation

A similar issue to those raised by monitoring may occur in connection with ongoing evaluation processes. If, for example, a service is to be evaluated by asking all or selected clients to complete questionnaires at the beginning and end of counselling, then the client should be aware that the questionnaires are to be used for research rather than, or as well as, diagnostic purposes, and consent should be obtained for any research use.

Complaints

Wherever possible, and always in the case of investigations undertaken within, or by, agencies and institutions, the client should have an effective avenue of complaint open to them if they feel that the investigation has infringed their dignity or is unsatisfactory on other grounds.

The person(s) dealing with complaints should be independent of the investigator(s).

Professional collaboration

Investigators and others must not claim authorship for work not actually done by them or for ideas not originated by them. Sources (e.g. other investigators' work) must be properly cited.

Accounts of investigations must acknowledge help given by other professionals and other relevant persons.

Alec McGuire
Chair, BAC Research and Evaluation Committee
May 1996

Author index

Persons and organizations as subjects are included in the subject index

Subject index